Special Edition Using Macromedia® Dreamweaver® UltraDev 4

NIIT

Contents

I
1. Introducing Dreamweaver UltraDev 4 7
2. The UltraDev 4 Environment 23

II Understanding Databases, ASP, JSP, and ColdFusion
3. Database Essentials 45
4. Understanding the Server Technology: Active Server Pages 61
5. Understanding the Server Technology: JavaServer Pages 81
6. Understanding the Server Technology: ColdFusion 101

III Designing Web Pages Using Dreamweaver UltraDev 4
7. Creating Sites and Documents 117
8. Working with Text in Documents 145
9. Creating and Managing Images 171
10. Linking Pages Together 189
11. Presenting Content in a Page 207
12. Building User Interactivity into a Page 237
13. Adding Multimedia Effects to a Web Page 255
14. Optimizing Your Work 283
15. Editing and Debugging in Code View 299
16. Setting Interface Preferences 321

IV Creating Dynamic Web Pages
17. Connecting to a Database 341
18. Dreamweaver UltraDev 4 Data Sources 359
19. Making a Web Page Dynamic 383
20. Building Dynamic Web Applications 407
21. Managing Site Access 431
22. Managing Your Web Site 453
23. Customizing Dreamweaver UltraDev 4 463

V Extending the Capabilities of Dreamweaver UltraDev 4
24. Introducing Extensions 483
25. Interface Extensions 495

VI Appendixes
A. Installing and Configuring Supporting Technologies 519
B. Dreamweaver UltraDev Web Sites and References 529
C. XML, HTML, and JavaScript Reference 535
D. Creating a Database Using Microsoft Access 551
Glossary 559

Index 569

que®

201 W. 103rd Street
Indianapolis, Indiana 46290

Special Edition Using Macromedia® Dreamweaver® UltraDev 4

Copyright © 2002 by Que

All rights reserved. No part of this book shall be reproduced, stored in a retrieval system, or transmitted by any means, electronic, mechanical, photocopying, recording, or otherwise, without written permission from the publisher. No patent liability is assumed with respect to the use of the information contained herein. Although every precaution has been taken in the preparation of this book, the publisher and author assume no responsibility for errors or omissions. Nor is any liability assumed for damages resulting from the use of the information contained herein.

International Standard Book Number: 0-7897-2577-0

Library of Congress Catalog Card Number: 2001094312

Printed in the United States of America

First Printing: October 2001

04 03 02 01   4 3 2 1

Trademarks

All terms mentioned in this book that are known to be trademarks or service marks have been appropriately capitalized. Que cannot attest to the accuracy of this information. Use of a term in this book should not be regarded as affecting the validity of any trademark or service mark.

Warning and Disclaimer

Every effort has been made to make this book as complete and as accurate as possible, but no warranty or fitness is implied. The information provided is on an "as is" basis. The authors and the publisher shall have neither liability nor responsibility to any person or entity with respect to any loss or damages arising from the information contained in this book.

Associate Publisher
Dean Miller

Executive Editor
Candace Hall

Development Editor
Sean Dixon

Managing Editor
Thomas F. Hayes

Senior Editor
Susan Ross Moore

Indexer
Tina Trettin

Proofreaders
Harvey Stanbrough
Maribeth Echard

Technical Editors
Eric Ladd
Matthew Pizzi
Doug Scamahorn
Nic Skitt

Team Coordinator
Cindy Teeters

Interior Designer
Ruth Harvey

Cover Designers
Dan Armstrong
Ruth Harvey

Contents

Introduction 2

This Book Is for You 2

How This Book Is Organized 2

How to Use This Book 3

I Getting Ready to Work with Dreamweaver UltraDev

1 Presenting Dreamweaver UltraDev 4 7

Introducing Dreamweaver UltraDev 4 8

The Evolution of Dreamweaver UltraDev 4 9
  Displaying Dynamic Content on the Web 10
  Responding to User Actions on the Client 10
  Macromedia's Web Page Design and Development Solution 11
  Enter UltraDev 1 12
  UltraDev 4 12

The Features of Dreamweaver UltraDev 4 13
  Database-Driven Dynamic Web Applications 13
  Built-In Support for Server-Side Processing 13
  Live Data View 15
  Customizable Environment 15
  The Dreamweaver Design Environment 15
  Site Management 18

Web Applications and UltraDev 4 19
  Personalized Web Sites 19
  Interactive Web Sites 20
  Intranets 20

Summary 21

2 The UltraDev 4 Environment 23

The UltraDev Workflow 24
  Designing a Page 24
  Creating Data Sources 25
  Adding Dynamic Functionality to a Page 25
  Extending the Functionality of a Page 26

The UltraDev Interface 26
  The Document Window 26

Menus and Toolbar Buttons 27
  The File Menu 27
  The Edit Menu 29
  The View Menu 31
  The Insert Menu 32
  The Modify Menu 33
  The Text Menu 34
  The Commands Menu 34
  The Site Menu 35
  The Window Menu 37
  The Panels on the UltraDev Interface 38
  The Help Menu 39
  The Status Bar 39

Summary 41

II Understanding Databases, ASP, JSP, and ColdFusion

3 Database Essentials 45

Database Fundamentals and Concepts 46
  Designing a Relational Database 46
  Mapping to a Table 48

Basic SQL Syntax 49
  Creating Databases and Tables 50
  Adding, Modifying, and Deleting Records 52

SELECT Statements   54
Arithmetic Operations   57
Generating Summary Data   58
Sorting Records   58
Stored Procedures   59

Summary   60

4 Understanding the Server Technology: Active Server Pages   61

Introduction to Active Server Pages   62
Identifying ASP Scripts   63
Objects in ASP   63

The Response Object   65
The Write Method   65

The Request Object   67
Cookies   67
HTTP Headers   68
Reading Cookies Using the Request Object   69

The Session, Application, and Server Objects   70
The Session Object   71
The Application Object   72

Databases and ASP   73
The Server Object   73
Creating a Connection to a Database   74
Retrieving Data from the Database   75
Inserting, Updating, and Deleting Records   77

Summary   79

5 Understanding the Server Technology: JavaServer Pages   81

What Is a JavaServer Page?   82
Models for Accessing JavaServer Pages   83
First Application Model   84
Second Application Model   84

JavaServer Page Syntax   85
Components of JavaServer Pages   86

Summary   99

6 Understanding the Server Technology: ColdFusion   101

Introducing ColdFusion   102
Work Flow: Web Server, ColdFusion Server, and Database   103

Working with Databases by Using CFML   104
Retrieving Data from a Database   106
Displaying Data on the Web Page   107
Inserting Data into a Database   110
Modifying Records in a Database   112

Summary   114

III Designing Web Pages Using Dreamweaver UltraDev 4

7 Creating Sites and Documents   117

Planning a Web Site   118
Planning the Site Structure   118
Planning for a Sample Site   118

Creating a New Site   119
Defining a Site   119
Working with the Site Window   125

Working with Documents   128
Opening Existing Documents   129
Saving Documents   130
Using the Different Views in UltraDev   130
Setting General Properties for a Document   131
Visual Aids   133
Viewing the Head Content   135

Page Layout 135
   Layout Tables and Cells 136
   Using the Property Inspector to Format Layout Tables and Cells 138

Design Considerations 140
   Browser Type and Version 140
   Platform 140
   Connection Speed 140
   Screen Dimension 141

Summary 141

Troubleshooting 141

Activity Corner 142
   Folders and Files 143

8 Working with Text in Documents 145

Adding Text and Objects to a Document 146
   Adding Dates 146
   Adding Special Text Characters 147
   Copying and Pasting HTML Source Code 148

Formatting and Editing the Text in a Document 148
   Formatting Paragraphs 149
   Changing the Font Color 149
   Changing the Font Size 149
   Changing the Font Style 150
   Changing the Alignment 151
   Performing a Spell Check 151
   Creating Simple and Nested Lists 153
   Searching and Replacing Text, Tags, and Attributes 156

Using HTML Styles and CSS 159
   Using HTML Styles 159
   Using CSS Styles 162

Summary 169

Activity Corner 169
   Applying HTML Styles to the `Sidebar.asp` File 169
   Applying HTML Styles to the `Aboutus.asp` and `Help.asp` Files 170
   Previewing Your Site 170

9 Creating and Managing Images 171

Working with Images 172

Image Formats 172
   Graphic Interchange Format 172
   Joint Photographic Experts Group 173
   Portable Network Graphics 173

Inserting Images into a Page 174

Inserting Rollover Images into a Web Page 176

Inserting Navigation Bars into a Page 177

Formatting Images 180
   Setting Image Properties 180
   Aligning Images 182
   Resizing Images 184

Working with Image Maps 184
   Creating an Image Map 185
   Modifying an Image Map 186

Using External Image Editors 186
   Setting an External Editor 186
   Opening an External Editor 188

Summary 188

Activity Corner 188

10 Linking Pages Together 189

Introducing Links 190
  Understanding Absolute and Relative Paths 190

Working with Links 193
  Creating a Link with the Property Inspector 193
  Changing and Updating Links 196
  Updating Link Information 196
  Using the Site Map to Create and Modify Links 196
  Named Anchors 198
  Adding More Functionality to Links 200

Creating a Jump Menu 202

Summary 204

Troubleshooting 204

Activity Corner 205

11 Presenting Content in a Page 207

Working with Tables 208
  Creating a Table 208
  Formatting a Table 209
  Inserting and Deleting Rows and Columns 214
  Splitting and Merging Rows and Columns 215
  Copying and Pasting Cell Content 218

Managing Data in a Table 218
  Sorting Table Contents 218
  Importing Tabular Data 219
  Exporting Tabular Data 220

Creating and Managing Layers 221
  Introducing the Layer Panel 221
  Selecting, Resizing, Moving, and Aligning Layers 222
  Setting Properties for a Layer 223
  Bringing Layers to Life 225
  Modifying Timeline Animations 227

Working with Frames 228
  Creating a Frame 228
  Saving Frames and Framesets 231
  Setting Frameset and Frame Properties 232
  Frame Content and Links 233

Summary 233

Activity Corner 234
  Creating a Layer Animation 234
  Creating the Contentpage.asp document 236

12 Building User Interactivity into a Page 237

How Forms Work 238

Using Forms 238
  Creating a Form 238

Working with Form Objects 240
  Creating Text Fields 241
  Inserting a File Field 243
  Inserting a Hidden Field 244
  Creating Buttons 244
  Inserting a Check Box 248
  Adding Menus and Lists 249

Processing Forms on the Server Side 250
  Processing Forms Using ASP 250

Summary 252

Activity Corner 252

13 Adding Multimedia Effects to a Web Page 255

Adding Flash, Generator, and Shockwave Media 256
    Adding Flash Objects to a Document 256
    Adding Shockwave Media to a Web Page 260
    Adding Generator Objects to a Web Page 261

Adding Fireworks Images to a Page 261
    Inserting Fireworks Files in UltraDev 261
    Editing Fireworks Files Placed in UltraDev 262
    Creating a Web Photo Album by Using Fireworks 263

Adding Sound Effects to a Page 264

Inserting ActiveX Controls and Java Applets 266
    Embedding Java Applets 267

Adding Client-Side Behaviors 267
    Behaviors in UltraDev 267
    Attaching a Behavior 268

Troubleshooting 280

Summary 281

Activity Corner 281
    Completing the `Navigation.asp` File 282

14 Optimizing Your Work 283

Managing Your Assets 284
    The Assets Panel 284

The History Panel 289
    Using the History Panel 290

Templates and Libraries 291
    Creating a Template 291
    Creating Editable and Noneditable Regions on a Template 293
    Creating Documents Based on Templates 293
    Working with Library Items 295

Troubleshooting 297

Summary 297

Activity Corner 297

15 Editing and Debugging in Code View 299

Editing HTML Becomes Easy 300
    The UltraDev Reference Panel 300
    Inserting Comments 302
    Roundtrip HTML 304
    Inserting and Editing a Script 305
    Viewing Script Functions 307
    Cleaning Up HTML Code and Microsoft Word HTML 308
    Formatting the HTML Source Code in Existing Documents 311
    Editing ColdFusion and Active Server Files in UltraDev 311
    Editing an HTML Tag in the Document Window 314

Debugging JavaScript Code 315
    Running JavaScript Debugger to Find Syntax Errors 315
    Using the JavaScript Debugger to Check for Logical Errors 316

Summary 319

16 Setting Interface Preferences 321

Choosing Your Style 322
    Setting the General Preference 322
    Setting Preferences for Code Colors 324

Setting Code Formatting Preferences 325
Setting Code Rewriting Preferences 326
Setting CSS Style Preferences 327
Setting File Types/Editors Preferences 328
Setting Font/Encoding Preferences 329
Setting Highlight Preferences 330
Setting Invisible Elements Preferences 330
Setting Layers Preferences 331
Setting Layout View Preferences 332
Setting Panels Preferences 333
Setting Preferences for Preview in Browser 333
Setting Quick Tag Editor Preferences 333
Setting Site Preferences 335
Setting Status Bar Preferences 336

Summary 337

IV Creating Dynamic Web Pages

17 Connecting to a Database 341

Database Connections 342
An Overview of ODBC, OLEDB, and JDBC 342

Creating and Managing Database Connections 344
ODBC Connections: DSN and DSN-less 345
Connecting a JSP Application to a Database 352
Performing a Final Check on the Database Connection 356
Managing Database Connections 356

Troubleshooting 357

Summary 358

Activity Corner 358

18 Dreamweaver UltraDev 4 Data Sources 359

Understanding Data Sources 360
Creating a Recordset 360

Creating and Managing Data Sources 366
Creating a Data Source for an Active Server Page 366
Creating a Data Source for a ColdFusion Page 371
Creating a Data Source for a JavaServer Page 374
Caching, Changing, and Deleting Data Sources 377

Summary 378

Activity Corner 378
Creating a Recordset in the `Contentpage.asp` File 378
Creating a Recordset in the `Songfetch.asp` File 379
Creating a Recordset in the `Search.asp` File 380

19 Making a Web Page Dynamic 383

Adding Dynamic Elements to a Web Page 384
Adding Dynamic Text to a Page 384
Displaying Dynamic Images on a Web Page 391
Displaying Dynamic Data Within Form Objects 392
Creating Dynamic HTML Attributes 399
Creating Dynamic Flash and ActiveX Controls 399

Adding More Functionality to the Dynamic Content 401
Displaying Record Counters 401
The Master-Detail Page 401

Summary   404

Activity Corner   404
   Adding the Show Region Server Behavior   406

20 Building Dynamic Web Applications   407

Adding a Search Feature to a Page   408
   A Sample Search Feature   408
   The Search Page   409
   The Results Page   411
   Creating a Detail Page   414

Adding, Updating, and Deleting Data in a Database   417
   Inserting Records into a Database   418
   Updating Records in a Database   422
   Deleting Records in a Database   426

Troubleshooting   429

Summary   429

Activity Corner   430

21 Managing Site Access   431

Preventing Unauthorized Access to a Site   432
   Creating a Registration Page   432
   Creating a Login Page   437
   Redirecting Unauthorized Users to Another Page   439

Copying and Pasting Access Rights to Other Pages   441

Logging Out of a Web Page   441

Summary   442

Activity Corner   442
   Completing the Registration Page   443
   Creating the Login Page   443

Completing the `Contentpage.asp`, `Search.asp`, and `Songfetch.asp` Pages   444
   Creating the `ViewCD.asp` Page   446
   Restricting Access to the `ViewCD.asp` Page   449
   Creating the `Placeorder.asp` Page   449
   Creating the `Editprofile.asp` Page   452

22 Managing Your Web Site   453

File Transfer and Synchronization   454
   File Transfer Between the Remote and Local Sites   454
   Synchronizing Files   454

Working in a Team   455
   Checking Files In and Out   456
   Creating Design Notes   458
   Reports   460

Checking Links and Fixing Broken Links   461

Summary   462

23 Customizing Dreamweaver UltraDev 4   463

Modifying the UltraDev Interface   464

Using the Keyboard Shortcut Editor   464
   Creating a Customized Shortcut Set   465

Customizing the Objects Panel   466
   Creating an Object   466
   Moving and Deleting an Object   466

Customizing the Menu System   467
   Reading the `menus.xml` File   467
   Editing the `menus.xml` File   469

Customizing Dialog Boxes   470

Customizing Data Formats 472

Customizing Server Behaviors 473
   Using the Server Behavior Builder 474
   Editing a Server Behavior 478

Summary 479

V Extending the Capabilities of Dreamweaver UltraDev 4

24 Introducing Extensions 483

The Concept of Extensions 484

The Document Object Model 485
   The Document Object Model in UltraDev 487

JavaScript in Extensions 489
   Using Tree Controls 489
   Installing Extensions 491
   Sharing Extensions 492

Summary 493

25 Interface Extensions 495

Extending Objects 496
   Functions to Implement Objects 498
   Implementing the Marquee Object 501

Extending Commands 505
   Functions to Implement Command Extensions 506
   The Justify Text Command 507

Extending Property Inspectors 508
   Functions to Implement Property Inspectors 509
   A Property Inspector for the Marquee Object 511

Extending Floating Panels 514
   Functions to Implement Floating Panels 514

Summary 515

VI Appendixes

A Installing and Configuring Supporting Technologies 519

Internet Information Server (IIS) 4.0 520
   Installing IIS 4.0 520

Installing SQL Server 7.0 521

ColdFusion Server 4.5 522
   Installing ColdFusion Server 4.5 522

Dreamweaver UltraDev 4.0 524
   System Requirements for Dreamweaver UltraDev 524
   Installing Dreamweaver UltraDev 525

Allaire JRun 3.0 526
   Requirements for Allaire JRun 3.0 526
   Installing JRun Server 3.0 526
   Configuring JRun Application Server 527

Windows DSN 528
   Configuring Windows DSN for SQL Server Databases 528

B Dreamweaver UltraDev Web Sites and References 529

JSP Sites 530

ASP Sites 531

ColdFusion Sites 532

Dreamweaver UltraDev Sites   533

HTML and XML Sites   534

C XML, HTML, and JavaScript Reference   535

XML Reference   536
   Creating XML Documents   537
   Rules for Creating XML Documents   539
   Defining the Document Structure   540
   The XML Parser   540

HTML Reference   541

JavaScript Reference   544
   Variables   545
   Operators   546
   JavaScript Entities   547
   Programming Constructs   548
   Functions   549
   Objects and Methods   549
   Event Handling   550

D Creating a Database Using Microsoft Access   551

Creating a Database   552
   Creating a Table   552
   Linking Tables   555
   Querying a Database   557

Glossary   559

Index   569

About the Author

About NIIT

NIIT is a Global IT Services and IT Training corporation. NIIT has more than 4,900 employees spread across 37 countries and has generated more than $270 million in revenue in the financial year 2000.

NIIT is actively involved in creating software solutions and learning solutions for markets worldwide. NIIT's software development procedure is controlled and managed through processes that are 100% ISO 9001-certified and assessed at SEI-CMM Level 5 for the maturity of our software processes—ensuring high-quality solutions which are delivered on-time and on-budget. NIIT's client list includes Hewlett-Packard, IBM, Microsoft, NETg, AT&T, Hitachi, Computer Associates, Red Hat, Oracle, Sony, Sun Microsystems, and Toshiba.

NIIT pioneered IT education and training in 1982. NIIT trains more than 350,000 career IT professionals through its network of more than 2000 training centers in more than 26 countries. NIIT has an alumni base of more than 1.5 million IT professionals.

NIIT has one of the world's largest learning content development facilities staffed with more than 900 learning content development professionals. Over the years, NIIT has developed a range of curricula for people with diverse requirements—from students seeking careers in computers, to IT professionals needing advanced training, to global corporate enterprises such as Microsoft, Arthur Andersen, PeopleSoft, Computer Associates, Tivoli Systems, Sun Microsystems, The World Bank, Thomson Learning, Pearson Education, and Oracle who require end-to-end learning solutions.

Acknowledgments

A book is born by the collective effort of many. To each person involved in the making of this book goes our heartfelt thanks for bringing this book to fruition.

We thank Anuradha Pradhyumnan for her thoughtfulness and endless patience that helped tide us over tough times. We are greatly appreciative of the efforts taken by Kavitha Ravipati to help us compose our thoughts and ideas into a presentable form. Her unrelenting demand for perfection and eye for detail helped greatly in bringing this book to its present form. Our thanks to Venkata Subramaniam for his patient handling of our technical queries, when we needed it the most. Our special thanks to Sindhu Bhairavi for her effective and efficient conversion of our word pictures into the graphic elements that have gone into this book. A special thanks to Shantanu Phadnis, for coordinating with the editorial and review team.

And, most importantly, to Kumar Krishnan, whose enthusiasm, faith, and support revitalized us each time we found ourselves in a tight spot. Kumar, thanks for making the writing of this book a pleasant and memorable experience.

We extend our heartfelt thanks to Sean Dixon, whose valuable suggestions and comments gave direction and focus to the book. We also thank Gayle Johnson and Eric Ladd for ensuring the technical accuracy of the book.

Finally, a hearty thanks to the rest of the project team for the music, jokes, and wholesome fun that kept us going.

INTRODUCTION

In this introduction

This Book Is for You 2

How This Book Is Organized 2

How to Use This Book 3

Welcome to Dreamweaver UltraDev 4! Macromedia's attempt to integrate Web site design and development has brought forth Dreamweaver UltraDev 4, a Web application-building tool that uses the ASP, JSP, and ColdFusion technologies behind the scenes to help you design powerful, dynamic Web sites. Dreamweaver UltraDev 4 builds upon the Dreamweaver architecture, with added features that enable database connectivity and auto-code generation for server-side programming. With Dreamweaver UltraDev 4, Web designers and Web developers can work together closely on a common platform.

If you have used Dreamweaver before, you will find the Dreamweaver UltraDev interface is strikingly similar. If you have been only designing Web sites and never ventured to implement features that require server-side coding, with Dreamweaver UltraDev 4 you can now do both. If you have already used Dreamweaver UltraDev 1, you will find an improved interface in version 4, with added server behaviors and better support for developing ColdFusion applications.

This Book Is for You

This book is targeted at both Web designers and programmers who want to use Dreamweaver UltraDev 4 to quickly develop Web applications. Even if you are new to Web designing or Web programming, you will find in this book all that you need to know about designing a Web site as well as adding dynamic features to it.

How This Book Is Organized

This book is divided into five parts. Each part covers a specific topic that you will need to know in order to use Dreamweaver UltraDev 4 to develop Web applications. Part I introduces you to the features of Dreamweaver UltraDev 4. If you already familiar with database concepts and server-side programming, you can skip Part II, which deals with database and server-side programming concepts that you will need to know to use Dreamweaver UltraDev 4 more effectively. Part III walks you through the process of Web page designing. Part IV deals with the tasks involved in connecting to a database, querying the database, and displaying dynamic data, apart from adding other dynamic features that require server-side programming. At the end of the every chapter in Parts III and IV, you will find the "Activity Corner" section. This section builds upon the features that you have learned in the chapter by guiding you through the process of creating a sample application. When you complete reading these two parts, you will have developed a complete dynamic Web application. Part V deals with writing programs to extend Dreamweaver UltraDev 4.

Part I, "Getting Ready to Work with Dreamweaver UltraDev 4," is an introduction to Dreamweaver UltraDev 4. Chapter 1, "Presenting Dreamweaver UltraDev 4," is a roadmap to the entire book. It introduces you to the current Internet scenario, explaining the concepts of static and dynamic content, as well as server-side and client-side scripting. It describes the features of Dreamweaver UltraDev 4 in brief and gives an overview of the kind of applications that can be built with Dreamweaver UltraDev 4. Chapter 2, "The UltraDev 4 Environment," introduces you to all the components of the Dreamweaver UltraDev 4 interface so that you can quickly start using the tool to create your Web applications.

Part II, "Understanding Databases, ASP, JSP, and ColdFusion," introduces you to the basics of relational databases as well as server-side programming. In Chapter 3, "Database Essentials," you will learn about the fundamental concepts of relational database design. You will also be introduced to using Structured Query Language (SQL) statements to create a database in SQL Server and retrieve data from it. You will also learn how to create a database, link database tables, and create queries to retrieve the records in the tables in Appendix D, "Creating a Database Using Microsoft Access." Chapters 4, 5, and 6 deal with the basics of ASP, JSP, and ColdFusion programming, respectively. They introduce you to all the fundamental concepts that you need to know about server-side scripting in order to make the maximum use of Dreamweaver UltraDev 4.

Part III, "Designing Web Pages Using Dreamweaver UltraDev 4," covers the entire range of activities that you need to do to design a page. It details the process of laying out a page, creating tables, forms, and frames, inserting images, ActiveX objects, and Java applets, as well as adding client-side behaviors. You will also learn about utilizing Dreamweaver tools to optimize your work. The "Activity Corner" sections in this part guide you through the process of designing a sample Web application.

Part IV, "Creating Dynamic Web Pages," deals with the tasks involved in adding dynamic content to a Web page. It explains the tasks involved in connecting to a database from ASP, JSP, and ColdFusion applications and retrieving records to display dynamic data. In the Activity Corner sections in this part, you will learn how to display dynamic data in the sample Web site that you designed in Part III. You will also be creating a shopping cart, and managing its contents as well as creating registration and login pages.

Part V, "Extending the Capabilities of Dreamweaver UltraDev 4," deals with developing extensions to enhance the features of Dreamweaver UltraDev 4. You will be introduced to the architecture and API functions of Dreamweaver UltraDev 4. You will learn to create simple interface extensions by writing programs using API functions.

The appendixes in this book contain a quick reference to XML, JavaScript, and HTML, listing of Web sites that provide information on ASP, JSP, and ColdFusion as well as steps to install and configure IIS 4.0, SQL Server 7.0, ColdFusion 4.5, Dreamweaver UltraDev 4, and Allaire JRun 3.0 to start you off with using Dreamweaver UltraDev right away.

How to Use This Book

This book uses various stylistic and typographic conventions to make it easier to use.

> **Note**
>
> When you see a note in this book, it indicates additional information that can help you better understand a topic or avoid problems related to the subject at hand.

> **Tip**
>
> Tips introduce techniques applied by experienced developers to simplify a task or to produce a better design. The goal of a tip is to help you apply standard practices that lead to robust and maintainable applications.

> **Caution**
>
> Cautions warn you of hazardous procedures (for example, actions that have the potential to compromise the security of a system).

Cross-references are used throughout the book to help you quickly access related information in other chapters.

→ For an introduction to the terminology associated with transactions, **see** "Understanding Transactions," **p. xxx**.

Many of the chapters in this book conclude with a "Troubleshooting" section that provides solutions to some of the common problems that you might encounter while you work with a particular topic. Throughout the main chapter text, cross-references such as these are included to direct you to the appropriate heading within the "Troubleshooting" section to address these problems.

Beginning in Chapter 7 and continuing through Chapter 21, there are also "Activity Corner" sections that help you get to work building actual applications with Dreamweaver UltraDev 4. The files associated with the Activity Corners are available on the Web. Go to www.quepublishing.com and type the ISBN for this book (0789725770) in the Search field to find these files.

PART 1

GETTING READY TO WORK WITH DREAMWEAVER ULTRADEV 4

1 Presenting Dreamweaver UltraDev 4 7

2 The UltraDev 4 Environment 23

CHAPTER 1

Presenting Dreamweaver UltraDev 4

In this chapter

Introducing Dreamweaver UltraDev 4   8

The Evolution of Dreamweaver UltraDev 4   9

The Features of Dreamweaver UltraDev 4   13

Web Applications and UltraDev 4   19

Summary   21

Introducing Dreamweaver UltraDev 4

Macromedia Dreamweaver UltraDev 4 is an integrated Web development environment for designing and building Web applications. UltraDev 4 supports three different application-building environments, better known as server technologies: Microsoft's Active Server Pages (ASP), Sun's JavaServer Pages (JSP), and Macromedia's ColdFusion. (ColdFusion was a product of Allaire Corporation but now is included in the Macromedia product line after the merger of Allaire with Macromedia.) Macromedia's Web site design and management tool, Dreamweaver 4, is integrated with UltraDev 4 to give you a visual environment for developing and managing Web applications.

With Dreamweaver UltraDev 4 (called UltraDev 4 for short), you can build dynamic Web applications that can connect to a database and display updated information as users request it. To connect to and retrieve information from a database, a Web application uses an application server associated with a specific server technology. The application server connects to the database, retrieves information from it, processes this information, and sends it to the browser, which then displays it to the user. To perform these tasks, the application server executes the instructions contained in server-side programs.

To write these programs, you require knowledge of a server technology, such as ASP, JSP, or ColdFusion, and the scripting language associated with that technology. For example, if you want to build a dynamic Web application by using the ASP server technology, you need to have a good knowledge of ASP and the associated scripting language, such as VBScript or JavaScript. Hand coding these server-side programs demands a lot of time and effort, in terms of understanding the technology and writing the programs.

The UltraDev 4 interface provides you with a set of easy-to-use application-building tools that shield you from the complexity of writing server-side programs for an ASP, JSP, or ColdFusion server.

With UltraDev 4, you can design your page without even needing to write Hypertext Markup Language (HTML) code. As you design your page in UltraDev's visual environment and add server-side logic using the application-building tools, the underlying code is automatically generated. For those developers who want to add custom-designed features to their Web applications, UltraDev 4 provides a set of tools that enable you to write your own code.

UltraDev 4 enables you to connect to a wide variety of databases, such as Informix, Microsoft Access, Microsoft SQL Server, Oracle, or Sybase. It supports servers such as Microsoft Internet Information Server, Allaire ColdFusion Server, IBM WebSphere, BEA WebLogic, and Netscape Enterprise Server. Other servers, such as Tango and servers that support PHP, can be added through plug-ins. UltraDev 4 works under both the Windows and Macintosh operating systems. In addition, the fact that it supports the ASP, JSP, and ColdFusion development environments makes it a true cross-platform solution.

The friendly and powerful user interface of UltraDev 4 brings the power of the Web effortlessly into the hands of the novice. All it takes is a few correct clicks and beginners will be well on their way to building Web applications.

For Dreamweaver 4 users, upgrading to UltraDev 4 is no effort at all, as UltraDev 4 shares all the features present in Dreamweaver 4, some of which are as follows:

- Code editing and debugging features, such as the O'Reilly code reference for HTML, JavaScript, and CSS, the JavaScript debugger, and the integrated code editor
- Interface options, such as the Code, Design, Split, and Layout views
- Page design features, such as the Web-safe color picker, Cascading Style Sheets (CSS), and templates
- Multimedia support with Fireworks and Flash integration
- Site management features, such as file transfer between the remote server and the local system, Design Notes, site reporting, and integration with the WebDAV protocol and the Visual SourceSafe version control system
- Asset management with the Assets panel
- Extension Manager, which allows you to download and install extensions from the Macromedia Web site

This book provides you with all the help you need to create Web applications, from designing Web pages to adding dynamic functionality to them and publishing a complete Web site. But before you get to know the features in UltraDev 4, it helps to understand the context in which this cross-server, cross-browser product was developed.

The Evolution of Dreamweaver UltraDev 4

The world of the Internet is changing rapidly. The Internet initially began as a platform for the simple dissemination and exchange of information. With the advent of the World Wide Web, the purpose and scope of the Internet has gradually gained new dimensions. The Web has transformed the Internet into a virtual business environment. Today customers are able to use the Web to search for products from online catalogs, place orders online, and provide feedback to businesses about their products and services.

With the changing role of the Internet, the way content is presented over the Web is also changing. A few years ago, Web sites were mostly static, which meant that the content on these sites consisted of general information pages that were updated very rarely. A static Web site afforded very little in terms of user interactivity.

However, with the Internet fast changing into a virtual business environment, static Web sites are giving way to dynamic Web applications. Two main features characterize these Web applications: a high degree of user interactivity and the capability to display dynamic content in response to user requests. In other words, dynamic Web applications display content containing up-to-date information that caters to changing user preferences. Examples of dynamic content are typically the results of a search operation, personalized welcome messages that appear when a user logs on to a Web site, and constantly changing information, such as stock prices.

Displaying Dynamic Content on the Web

With the change in the type of content that is presented over the Web, the technologies that are used to render this content are also changing. To understand the context in which these technologies have originated, it is essential to first understand the way the Internet works.

The Internet works on the client/server model. In this model, the client requests a Web page from the server and the server responds to the client's request by sending the required Web page. The client in this case is a Web browser and the server is a Web server. The Web server plays a key role in determining what kind of content can be displayed on a Web page. To display static content, all that a Web server needs to do is fetch the page that is requested by the browser when the user types a Uniform Resource Locator (URL) in the browser. The page that the Web server looks for is typically an HTML page that contains information about the way the browser must render the page.

However, the Web server and HTML are severely limited when it comes to displaying dynamic content. Many server-side processing tasks are involved in displaying dynamic content, such as connecting to databases, retrieving data from them, processing the retrieved data, and then passing this data to the browser in an HTML format. The Web server is not fully equipped to carry out these tasks on its own. HTML also does not have capabilities to perform such tasks. Therefore, server-side programs, or scripts, are required to take care of these server-side processing tasks.

In the early days of dynamic Web pages, server-side processing was achieved by writing server-side scripts, known as Common Gateway Interface (CGI) scripts, in Perl or C. These scripts were applications that allowed the server to process data received from the browser. Although CGI scripts offered database features and helped to create customizable Web sites, they also suffered from certain shortcomings. They were very slow, required an interpreter to be installed on the server, and did not lend themselves to modification easily.

Other server-side technologies arrived on the scene to address the shortcomings of CGI scripts. The first of these technologies was Active Server Pages, which has been followed by JavaServer Pages and ColdFusion. These technologies come with a set of application-building tools. Of these tools, the application server and the scripting language play a key role in enabling dynamic content. See Part II of this book for more information on these technologies.

Responding to User Actions on the Client

Displaying dynamic content in response to user requests is only part of the interactivity offered by a Web page. Interactivity also refers to the capability of a browser to respond to simple user actions, such as pointing to a particular element on the Web page or entering form data.

To respond to such user actions, certain simple processing tasks are required that need not be directed to the server and can be carried out on the browser's end. Executing such simple processing tasks on the client side enables quick responses to user actions, as the waiting time spent in communicating with the server is reduced. The load on the server is also reduced. For example, when a user fills a form on a Web page, the validation of input data can be done on the client side to give faster feedback to the user. Nowadays, Web sites are designed to enable quick responses in spite of slow connection speeds. Therefore, when creating a Web site, developers decide which processing tasks need to be done on the client or the server and build the Web site accordingly.

A browser cannot carry out client-side processing tasks on its own. It relies on client-side scripts, which contain the instructions necessary to respond to user actions. In client-side programming parlance, user actions are known as *events*. Execution of client-side scripts is event-based, which means that the browser executes the code contained in these scripts only when the events mentioned in these scripts occur on the browser. Client-side scripts are written using scripting languages, such as VBScript or JavaScript, which are then embedded within an HTML page.

Although client-side scripts provide browsers with enhanced capabilities to respond to user actions, they pose a major problem in terms of security. It is quite possible for a user to change the client-side code contained in an HTML page, because the scripts embedded in the HTML page are downloaded along with the page. In addition, client-side scripts do not possess advanced capabilities, such as connecting to a database and retrieving information. Therefore, it is necessary to augment the functionality of a Web page containing client-side scripts with server-side scripts as well.

MACROMEDIA'S WEB PAGE DESIGN AND DEVELOPMENT SOLUTION

In the days of static content, HTML editors ruled the roost, featuring the What You See Is What You Get (WYSIWYG) interface, which relieved designers from much of the tedium of hand coding. These editors sported a Graphical User Interface (GUI) that greatly improved the look and feel of the work environment and was efficient enough to automatically generate HTML tags with a few clicks. Some editors also provided sophisticated link-management features.

However, HTML editors suffered from the major drawback of generating browser-specific code, such as the MARQUEE tag, which worked only in Internet Explorer 3, and the MULTICOL tag, which worked only in Netscape Navigator. The code these editors generated was difficult to debug and occupied a lot of memory as well. There was no standard code that would run well in all browsers. Therefore, when the Web development community began to feel the need for the standardization of HTML, the World Wide Web Consortium (W3C) was created to set the standards. Macromedia's Dreamweaver 3 was one of the few versatile WYSIWYG tools that provided a platform to implement HTML as per the W3C specifications. Dreamweaver 3 also provided support for Cascading Style Sheets (CSS) and layers. CSS and layers give designers more control over the style and positioning of page elements. These can be combined with JavaScript to add powerful client-side interactivity to a Web page. Dreamweaver 3 came with a set of prewritten client-side scripts that combined the power of CSS, layers, and JavaScript to give designers a ready-made solution to add interactive features to their Web sites.

Features such as site management and team collaboration gave designers greater control over their sites and better coordination within their development teams.

Enter UltraDev 1

Although Dreamweaver 3 took into consideration all aspects of client-side scripting, server-side scripting remained largely in the hands of programmers who had proficiency in using server technologies, such as ASP, ColdFusion, and JSP. Web designers and Web developers worked separately to create pages. Designers designed the look of Web pages and added client-side interactivity to them, whereas developers added the server-side logic to these pages. The eventual merger of client-side page design and server-side programming logic often led to the discovery of errors in integration well after the site was hosted. There was no common platform from which both client-side page design and server-side programming could be achieved.

Macromedia took its first step toward combining client-side page design and server-side programming in a single product with its acquisition of Elemental Software, the maker of Drumbeat, in February 1999. Drumbeat was a Web application development program that supported the creation of ASPs and JSPs. Macromedia combined the features available in Drumbeat with all the features of Dreamweaver 3 to create a new product, Dreamweaver UltraDev 1. This product sported the familiar Dreamweaver interface with all the Web page design features of Dreamweaver 3 and the server-side programming features of Drumbeat. It became the first Web development tool to pioneer an integrated development environment for building ASP, JSP, and ColdFusion applications. It relieved the developer of having to write code for server-side development and brought the Web designer and the developer into a common authoring environment.

UltraDev 1 provided developers with some basic server-side scripts, leaving them wishing for more complex ones. The interface components in UltraDev 1, such as the Data Bindings and Server Behaviors panels, were not integrated smoothly with the Dreamweaver interface. Moreover, UltraDev 1 had problems implementing application development features for ColdFusion. Therefore, the Web developer community was left wishing for more from the UltraDev product.

UltraDev 4

Soon after Macromedia released its next version of Dreamweaver, version 4, it went on to release the next version of UltraDev 1. This new version addressed the shortcomings of UltraDev 1. It added onto UltraDev 1 by building on features such as hand coding, remote database connectivity, server behaviors, and extensibility. This improved version contained all the features of Dreamweaver 4 and therefore was released as Dreamweaver UltraDev 4.

Hand coding is improved in UltraDev 4. The integrated text editor provides features such as syntax coloring, auto-indenting, and punctuation-balancing.

The remote database connectivity feature is also improved in UltraDev 4. In UltraDev 1, Macintosh users had difficulty connecting to a database. However, in UltraDev 4 database connections are achieved using the Hypertext Transfer Protocol (HTTP), which makes it easy for both Macintosh and Windows users to connect to databases. UltraDev 4 allows you specify a one-time connection to be used both at design time and runtime. There is no need to set up ODBC or JDBC drivers on the development machine in order to connect to the database.

→ For more information on JDBC and ODBC drivers, **see** "An Overview of ODBC, OLEDB, and JDBC," **p. 342**.

New in UltraDev 4 are server behaviors that help you regulate site access, as well as live objects that help you create recordset navigation bars and database update forms.

With UltraDev 4, you can streamline your Web development process by connecting to Microsoft Visual SourceSafe, the leading version control system. UltraDev 4 also provides integration with the Web-based Distributed Authoring and Versioning (WebDAV) protocol. WebDAV is a set of standard extensions to HTTP that manage metadata, namespaces, and versions to prevent overwrites.

The Features of Dreamweaver UltraDev 4

The following sections discuss in brief the features of UltraDev 4 that help you create dynamic Web applications. They also describe all the features of Dreamweaver 4 that are integrated with UltraDev 4.

Database-Driven Dynamic Web Applications

UltraDev 4 enables you to create database-driven Web applications with its single-point remote database connectivity feature. This feature allows you to specify a direct connection instead of specifying separate connections on the server and your machine. This single connection comes in handy during both design time and runtime. At design time, UltraDev uses this connection to let you preview the data retrieved from the database, and at runtime it uses the same connection to display the retrieved data on the browser. You specify the database connection once in UltraDev 4, and it retains this connection for subsequent sessions. You create the database connection by means of an easy-to-use interface that hides all of the technical details involved in writing server-side scripts to connect to a database. Information from databases can be added to your page instantaneously through the Data Bindings panel, which shields you from the complexity of writing code to do so.

Built-In Support for Server-Side Processing

UltraDev 4 supports servers such as Microsoft Internet Information Server (IIS), Allaire ColdFusion, IBM WebSphere, BEA WebLogic, and Netscape Enterprise Server. Other servers, such as Tango and servers that support PHP, can be added through plug-ins. Support for server-side scripting languages allows you to build applications for most ASP, JSP, and ColdFusion servers.

You can add server-side logic to your Web page by using the server-side behaviors available in the server behavior library. A set of predefined objects enables you to incorporate certain common features in your Web applications, such as recordset navigation bars and recordset statistics. Updating a database becomes easy with the Insert Record, Update Record, and Delete Record server behaviors. You can regulate site access by using the User Authentication server behavior, which allows you to password protect sites. Figure 1.1 shows the Server Behaviors panel with a list of the built-in server behaviors.

Figure 1.1
The Server Behaviors panel not only comes with a set of pre-defined server behaviors, but also allows for creating customized behaviors.

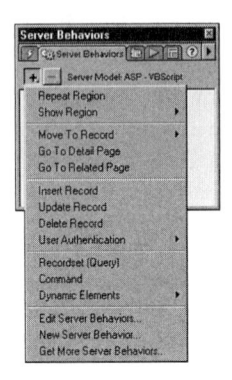

You can add these server behaviors to your Web pages by means of simple point-and-click actions, thus eliminating the need to write complex programs. Also, you can add these server behaviors to your page without needing to write server-side includes. You can also create your own server behaviors by using the server behavior builder. You can record server behaviors you use often so that the next time you apply them you can save a lot of time and effort.

→ For more information on server behaviors, **see** "Adding Dynamic Elements to a Web Page," **p. 384**.

The single-platform support for building ASP, JSP, and ColdFusion Markup Language (CFML) pages provides developers with a welcome break from the normal practice of switching to different development environments to meet client needs. To build ASP, JSP, and ColdFusion sites from UltraDev 4, it is not mandatory to know the respective scripting languages. All you need to do is specify the required server technology, and UltraDev 4 generates the code for you. However, a little bit of scripting knowledge comes in handy when you need to troubleshoot problems. This book provides you with the basic scripting knowledge necessary to understand and debug your scripts.

With the Roundtrip Server Markup feature, UltraDev 4 recognizes the code in ASP, JSP, and ColdFusion tags and doesn't mark them as errors. When you add server behaviors and other objects to your pages, the code is generated automatically, which eliminates the need to upload any extra files to your server.

Ask Your Favorite Bookseller About
The New Perl Resource Kit from O'Reilly

If you're serious about tapping the power of Perl, check out the new "must-have" in Perl programming: The *Perl Resource Kit* from O'Reilly. Available in both UNIX and Win32 editions. The *Perl Resource Kit* is the most comprehensive and useful collection of Perl software and documentation ever made available.

Both kits include multiple tutorial and reference books, with over 1,000 pages of invaluable documentation, plus essential Perl software tools all on one convenient CD-ROM, including:

- *A snapshot of the entire Comprehensive Perl Archive Network (CPAN). The Resource Kit's CPAN Connector automatically determines whether a newer version of any module exists on CPAN online.*

The UNIX edition includes:

- *A Java™/Perl interface, written specifically for the kit by Larry Wall, creator of Perl.*

The Win32 edition includes:

- *New software written by Dick Hardt, creator of Perl for Win32, including a Win32 debugger.*

**Ask your favorite bookseller about The Perl Resource Kit today!
For more information go to http://perl.oreilly.com or call 800-998-9938 or 707-829-0515.**

Part # 8019B

HOW TO GET
MORE
OUT OF...

Ask your favorite bookseller about *The Perl Resource Kit* today! For more information go to

http://perl.oreilly.com
or call 800-998-9938
or 707-829-0515

O'REILLY™

Live Data View

The live data feature of UltraDev 4 enables you to view dynamic data at design time. After you have specified a data source, you can bind the required field from the data source to the page element where you want the live data to appear. In the Design view, the bound data source appears within a placeholder. When you switch to the Live Data view, you can see the actual value of the field you have bound.

The Live Data view helps you to figure out inconsistencies during design time instead of waiting for them to crop up after the page is published. As live data appears in the edit mode, you can continue formatting dynamic data during preview. Another notable feature of dynamic data formatting is that you can apply format styles without having to write code.

The SQL query editor of UltraDev 4 allows you to test any SQL statements that you might write to query your database. It provides drag-and-drop features to reduce the amount of time you have to spend typing out queries.

Customizable Environment

The live data preview is customizable. Similarly, keyboard shortcuts, menus, objects, behaviors, and data formats are also customizable. You can customize keyboard shortcuts by using the keyboard shortcut editor. You can add an entire menu or remove menu items by making changes to a single XML file, which contains the structure for the menus.

You can extend the capabilities of UltraDev 4 to suit a variety of user requirements. UltraDev 4 has a flexible extensibility model. Because many features of UltraDev 4 are written in XML and JavaScript, it is easy to develop your own extensions. Extension Manager, which comes with UltraDev 4, is a versatile tool for installing and managing extensions. At Macromedia Exchange, (http://www.macromedia.com/exchange/ultradev/), you can find an impressive collection of objects, behaviors, and commands contributed by the UltraDev Web developer community. You can also participate in discussion forums at this site.

The Dreamweaver Design Environment

UltraDev 4 includes the Layout view feature of Dreamweaver, using which you can create complex tables that are browser-compatible. The Layout view gives you complete control over the way your page elements are presented in the form of tables, without the hitches inherent in using tables. Complex page design becomes easy with the capability to directly drag and drop cells on the page and precisely position elements. Using the layout feature, complex nested tables can be un-nested easily.

The integrated text editor features syntax coloring for ASP, JSP, JavaScript, HTML, and CFML tags. As you type code, the syntax coloring feature automatically colors different elements, such as keywords and tags, in different colors. This helps you identify different code elements while debugging. You can also edit non-HTML documents, such as JavaScript, XML, and other text files, in the text editor. The Code View toolbar in the text editor contains a drop-down list that enables you to easily navigate to JavaScript functions and edit them.

The editor also recognizes non-HTML files, such as `global.asa`, `application.cfm`, and server-side includes. You have the flexibility of indenting multiple selected lines as well as enabling or disabling word wrap and line numbering. UltraDev 4 also comes with a trial version of BBEdit 6.0 for Macintosh users and HomeSite 4.5 for Windows users.

> **Tip**
> If you still prefer your favorite text editor to the native editor of UltraDev 4, you can set your preferred editor as the default editor by using the Preferences option of the Edit menu.

With the Roundtrip HTML feature, changes made to the code in the Code view are instantly reflected in the Design view, eliminating the need to open a separate browser window to view the changes. You can save time and maintain control over your code as well. You can edit HTML code in BBEdit or HomeSite and view the resuts in Dreamweaver without overwrites to handwritten tags.

The split view improves the process of page design. Using the split view, you can see the page design and the code in two panes in the same window. When you select an element in the Design view, the corresponding tag is highlighted in the Code view. Figure 1.2 illustrates the split view feature.

Figure 1.2
The split view allows you to see the Code view and the Design view simultaneously.

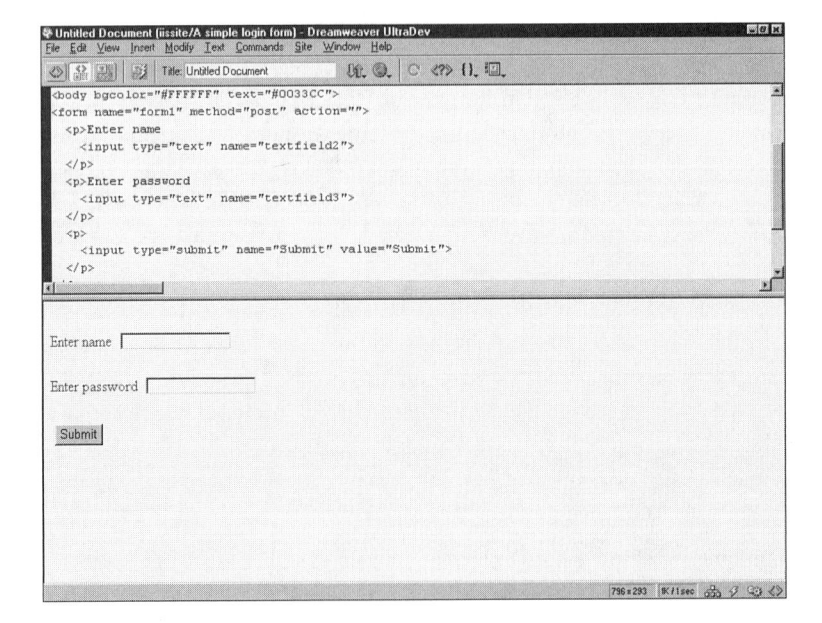

While you are designing a particular element, you can edit the code associated with the element in Quick Tag Editor. Figure 1.3 shows the Quick Tag Editor. You can also use the drop-down list in the Code View toolbar to navigate quickly to the code you want to edit.

Figure 1.3
Quick Tag Editor allows you to edit one element at a time.

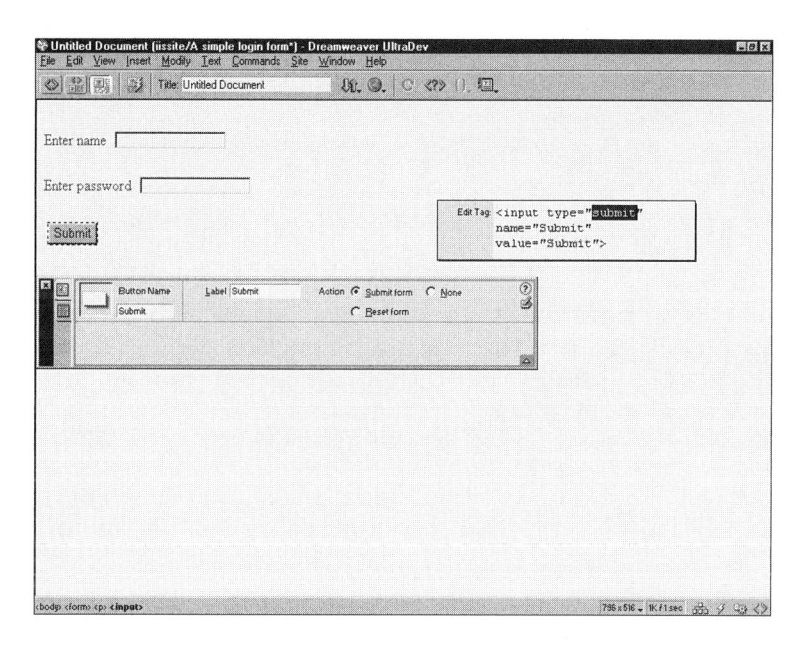

Editing graphics becomes easy as Fireworks is integrated with UltraDev 4. This integration provides you with a quick way of opening and editing graphics in Fireworks. You just need to double-click the graphic while holding down the Ctrl or Command key (depending on whether you are working on a Windows or Macintosh computer, respectively) to open the source file in Fireworks. Fireworks and UltraDev 4 recognize and preserve each other's code. Therefore, changes made to any graphic element can be incorporated easily in an UltraDev 4 page without making changes to HTML tables.

Support is also provided for Macromedia Flash, Freehand, Shockwave, Generator, QuickTime, and Real content, which helps you insert these movie files and objects into UltraDev 4 pages.

UltraDev 4 complies fully with W3C standards, supporting HTML styles and CSS. Using CSS and HTML styles, you can apply custom-defined fonts, colors, margins, and other styles to selected elements across documents in your Web sites. The Web-safe eyedropper allows you to pick colors from anywhere on the screen and apply the nearest Web-safe matching color to page elements.

You can easily add Flash effects to your page using the built-in Flash text and buttons. You can insert a set of predefined Flash objects by using the Objects panel. These Flash objects make ready-made vector graphics available to your site, which makes your site attractive without compromising on download time.

Note

You can download a number of free Flash button styles from Macromedia Exchange at the URL http://www.macromedia.com/exchange/ultradev/.

UltraDev 4 integrates well with Adobe Photoshop and Microsoft Office. You can import data delimited by tabs, spaces, commas, or other special characters from text files. Word HTML files can be imported into UltraDev 4. The Clean-up Word HTML feature automatically removes nonstandard tags from Word HTML documents as well as proprietary XML and CSS tags.

The History palette allows you to undo and redo actions. It also enables you to combine a number of steps into a single command that you can apply to other pages later.

You can use templates to optimize your work. Templates allow you to apply a consistent design to all pages across your site. You can specify editable and noneditable regions in a template, where editable regions can be identified by a bounding rectangle that contains the name of the editable region.

The Assets panel scans for all types of site media in your site and pools them in a single location. You can also preview multimedia files, URLs, templates, library items, colors, and scripts in the Assets panel. You can organize these assets by saving them as favorites. This helps you reuse them in other documents across multiple sites.

The live JavaScript debugger feature allows you to debug code as it executes in your browser. You can use this feature to test how JavaScript code behaves in different browsers. You can set breakpoints inside an HTML page or a JavaScript file and step through code to detect bugs. The integrated code reference feature has compiled information from O'Reilly publications such as *HTML: The Definitive Guide*, *CSS: The Definitive Guide*, and *JavaScript: The Definitive Guide* on the usage of the respective languages. You can catch a quick glimpse of JavaScript, HTML, and CSS usage either by typing in a keyword in the O'Reilly Reference window or by highlighting code in the Code view and clicking on the Reference tool button.

SITE MANAGEMENT

The Site window in UltraDev 4 helps you to build and manage sites. Creating files, adding links, and moving and removing links can all be done through this single window. You can see the site map in the Site window, which helps you track missing or broken links. FTP is integrated with the Site window to give you a faster and simpler way to upload files to the remote server. You can also synchronize files between the local machine and the remote server.

The site reporting feature helps you to find problems, such as untitled pages or missing links, in your HTML pages. To access the erroneous code, all you need to do is click the reported error.

The XML-based Design Notes tool in UltraDev 4 helps improve team collaboration. Users can attach workflow status and comments to every file a team member has changed or updated by using Design Notes. The integrated e-mail facility also enhances team collaboration.

Web development in a collaborative work environment becomes easier as UltraDev 4 allows integration with the Microsoft Visual SourceSafe version control system. You can upload application files to Visual SourceSafe and manage file check-in and check–out among team members. You can connect to Web servers, such as Windows IIS5 and Apache, that support the WebDAV protocol, and to WebDAV-compliant content management systems, such as Broadvision, Vignette, Documentum, and ATG.

Web Applications and UltraDev 4

Web applications are powering businesses today. Be it dotcom companies that aim to create interactive and personalized Web sites or organizations that venture into intranet technology to streamline their business processes, data-driven applications are the key to implementing their strategies. Web developers and designers are leveraging the power of dynamic sites to provide a meaningful browsing experience to the user.

Web applications range from simple registration forms toonline shopping malls and online training and testing programs. For building each of these types of Web applications, an integrated and flexible development environment that provides a cross-platform and scalable solution is required.

Personalized Web Sites

As the name implies, personalized Web sites display customized information where the user decides the extent of personalization. This attracts a lot of users, as they can do away with subjects that are irrelevant to them. Personalization gains more relevance in the context of addressing a global audience. When the site addresses a global audience, regional differences can be overcome by tailoring the Web site to suit different user preferences.

The logic underlying personalized Web sites is to store the settings that the user makes to that Web site in a database. The next time the user logs on, this information is retrieved and used to display the Web page the way the user customized it. The real challenge here is that of making the site work when the same user logs on from another machine with a different browser or with totally different settings.

You can create personalized Web sites with UltraDev 4 by using server behaviors to create a registration and logon page that accepts and stores data a user enters in a database from which the data can be retrieved the next time the user logs in to the site.

→ For more information on creating the logon page, **see** "Creating a Logon Page," **p. 437**.
→ For more information on creating the registration page, **see** "Creating a Registration Page," **p. 432**.

Interactive Web Sites

Gone are the days of good old static pages where Web sites displayed reams of text interspersed with only a few images. Today, Web sites are loaded with multimedia files that engage the user with their many interactive features. The content on these sites is updated on a day-to-day basis. The introduction of sound has added a new dimension to the silent realm of the Web. The addition of an audio component has made Web sites accessible to people with visual disabilities.

Discussion forums, e-commerce sites, and educational sites are some of the interactive sites that have become immensely popular today. Discussion forums help bring people with common interests together. They provide a single platform to share and disseminate information. Features such as posting queries and viewing the results by sorting according to date and topic are possible only with a technology that provides an integrated database search-and-retrieval solution. The information to be displayed on the Web page can be stored in a database and then retrieved by means of a query.

E-commerce sites such as shopping malls and online bookstores allow users to select products according to their preferences by using a similar database approach. Online educational testing systems use this approach to conduct tests whereby the test questions are stored in a database. Score information is updated in the database and then delivered to the user on request.

You can build all of these features, which are achieved by means of database interactions, into your Web pages by using the panels in UltraDev 4. You can use the Data Bindings panel in UltraDev 4 to create a recordset that displays specific records from a database based on a query entered in the SQL query editor. To update user queries and answers in the database, you can use server behaviors such as Update Record.

Intranets

Businesses are using intranets to improve organizational productivity and communication. They use intranets to share up-to-date critical information among their employees. Intranets address every aspect of an organization's concerns, such as employee information management, knowledge management, sales and product management, and financial management. Employees can look to their corporate intranets for anything ranging from information on their pay details to documents containing organizational policies and procedures. An intranet of an organization can be used as a knowledge management tool by making a knowledge database available to employees where their account of the knowledge and experience gained in their areas of expertise can be stored. Status reports on the financial performance of businesses in an organization can also be made available on an intranet. Product inventory status and sales trends can also be shared throughout the organization using an intranet.

Intranets are able to bring employees and information closer together by following the same database approach discussed in the previous section on interactive Web sites. Maintaining updated information in a database and making that available to organizational units spread across geographical areas is vital to the success of an intranet.

UltraDev 4 helps you to create intranets using its information retrieval and site management features that will be discussed in detail in the chapters to follow. Database processing functions are well encapsulated in the interface, providing you a clean design environment to work with. UltraDev 4 not only provides all the basic features needed to develop dynamic Web applications, but also makes provisions for developers to add more functionality to their applications. The following chapters in this book will guide you to make effective use of UltraDev 4 and add the best of features to your Web application.

Summary

UltraDev 4 is a Web application design and development tool that adds dynamic functionality to your Web pages. It builds on Dreamweaver capabilities to provide server-side dynamism to your Web pages. Web designers can migrate to UltraDev 4 if they want to add server-side code to their Web pages. Developers who had to switch over to different application-building environments to suit client needs can now use a common development environment to build JSP, ASP, and ColdFusion applications.

UltraDev 4 has code generation capabilities that eliminate the need to write code to create pages for ASP, JSP, or ColdFusion environments. Low-level details involved in connecting to and interacting with a database are well encapsulated in the UltraDev 4 interface.

Because UltraDev 4 includes all of the Dreamweaver features, you get a holistic Web development environment that provides you with tools that assist you from the stage of designing a page to making it dynamic and publishing it.

CHAPTER 2

THE ULTRADEV 4 ENVIRONMENT

In this chapter

The UltraDev Workflow   24

The UltraDev Interface   26

Menus and Toolbar Buttons   27

Summary   41

The UltraDev Workflow

The process of building Web applications has two marked phases, one of creating a page design and the other of adding dynamic functionality to the page.

The tools and features of UltraDev aid in the entire process of developing dynamic Web applications, from the page design phase to that of hosting the Web application on a server. As Web development happens in a step-by-step process, it helps to learn how the UltraDev environment models the development process.

This section gives an overview of the various tasks required to build Web applications. It also gives a brief description of the various tools that UltraDev provides in order to carry out these tasks.

There are four distinct phases in the UltraDev workflow pattern. These phases are as follows:

1. Design and lay out a page.
2. Specify sources of data from which dynamic content will be added to the page.
3. Add dynamic content to the page.
4. Extend the functionality of the page.

Designing a Page

Page design in UltraDev follows an approach similar to Dreamweaver. You can use layers or tables for page layout. After you lay out a page, you can add elements, such as text, images, and forms, to the page. Forms are an important component of dynamic Web applications because they are essential for including interactivity in a page.

If pages are going to have dynamic content displayed in them, it is best to decide in advance what elements in a page are going to be dynamic. This allows the designer to decide on alternative design strategies to be applied to the dynamic elements. One such design decision can be the space that must be allotted to the dynamic elements.

For example, if you plan to include a logon feature in your Web site, you can also display a personalized welcome message to greet the user by name after the logon is successful. In this case, the welcome message will have a dynamic text, which contains the name of the user. Deciding on the portion of the welcome message that contains the dynamic text allows you to decide on the space that must be allotted to this dynamic text.

Note Before you can make text or other page elements dynamic, it is necessary to create a database connection.

You should take care to ensure that the part where a dynamic element is going to appear is appropriately labeled. This makes the type of content that will appear in that element clear to the designer. As for the user who is going to view the page, labels for dynamic content explain more clearly what the information is all about.

The Live Data view allows you to see how the page will look with the actual data. As dynamic content can be previewed in the Live Data view, you can make format-related changes to the live data, depending on how the appearance of the live data affects the other elements in the page.

→ For an in-depth discussion of page layout, **see** "Page Layout," **p. 135**.

CREATING DATA SOURCES

Dynamic Web applications require a data source from which they can retrieve and display up-to-date information. Therefore, the primary step in creating dynamic pages is to identify a data source. Data sources can be databases or browser-submitted variables, such as request, application, and session variables.

→ For information on browser-submitted variables, **see** "Creating and Managing Data Sources," **p. 366**.

If you are using a database as source of data, you need to create a *recordset* in UltraDev. The recordset is a collection of fields from the specified database that the application server uses for faster data retrieval. You can use the Data Bindings panel to create a recordset. You can also use the Data Bindings panel to define other data sources, such as request, application, and session variables.

Figure 2.1 shows the Data Bindings panel that displays the data sources that can be created for an ASP server.

Figure 2.1
When you click the + button on the Data Bindings panel, it displays the options that are used to define data sources.

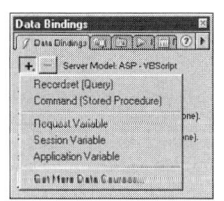

ADDING DYNAMIC FUNCTIONALITY TO A PAGE

After you have specified the data sources you want to use, the next phase involves binding the dynamic data to the elements in the page. Adding dynamic data is a simple process of dragging and dropping the required data onto the page element where you want the data to appear. UltraDev generates the server-side script when you choose the data source in the Data Bindings panel. This code directs the server to retrieve the specified data and display it on the Web page during runtime.

Extending the Functionality of a Page

Adding dynamic content by using the Data Bindings panel alone does not give your page all the functionality that you would want. You can add server behaviors and live objects to give your page more functionality. A server behavior, such as Repeat Region, allows you to display multiple records in your page, whereas a live object, such as Recordset Navigation Status, displays a record counter on your Web page.

UltraDev comes with a set of predefined objects, which you can use to introduce dynamic functionality to the page. However, if you want to create more server behaviors that give your page added functionality, you can create your own using the UltraDev Application Programming Interface (API). There are a number of freeware and shareware extensions available at Macromedia Exchange. One such extension is the Horizontal Looper 2 extension that allows you to specify the number of columns and rows you want to display on the Web page.

The UltraDev Interface

The UltraDev interface is simple and flexible, although seemingly not so the moment you open the application.

Though a number of windows appear after you start UltraDev 4, you can keep the interface as simple as you want. You can move, resize, or close the many windows that are open. You can also minimize and restore commonly used windows.

After you start UltraDev, you observe that there is a single main window on which there are a number of smaller windows. This main window is called the Document window. The other windows are the Objects panel, the Property inspector, and the Data Bindings panel. These panels are also known as *floating panels*. You can open many other floating panels by using the Window menu. If you open too many floating panels at the same time, the UltraDev interface can become cluttered. However, you can keep the interface clean by combining two or more panels into a single panel. This process of combining panels is called *docking*. In the sections that follow, each element of the UltraDev interface is explained briefly to give you an idea of the purpose served by each.

Figure 2.2 shows various components of the UltraDev interface.

The Document Window

The Document window comprises the Title bar, Menu bar, toolbar, design area, and Status bar.

The Title bar of the Document window contains the title of the current page. Next to the title, you will find the file name and the local folder in which it is stored displayed in parentheses. The design area is the place where you will create and edit the documents in your site.

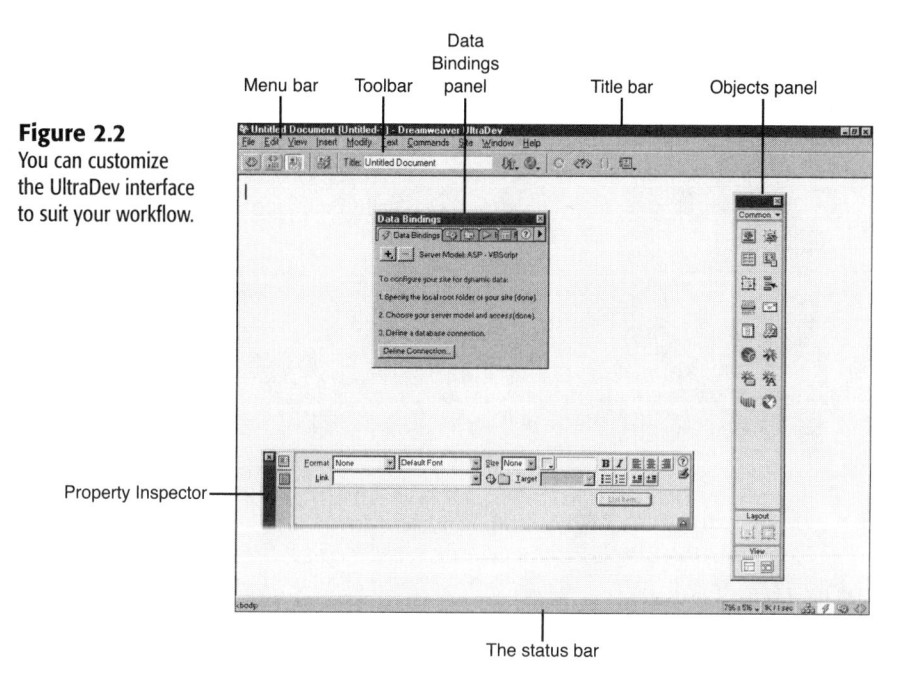

Figure 2.2
You can customize the UltraDev interface to suit your workflow.

Labels on figure: Menu bar, Toolbar, Data Bindings panel, Title bar, Objects panel, Property Inspector, The status bar

> **Tip**
> The title of your current document appears in the Title field on the toolbar. You can edit the title directly in this field.

MENUS AND TOOLBAR BUTTONS

The menu system in UltraDev provides a single-point entry to access all of the tools in UltraDev. If you familiarize yourself with all of its options, you will find it easier to navigate the interface.

This section provides a brief description of all the menu options available in UltraDev. Some of the menu options are replicated as buttons on the toolbar; these buttons are mentioned where relevant. You will find detailed instructions on how to use the various menus and buttons in the relevant chapters of Parts III and IV.

THE FILE MENU

The File menu contains options to create and manage documents. Figure 2.3 displays these options. Notice that some options have been disabled.

Chapter 2 The UltraDev 4 Environment

Figure 2.3
A closer look at the File menu reveals sets of options addressing related functions. An engraved line separates each set.

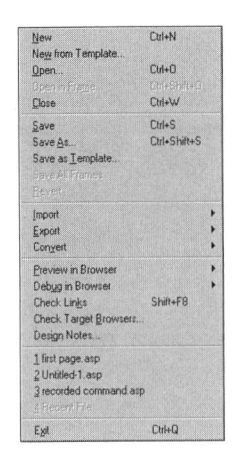

Table 2.1 lists and briefly describes each option.

TABLE 2.1 File Menu Options

Option	Description
New	Creates a new file.
New from Template	Creates a template-based file.
Open	Opens an existing document.
Open in Frame	Opens a file in a particular frame.
Close	Closes the current document.
Save	Saves a file.
Save As	Saves the current document with a name you define.
Save As Template	Saves a file as a template.
Save Frame	Saves a particular frame as a separate file.
Save All Frames	Saves all your frames at once.
Save Frame As Template	Saves a frameset as a template.
Import	Import data from an XML file and adds that data to the editable region of a template. You can also import Word HTML files and other text files containing tabular data.
Export	Exports the data contained in the editable regions of a template to an XML file. You can create new CSS style sheets by exporting CSS styles from the current document. You can also export tabular data to file formats that accept data delimited by commas, colons, semicolons, spaces, or other user-defined delimiters.

TABLE 2.1 CONTINUED

Option	Description
Convert	Converts CSS styles to HTML tags and layers to tables so you can view them in version 3.0 browsers.
Preview in Browser	Displays your current document in the default browser.
Debug in Browser	Starts the JavaScript debugger while displaying the current page in the default browser window.
Check Links	Searches the current document or the entire site for broken links and orphaned files and displays information about the search results.
Check Target Browsers	Checks whether the target browser supports all the HTML tags in the current document.
Design Notes	Attaches status and other extra information to your documents as well as elements in your documents, such as images, applets, ActiveX controls, and Flash movies.
Exit	Exits UltraDev 4.

> **Note**
> The Open in Frame, Save Frame, Save All Frames, and Save Frame as Template options are available on the File menu only when you open a document that contains frames.

> **Note**
> The functionality of the Preview in Browser and Debug in Browser options is present in the Preview/Debug button on the toolbar.

> **Tip**
> You can also access the Design Notes option by clicking the File Management button on the toolbar.

The Edit Menu

This menu provides document-editing options such as Cut, Copy, Paste, Clear, Undo, and Redo. It also has other editing features, which are outlined in Table 2.2. Figure 2.4 shows the options that are on the Edit menu.

Figure 2.4
Use the Edit menu for design editing as well as code editing.

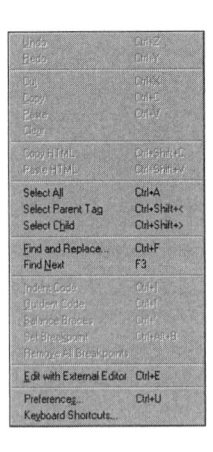

TABLE 2.2   EDIT MENU OPTIONS

Option	Description
Copy HTML	Copies the HTML code of document elements from Design view to other external text editors.
Paste HTML	Pastes HTML code copied from other external text editors.
Select Parent Tag	Selects the appropriate parent tags as you edit HTML code.
Select Child	Selects the appropriate child tags as you edit HTML code.
Indent Code	Indents code when you work in Code view.
Outdent Code	Outdents code when you work in Code view.
Balance Braces	Checks whether all opening braces in your code have closing braces.
Set Breakpoints	Stops the execution of the code at particular points so you can examine it.
Remove All Breakpoints	Removes all previously set breakpoints.
Edit with External Editor	Allows you to choose an external editor to edit your code.
Preferences	Allows you to set preferences for various interface features of UltraDev.
Keyboard Shortcuts	Allows you to create and edit shortcut keys for carrying out various tasks in UltraDev as well as BBEdit or HomeSite.

Tip

You can set and remove breakpoints by clicking the Code Navigation button on the toolbar.

Note

After you set an external editor with the Edit with External Editor option, the option name changes to Edit with `<editor name>`.

The View Menu

The View menu allows you to have flexibility over the way your working design environment looks. You can use the various options in this menu to aid you in the design process. Figure 2.5 shows the options of the View menu. Table 2.3 shows the options of the View menu.

Figure 2.5
Use the View menu to switch between various views.

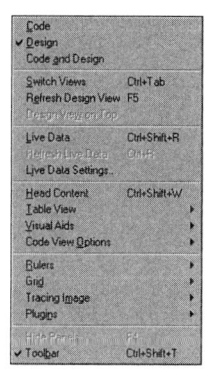

TABLE 2.3 VIEW MENU OPTIONS

Option	Description
Code	Allows you to design your page by manually writing the code for the page.
Design	Allows you to work in a visual environment without manually writing code.
Code and Design	Allows you to work in a split view with both the Code and Design views open.
Switch Views	Allows you to switch easily between the Code and Design views to see the changes made to either view immediately.
Refresh Design Views	Allows you to view the changes made to the code written in an external editor in the Design view.
Design View on Top	Allows you to keep the Design view on top when you are in the split view. The Code view appears below the Design view.
Live Data	Allows you to view the actual data that normally appears on the browser.
Head Content	Allows you to view and edit the content that appears in the HEAD tag.
Table View	Allows you to switch between the standard and the layout views.
Visual Aids	Allows you to use visual aids such as table, layer and frame borders, and image maps.
Code View Options	Allows you to set word wrap, line numbering, auto indenting, and syntax coloring in Code view.

TABLE 2.3 CONTINUED

Option	Description
Rulers	Shows or hides the ruler and displays the ruler dimensions in pixels, inches, or centimeters. If you change the origin of the ruler by dragging the ruler-origin icon found on the ruler, you can reset the origin by using the Reset Origin suboption.
Grid	Shows or hides the grid. You can snap layers to the grid by using the Snap to Grid suboption. Set the properties for the grid by using the Edit suboption.
Tracing Image	Allows you to view a tracing image in your document. Tracing images can be placed in the background of a document and used to re-create the image in the document.
Plugins	Plays plug-ins.
Hide Panels	Hides all open panels.
Toolbar	Shows or hides the toolbar.

Note: You can use the Show Code View, Show Design View, and Show Code and Design View buttons on the toolbar to switch quickly between views.

Note: These options are available from the View Options button on the toolbar.

THE INSERT MENU

The Insert menu is self-explanatory to a large extent. It lets you insert elements, such as images, layers, tables, frames, and more. The functionality of the Insert menu is replicated in the Objects panel, which is discussed a little later in the chapter. Figure 2.6 shows the options of the Insert menu.

Figure 2.6
Use the Insert menu to insert objects such as images, tables, layers, frames, and more.

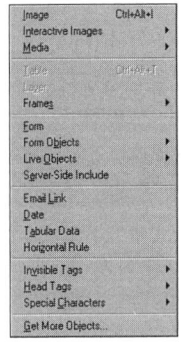

THE MODIFY MENU

This menu, as the name suggests, has options that enable you to specify or change various properties of elements in your pages. Figure 2.14 shows the options in the Modify menu. Table 2.4 briefly lists and describes these options.

Figure 2.7
Use the Modify menu to set properties for the page.

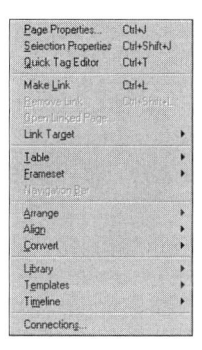

TABLE 2.4 MODIFY MENU OPTIONS

Option	Description
Page Properties	Allows you to specify the background image, colors for background, text, and links, and margin height and width for your page.
Selection Properties	Invokes the Property inspector, which sets the properties for the selected element.
Quick Tag Editor	Allows you to hand code the properties of a particular tag for a selected element. You can change the width and height of a selected image by rewriting the width and height attributes of the `<img src>` tag.
Make Link	Creates links for an element from the Insert menu.
Remove Link	Removes a particular link from a page.
Open Linked Page	Opens the page referred to by a link.
Link Target	Loads the target page in the same window or in a different window.
Table	Modifies table properties. You can add rows and columns to a table, increase or decrease row or column span, and adjust cell height and width.
Frameset	Splits existing frames. You can also edit the content that appears in browsers that do not support frames.
Navigation Bar	Modifies the properties of the Navigation Bar live object.
Arrange	Arranges the order of layers and control layer overlaps.
Align	Align a table with other elements on the page, such as text and images.
Convert	Converts layers to tables and vice versa.

Table 2.4	Continued
Option	**Description**
Library	Adds frequently used items to the library and updates pages with the library items.
Templates	Allows you to apply a particular template to the page, remove a template that has been attached, or create and remove editable regions in a template.
Timeline	Allows you to add objects, frames, keyframes, and behaviors to or remove them from the timeline.
Connections	Allows you to connect to a database.

The Text Menu

Then Text menu consists of options that allow you to format the text on the page. You can indent and outdent text, apply paragraph styles, change font size, align text, and check spelling using this menu. Figure 2.8 shows the options in this menu.

Figure 2.8
Use the Text menu to format text by applying styles.

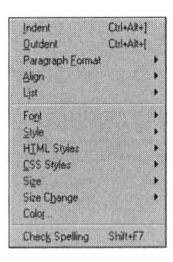

Using this menu, you can indent or outdent text, apply predefined paragraph formats, align text, and apply fonts to text. You can also apply HTML styles to your document by using the HTML styles option. This option allows you to create new styles by defining features, such as the text color, font size, and style, and decide whether to apply these styles by clearing the existing styles or by adding the new styles to the existing styles. Using the CSS styles option, you can create and edit CSS styles. You can also run the spell checker by using the Check spelling option.

The Commands Menu

The Commands menu provides a simple way to automate sets of tasks. The options in this menu appear as shown in Figure 2.9. Table 2.5 gives you a list of the menu options and a brief description of what purpose each serves.

Figure 2.9
The Commands menu provides you with macro-like functionality.

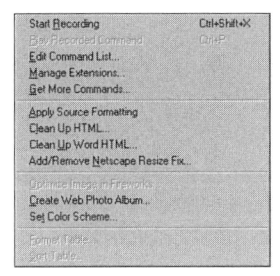

TABLE 2.5 COMMANDS MENU OPTIONS

Option	Description
Start Recording	Records a set of actions as a single command that can be later used like a macro.
Play Recorded Command	Runs a recorded command.
Edit Command List	Edits history steps that have been saved as a command.
Manage Extensions	Launches the Extension Manager, which you can use to install and remove extensions.
Get More Commands	Downloads extensions from Macromedia Exchange.
Apply Source Formatting	Applies customized formats to code.
Clean up HTML	Removes redundant nested tags and empty tags.
Clean up Word HTML	Removes proprietary tags from Word documents.
Add/Remove Netscape Resize Fix	When you use layers in your page, you must choose this option so that the layers do not lose their positions when viewed in Netscape Navigator 4.0.
Optimize Image in Fireworks	Allows you to change the optimization settings of images created in Fireworks.
Create Web Photo Album	Allows you to create a Web site containing images from your local folder. This option works only if you have Fireworks installed on your system.
Set Color Scheme	Sets default colors for text, links, visited links, and active links.
Format Table	Selects format styles for your table.
Sort Table	Sorts the data in a table.

THE SITE MENU

The Site menu consists of options that let you create and edit sites. You can open the Site window from this menu. Figure 2.10 shows the options of the Site menu.

Figure 2.10
Use the Site menu to manage sites.

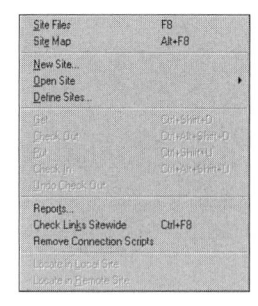

The Site window is a central location from which you can view and manage all the files in your site. Using this window you can create a new document or a site, view the site map, transfer files between your local machine and the Web server, manage the links in your site, and share files among your team members. Table 2.6 briefly lists and describes the Site menu options.

TABLE 2.6 SITE MENU OPTIONS

Option	Description
Site Files	Opens the Site window.
Site Map	Displays the site map in the Site window.
New Site	Defines a new site.
Open Site	Opens an existing site.
Define Sites	Edits the definitions of existing sites.
Get	Transfers files from the remote server.
Check Out	If you are working as a team, this option allows you to transfer a file from the remote server to your local root folder for editing. When you check out a file, it is locked so that other members do not edit it at the same time. The Checked out By column in the Site window indicates the name of the team member who has transferred the file from the remote server to edit on their local machines.
Put	Transfers files to the remote server.
Check In	Transfers a checked-out file to the remote server after you finish editing the file. This releases the file so that other team members can edit it.
Undo Check Out	Undoes the last check out from the remote server.
Reports	Allows you to generate and save reports on the status of files.

TABLE 2.6 CONTINUED

Option	Description
Check Links Sitewide	Checks the entire site for missing or broken links.
Remove Connection Scripts	Removes connection scripts uploaded to the server.
Locate in Local Site	Locates files in the local site. The specified file is highlighted in the left pane of the Site window.
Locate in Remote Site	Locates files in the remote site. The specified file is highlighted in the right pane of the Site window.

→ For more information on site definition, **see** "Creating a New Site," **p. 119**.

THE WINDOW MENU

The Window menu helps you organize your work area. You can open the Property inspector, Site Window, Launcher bar, and all the panels by using this menu. Figure 2.11 shows the options in the Window menu.

Figure 2.11
Use the Window menu to keep your work area uncluttered.

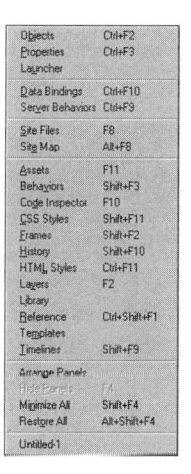

To open any window, you can choose the respective window from the Window menu. After a window is open, you see a tick mark against the name of the window on the Window menu. Clicking on the tick mark closes the window.

> **Note**
>
> You cannot create a new Document window from the Window menu. However, you can restore minimized Document windows by choosing the document title that appears on the menu.

> **Caution**
>
> In an effort to keep your workspace uncluttered, you might want to close all open windows. You must either keep the Site window or one Document window open to continue working with UltraDev. UltraDev will exit if you try to close the last Document window after closing the Site window. However, if the Site window is open, you can close the last Document window.

The Panels on the UltraDev Interface

The most important functions in UltraDev are presented through the following panels, which are listed as options in the Window menu:

- Use the Objects panel to insert elements on your page, such as special characters, images, tables, server-side includes, Flash buttons, Flash text, form objects, frames, meta tags, named anchors, server objects, java applets, ActiveX controls, and so on.
- Use the Properties panel, better known as the Property inspector, to set and change the properties of any element on the page.
- Use the Launcher as a quicker way to open the Site window, the Data Bindings panel, the Server Behaviors panel and Code Inspector, without accessing these using the menu bar or the icons on the status bar. You can customize the Launcher by adding panels to the Launcher to suit your workflow.
- Use the Data Bindings panel to create and edit data sources for your Web application.
- Use the Server Behaviors panel to add server-side logic to your Web application.
- Use the Assets panel to keep track of the assets in your document, such as images, colors, URLs, and so on.
- Use the Behaviors panel to add client-side dynamism to your page, such as playing sound, showing pop-up messages, swapping images, and so on.
- Use the Code Inspector to write and edit HTML and JavaScript code. It is very similar to working in the Code view.
- Use the CSS Styles panel to create, edit, and apply CSS styles to your document.
- Use the Frames panel to select frames and change their attributes easily.
- Use the History panel to redo and undo any changes made to your document.
- Use the HTML Styles panel to create and apply custom styles that use 3.0 compatible HTML tags to a particular selection or a paragraph in the document.
- Use the Layers panel to view and arrange the layers in your document.
- Use the Library panel to create libraries of commonly used items and update them across documents.
- The Reference panel contains the O'Reilly code reference for HTML, JavaScript, and CSS.
- Use the Templates panel to create and edit templates.

MENUS AND TOOLBAR BUTTONS | 39

> **Note**
>
> When you choose the Templates option from the Window menu, the assets panel displays with the Template icon activated, indicating the selection.

- Use the Timelines panel to create timeline animations on your page.

You can arrange and hide open panels by using the Arrange Panels and Hide Panels options. You can also minimize and restore windows using the relevant options on the window menu.

> **Tip**
>
> All floating panels, except the Property inspector and the Launcher, can be docked. *Docking* is combining one or more panels to form a single tabbed panel. You can dock two panels by dragging the tab of one panel and dropping it in another panel. You can create a single panel with multiple tabs, each tab indicating a different panel. This helps prevent cluttering of the workspace with too many panels.

PART
I
CH
2

THE HELP MENU

The Help Menu in UltraDev gives you a guided tour of UltraDev as well as a tutorial that helps you build a simple Web application. The UltraDev Exchange option takes you to Macromedia exchange from where you can share and download extensions. Figure 2.12 shows the Help menu system.

Figure 2.12
The Help menu allows you to connect to Macromedia Exchange. It features a guided tour that gives you an overview of the features of UltraDev 4.

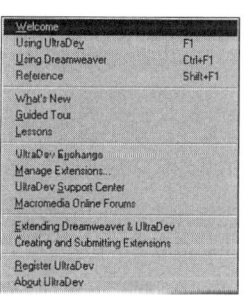

The Manage Extensions option launches the Extension Manager, which you can use to install extensions.

THE STATUS BAR

The Status bar in the Document window comprises the Tag selector, the Window Size pop-up menu, the Document Size and Estimated download Time indicator, and the Launcher bar. Figure 2.13 shows the components of the Status bar.

Figure 2.13
Click the Tag selector to highlight a section of your document.

The Tag selector • Window Size pop-up menu • The Launcher bar • Document Size and download time indicator

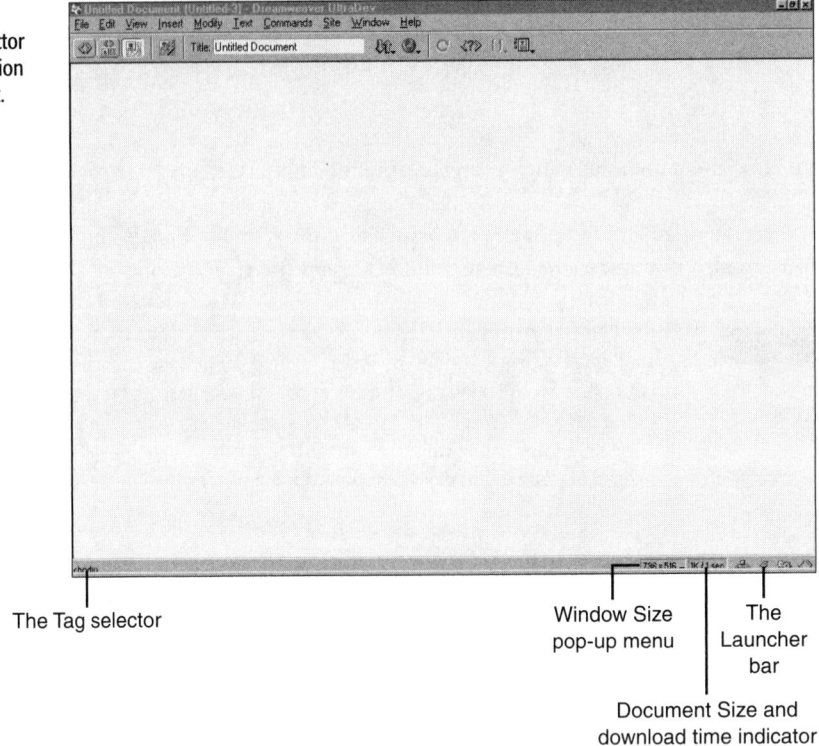

The Tag selector displays the parent tags associated with the elements on the page. You can click on a parent tag to highlight its contents on the page.

The Launcher bar can be used as a quick means of accessing the Site Window, the Data bindings panel, the Server Behaviors panel, and Code Inspector.

The Window Size pop-up menu contains a list of the different browser screen dimensions to which you can resize the window. You can use this pop-up menu to choose a particular size at which your document will look its best in the browser. You can also edit the predefined sizes or add a new size to the pop-up menu by choosing the Edit Sizes option from the pop-up menu.

The Document Size and Estimated Download Time indicator calculates the size of the document inclusive of all objects such as images and plug-ins. It also estimates the time that a document of a particular calculated size will take to download. This indicator helps you to design documents that will take no longer than a few seconds to download.

Summary

The UltraDev 4 workflow consists of four phases: creating a site design, connecting to a database, adding dynamic functionality, and extending the functionality of the page. UltraDev 4 has tools and features that help you through these phases to create dynamic Web applications.

The UltraDev 4 interface is an easy-to use interface that can be organized in a way that suits your work style best. The UltraDev 4 interface consists of the Document window, the Menu bar, the toolbar, the Status bar, and floating panels.

Most of the options available in the menu system are available in the floating panels and the buttons. UltraDev, on the whole, provides a GUI interface that reduces the time and effort spent in building dynamic Web applications.

PART II

UNDERSTANDING DATABASES, ASP, JSP, AND COLDFUSION

3 Database Essentials 45

4 Understanding the Server Technology: Active Server Pages 61

5 Understanding the Server Technology: JavaServer Pages 81

6 Understanding the Server Technology: ColdFusion 101

CHAPTER 3

DATABASE ESSENTIALS

In this chapter

Database Fundamentals and Concepts 46

Basic SQL Syntax 49

Summary 60

Database Fundamentals and Concepts

In an era of information explosion, management of data has become a prime concern for many. One of the most reliable solutions for data management is the database approach. A *database* is a collection of information that is organized for easy access, management, and modification.

Database creation and management can be done most effectively with the help of database management systems (DBMS). *Database management systems* are computerized record-keeping systems that enable you to organize, store, and retrieve the data stored in a database. In most cases, sets of data are logically related to each other. To store this logically related data, you can use a relational database. In a relational database, the data is stored in the form of tables, which are related to each other. You can query and view the information stored in these tables in different ways without changing the structure of these tables. To manage a relational database, relational database management system (RDBMS) is used. There are various RDBMS available, such as Access, FileMaker Pro, Sybase, Informix, Oracle, and SQL Server.

Most Web sites are database-driven. Creating such Web sites requires the back-end database support of a full-fledged database management system. UltraDev does not provide any feature to create such a database. Therefore, you need to set up a database server and create a database yourself. The database server that you will be using to create and work with databases in this chapter is SQL Server 7.0.

→ To learn more about how to set up SQL Server, **see** "Installing SQL Server 7.0," **p. 521**.

You can also create databases by using a database application, such as Microsoft Access, that has an easy-to-use graphical user interface.

→ To learn more about how to create databases in Microsoft Access, **see** "Creating a Database," **p. 552**.

Let's take an online university that offers courses on a variety of subjects as an example. Administering this site involves maintaining a list of courses offered by the site and keeping a record of all the students who register for these courses. Therefore, the course information and the student information together form the database for the site.

Designing a Relational Database

The first step toward creating and managing a database is to design the database. Designing a database means determining the most efficient method to store data. Effective data storage enables easy modification and retrieval of data. Therefore, before you get into the intricacies of a database, you must first understand the basic elements involved in any relational database design.

Entities

An *entity* is an object about which you need to store data. An object can be a person, a place, a thing, or a concept. In the previous example of the online university, the two entities that are involved are course and student. Every entity has a distinct set of characteristics that can be easily identified. In a relational database model, entities are represented as tables.

ATTRIBUTES

Attributes are the properties of an entity that describe the entity. Attributes provide information about the entity. For example, name, registration number, date of birth, email address, and phone numbers are the attributes of the student entity. In a relational database model, attributes are represented as fields in a table.

RELATIONSHIPS

Relationships represent a logical connection between two separate entities. Relationships between entities are of three types:

- One-to-One
- One-to-Many
- Many to Many

ONE-TO-ONE

Two entities have a *One-to-One* relationship if for each instance of one entity there exists only one instance of the other entity. For example, a school can have only one principal and a person can be the principal of only one school. Figure 3.1 displays a One-to-One relationship.

Figure 3.1
In a One-to-One relationship, an instance of an entity is logically related with only one instance of another entity.

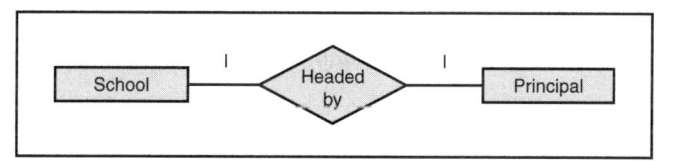

ONE-TO-MANY

A *One-to-Many* relationship exists between two entities when for each instance of the first entity there can exist zero or more instances of the second entity and for every instance of the second entity there is only one instance of the first entity. For example, in a university, an instructor might handle more than one class during an academic year. Figure 3.2 displays a One-to-Many relationship.

Figure 3.2
In a One-to-Many relationship, one instance of an entity is related to zero or more instances of another entity.

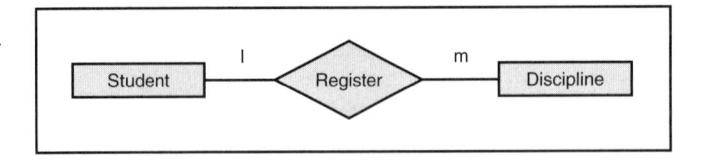

```
Student  ──1──  ◇Register◇  ──m──  Discipline
```

MANY-TO-MANY

A *Many-to-Many* relationship exists between two entities when for each instance of the first entity there can be multiple instances of second entity and for every instance of the second entity there can be multiple instances of the first entity. For example, at a given point of time a student can register for more than one major and many students can enroll for the same major. Figure 3.3 displays a Many-to-Many relationship.

Figure 3.3
In a Many-to-Many relationship, multiple instances of an entity are related to multiple instances of another entity.

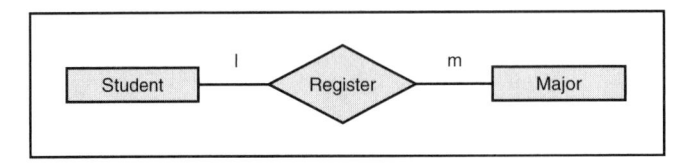

```
Student  ──1──  ◇Register◇  ──m──  Major
```

MAPPING TO A TABLE

You will now see how the three concepts used in database modeling, entities, attributes, and relationships, are implemented in a relational database. In a relational database, entities and attributes are mapped to tables and columns.

The two entities of the online university database, student and course, can be mapped to simple tables, as shown in Figures 3.4 and 3.5.

Figure 3.4
The Course Details table is used to store various details of the courses offered by the online university.

Course Id	Course Name	Course Description
C001	Outlook 2000 Level 1	This course covers the basics of Outlook 2000.
C002	Windows 2000 Level 1	This course covers the basics of Windows 2000.
C003	FrontPage 2000 Level 1	This course covers the basics of FrontPage 2000.
C004	Access 2000 Level 1	This course covers the basics of Access 2000.

Figure 3.5
The Student Details table is used to store the details of the students of the online university.

Student Id	Password	Student Name	DOB	Sex	Course Id	Email Id	Phone No	Marks
S001	moonwalker	Don Allen	03/05/78	M	C004	Don78@hotmail.com	317-581-6789	50
S002	maryson	Mary Robinson	05/09/77	F	C004	Maryrob@hotmail.com	987-876-9876	75
S003	custard	Cathrine Shields	10/22/79	F	C002	Cathy79@hotmail.com	187-894-9875	0
S004	victory2000	Victor Robinson	07/14/79	M	C003	Victor77@hotmail.com	789-876-9876	60

Each row in a table represents an instance of the entity and each column represents an attribute of the entity. In the Student Details table, each row represents one student and each column holds specific information about each student, such as student id, name, date of birth, and so on. Rows and columns are referred to as *records* and *fields*, respectively. The information stored in a field is called a *value*. For example, the first student's name, Don Allen, is a value in the Name field.

Fields in a table might or might not contain values. For example, in the Student Details table, the Student Name field must contain a value, because every student will have a name, whereas the Phone No. field might not contain any value, because not every student might have a phone number. You can specify the properties of a field in a table at the time you define the table structure. You can also specify the data type of each field in a table while defining the table structure.

Every table must have a field (or a combination of fields) that uniquely identifies each record in the table. The field (or combination of fields) that enables you to enforce the uniqueness of every record in a table is called the *primary key*. For example, the Student ID field is the primary key that uniquely identifies every record in the Student Details table.

Because the tables are logically related to each other, there must be a method by which you can link these tables. This link can be established with the help of foreign keys. A *foreign key* is a field in a table that exists as a primary key in another table. For example, the Course ID field is a primary key in the Course Details table and a foreign key in the Student Details table. Foreign keys help maintain referential integrity across tables. *Referential integrity* ensures that for every foreign key value there is a matching primary key value. For example, a course ID entered in the Student Details table must have a corresponding course ID in the Course Details table.

Basic SQL Syntax

The Structured Query Language (SQL, pronounced "sequel") is the standard language used by all RDBMS to define, retrieve, and manipulate data. Each RDBMS has its own version of SQL, which is derived from the standard SQL. The variations can be in syntax or keywords. In the following sections, you will learn to use Transact SQL (T-SQL), which is the version of SQL used in SQL Server7.0. Most of the T-SQL statements discussed in this chapter are similar to the standard SQL (ANSI SQL). However, a note has been added to all the T-SQL statements whose syntax differs from the standard SQL (ANSI SQL). In SQL Server, you enter SQL statements in the SQL Server Query Analyzer window.

Creating Databases and Tables

The first step toward implementing the database design is to create a database. To create a database use the following command:

```
CREATE DATABASE database_name
```

For example, to create a database with the name university, you need to give the following command:

```
CREATE DATABASE university
```

> **Note**
>
> By default, only system administrators have permission to create databases. (This permission can be transferred to others, however.) You must be in the Master database to create a database. The *Master* database is the default database created by SQL Server at the time of its installation.
>
> The USE keyword can be used to switch from one database to another.
>
> The database name must be unique to the server and can be up to 128 characters in length.

After creating the database you need to explicitly tell SQL Server that you want to use the database. To do this use the following command:

```
USE database_name
```

For example, to use the university database you need to use the following command:

```
USE university
```

If you do not need the database, you can delete it. Use the following command to delete a database:

```
DROP DATABASE database_name
```

For example, to delete the university database you need to use the following command:

```
DROP DATABASE university
```

> **Note**
>
> Only the system administrator and the database owner have permission to delete a database. When you delete a database, all database objects within the database will also be deleted.

After you create a database, you can create tables and other objects in the database to implement the database model. Tables are objects in a database, which actually stores the data. The syntax used for creating a table is as follows:

```
CREATE TABLE table_name
(column_name data type [NULL|NOT NULL] table_constraint)
```

In this statement, `table_name` is the name of the table and `column_name` is the name of the column in the table. Names of tables and columns must be meaningful so that they describe their content.

Data type specifies the kind of data that a column holds. Some of the data types supported by SQL Server are as follows:

- `int`—Stores numeric data. Numeric data consists of positive as well as negative numbers. 122, –56, and 0 are all examples of numeric data.
- `char(#)`—Stores a specified number of characters. Character data can consist of letters (A–Z), numbers (0–9), and special characters (!, @, #, $, %, ^, &, and *), or any combination of these. Use the char data type when the length of values in the rows of a column is almost the same.
- `varchar`—Stores a string in a column where the length of the string varies in each record.
- `datetime`—Stores date and time values.
- `money`—Represents monetary data.

The keywords `NULL|NOT NULL` specify whether a column can contain null values. By default, SQL Server allows null values in columns.

Finally, use `table_constraint` to ensure the integrity of the data entered in the columns. For example, you can use the primary key constraint on the `course_id` field to ensure that no two courses have the same `course_id`. Similarly, a foreign key constraint can be used to ensure referential integrity between tables.

> **Note**
>
> A SQL Server database can contain up to two billion tables. Table names must be unique in a database. Table names in SQL can be up to 128 characters. If the name consists of two words, there should not be any space between them. A table can contain up to 1,024 columns and column names must be unique within a table.

You can now create the course details and student details table by using the CREATE TABLE statement:

```
CREATE TABLE course
(
course_id char(4) NOT NULL PRIMARY KEY,
course_name char(30) NOT NULL,
course_desp varchar(50) NULL
)
```

```
CREATE TABLE student
(
stud_id char(4) NOT NULL PRIMARY KEY
password char(15) NOT NULL,
stud_name char(20) NOT NULL,
dob datetime NOT NULL,
sex char(1) NOT NULL,
email_id char(15),NULL
phone_no int NULL,
course_id char(4) NOT NULL REFRENCES course(course_id),
marks int NULL
)
```

In this `CREATE TABLE` statement, the `REFRENCES` keyword creates a foreign key constraint on the `course_id` field.

Adding, Modifying, and Deleting Records

Now that the tables are ready, you can learn the SQL statements used to add, modify, and delete records from a table. `INSERT`, `UPDATE`, and `DELETE` are the three SQL statements used to add, modify, and delete records, respectively. These three statements are collectively known as *Data Manipulation Language (DML)* statements.

Adding Records

After you create a table, you can add records to the table by using the `INSERT` statement. You can use the `INSERT` statement to enter a single record or multiple records into a table.

Note: The table owner is the only person allowed to insert records into a table. However, this permission can be transferred to others.

When you add a record to a table, you can either enter values for all the fields in the table or enter values for only specific fields in the table.

The following syntax is used to enter values for all the fields in a table:

```
INSERT INTO table_name VALUES(value1, value2, value3,...)
```

For example, to enter a record into the course table you need to use the following statement:

```
INSERT INTO course VALUES('C005', 'Office 2000 level-1',
            'this course covers the basics of office 2000')
```

Caution: The names assigned to a database and database objects are case-sensitive. Therefore, you need to be careful when referring to these in your SQL statements.

To enter values for only specific fields in a table the following syntax is used:

```
INSERT INTO table_name[(field1, field2, field3...)] VALUES (value1, value2, value3,...)
```

For example, to add a record to the course table with only the `course_id` and `course_name`, you need to use the following statement:

```
INSERT INTO course(course_id, course_name)
VALUES('C005', 'Excel 2000 Level-1')
```

> **Note**
>
> Values entered into `char`, `varchar`, and `datetime` fields should be enclosed within single quotes.

The `INTO` keyword in the `INSERT` statement is optional and is usually used to improve the readability. However, the `INTO` keyword is not optional in the case of ANSI SQL.

> **Caution**
>
> Take the following precautions when inserting records into a table:
> - The value entered into a column must match the data type of the column.
> - `NULL` values must not be entered into `NOT NULL` columns.
> - Data entered into a column must not violate any constrains set for the column.
>
> Violating these rules will return an error message.

Updating Records

You can modify the data in one or more rows of a table by using the UPDATE statement. The syntax for the UPDATE statement is as follows:

```
UPDATE table_name
SET column_name=value
WHERE condition
```

For example, the following statement modifies the name of the course C004 from 'Access 2000 Level 1' to 'Project 2000 Level 1':

```
UPDATE course
SET course_name='Project 2000 Level 2'
WHERE course_id='C004'
```

An UPDATE statement without the WHERE condition modifies all the records in the table. For example, the following statement modifies the name of all the courses to 'Project 2000 Level 1':

```
UPDATE course
SET course_name='Project 2000 Level 2'
```

> **Caution**
> The precautions that are taken while inserting a record, such as checking for the data types, NULL and NOT NULL values, and constraints, must also be taken while updating records. You must also make sure to include the WHERE condition in the UPDATE statement until and unless you want the UPDATE statement to modify all the records in the table.

DELETING RECORDS

Use the DELETE statement to delete one or more records from a table. The basic syntax for deleting a row is

```
DELETE table_name
WHERE condition
```

> **Note**
> The syntax of the DELETE statement in ANSI SQL is slightly different from that of T-SQL. The syntax for a deleting a row in ANSI SQL is
> ```
> DELETE FROM table name
> WHERE condition
> ```

For example, the following statement deletes the row from the course table where the course_id is 'C004':

```
DELETE course
WHERE course_id='C004'
```

You can also delete all the rows in the course table by using the following statement:

```
DELETE course
```

SELECT STATEMENTS

You can retrieve the data stored in tables with the help of SELECT queries.

Queries retrieve a set of rows and columns from one or more tables. This set of rows and columns returned on querying a database is called a *recordset*. You can query a database on SQL Server by using the SELECT statement. The SELECT statement retrieves data stored in specific columns of one or more tables to form a recordset. The basic syntax for a SELECT statement is

```
SELECT column_name FROM table_name
```

For example, the following statement displays a list of all course names from the course table with their respective course descriptions:

```
SELECT course_name, course_desp FROM course
```

The SELECT statement can also include all fields of a table into a recordset. To do this, use the asterisk (*) symbol along with the SELECT statement.

For example, the following statement retrieves all the records from the course table and displays the data of all the columns in the table:

```
SELECT * FROM course
```

Conditional Search

You can also retrieve specific records that satisfy a condition by using the WHERE clause in the SELECT statement.

The conditions that can be specified along with the WHERE clause are classified into various categories, such as comparison operators, logical operators, and range operators.

Comparison Operators

Table 3.1 provides a list of comparison operators that can be used along with the WHERE clause.

TABLE 3.1 COMPARISON OPERATORS

Operator	Description
=	Equal to
>	Greater than
<	Less than
>=	Greater than or equal to
<=	Less than or equal to
!>	Not greater than
!<	Not less than
<>, !=	Not equal to

The following statement retrieves only those records from the course table that have the course_id 'C002':

```
SELECT * FROM course
WHERE course_id='C002'
```

The following statement displays a list of all students who were born before 1/6/1980:

```
SELECT * FROM student
WHERE dob < '1/6/1980'
```

Logical Operators

You can specify more than one condition in the WHERE clause by using logical operators such as AND, OR, and NOT. The logical operators enable you to combine multiple SELECT statements into a single statement.

The AND operator is used when you want all the conditions to be satisfied by every record in the recordset.

For example, the following statement returns a list of all female students born before 1/2/78:

```
SELECT * FROM student
WHERE dob < '1/2/78' AND sex = 'F'
```

Use the OR operator when every record in the recordset needs to satisfy only one of the specified conditions. For example, the following statement returns a list of students born either on 2/2/78 or on 2/2/76.

```
SELECT * FROM student
WHERE dob= '2/2/78' OR dob='2/2/76'
```

Use NOT operator when you want to specify a condition that must not be satisfied by the recordset.

For example, the following statement returns a list of only the female students born after 1/2/78.

```
SELECT * FROM student
WHERE sex='F' AND NOT dob < '1/2/78'
```

RANGE OPERATORS

SQL Server provides range operators to fetch data that fall between a range of values. BETWEEN and NOT BETWEEN are the two range operators provided by SQL Server.

Use the BETWEEN operator with the WHERE clause to specify a range of values. Use the NOT BETWEEN operator with the WHERE clause to find values that do not fall within the specified range.

The following statement returns a list of students whose date of birth falls between 1/1/75 and 1/1/80:

```
SELECT * FROM student
WHERE dob BETWEEN '1/1/75' AND '1/1/80'
```

> **Note**
>
> The records fetched using the range operators include the upper and lower range value. The SELECT statements executed using the BETWEEN operator can also be executed by using the >= and =< operators.

STRING OPERATORS

You can fetch records containing columns that match a wildcard pattern by using the LIKE keyword along with the WHERE clause. Table 3.2 displays a list of wildcard patterns that can be used with the LIKE keyword.

TABLE 3.2 WILDCARD PATTERNS

Wildcard Pattern	Description
%	Zero or more characters
_	A single character
[ ]	Any single character within the specified range. For example, [pqrst] or [p-t].
[^]	Any single character not within the specified range. For example, [^pqrst].

The following statement displays a list of all students whose names start with *Ma*:

```
SELECT * FROM student
WHERE stud_name LIKE 'Ma%'
```

To list the students whose names end with *y* but do not begin with *M*, the following statement can be used:

```
SELECT * FROM student
WHERE stud_name LIKE '[^M]%y'
```

ARITHMETIC OPERATIONS

You can perform arithmetic operations using the various arithmetic operators provided by SQL Server.

In SQL Server, arithmetic operations such as addition, subtraction, division, and multiplication can be performed on columns that support data types such as int and money.

The following are the arithmetic operators supported by SQL Server:

- \+ for addition
- \- for subtraction
- * for mutiplication
- / for division

All the above-mentioned operators can be used with the int and money data types. The order of precedence of these operators is *, /, +, and -, which means that * is evaluated first, / second, and so on. However, you can change this order by using parentheses; operations enclosed within parentheses are evaluated first. Apart from these operators, SQL supports another operator called the modulo operator (%) which returns the remainder of two divisible numeric values. The modulo operator cannot be used with the money data type.

This statement

```
SELECT stud_id, marks + 2
FROM student
```

adds 2 to all the values in the marks column and displays the recordset.

Generating Summary Data

SQL Server also provides aggregate functions to produce summary values, such as the sum, average, minimum, maximum, and count of the values that are stored in various columns of a table.

For example, the following statement displays the sum of marks scored by the students who have registered for the course C002:

```
SELECT SUM(marks)
FROM student
WHERE course_id='C002'
```

To know the maximum mark scored in course C002, use the following statement:

```
SELECT MAX(marks)
FROM student
WHERE course_id='C002'
```

To know the minimum mark scored in course C002, use the following statement:

```
SELECT MIN(marks)
FROM student
WHERE course_id='C002'
```

Use the following statement to know the average marks scored by the students in course C002:

```
SELECT AVG(marks)
FROM student
WHERE course_id='C002'
```

Find the total number of students who have registered for course C002 by using the following statement:

```
SELECT COUNT(stud_id)
FROM student
WHERE course_id='C002'
```

Whenever you use an aggregate function to display summarized data, SQL displays only the resultant value without any heading for the value. However, you can provide a descriptive heading for the aggregate values by using an alias, as shown in the following example:

```
SELECT AVG(marks) AS Avgscore
FROM student
WHERE course_id='C002'
```

In this example, the average score of the students are displayed along with the heading "Avgscore".

Sorting Records

The records in a recordset can be sorted by a particular field name by using the ORDER BY clause. For example, to sort the records in the recordset based on the student name field, use the following statement:

```
SELECT * FROM student
ORDER BY stud_name
```

The default order in which the ORDER BY clause sorts records is ascending order (1,2,3,… or A,B,C,…). To sort the records in descending order, use the DESC keyword as follows:

```
SELECT * FROM students
ORDER BY stud_name DESC
```

STORED PROCEDURES

While working with SQL statements, you might have to enter the same SQL statement repeatedly to perform a particular activity. For example, every time you want to view the list of records in the student table, you have to enter the following statement in the SQL Server Query Analyzer window:

```
SELECT * FROM student
```

However, if you do not want to repeatedly enter the SELECT statements, you can make use of stored procedures. A *stored procedure* is a collection of SQL statements referred to by a common name. A stored procedure is stored in a database in a compiled form and therefore it can be executed when required. You can create a stored procedure by using the CREATE PROCEDURE statement.

For example, you can use the following statement to create a stored procedure for the preceding SELECT statement:

```
CREATE PROCEDURE stud
AS
SELECT * FROM student
```

The above statement creates a stored procedure called stud, which can be used to display the records stored in the student table. Every time you want to view the list of records in the student table, you can execute this stored procedure by using the EXECUTE statement, as follows:

```
EXCECUTE stud
```

You can also use stored procedures to display only specific records from a table that satisfy a given condition. For example, at the time of executing the stored procedure, you can choose to view the list of students born on a specific date. To do this, you must pass parameters to the stored procedure. A parameter is an argument whose value can be passed to the stored procedure at the time of executing the stored procedure. Parameter names must be preceded by the @ symbol.

You can use the following stored procedure to display the details about students born on a particular date:

```
CREATE PROCEDURE birthday (@bdate datetime)
AS
SELECT * FROM student
WHERE dob=@bdate
```

In this statement, bdate is the parameter passed to the stored procedure, birthday. To assign a value to the bdate parameter at the time of executing the stored procedure, you can use the following statement:

EXECUTE birthday'2/28/70'

> **Note:** Apart from simple SQL statements, stored procedures can contain program flow control structures and advanced SQL statements used for error handling.

SUMMARY

A database is a collection of related information that is organized to enable effective storage, manipulation, and deletion of data. Database creation and management can be done with the help of database management systems, such as Access, Sybase, Informix, Oracle, and SQL Server.

Understanding the concepts involved in database design, such as entities, attributes, and relationships, help in designing a database structure.

You can add, modify, and delete the data stored in a database with the help of SQL statements. SQL statements enable you to modify and delete data based on specific conditions, too. SQL statements also enable you to fetch summarized data from databases.

CHAPTER 4

UNDERSTANDING THE SERVER TECHNOLOGY: ACTIVE SERVER PAGES

In this chapter

Introduction to Active Server Pages   62

The `Response` Object   65

The `Request` Object   67

The `Session`, `Application`, and `Server` Objects   70

Databases and ASP   73

Summary   79

Introduction to Active Server Pages

UltraDev supports ASP, one of the most popular technologies for creating dynamic Web applications. Dynamic Web applications require a server that can process requests generated dynamically by a browser. The browser can request either static or dynamic content from the Web server. Whereas the Web server can send static HTML pages that have been requested by the browser, it cannot send dynamic content unless an application server associated with a server technology, such as ASP, is installed on it. In the context of dynamic Web applications, the role of the Web server is to process an ASP page and send the results to the browser. To create dynamic Web applications from UltraDev, you need a Web server, which runs an application server that supports ASP pages. ASP pages can run on Web servers such as Internet Information Server (IIS) and Personal Web Server (PWS). (PWS is a scaled-down version of IIS.) Whereas you can only install IIS on Windows NT and Windows 2000, you can install PWS on Windows 95, 98, and NT Workstation.

UltraDev supports ASP 2.0. To use ASP 2.0 with UltraDev, you must install IIS 4.0 on a Windows NT Server. You can also use ASP 3.0 with UltraDev if you have access to IIS 5.0, which ships with Windows 2000.

> **Note**
> To use ASP without IIS or PWS, you can use products such as iASP and Chili!ASP. These products can run on Web servers such as Apache, Java Web Server, and Netscape Enterprise Server.

ASP allows you to write code with embedded application logic that performs the tasks involved in generating dynamic content. These tasks involve connecting to databases and retrieving information from them. With ASP technology, you can write ASP pages, which are programs or scripts embedded in an HTML page. These programs are also known as server-side scripts, as they run on a Web server.

> **Note**
> Apart from server-side scripts, an HTML page can contain client-side scripts embedded within it. Client-side scripts are written in scripting languages such as JavaScript and VBScript. These scripts are embedded in an HTML page within the <SCRIPT> and </SCRIPT> HTML tags. A server does not process client-side scripts. It simply passes the page containing these scripts to the browser, which takes care of processing the code. The difference between server-side scripts and client-side scripts lies mainly in this fact that they are executed at different ends.

ASP is an open technology, which implies that you can write ASP scripts by using VBScript, JScript, JavaScript, PerlScript, or Python. ASP scripts are text files, so you can write these scripts by using any text editor, such as Notepad for Windows or Simple Text for the Macintosh. You can also write and edit ASP code with the native code editor of UltraDev.

ASP can be combined with the Extensible Markup Language (XML), Component Object Model (COM), and HTML to give additional functionality to Web applications. ASP is packaged with a set of related built-in objects and components, which are described in the following sections.

When you develop Web applications in UltraDev by using ASP, you do not have to hand code ASP scripts. UltraDev generates the ASP code that contains instructions for performing the tasks required to develop dynamic Web applications, such as connecting to a database or retrieving information from it. However, it helps to understand the code in these ASP scripts to be able to appreciate what the code actually accomplishes. In addition, it helps if you want to add any customized functionality to your Web application. The following sections help you to familiarize yourself with ASP scripts and also understand how they work.

Identifying ASP Scripts

The scripts in an ASP page are embedded within a tag that consists of a percentage symbol delimiting the left and right angular brackets. Anything written between the <% tag and the %> tag is interpreted by the server as server side code that needs to be processed to send the results containing dynamic content to the browser in an HTML format. The server does not parse the HTML statements written outside these tags. The first line in an ASP page differs depending on the language you want to use. The general syntax for the first line in an ASP page is as follows:

```
<%@ Language=VBSCRIPT %>
```

or

```
<%@ Language=JavaScript %>
```

> **Tip**
>
> Alternatively, you can start an ASP code block by using the <SCRIPT> tag. This tag contains an extra attribute called RUNAT, which indicates that the code within the tag must run on the server. If this attribute is not specified, the code runs on the browser.
>
> An ASP page containing the <SCRIPT> tag instead of the <% and %> tags is written as follows:
>
> ```
> <SCRIPT LANGUAGE=JAVASCRIPT RUNAT=SERVER>
> ...
> ...
> </SCRIPT>
> ```

Objects in ASP

Objects in ASP are modeled on the popular object-oriented development model. Just as the real world is made up of entities that possess certain attributes, programs in the object-oriented model also possess some attributes that are modeled after entities. For example, in the real world, a computer is an object possessing certain attributes or characteristics, such as color and shape and functionality (the ability to compute, for example). Specific instances of this generalized object are a Windows desktop PC, a Macintosh machine, and so on. These instances possess their individual characteristics, although they share certain general characteristics with the parent entity, computer.

In the world of object-oriented programming, blocks of generalized programs are modeled after entities. Such generalized code blocks are called *objects*. Like real-life objects, these objects have functionality or behavior associated with them. The functionality or behavior of an object is called a *method* in object-oriented programming. These objects also possess attributes, which can be equated to the characteristics possessed by a real-world object. Just as real-world objects are used only when there is a need, these objects are also executed only when there is a need. A need arises at the request of a user action, otherwise known as an *event*. The benefit of following the object-oriented method in writing programs is that low-level details can be encapsulated and code can be reused and extended.

ASP consists of five built-in standard objects that are executed when an event occurs. These objects possess certain attributes and methods. Apart from these attributes and methods, these objects also contain collections. A *collection* consists of sets of information represented as name and value pairs. An example of a name and value pair is the string that you can see in the URL text box of a browser. For example, in the string `?firstname=Peter&lastname=Wright`, the name and value pair is represented by `firstname` and `Peter`, respectively. You can associate a name and value pair with form fields and their values.

The following list summarizes the purpose of the five objects of ASP:

- The `Application` object—Contains global application-level information that can be shared by several applications running at the same time.
- The `Request` object—Retrieves the information that a user sends from a browser. Form data, query string data, and information from cookies are some examples of information that can be sent from a browser. The Request object can also be used to access information from environment variables. An example of an environment variable is the name of the Web server used by the client computer.
- The `Response` object—Sends processed information to the browser. It decides when and how the results should be sent to the browser. The Response object can be used to redirect the user to another page as well as write cookies to the browser.
- The `Server` object—Creates objects that control server functions, such as opening or closing a connection with a database and reading information from files. The methods and properties of this object can be used for carrying out commonly performed tasks.
- The `Session` object—Maintains information about the current session of a single user who is accessing a particular Web application. Information, such as a user's login name and the contents of the user's shopping cart, for a session is maintained in this object.

> **Note**
>
> ASP 3.0 consists of two more built-in objects, `ObjectContext` and `ASPError`. The `ObjectContext` object is used to manage transactions in Microsoft Transaction Server. The `ASPError` object is used to provide information about errors that might be generated while running ASP scripts.

The following sections discuss the five standard objects in ASP: `Response`, `Request`, `Application`, `Session`, and `Server`. The `ObjectContext` and `ASPError` objects are outside the scope of this chapter and therefore have not been covered in detail. To find more information on these objects, refer to Appendix B, which lists Web sites containing information on ASP.

THE Response OBJECT

The `Response` object is used to send output from a server to a browser. This output can be text that will be displayed on the browser, embedded HTML that can be rendered by the browser, or data that will be stored on the computer where the browser is present.

THE Write METHOD

The most commonly used method of the `Response` object is the `Write` method. Using this method, you can send data to be displayed on the browser.

The following is the syntax for the `Write` method:

`Response.Write (expression)`

or

`Response.Write expression`

The expression mentioned in the preceding syntax can be a character, an integer, or text, each of which is expressed as string.

Listing 4.1 shows a sample program that displays the `Welcome to ASP` message on the browser screen.

LISTING 4.1 AN EXAMPLE FOR THE Write METHOD

```
<html>s
<head>
<title>Introducing ASP</title>
</head>
<body bgcolor="#FFFFFF" text="#000000">
<% Response.Write ("Welcome to ASP") %>
</body>
</html>
```

Writing the `<% = expression %>` tag is equivalent to writing the `<% Response.Write (expression) %>` tag. Therefore, in the preceding code, if the `<% Response.Write ("Welcome to ASP") %>` tag is replaced by the `<% ="Welcome to ASP" %>` tag, the generated output is the same.

> **Caution**
>
> The `<% = expression %>` tag works if it is the only instruction in a code block. If it is part of a series of instructions in a code block, such as the one given in the following code, an error results.
>
> ```
> <% dim greeting
> greeting = "hello"
> =greeting %>
> ```
>
> The preceding code works if it is modified as follows:
>
> ```
> <% dim pub
>   pub="hello" %>
> <%=pub %>
> ```

The other methods of the `Response` object are listed in Table 4.1.

TABLE 4.1 THE METHODS OF THE Response OBJECT

Method	Description
AddHeader	Adds a name/value pair to the HTML header.
AppendToLog	Adds a string to the end of the Web server log entry for the current request.
BinaryWrite	Writes binary information to the current HTTP output stream.
Clear	Clears HTML output that is not sent from the buffer and then deletes the buffer.
End	Stops the execution of the current ASP script.
Flush	Similar to the `Clear` method, except that it sends output from the buffer to the client and then flushes the buffer.
Redirect	Redirects you to a different URL.

Table 4.2 lists the properties of the `Response` object.

TABLE 4.2 PROPERTIES OF THE Response OBJECT

Property	Description
Buffer	Turns buffering on and off.
Status	Changes the value of the status line returned by the server.
Expires	Specifies the duration for which a cached page can remain on a browser before it expires.
ExpiresAbsolute	Specifies the date and time when a cached page expires.
ContentType	Specifies the content type of the page sent from a server. A content type is indicated by a combination of the type of content and the associated file type. text/html, image/gif, and image/jpeg are some examples of content types. The default content type is text/html.

Cookies

Cookies are information bits written on the client computer by the Web server. These information bits convey information about a user session, which can be used when the user visits the Web site again.

The types of information that a cookie can store can be anything from form data to information such as the search keywords typed during a particular search. For example, the Remember Me checkboxes that you see in login pages are used to enable cookies that store your username and password. These cookies enable you to automatically log on the next time you visit the page.

Cookies are sent to the client computer through response headers. They can be created using the `Cookies` collection of the response header. The syntax for writing cookies is as follows:

```
Response.Cookies(cookiename)= cookieinformation
```

For example, to create a cookie called `searchword` that contains the search keyword, `ASP`, the following statement can be used:

```
<%Response.Cookies("searchword")= "ASP"%>
```

The Request Object

In a *client/server* model, such as the Internet, the server processes the ASP page requested by a browser and sends the results to the browser. When the browser sends a request to the server, it sends data along with the request. This data can include, for example, form data or header data.

Form data refers to the data that is entered in a form on the browser. Data, such as user name and password, entered by users in the login form to log on to their mail accounts is an example of form data. This form calls an ASP page on the server. This ASP page reads the form data and then sends a query to the database to check whether the username and the password are correct.

Form information can be sent to the server by using two methods, `GET` and `POST`. If the form uses the `GET` method, the form data is passed through a query string. A *query string* is a string appended to the URL of the requested page. This string contains name and value pairs associated with form fields. For example, when a user types Don in the `firstname` field and Allen in the `lastname` field, the URL that is sent is as follows:

```
http://www.myserver.com/formprocess.asp?firstname=Don&lastname=Allen
```

In this URL, the query string is the string that starts with the question mark and contains two name and value pairs, `firstname` and `Don` and `lastname` and `Allen`.

When a form submits form information through the `POST` method, it does not use the query string to pass data. It instead uses HTTP headers.

> **Note**
>
> When sensitive information has to be passed from a form, it is best to use the POST method. For example, when login information is passed using the POST method, the password is not displayed along with the URL. Unlike the GET method, the POST method allows more than 1 KB of data to be passed from the browser to the server. So, it is advantageous to use the POST method.

To read form data, the ASP page uses the Request object. The Request object has two collections, QueryString and Form. The QueryString collection is used to access data passed through a querystring and the Form collection accesses data passed by the POST method.

The following is the syntax for the use of these two collections with the Request object:

```
Request.QueryString (Variablename)
```

or

```
Request.Form (Variablename)
```

To display the value of the firstname field discussed in the previous example, the two collections of Request object can be used as follows:

```
<% =Request.QueryString ("firstname") %>
```

or

```
<% =Request.Form ("firstname") %>
```

The preceding two statements read the value, Don, contained in the firstname field of the form and display the same on the screen.

Listing 4.2 shows a sample program that demonstrates the use of the Request object. This program reads the username from the name form field and displays the same.

LISTING 4.2 USING THE Request OBJECT

```
<%@ Language = VBSCRIPT %>
<% dim readname
readname = Request.Form ( "name")
Response.Write " The username entered on the form is " & readname %>
```

HTTP HEADERS

In a client/server transaction, when the browser sends information to the server, it not only sends data supplied by the user but also sends some additional information. This information can include the name of the browser, the operating system on which it is running, and the URL of the page that requests the ASP page. Each additional piece of information about the client is known as a *request header*. When the server processes this request and sends the results to the browser, it also sends additional information about the sent page through a *response header*. The request and response headers are together called as the *HTTP headers*.

Some of the standard HTTP request headers that are commonly used are HTTP_ACCEPT, HTTP_HOST, and HTTP_USER_AGENT. HTTP_ACCEPT contains a list of the Multi-Purpose Internet Mail Extensions (MIME) types supported by the browser. HTTP_HOST contains the name of the computer on which the browser is running. HTTP_USER_AGENT contains information such as the type and version of the browser and the operating system on which the client is running.

You can read HTTP headers by using the ServerVariables collection of the Request object. Table 4.3 gives a list of the other collections of the Request object.

TABLE 4.3 FIVE TYPES OF Request COLLECTIONS

Collection	Description
Form	Retrieves data that has been sent from a form by the POST method.
Cookies	Reads the values set in cookies on the browser.
QueryString	Retrieves data that has been sent from a form by the GET method.
ClientCertificate	Read the values from the certification fields sent by the client.
ServerVariables	Stores values of environmental variables.

To read all the HTTP headers sent by a browser, you can use the following statement:

```
<% Request.ServerVariables ("ALL_RAW") %>
```

To read a specific HTTP header, such as the HTTP_USER_AGENT header, use the following statement:

```
<% Request.ServerVariables ("HTTP_USER_AGENT") %>
```

Listing 4.3 shows a sample program that reads values from the ServerVariables collection and displays them onscreen.

LISTING 4.3 AN EXAMPLE FOR THE ServerVariables COLLECTION

```
<%@ Language = VBSCRIPT %>
<% dim s
  s= Request.ServerVariables("HTTP_USER_AGENT")
  Response.Write s & "<HR>" %>
```

READING COOKIES USING THE Request OBJECT

You can read cookies stored on the client by using either the ServerVariables collection or the Cookies collection of the Request object.

To display the cookies on a client by reading the HTTP_COOKIE header, use the following statement:

```
<% =Request.ServerVariables ("HTTP_COOKIE") %>
```

You can read cookies by using the `Cookies` collection of the `Request` header as follows:

```
dim variable
variable=Request.Cookies (cookiename)
```

For example, to read a cookie that has the name, `searchword`, use the `Request` object as follows:

```
<% dim readcookie
readcookie= Request.Cookies ("searchword")%>
```

Listing 4.4 shows a sample program that reads the user name entered in the `name` form field and stores it in a cookie called `usernamecookie`.

LISTING 4.4 AN EXAMPLE FOR WRITING A COOKIE

```
<%@ Language = VBSCRIPT %>
Response.Cookies ("usernamecookie")= Request.Form ("name")

%>
```

Listing 4.5 shows a sample program that reads the value stored in the `usernamecookie` and displays the same in a welcome message.

LISTING 4.5 AN EXAMPLE FOR READING A COOKIE

```
<%@ Language = VBSCRIPT %>
<%
dim readcookie
readcookie = Request.Cookies ("usernamecookie")
Response.Write " Welcome    " & readcookie & "  !"
%>
```

THE `Session`, `Application`, AND `Server` OBJECTS

When a user browses through the different pages of a Web site, the Web server serves each page requested by the user without saving the information of the page it served last. This means that the information that was obtained from a user from an earlier page is lost when the next page is served in the same session. Such a transaction is named the *stateless* transaction. However, dynamic Web pages should be able to maintain state between two user requests in a single session. These Web pages try to maintain state by using either cookies or the `Session` and `Application` objects.

Although cookies help to preserve simple data, such as numbers and strings, they cannot preserve complex data such as arrays and objects. To preserve such complex data, you can use the `Session` and `Application` objects.

The Session Object

The `Session` object contains session variables, which store the values retrieved from a particular session. Session variables can be created with the following syntax:

`Session(sessionvariable)=value`

For example, in the following statement, a session variable called `name` is created, which contains the value, `Don Allen`:

`<% Session("name")="Don Allen" %>`

This name is available across pages in a particular user session. A personalized welcome message is displayed on the browser screen as soon the user logs on.

The following is the syntax used to read the values stored in a session variable:

`readsessionvariable=Session(sessionvariable)`

Listing 4.6 shows a sample program that creates a session variable to store the name entered by a user in the form field called `name`.

LISTING 4.6   CREATING A SESSION VARIABLE

```
<%@LANGUAGE=VBSCRIPT%>
<HTML>
<TITLE> FORM WHERE USER ENTERS HIS NAME </TITLE>
        <%
        Dim string
        string=Request.form("name")
        Session("username")=string
        %>
</HTML>
```

Listing 4.7 shows how the `username` session variable created in the preceding listing is read and how its contents are displayed on the next page that is requested.

LISTING 4.7   READING A SESSION VARIABLE

```
<%@LANGUAGE=VBSCRIPT%>
<HTML>
        <%
        Dim readname
        readname=Session("username")
        Response.Write "Welcome   " & readname & "   !"
        %>
</HTML>
```

Apart from storing string variables, the `Session` object can store object variables, in which case the syntax of a session variable is as follows:

`Set Session (sessionvariable)= Instance of an object`

For example, the following line of code creates an instance of the `Connection` object of the ADODB component and stores this instance in a session variable called `databaseconnection`. To create an instance of any object, the `CreateObject` method of the `Server` object must be used.

```
Set Session("databaseconnection")=Server.CreateObject("ADODB.connection")
```

The methods of the `Session` object are listed in Table 4.4.

TABLE 4.4   METHODS OF THE Session OBJECT

Method	Description
Abandon	Deletes a `Session` object.
Contents.Remove	Removes a session variable from the `Contents` collection.
Contents.RemoveAll	Removes all session variables from the `Contents` collection.

The properties associated with the `Session` object are listed in Table 4.5.

TABLE 4.5   PROPERTIES OF THE Session OBJECT

Properties	Description
CodePage	Specifies the page that will display dynamic content.
LCID	Contains the location identifier.
SessionId	Contains the identifier for a given session.
Timeout	Contains the timeout period for a session in minutes.

The collections of the `Session` object are listed in Table 4.6.

TABLE 4.6   COLLECTIONS OF THE Session OBJECT

Collection	Description
Contents	Stores the session variables that are added to the session through script commands.
StaticObjects	Stores the objects created with the `<object>` tag in the current session.

THE Application OBJECT

Whereas the `Session` object stores information about a particular session, the `Application` object stores global information that can be accessed by all sessions that are running simultaneously on different clients. The `Application` object can store complex data types like the `Session` object. Information for an entire session is maintained in the `Application` object, which can be seen by all users who are browsing the site. For example, the number of hits a page receives can be stored in an application variable and updated every time a user visits the site. This information will be available to all users who are visiting the page.

The syntax for creating an application variable is as follows:

```
Application (applicationvariable)=value
```

The `Application` object contains similar collections as the `Session` object. It contains the `Remove` and `RemoveAll` methods of the Session object. In addition to these methods, the `Application` object contains two more methods, `Lock` and `Unlock`. The `Lock` method prevents clients from modifying the properties of the `Application` object, whereas the `Unlock` method allows clients to modify the properties of the `Application` object.

THE Server OBJECT

The `Server` object provides basic methods and properties that carry out common tasks on the Web server. For example, this object is used most commonly to create instances of server components. The `Server` object has methods such as `CreateObject`, `HTMLEncode`, `URLEncode`, and `Execute`.

The `CreateObject` method is used with the `Set` statement to create instances of component objects. The following is the syntax for the `CreateObject` method:

```
Set <instanceofobject> = Server.CreateObject("Class.Component")
```

The `HTMLEncode` method is used to display HTML tags on the browser without interpreting them. When you apply the `HTMLEncode` method to an HTML tag, this method replaces the < and > tags with < and >, respectively. When the browser encounters these characters, it displays the text within these characters without interpreting them. Therefore, you can see the HTML code on the screen.

The `Execute` method is used to execute an .asp file.

DATABASES AND ASP

You can connect to any database that supports Open Database Connectivity (ODBC) by using ASP. Apart from databases such as Oracle, Access, SQL Server, and Paradox, which are ODBC-compliant, ASP can access Excel spreadsheets and delimited text files that are also ODBC-compliant. ODBC is a solution to create a common interface to access databases that present data in different formats. Using ODBC, an application can query a database without using a low-level Application Programming Interface (API).

> **Note**
> A *low-level API* consists of function calls that interact directly with the hardware components of a computer, such as I/O ports. To understand how these low-level function calls work, you need to have a good understanding of the role binary and hexadecimal numbers play in interacting with hardware.

ODBC has a shortcoming in terms of not being able to fully encapsulate low-level programming. Programmers still have to use low-level function calls to communicate with databases if they use ODBC. So, Object Linking and Embedding Database (OLE DB) was introduced to enable you to connect to all types of data sources, both ODBC-compliant and non-ODBC compliant. OLE DB introduces an ODBC driver to access the ODBC data sources.

ASP connects to databases by using ActiveX Data Objects (ADO), a component that comes packaged with ASP. ADO allows ASP to connect to OLE DB, which in turn can access ODBC-compliant databases. ADO consists of six objects, using which an ASP page can connect to and query databases. Table 4.7 shows the objects in the ADO component.

TABLE 4.7   THE OBJECTS IN THE ADO COMPONENT

Object	Description
Connection	Connects an application to a database.
Recordset	Creates a recordset, which is a set of rows from a table. You can use a recordset to read, modify, or insert data.
Error	Stores errors that are generated while connecting to a data source.
Command	Creates a recordset object by combining the Recordset and Connection objects.
Parameter	Stores the parameters needed by the Command object.
Field	Stores the data of a field in a table.

CREATING A CONNECTION TO A DATABASE

Before creating a connection to a database through ASP, you need to create a System Data Source Name (DSN), which gives the ASP page the information about the kind of database that it is connecting to.

→ To learn more about creating a DSN, **see** "A DSN Connection," **p. 345**.

For the purpose of understanding the following sections, let us assume that a DSN called mydsn has been created to an Access database called employee.mdb.

To create a connection to a database from your ASP page, you use the Connection object of the ADODB component. This object retrieves and stores information regarding the database from the system DSN. The Connection object is created with the CreateObject method of the Server object. The following is the syntax for creating a connection to a database:

```
<%Dim connect
Set connect = Server.CreateObject("ADODB.connection")%>
```

The preceding statement creates a Connection object called connect. This connection object stores the DSN so that it is able to read the database information. The following statement accomplishes this:

```
<%connect.ConnectionString = "DSN.mydsn" %>
```

After a connection is created, it has to be opened to read or write to the database. The `Open` method of the `Connection` object is used for this purpose. The following is the syntax for opening a connection:

```
<% connect.Open %>
```

The preceding statement opens the connection that was created earlier.

The steps for creating and opening a connection can be summed up as follows:

```
<% Dim connect
Set connect = Server.CreateObject("ADODB.connection")
connect.ConnectionString = "DSN.mydsn"
connect.Open
%>
```

After you open a connection and retrieve data from the database, you need to close the connection. The `Close` method is used to close a connection, This method releases the memory occupied by the `Connection` object. The following statements accomplish this:

```
<% connect.Close
Set connect = Nothing %>
```

Retrieving Data from the Database

ASP stores the data retrieved from a database in an object called `Recordset` that is part of the ADODB component. This `Recordset` object can contain either specified rows in a table or the entire table. To read data from a database, an instance of the `Recordset` object has to be created. The syntax for this is as follows:

```
<% Dim recordsetobj
Set recordsetobj = Server.CreateObject ("ADODB.Recordset") %>
```

After creating a recordset object, it has to be filled with records retrieved from the database. To do this, the `Open` method is used. The syntax for the `Open` method is as follows:

recordsetobjectname.Open *source, connection, cursortype, locktype, commandtype*

The `Open` method has five arguments. The first argument, *source*, refers to the name of the data source. The second argument, *connection*, refers to the name of the connection object that is created. The third argument, *cursortype*, specifies the way the cursor moves through a recordset. The fourth argument, *locktype*, indicates the access rights for a table and the last argument, *commandtype*, describes the source that is specified as the first argument.

Assume that the `employee.mdb` database contains a table called `employeemaster`. To retrieve records from this table by using the `Recordset` object, use the following syntax:

```
<% recordsetobj.Open "employeemaster", connect, adOpenForwardOnly, adLockReadOnly,
adCmdTable %>
```

`employeemaster` is the name of the source and `connect` is the name of the connection object that was created earlier. The `adOpenForwardOnly` parameter is a constant that indicates that the cursor can only move forward through a recordset. The `adLockreadOnly` parameter is another constant that indicates that data can only be read from a table. The `adCmdTable` parameter is a constant that indicates that the type of the data source specified in the first argument is a table. These constants are defined in the `adovbs.inc` file, which is installed when you install IIS or PWS. You can find this file in `C:\Program Files\Common Files\System\ado`. To use the constants defined in this file in an ASP page, you need to include this file in that page. Before including the file in your ASP page, you need to copy it to the directory where all your site files are located. The syntax for including this file is as follows:

```
<!-- #include virtual="path_of_the_file/adovbs.inc" -->
```

Listing 4.8 in the next section shows a sample program that uses this file.

Reading from a Recordset

After a recordset is filled with data that is retrieved from a database, this data has to be read so that it can be displayed onscreen.

The following is the syntax for reading data from a recordset:

```
recordsetobjectname ("fieldname")
```

For example, consider that the recordset contains a field called `employeename`. The value from this field can be read as follows:

```
recordsetobj("employeename")
```

To traverse through the records in a recordset, the `Recordset` object uses a pointer that moves to each record in the recordset. The `Recordset` object has methods that direct the pointer to move in a particular direction. Table 4.8 lists these methods.

TABLE 4.8 METHODS OF THE Recordset OBJECT

Method	Description
MoveNext	Moves the recordset pointer to the next record in a recordset.
MovePrevious	Moves the recordset pointer to the previous record in a recordset.
MoveFirst	Moves the recordset pointer to the first record in a recordset.
MoveLast	Moves the recordset pointer to the last record in a recordset.
Move recordnumber	Moves the recordset pointer to a specified record in a recordset.

However, these methods need to be applied depending on the current position of the pointer. For example, if the pointer is already in the first record, you cannot use the `MovePrevious` method.

The `Recordset` object has two properties, `EOF` and `BOF`. The `EOF` property specifies whether the pointer is at the end of the recordset and the `BOF` property specifies whether the pointer is at the beginning of the recordset.

To close a recordset after it used, the `Close` method is used. This method releases the memory occupied by the `Recordset` object. The following is the syntax for closing a recordset:

```
recordsetobj.Close
Set recordsetobj = Nothing
```

Listing 4.8 shows the code required for the entire sequence of connecting to a database and displaying records from it. In the listing, the database that is used is `employee.mdb` and the table from which the recordset is created is `employeemaster`. The fields from this table that are added to the recordset are `employeename`, `salary`, and `age`.

LISTING 4.8 RETRIEVING AND DISPLAYING RECORDS FROM A DATABASE

```
<% @ Language = VBSCRIPT %>
<!-- #include virtual="/adovbs.inc" -- >
<% Dim connect
Set connect = Server.CreateObject("ADODB.connection")
connect.ConnectionString = "DSN.mydsn"
connect.Open
Dim recordsetobj
Set recordsetobj = Server.CreateObject ("ADODB.Recordset")
recordsetobj.Open "employeemaster", connect, , , adCmdTable
Do while NOT recordsetobj.EOF
        Response.Write " Name:" & recordsetobj ("employeename")
        Response.Write("<BR>")
        Response.Write "Salary:" & recordsetobj (        "salary")
        Response.Write("<BR>")
        Response.Write "Age:" & recordsetobj ("age")
        recordsetobj.MoveNext
Loop
connect.Close
Set connect = Nothing
recordsetobj.Close
Set recordsetobj = Nothing %>
```

INSERTING, UPDATING, AND DELETING RECORDS

The `Recordset` object can be used for inserting records into a database. The `AddNew` and `Update` methods of the `Recordset` object will enable you to insert records.

The `AddNew` method creates a new record, whereas the `Update` method adds that record to a database. Unless you call the `Update` method explicitly, the newly created record is not added to the database.

For example, consider the `employeetable` table that contains fields, such as `salary` and `age`, apart from the `employeename` field. Using the `Recordset` object that was created earlier, you can create and add a new record to the `employeetable` table. The syntax for adding a new record to the `employeetable` table is as follows:

```
<%recordsetobj.AddNew
recordsetobj("employeename") = "Bob"
recordsetobj("employeesalary") = "$10,000"
recordsetobj("age") = "35"
recordsetobj.Update %>
```

The preceding statements add the values Bob, $10,000, and 35 to the employeename, employeesalary, and age fields, respectively.

An alternate way of adding values to fields is as follows:

```
recordsetobj.AddNew
Array ("employeename", "employeesalary", "age"), Array ("Bob","$10,000","35")
```

Listing 4.9 shows a sample program to insert records into a database. In this program, the names of the form fields are name, salary, and age.

LISTING 4.9 A SAMPLE PROGRAM TO INSERT RECORDS

```
<% @ Language = VBSCRIPT %>
<!-- #include virtual="/adovbs.inc" -- >
<%
        Dim connect
        Dim recordsetobj
        Set connect = Server.CreateObject("ADODB.connection")
        connect.ConnectionString = "DSN.mydsn"
        connect.Open
        Set recordsetobj = Server.CreateObject ("ADODB.Recordset")
        recordsetobj.Open "employeemaster", connect, adLockOptimistic, adcmdTable
        recordsetobj.AddNew
        recordsetobj("employeename") = Request.Form ("name")
        recordsetobj("salary") = Request.Form ("salary")
        recordsetobj("age") = Request.Form ("age")
        recordsetobj.Update
        connect.Close
        Set connect = Nothing
        recordsetobj.Close
        Set recordsetobj = Nothing
%>
```

The methods for updating records in a database are the same as that used for adding records except that before using the AddNew method, you need to move the record pointer to the record you want to update. After you move to the required record, you can use the AddNew method followed by the Update method. You can use the CancelUpdate method to undo any updates that are made to records. The following syntax shows the usage of the Update and CancelUpdate methods:

```
recordsetobj("salary")= Request.Form ("salary")
        If recordsetobj("salary") = " " then
                recordsetobj.CancelUpdate
        Else
                recordsetobj.Update
```

DELETING RECORDS FROM A DATABASE

To delete records from a database, you can use the Delete method of the Recordset object. The logic is to move the record pointer to a particular record and then use the Delete method.

The syntax for using this method is

recordsetobjectname.Delete

Summary

ASP is a technology with which you can create dynamic Web pages. To run ASP, you need a Web server. You can create ASP pages if you know any of the scripting languages such as VBScript or JavaScript. You can write ASP in any text editor, such as Notepad or the native editor of UltraDev 4.

ASP 3.0 consists of seven built-in objects: `Response`, `Request`, `Application`, `Session`, `Server`, `ObjectContext`, and `Error`. The `Response` and `Request` objects are most commonly used in Web applications. While the `Response` object is used to send output to a browser, the `Request` object is used to read information sent by the browser. The `Server` object can be used to open a database connection while the `Session` and `Application` objects are used to maintain state in a single session and across all current sessions, respectively.

To interact with databases, ASP comes with a component called ADO, which consists of objects such as `Connection` and `Recordset`. The `Connection` object opens a connection with a database while the `Recordset` object creates a recordset consisting of rows retrieved from a table in a database. The `AddNew`, `Update`, and `Delete` methods of the `Recordset` object are used to add, update, and delete records in a database.

CHAPTER 5

UNDERSTANDING THE SERVER TECHNOLOGY: JAVASERVER PAGES

In this chapter

What Is a JavaServer Page? 82

JavaServer Page Syntax 85

Summary 99

What Is a JavaServer Page?

JavaServer Pages (JSP) is a solution provided by Sun Microsystems to create dynamic and user-interactive Web sites. Dynamic Web applications require a server to process requests generated dynamically by a browser. A browser can request either static or dynamic content from the Web server. The request from the browser goes to the Web server, which locates the Web page and sends it to the browser. The browser then displays this page. The Web server can only send static HTML pages that have been requested by the browser; it cannot send dynamic content unless an application sever is installed on it. Web technologies such as Common Gate Interface (CGI), Servlets, Active Server Pages (ASP), ColdFusion, and JavaServer Pages (JSP) can be used to generate dynamic content.

Dreamweaver UltraDev provides support to build dynamic Web applications by using the JSP server technology. In the context of dynamic Web applications, the role of the Web server is to process a JSP page and send the results to the browser. Although UltraDev generates JSP code as you build these applications, an understanding of the basics of JavaServer Pages will help you in making effective use of UltraDev. In this chapter, you will learn what JavaServer Pages are, how they work, and how you can use them.

JSP is one of the latest and few server-side scripting technologies used for developing Web applications. Scripts that run on the Web server in a *client/server system* are called *server-side scripts*. On the other hand, programs that are executed on browsers are called *client-side scripts*. JSP scripts are server-side scripts that are processed completely on the Web server and the output in the form of HTML pages is sent to the Web browser.

JSP provides Web developers an efficient way to develop and maintain dynamic Web pages. It enables them to change the overall layout or appearance of Web pages without changing the logic, which generates dynamic content. It also enables Web developers and designers to combine HTML tags with *JSP tags* to produce dynamic output The HTML tags are processed by the browser to display a page, whereas the JSP tags are used by the Web server to generate dynamic content. JSP tags separate Web content authors from the Web developers.

A JSP page is similar to any HTML page, except that it contains additional bits of code, such as JavaBeans, Java Database Connectivity (JDBC) objects, Enterprise JavaBeans (EJB), and Remote Method Invocation (RMI) objects, which execute application logic to generate dynamic content. Consider a JSP page that contains HTML code to display static text and graphics and JDBC objects to access databases. This JSP page, when displayed, contains both the static content and the dynamic information from the database. The Web-based applications built using JSP technology are platform independent. They can work with a wide variety of Web servers, browsers, and development tools efficiently.

A JSP page can also contain JavaBean components. A *JavaBean component* is a reusable and portable software component developed using the Java programming language. A JavaBean component has properties, methods, and events. When a JavaBean is used with *servlets* and JSP pages, it forms the business logic of an application.

To understand the benefits of JSP, you must first understand the difference between component-centric and page-centric Web development. In *page-centric* Web development, the logic for the layout, design, and content display of a specific page is embedded within the page. The page-centric model was easy to learn and therefore it was widely used. However, to build complex and scalable Web applications, people started looking for alternatives to the page-centric model. That's when the JSP technology emerged as a component-centric platform. In *component-centric* Web development, the logic for dynamic content generation is not embedded within a page, but is implemented through servlets or beans.

The component-centric nature of JSP allows non-Java developers, who work on the content presentation, and Java developers, who work on the content generation, to work independently. For example, an experienced Java developer develops a JavaBean for user name and password verification, a non-Java developer can use this to verify and display usernames and passwords without writing any code.

JSP pages can run on Web servers such as Microsoft Internet Information Server (IIS), Java Web Server (JWS), and Apache. By default, JSP uses Java as its scripting language. The other languages that can be used with JSP are JavaScript and VBScript. However, JSP with Java is more efficient.

The JSP technology is built on the Servlet Application Program Interface (API). This technology enables users to control the appearance of Web pages and generate dynamic content by using servlets. Users can extend the capabilities of a Web server by using servlets, which are server-side Java applications. These applications are invoked by a user request, and they respond to the request with an HTML reply. Servlets use Servlet Application Program Interface (Servlet API) and its classes and methods to modify a Web page before it is sent to the user. Servlets are loaded and run on a Web server and are similar to applets that run on a browser on the client side.

JSP provides a few server-side tags that allow developers to deliver dynamic content with minimal use of server-side scripting language. HTML designers and developers who are not familiar with scripting can use these tags for generating simple output without learning Java.

Models for Accessing JavaServer Pages

In JSP, the HTTP requests are processed in two different ways depending on the JSP model that is used. The difference between these two models is the location at which the request is processed.

The first JSP model is a two-tier model. In this model, the Java application uses a JDBC driver to access information from the database directly. The JSP page processes the request as well as generates the response and sends it to the browser. The second JSP model is a three-tier model. In this model, the Java application uses two components, one that processes the request and another that generates a response. You will learn more about the JSP models in the following sections of this chapter.

First Application Model

In the first model, as shown in Figure 5.1, the JSP server receives a request from a Web browser and sends it directly to a JSP page.

The first application model is shown in Figure 5.1.

Figure 5.1
In the first application model, a single component (the JSP page) processes the request and generates a response for the client.

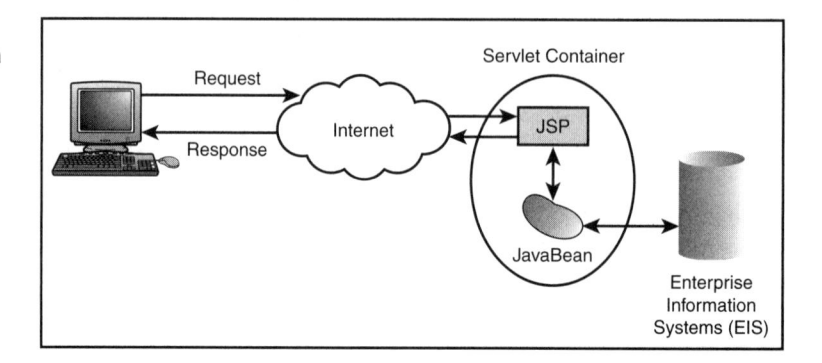

The JSP page then processes the request and generates a response for the client. Sometimes, the JSP page calls JDBC or *Java Blend components* to get information directly from a database and generates the requested content.

The Web server then creates standard HTML content and sends it to the browser. This model is easy and fast to program. In this model, the page author can easily generate dynamic content based on the request. This model is not advisable in situations where a large number of simultaneous clients are accessing the same Web resource.

> **Caution**
> If the JSP page accesses a database, it might generate many connections to the database, which can affect the performance of the databaseserver. This results in slower connections to the database and the speed with which the database server responds is also reduced.

Although the first model is simple and fast to program, it is not advisable to use this model for complex and large-scale applications.

Second Application Model

One of the two components in the second application model is the presentation component. *Presentation components* are JSP pages that generate HTML or XML content as output. These components are responsible for the presentation of the content and the user interface. The other component is the front component, which is also known as the *controller*. This component is responsible for creating any beans or objects used by the presentation component. The front component can either be a servlet or a JSP page. Depending on the user's action, the front component decides on the presentation component to which the request must be forwarded.

If the front component is a servlet, as shown in Figure 5.2, the Web browser sends the client request directly to the servlet. This servlet requests dynamic content from a JavaBean or Enterprise JavaBean. This dynamic content is embedded in a bean that is instantiated by the servlet. The presentation component, the JSP page, accesses the dynamic content from this bean and sends the results as HTML content to the browser. Front components are not responsible for any content presentation. In this model, there is a clear distinction between the presentation and front components.

The second application model is shown in Figure 5.2.

Figure 5.2
In the second application model, the presentation component (the JSP page) processes the request and the front component generates a response for the client.

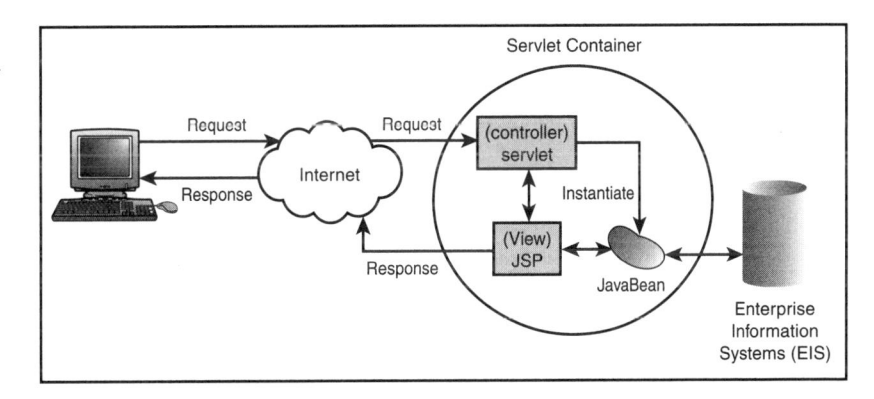

JAVASERVER PAGE SYNTAX

JSP is a collection of Java objects and simple scripting syntax. The syntax is used to communicate between the objects and the JSP server. Before we look at the JSP syntax, it is important to understand the usage of objects in JSP.

JSP consists of nine implicit objects that are used explicitly in servlets. The implicit objects are visible only within the system-generated jspService() method. These objects possess certain attributes and methods. Apart from these attributes and methods, these objects also contain collections.

The following list summarizes the purpose of the nine objects of JSP:

- request—Retrieves the information that a user sends from a browser. Form data, query string data, and information from cookies and server variables are some types of information that can be sent from a browser. These types of information are also called collections.
- response—Sends output from a server to a browser. This output can be text that is displayed on the browser, embedded HTML that can be rendered by the browser, or data that will be stored on the computer where the browser is located. Just like the reponse

object in ASP, the `response` object in JSP also has some methods and properties. The `response.setHeader()`, `response.setDateHeader()`, `response.sendRedirect()`, and `response.addCookie()` are some of the methods of the response object.

- `pageContext`—Stores information about the page. Each JSP page has a `pageContext` object. This object is created every time a user visits the page and is destroyed after the page is executed. Therefore, you can use this object to store and display information that needs to be maintained for the lifetime of a page. It contains the following methods: `findAttribute()`, `getAttribute()`, `getAttributes()`, `setAttribute()`, and `removeAttribute()`.

- `session`—Stores the values retrieved from a particular `session` in session variables. Session variables are used to store and display information about the user's interaction with the server, such as user's name, the duration of user's visit, user preferences, and so on. Some of the methods used by the session object are `getAttribute()`, `setAttribute()`, and `removeAttribute()`.

- `application`—Stores global application-level information that can be shared by several applications running simultaneously on different browsers. Global information, such as the page counter and number of hits for a page, are stored in application variables. These application variables are available to all users using the application. The information in this object is updated every time a user visits the site and is made available to all the users who are visiting the site. This object contains the `getAttribute()` and `setAttribute()` methods of the `Session` object. The `getAttribute()` method is used for retrieving the values of a variable, whereas the `setAttribute()` method is used for setting the values of a variable.

- `out`—Sends a stream of output to the browser. This object is used in scriptlets. This object uses the `out.println` method to send the output to the browser.

- `config`—Stores information such as the name of the servlet and the names of the initialization parameters in the servlet. This is a rarely used object in JSP. The config object uses the `getServletName()`, `getServletContext()`, `getInitParameter()`, and `getInitParameterNames()` methods to store information about the servlet configuration.

- `page`—This object is rarely used in JSP. This object is used just like the "this" object, to refer to the current instance of the JSP or the JSP page itself.

- `exception`—Stores information about the errors on a JSP page. You can use this object with the page directive on an error page. The exception object uses the three methods: `getMessage()`, `printStackTrace()`, and `toString()`.

COMPONENTS OF JAVASERVER PAGES

The components that make up a JavaServer Page can be classified into directives, declarations, JSP tags, expressions, and scriptlets. These components are discussed in detail in the subsequent sections.

JSP technology also enables you to access reusable components, such as JavaBean components, from within a JSP page. A JavaBean component can be used with JSP pages to separate code from layout. Generally, JSP tags are used for content access and presentation and JavaBean components are used for the programming code that generates dynamic content. As with any other component, a JavaBean component also has properties, methods, and events. The properties and methods of a JavaBean are used to exchange data and provide services. An event is used to trigger a method.

JSP Directives

A JavaServer page uses a JSP directive to pass information about the page may be the language, method, and type of content to the JSP server. JSP directives set global values, such as class declarations or methods, and page-level instructions. In addition, JSP directives can output content types, including data from external files, and specify custom tag libraries. JSP directives include the page, include, and taglib directives. The page directive enables you to provide information about the JSP page. The include directive enables you to include a file in a JSP page. The taglib directive enables you to define custom tags in a JSP page. Of these, the page and include directives are the most important. JSP directives are enclosed within the <%@ and %> delimiters.

The syntax for a JSP directive is as follows:

```
<%@ directive attribute= "value" ... %>
```

> **Note:** Generally the first line of a JSP page indicates the location from where Java programming language extensions can be accessed.

An example of a first line of a JSP page that imports the classes available in the UTIL package of JDK is as follows:

```
<%@ page import="java.util.*"%>
```

You will learn more about these directives in the subsequent sections of this chapter.

page Directives

The JSP page directive is a JSP tag that enables you to set attributes that apply to a JSP page. You will find this directive in most of JSP source files. The global attributes for a particular page are defined here. You can have any number of page directives within a JSP page.

The syntax for a JSP <%@ page %> directive is as follows:

```
<%@ page
    [language="java"]
    [extends="package.class"]
    [import="{package.class|package.*}, ..."]
    [session="true|false"]
    [buffer="none|8kb|sizekb"]
    [autoFlush="true|false"]
```

```
        [isThreadSafe="true|false"]
        [info="text"]
        [errorPage="relativeURL"]
        [contentType="mimeType[ ;charset=characterSet ]"|
➥           "text/html ; charset=ISO-8859-1" ]
        [isErrorPage="true|false"]
%>
```

JSP page directives have many attributes, of which some are mandatory. The mandatory attributes have default values. The page directives include attributes for setting the scripting language for the page (the default being Java), importing Java classes to use them in scriptlets, specifying buffer size, configuring output buffering, and so forth.

The following list summarizes the purpose of the attributes of a page directive:

- language—Specifies the language used in the JSP file.
- extends—Describes the parent class from which the JSP file is extended.
- import—Defines the packages available for the JSP file.
- session—Determines the availability of session data.
- buffer—Determines whether the output is buffered.
- Autoflush—Determines whether the output must be flushed automatically or must throw an exception when the buffer is full. By default, the value is true, which indicates that the buffer is flushed automatically.
- IsThreadSafe—By default, the value is true, which indicates normal servlet processing, where the JSP engine can process multiple requests simultaneously with a single servlet instance, provided the instance variables are synchronized. If IsThreadSafe is set to False, the JSP engine processes client requests one at a time.
- Info—Defines the page information that can be accessed using the Servlet.getServletInfo() method of the page.
- ErrorPage—Specifies the relative path that can handle exceptions.
- IsErrorPage—Marks a page as an error page. By default, this attribute is set to false.
- ContentType—Specifies the MIME type and the character set.

Tip

You can place page directives anywhere in a JSP file, but it's good programming style to place them at the top of the file.

An example of a page directive that imports the classes available in the SQL package of JDK and sets the buffering to 8KB is as follows:

```
<%@ page import="java.sql.*", buffer="8kb"%>
```

include DIRECTIVES

The JSP `<%@ include %>` directive is a JSP tag that allows you to include a file in a JSP file. This file is placed where the directive is located in the JSP file. The included file can be a text file, HTML file, or a JSP file. This directive enables you to include content from other files, such as copyright information, scripting language files, HTML headers and footers that are stored in separate files, or anything you might want to use from other applications.

When you use the `<%@ include %>` directive, the text of the included file is directly added to the JSP file. If the included file is a JSP file, its JSP elements are translated and included in the calling JSP file. Then, the process of translation continues with the next line of the calling file. The `<%@ include %>` directive saves a lot of time, as you can maintain this file in a central location and update it in order to effect updates in each JSP page.

> **Caution**
>
> Before you include a file by using the `<%@ include %>` directive, you must take care that the included file does not contain any `<html>` or `<body>` tags. If the included file contains `<html>` or `<body>` tags, they will conflict with the similar tags that are in the calling JSP file.

The syntax for the JSP include directive is as follows:

```
<%@ include file="relativeURL" %>
```

In the following example, the `<%@ include %>` directive is used to include the contents of the file scriptintro.html within the JSP page:

```
<%@ include file = "scriptintro.html" %>
```

In the following example, the `<%@ include %>` directive is used to include the contents of the header file within the JSP page. If you view this JSP page in a browser, you will find the contents of the header file, header.jsp, in the JSP page.

```
<HTML>
<BODY>
<BR>Including header, contents of header.jsp, in every page.<BR>
<%@ include file="header.jsp" %>
</BODY>
</HTML>
```

taglib DIRECTIVES

The `<%@ taglib %>` directive is a JSP tag, which declares that the JSP page uses a custom tag library, names the tag library that defines the custom tags, and specifies the associated tag prefix. The tag library enables you to create your own custom tags and specify a prefix for the custom tags. The tags in the tag library can be called from anywhere within the JSP page. The prefixe for each custom tag must be unique. The syntax for this directive is as follows:

```
<%@ taglib uri = "URIToTagLibrary" prefix = "tagPrefix" %>
```

> **Caution**
> If you are using more than one `taglib` directive in a JSP file, the prefix defined for each directive must be unique.

The `<%@ taglib %>` directive declares that the JSP file uses custom tags, names the tag library that defines the custom tags, and specifies the tag prefix. The `uri` attribute in the preceding syntax refers to a Uniform Resource Indicator that uniquely identifies the custom tag library, URI*ToTagLibrary*. The prefix attribute defines the prefix that is used to distinguish a custom tag instance.

> **Caution**
> Do not use `jsp`, `java`, `jspx`, `javax`, `servlet`, `sun`, and `sunw` as tag prefixes in custom tags, as they are reserved by Sun Microsystems.

> **Caution**
> Place the `taglib` directive before the custom tag in a JSP file so that the Web server interprets the custom tags and displays them as plain HTML text.

JSP Declarations

JSP declarations are similar to the declarations used in Java. A *declaration* enables you to define a method or a global variable in a JSP page that can be used from anywhere within the page. Declarations can only be used for defining and not for generating output. They are enclosed between the `<%!` and `%>` tags. The syntax for a JSP declaration is as follows:

```
<%! declaration; %>
```

The declaration syntax can contain more than one method or variable within one declaration element. You must separate these methods and variables by semicolons. The methods and variables of a declaration statement are initialized when the JSP page is initialized. After the JSP page is initialized, these declarations are available for scriptlets and expressions. You must always end a declaration with a semicolon.

In the following example, a declaration is used to declare the integer x and set its value to 0.

```
<%! int x = 0; %>
```

In the following example, a declaration is used to declare the new price of the book after a discount of 25%.

```
<%! Newbookprice = Oldbookprice-((Oldbookprice*25)/100);%>
```

JSP Expressions

A JSP expression contains any expression that is valid in the scripting language specified in that page. The JSP expression defined between the `<%=` and `%>` tags is evaluated and the

> **Note**
>
> In a scriptlet, end each line with a semicolon only if the scripting language requires it. For example, semicolons are used in Java and JavaScript languages, but not used in VBScript.

The following is an example of a scriptlet that uses a scripting, which requires a semicolon:

```
<HTML>
<BODY>
<% for(int i=1; i<11; i++) { %>

<% int c = i%2; %>

<% if (c==0) {%>

The <%=count%> number is: <U> <%= i %> </U><BR>

<%count=count+1; %>

<% } %>
</BODY>
</HTML>
```

You can combine scriptlets with static elements of a page to generate a dynamic page. The following is an example of a scriptlet and HTML. In this example we are assuming that there is a boolean variable named "magic" available. If you set it to true, you will see the output `Welcome to the Magic world`. If you set it to false, you will see a different output, `Try again world`.

```
<HTML>
<BODY>
<%
if (magic ) {
%>
<P>Welcome to the Magic world
<%
} else {
%>
<P>Try again world
<%
}
%>
</BODY>
</HTML>
```

You can use any of the JSP objects or classes imported by a page directive declared in a declaration or named in a `<jsp:usebean>` tag in your JSP scriptlet.

```
<jsp:useBean> id="login" class="log.class" scope="request">
</jsp:useBean>
<%
if (login.verify()) {
%>
 <jsp:forward page = "Welcome.jsp"/>
<%
```

```
} else {
%>
 <jsp:forward page = "login.jsp"/>
<%
}
%>
```

> **Caution** You must always end the scriptlet with the %> tag before you switch to any text, HTML tag, or JSP tag.

JSP ACTIONS

Actions are elements that perform server-side tasks without any coding. They are also referred to as JSP tags or JSP bean tags. In the JSP model, most JSP tags assume that the user is working with information that resides in a bean. Java Web servers use JSP tags to generate dynamic content. JSP tags are case sensitive and they can be used to perform a variety of functions, such as calling a JavaBean, connecting to a database, or executing standard Java codes.

Most of the processing in JavaServer Pages is implemented through JSP-specific tags, which are XML-based. The standard tags used in JSP 1.0 are referred to as *core tags*. The best thing about tags is that they are easy to use and can be shared between applications.

Some of the standard tags are jsp:forward, jsp:request, jsp:setProperty, jsp:getProperty, jsp:include, and jsp:plugin.

THE <jsp:forward> TAG

The <jsp:forward> tag forwards the client request from a JSP file to a HTML file, JSP file, or servlet for processing. This tag accepts two attributes, page and param name.

The syntax for the <jsp:forward> tag is as follows:

```
<jsp:forward page = "{relative URL | <%=expression%>}"
        {/>
        >[<jsp:param name = "parametername" value = "{parameter value|
<%=expression%>}"/>] +
</jsp:forward>}
```

The following list summarizes the purpose of the attributes of the <jsp:forward> tag:

- page—Represents the relative URL of the file to be forwarded.
- param name—Specifies the name of the parameter to be forwarded.

In the following example, the <jsp:forward> tag is used to forward the header.html file to a JSP file:

```
<jsp:forward page="header.html"/>
        <jsp:param name="bookname" value="Dreamweaver UltraDev 4"/>
</jsp:forward>
```

THE <jsp:plugin> TAG

The `<jsp:plugin>` tag enables you to download a Java plug-in to the browser for executing an applet or a bean. This tag generates an `<object>` element or an `<embed>` element resulting in an HTML file that is sent to the browser.

The attributes of the `<jsp:plugin>` tag can specify whether the object is a bean or an applet. In addition, they can specify the name for the instance of the bean or applet and pass parameter names and values to them. The other attributes locate the code and position the object in the browser window. The URL from which the plug-in software is downloaded can also be specified using these parameters.

The syntax for the `<jsp:plugin>` tag is as follows:

```
<jsp:plugin
    type ="bean|applet"
    code = "classFileName"
    codebase = "classFileDirectoryName"
    [name = "instanceName"]
    [archive = "URIToArchive,…. "]
    [align = "bottom|top|middle|left|right"]
    [height = "displayPixels"]
    [width = "displayPixels"]
    [hspace = "leftRightPixels"]
    [vspace = "topBottomPixels"]
    [jreversion = "JREVersionNumber|1.1"]
    [nspluginurl = "URLToPlugin"]
    [iepluginurl = "URLToPlugin"] >
    [<jsp:params> <jsp:param name = "parameterName" value = "parameter Value>
+</jsp:params>]
    [<jsp:fallback> text msg for the user </jsp:fallback>]
</jsp:plugin>
```

The following list summarizes the purpose of the attributes of the `<jsp:plugin>` tag:

- type—Specifies the type of object, bean, or applet the plugin software will execute.
- code—Specifies the name of the applet or bean file the plugin software will execute.
- codebase—Specifies the path to the directory that contains the code of the applet.
- name—Defines a name for the instance of the applet or the bean.
- archive—Specifies the paths to locate the archives that must be loaded before executing the applet or the bean.
- align—Defines the position of the image displayed by the applet or the bean in the JSP page.
- height—Specifies the height of the image displayed by the applet or the bean in pixels.
- width—Specifies the width of the image displayed by the applet or the bean in pixels.
- hspace—Specifies the amount of space, in pixels, to the left and right of image displayed by the applet or the bean.
- vspace—Specifies the amount of space, in pixels, at the top and bottom of the image the applet or the bean displays.

result obtained is converted to a string. This string is then inserted into the JSP file and displayed dynamically. If a result cannot be converted to a string, an error occurs.

Generally, expressions display simple values of variables or return values of bean methods. The syntax for a JSP expression is as follows:

```
<%= expression %>
```

The following code generates the first five even numbers. In this example, `<%= i %>` is an expression and `<% int count=1; %>` is a declaration:

```
<%@ page import="java.util.*" %>
<HTML>
<HEAD>
<TITLE>THIS IS A SAMPLE JSP PAGE </TITLE>
</HEAD>
<BODY>
<H1><CENTER>Even Numbers</CENTER></H1>
<H2>
<% int count=1; %>

<% for(int i=1; i<11; i++) { %>

<% int c = i%2; %>

<% if (c==0) {%>

The <%=count%> number is: <U> <%= i %> </U><BR>

<%count=count+1; %>

<% } %>

<% } %>
</H2>
</BODY>
</HTML>
```

> **Caution**
> Unlike a JSP declaration, a JSP expression must not end with a semicolon. If you end a JSP expression with a semicolon, it will flag an error.

JSP SCRIPTLETS

JSP scriptlets are small blocks of Java code included in JSP pages. Scriptlets allow you to declare variables or methods and write any number of valid scripting language statements within the `<%` and `%>` tags. In short, a scriptlet is a code fragment executed at the time of client request. The syntax for a scriptlet is as follows:

```
<% code fragment %>
```

- **jreversion**—Specifies the version of the Java Runtime Environment (JRE) that the applet or the bean requires.
- **nspluginurl**—Specifies the URL from where the user can download the JRE plugin for Netscape Navigator.
- **iepluginurl**—Specifies the URL from where the user can download the JRE plugin for Internet Explorer.
- `<jsp:params> <jsp:param name = "parameterName" value = "parameter Value"> +</jsp:params`—Specifies the parameters and values to be passed to the applet or the bean.
- `<jsp:fallback> text msg for the user </jsp:fallback>]`—Specifies the text message to be displayed if the applet or bean does not start.

The `type`, `code`, `codebase`, `name`, and `archive` attributes are mandatory. The remaining attributes are optional.

In the following example, the browser downloads a Java plugin to execute the applet.

```
<jsp:plugin
    type ="applet"
    code = "car.class"
    codebase = "carmodels.html" >
    <jsp:params> <jsp:param name = "carcolor" value = "red"> </jsp:params>
    <jsp:fallback> Failed to load the applet </jsp:fallback>
</jsp:plugin>
```

THE `<jsp:include>` TAG

The `<jsp:include>` tag enables you to include a static or a dynamic file in a JSP file. If you are including a static file, then the include tag includes the content of the static file in the calling JSP file. If you are including a dynamic file, the include tag acts on the request, processes it, and sends a result that is included in the JSP page. The difference between the include directive and the include tag is that in the include directive the file is inserted only after the JSP file is translated into a servlet. However, in the case of an include tag the file is included at the time of a request.

The syntax for the `<jsp:include>` tag is as follows:

```
< jsp:include page = "{relativeURL | <%= expression %>}"
        flush = "true" >
        <jsp:param name ="parameter name"
        value ="{parameter value| <%= expression %>}" />+
</ jsp:include>
```

If the included file is dynamic, you can use a `<jsp:param>` clause as shown in the preceding syntax. You can use this clause to pass the name and value of a parameter to the dynamic file.

The following list summarizes the attributes of the `<jsp:include>` tag:

- `page`—Represents the relative URL of the file to be included.
- `param name`—Represents the name of the parameter. This attribute takes a case-sensitive literal string.
- `value`—Indicates the value of the parameter. The `value` attribute takes either a case-sensitive literal string or an expression evaluated at request time.
- `flush`—Enables you to specify whether the buffer should be flushed. It is advisable to set the `flush` attribute to `true` so that the buffer is automatically flushed when it is full.

An example to include the contents of an existing `registration.html` file in a JSP file is as follows:

```
<jsp:include page="registration.html"
flush = "true" >
    <jsp:param name="fname" value="Don"/>
</jsp:include>
```

> **Note**
>
> If you want to send more than one parameter to the included file, you can use more than one `<jsp:param>` clause.

THE `<jsp:usebean>` TAG

You can initiate the use of a bean in a JSP page by using the `<jsp:usebean>` action tag. The syntax for the `<jsp:usebean>` tag is as follows:

```
<jsp:usebean id="beanInstanceName"
    scope="page|request|session|application"

    {class="package.class" |
    type="package.class" |

    class="package.class" type="package.class" |

    beanName="{package.class | <%= expression %>}" type="package.class"
    }
    {/> | > other elements </jsp:usebean>
    }
```

This tag accepts three attributes: `id`, `class`, and `scope`. The following list summarizes the purpose of these three attributes:

- `id`—Specifies the name of the bean instance.
- `class`—Specifies the JavaBean class.

- scope—Specifies the scope of the bean and the context in which the bean should be made available. Depending on the scope declared for the bean, the <jsp:usebean> tag might or might not generate a new instance of the bean within the page. This attribute of the <jsp:usebean> tag sets the scope of the associated bean to a page, a request, a session, or an application:
    - page—The default value of scope is page. This scope is page-dependent. In this case, an object can be accessed by a single client and only from the page on which it is created. The page beans will be destroyed after the output is sent to the browser.
    - request—This scope is request-dependent. In this case, the object can be accessed by a single client and only for the lifetime of the single client request. The request beans are destroyed after the output is sent to the browser. JSP allows you to execute more than one page during a single client request.
    - session—This scope is session-dependent. In this case, the bean instance remains for the lifetime of the session unless the user purposely destroys it. To make the bean available for the current session, the <jsp:usebean> tag creates a new instance of the bean for the session or retrieves the current instance of the bean.
    - application—This scope is application-dependent. In this case, the bean instance remains for the lifetime of an application. If the application is reloaded or server is restarted then the bean instance expires.

In the following example, the JSP code generates a bean instance defined in the tryBeanClass class and names the reference as tryBeanInstance. The scope is request so this instance exists only for the life cycle of a single HTTP request for the JSP page:

```
<jsp:usebean ID="tryBeanInstance" CLASS="tryBeanClass" SCOPE="request">
...body...
</jsp:usebean>
```

Note: Beans can be either JavaBeans or EJB components.

The <jsp:usebean> tag declares the usage of an instance of a JavaBeans component

In the following example, the JSP code generates a bean instance defined in the sampleBean class and names the reference as myBean. The scope is set to session so this instance remains for the lifetime of a session. In this example the expression <%= mybean.convertToRupees()%> converts the amount in dollars to rupees:

```
<jsp:useBean id="myBean" class="sampleBean" scope="session"/>
<HTML>
<BODY>
You entered<BR>
dollars: <%=request.getParameter("bookprice")%><BR>
in Rupees: <%= mybean.convertToRupees()%><BR>
</BODY>
</HTML>
```

THE `<jsp:setProperty>` TAG

Some components of beans can be created and used immediately but some need to be initialized before they are used. The `<jsp:setProperty>` tag enables the user to set the properties of beans to the values that the user specifies or to values passed by an HTTP request. The syntax for the `<jsp:setProperty>` tag is as follows:

```
<jsp:setProperty name="beanInstanceName"
    {property="*" |    property="propertyName"
    [param="parameterName"] | property="propertyName"
    value="{string | <%= expression %>}" } />
```

The `<jsp:setProperty>` tag accepts four attributes: name, property, value, and param. The name and property attributes are mandatory and the value and param attributes are optional.

The following list summarizes the purpose of the attributes of the `<jsp:setProperty>` tag:

- name—Specifies the name of the object or the bean instance defined previously in the `<jsp:usebean>` tag.
- property—Specifies the name of the bean property whose value is to be displayed in the results page.
- value—Initializes the bean property to the value that a user specifies.
- param—Sets the bean property to the value passed by an HTTP request.

> **Caution**
> Both the `value` and param attributes cannot be used in the same `<jsp:setProperty>` tag. If they are used in the same `<jsp:setProperty>` tag, an error is generated.

> **Tip**
> The `<jsp:setProperty>` tag is used in the body of a `<jsp:usebean>` tag. If you want to use the `<jsp:setProperty>` tag within a JSP page, you must first define a bean with a proper scope by using the `<jsp:usebean>` tag.

THE `<jsp:getProperty>` TAG

After the components of beans are created and initialized, the user can use them to generate dynamic content within a JavaServer page. The `<jsp:getProperty>` tag converts the value of a bean instance property into a string and places it in the implicit object, out.

The `<jsp:getProperty>` tag displays a property of a bean that is already defined on the page or defined as a session or an application bean earlier. The syntax for the `<jsp:getProperty>` tag is as follows:

```
<jsp:getProperty name="beanInstanceName" property="propertyName" />
```

The `<jsp:getProperty>` tag accepts two attributes, name and property. These attributes are mandatory. The name attribute specifies the name of the object or the bean instance previously defined in the `<jsp:usebean>` tag. The `property` attribute specifies the name of the bean property whose value is to be displayed in the results page.

> **Tip**
>
> You can mix HTML tags with `<jsp:getProperty>` tags to dynamically generate and format HTML content.

Assume that a bean by the name RegInfo is already defined as an application bean earlier. In the following example, the `getProperty` tag is used to display the value of the username property of the `RegInfo` bean.

```
<b>
User Name: <jsp:getProperty name="RegInfo" property="userName" />
</b>
```

SUMMARY

In this chapter, you learned what a JavaServer Page is and how is it better than other server-side scripting technologies. You also learned about the components of JavaServer Pages that include directives, declarations, JSP tags, expressions, and scriptlets. Next, you learned about the three types of directives and a few JSP tags.

You learned about the advantage of tags and developing custom tag libraries. The idea of developing customized tag libraries will encourage Web developers and designers to create their own tag libraries for common functions. Very soon, Web developers and designers will start using JavaServer pages to create portable Web applications that can run on different Web and application servers.

In addition, you learned about the different JSP application models. Finally, you learned how JSP technology speeds the development of dynamic Web pages.

JSP technology has made development of dynamic Web pages much easier and faster. JSP technology uses tags, and reusable components such as JavaBeans and Enterprise JavaBeans to separate the process of content generation and presentation.

CHAPTER 6

UNDERSTANDING THE SERVER TECHNOLOGY: COLDFUSION

In this chapter

Introducing ColdFusion   102

Working with Databases by Using CFML   104

Summary   114

Introducing ColdFusion

UltraDev supports one of the latest server technologies available in the field of Web application development—ColdFusion. ColdFusion, a product of Allaire Corporation, is a Web application server that enables you to build dynamic Web sites. Although a product of Allaire Corporation, ColdFusion is now owned by Macromedia. In ColdFusion, Web applications are created using ColdFusion Markup Language (CFML). Similar to HTML, CFML is also a tag-based scripting language. The pages created using CFML are similar to HTML pages, except that CFML pages contain server-side scripts that dynamically control data integration and presentation.

Unlike static Web sites, the primary focus of dynamic Web sites is on programmatic design and logic required to maintain online transactions. CFML enables you to include this logic with the help of CFML tags. Like other programming languages, CFML enables you to work with variables and program flow controls. It also enables you to interact with a database by using SQL statements. A simple feature, which requires numerous lines of complex coding in ASP or JSP, can be easily implemented using a single CFML tag. You can code CFML pages in Notepad or any other HTML editor and they should have a .cfm extension.

ColdFusion Server runs as a multithreaded process, providing excellent features for database support, load balancing, and failover. ColdFusion Server contains a comprehensive server administration tool called ColdFusion Administrator. Using ColdFusion Administrator, server managers can easily administer ColdFusion servers, applications, and DSNs remotely. ColdFusion also provides an integrated development environment called ColdFusion Studio (licensed separately from ColdFusion Server) that incorporates visual programming and debugging tools. ColdFusion server supports Windows 95/98, Windows NT, Solaris, HP-UX, and Linux operating system platforms.

ColdFusion Server is available in three editions: Enterprise, Professional, and Express. The Enterprise edition of ColdFusion is designed for large-scale transaction-intensive e-business applications that demand high security, load balancing, and server failover features. This edition also enables you to extend ColdFusion applications with a range of technologies, such as C++, COM, CORBA, EJB, and CFX. The Enterprise edition provides support for native drivers, such as Sybase, Informix, DB2, and Oracle, and is available for the HP-UX and Solaris systems. All these advanced features are supported only by the Enterprise edition of ColdFusion and not by the other two editions. Although the Professional edition does not support these features, it supports all the basic features of ColdFusion and therefore you can use it with UltraDev for developing Web applications. The last edition of ColdFusion, called ColdFusion Express, is a free edition. This edition supports all the features the Professional edition supports, but it cannot be used with UltraDev because it does not support certain tags, such as CFSCRIPT, that are widely used by UltraDev in many of its Server Behaviors.

The UltraDev CD comes with a single-user and scaled-down version of the ColdFusion Enterprise edition. You can use this edition to develop and access ColdFusion applications locally through an http://localhost or through a 127.0.0.1 IP address. You can install this Enterprise edition on a Windows 95, 98, NT, or 2000 machine that has a Web server running on it.

→ To learn how to install the version of ColdFusion server that comes along with UltraDev, **see** "Installing ColdFusion Server 4.5," **p. 522**.

After you install the ColdFusion Server, you can configure UltraDev to connect to the ColdFusion server by using the Site Definition dialog box of UltraDev. This configuration allows you to add dynamic features to a Web site by using various options available in Ultradev. For every feature that you add to your Web page, UltraDev generates the relevant ColdFusion tags and functions automatically. However, it will be of help if you understand some of the basic CFML tags generated by UltraDev. Therefore, the following sections introduce you to some of the basic ColdFusion tags that are generated automatically for some of the commonly used server behaviors in UltraDev. Apart from the tags mentioned in this chapter, ColdFusion supports more than 70 server-side tags, 200 functions, and 800 third-party components. To learn about these tags, functions, and third-party components, you can refer to the Allaire Web site.

→ To learn how to connect UltraDev to a ColdFusion Server, **see** "Application Server Information," **p. 123**.

Work Flow: Web Server, ColdFusion Server, and Database

Information requests and processing take place on the Web basically between the client, which is the Web browser, and the host, which is the Web server. The Web server processes requests sent by a Web browser. If the request is for static data, such as an HTML file, the Web server sends the requested HTML file to the browser. But if the request is for a .cfm file, as shown in Figure 6.1, the Web server passes the file to ColdFusion Server. ColdFusion Server processes the CFML tags in the .cfm file and returns only HTML and other client-side technologies, such as CSS and JavaScripts, to the Web server. The Web server then passes the page to the Web browser.

> **Note**
> The Web server and the ColdFusion Server can exist on the same machine or on different machines.

Figure 6.1
The ColdFusion server processes the .cfm file and returns an .html file to the Web server.

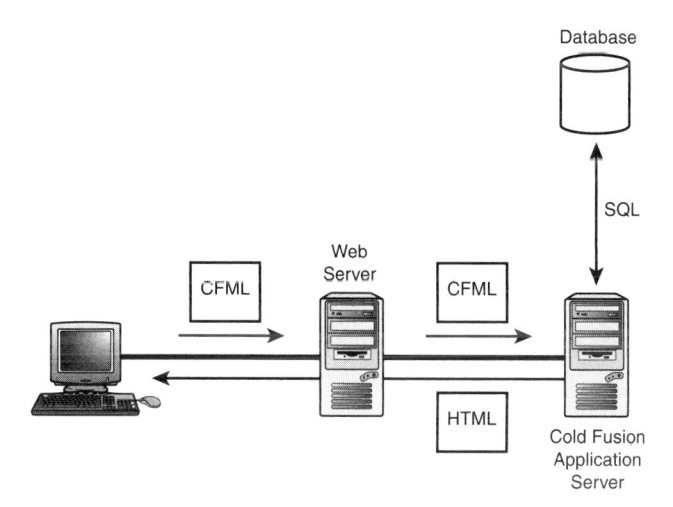

Working with Databases by Using CFML

The first step toward building a dynamic Web site is to connect the Web site to a database. You can connect ColdFusion to any database that supports *Open Database Connectivity* (ODBC). ODBC is an interface that is used to connect a database to an application by using a *Data Source Name (DSN)*.

→ To learn more about ODBC, **see** "Databases and ASP," **p. 73**.

> **Note**
> ColdFusion applications are not limited to ODBC databases. They also enable you to retrieve data by using *OLE-DB* and native *database drivers*. In addition, they enable you to assess information from mail servers that support *Post Office Protocols (POP)*.

A DSN contains information that is required to connect to a database. This information includes the database name, the name of the server on which the database exists, and the user name and password that are required to connect to the database. For example, to access the database `bookstore` on the server `serve1`, with `newuser` as the user name and `mypassword` as the password, you can create a DSN called `storeconnect`.

> **Note**
> The name given to a DSN must be a single word and must begin with a letter of the alphabet. DSN names can contain only letters, numbers and underscore. DSN names must not contain any special characters.
>
> All DSNs need not necessarily contain a username and password. For example, a DSN created for a Microsoft Access database does not require a username and password.

To create a DSN in ColdFusion, perform the following steps:

1. Choose Start, Programs, ColdFusion Server, Cold Fusion Administrator. If a username and a password are assigned at the time of installing the ColdFusion server, the administrator prompts you to enter them. Enter the username and the password and click OK. The ColdFusion Administrator page is displayed, as shown in Figure 6.2.
2. Click the ODBC option in the ColdFusion Administrator page. The ODBC Data Sources Available to ColdFusion page is displayed, as shown in Figure 6.3.
3. In the Data Source Name text box, type a name for the DSN that you want to create. For example, to create a DSN called `storeconnect`, type **storeconnect** in the Data source Name text box.
4. From the ODBC driver drop-down list, select an ODBC driver and click the Add button. For example, if you are using an Access database, choose the Microsoft Access Driver (*.mdb) option and click Add. The Create ODBC Data Source page is displayed as shown in Figure 6.4

WORKING WITH DATABASES BY USING CFML | 105

Figure 6.2
Use the ODBC option in the ColdFusion Administrator page to add a new DSN.

Figure 6.3
Use the ODBC Data Sources Available to ColdFusion page to specify the name of the new DSN.

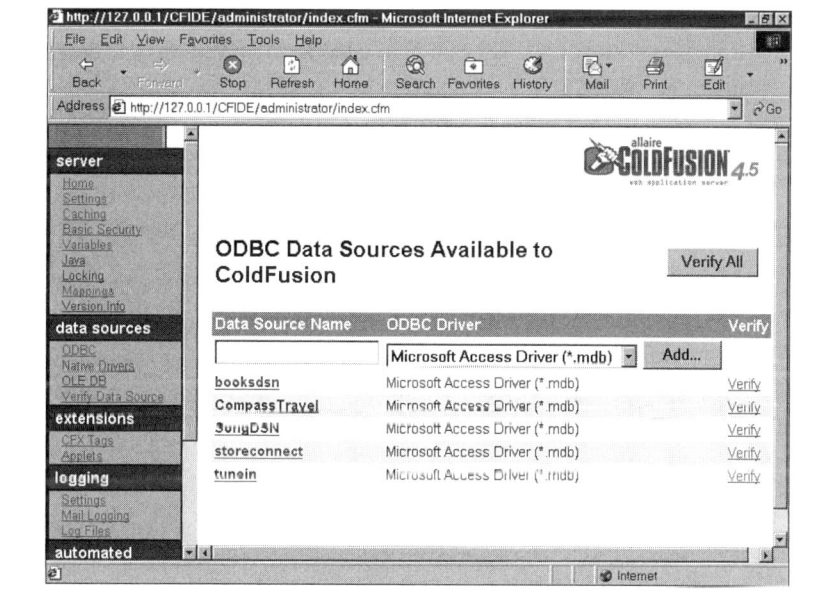

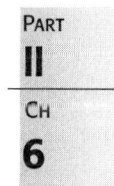

PART
II
CH
6

Figure 6.4
Use the Create ODBC Data Source page, to specify the location of the database to which the DSN must connect.

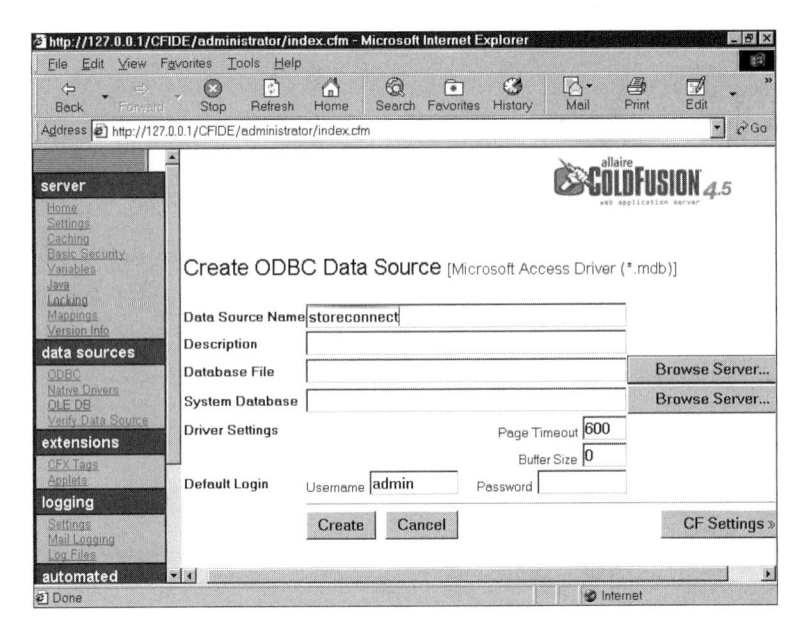

5. In the Database File text box, enter the path to the database to which you want to connect and click OK. Alternatively, you can click the Browse Server button to browse to the database.
6. Click the Create button to create the new data source. The new data source is added to the list of data sources.
7. Click the Verify button next to the newly added data source. If the data source is created successfully, a message is displayed informing you that the data source connection is verified successfully.

Retrieving Data from a Database

After you have created a DSN, you can search the information stored in the database with the help of the <CFQUERY> tag provided by ColdFusion.

A simple CFQUERY requires parameters such as the query name and the data source name. The following is the syntax for the <CFQUERY> tag:

```
<CFQUERY NAME="query_name" DATASOURCE="datasource_name">
query statement using SQL
</CFQUERY>
```

For example, to retrieve a list of all books stored in the books table of the bookstore database, the following code can be used:

```
<HTML>
<HEAD>
<TITLE>BOOKS DETAIL </TITLE>
</HEAD>
```

```
<BODY>
<CFQUERY NAME="booksdetail" DATASOURCE="storeconnect">
SELECT * FROM book
</CFQUERY>
</BODY>
</HTML>
```

> **Note** Attribute values of CFML tags must be enclosed within quotes ("). The datasource must exist in the ColdFusion Administrator for the query to be executed successfully.
>
> The `<CFQUERY>` tag can also be placed above the HTML code snippet tag so that the database information retrieved by the `<CFQUERY>` tag can be used in any place in the HTML code. UltraDev also places the `<CFQUERY>` tag as the first tag in the code before the HTML section.

UltraDev generates the `CFQUERY` tag whenever you use insert, update, or delete server behaviors. It is also generated whenever you define a recordset for a page by using the Data Bindings panel in UltraDev.

→ To learn more on insert, update, and delete various server behaviors, **see** "Building Dynamic Web Applications," **p. 407**.

Displaying Data on the Web Page

Information can be displayed on the Web page with the help of the `<CFOUTPUT>` tag. This tag displays text and values stored in variables, as shown in the following code:

```
<HEAD>
<TITLE>BOOKS DETAIL </TITLE>
</HEAD>
<BODY>
<CFSET city="Texas">
<CFOUTPUT>
My favorite city is #city#.
</CFOUTPUT>
</BODY>
</HTML>
```

In the preceding example, the `<CFSET>` tag declares a variable called `city`. The variable `city` is assigned the value `Texas`. The `<CFOUTPUT>` tag displays the value stored in the variable, `city`. In CFML, variable names are enclosed within # marks.

The `<CFQUERY>` tag enables you to retrieve the data stored in a database. The data retrieved from the database using the `<CFQUERY>` tag can be stored as query variables. You can use the value of the query variables by referencing them in the `<CFOUTPUT>` tag block. The `<CFOUTPUT>` tag uses the QUERY attribute to define the query variable that you want to display on the Web page. For example, to display the data retrieved by the `booksdetail` query on the Web page, the following code can be entered after the `<CFQUERY>` tag:

```
<CFOUTPUT QUERY ="booksdetail" >
#bookid#<BR>
```

```
#title#<BR>
#price#<BR>
</CFOUTPUT>
```

The query variables that are defined in the preceding code store values retrieved from the query mentioned in the QUERY attribute of the <CFOUTPUT> tag.

> **Caution:** If you want the variables to refer to the values stored in the fields in a database, then variable names must be the same as the field names.

UltraDev generates the <CFOUTPUT> tag whenever you try to display any content on a Web page.

Displaying Formatted Output

The output of a query can be formatted using HTML tags. For example, to display the bookid in bold font, the following code can be used:

```
<CFOUTPUT QUERY ="booksdetail">
<B>#bookid#</B> <BR>
#title# <BR>
#price# <BR><BR>
<BR></CFOUTPUT>
```

ColdFusion returns a formatted output for every record fetched by the SELECT statement.

Figure 6.5 displays the output of this code viewed on the browser.

Figure 6.5
Use the <CFOUTPUT> tag to display a formatted output.

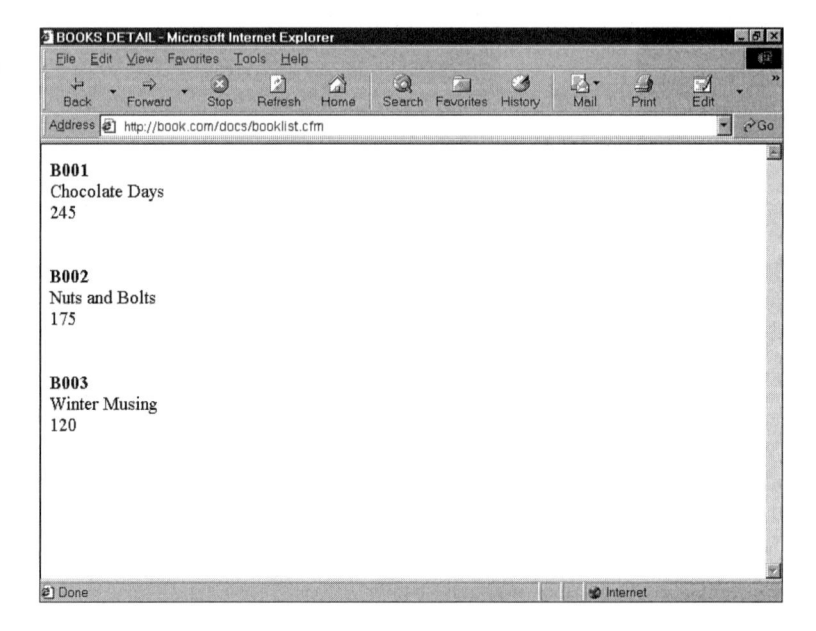

Every item within the <CFOUTPUT> tag repeats itself until all the records in the recordset are accounted for. Therefore, you need to be careful with the use of HTML tags within the <CFOUTPUT> tag. For example, the following code will display the output shown in Figure 6.6:

```
<CFOUTPUT QUERY ="booksdetail" >
<H2> Book List </H2>
#bookid#<BR>
#title#<BR>
#price#<BR>
<BR>
<BR>
</CFOUTPUT>
```

Figure 6.6
Placing an HTML tag within a <CFOUTPUT> tag repeats the content of the HTML tag for every record.

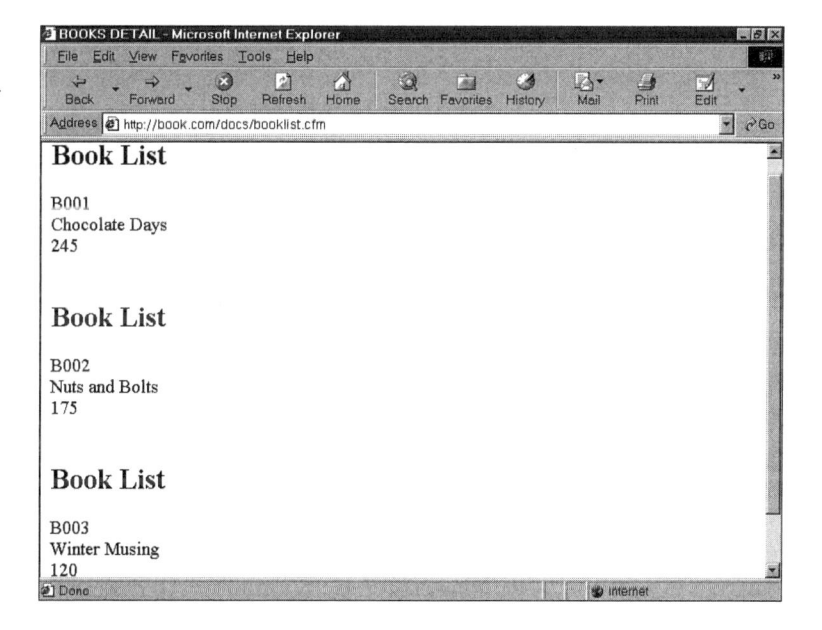

As shown in Figure 6.6, the heading "Book List" repeats itself after every record because the HTML tag <H2> Book List </H2> is placed within the <CFOUTPUT> tag. This problem can be resolved by placing the HTML tag outside the <CFOUTPUT> tag, as shown in the following code:

```
<H2> Book List </H2>
<CFOUTPUT QUERY ="booksdetail" >
#bookid#<BR>
#title#<BR>
#price#<BR>
<BR>
<BR>
</CFOUTPUT>
```

The above code will display the heading followed by a list of book titles, as shown in Figure 6.7.

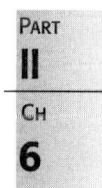

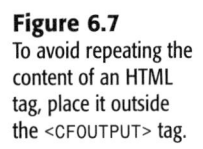

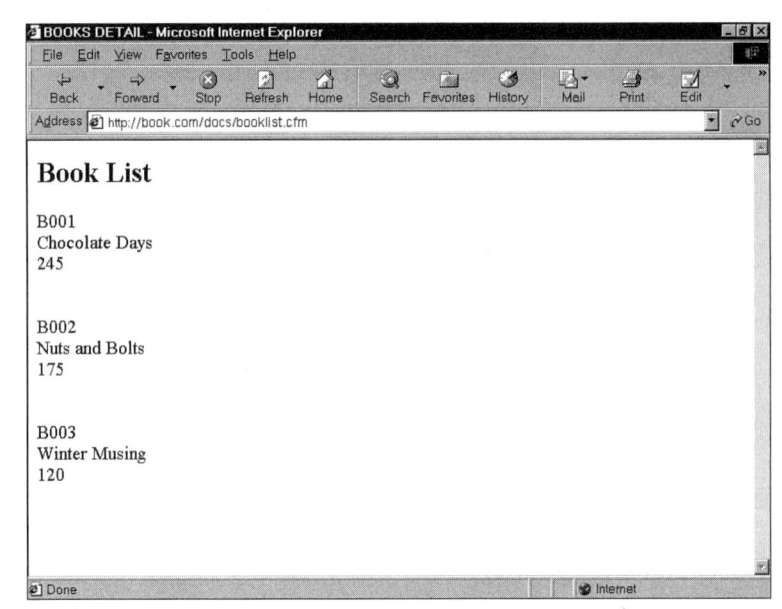

Figure 6.7
To avoid repeating the content of an HTML tag, place it outside the <CFOUTPUT> tag.

USING VARIABLES WITH <IMG>, <SRC>, AND <A HREF> TAGS

ColdFusion variables can be used to specify attribute values for the <IMG> or <A HREF> tags used in HTML.

For example, if there is a field called image in the book table that contains URLs for the pictures of each book, then the following code can be used to display the picture of each book along with its title:

```
<CFOUTPUT QUERY ="booksdetail" >
<B>Book title: #title#</B> <BR>
<IMG SRC="#image#"> <BR>
</CFOUTPUT>
```

Similarly, if there is a field called view that contains URLs pointing to the location on the Web site where a brief description of each title is stored, then you can use the following code to display the description of each title when it is clicked:

```
<CFOUTPUT QUERY ="booksdetail" >
<B> <A HREF="#view#"> Book title: #title#</B> <BR>
</CFOUTPUT>
```

INSERTING DATA INTO A DATABASE

CFML tags can also be used to insert data into a database. To enable a user to insert data into a database, you need to first design an HTML form in which the user can enter the information.

For example, to create a form that will enable a user to enter values into the book table, you can use the following HTML code:

```
<HTML>
<HEAD>
<TITLE>BOOKS DATA ENTRY FORM</TITLE>
</HEAD>
<BODY>
<FORM METHOD="POST" ACTION="addrecord.cfm">
Book ID: <INPUT TYPE="TEXT" NAME="bookid"> <BR>
Title: <INPUT TYPE="TEXT" NAME="title"> <BR>
Price: <INPUT TYPE="TEXT" NAME="price"> <BR>
<INPUT TYPE="SUBMIT"><BR>
</FORM>
</BODY>
</HTML>
```

In the preceding example, the filename addrecord.cfm, which is passed as a value for the ACTION attribute, specifies the file to which the browser will pass the information when the user clicks the submit button. The names of the input fields in the form are the same as the names of the fields in the table.

After designing the form, you can create the addrecord.cfm file that adds the data entered into the form to the database. The <CFINSERT> tag is used to enter the data into a database.

For example, the contents of the addrecord.cfm file will be as follows:

```
<CFINSERT DATASOURCE="storeconnect" TABLENAME="book">
```

The preceding code is simply one line because the names of the input fields are the same as the names of the fields in the table. If the names of the input fields differ from the names of the fields in the table, for example, if the names of the input fields are id, booktitle, and price, the <CFQUERY> tag must be written as follows:

```
<CFQUERY NAME="addbook" DATASOURCE="storeconnect">
INSERT INTO book(bookid, title, price)
VALUES ('#Form.id#','#Form.booktitle#', '#Form.price#')
</CFQUERY>
```

In this code, the variables #Form.id#, #Form.booktitle#, and #Form.price# are referred to as form variables. When a form is submitted, a form variable is passed for every form control that contains a value.

UltraDev generates the <CFINSERT> tag when you use the Insert Record server behavior.

While inserting records into a database table using a form, you might have to validate the data entered into the form. You can perform such validations by using the <CFIF> and <CFELSE> tags. For example, if no value is entered in the title field of the form, you can display a message prompting the user to enter a value in the title field by using the following code:

```
<CFIF Form.bookid EQ "">
Please enter the book id!
</CFIF>
<CFIF Form.title EQ "">
Please enter the book title!
```

```
</CFIF>
<CFIF Form.price EQ "">
Please enter the price of the book!
</CFIF>
<CFELSE>
<CFQUERY NAME="addbook" DATASOURCE= "storeconnect">
INSERT INTO book(bookid, title, price)
VALUES ('#Form.bookid#','#Form.title#', '#Form.price#')
</CFQUERY>
Your record is added successfully!
</CFIF>
```

> **Note** Table names and columns names specified in SQL statements must exist in the database. Otherwise, the query will fail.

Modifying Records in a Database

You can use a combination of HTML and CFML tags to modify the records in a database. To enable a user to modify the records in a database, you need to display a list of all the records available in the database. For example, the following code displays the records in the book table:

```
<HTML>
<HEAD>
<TITLE>BOOKS DETAIL </TITLE>
</HEAD>
<BODY>
<H1> BOOK LIST</H1>
<CFQUERY NAME="booksdetail" DATASOURCE="storeconnect">
SELECT * FROM book
</CFQUERY>
<CFOUTPUT QUERY="booksdetail">
Book Id: #bookid# <BR>
Title: #title# <BR>
Price: #price# <BR>
</CFOUTPUT>
</BODY>
</HTML>
```

To enable the user to modify the records that are displayed, an option must be given to edit the value of the record. To do this, you can use <CFOUTPUT> tag as follows:

```
<CFOUTPUT QUERY="booksdetail">
Book Id: #bookid# <BR>
Title: #title# <BR>
Price: #price# <BR>
Click here to <A HREF="editbook.cfm?bookid=#bookid#">
edit the book information.</A><br><br>
</CFOUTPUT>
```

In the preceding example, when the user clicks the link to edit the information for a specific book, the `editbook.cfm` file is invoked. The ID of the book for which the information has to be modified needs to be passed to the `editbook.cfm` file. This is done by specifying the name of the variable, `bookid`, and the value stored in the variable, `#bookid#`, in the URL of the page. A question mark separates the URL information from the variable information.

For example, if the user decides to edit the information of the book, B012, then the URL of the `editbook.cfm` page will contain the following information:

```
editbook.cfm?bookid=B012
```

The `editbook.cfm` file displays a form with the current information of the book, which needs to be edited. The following code is written in the `editbook.cfm` file:

```
<HTML>
<HEAD>
<TITLE>EDIT BOOK DETAIL </TITLE>
</HEAD>
<BODY>
<CFQUERY NAME="editbook" DATASOURCE="storeconnect">
SELECT * FROM book
WHERE bookid='#URL.bookid#'
</CFQUERY>
<CFOUTPUT QUERY="editbook">
<FORM METHOD="POST" ACTION="updatebook.cfm">
<INPUT TYPE="HIDDEN" Name="bookid" VALUE="#bookid#"><BR>
Title:<INPUT TYPE="TEXT" NAME="title" VALUE="#title#"><BR>
Price:<INPUT TYPE="TEXT" NAME="price" VALUE="#price#"><BR>
<INPUT TYPE="SUBMIT">
</FORM>
</CFOUTPUT>
</BODY>
</HTML>
```

The preceding code displays the results of the `editbook` query in a form. The title and price of the book are displayed as editable fields. The `bookid` is hidden as this value cannot be changed.

After the user edits the book information and submits the form, the browser passes the information to the `updatebook.cfm` file, which finally updates the book table with the new values.

The `updatebook.cfm` file contains the following code:

```
<HTML>
<HEAD>
<TITLE>UPDATE BOOK DETAIL </TITLE>
</HEAD>
<BODY>
<CFQUERY NAME="updatebook" DATASOURCE="storeconnect">
UPDATE book
SET
title='#Form.title#',
price='#Form.price#'
WHERE bookid='#bookid#'
</CFQUERY>
The book details have been updated
</BODY>
</HTML>
```

Summary

ColdFusion provides an application development environment to build dynamic Web sites with the help of CFML. CFML is a tag-based programming language, used to write server-side scripts. These scripts take care of dynamic data integration, application logic, and interface design. CFML enables Web applications to communicate with databases with the help of SQL. CFML also provides a list of tags and functions that can be used effectively to build dynamic Web sites. The user friendly visual environment of UltraDev can be integrated with the simple tag-based scripting language of ColdFusion to create excellent dynamic Web sites.

PART III

DESIGNING WEB PAGES USING DREAMWEAVER ULTRADEV 4

- **7** Creating Sites and Documents 117
- **8** Working with Text in Documents 145
- **9** Creating and Managing Images 171
- **10** Linking Pages Together 189
- **11** Presenting Content in a Page 207
- **12** Building User Interactivity into a Page 237
- **13** Adding Multimedia Effects to a Web Page 255
- **14** Optimizing Your Work 283
- **15** Editing and Debugging in Code View 299
- **16** Setting Interface Preferences 321

CHAPTER 7

CREATING SITES AND DOCUMENTS

In this chapter

Planning a Web Site   118

Creating a New Site   119

Working with Documents   128

Page Layout   135

Design Considerations   140

Summary   141

Troubleshooting   141

Activity Corner   142

Planning a Web Site

A lot of planning goes into creating a Web site. Before you create a Web site, you need to be sure about the goal of your Web site and the target audience you intend it to reach. If you know these things, you can decide on the design features of the Web site and plan accordingly. For example, the approach to designing an online dictionary is entirely different from how you would approach the design of an e-commerce Web site capable of handling monetary transactions.

A clear understanding of the target audience helps you decide which technologies you need to support your Web site. If you are developing an intranet and you know the system configuration of the target audience, you can develop a site that best suits that configuration. In UltraDev, you can develop applications using ASP, JSP, or ColdFusion. The requirements of the target audience help you decide which technology you should use. For example, if you are developing an intranet for a company that uses an IIS server to host the intranet, you must choose ASP to develop this intranet in UltraDev. You can choose ColdFusion only if you have ColdFusion Server installed on IIS.

Planning the Site Structure

After you have decided the goal of your Web site and which support technologies you need to develop the site, the next step is to put together a plan for creating the Web site. This plan will map out the design features of the Web site, the structure of the site, and the implementation details, such as the directory structure and file naming conventions.

Before you begin working in UltraDev, you can design the layout of the Web site on a paper or create a mock-up of the site with software such as Macromedia Fireworks. This helps you plan the site structure in terms of the number of pages the site will have and the features that must be present.

The next step is to decide on the folder structure. Before you begin to create a site in UltraDev, you should create a folder structure on paper and decide which components of the Web site that will go into each folder. You can also decide on the subfolders that you want to create within your main folder so that you can place related elements in these subfolders. Provide meaningful names for the folders so that you can identify them easily.

For example, if you are planning to create a Web site that allows people to buy books in a variety of categories online, you can create folders that correspond to each category of the books that will be displayed on the site. You can name each of these folders after the category of the books, such as fiction, science, arts, and so on. It is best to keep these names short and simple.

Planning for a Sample Site

Consider the example of the bookseller Web site in a little more detail. Such a Web site will cater to a global audience with varied preferences regarding the type of books that they want to buy. Such a site is an ideal candidate for the incorporation of dynamic features.

When you plan for this site, you need to decide on the server technology that you will use to develop the site and the features that the Web site will have. Because your site caters to a global audience, it is possible that the site will reach a huge number of users as it becomes popular. Therefore, the Web site needs to be hosted on a robust Web server that can handle simultaneous requests from a large number of users. The choice of server technology depends on the Web server on which the site will be hosted.

You can use the ASP, JSP, and ColdFusion technologies on both Windows and non-Windows servers. Non-Windows servers support third-party implementations of ASP. JSP is available on a large number of both Windows and non-Windows servers. Windows, Solaris, and Linux Web servers support ColdFusion. If scalability is an issue, ColdFusion is a better choice than ASP. If portability is an issue, JSP is the best choice.

Consider that this Web site uses a Windows-based Web server, such as IIS 4.0, simply because Windows-based servers are among the most common robust Web servers available today. This site uses the ASP technology instead of ColdFusion or JSP because the application server associated with the ColdFusion or JSP technologies must be installed on the Web server to be able to use them with that server. After deciding on these aspects, the next step is to create this site.

CREATING A NEW SITE

To begin creating a new site in UltraDev, follow these steps:

1. Create a local folder for every new site that you create. You can use this local folder for creating and editing new files. The local folder can act as a temporary storage location for your site before you publish it to the Web. This local folder is also known as the *local root folder*.

2. Specify a Web server and create a remote folder on it. The remote folder on the Web server will have your site files. The Web server publishes these site files and serves your site to the target audience. You need to ensure that the folder structures on the local machine and on the Web server are exactly alike.

3. Specify an application server. This application server can be any server that supports the ASP, JSP, or ColdFusion technologies. You need to specify the server technology at the time you create the site so that UltraDev can use this information to connect to the application server at design time. You also need to specify the scripting language that UltraDev will use to generate the underlying code as you develop Web applications.

DEFINING A SITE

After you have decided which Web and application servers you want to use, you can define your site by using the Site Definition dialog box. To display this dialog box, choose the Define Sites option from the Site menu. Figure 7.1 shows the Site Definition dialog box.

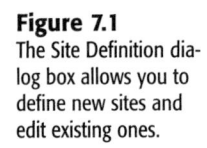

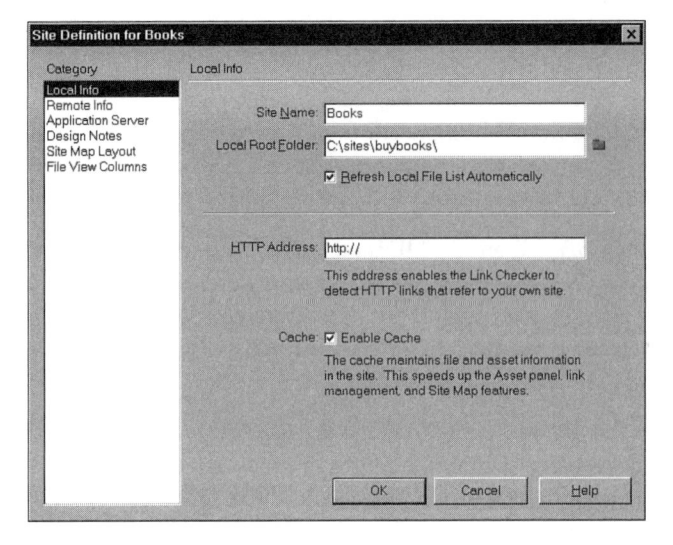

Figure 7.1
The Site Definition dialog box allows you to define new sites and edit existing ones.

LOCAL INFORMATION

You use the Local Info category of the Site Definition dialog box to provide information about the local folder that will hold your site files.

The first piece of information that you need to specify in this category is the name of the site. The site name is only for your reference. When you are working on multiple sites in UltraDev, choosing a simple, meaningful name for each site helps you easily distinguish the sites from one another. In Figure 7.1, the name Books is given as the name for the sample site in the Site Name text box.

Next, you need to specify the local folder, which is the folder on your local hard disk in which UltraDev stores all the files and folders of the site on which you are working. When you preview your Web site on a browser, UltraDev retrieves the files to display on the browser from the local folder. To specify the local folder, click the folder icon next to the Local Root Folder text box and browse to the folder. In Figure 7.1, the local folder where the files of the Books site will be stored is called buybooks. This folder has been created exclusively for this sample site. This folder is in the sites folder on the C: drive of the development computer.

To automatically refresh the local file list that appears in the Site window, you need to select the Refresh Local File List Automatically option. For example, if you have created, copied, deleted, or renamed any files or subfolders in the local folder, the file list in the Site window is refreshed automatically. If you do not select this option, you need to manually refresh the local file list by clicking the Refresh button that appears on the toolbar of the Site window.

> **Caution**
>
> When you specify the local folder, make sure that this folder is not shared by another site on which you are working. In other words, each new site that you create must have a unique local folder that is dedicated only to it.

In the HTTP Address text box, specify the URL of your Web site. This enables UltraDev to check for links that are created using absolute URLs. An *absolute URL* is the complete URL of the page that resides on the remote root folder of the Web server. However, you can also specify just `http://` in this text box, which refers to the local root folder that contains the site files.

→ For more information on absolute URLs, **see** "Absolute Paths," **p. 191**.

The Enable Cache option allows you to create a cache for your site. It is best to select this option, because a cache speeds up link checks and updates. When you enable caching, UltraDev creates a cache file that is updated whenever you add, remove, or modify links. If the Enable Cache option is not selected, UltraDev prompts you to create a cache before it creates the site.

SERVER INFORMATION

The Remote Info category, as shown in Figure 7.2, allows you to specify information about the Web server to which you want to connect.

Figure 7.2
In the Remote Information category, specify the details about the remote Web server on which your site is hosted.

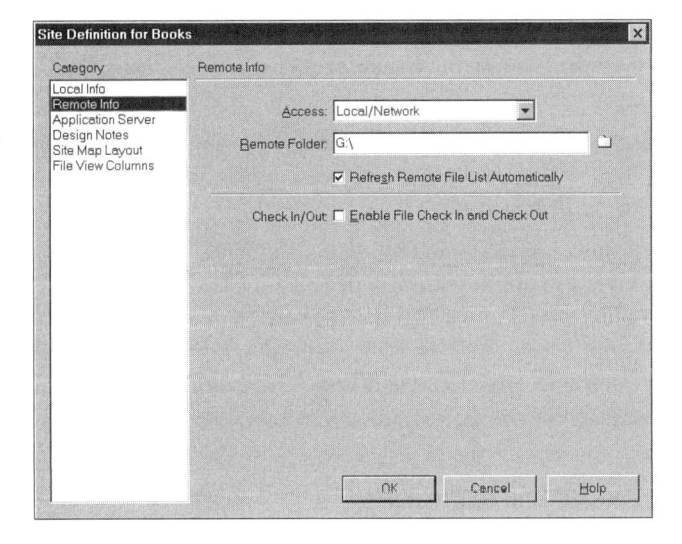

When you select this category, the Access drop-down list is displayed. This drop-down list has five options: None, Local/Network, FTP, SourceSafe Database, and WebDAV. When you select each of these options, the information related to each option is displayed.

If you have the Web server on your local machine, you can select the None option. You can also use this option if you are not planning to upload the local root folder to a Web server.

If you are connecting to a Web server on the local machine or a network machine, you can choose the Local/Network option. After you select this option, you need to specify the location of the remote folder. This remote folder can be located either on the local or remote machine. In Figure 7.2, the remote root folder is mounted on a network drive called G:\. The protocol used to upload the local files to this remote folder is HTTP.

If you are part of a development team, you can select the Check In/Out option. Using this option, you can transfer files to and from the remote server. When you transfer a file from the remote server to your local machine to edit the file (which is known as checking out a file), it is locked. More than one team member cannot edit the same file at the same time; if you are editing a file, the other team members are locked out of that file. Only after you check a file you have been editing back in to the remote server can other members of your team edit that file. As long as you are editing the file, the name that you specify in the Check Out Name text box of the Remote Info Category appears in the Checked Out By column in the Site window. You can specify your e-mail address in the Email Address text box. When team members want you to release a file you have checked out, they can send a mail to you by clicking your name, which appears in the Checked Out By column. This opens their default mail program with the your mail address in it.

→ To learn more about the Check In/Out feature, **see** "Checking Files In and Out," **p. 456**.

The other option in this category is The Refresh Remote File List Automatically option. This option is similar to the Refresh Local File List Automatically option in the Local Info category.

CONNECTING TO AN FTP SERVER

File Transfer Protocol (FTP) is one of the most efficient protocols available to publish files to a remote server. To publish your files to a remote server by using the FTP protocol, this remote server must be running an FTP server program. An FTP client program must also be running on your computer. This FTP client must establish a connection with the FTP server; the server connects back to the client. After both connections are established, you can publish your site files to the remote server. UltraDev contains an FTP client program that you can use to connect to an FTP server.

To establish a connection from UltraDev to an FTP server, you must select FTP from the Access drop-down list in the Remote Info category of the Site Definition dialog box. When you select this option, a list of options is displayed that enable you to specify connection details.

In the FTP Host text box, specify the name of the FTP server. The name of the server can be either the IP address or hostname of the server. When you specify the hostname, the protocol must not be mentioned just before the hostname. For example, if you want to connect to a remote site named buybooks.com by using FTP, you must enter **ftp.buybooks.com** in the FTP Host text box, not ftp://ftp.buybooks.com.

The next option is Host Directory, in which you must specify the root directory on the server. To ensure proper file uploads, the structure of the remote root folder must be similar to that of the local folder. A root folder must be created on the FTP server before you can specify a connection to it.

You can specify a login name and password to connect to the Web server. You can get the information about the hostname and host directory of the FTP server and the login name and password to connect to the FTP server from the system administrator of the FTP server.

You can also save your password by selecting the Save check box. You must select the Use Firewall option if your computer is behind a firewall. When your computer is behind a firewall, the FTP server might not be able to establish a connection with your computer. This prevents file transfer between the FTP server and client. In such a case, you can select the Use Passive FTP option, which enables your computer to establish a second connection with the FTP server by which file transfer can happen more smoothly.

APPLICATION SERVER INFORMATION

The Application Server category, as shown in Figure 7.3, enables you to specify information about the application server that you will use with UltraDev.

Figure 7.3
The Application Server category allows you to connect to ASP, JSP, or ColdFusion servers.

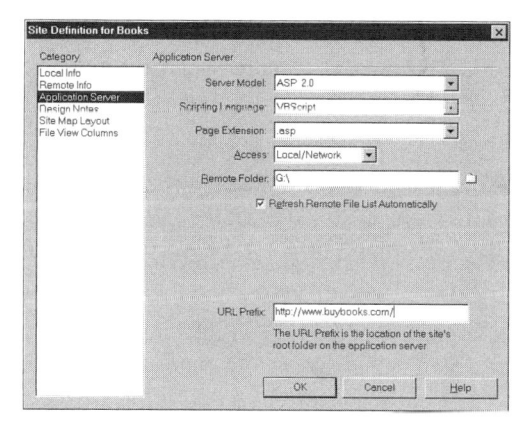

In the Server Model drop-down list, select the server model you want to use. If you select the ASP server model, you can choose either VBScript or JavaScript from the Scripting Language drop-down list.

If you select the JSP or ColdFusion model, the Scripting Language drop-down list displays Java or CFML, respectively.

The Page Extensions option enables you to select .asp, .jsp, or .cfml as the page extension, instead of the .htm and .html extensions. If you select the .htm or .html extensions, documents that contain dynamic content are not rendered properly.

If the application server and the Web server are on the same machine, then the Access and Remote Folder options contain the same information as specified in the Remote Info category, and you need not make any changes to these options. If the application server is not on the same computer as the Web server, you need to specify whether you are connecting to the application server through FTP or through a local or network drive by selecting the appropriate option from the Access drop-down list. If the application server is on your development computer, select None from the drop-down list. After this, you also need to specify a folder on the application server that contains all the files on your site. If the application server is on your development computer, the path to the folder that you specify here will be the same as the path of the local root folder. UltraDev shows live data by using the application server. Therefore, the files that you create in your local folder must also be uploaded to the folder on the application server.

The URL Prefix option is an important piece of information that you need to specify if you want to preview the Web site in a browser or use the live data view in UltraDev. This prefix is the domain name of the server where the site is hosted and must be mapped to the home directory on the server. When you configure a Web server that runs on your development machine, you create a home directory on your Web server that holds all the files that you intend to publish. This home directory is mapped to the domain name that you create for your site in the Web server.

The URL prefix that you specify is the prefix that browsers use to connect to the site. By default, the http://localhost/ prefix is displayed in the URL Prefix text box. When your copy of UltraDev and the Web server run on the same machine, you can use this default prefix as the URL prefix.

Figure 7.3 shows the Application Server category of the Site Definition dialog box. From the Server Model drop-down list, ASP is selected for the sample site Books. VBScript is set as the default scripting language. The page extension is set to .asp, because the server model is ASP. The application server is the same as the Web server for this site, because the Web server that this sample site uses is IIS. Therefore, the information in the Access and Remote Folder fields is the same as that in the Remote Info category. In the URL Prefix text box, the domain name of the computer on which the application server runs is specified as http://www.buybooks.com/.

> **Note**
>
> If you want to edit the site definition at any point in time, you can use the Define Sites dialog box. To display this dialog box, choose the Define Sites option from the Site menu. This dialog box contains a list of the sites that you have created. You can select the site that you want to edit and click the Edit button to display the Site Definition dialog box.

WORKING WITH THE SITE WINDOW

After you have defined your site and closed the Site Definition dialog box, the Site window opens. The Site window, as discussed in Chapter 2, is a central location from which you can manage your entire site. The left and right panes of the Site window show the file structures on the remote and local sites, respectively. Figure 7.4 shows the file structure in the Site window.

Figure 7.4
Use the Site window to manage your site files.

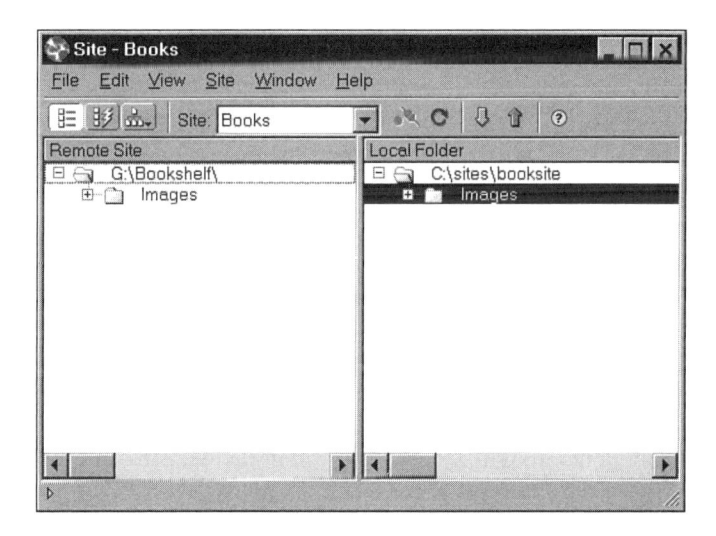

> **Tip**
>
> When you are working with the files on your local site and you find that your workspace is cluttered, you can customize the Site window to display only the Local Folder pane by clicking the triangle button ▷ located at the bottom of the Site window.

CREATING NEW DOCUMENTS BY USING THE SITE WINDOW

After the plan is ready for your Web site, you can start creating your site files by using the Site window. If you want to use image files and other media files in your site, you can copy them to the local root folder by using the Site window.

To create a new document in the local folder, select the local folder in the Local Folder pane of the Site window. If you are a Windows user, right-click on this folder, and and choose New File from the context-sensitive menu. Macintosh users must control-click on the local folder to get the context-sensitive menu. Figure 7.5 shows the context-sensitive menu in the Site window.

Figure 7.5
You can manage your files in the local root folder by using the context-sensitive menu.

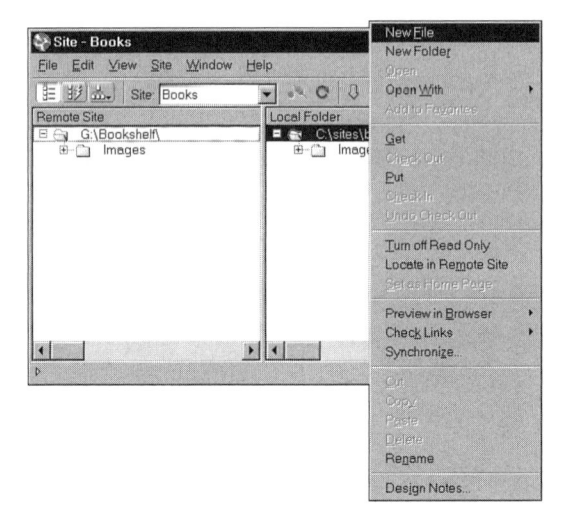

By default, the left pane of the Site window shows the files on the remote folder. You can change this view to display the site map by clicking the Site Map button on the Site window toolbar. When you click this button, it displays two options, Map Only and Map and Files. If you choose Map Only, the Site window will show only the site map. If you choose Map and Files, the site map is displayed in the left pane and the files on the local folder are displayed in the right pane.

> **Note**
>
> Before you can view the site map, UltraDev prompts you to create a home directory. Only after you create a home directory can you view the site map. The following section discusses the creation of a home directory.

CREATING YOUR HOME PAGE

When you click the Site Map button, a dialog box prompts you to create a home page for your site. When you click the Define Sites button in this dialog box, the Site Definition dialog box appears. In this dialog box, you can specify the home page by selecting the Site Map Layout category. Click the folder icon next to the Home Page text box and browse to the file that you want to set as the home page. Figure 7.6 shows the Site Map Layout category of the Site Definition dialog box.

Figure 7.6
You can change settings for the site map view by using the Site Map Layout category.

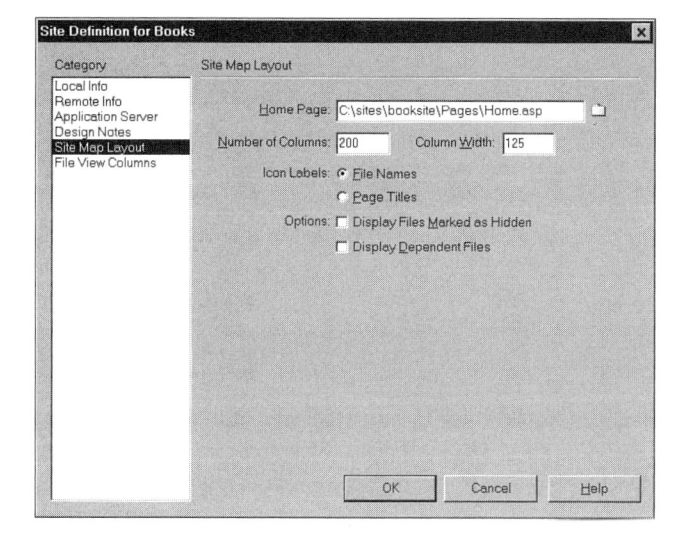

THE SITE MAP VIEW

You can use the site map view to display the files on your local site. In this view, you can see how the files that compose your site are linked. You can also create new links and remove or edit links. Figure 7.7 shows the Site Map view.

Figure 7.7
The Site Map view gives an accurate picture of how documents in a site are linked to each other.

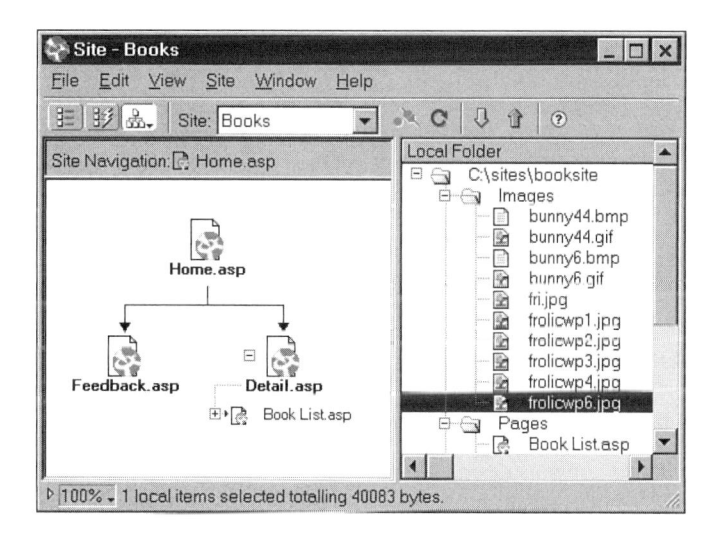

→ For more information on creating links, **see** "Working with Links," **p. 193**.

Changing the Site Map Layout

You can adjust the site map layout by setting options in the Site Map Layout category of the Site Definition dialog box. In this dialog box, you can set the number of columns per row, which determines the number of icons that are displayed per row of the site map. For example, if you specify the number of columns in the Number of Columns field of the Site Definition dialog box as 4 and then view a site map that contains five files linked from a document, only four of these files are displayed in one row. The fifth file is displayed in the next row. Therefore, to accommodate more files per row, you need to increase the number of columns per row.

You can also change the width of an icon and its label by specifying a value, in pixels, in the Column Width text box. If you specify a width that is less than the length of the icon, the icon label is partially displayed in the site map view. In addition, you can choose to display hidden and dependent files. *Hidden files* are files that you might want to hide so that you do not accidentally delete them. If you hide an file, it is not listed in the local site files list in the site window. The hidden file still exists in your site, however, and is linked to other pages.

> **Note**
> *Dependent files* are non-HTML files, such as images, that are loaded by the browser along with the main page. By default, dependent files are hidden.

> **Tip**
> You can hide certain files in the site map view to keep the site map focused and lean. To display or hide a file in Windows, select the file and choose Show/Hide Link from the View menu of the Site window. On a Macintosh, you need to choose Site, Site Map View, Show/Hide Link to display or hide a file. To display dependent files in Windows, choose View, Show Dependent Files. On a Macintosh, choose Site, Site Map View, Show Dependent Files to display dependent files.

Working with Documents

A *document* is a Web page of your site. It can contain static elements, such as text, images, and links, as well as dynamic content, such as Flash movies, rollover images, and recordset navigation bars.

A document also contains design elements, such as frames, layers, and tables. Frames partition your Web page into multiple sections. You can display content in each of these sections. Frames enable the user to scroll through particular sections of a page while keeping the other sections static. Layers enable you to have greater control over the positioning of elements in your page. Tables, of course, allow you to present content in a tabular structure.

→ To learn more about tables, layers, and frames, **see** "Presenting Content in a Page," **p. 207**.

Layout tables and cells are a feature provided by UltraDev to create tabular structures easily. Layout tables and cells are discussed in later sections of this chapter.

You can create a document either from scratch or by using templates. To create a new document from scratch, choose New from the File menu on the Document window. When you create a new document in the Code view, HTML tags, such as `<html>`, `<body>`, and `<title>`, are automatically created.

> **Note**
>
> If you have only the Site window open and no Document windows open, choose either New File or New Window from the File menu on the Site window. When you choose New File, a new file appears in the Site window with the default name untitled. You can edit this default name. You must double click this file to open it in a Document window. When you choose New Window from the File menu on the Site window, a new Document window opens.

→ To learn how to create documents from templates, **see** "Creating Documents Based on Templates" **p. 293**.

After you create a blank document, you can define certain basic properties for the document, such as the text and background colors. After defining these properties, you can begin designing your document by deciding on the layout of the page and then adding elements, such as text, images, forms, and so on. Before you can start designing the document layout and adding elements to your document, it helps to familiarize yourself with a few basic operations that you need to know to proceed with designing your page. The following sections discuss these operations. The rest of the chapters in Part III help you continue the design process by adding elements to your documents.

OPENING EXISTING DOCUMENTS

To open an existing document, choose Open from the File menu. When you open a document, it is displayed either in Code or Design view, depending on which is currently enabled.

In UltraDev, you can also open plain-text and JavaScript files and edit them. When you open a plain-text file, all three views are disabled. The document window performs the functions of a text editor, enabling you to perform basic edit operations on the text file.

If you want to import a Word document into UltraDev, choose File, Import, Import Word HTML and browse to select the document. A Word file can be imported into UltraDev only if it is saved as an HTML file. If you want to import tabular data into UltraDev, you need to choose File, Import, Import Tabular Data.

→ To get help on how to import tabular data, **see** "Importing Tabular Data," **p. 219**.

> **Note**
>
> UltraDev cannot directly import Excel spreadsheets. It can only import text files that have tabular data delimited by tabs, colons, semicolons, or user-defined delimiters.

Saving Documents

When you save a document by choosing the Save option from the File menu, UltraDev saves the document with the `.asp`, `.jsp`, or `.cfml` extension, depending on the server technology that you have specified. When you save a file, you need to ensure that you save it in the local root folder.

> **Caution**
>
> When you save documents in UltraDev, you can include spaces, numerals, or characters such as colons and slashes in the document names. Although this does not create problems when you view the documents from the local folder, viewing them from the remote folder can cause problems. When these documents are uploaded to the server, the document names undergo changes, upsetting links. For example, if you upload a document named `index page.asp`, which contains a space, to a remote site, the Web server on the site converts this name to `index%page.asp`. Therefore, it is better to avoid spaces or special characters, such as periods, semicolons, or apostrophes, in your document names. It is common practice to indicate a space with an underscore. It is recommended that you follow this practice when naming your documents.

Using the Different Views in UltraDev

You can design your page in UltraDev by using five different views. If you want to use a WYSIWYG environment to design your page, choose the Design view by clicking the Design View button on the toolbar. As you design your page in the Design view, the underlying code is generated automatically.

If you want to write HTML code to generate your page design, click the Code View button on the toolbar to switch to the Code view. You can also see both the Code and Design views simultaneously by clicking the Show Code and Design button on the toolbar. When you click on an element in Design view, the corresponding tag is selected in Code view. As you make changes in Code view, you see the effect in Design view. You can adjust the split between the Code and Design views by dragging the horizontal divider between the two views.

The Design view includes two views, Standard and Layout. The Standard view enables you to create layers, frames, and tables in your document. The layout view enables you to design your page layout by using layout tables and cells. When you design your page by using the layout tables and cells, the `<table>` tag is inserted into the HTML code for your page. With layout tables and cells, you can create tabular structures that are similar to tables, but these structures are more flexible than tables. In the following sections of this chapter, you will learn how layout tables lend themselves to creating flexible tabular structures. In the Layout view, you cannot insert layers or tables into your document. However, you can insert text, images, and other media into the layout cells of the Layout view.

When you want to use layout tables in your document, you must switch to the Layout view. However, if you want to insert layers or frames into your document, you must switch to the Standard view. You can switch between the layout view and the Standard view by clicking the appropriate button on the Objects panel. Figure 7.8 shows the Objects panel with the Layout View icon enabled.

Figure 7.8
When Layout View is enabled, the layout cells and tables are automatically enabled.

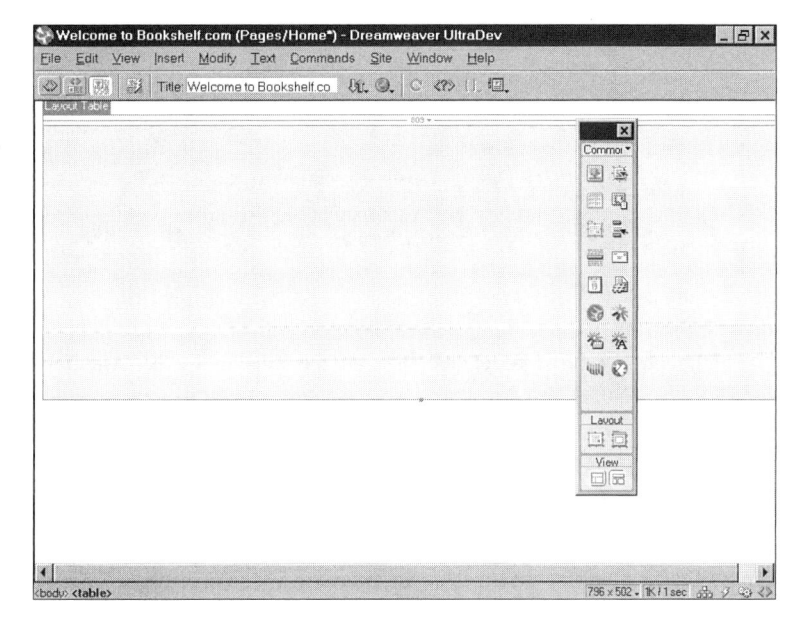

Setting General Properties for a Document

You can set general properties for your page, such as title, text color, and background image, by using the Page Properties dialog box. To see this dialog box, choose the Page Properties option from the Modify menu. Figure 7.9 shows the Page Properties dialog box.

You can specify the title for your document in the Title text box. You can also specify the background color and image for the document. When you specify the background image, it is a good practice to specify the background color also. If you do so, when the page is viewed in a browser, the background color will begin filling up the browser window before the image downloads. When the background image is completely downloaded, it replaces the background color. If the background image does not fill the entire browser window, it tiles to fill the entire browser window by default. You can use Cascading Style Sheets to prevent image tiling by using the Style Definition Background Panel of the CSS Style Definition dialog box in UltraDev.

Figure 7.9
Use this dialog box to set properties for your page.

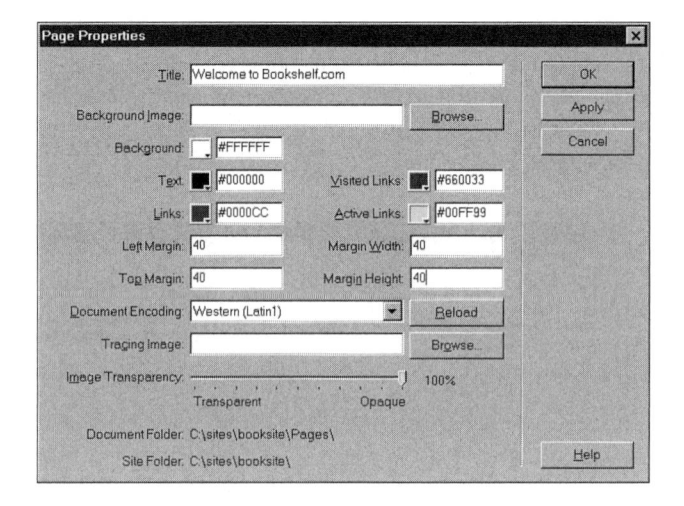

→ To learn how to use the Style Definition Background Panel of the CSS Style Definition dialog box, **see** "Creating a CSS Style Sheet," **p. 164**.

To set the background color, you can use the color picker, also known as the *eye-dropper*. To display the color picker, you need to click the color palette next to the Background option. After clicking the color picker, move the mouse pointer to move the color picker to point to any color in the color palette.

You can also move the color picker to any part of the computer screen to select a color from the screen. After moving the color picker to the required color, click the color to set it as the background color.

> **Tip**
> When you choose a color, it is always better if it is a Web-safe color, because a Web-safe color does not change its shade when viewed on different monitors and browsers. You can convert your color to a Web-safe color by selecting the Snap to Web Safe option from the pop-up menu that appears when you click the triangular button on the upper right corner of the color picker. The color you pick is converted to a Web-safe color and added to the Background color box.

You can select Web-safe colors for text, links, visited links, and active links from the Page Properties dialog box.

In the Page Properties dialog box, you will find four options for specifying document margins: Left Margin, Top Margin, Margin Width, and Margin Height. These options are used to set the top and left margins for a document when it is displayed on the browser. Internet Explorer supports the left margin and top margin attributes in the <body> tag, whereas Netscape Navigator supports margin height and margin width attributes in the <body> tag. UltraDev allows you to set values for all the four options to ensure that the margins you have set work for both Internet Explorer and Netscape Navigator.

> **Note**
> You can specify 0 in all four fields if you do not want margins to appear on the page when it is displayed on the browser.

You might want to create customized Web pages that can display characters in the language of the target audience. The Document Encoding drop-down list of the Page Properties dialog box contains options from which you can choose the character encoding for the language in which you want the Web page to be displayed on the browser. You can select Other if the option you are looking for is unavailable. Selecting this option lets you create a document with the encoding used by your operating system. For example, if you have installed the English version of Windows NT on your computer, then the document encoding used by the Windows NT operating system is Western European (Windows).

The Tracing Image option in the Page Properties dialog box enables you to specify a tracing image for the page. A tracing image helps to recreate the design of the image on your page. After you set the tracing image, it appears on the Document window. You can design the various elements, such as layers, images, forms, and tables, according to the appearance of the tracing image. If you want an image to appear in your document in a rectangular area that occurs at the same position and has the same size as a rectangle on a tracing image, you can draw a layer over the rectangle and adjust the size of the layer to fit the size of the rectangle. Insert the image in this layer. The tracing image appears only during design and not on the browser. The Image Transparency option lets you set the opacity of the image. The tracing image will appear dark or light on your document window depending on the opacity you set.

VISUAL AIDS

When you are designing your document, you can use the visual aids available on the UltraDev interface. Frame, layer, and table borders, image maps, and the grid and ruler are the visual guides that help you design your page more effectively. A grid enables you to precisely position layers. A ruler come in handy when you resize tables and also helps you decide upon spaces between elements.

You can view the grid and ruler by choosing the appropriate options from the View menu. To view the grid, choose View, Grid, Show Grid. The Show Grid option is a toggle option, so you can hide the grid by choosing this option again. To view the ruler, choose View, Rulers, Show, which is also a toggle option. You can set the ruler to show dimensions in pixels, centimeters, or inches. To do this, select the appropriate option from the Ruler option of the View menu. By default, the ruler's origin is at pixel 0. You can set the ruler origin to a number less than zero by dragging the ruler icon across the page and positioning it at the point where you want the ruler origin to appear. You can set the origin to its default value by choosing Rulers, Reset Origin from the View menu.

Many elements that you use in your document are not visible to users when they see the document on the browser. Such elements typically are comments that you insert in your document for your reference, named anchors that you use to link elements within a page, or client-side scripts that you embed in your document.

Although these elements are invisible on the document when it is displayed in the browser, it helps to view them while designing the document so that you can edit these elements if you want. UltraDev uses marker icons to display these invisible elements. You can choose to show or hide these invisible elements by choosing View, Visual Aids, Invisible Elements. You can choose to show or hide certain invisible elements by setting preferences using the Preferences dialog box. To display this dialog box, choose Edit, Preferences. In the Invisible Elements category, select those invisible elements that you wish to show when you select the Invisible Elements option from the View menu. Figure 7.10 shows the invisible elements in the Design view.

Figure 7.10
The invisible element shown in the figure is a comment.

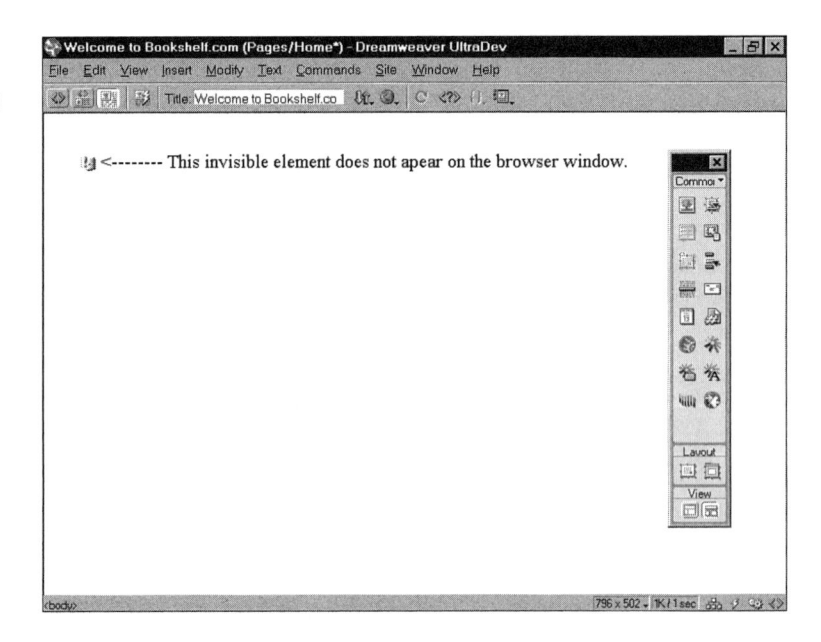

> **Note**
>
> You can use the Tag selector that appears on the status bar to edit code associated with an element on your document. Right-click the required tag to open the quick tag editor and edit the tag.

Viewing the Head Content

An HTML document consists of two sections, the head section, which contains important information about the document, and the body section, which contains information to be displayed on the document. Some of the important elements of the head section are Title, Meta, Keywords, Refresh, Link, and Base. The body section contains all of the elements, such as text, images, and tables, visible on the browser.

By default, you cannot view the head content in Design view. However, to set properties for the head content in Design view by using the Property inspector, you must make it visible. To view the head content, choose View, Head Content. The head content appears below the toolbar, as shown in Figure 7.11.

Figure 7.11
This figure displays the Title element and Meta elements in the head content display area.

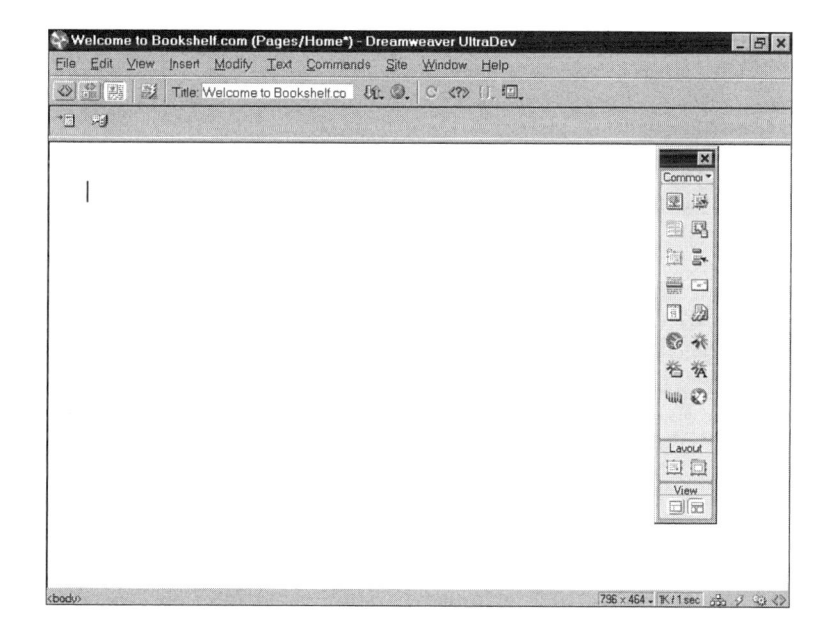

→ For more information about the elements in the head section and their properties, **see** "HTML Reference," **p. 541**.

Page Layout

Page layout involves deciding the location of text and images in your documents. UltraDev provides you with an easy way to create the page layout by using layout tables. Layout tables give you more flexibility in creating complex page layouts, which is not possible by using normal tables. Tables were originally intended to display tabular data. Therefore, they are not suited well for creating a page layout. However, layout tables give you a better control over laying out a page than normal tables. For example, when you use normal tables, it is not possible to design cells with unequal heights within a row. When you specify the height of a particular cell, the heights of the other cells in that row also change according to the height of the changed cell. But, when you create layout tables, specifying the height for a particular layout cell does not affect the height of other layout cells. Therefore, you have more flexibility in designing complex tabular structures when you use layout tables instead of normal tables. Using layout tables, you can position elements in your document as you do using a table. However, layout tables save you from the common problems associated with creating tables for page layout. You can easily adjust cell widths, move cells, and nest tables by using layout tables.

After you create your page layout in the Layout view, you can switch to the Standard view to insert layers.

Layout Tables and Cells

A layout cell marks out an area where the content will appear on your page. A layout cell always appears inside a layout table. When you are in Layout View, you first draw a layout table and then draw layout cells within the table. However, if you draw a layout cell first, UltraDev automatically draws a layout table around it.

You can draw multiple layout tables below each other or nested tables within one another. When the content in a cell is bigger than the cell width, the cell width automatically increases. This increase in the size of a cell affects the other cells around it. Therefore, if you use a single layout table for your entire page, you might not be able to control the page layout. To overcome this, it is better to have multiple layout tables, as changes in the content area in one table do not affect the cells in the other table.

To draw a layout table, click the Layout Table button on the Objects panel. The mouse pointer changes to a + sign. You can then position the pointer on your document and click and drag to draw a layout table.

> **Note**
> When you draw a new layout table on a blank document, it is automatically snapped to the upper-left corner of the Document window. If you already have content on your table, you can draw a table only below the existing content.

To create a nested layout table, click the Draw Layout Table button in the Objects panel and place the mouse pointer within the gray area of an exiting layout table. Then, click and drag the pointer to the desired height and width to create a nested layout table.

To draw a layout cell, click the Layout Cell button in the Objects panel and click and drag the mouse pointer inside a layout table.

> **Tip**
>
> If you are a Windows user, hold the Ctrl key and draw the layout cells to avoid clicking the Layout Cell button each time you want to draw a new layout cell. Macintosh users need to hold down the command key to draw multiple layout cells.

After you draw layout cells, you can click inside a cell to insert text. You can also insert other elements, such as images, into a layout cell. You cannot add content to the gray areas of a layout table.

If the height of the content in a cell is less than the cell height, you can clear the extra space to make the cell height fit the content. To clear this extra space, click the cell you want to adjust and select Clear Cell Heights option from the Column Header drop-down list that appears on the upper border of the layout table. When you clear the cell heights for a particular cell, you might find that some of the neighboring cells shrink. However, you can resize those neighboring cells back to their original size by specifying their width and height in the Property inspector. Figure 7.12 shows the menu using you can use to clear cell heights.

Figure 7.12
The number that appears on top of the Column Header menu indicates the width of the cell in pixels.

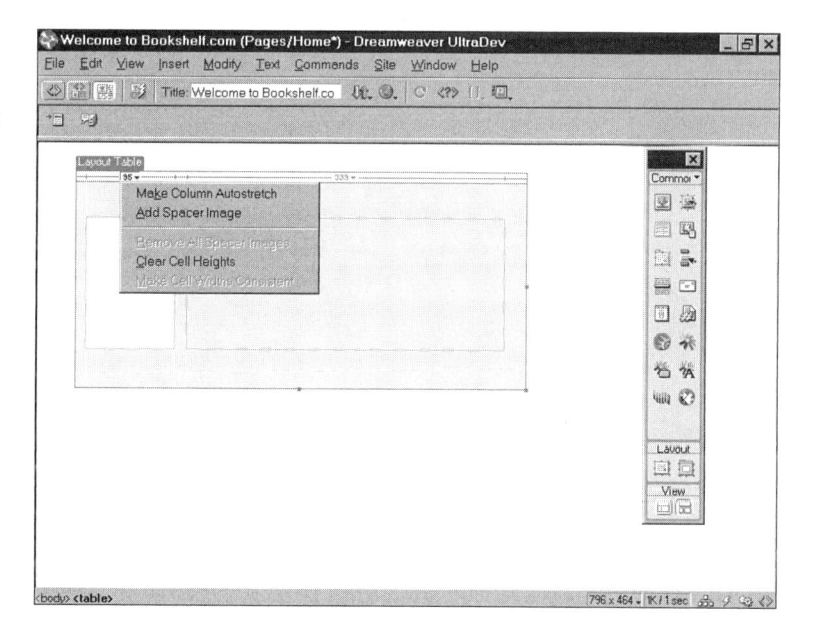

To resize a cell, click the cell and drag the selection handles to the required width and height. You can use the ruler to help you decide on the precise width and height of the cell.

To move a cell, select the cell, place the mouse pointer at the selection border, and drag the cell to the desired position on the table. Alternatively, you can hold down the Shift key and press the arrow keys to move the cell 10 pixels at a time.

Using the Property Inspector to Format Layout Tables and Cells

You can format layout cells and tables by using the Property inspector. You can adjust the height and width of a table, set the background color for a table or cell, align content within a cell, and adjust cell spacing and padding within a table. You can also set spacer images in tables that have the autostretch property enabled. When the autostretch property is enabled, the size of the table expands according to the size of the browser window.

To format a layout cell or a table, first select the cell or table so that selection handles appear around it. Next, choose Properties from the Windows menu to display the Property inspector. Figure 7.13 shows the Property inspector displaying the properties of a layout table.

Figure 7.13
The Property inspector has two tabs, one that enables you to set properties by selecting predefined options and another that enables you to set properties by choosing HTML tags.

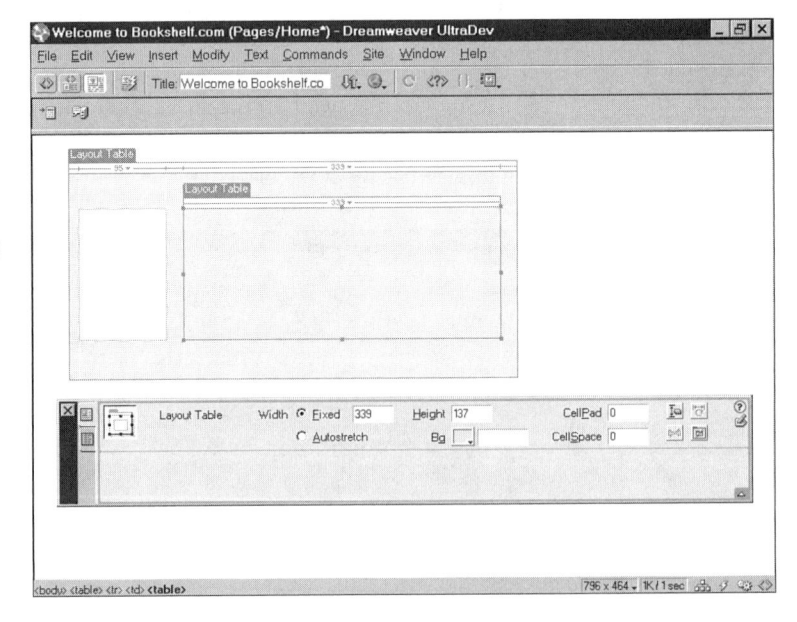

You can set a fixed width and height to a layout table or cell or make them stretch according to the content in them. To set a fixed height and width, select the Fixed option in the Property inspector and then type the values in the respective text boxes.

Even if you have set a fixed width for a cell, you will find that the cell width changes to accommodate a larger content. The number on the Column Header changes to show two numbers, one indicating the fixed width and another indicating the actual width. If you click the Make Cell Widths Consistent icon in the Property inspector, the fixed cell width changes to reflect the current width of the cell.

If you want to automatically resize the width of layout cells and tables depending on the size of the browser window, you can select the Autostretch option. Within a layout table, you can set only one cell to be an autostretch cell.

When you set the Autostretch option for a particular layout cell or a table, there is always a chance of the other tables or cells changing their size or disappearing from the browser window, a problem that happens especially in Netscape Navigator. To overcome this problem, UltraDev enables you to specify a spacer image. A *spacer image* is a transparent 1 pixel by 1 pixel GIF image that controls the spacing in autostretch tables and cells. This image maintains the width that has been set for a layout table and cell. When you select the Autostretch option without setting up a spacer image, a dialog box prompts you to set up a spacer image. You need to specify a name and a location for the spacer image in this dialog box. If you have already created a spacer image, you can add it to autostretch layout cells by choosing the Add Spacer Image option from the Column Header pop-up menu that appears on the top of the cell.

To set the background color of a layout table or cell, you can choose a color from the color-picker that appears near the Bg drop-down list of the Property inspector. Alternatively, you can type in a *hexadecimal color* in the text box. A *hexadecimal color* is a color code used to create colors that can be displayed on browsers. A hexadecimal color is represented by six digits. The first two digits represent red, the second two represent green, and the last two digits represent blue. Each digit can take a hexadecimal value from 0 to F. The hexadecimal representation of a color is preceded by a # symbol. For example, to create a dark blue color, you must enter #000099 in the text box next to the Bg color-picker.

You can set the horizontal alignment of the layout cell content to left, right, or center. You can also set the horizontal alignment to default, which aligns the content to the left. You can set the vertical alignment of the content in a layout cell to the top, middle, or bottom of the cell. You can also set the content to default, which aligns the content to the middle of the cell or set it to baseline, which aligns the content to the top of the cell. These options are available only for a layout cell and they do not appear in the Property inspector of a layout table.

You can select the No Wrap checkbox to prevent the contents of a cell from wrapping around to the next line.

You can set cell padding and cell spacing for a layout table. *Cell padding* is the space between the content and the borders of a cell and *cell spacing* is the space between cells. You can specify pixel values for cell padding in the CellPad text box and cell spacing in the CellSpace text box.

If you have a table nested within a table, you can remove the nesting without destroying the contents of the nested table. To do this, select the nested table and click the Remove Nesting icon in the Property inspector. After the nesting is removed, the contents of the nested table appear as a part of the parent table.

To remove spacer images from a layout table, click the Remove All Spacers icon in the Property inspector of the layout table.

Design Considerations

Before you design a page, you need to take into account various factors that affect the look of your site on a browser. These factors include the type and version of the browser, the platform on which the browser runs, connection speeds, and the screen dimensions.

Browser Type and Version

Although Internet Explorer and Netscape Navigator are the most popular browsers today, some people might use text-only browsers. Therefore, it is always better to create cross-browser compatible sites. People also use different versions of browsers, and all features of a Web site are not supported by all versions. Whereas a feature such as Cascading Style Sheets is supported by Netscape Navigator 4.x is not supported by Netscape Navigator 3.x. To overcome such problems, a possible solution is to create cross-browser versions of those pages that contain such content. For example, if you are planning to use frames in a page, it is always better to create a framed as well as a frameless version of the page, because not all browsers support frames. When you use images in a page, always use the ALT attribute so that a text-only browser can display meaningful content in areas where it cannot display images.

Platform

Font sizes tend to differ on the Windows and Macintosh platforms. Therefore, it is best to test your site on both platforms and use an optimum font size that works well on both. Similarly, it is also better to use standard fonts because not all users might have the fonts that your Web site uses. If you want to use a variety of fonts, it is best to specify a standard font, such as Arial, Courier New, Georgia, or Times New Roman, which are available in both Windows and Macintosh computers, as an alternative font.

Connection Speed

Different users connect to the Internet at different connection speeds. It is best to design a site that downloads quickly, regardless of the connection speed. For this, it is essential to keep the size of your Web pages small. Graphics and sound files take a long time to download due to their large file sizes. Therefore, you need to decide on ways to use these elements without affecting download time. Compressing audio files is one way you can overcome large file sizes. *Motion Pictures Expert Group (MPEG) compression* is the international standard for compression formats. Files compressed with MPEG compression result in smaller file sizes when compared to the uncompressed formats. MPEG files, although small in file size, produce sound of high quality. For example, if you compress a .avi file using the MPEG format, the file is compressed in the ratio 20:1. If you are planning to use a lot of images in your site, specify the width and height attributes for every image, as this helps in rendering the page easily. When the browser comes across these attributes, it knows exactly where the images will appear and begins rendering the text around the images. This reduces download time and also holds the user's attention.

Screen Dimension

It is best to design a site that works with the lowest common resolution base. If you design a site with a high resolution, users who use a lower resolution screen will not be able to view all the content of the site. It is preferable to use a resolution not greater than 800×600.

Summary

This chapter dealt with the creation of a Web site. Before creating a Web site, it is always better to plan in advance the site structure and the support technologies that will be used by the Web site. These decisions can be taken if the target audience and goal of the Web site are clearly laid down.

To create a Web site in UltraDev, you need to first define it. Defining a Web site refers to specifying the location of the local folder, the Web server, and the application server. The application server, the Web server, and your copy of UltraDev can be on different machines. The site definition must clearly specify how you are going to connect to the Web server and the application server.

After you define your site, you can create documents for your site. Before creating text or images on your document, you can layout the page using layout cells and tables, which will help you decide on the location of elements on the document. To simplify document layout, UltraDev has the Layout view, using which you can layout complex pages easily. You can design your layout using layout tables and cells. You can format these tables and cells by using the Property inspector.

While designing your page, you need to take into consideration many factors that will affect the appearance of your site. Factors, such as the browser type and version, the platform on which the browser runs, the screen dimensions of the browser, and the connection speed of the modem, can greatly affect the way your Web site will ultimately appear on the browser. You need to look at design solutions, which will help you tackle these issues.

Troubleshooting

Connecting to a Remote Server

I can't connect to the remote server.

You might encounter problems with the connection if you do not specify the path correctly in the URL Prefix text box. Remember that the domain name you specify in the URL Prefix text box must exist on the remote server before you attempt connecting to it. This domain name must be mapped to your home directory on the Web server. If this mapping is not done, you will not be able to establish a connection with the remote server.

I can't connect to the FTP server.

The FTP implementation in UltraDev is slightly different from standard FTP applications. You cannot navigate through the folder structure of the remote system to locate your root folder. You need to specify the remote root folder directly while specifying the connection. If you are having problems transferring files to the FTP server, you can view the FTP log by choosing Window, Site FTP Log from the Site window in a Windows machine. In a Macintosh machine, you need to choose Site, FTP Log to display the FTP log.

ACTIVITY CORNER

In this section, you begin building a simple Web application by using the concepts and skills you learned in this chapter. You will create a Web site called TuneIn.com that enables users to browse and listen to songs of their choice. This Web site also provides the option of allowing users to place an order for customized CDs that contain the songs selected by the users. To place an order for a customized CD, the user must first register with the site. Users can also log on to the site and edit their profile. After the users log on to the site, they can place an order for a customized CD. The site allows users to pay with a credit card or check. These are the broad features that the site provides. The files and folders necessary for creating this sample Web site can be found by browsing to www.quepublishing.com and typing **0789725770** for the ISBN to go to the info page for this book.

Before you begin to create this site, you need to have access to database systems, such as Access, a Web server, and an application server. If you plan to use the ColdFusion application server that ships with the UltraDev CD, make sure you install it on a system that has a Web server, such as IIS or PWS. If you want to use JSP, you can use the copy of JRun that ships with the UltraDev CD. You must have access to a Web server, such as IIS or PWS, to run JRun. If you are planning to use ASP for developing your Web site, you can use Web servers, such as IIS or PWS, that double as application servers. This Wet site is built assuming that you are connecting to a Web server that uses the HTTP protocol.

After installing the required Web server and application server on either your development computer or a remote system, you can proceed with the creation of the Web site. Create a folder on your local disk called TuneInSite. This folder is the local root folder where you will store your site files before uploading them to the remote root folder. In addition, create a remote root folder on the computer on which your Web server is running. Name this folder TuneInSite.

To begin creating this site, you need to first define the site in UltraDev by using the Site Definition dialog box. Perform the following steps to complete the site definition:

1. Choose Site, New Site. The Site Definition dialog box is displayed.
2. In the Local Info category, specify **Music_site** in the Site Name text box.
3. In the Local Root Folder text box, type the path to the TuneInSite folder.

4. In the HTTP Address text box, type **http://www.tunein.com**, which is the URL that your completed Web site will use.
5. In the Remote Info category, select Local/Network from the Access drop-down list.
6. Select the Refresh Remote File List Automatically option.
7. In the Application Server category, specify the required information in the Server Model, Scripting Language, and Page Extension fields.
8. From the Access drop-down list, select the Local/Network option.
9. Specify the location of the remote folder, TuneInSite, in the Remote Folder text box.
10. Select the Refresh Remote File List Automatically option.
11. In the URL Prefix text box, type **http://www.tunein.com/**.

The site definition is now complete. You can check the Site window to see whether the local and remote folders are listed.

FOLDERS AND FILES

After defining the site, create the folders and files you need for the site. To store the images that you will use in the site, create a folder called Images in the local root folder. To store the documents that contain features that allow the users to log on to the site, register with the site, and edit their profile, create a folder called Userdetails in the local root folder. To store the documents that will display the results of a search operation initiated by the user, create a folder called Songresults in the local root folder.

Before you start creating the documents in your site, it is necessary to visualize the look and feel of the first document of the site, as it introduces the broad level features of your site. This document will be set as the home page of your site. The subsequent documents in the site depend on the features contained in this first document. Name this first document Musichome. It will contain the following features:

- A search feature that allows users to search for songs based on a keyword. This keyword can either be a composer name or a song name.
- A list of song categories. When the user chooses a category, the list of songs available in that category is listed.
- A list of new song releases as well as a list of songs that are topping the charts.
- Logon and registration.
- Profile modification.
- A section that describes the Web site in detail.
- A help section where users can find answers to queries that they might have.

To implement these features in the first document, divide the first document into three sections by using three frames. Each of these frames contains a file. Name these three files Navigation, Sidebar, and Contentpage, respectively.

To create the Musichome, Navigation, Contentpage, and Sidebar files and set the Musichome file as the home page, perform the following steps:

1. Create a new document by selecting New Window from the File menu in the Site window.
2. The new blank document is displayed in the Document window. Save this document as Musichome with the required file extension in the TuneInSite folder on your local disk.
3. Repeat steps 1–2 to create the other three files, Navigation, Sidebar, and Contentpage.
4. To set the Musichome file as the home page, open the Site Definition dialog box, select the Site Map Layout category and browse to the Musichome file by clicking the folder icon next to the Home Page text box.

The home page is now set. Next, you can begin designing the page by adding elements to the document. The activity corner sections in subsequent chapters proceed with designing the page, connecting the page to a database, and adding dynamism to the page.

CHAPTER 8

WORKING WITH TEXT IN DOCUMENTS

In this chapter

Adding Text and Objects to a Document   146

Formatting and Editing the Text in a Document   148

Using HTML Styles and CSS   159

Summary   169

Activity Corner   169

Adding Text and Objects to a Document

A *Web site* is a collection of Web pages that are called documents. A *document* is any page of a Web site that contains text, images, animations, links to other documents, and audio. In the preceding chapter, you learned to plan and create a site. In this chapter, you will learn to create documents and format the text in documents.

If you want the maximum number of people to visit your site, it is very important to present the content in an interesting and visually appealing manner. The type of content and its presentation style are equally important for creating Web pages. Using UltraDev, you can easily add a variety of content to Web pages.

Text formatting is one of the most important tasks in Web page designing. It involves tasks such as changing the text's font type, size, and color, and adding special characters, e-mail links, and date and time.

In UltraDev, you can enter text directly into the Document window as you do in a word processor. You can also copy content from other documents and paste it into the Document window. The Document window displays the documents approximately as they will appear on the Web page. You can also insert dates, special characters, images, horizontal rules, tables, and layers into a Document window.

> **Note:** UltraDev does not preserve the formatting of text copied from other applications, but it does preserve line breaks.

Adding Dates

The Date option on the Insert menu lets you insert the current date in a chosen format. In addition, this option lets you format the existing date. To insert the current date into a Document window, choose Insert, Date. The Insert Date dialog box is displayed, as shown in Figure 8.1.

Figure 8.1
The options in the Insert Date dialog box allow you to choose a format for the name of the day, the date, and the time.

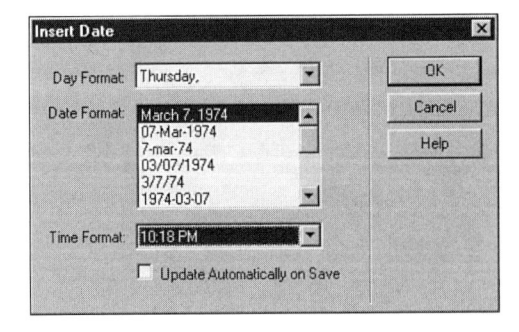

> **Tip**
> The Insert date button in the Common category of the Objects panel also lets you insert the current date in a chosen format.

The options in the Insert Date dialog box are summarized in Table 8.1.

TABLE 8.1 THE INSERT DATE DIALOG BOX OPTIONS

Option	Description
The Day Format drop-down list	Lets you select a format for the day.
The Date Format drop-down list	Lets you select a format for the date.
The Time Format drop-down list	Lets you select a format for the time.
The Update Automatically on Save check box	Lets you update the inserted date automatically. If this option is not selected, the inserted date becomes plain text and does not get updated automatically.

ADDING SPECIAL TEXT CHARACTERS

Many symbols and characters, such as © and ®, are not present on the keyboard. To insert such a character, place the cursor where you want the character to appear and then choose Insert, Special Characters. A list of special characters is displayed, as shown in Figure 8.2. You can choose a character from this list to insert it into the specified location.

> **Tip**
> The Character category of the Objects panel also lets you insert special characters.

Figure 8.2
The Special Characters option of the Insert menu lets you add special characters to your document.

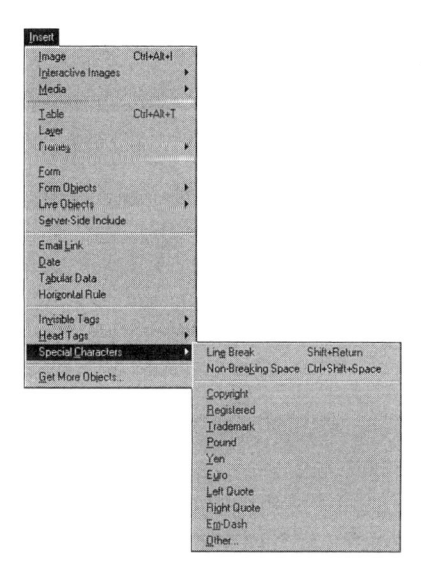

Special characters, such as the copyright, registered, trademark, and ampersand symbols, are displayed in the form of *HTML entities* in Code view. For example, the copyright symbol in Design view is represented as &copy in Code view.

Avoid using special characters such as bullets and others that are not supported in standard HTML text.

Copying and Pasting HTML Source Code

UltraDev lets you copy HTML source code from another application and paste it in the Document window. In addition, you can copy the source code from the Code view of a Document window and paste it in Design view.

The HTML code can be pasted as text or as code, depending on how you choose to copy and paste it.

If you want the HTML source code for a table to appear as text in a Document window, copy the code and paste it in Design view of the Document window.

If you want the HTML source code for a table to appear as a table in a Document window, copy the code and paste it in Code view of the Document window.

Formatting and Editing the Text in a Document

There are several ways to format the text in an UltraDev document, such as using the Property inspector or the Text menu to set font characteristics, using HTML styles, and using CSS to redefine HTML tags.

The Property inspector (see Figure 8.3) and the Text menu let you change the text's font characteristics on the page. HTML styles let you format text by defining various features, such as the text color, font size, and font style. Cascading Style Sheets (CSS) is a very important file used by Web designers for text and page formatting.

Figure 8.3
The Property inspector displays the formatting characteristics for the selected text.

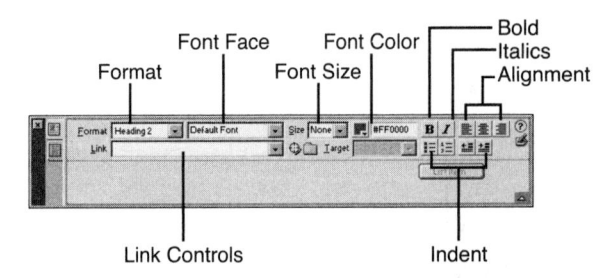

In the following sections, you will see how to enhance your text with bold, italics, and other formatting options.

First, let's look at how to change the color and size of the text in a document. You should be careful when you are selecting background colors and text colors.

> **Note**
> The Indent and Outdent options on the Text menu let you indent or outdent the selected text.

Formatting Paragraphs

Choose Text, Paragraph Format. You can choose an option from the list of paragraph formats, such as Heading 1, Heading 2, and Preformatted Text, that is displayed.

Choose None from the list to remove an existing paragraph format.

Changing the Font Color

UltraDev's Color dialog box lets you change the font color of the text in a Document window. To change the color of the text, select the text and choose Text, Color. The Color dialog box is displayed, as shown in Figure 8.4. Select a color and then click OK.

Figure 8.4
You can either choose a color from the basic colors available or define your own custom color in the Color dialog box.

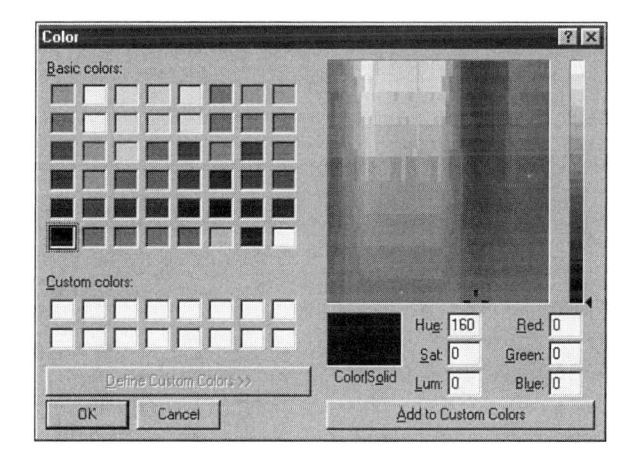

If you have not selected any text, the color change applies to the text that is added after you change the color.

You should be careful when you are selecting background colors and text colors. Do not choose very flashy colors such as orange and yellow, or the visitor can get distracted from whatever you are trying to say.

Changing the Font Size

The Size option of the Text menu lets you set a font size for the text in a Document window. Choose Text, Size. A list of font sizes is displayed, as shown in Figure 8.5. You can choose the desired font size from this list.

Figure 8.5
This list contains the seven standard HTML text sizes.

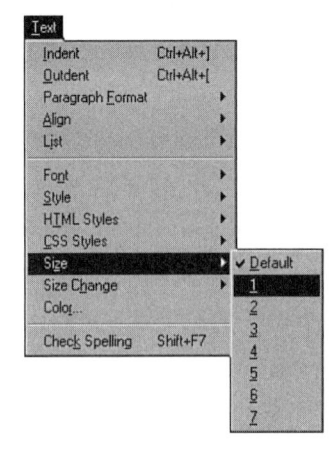

The Size Change option on the Text menu lets you increase or decrease the existing font size of selected text. After you choose Text, Size Change, a list of various font sizes is displayed, as shown in Figure 8.6. You can choose the desired size from this list.

Figure 8.6
The list of seven items lets you increase or decrease the font size.

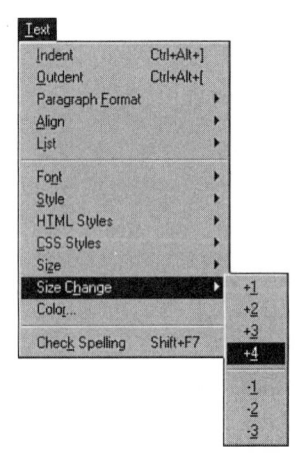

Changing the Font Style

The Style option on the Text menu lets you apply formatting, such as bold, italic, code, and underline, to the text in a document. When you choose this option, a list of 13 font styles is displayed, as shown in Figure 8.7. You can choose a style from this list to apply it to the selected text in document.

> **Tip**
> If you want a quick change in style, select the text, right-click the selection, and choose Style. A list of styles is displayed.

FORMATTING AND EDITING THE TEXT IN A DOCUMENT | 151

Figure 8.7
A list of 13 font styles.

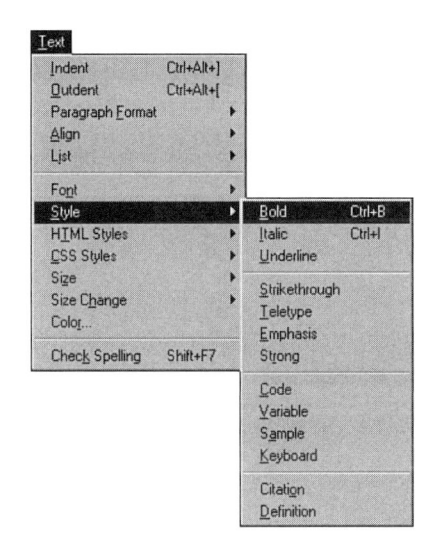

PART
III

CH
8

CHANGING THE ALIGNMENT

The Align option on the Text menu lets you change the alignment of text. Select the text to be formatted, and then choose Text, Align. The Align options list is displayed, as shown in Figure 8.8. Choose the alignment you want. The selected text is aligned.

Figure 8.8
The Left, Center, and Right options in the Align options list lets you left-align, right-align, or center text.

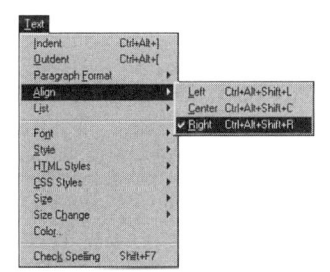

PERFORMING A SPELL CHECK

UltraDev provides you with built-in spell checking commands to check spellings and find and replace words in a document. It is a good practice to check spellings in a document before you close it.

> **Tip**
> Transfer your text to HTML only after it has gone through a spell check and has been proofread by someone.

You can run the UltraDev spell checker by using the Check Spelling option on the Text menu. When you choose this option, the Check Spelling dialog box is displayed, as shown in Figure 8.9. This dialog box lets you add a new word to your Personal dictionary, select a word from the Suggestions list box, or replace a selected word with the word specified in the Change To text box. In addition, you can tell the spell checker to ignore a word's spelling.

Figure 8.9
The Check Spelling option checks the spelling in the current document. It ignores HTML tags and attribute values.

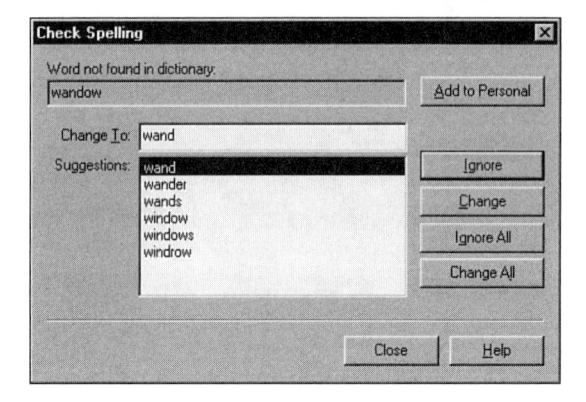

If any correct word is identified as an error, you can add this word to your Personal dictionary so that it will not be flagged as an error in the remaining part of the document.

Table 8.2 describes the options available in the Check Spelling dialog box.

TABLE 8.2   THE CHECK SPELLING DIALOG BOX OPTIONS

Option	Description
Ignore	Ignores the spelling of the selected word.
Ignore All	Ignores the spelling of all the occurrences of the selected word.
Add to Personal	Lets you add the selected word to the Personal dictionary.
Change	Replaces the selected word with the word specified in the Change To text box or the selection in the Suggestions list box.
Change All	Replaces the selected word and all other occurrences of the word with the word specified in the Change To text box or the selection in the Suggestions list box.

By default, the Check Spelling option on the Text menu uses the U.S. English spelling dictionary. To change the default dictionary, you need to use the Preferences dialog box. To display this dialog box, choose Edit, Preferences. In this dialog box, select the dictionary you want to use as the default dictionary from the Spelling Dictionary drop-down list. (The dictionaries listed are available in the Dreamweaver UltraDev 4/Configuration/Dictionaries folder.)

FORMATTING AND EDITING THE TEXT IN A DOCUMENT | 153

> **Note**
>
> If you want to add or remove words from your Personal dictionary, you can edit the Personal.dat file in a text editor. This file is located in the Dreamweaver UltraDev 4/Configuration/Dictionaries folder.

PART
III

CH
8

CREATING SIMPLE AND NESTED LISTS

A list is used to represent a series of similar items in an organized manner. Users can access information from lists easily because the information is presented in an orderly way.

In UltraDev, you can create various kinds of standard HTML lists. HTML supports five types of lists: ordered, unordered, definition, directory, and menu. In UltraDev, you can create ordered, unordered, and definition lists. The text in a list can be either existing text or new text.

CREATING AN ORDERED LIST

Ordered lists are also called numbered lists because the items in the lists are marked with numbers, as shown in Figure 8.10. In these lists, the items are arranged either in a sequence or in order of importance. The list starts with number 1 by default.

> **Note**
>
> The Reset Count To option in the List Properties dialog box lets you specify different start values. This numbering continues for the items in the list until you change it. See the later section "Setting List Properties" to learn more about the List Properties dialog box.

Figure 8.10
An example of an ordered list.

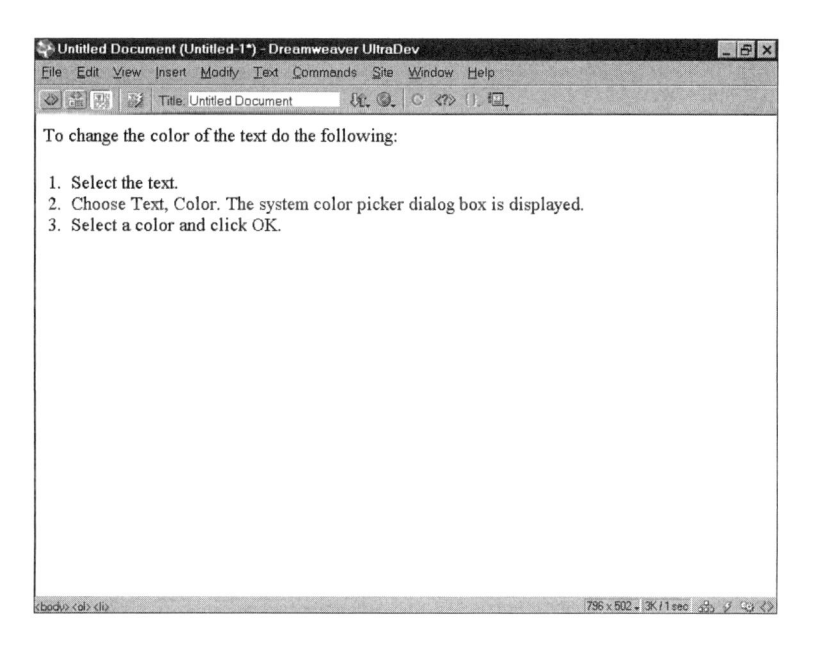

> **Note:** The Code and Design option on the View menu allows you to work in a split view with both the Code and Design windows open.

To create a new ordered list, follow these steps:

1. Choose View, Design to open Design view. This view allows you to work in a visual environment.
2. In Design view of the Document window, place the cursor where you want to add the list of new items.
3. Choose Text, List, Ordered to display the number of the first item in the list. You can also click the Numbered List button in the Property inspector to display this list.
4. Type the text for the list item, and then press Enter to move to the next list item.
5. After you finish adding all the elements in the list, press Enter twice to end the list.

> **Note:** On a Macintosh machine, to move to the next item in a list, press the Return key instead of Enter.

CREATING AN UNORDERED LIST

Unordered lists are also called bulleted lists because the items in the lists are marked with bullets, as shown in Figure 8.11. Bulleted lists can be used for items that need not be displayed in a particular order.

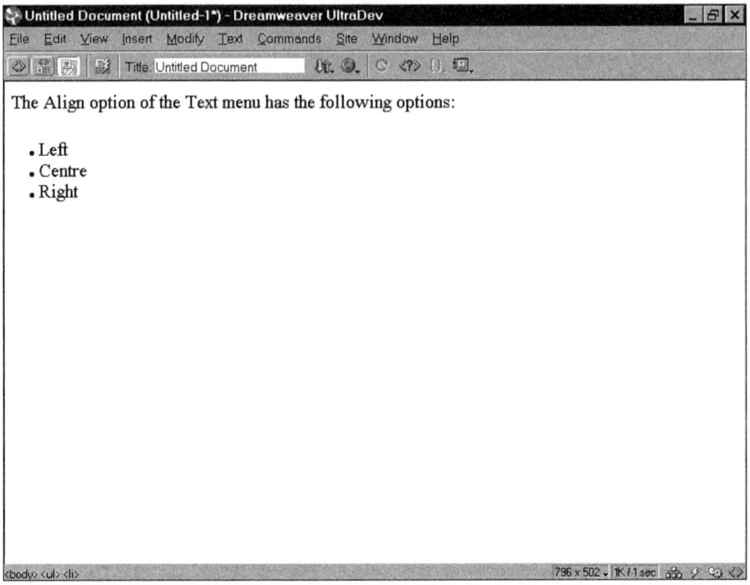

Figure 8.11 An example of an unordered list.

A bullet can be square or round. In these types of lists, the text is automatically indented, single-spaced, and preceded by bullets.

> **Note** Unordered or bulleted lists are the most commonly used lists on the Web.

To create an unordered list, follow these steps:

1. In Design view of the Document window, place the cursor where you want to add a list of new items.
2. Choose Text, List, Unordered or click the Bulleted List button in the Property inspector.
3. Enter a list item, and then press Enter to begin another list item.
4. Press Enter twice to complete the list.

> **Note** Definition lists do not use leading characters such as bullets or numbers. They are used when glossaries, terms, or descriptions are to be included in a Web page.

Creating a Nested List

In UltraDev, you can also create nested lists. A nested list has one main list that contains other lists.

Figure 8.12 shows a bulleted list nested within a numbered list.

Figure 8.12
The numbered list is the main list, and it contains a bulleted list.

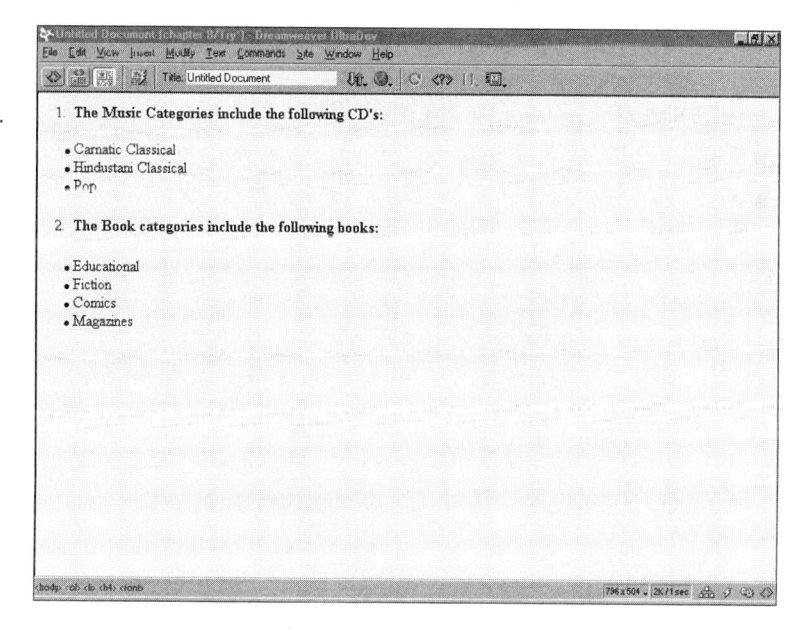

To create a nested list, do the following:

1. In Design view of a Document window, select the list of items to be presented as a nested list.
2. Choose Text, Indent to indent the selected text, which forms a part of the existing list.
3. UltraDev creates a separate list with the HTML attributes of the main list. You can apply a new list type to the nested list by following the steps given for creating a new ordered list or unordered list.

Setting List Properties

You can change a list's properties to enhance its appearance. The List Properties dialog box lets you do this. Choose Text, List, Properties to display the List Properties dialog box, shown in Figure 8.13.

Figure 8.13
The List Properties dialog box.

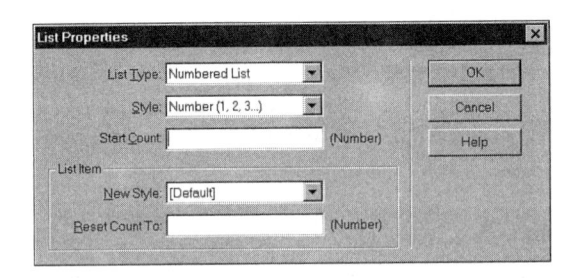

> **Tip**
>
> You can also display the List Properties dialog box by right-clicking a list item and choosing List, Properties or by clicking the List Item button in the Property inspector.

The List Properties dialog box has the following options:

- List Type: Lets you change the list type by selecting the appropriate type.
- Style: Lets you specify the style of numbers or bullets used for a numbered or bulleted list. If the list type is a bulleted list, this option lets you choose a round or square bullet. If the list type is a numbered list, this option lets you choose the Number, Roman Small, Roman Large, Alphabet Small, or Alphabet Large types.
- Start Count: Lets you set a starting value for a numbered list.
- New Style: Lets you specify a different bullet type or number type for a list.
- Reset Count To: Lets you create nonsequential numbered lists.

Searching and Replacing Text, Tags, and Attributes

UltraDev's Find and Replace option lets you search the current document, a selected file, a directory, or an entire site for text or HTML tags and attributes.

Searching for Text

To search for text within a document, do the following:

1. Choose View, Design to display Design view.
2. Choose Edit, Find and Replace. The Find and Replace dialog box is displayed, as shown in Figure 8.14.

Figure 8.14
The Find and Replace dialog box.

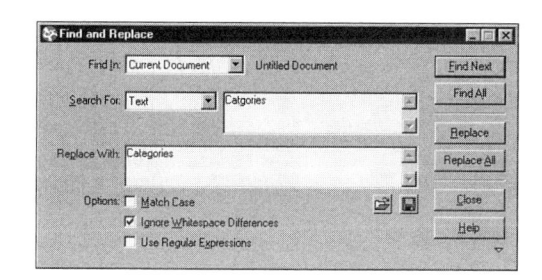

3. Select the file that you want to search from the Find In drop-down list. If you want to restrict your search to the active document, choose Current Document. Choose Selected Files if you want to search the files that are currently selected in the Site window. If you want to search all documents in the current site, choose Current Site from the drop-down list. Choose Folder if you want to search a specific group of files.
4. Select the kind of search you want to perform from the Search For drop-down list.
5. Type the text you want to search for in the text field next to the Search For drop-down list.
6. In the Replace With text box, specify the replacement text, if any.
7. Click Find Next to find the next instance of the text in the current document. Click Find All to generate a list of all the instances of the text. Click Replace to replace the instance of the text with replacement text. Click Replace All to replace all the instances of the text with the specified replacement text.

Searching for Tags

The Specific Tag option in the Find and Replace dialog box lets you search for tags, attributes, and attribute values.

To search for tags within a document, follow these steps:

1. Select View, Design to be able to work in Design view. This option allows you to work in a visual environment.
2. Choose Edit, Find and Replace. The Find and Replace dialog box is displayed.
3. Select the file you want to search from the Find In drop-down list.

4. Choose Specific Tag from the Search For list box. The Find and Replace dialog box displays some additional options, as shown in Figure 8.15. Select the tag you want to search for in the drop-down list next to the Search For drop-down list. If you only want to find all occurrences of the specified tag, press the – button and move on to step 6. Otherwise, continue with step 5.

Figure 8.15
The Find and Replace dialog box also lets you search for tags within a document.

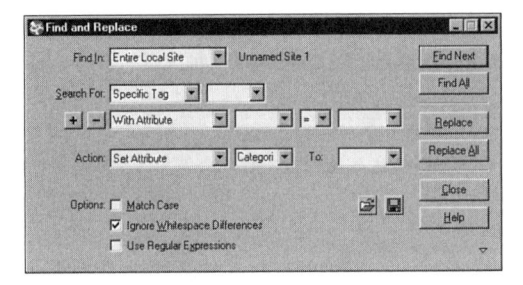

5. The list box next to the + and – buttons contains items that let you choose attributes. Select With Attribute to choose an attribute that must be in the tag for it to match. Select Without Attribute to choose an attribute that cannot be in the tag for it to match.

Tip

The list boxes next to the list box containing the With Attribute option, as shown in Figure 8.15, allow you to search for a tag with its attribute containing a specific value. If you want to search for the <body> tag with the attribute bgcolor equal to the value #000066, you need to select the body option from the list box next to the Search For list box. Then, select the With Attribute option from the list box next to the – button, the bgcolor option from the second list box, the = option from the third list box list box, and type #000066 in the fourth list box. If you want to specify more attributes, you can click the + button and follow the same procedure as described above.

6. If you want to replace the attribute of a tag with another attribute, you need to select the Set Attribute option from the Action list box, select the attribute option from the second list box, and type the value in the To list box.
7. Click Find Next to find the next instance of the tag in the current document. Click Find All to generate a list of all the instances of the tag.
8. Click Replace to replace the instance of the found text or tag with the replacement tag. Click Replace All to replace all instances of the tag with the specified replacement tag.

SAVING A SEARCH

The Save Query button in the Find and Replace dialog box lets you save search patterns for later use. This button is identified with a floppy disk icon. To save a search pattern, follow these steps:

1. Select Edit, Find and Replace. The Find and Replace dialog box is displayed.
2. Type the text you want to search for in the text field next to the Search For drop-down list. Click the Save Query button. The Save Query dialog box is displayed, as shown in Figure 8.16.

Figure 8.16
The Save Query dialog box.

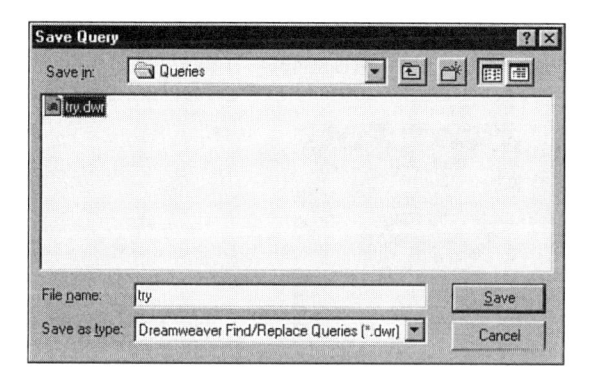

3. Type a name for the search pattern in the File name text box.
4. Click Save to save the search.

> **Note**
> By default, the queries are saved in the Configuration/Queries folder of the Dreamweaver UltraDev 4 application folder.

USING HTML STYLES AND CSS

A *style* is a set of formatting attributes that controls the appearance of the text in a document. Using a style, you can change various formatting properties at the same time.

Each style has a unique name. By applying the style name to a selected piece of text, you can change several formatting properties of the selected text at the same time. All the styles and formatting specifications are stored in a page styling template. This template is known as a *style sheet*.

UltraDev allows you to use HTML styles, CSS styles, and manually created HTML formatting styles within a page.

USING HTML STYLES

An HTML style is a combination of several standard HTML tags. In UltraDev, you can apply HTML styles to the text in a document by using the HTML styles option. This option allows you to create new styles by defining various features, such as the text color, font size, and font style. The HTML styles option also lets you apply new styles to text by clearing or adding to the existing styles.

Manual HTML formatting and HTML styles use the standard HTML tags to format text and are supported by most Web browsers.

CREATING A NEW HTML STYLE

To create a new HTML style, you use the Define HTML Style dialog box, shown in Figure 8.17. To display this dialog box, choose Text, HTML Styles, New Style. The options in this dialog box let you apply or edit an HTML style.

Figure 8.17
The Define HTML Style dialog box lets you set font and paragraph attributes.

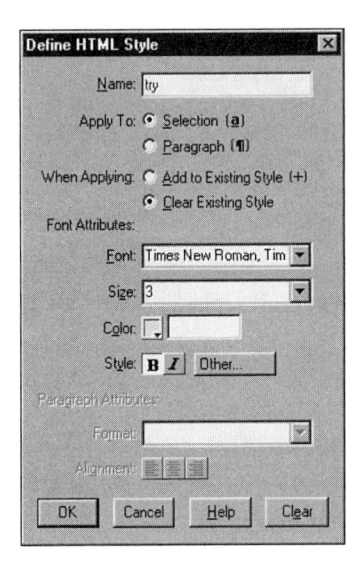

Table 8.3 describes the options available in the Define HTML Style dialog box.

TABLE 8.3   THE DEFINE HTML STYLE DIALOG BOX OPTIONS

Option	Description
Name	Lets you name the new style.
Apply To	Lets you apply the selected style to a selection or an entire paragraph.
	Select the Selection check box if you want to apply the HTML style to a selected piece of text.
	Select the Paragraph check box if you want to apply the HTML style to an entire paragraph.
When Applying	Lets you either add the new style to the existing style or apply the new style by clearing the existing style.
	Select the Add to Existing Style check box if you want to add the new HTML style to the existing styles in the text.
	Select the Clear Existing Style check box if you want to remove the existing style and replace it with the new HTML style.

Using HTML Styles and CSS

Table 8.3 Continued

Option	Description
Font Attributes	Lets you set font attributes, such as font type, font size, and font color.
Paragraph Attributes	Lets you configure paragraph attributes, such as format and alignment.

Note

If you are using HTML styles, CSS styles, and external CSS styles in your document, UltraDev gives first priority to HTML styles and then to CSS styles and then to external CSS styles.

Applying an Existing HTML Style

To apply an existing HTML style, you need to use the HTML Styles panel. panelIt also lets you create, delete, and edit HTML styles. To display the HTML Styles panel, shown in Figure 8.18, choose Window, HTML Styles.panel

Figure 8.18
HTML Styles panel lets you create, delete, and edit HTML styles.

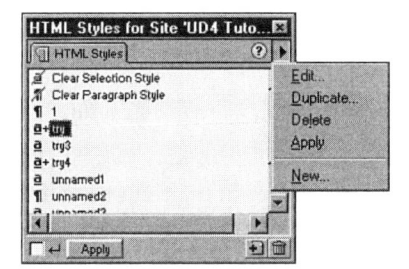

To apply an HTML style to the text in a document by using the HTML Styles panel, you need to select the text and then select the style you want to apply. If the Auto Apply check box in the lower-left corner of the panel is selected, the HTML Styles panel automatically applies the style to the selected text. If the Auto Apply check box is not selected, you need to click the Apply button to apply the style. Using the Auto Apply button is faster than manually applying the style. Table 8.4 describes the options available in the HTML Styles panel.

Table 8.4 The HTML Styles Panel Options

Option	Description
The context menu	An arrow mark to the upper-right corner of the panel represents the context menu. Alternatively, you can right click anywhere in the panel to view the context menu. The options on this menu let you duplicate, delete, apply, define, and edit a new style.
The Auto Apply check box	This option lets you apply a selected style automatically.

Table 8.4 Continued

Option	Description
The Apply button	This option lets you apply a selected style manually. The Apply button is enabled only when the Auto Apply check box is not selected.
New Style	A plus sign in the lower-right corner of the panel represents the New Style button. This option lets you create a new HTML style.
Delete Style	A trash can icon in the lower-right corner of the panel represents the Delete Style button. This option lets you delete a selected style from the HTML Styles panel.

Sharing Your HTML Style with Other Users

Consider a team of three users who are designing different pages of a Web site. All three of them have to use the same HTML styles to maintain consistency across the Web site. The HTML styles are placed in a central location to allow the team to apply the same style to all pages.

Choose Window, Site Files. The Site window in Site Files view is displayed. The Site window is a central location from where you can manage your entire site.

The left and right panes of the Site window display the file structures on the remote and local sites, respectively.

Open the Site Root folder, with the Library folder in the right pane. In the Library folder, you will notice a file called `styles.xml`. It contains all your HTML styles for the site. Select the file styles.xml and right-click to see the options. These options allow you to put, get, check in, check out, and copy this file as you would do with any other file in your site. You can use the Design Notes option to create design notes for the `styles.xml` file.

→ To learn how to create design notes, **see** "Creating Design Notes," **p. 458**.

Using CSS Styles

Cascading Style Sheets (CSS) is a very important file used by Web designers for text and page formatting. Cascading Style Sheets are external text files that contain styles and formatting details that let you apply text and page formatting. CSS style sheets define the formatting for all text in a particular class. These styles can also be used to redefine the formatting for a particular tag. You can use the options in the CSS Styles palette to create and edit CSS style sheets.

Generally, CSS style sheets reside in a document's HEAD region. CSS style sheets have an advantage over HTML style sheets. If you make changes to a CSS style sheet linked to multiple documents, the formatting of all the documents linked to that style sheet is automatically updated.

USING HTML STYLES AND CSS | 163

> **Note**
> Cascading Style Sheets are currently supported by Netscape Navigator 4.0 and later and Microsoft Internet Explorer 3.0 and later.

USING THE CSS STYLE PANEL

The CSS Styles panel lets you create, delete, and edit CSS styles. To display the CSS Styles panel, shown in Figure 8.19, choose Window, CSS Styles panel.

Figure 8.19
The CSS Styles panel is similar to the HTML Styles panel.

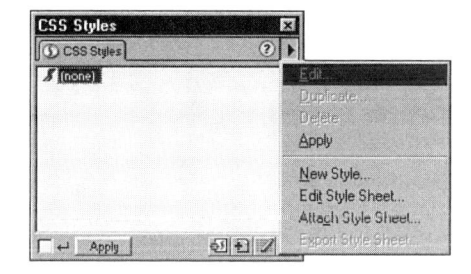

Table 8.5 summarizes the options available in the CSS Styles panel.

TABLE 8.5   THE CSS STYLES PANEL OPTIONS

Option	Description
The context menu	An arrow mark to the upper-right corner of the panel represents the context menu. Alternatively, you can right click anywhere in the panel to view the context menu. The options on this menu let you duplicate, delete, apply, define, and edit a new style.
The Auto Apply check box	This option lets you apply a selected style automatically.
The Apply button	This option lets you apply a selected style manually. The Apply button is enabled only when the Auto Apply check box is not selected.
New Style	A plus sign in the lower right corner of the panel represents the New Style button. This option lets you create a new CSS style.
Attach Style Sheet	This option is represented by an icon in the lower-right corner of the CSS panel. It lets you link to an external style sheet.
Edit Style Sheet	A pencil icon in the lower-right corner of the CSS panel represents the Edit Style Sheet button. This option lets you edit any of the styles in the current document or in an external style sheet.
Delete Style	A trash can icon in the lower-right corner of the panel represents the Delete Style button. This option lets you delete a selected style from the CSS Styles panel.

CREATING A CSS STYLE SHEET

To create a CSS style sheet, do the following:

1. Choose Window, CSS Styles. In the CSS Styles panel that is displayed, click the New Style button. The New Style dialog box is displayed, as shown in Figure 8.20.

Figure 8.20
The New Style dialog box.

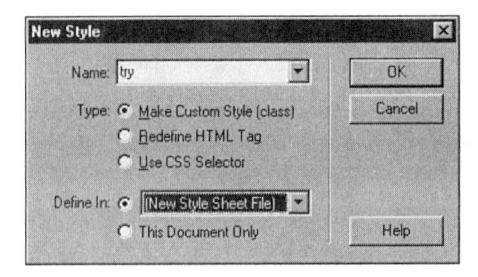

The New Style dialog box has the following options:

- Name: Lets you type a name for the new CSS style.
- Type: Lets you choose one of three check boxes that define the type of the CSS style:

    The Make Custom Style (class) check box creates a style that can be applied as a CLASS attribute to a block of text. Custom style names must begin with a period (.).

    The Redefine HTML Tag check box lets you set the default style of a specific HTML tag.

    The Use CSS Selector check box lets you define the formatting for a particular combination of tags.

- Define In: Lets you create your styles in an external file or in the document in which you are working. The (New Style Sheet File) option lets you add the style to a new style sheet. Select the This Document Only check box to keep the styles defined within a document.

2. Enter a name for the new CSS style in the Name text box. Select a tag or selector for the new CSS style. Select the location in which the style will be defined.
3. Click OK. The Style Definition dialog box is displayed, as shown in Figure 8.21. The Style Definition dialog box divides the various Style properties into a list of items under the Category list box. You can choose the formatting settings for the new CSS style by clicking each item in the Category list box.
4. Click OK.

After you have created a CSS style, you can apply it to any text. To apply a CSS style, you need to select the text and then select the style from the CSS Styles panel. If the Auto Apply check box in is selected, the CSS Styles panel automatically applies the style to the selected text. If the Auto Apply check box is not selected, you need to click the Apply button to apply the style.

Figure 8.21
The CSS Style Definition dialog box.

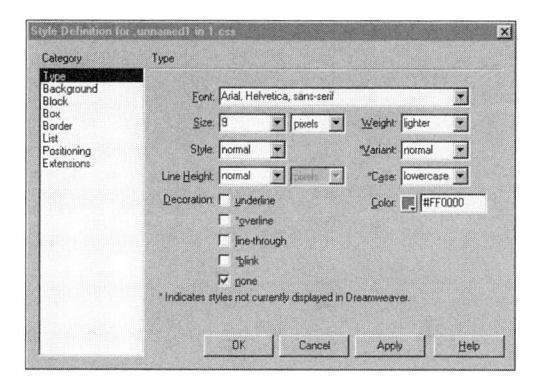

You can also edit an existing CSS style. To edit an existing CSS style, open the CSS style panel and double-click the style you want to edit. In the Style Definition dialog box that is displayed, make the required changes to the style, and click the Apply button to apply the style to selected text, if any, on the document and then click OK to save the changes to the style.

You can set CSS Style attributes for objects in your document by using the items in the Category list box of the Site Definition dialog box. The following list describes the items:

- The Type item of the Category list box (see Figure 8.22) lets you define style attributes for text objects. It allows you to define font size, font style, font color, case, and line spacing for text objects.

- The Background item of the Category list box, shown in Figure 8.22, lets you define the background attributes for objects. It allows you to choose the background color, the background image, and the horizontal and vertical positions of the background image.

Figure 8.22
The Background item lets you define basic background settings.

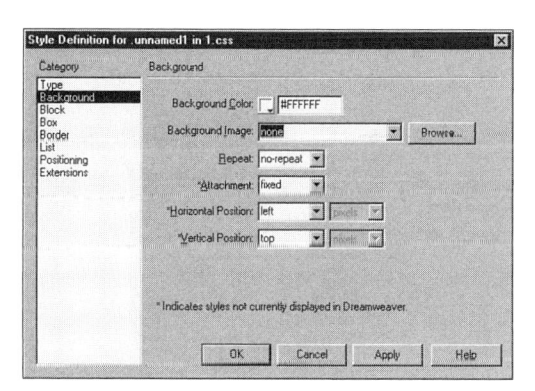

- The Block item, shown in Figure 8.23, lets you define the spacing, alignment, and indentation attributes for a block of text.

Figure 8.23
The Block item lets you define basic block settings.

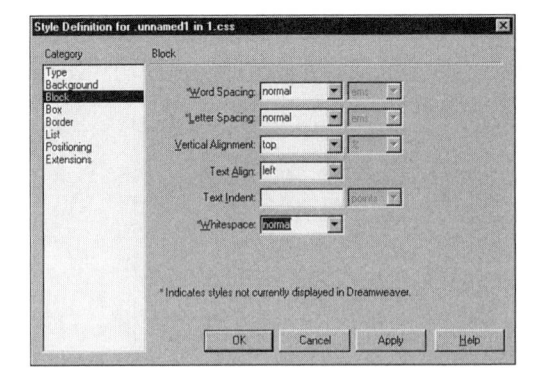

- The Box item of the Category list box, shown in Figure 8.24, lets you define the settings for styles that control the placement of elements on the page.

Figure 8.24
The Box item lets you define basic properties for a block of text.

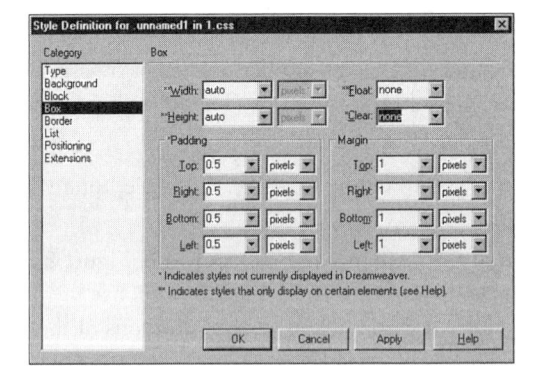

- The Border item, shown in Figure 8.25, lets you define settings, such as border size and color.

Figure 8.25
The Border item lets you define basic settings for borders around elements.

- The List item of the Category list box, shown in Figure 8.26, lets you define settings for a list, such as list type and bullet type.

Figure 8.26
The List item lets you define basic settings for a list.

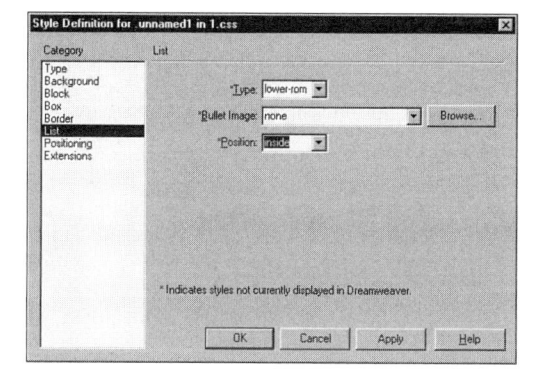

- The Positioning item of the Category list box, shown in Figure 8.27, lets you change the tag or selected block of text into a new layer.

Figure 8.27
The Positioning item lets you define the position and clipped regions of layers.

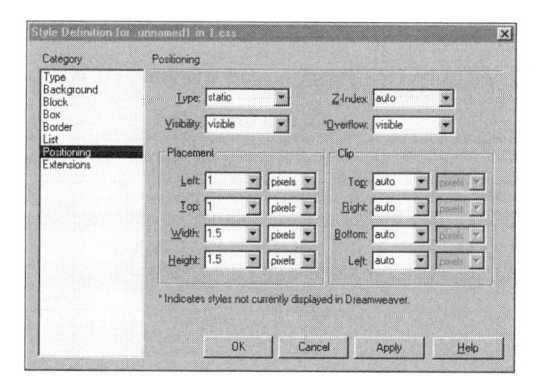

- The Extensions item of the Category list box, shown in Figure 8.28, lets you define attributes that are not consistent across browsers, such as page breaks, filters, and cursor shapes.

Figure 8.28
The Extensions item lets you define basic block settings for a CSS style.

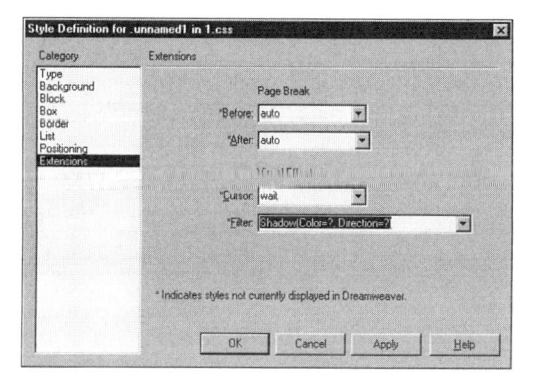

Converting CSS Styles to HTML Tags

Cascading Style Sheets are supported by Netscape Navigator 4.0 and later and Microsoft Internet Explorer 3.0 and later. If you use CSS styles with older browsers, you will not be able to view CSS-formatted pages properly. In such cases, you can use the Convert to 3.0 Browser Compatible dialog box to convert CSS styles, wherever possible, to HTML tags.

Choose File, Convert, 3.0 Browser Compatible to display the Convert to 3.0 Browser Compatible dialog box, shown in Figure 8.29.

Figure 8.29
The Convert to 3.0 Browser Compatible dialog box.

Select CSS Styles to HTML Markup to convert the CSS styles, wherever possible, to HTML tags. Table 8.6 lists the attributes that can be converted into HTML tags. Any CSS attribute that cannot be converted to HTML is removed and is not listed in the table.

TABLE 8.6 LIST OF CSS ATTRIBUTES THAT CAN BE CONVERTED TO HTML TAGS

CSS Attribute	Converted To
color	FONT COLOR
font-family	FONT FACE
font-size	FONT SIZE = "[1-7]"
font-size: oblique	I
font-size: italic	I
font-weight	B
list-style-type: square	UL TYPE = "square"
list-style-type: circle	UL TYPE = "circle"
list-style-type: disc	UL TYPE = "disc"
list-style-type: upper-roman	OL TYPE = "I"
list-style-type: lower-roman	OL TYPE = "i"
list-style-type: upper-alpha	OL TYPE = "A"
list-style-type: lower-alpha	OL TYPE = "a"
list-style	UltraDev or OL with TYPE as appropriate
text-align	P ALIGN or DIV ALIGN as appropriate
text-decoration: underline	U
text-decoration: line-through	STRIKE

Summary

In this chapter, you learned to create documents and format the text in them. You learned to change the font, size, color, and alignment of selected text. In addition, you learned to use the Text, Style submenu to apply formatting such as bold, italic, code, and underline to the text in a document. You also learned to create and apply HTML and CSS styles to your document by using the HTML and CSS Styles palette. In addition, you learned to convert CSS styles to HTML tags.

Activity Corner

In this activity corner section, you will create and apply HTML styles to the text in the Help.asp, Aboutus.asp, and Sidebar.asp files. A point to note before proceeding with the activity corner section: For the sake of uniformity, all the filenames in the activity corner sections across chapters are referred with the extension .asp. In this section and in subsequent sections, you will be copying some base files from the Web to develop your application. These base files are also .asp files. If you use ColdFusion or JSP to develop this application, rename the files with the appropriate extension after copying them from the Web.

Before applying the HTML styles to the documents, copy the Help_base.asp, Aboutus_base.asp, and Sidebar_base.asp files from the Web to your local root folder. Save the Help_base.asp as Help.asp, Aboutus_base.asp as Aboutus.asp, and Sidebar_base.asp as Sidebar.asp. When you try to save the Sidebar_base.asp as Sidebar.asp, UltraDev displays a dialog box to ask if the file can be overwritten. Click the Yes button to overwrite the file.

Applying HTML Styles to the Sidebar.asp File

After copying these files, you can proceed to create the HTML styles for the Sidebar.asp. The Sidebar.asp file contains a layout with some text. You now need to create two HTML styles named Link_style and Sidebar_style and apply these styles to the text in the Sidebar.asp file. To create these two styles and apply them, perform the following steps:

1. Choose Windows, HTML Styles to open the HTML Styles panel.
2. Click the New Style button on the HTML Styles panel. The Define HTML Style dialog box is displayed.
3. In the Name text box of the Define HTML style dialog box, type the text **Link_style**.
4. Select the Selection radio button.
5. Select the Clear Existing Style radio button.
6. Choose Verdana from the Font drop-down list. Select 2 from the Size drop-down list and type **#999999** in the Color text box.
7. Click OK to close the Define HTML Style dialog box.
8. Next, create another HTML style named Sidebar_style. The font for the Side_bar style must be Verdana, the font size must be 3, and the text color must be #CCCCCC.
9. Select the Auto Apply check box at the bottom of the HTML Style panel.

10. Select the text Categories and click the `Sidebar_style` in HTML Style panel. Do the same for the text Search. Next, apply the `Link_style` to the rest of the text on the `Sidebar.asp` document.

After applying these styles, choose Modify, Page Properties to open the Page Properties dialog box. In the Links, Visited Links, and Active Links text boxes, specify the color as `#999999`.

Applying HTML Styles to the `Aboutus.asp` and `Help.asp` Files

To apply an HTML style to the text in the `Aboutus.asp` and `Help.asp` files, you need to create an HTML style named `Text_style`. Specify the font of this new style as Verdana, font size as 2 and font color as `#000066`. Select the text in the `Aboutus.asp` file and apply this style. Do the same for the text in the `Help.asp` file.

Previewing Your Site

To preview the site you are developing, it is better to open the `Musichome.asp` file in a new browser window that is not resizable. This is done to maintain the look and feel of the site when viewed in different browsers and screen resolutions.

To open the Musichome.asp file from a new browser window, copy the `Start.htm` file from the Web to your local root folder. Then, open your browser and type `http://www.tunein.com/Start.htm` in the URL window. You can also preview your site by opening the `Start.htm` file in the Document window and pressing F12.

CHAPTER 9

CREATING AND MANAGING IMAGES

In this chapter

Working with Images   172

Image Formats   172

Inserting Images into a Page   174

Inserting Rollover Images into a Web Page   176

Inserting Navigation Bars into a Page   177

Formatting Images   180

Working with Image Maps   184

Using External Image Editors   186

Summary   188

Activity Corner   188

Working with Images

Images significantly affect the visual impression your Web sites make. However, you need to be careful about using images in a Web page because they can adversely affect the download time of the page. There are several questions that you must answer before inserting images into your documents:

- Does your site really require images?
- What purpose do the images serve? Do the images match the content or add value to the content?
- How many images do you need?
- Where should you place the images?
- What should the size and file format of the image be?

You must look carefully at the purpose of your Web site to decide whether it really needs images to be effective. For example, if the goal of your Web site is to provide online shopping, then the site should probably contain images of the products you are selling so that users can preview items before they decide whether to buy them. You always need to be careful, however, not to include so many large images that you increase download times unreasonably for the users. The file format you choose for your images can be very important. If the images you want to use are large, it is best to choose a file format that gives maximum compression for faster download times. Where you put the images can also be important. When the number of images becomes large, you can place these images separately from the principal information pages. Users can get to information like product details without needing to download the images along with that information. They can choose to download the images in separate pages or windows. The following sections help you choose the best file format for your needs and show you how to work effectively with images in your Web pages.

Image Formats

Graphic file formats are of various types, such as GIF, JPEG, PNG, TIFF, PCX, and so on. Of these file formats, GIF, JPEG, and PNG are best suited for the Web. Whereas Graphic Interchange Format (GIF) and Joint Photographic Experts Group (JPEG) are very popular formats and are supported by most of the Web browsers, the Portable Network Graphics (PNG) file format is relatively new. However, it is quickly gaining popularity, as will be discussed shortly.

Graphic Interchange Format

GIF is one of the two widely used graphic file formats on the Web. This is because browsers can easily download and decompress GIF images; GIF supports only 256 colors.

GIF file compression is *lossless*, which means that there is no loss of information when GIF files are compressed. A GIF image looks the same decompressed as it did before compression.

Although GIF images support only 256 colors, you can use them to provide various graphical effects to a Web site, such as transparent backgrounds, interlacing, and animations. You can use GIFs for images that have large areas of *flat colors*, which do not contain gradations or shades. For example, you can use them to create logos, navigation buttons, and other images that contain flat colors.

JOINT PHOTOGRAPHIC EXPERTS GROUP

You can use the JPEG format for photographs and other images that have a *continuous shading tone*, that is, images containing a multitude of colors and shades. These images are usually true color images with a 24-bit color depth. JPEG provides support for 24-bit color depth, using a color palette of 16.7 million colors. Therefore, images compressed with JPEG have a superior quality when compared to GIF images. Although JPEGs offer an increase in image quality, download times also increase for JPEG images. To overcome this, you can increase the compression percentage of the JPEGs. However, you must be careful when compressing JPEG images. JPEG images are compressed using the lossy compression method, so JPEG image quality degrades with compression. For example, if you compress an image to about 90% of its original size, you might get a smaller file size and faster download, but the quality of the image suffers. Therefore, you need to strike a balance between the size and quality of JPEG images.

PORTABLE NETWORK GRAPHICS

The PNG graphic file format allows you to overcome the drawbacks of both the GIF and JPEG file formats. Like JPEG, PNG supports true color, which gives it an edge over GIF when used with photographs. In addition to true color 24-bit images, PNG supports grayscale (256 shades of gray) and 8-bit images. It also supports what is known as the *alpha channel*. An alpha channel gives information about the transparency of an image. For every pixel in an image, the alpha channel stores information about the transparency of that pixel. Because PNG supports alpha channel, you can create images with shadow and fading effects. The alpha channel support in PNG images is better than that for GIF images. Whereas GIF images can be either completely opaque or completely transparent, PNG images can be partially transparent, because PNG supports up to 254 levels of transparency. PNG images have an edge over JPEG images because PNG uses the lossless compression method. Compressing a PNG image does not reduce its quality.

PNG also supports *indexed colors*, which allow a browser to render graphics accurately. When you compress a file using the PNG compression format, you have an option of creating indexed colors. When you create indexed colors, the colors in the image file are counted and assigned a number. These colors and their numbers are stored in a color palette. When a PNG image loads in the browser, the color palette also loads, thus allowing the browser to render the image correctly.

Although PNG has many advantages over GIF and JPEG images, it still doesn't have full support by all browsers. PNG was released as a W3C specification in 1996. Most browsers up to that time did not support the format. Browser versions released after 1996 have gradually begun to support PNG. Internet Explorer 5.0 for Windows has partial PNG support, whereas IE 5.0 for the Macintosh fully supports PNG. Netscape Navigator versions beginning with 4.04 support PNG.

INSERTING IMAGES INTO A PAGE

You can insert an image into a page in UltraDev by using the Select Image Source dialog box. To insert an image into your document, follow these steps:

1. Place the cursor at the position on the page where you want to insert the image.
2. Choose Insert, Image to display the Select Image Source dialog box, as shown in Figure 9.1.

Figure 9.1
Use the Select Image Source dialog box to select the image you want to insert into the Web page.

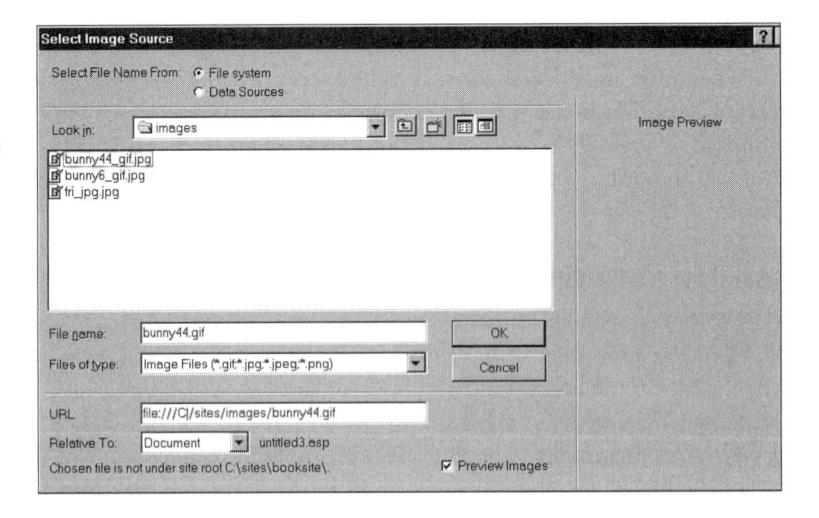

3. The Look in drop-down list allows you to select an image from anywhere within your file system. By default, it lists the images in the local root folder. If the image that you want to use is in a subfolder of the local root folder, you can double-click that subfolder to view the image files. If the image is in a folder other than the local root folder, select that folder from the Look in drop-down list. When you select the image that you want to insert, a preview of the selected image appears on the right side of the dialog box. Click OK to insert the image. Figure 9.2 shows the Select Image Source dialog box with the preview of the selected image.

4. If the image file that you selected is not within the local root folder, a warning message prompts you to copy the image file to the local site folder. Click Yes in the message box to copy the image to the local site folder. The Copy File As dialog box appears.

INSERTING IMAGES INTO A PAGE | 175

Figure 9.2
You can preview the image in Select Image Source dialog box before inserting it in the page.

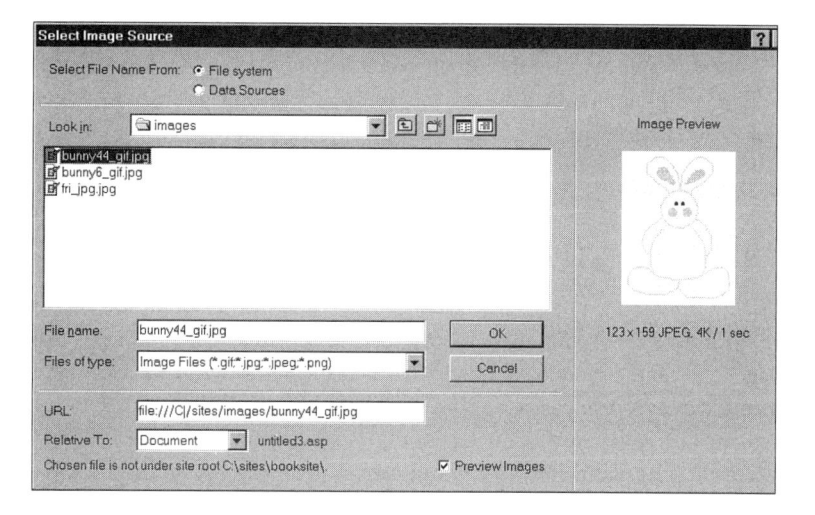

> **Caution**
> If you do not copy an image to the local site folder, it does not appear when you publish your site. It is always better to have all the images you plan to use for your site in the local root folder, preferably within a subfolder of the local root folder. So, before you begin inserting an image, make sure you have all the images in the required subfolder of the local root folder.

5. In the Copy File As dialog box, type a name for the image file in the File Name text box and click Save. The Copy File As dialog box closes and the image appears at the position you specified, as shown in Figure 9.3.

Figure 9.3
The image that you select is inserted at the position of the cursor.

You can also use the Insert Image button in the Objects panel to insert an image. When you click this button, the steps that you must follow to insert the image are the same as those that you follow after you choose the Image option from the Insert menu. Alternatively, you can drag and drop an image from the Assets panel or the desktop. When you use the Assets panel to insert an image, you can insert only those images that are in the local root folder of the current site, because the Assets panel lists only those images that are in the current site. When you drag and drop an image from the desktop, the warning message that the image is not in your local root folder appears, prompting you to save the file to the local root folder before inserting it into your document.

INSERTING ROLLOVER IMAGES INTO A WEB PAGE

Rollover images are images that change when you move the mouse pointer over them. Rollover images are made up of two images, a primary image that is displayed when the page loads and a secondary image that is displayed when the mouse pointer moves over the primary image. You can use rollover images to give a live feeling to a page. For example, you can create a rollover effect with the two images shown in Figure 9.4 to show the effect of a touch-me-not plant. Before you can create a rollover image to bring about the effect of the touch-me-not, you must first create the primary and secondary images. In Figure 9.4, the primary image is in a file called `open_leaf.jpg`, and the secondary image is in a file called `close_leaf.jpg`.

Figure 9.4
Create a rollover effect for images by using primary and secondary images.

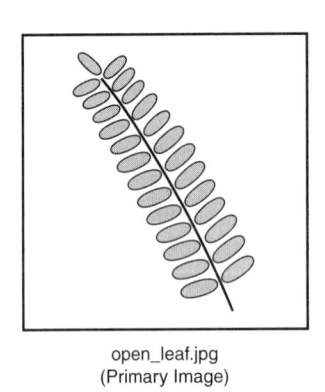

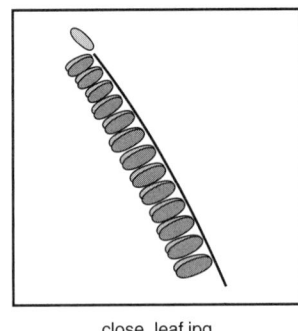

open_leaf.jpg
(Primary Image)

close_leaf.jpg
(Secondary Image)

Apart from giving a live feeling to your Web pages, you can use rollover images to attract a user's attention to the clickable areas on your pages.

To insert a rollover image into a document, perform the following steps:

1. Place the cursor at the position where you want to insert a rollover image and choose Insert, Interactive Images, Rollover Image. The Insert Rollover Image dialog box appears, as shown in Figure 9.5.

2. In the Image Name text box of the Insert Rollover Image dialog box, type a name for the rollover image. For example, to show the rollover effect for a touch-me-not, specify a name such as tmnPlant.

Figure 9.5
Use the Insert Rollover Image dialog box to insert rollover images.

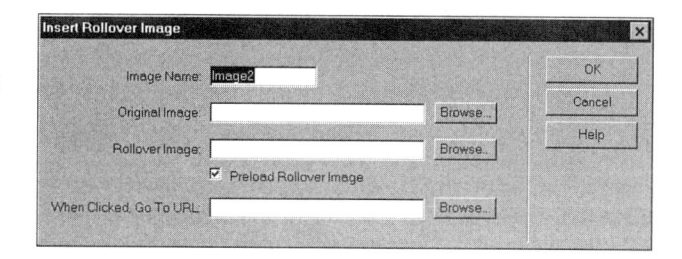

3. In the Original Image text box, type the name of the primary image that should appear as soon as the page loads. Alternatively, you can click the Browse button to select an image. To show the rollover effect of the touch-me-not, type `open_leaf.jpg` in the Original Image text box.

4. In the Rollover Image text box, enter the name of the secondary image that must appear when the mouse pointer moves over the primary image. Alternatively, you can click the Browse button to select a rollover image. Type `close_leaf.jpg` in the Rollover Image text box to specify this image as the secondary image.

5. Check the Preload Rollover option if you want the image to be preloaded into the browser's cache. When images are preloaded on the browser, they appear more quickly and thereby give a better rollover effect.

6. In the When Clicked, Go to URL text box, enter the path of the file that you want to display when the user clicks the rollover image.

7. Click OK to close the Insert Rollover Image dialog box.

You can preview the rollover effect of the image in the browser by pressing the F12 key.

INSERTING NAVIGATION BARS INTO A PAGE

Navigation bars allow users to navigate from one page to another. A navigation bar consists of a series of images whose states change based on the actions performed by a user.

To create a navigation bar, first you need to create the images that can be used as elements in the navigation bar. Use a graphics application such as Adobe Photoshop or Paint Shop Pro to create the images. For example, Figure 9.6 shows a series of images that you can use to create a navigation bar.

Figure 9.6
Use a related set of images such as these to create a navigation bar.

Each element of a navigation bar can have different states based on the actions performed by a user. UltraDev enables you to create four states for each element in the navigation bar: Up, Over, Down, and Over While Down. The following list summarizes each state:

- **Up**   This is the default state of an element, displayed when a page loads on a browser.
- **Over**   This state appears when the mouse pointer is placed over the element. The pop-up state of a toolbar button is an example of the Over state.
- **Down**   This state appears after the user clicks the element. For example, when a user moves to a new page by clicking an element on the navigation bar and the navigation bar is still displayed in the next page, the color of the clicked element can change to a different color to indicate that the user has selected that option.
- **Over While Down**   This state appears when the mouse pointer moves over the Down state of the element. For example, if an element is already selected and is in a depressed state, then you can change the element to appear grayed out when the user moves the mouse pointer over it.

It is not necessary for an element to show all four states. For example, an element can just show the Up, Over, and Down states. Figure 9.7 shows the navigation element home in the Up, Over, and Down states.

Figure 9.7
These are images of the Home button in the Up, Down, and Over states.

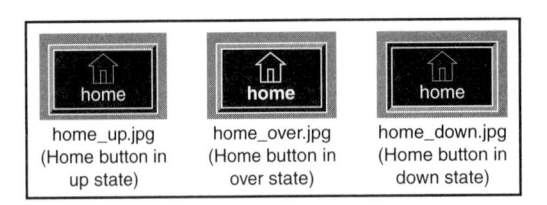

home_up.jpg (Home button in up state)   home_over.jpg (Home button in over state)   home_down.jpg (Home button in down state)

Before you begin creating a navigation bar such as the one shown in Figure 9.6, you need to create the images for all the states of each element in the navigation bar. Figure 9.7 shows the images for the Up, Over, and Down states of the home navigation element. After these images are ready, you can add the elements to the navigation bar and associate the images for each navigation bar element with each of its states. Perform the following steps to insert a navigation bar into your Web page:

1. Choose Insert, Interactive Images, Navigation Bar. The Insert Navigation Bar dialog box appears, as shown in Figure 9.8.
2. Enter a name for the navigation bar element in the Element Name text box. To specify a name for the first element, home, type **home** in the Element Name text box.
3. In the Up Image text box, type the path of the image to be displayed for the up state of the element. Alternatively, you can also click the Browse button to select an image. The Up state is required for all elements. All other states are optional. If the image file associated with the Up state of the home element is home_up.jpg, type this filename in the Up Image text box.

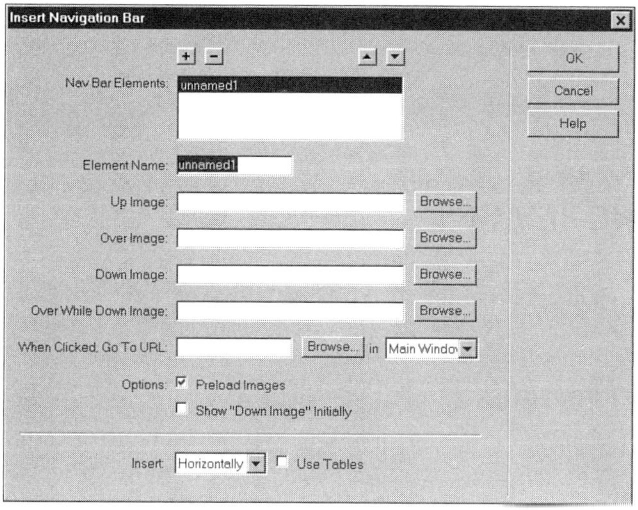

Figure 9.8
Use the Insert Navigation Bar dialog box to insert a navigation bar.

4. Type the paths of the images to be displayed for the Over, Down, and Over While Down states in the Over Image, Down Image, and Over While Down Image text boxes, respectively. Alternatively, you can click the Browse button to select the images. If the image files associated with the Over and Down states of the home element are named `home_over.jpg` and `home_down.jpg`, respectively, type these filenames in the Over Image and Down Image text boxes.

5. Enter the URL of the file that must be opened when the element is clicked, in the When Clicked, Go To URL text box. Along with the URL you can also specify the target window in which the linked file must open.

6. Check the Preload Image option to download the image into the browser's cache to display the image faster.

7. Check the Show Down Image Initially option to display the down state of the element when the page downloads.

8. Select an option from the Insert drop-down list to insert the navigation bar either horizontally or vertically, based on your preference.

You must perform steps 2–7 for every element you add to the navigation bar. Therefore, to complete the navigation bar shown in Figure 9.6, you repeat steps 2–7 for the rest of the elements shown in the figure. You can add elements to and remove them from the navigation bar by clicking the + and – signs in the Insert Navigation Bar dialog box. You can also change the order of the elements in the navigation bar by using the up and down arrows. However, each Web page can have only one navigation bar.

After you insert a navigation bar, you can modify the properties of the navigation bar at any time by using the navigation bar element list. To display this element list, choose Modify, Navigation Bar. Modify the element list and its properties in the Insert Navigation Bar dialog box. The new properties will be applied to the navigation bar.

> **Note**
> Although you can modify the navigation bar, you cannot change the alignment of the navigation bar elements. Moreover, you do not have the option of specifying whether the navigation bar elements can appear in a table when you modify the navigation bar.

FORMATTING IMAGES

UltraDev provides you with the flexibility to change or set properties for an image. You can resize and align images by using the Property inspector of the image. In addition, you can create hyperlinks and set borders for images by using this window.

SETTING IMAGE PROPERTIES

You can set various properties for an image by using the Property inspector. To view the Property inspector of the image, select the image and choose Window, Properties. By default, the Property inspector displays only some of the most commonly used properties of an image. However, you can expand the window by clicking the expander arrow in the lower right corner of the window.

As soon as you insert an image into a page, the height and width of the image are displayed in the W and H text boxes of the Property inspector, as shown in Figure 9.9.

Figure 9.9
Use the Property inspector to set properties for the image.

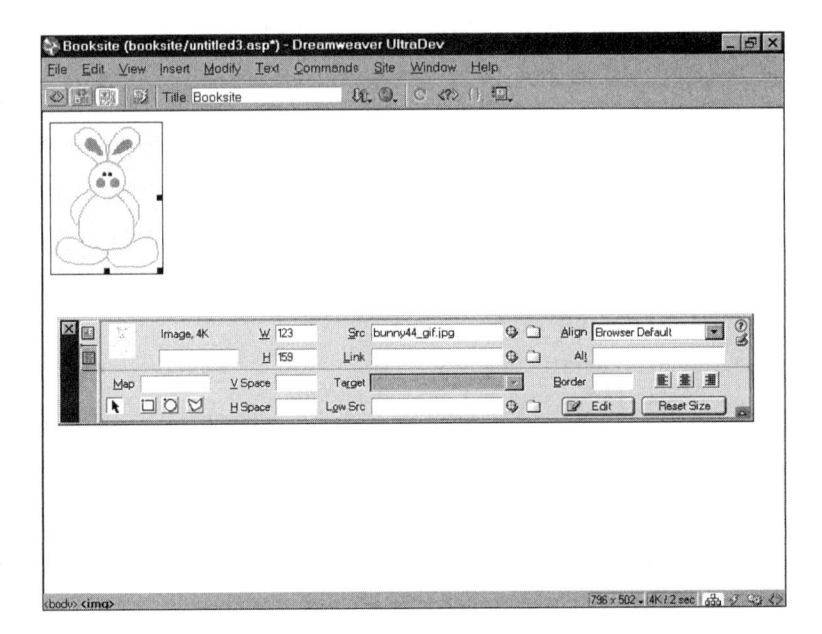

The W and H attributes of an image allocate space for the image on the page when the page is downloaded. You can change the width and height of an image by specifying new values in the W and H text boxes. By default, the width and height values are measured in pixels. You can also specify other units, such as pt (point), in (inches), mm (millimeter), and cm (centimeter). You can restore the original width and height of the image by clicking the field labels. You can also use the Reset Size button to restore the image to its original size.

> **Note**
> Changing the width and height of an image only scales the display of that instance of the image. It does not change the size of the image or the download time of the image, because the browser downloads the image file in its original size before scaling the image. To reduce the actual size of the image file you need to use an image editing application such as Adobe Photoshop or Paint Shop Pro.

Along with the width and the height of an image, the Property inspector also displays the source file of the image. You can change the source file for the image by entering the path of the new source file in the SRC text box or by clicking the folder icon and browsing for the source file. Alternatively, you can drag the Point to File icon to a file in the Site window to select the source file.

The Link option in the Property inspector enables you to set a hyperlink for an image. You can either specify the URL of the file to which the image must link or click the Browse button to select the document to which the link needs to be established.

The Align option enables you to set the alignment of an image with respect to other elements in the same line as that of the image. You can align the images horizontally by using the Align Left, Align Center, and Align Right buttons in the Image Property inspector.

Images that are inserted into a Web page cannot be viewed in text-only browsers. Therefore, UltraDev provides you the Alt option that enables you to specify a text that can appear instead of the image in text-only browsers. This option is also useful for browsers that have been set to download images manually. In some browsers, the text is displayed when the user points to the image.

You can set horizontal and vertical spacing around an image by using the V Space and H Space options in the Property inspector of the image. The V Space option enables you to add space, in pixels, to the top and bottom of the image. The H space option adds space to the left and right of the image.

The Target option enables you to specify the frame or the window in which the linked page must be displayed. This option is enabled only if a link is created for the image. By default, the following reserved target names appear in the Target drop-down list:

- **_blank** Allows you to open the linked file in a new browser window
- **_parent** Allows you to open the linked file in the window of the frame that contains the link
- **_self** Allows you to load the linked file in the same frame or window where the link exists
- **_top** Allows you to load the linked file into a full browser window

Using the Property inspector of an image, you can also draw a boundary around the image by applying a border. You can specify the size of the border for an image in the Border text box. You can apply borders for linked and unlinked images. The border color for a linked image is the same as the color set for links in the Page Properties dialog box. The border color for an unlinked image is the same as the color of the text in the paragraph in which the image is inserted. If you do not need a border for an image, enter **0** in the Border text box.

The Edit button enables you to edit an image in an image editor. After you edit the image and save the file, UltraDev automatically updates the image in the Document window.

ALIGNING IMAGES

When you add text beside an image or insert an image beside an existing line of text, the text moves to the bottom edge of the image. However, you can change this alignment by using the various alignment options provided in the Align drop-down list box of the Property inspector of the image, as shown in Figure 9.10.

Figure 9.10
Use the various alignment options available in the Property inspector to set the alignment of the image.

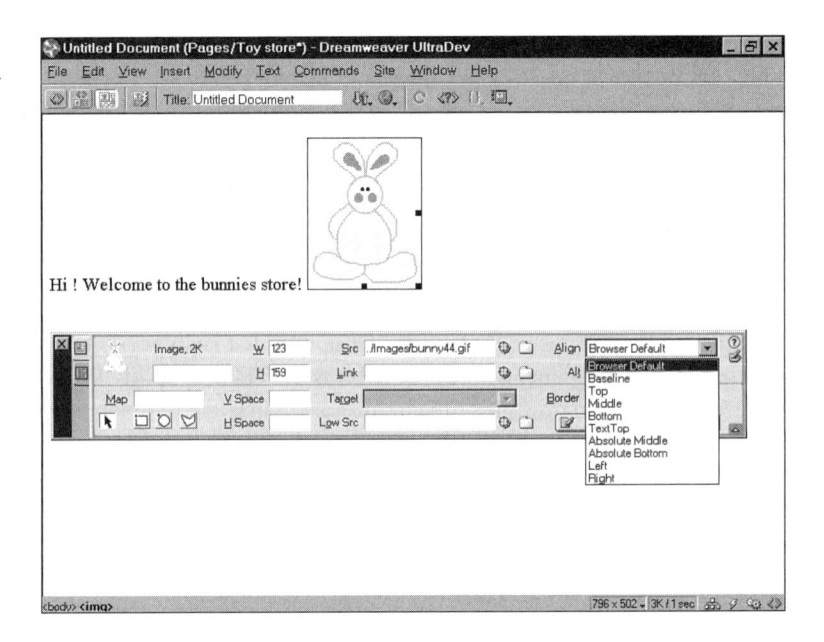

The Top, Middle, and Bottom or Baseline options enable you to align the text to the top, middle, and bottom of an image, respectively, as shown in Figure 9.11.

> **Note**
> Netscape introduced the baseline option. This option has the same effect as the bottom option. Although the bottom and baseline options are the same, the baseline option is included in UltraDev to support users familiar with Netscape Navigator conventions.

Figure 9.11
You can see the text aligned to the top, middle, and bottom of the image.

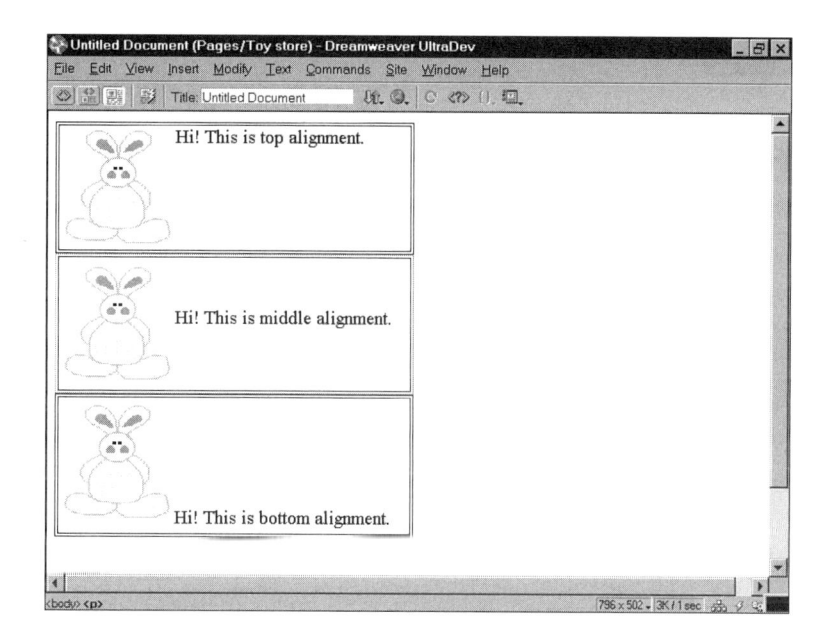

The Right and Left options of the Align drop-down list enable you to wrap a text around an image. The Right option places the image to the right margin and wraps all the text around it to the left. However, if there is any text before and after the image, the image is moved to a new line. Similarly, the Left option places the image to the left margin and wraps all the text around it to the right. Table 9.1 briefly describes the other alignment options.

TABLE 9.1   ALIGNMENT OPTIONS

Option	Description
Browser Default	Aligns the baseline of the text to the bottom edge of an image. This default alignment varies from browser to browser.
Text Top	Aligns an image to the top of the tallest character in the same line.
Absolute Middle	Aligns an image to the absolute middle of the current line.
Absolute Bottom	Aligns the baseline of the selected image to the absolute bottom of text on the same line. This adjusts letters such as "j," "y," and "g" so that the descenders (the lower portions of these letters) are aligned within the same line as the image.

> **Note**
> The Text Top option aligns an image only to text in the same line, whereas the Top option aligns an image to the text or other images in the same line.

Resizing Images

UltraDev enables you to visually resize elements, such as images, Flash movies, plugins, applets, and ActiveX controls, in the Document window. Resizing helps you in making minor adjustments to the layout of the Web page.

> **Note**
> Resizing images can produce weird results depending upon the kind of image. Resizing vector-based elements, such as Flash movies that are scalable, does not distort the elements. However, resizing GIF, JPEG, and PNG images can distort the images.

To resize an image, first you need to select the image. As soon as you select the image, the selection handles appear at the bottom, right, and bottom-right corners of the image. Perform any one of the following actions to resize an image:

- Drag the right selection handle to resize the width of the image.
- Drag the bottom selection handle to resize the height of the image.
- Drag the bottom-right selection handle to resize both the height and width of the image.

You can visually resize an image only up to 8×8 pixels. To further reduce the size of an image you need to manually enter the values in the W and H text boxes of the Property inspector of the image.

Working with Image Maps

An *image map* is an image that can be divided into various regions called *hotspots*, where each hotspot points to a different URL. For example, you can use a geographic map of a country as an image map and define each state in the country as a hotspot. These hotspots can be links to pages where details on the selected state are specified. The hotspot on an image map can either be a rectangle, oval, circle, polygon, or a point. Some of the shapes provided by UltraDev are rectangle, circle, and polygon.

Image maps are of two types, *client-side* and *server-side*. In a client-side image map, when a user clicks a hotspot of the image map, the browser passes the URL of the document to the server, whereas in a server-side image map the browser sends the coordinates of the area clicked to the server. The server in turn interprets these coordinates and sends the document to the browser. The client-side image map is faster because each time an image is clicked the coordinates need not be sent to the server to be interpreted. However, not all browsers support client-side image maps. Currently, Netscape Navigator, Internet Explorer, OmniWeb, and NCSA Mosaic versions 2.1 and 3.0 support client-side image maps. With browsers that cannot support client-side image maps, server-side image maps can be used.

CREATING AN IMAGE MAP

In UltraDev, you can create a client-side image map by using the Property inspector. When you use the Property inspector, the code for a client-side image map is generated automatically. If you want to create a server-side image map, you need to create a map file with an extension .map and place the file in the /cgi-bin/imagemap/ folder on the server. This map file contains information about the hotspots present on the image and the document to which each hotspot must link. In the HTML document that contains the image that acts as an image map, you must include the ISMAP keyword within the <img> tag. The ISMAP keyword tells the browser that the image must act as an image map. You must then create a link from this image to the map file that resides on the server.

It is easier to create a client-side image map than a server-side image map when you do not have access to the cgi-bin directory on the Web server. In UltraDev, you can easily create a client-side image map as follows:

1. Select the image to create an image map. Choose Windows, Properties to display the Property inspector of the image.
2. In the Map text box of the Property inspector, enter a name for the image map.
3. Define hotspots on the image by using the Rectangular, Oval, or Polygon hotspot tools. For example, if you want to create a rectangular hotspot on the image, click the Rectangular Hotspot Tool button on the Property inspector.
4. Next, place the mouse pointer over the area on the image where you want to create the hotspot. The mouse pointer changes to a + sign. Drag the mouse pointer to create a rectangle. You first get an outline of the rectangle as you drag the mouse pointer. When you release the mouse pointer, the rectangle is filled in.
5. To create a circular hotspot on the image, click the Oval Hotspot Tool button (although this tool draws a circle, it is called the Oval Hotspot Tool) and use the same method as you would to draw a rectangle. The method to create a polygon hotspot is slightly different. You need to first define the two points of the polygon by clicking on each point when the mouse pointer changes to a + sign. When you define the first two points, a line appears that links the two points. You must then define the third point in the polygon by clicking that point. When you define the third point, you get a triangle. You can expand the triangle by clicking the mouse pointer on nearby areas.
6. After you define a hotspot, the hotspot Property inspector is displayed.
7. In the Link text box of the hotspot Property inspector, type the URL of the file that must be opened when the user clicks the hotspot. Alternatively, you can click the folder button to browse to the file.

8. In the Alt text box, type the text that must be displayed instead of the image in text-only browsers.
9. Repeat steps 3–5 for every hotspot you create on the image.
10. Use the Target drop-down list to specify the window or the frame in which the linked file must open.
11. After you finish creating all hotspots, preview the image map by pressing F12.

Modifying an Image Map

You can resize and move hotspots on an image map. To resize a hotspot, click the hotspot to select it. Selection handles appear around the hotspot. Drag a selection handle to resize the hotspot. You can select multiple hotspots by holding down the Shift key and clicking each hotspot. You can also use the Ctrl-A key combination to select all the hotspots in an image. However, you must first select the image before using these key combinations.

To move a hotspot, select the hotspot and drag it to the desired location. Alternatively, you can use the arrow keys to the move the hotspot by 1 pixel a key press or hold down the Shift key and press the arrow keys to move the hotspot by 10 pixels a key press.

You can copy an image map from one document to another. You can also copy hotspots from one image to another.

Using External Image Editors

While working with images, you might want to edit the images in an image editor application. UltraDev enables you to edit images in an external graphic editor while working in UltraDev. After you edit the image and save the file in the external graphic editor, UltraDev automatically updates the image in the document window.

Setting an External Editor

UltraDev enables you to set preference for external graphic editors based on specific file formats. For example, you can set preferences to start Adobe Photoshop when you need to edit GIF images and Paint Shop Pro when you need to edit JPEG images. You can also specify more than one editor for a specific file format.

To set preferences for an external editor, you need to perform the following steps:

1. Choose Edit, Preferences to display the Preferences dialog box as shown in Figure 9.12.
2. In the Preferences dialog box, select the File Types/Editors option from the category list. The File Type/Editors page appears, as shown in Figure 9.13.
3. From the Extensions list box, select the type of file for which you want to set an external editor.
4. Click the + sign above the Editor list box to select the graphic editor that must open when you want to edit the specified file type. The Select External Editor dialog box is displayed.

Figure 9.12
Use the Preferences dialog box to set editors for various file types.

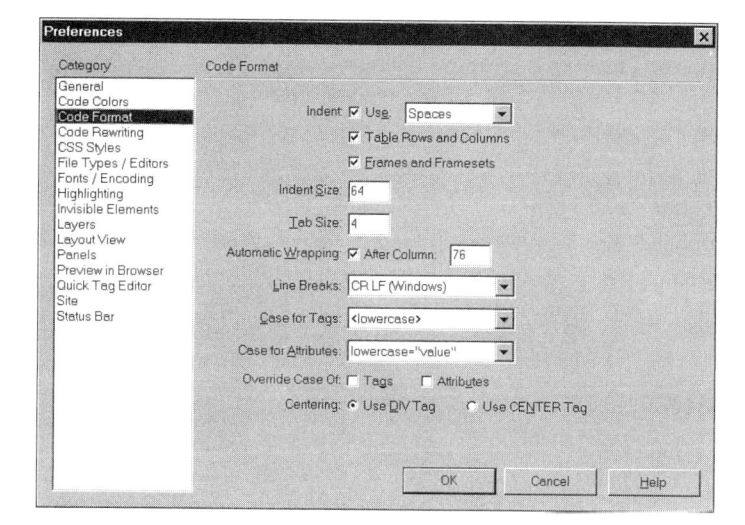

Figure 9.13
Use the File Type/Editors page of the Preferences dialog box to specify the default editor for each file type.

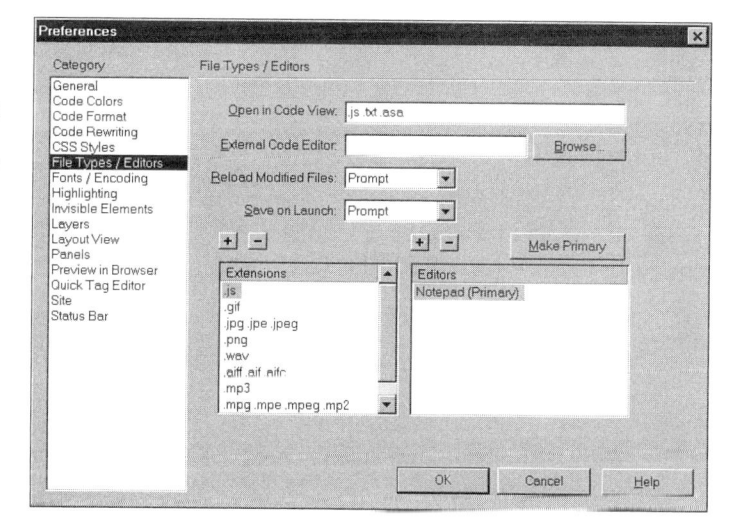

5. In the Select External Editor dialog box, browse to select the application you want to start and click Open. The selected editor is added to the Editors list.
6. Click the Make Primary Editor button to specify the selected editor as the primary editor.

You can add multiple editors to the Editors list by repeating steps 3–5.

You can also add new file types to the extensions list. To add a new file type, open the File Types/Editors page in the Preferences dialog box and click the + sign above the Extensions list. A text box is displayed in the Extension list that prompts you to enter the new file type for which you want to launch an external editor. Enter the file type and perform the steps mentioned earlier to specify the application that must be launched to edit the specified file type.

Opening an External Editor

After you set the editor preferences for the various file types, you can edit an image in an external editor while working with the document in UltraDev. To edit an image, select the image and click the Edit button in the Property inspector. UltraDev automatically launches the external editor according to the preferences you have set. You can also edit an image by right-clicking the image and selecting an image editor from the Edit With menu.

Summary

Images enhance the look of a Web site. They also enable you to add value to the content of the Web site. However, when you are working with images, proper planning and decision-making is required because images affect the download time of a Web site to a great extent. Therefore, you must take utmost care while adding images of various sizes and formats to a Web site. Apart from providing visual effects, images can also be used to provide good navigation facilities within a Web site.

Activity Corner

In the TuneIn.com site, two main images, TopPanel.jpg and SideBar.jpg, are used. The TopPanel.jpg file contains the name and logo of the site. This image will be set as the background image for the Navigation.asp file. The SideBar.jpg file is used as the background image for the Sidebar.asp file.

To set the background images for the Navigation.asp and Sidebar.asp files, follow these steps:

1. Copy TopPanel.jpg and SideBar.jpg to the Images folder in your local root folder.
2. Open the Navigation.asp file. Choose Modify, Page Properties.
3. In the Page Properties dialog box, type **Top Panel** in the Title text box.
4. Type **\Images\TopPanel.jpg** in the Background Image text box. Click OK to close the Page Properties dialog box. The background image for the Navigation.asp file is set.
5. Open the Sidebar.asp file. Choose Modify, Page Properties. In the Page Properties dialog box, specify the title for the page as **Search Bar**. Specify **\Images\SideBar.jpg** in the Background Image text box.
6. Click OK to close the Page Properties dialog box. The background image for the Sidebar.asp file is set.

CHAPTER 10

LINKING PAGES TOGETHER

In this chapter

Introducing Links   190

Working with Links   193

Creating a Jump Menu   202

Summary   204

Troubleshooting   204

Activity Corner   205

Introducing Links

Links help you design a flexible site that can be resourceful as well as lean. By means of links you can create many information access points in your documents. You do not have to create as many documents as there are information points because each information point can link to the same document. For example, consider a Web site that enables users to buy books. This Web site might contain various sections that allow the user to browse the available books, add books to a shopping cart, place orders for the books, rate the books, and so on. Such a Web site will also ideally carry a section on the latest book releases. A user might want to access information on the latest book releases from any section of the Web site. To enable this, you can create information access points from every section of the Web site to the document that contains this information by means of links. Thus, a single well-thought-out document will suffice to present all the information that a user might look out for from various points in the site.

UltraDev provides you with several ways to create and manage links. You can create links from text or images present anywhere in a document, whether they are in a table, layer, or frame. Using the link tools available in UltraDev, you can create links to documents located on other sites, multimedia files, and downloadable software. You can also add behaviors to your links. You can use these behaviors to perform functions such as describe the destination of a link on the status bar, open a linked image in a new browser window, or display links in a drop-down menu called a *jump menu*.

> **Tip**
> Before you start creating links, it helps to decide in advance the number of documents in your site as well as the content in each document. You can then create all the documents you want to link before actually creating the links. UltraDev allows you to create links to documents that are yet to be created.

Understanding Absolute and Relative Paths

When you create links from a document, you need to be clear about the location of the target document and the path you need to specify to access that document. Your target document can be located within the same folder as your current document, in a folder within the root folder of your site, or on a different site altogether. In order to specify the location of target document, you can use either the absolute path method or the relative path method. When you use the absolute path method, you specify the complete path to refer to the location of the target document. When you use the relative path method, you specify only a partial path to refer to the location of the target document.

Absolute Paths

You can use the absolute path method to link to documents that reside on a server different from your site's server. An *absolute path* contains the complete URL of the linked document. This path contains the protocol used to request the document followed by the complete path of the target document. The following is an example of an absolute path:

```
http://www.example.com/folder/targetfile.htm
```

> **Caution**
> If you use an absolute path to link to a document located within your site, moving your site to another server will cause the absolute path links to break. In such a case, it is always better to use relative paths.

Relative Paths

A *relative path* does not specify the complete path of the target document. It contains the path from a specific folder in the folder hierarchy. Depending on the starting point specified in the path, which can be either the current document folder or the site root folder, the path can be document-relative or root-relative.

You can use a *document-relative* path to link to a document present in the same folder as the current document, in a subfolder of the current document folder, or in the parent folder of the current folder. To link to a document within the same folder as the current document, the path must contain only the name of the document. To link to a document within the subfolder of the current document's folder, the path must begin with the name of the subfolder. To link to a document in the parent folder of the current folder, the path begins with ../ followed by the name of the document.

Figure 10.1 uses a sample site structure to illustrate document-relative paths. Table 10.1 shows the paths to be used from Home.asp, located in the Pages folder of the Booksite root folder, to link to the various documents illutrated in Figure 10.1.

TABLE 10.1   DOCUMENT-RELATIVE PATHS

Document	Path to Link to Document
Feedback.asp	Feedback.asp
Booklist.asp	books/fiction/Booklist.asp
Logo.gif	../images/Logo.gif

Figure 10.1
The booksite folder is the root folder.

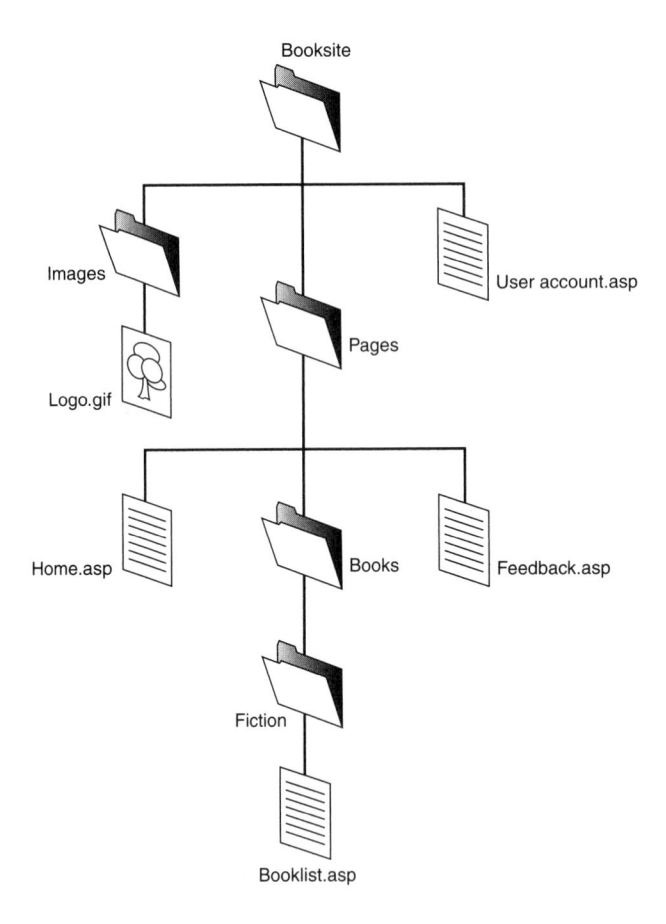

[Diagram showing folder hierarchy: Booksite (root) contains Images folder, Pages folder, and User account.asp. Images folder contains Logo.gif. Pages folder contains Home.asp, Books folder, and Feedback.asp. Books folder contains Fiction folder. Fiction folder contains Booklist.asp.]

The advantage of using a document-relative path is that when you move a folder, the links to documents within that folder are not affected. For example, in the site structure outlined in Figure 10.1, if you move the Pages folder to a different location, the links between documents in that folder are not affected by the move.

A *root-relative* path contains the path from the root folder of the site. It begins with a forward slash, followed by the path to the document. For example, to link to the Useraccount.asp document shown in Figure 10.1, which is in the root folder, you must use the root-relative path, which is /Useraccount.asp. The advantage of using a root-relative path is that when you move a document that contains links to other documents, the links to the target documents are still valid.

> **Note** When you move or rename the target files linked by a root-relative path, you must update the links. For example, if you move the Useraccount.asp file to the Pages folder, you must update the links to this document by changing the path from /Useraccount.asp to /Pages/Useraccount.asp.

Working with Links

In UltraDev, you can create links by using the Property inspector or the Make Link option of the Modify menu. You can also use the site map to view, create, and manage links. With these visual tools, you can specify the exact location of a file without having to type the complete path of the file. You can also create e-mail, null, and script links. An e-mail link allows you to open an e-mail program. The feedback sections that you find on Web sites usually contain an e-mail link. When you click the link, an e-mail program opens up automatically, bearing the recipient's name. A null link allows you to attach behaviors to text. For example, if you want introduce sound effects when a user clicks a text element on your document, you can attach a null link to the text and then attach the Play Sound behavior to the text. You can use a script link to perform form validations and other processing tasks by calling JavaScript code. For example, when a user clicks a link to visit a page that requires a plug-in to run, you might want to display a message that informs the user that a plug-in needs to be installed. To do this, you can create a script link, which calls the JavaScript code that informs the user about the plug-in requirement.

Creating a Link with the Property Inspector

To create a link to another document from any element in the current document, such as text, an image, or an object such as date, select the element and choose Window, Properties. The Property inspector is displayed as shown in Figure 10.2. In the Link text box of the Property inspector, specify the location of the target document. Choose an option from the Target drop-down list to indicate where the document will be loaded.

Figure 10.2
You can use the Point-to-File icon or the folder icon to select your target document.

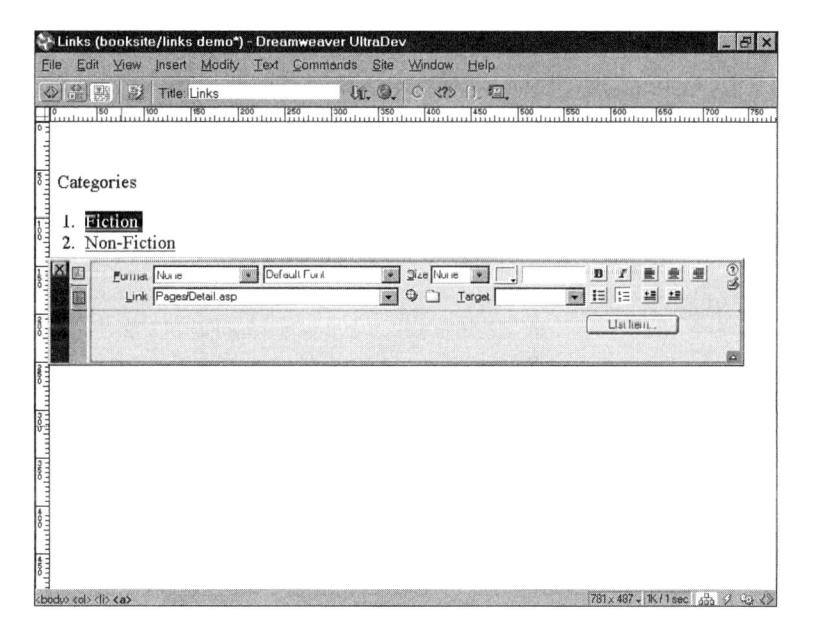

To specify the location of the target document, you can use any of the following three methods in the Property inspector:

- Enter the path of your target document in the Link text box. To create external links, you need to type the absolute path of the target document.

> **Note**
>
> If you want to create links to files before actually creating the files, you can specify the path to these files in the Link text box. Later, you can actually create the files.

- Click the folder icon to browse to the file to which you want to link. Figure 10.3 shows the Select File dialog box that you use to browse to the file. The path of the document appears in the URL text box of the Select File dialog box. You can specify whether the path should be document-relative or root-relative by selecting the appropriate option from the Relative To drop-down list of the dialog box.

Figure 10.3
Use this method to browse to documents that exist in different folder levels in the folder hierarchy.

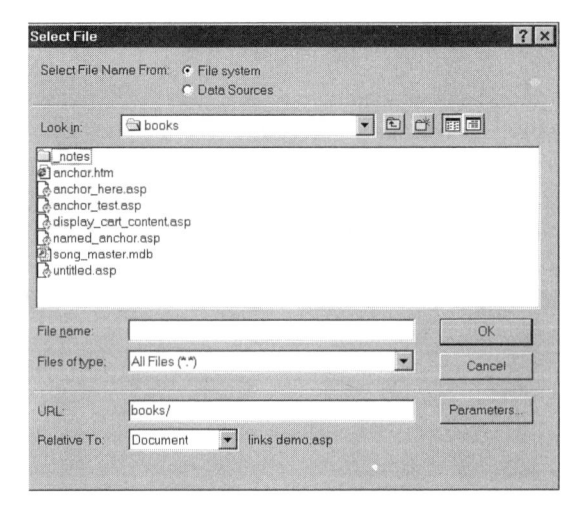

> **Note**
>
> The path type that you select from the Relative To drop-down list the first time you create a link is set as the default path type for any future links. You can change this default path by specifying a different path the next time you create a link.

- Click and drag the Point-to-File icon to any of the files in the Site window, as shown in Figure 10.4. When you reach the required file, the link is created and the path appears in the Link text box.

WORKING WITH LINKS

> **Note**
> Ensure the Site window is opened and maximized before you use the Point-to-File icon. Another point to note is that the target files must be created before you use this option.

Figure 10.4
The Point-to-File icon is a quick and easy way to create links.

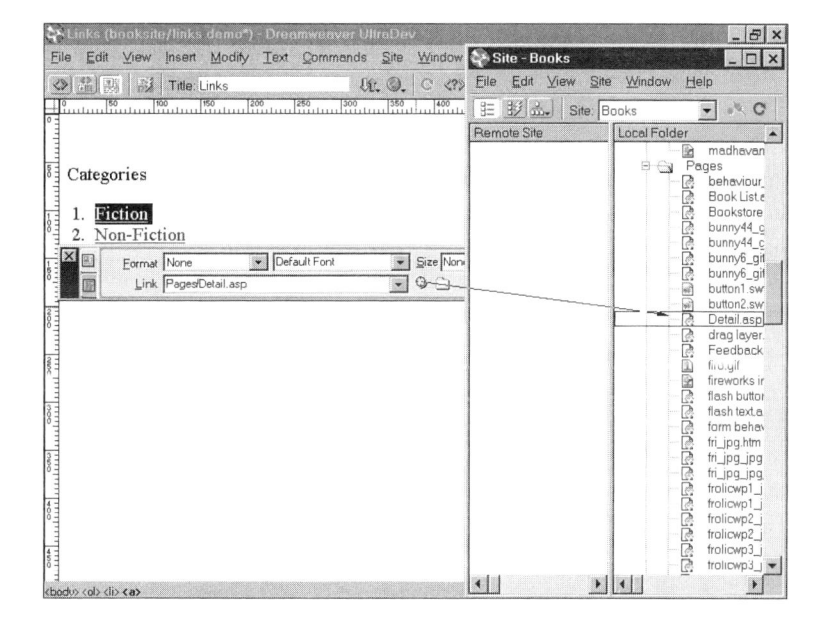

> **Tip**
> If you want to create a link from any text in the document, you can activate the Point-to-File icon even without using the Property inspector. To do so, select the text from which you want to create a link, hold down the Shift key, and drag the mouse pointer to either an open document and or any document listed in the Site window. The Point-to-File icon is activated and the link is created.

In addition to specifying the path of the target document, you need to specify where the target document should be loaded. To do this, choose any of the four options from the Target drop-down list of the Property inspector. The following list describes these options:

- **_blank** If you choose this option, the linked document loads in a blank, unnamed browser window.
- **_parent** This option is applicable when your document contains frames. If you choose this option, the linked document loads in the parent frameset or in the frame that contains the link.

- `self` If you choose this option, the linked document loads in the same window or frame as the link.
- `_top` If you choose this option, the linked document loads in the full browser window. If there are any frames, they are all removed.

Changing and Updating Links

You can set preferences in UltraDev to automatically update links whenever you move or rename the target documents. These preferences let you specify whether UltraDev should automatically update links or prompt you to update selected or all links. To set preferences, you need to choose Edit, Preferences and select the General category in the Preferences dialog box. In the Update Links when Moving Files drop-down list in the General category, select the Always option if you want UltraDev to automatically update links or select the Prompt option to set UltraDev to notify you before updating links.

UltraDev creates a cache file to make faster link updates. Recall that UltraDev prompts you to create a cache when you define a site. This cache file maintains information about the links in a site. When you add or modify links, the information in the cache file is automatically updated. This information speeds up the process of link updates.

Updating Link Information

There might be situations when you want to change those links that point to a specific target document in a site. To change the target document pointed to by these links, you need to use the Change Link Sitewide dialog box. To display this dialog box, choose Site, Change Link Sitewide in the Site window. The name of the current target document appears in the Change All Links To text box of the Change Link Sitewide dialog box. Type the name of the new target document in the Into Links To text box. In Figure 10.5, all those links that point to a target document named `Detail.asp` are changed to point to another target document named `List.asp`.

Figure 10.5
You can change e-mail, null, and script links by using this dialog box.

Using the Site Map to Create and Modify Links

The site map gives a visual representation of the links between documents in your site. Therefore, it is easy to manage the links in your site by using the site map. You can gauge the level of nesting between documents and add or delete links accordingly.

CREATING A LINK BY USING THE SITE MAP

You can create a link from the site map by using the Point-to-File icon present next to the folder icon in the Site Map view. Using the site map to create links helps when you want to lay out a visual map of your site structure before you actually create the content in your documents.

To create a link by using the site map, you need to display the site files and site map in the right and left panes of the Site window. To do this, select the Map and Files option of the Site Map button. Select the file in the site map from which you want to create a link to a file in the site files list. When you select the file, the Point-to-File icon appears next to the file icon. Drag the Point-to-File icon to the target file in the site files list. Figure 10.6 shows how to create a link from the site map to a file in the site files list. You can also use the Point-to-File icon to link to any other file within the site map structure. Figure 10.7 shows how to create a link from the site map to another file in the site map structure.

Figure 10.6
Use the Point-to-File icon to link to the required document.

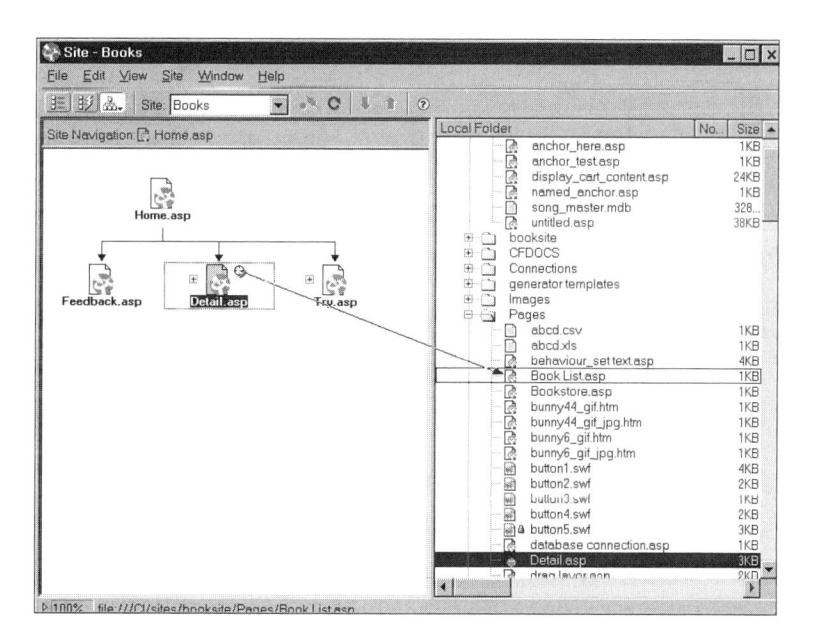

MODIFYING LINKS FROM THE SITE MAP

To modify an existing link, select the target document that you want to change from the site map and choose Site, Change Link in the Site window. In the Select HTML File dialog box that appears, type the URL of the file to which you want to link. Alternatively, you can browse to the file.

To open the source of a link in order to verify the element from which the target document is linked, select the file whose source you want to verify and choose Site, Open Source of Link. The source document that contains the link is displayed and the element containing the link is highlighted.

Figure 10.7
The site map is automatically updated to reflect the newly created link.

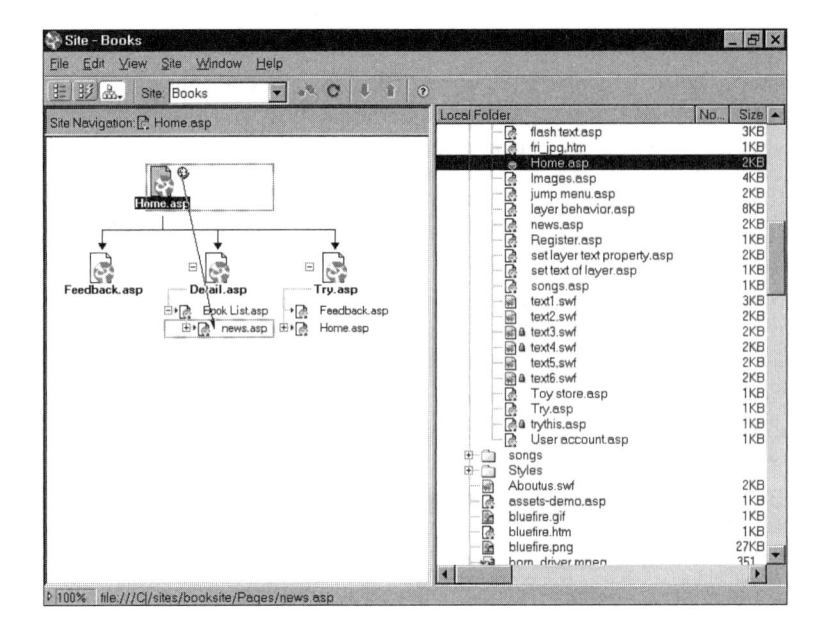

To remove a link to a target document, select the document in the site map and choose Site, Remove Link in the Site window.

> **Note:** In Macintosh machines, the Change Link, Open Source of Link, and Remove Link options are available in the Site Map View option of the Site menu in the Site window.

Named Anchors

Named anchors let you create links from one part of your document to another in the same document. These types of links are helpful when a Web page is too lengthy. They eliminate the need to scroll a page up and down to view all of its contents. Using named anchors, you can set markers at specific locations in your document and then link the rest of your document to these named anchors.

Creating links within a document involves two steps, creating a named anchor and creating a link to the named anchor.

Creating a Named Anchor

Open a document in which you want to create a named anchor. Select a location in this document to which you want to create a link. Choose Insert, Invisible Tags, Named Anchor, or choose the Invisibles category from the Objects panel, and click the Named Anchor button.

In the Insert Named Anchor dialog box, type a name for the anchor in the Anchor Name text box and click OK in the Insert Named Anchor dialog box.

As soon as you create an anchor, the anchor marker appears at the selected location. An anchor marker is an invisible element and it appears only if the Named Anchors check box of the Preferences dialog box is checked and the Invisible Elements option in the View menu is enabled. To enable the Invisible Elements option, choose View, Visual Aids, Invisible Elements.

Linking to the Named Anchor

In Design view, select the element from which you want to create a link to a named anchor. To create a link from an element to a named anchor, use the Property inspector.

To link to a named anchor using the Property inspector, select the element from which you want to create a link and type the anchor name in the Link text box of the Property inspector. If the named anchor and the element from which you want to link to the named anchor are in the same document, precede the anchor name with a # sign. However, if the named anchor is in another document, type the path to the target document that contains the named anchor followed by the # sign and the anchor name. For example, to link an element in a document named home.htm to an anchor called anchor1 in a document called linkto.htm that is in the same folder as home.htm, select the element in the home.htm document and type **linkto.htm#anchor1** in the Link text box of the Property inspector of the selected element.

You can use the Point-to-File icon to link a text element to a named anchor. To activate the Point-to-File icon from a text element, select the text, press Shift, and drag the mouse pointer from the selected text to the anchor to which you want to create a link. You can do the same to link to a named anchor in another open document. Figure 10.8 shows the process of creating a link to a named anchor.

Figure 10.8
The Point-to-File icon appears when you press Shift and drag to the selected element.

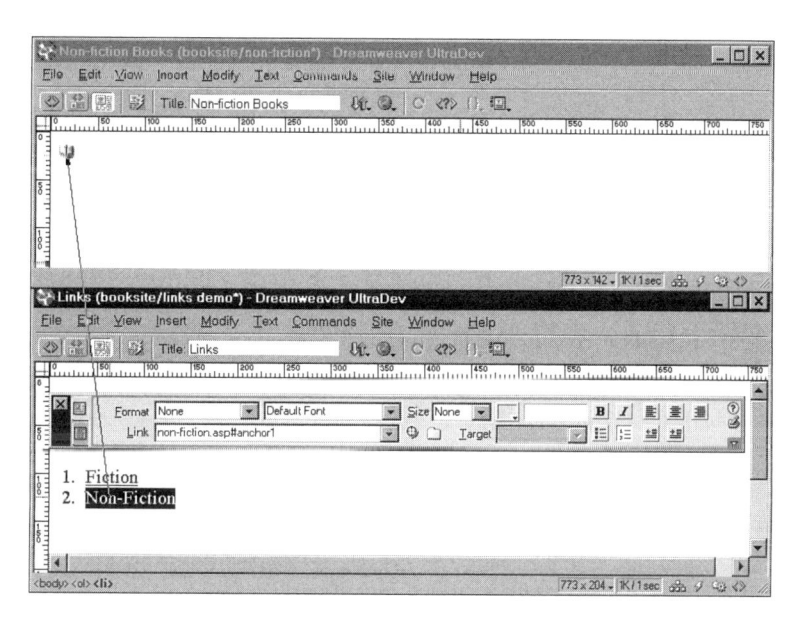

Note

When you link to an anchor in another open document, the anchor name in the Link text box of the Property inspector displays the document name followed by the anchor name.

Adding More Functionality to Links

The function of links need not be limited in scope. They can perform more functions beyond simply taking a user to a different document. You can use null links to attach various behaviors to links, such as opening an image in a browser window equal to its size or displaying a message in the status bar when a link is clicked. You can attach Javascript code to links by means of script links. You can use e-mail links to enable users to send e-mail messages by clicking a link.

Null Links

Use null links to attach behaviors to page elements, such as text and images. You cannot attach behaviors to plain text. Therefore, you must create a null link to the text if you want to attach a behavior. Similarly, some behaviors can be attached to images only if they contain a null link.

→ To learn more about attaching behaviors to links, **see** "Attaching a Behavior," **p. 268**.

A null link does not indicate the name of any target document. The procedure for creating a null link is no different from that of a normal link, except that you type a # sign in the Link text box of the Property inspector instead of specifying a file name. Alternatively, you can type `javascript:;` in the Link text box.

Tip

Using the `javascript:;` method is preferable when creating null links, because if you use the # sign to create a null link that is at the middle or bottom of a page, clicking the null link takes you to the top of the page containing the null link.

Script Links

You can create script links that execute JavaScript code or call a JavaScript function. You can therefore use script links to perform calculations, validate forms, or display messages when a user clicks a link. To create a script link, you need to type `javascript:` followed by JavaScript code or a function call in the Link text box of the Property inspector.

For example, you can write a JavaScript function that allows a user to follow a link to visit a particular document only if she is a valid user. This function validates the user and displays a message if the user is not a valid user. If the user is valid, the link takes the user to the target document. Assume that you have written a function called `verify_user()`. To call this function when the user clicks the link, type `javascript:verify_user()` in the property inspector, as shown in Figure 10.9.

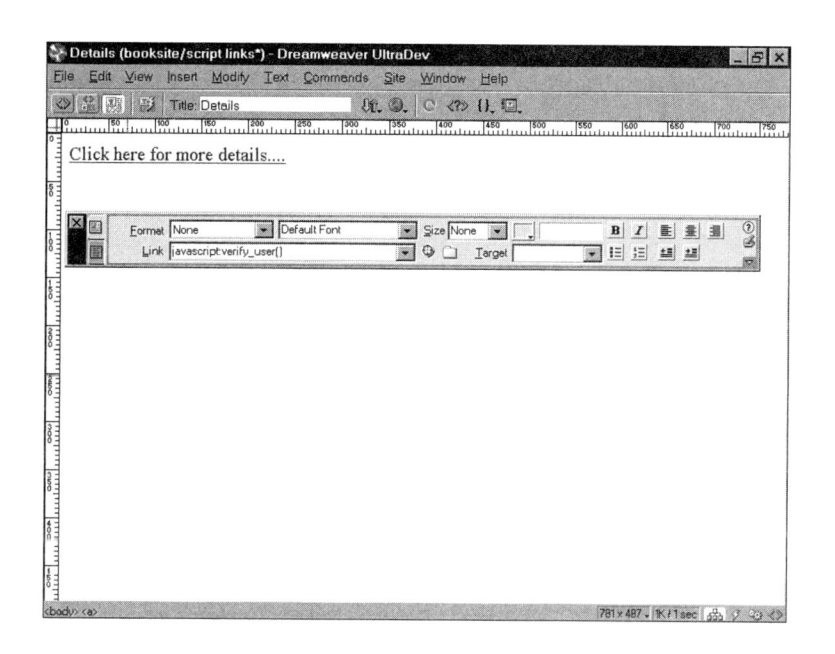

Figure 10.9
Use the Property inspector to create script links.

E-MAIL LINKS

You must have seen feedback sections on Web sites that contain e-mail addresses of persons to whom you can send feedback. These e-mail addresses contain e-mail links. When you click such a link, the mail program associated with the browser automatically opens.

In UltraDev, you can create an e-mail link by using the Property inspector or the E-mail link option of the Insert menu. To create an e-mail link, select the text and type `mailto:` followed by the address of the recipient in the Link text box of the Property inspector. There should be no space between `mailto:` and the address, as shown in Figure 10.10.

Alternatively, you can create an e-mail link by clicking the Insert E-mail Link button from the Common category of the Objects panel. Before clicking this button, place the cursor at the point where you want the e-mail link to appear. When you use this method, you do not have to type the text before inserting the e-mail link. After you click the Insert E-mail Link button in the Objects panel, the Insert Email Link dialog box appears, as shown in Figure 10.11.

The Insert E-mail Link dialog box enables you to specify the text that must contain the e-mail link as well as the e-mail address of that link. Type the text that must contain the e-mail link in the text box named Text in the Insert E-mail Link dialog box. In the E-mail text box, specify the e-mail address. When you type the e-mail address in the Insert E-mail Link dialog box, you do not have to type `mailto:` before the e-mail address because UltraDev automatically inserts mailto: in the <a> tag. After you click the OK button in the Insert E-mail Link dialog box, you can see the text containing the e-mail link inserted into the document.

Figure 10.10
This link opens a mail program that displays the address given in the link in the recipient's address field.

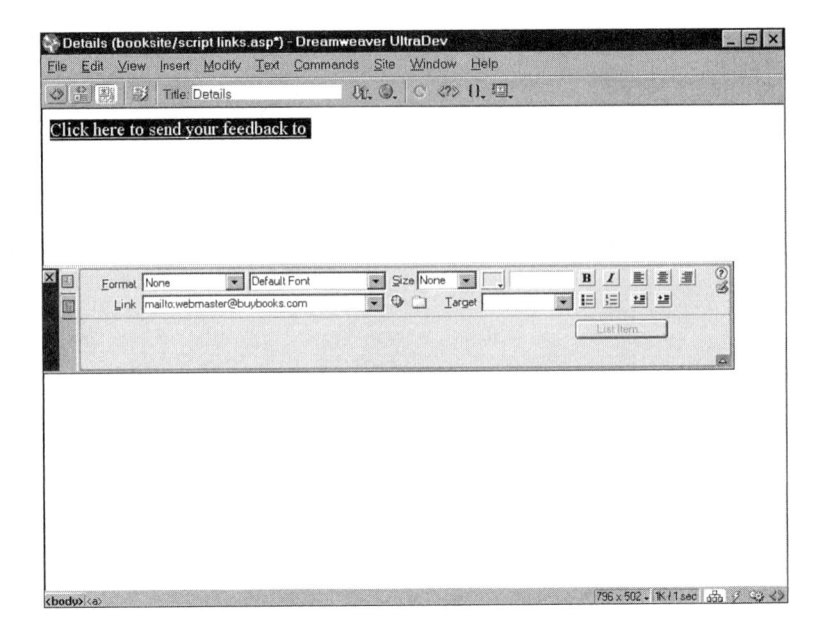

Figure 10.11
Use this dialog box to create an e-mail link.

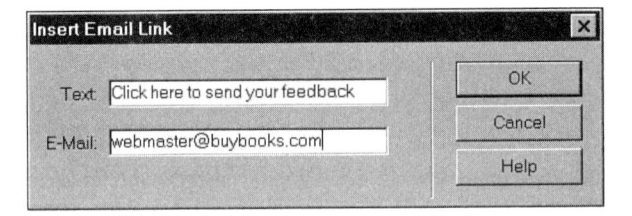

CREATING A JUMP MENU

You can group a set of related links by using a jump menu. A *jump menu* is a drop-down menu where each option of the menu links to a different document. A jump menu can contain the following components:

- A description of the category of menu options that serves as a menu selection prompt
- A list of menu options, each of which links to a document
- A Go button

The following are the steps for creating a jump menu:

1. Choose Windows, Objects to display the Objects panel.
2. Click the Insert Jump Menu button from the Forms category of the Object panel. The Insert Jump Menu dialog box appears, as shown in Figure 10.12.

Figure 10.12
This dialog box is displayed only the first time you create a jump menu.

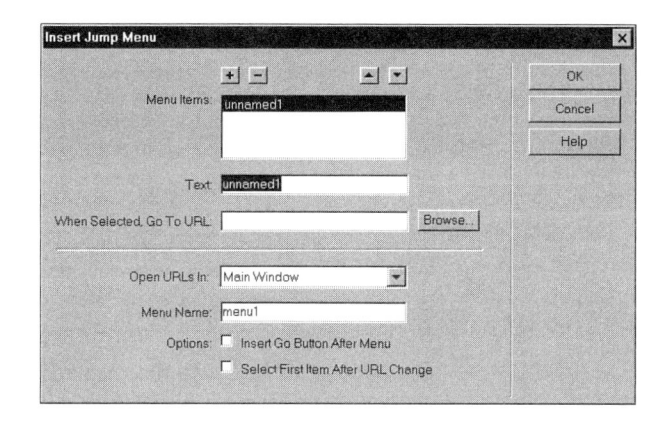

3. In the text box named Text, type the name of the menu selection prompt and click the + button. This adds the prompt as the first item to the menu.

4. To add other items, type the name of each item in the Text text box and specify the target document in the When Selected, Go To URL text box. Click the + button to add each menu option to the list.

5. From the Open URLs In drop-down menu, choose the area in which the target document must appear. This drop-down menu displays only the Main Window option if there are no frames in your document. If you have frames and you want them to appear in the drop-down menu, you need to name the frames.

6. Select the Select First Item After URL Change checkbox to reset the selection prompt after the user chooses an option.

7. Select the Insert Go Button After Menu option to insert a Go button next to the jump menu. Normally, when the user re-selects an item that she has already chosen once from the jump menu, the URL doesn't load again. A Go button helps the user to open an already selected link from the jump menu.

8. To change the order of the menu options, click the appropriate triangular buttons that are next to the + and – buttons in the Insert Jump Menu dialog box.

To edit the jump menu items, you can use the Property inspector. The Property inspector allows you to make changes to the order of the items as well as the target documents associated with each item. Click the List Values button in the Property inspector to display the List Values dialog box. In this dialog box, you can make changes to the list order and also specify different target documents. Figure 10.13 shows the List Values dialog box and the Property inspector for a jump menu.

Figure 10.13
You can make changes to the list order and specify different target documents in the List Values dialog box.

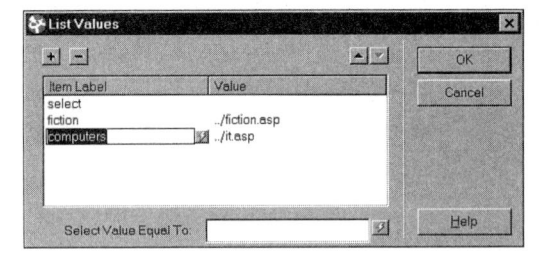

Summary

This chapter dealt with creating links and modifying them. You can use the Property inspector to create links and specify where the target document should be loaded. Using the Point-to-File icon is a faster way to create links. However, to use this method, you need to keep either the Site window or the target document open.

You can create e-mail and script links by using the Property inspector. You can attach behaviors to links by using null links. You can create a jump menu to group a set of related links together.

Troubleshooting

Repairing Broken Links

A specific link in a particular document doesn't work.

Check for the following:

- Ensure that the path is correct.
- Ensure that the file you are linking to exists.
- Ensure that you have updated all the links to folders or files that you have moved or renamed.
- Ensure that you have uploaded all the files to the server before previewing them. If you do not want to preview files using the application server, choose Edit, Preferences. In the Preferences dialog box, select the Preview in Browser category and uncheck the Preview Using Application Server check box.

Activity Corner

In this activity corner section, we will create some of the links between the documents in the TuneIn.com site. The Sidebar.asp file lists five categories of songs. When the user clicks any of these five categories, the songs available in that category must be displayed. To do this, link each of the categories in the Sidebar.asp file to the Songfetch.asp file. This file dynamically displays the list of songs belonging to a category selected by the user. The Sidebar.asp file also contains a text called "Home." When the user clicks this text, the Contentpage.asp file must be displayed.

To create a link to the **Songfetch.asp** file from each category in the Sidebar.asp file, perform the following steps:

1. Open the Sidebar.asp file. Select the text "Merry."
2. Open the Property inspector and type **Songresults/songfetch.asp** in the Link text box.
3. Perform steps 1–2 to set the links for the rest of the categories represented by the text "Foot Tapping," "Soul Stirring," "Mystical," and "Melancholy" in the sidebar.asp file.

To create a link from the text "Home" to the Contentpage.asp file, select the text and type **/Contentpage.asp** in the Link text box of the Property inspector.

CHAPTER 11

PRESENTING CONTENT IN A PAGE

In this chapter

Working with Tables   208

Managing Data in a Table   218

Creating and Managing Layers   221

Working with Frames   228

Summary   233

Activity Corner   234

Working with Tables

Tables provide a useful method of displaying information on a Web page. Tables allow you to summarize large amounts of data and present the data in a structured format on the Web page, which makes data access quick and easy. You can design your page by using tables. Chapter 7, "Creating Sites and Documents," discussed using the Layout view to create tables. This chapter focuses on creating tables in the Standard view.

Creating a Table

To create a table, place the cursor at the position where you want the table to appear in the document and choose Insert, Table. The Insert Table dialog box appears, as shown in Figure 11.1. Table 11.1 briefly describes the options available in the Insert Table dialog box.

Figure 11.1
Use this dialog box to specify properties for the table.

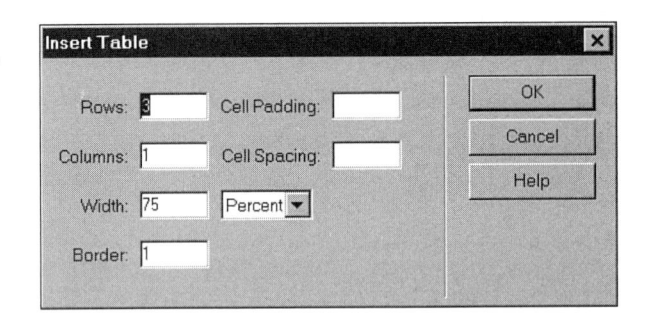

> **Note**
> To enable the Table option in the Insert menu, you must be in the Standard view.

Table 11.1   Options in the Insert Table Dialog Box

Option	Description
Rows	Specifies the number of rows
Columns	Specifies the number of columns
Width	Sets the width of the table in pixels or as a percentage of the browser screen
Cell Padding	Specifies the spacing between the cell content and the cell boundary
Cell Spacing	Specifies the spacing between the cells in the table
Border	Specifies the number of pixels for the table border

After you specify the various attributes for the table in the Insert Table dialog box, UltraDev creates a simple table with the specified attributes at the cursor position.

You can add information to the inserted table in the form of text or images. You can enter text into the table either by directly typing the information or by pasting the information copied from another document.

To insert text into a cell of a table, place the cursor in the cell and type the text. After you enter text in one cell, you can move to other cells in the table by using the Tab key or the arrow keys.

> **Caution**
> Pressing the Tab key in the last cell of the table adds a new row to the table.

UltraDev also enables you to import data from other applications into a table. You learn how to do this in the following sections.

You can clear the contents of an entire table or the contents of specific rows and columns in the table by selecting the contents and choosing the Clear option from the Edit menu. Alternatively, you can select the contents and press the Delete key.

Formatting a Table

The Table option of the Insert menu enables you to create a simple table with a specified number of rows and columns. You can further modify and enhance the look of this table by adding background colors and images to the table. You can also set properties for each cell in the table.

Setting Properties for an Entire Table

The Property inspector of the table enables you to add additional features to your table. To view the Property inspector, you need to select the table and choose Window, Properties. The Property inspector is shown in Figure 11.2.

Figure 11.2
Use the Property inspector to add or modify the properties of a table. The Property inspector provides various options to change or set properties for a table.

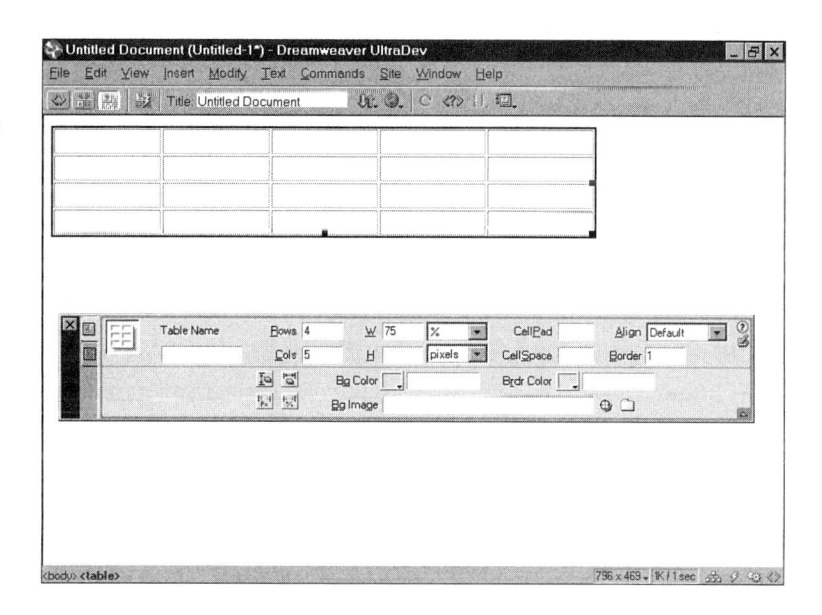

The W and H options in the Property inspector enable you to specify the width and height of the table in pixels or as a percentage of the browser window. If you set the width and height as a percentage of the browser window, the table automatically resizes itself in proportion to the browser window.

The Rows and Cols options enable you to specify the number of rows and columns for the table.

The Align drop-down list provides various options to align the table to other elements in the same paragraph as that of the table. The Left align option aligns the table to the left and moves the other elements to the right. The Right align option aligns the table to the right and moves all the other elements to the left. You can also align the table to the center by using the Center align option. In addition, you can allow the table to be aligned to the browser default by using the Default option.

The Border option in the Property inspector enables you to set the width of the border for the table in pixels. Generally, most browsers display the table border as a line with a three-dimensional effect. You can also set a color for the table border by using the Brdr Color option.

You can apply a background image or background color for the table by using the Bg Image and Bg Color options, respectively.

The Clear Row Heights and Clear Column Widths options enable you to clear the values specified for row heights and column widths.

The Convert Table Width to Pixels and Convert Table Width to Percent options enable you to convert the table width from a percentage of the browser window to the current width in pixels and vice versa.

You can specify the spacing between the cell content and the cell boundary by using the CellPad option. You can use the Cell Spacing option to set the spacing between the cells in the table.

> **Note**
>
> If you do not specify values for cell spacing and cell padding, UltraDev, Internet Explorer, and Netscape Navigator will display the table with a cell spacing of 2 pixels and cell padding of 1 pixel.

Setting Properties for Specific Cells, Rows, and Columns

To set properties for specific cells, rows, or columns in a table, you must first select them.

To select a cell, press the Ctrl key and click the cell. To select a row or a column, place the insertion point to the left of the row or on top of the column and click when an arrow appears, as shown in Figure 11.3.

Figure 11.3
Select the column when this arrow appears on top of the column.

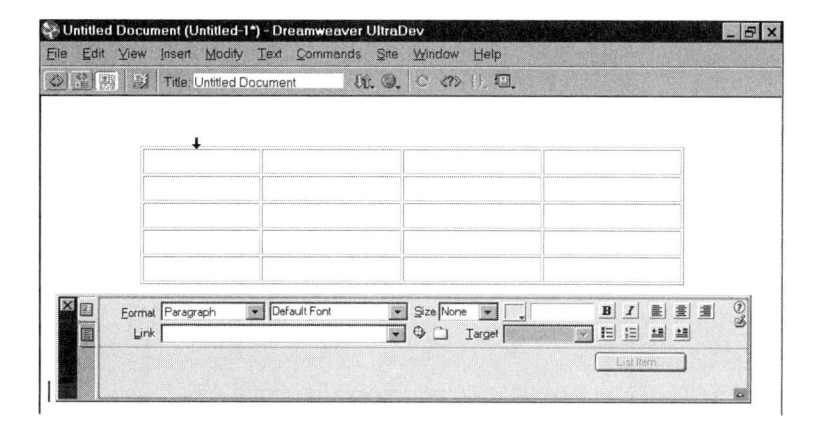

To select a set of continuous cells, you can click a cell and drag to the destination cell. Alternatively, you can also click the cell, hold down the Shift key, and click another cell to select all the cells between these two cells. Figure 11.4 shows a selection of continuous cells.

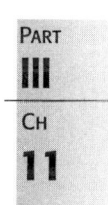

Figure 11.4
Select continuous cells by holding the Shift key as you select them.

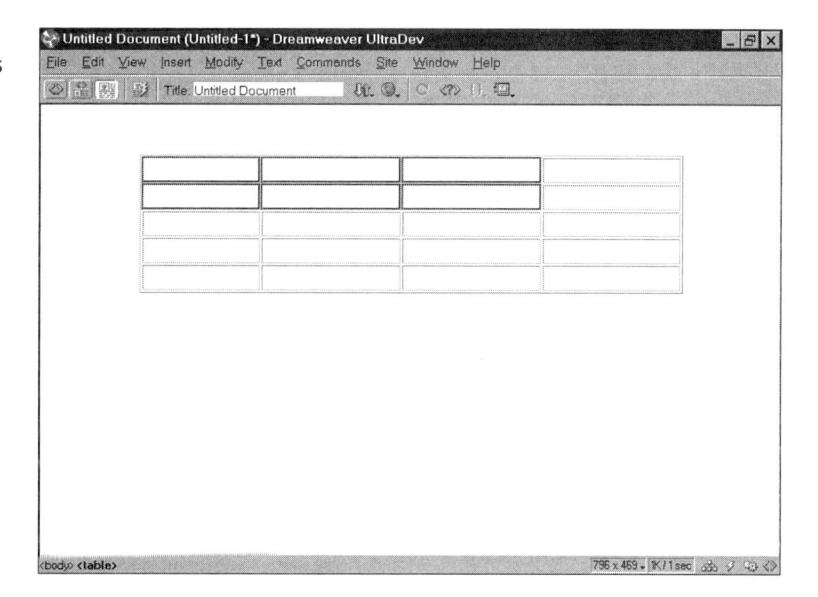

You can also select multiple cells that are not continuous by pressing the Ctrl key and clicking all the cells that you want to select. Figure 11.5 shows a selection of cells that are not continuous.

Figure 11.5
Select noncontinuous cells by holding the Ctrl key while selecting each cell.

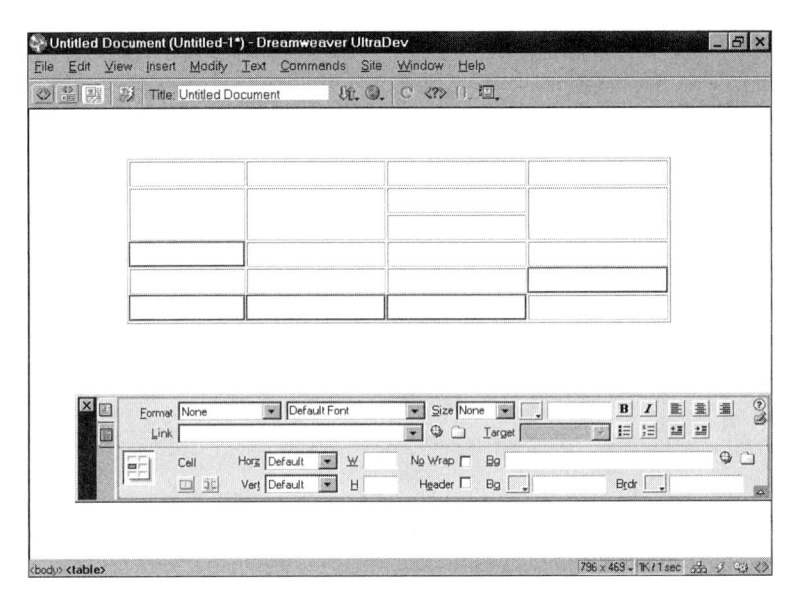

After you select the cells, rows, or columns to be formatted, you can format them by using the Property inspector. Figure 11.6 displays the Property inspector.

Figure 11.6
Use the Property inspector to format selected cells, rows, and columns of a table.

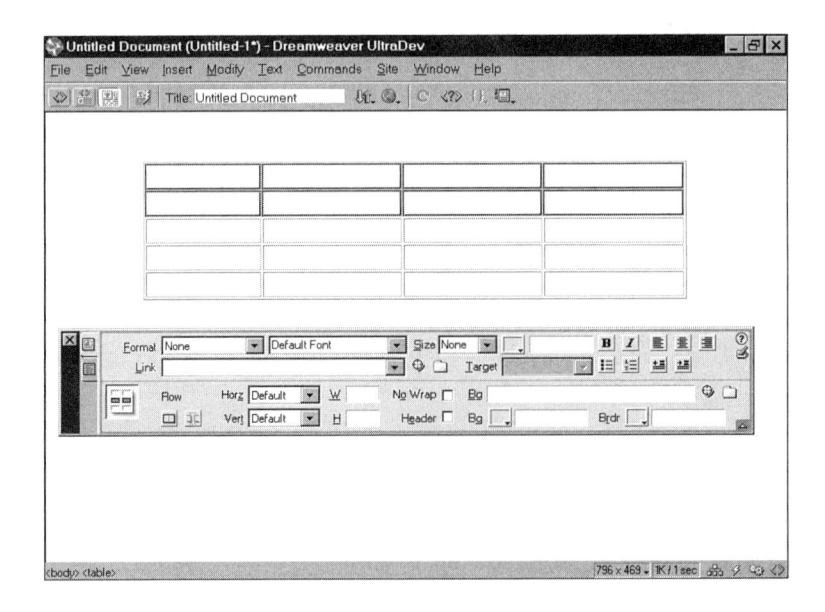

To align the content of a cell along the horizontal or vertical axes, you can use the Horz and Vert drop-down lists in the Property inspector. The Horz drop-down list enables you to align the content of a cell to the right, left, or to the center of the cell. You can also align the content to the browser's default, which is left for regular cells and center for header cells.

The Vert drop-down list enables you to align the content of a cell to the top, bottom, baseline, and to the center of the cell. You can also align the contents to the browser's default, which is center.

The W and H options enable you to specify the width and height of a cell in pixels. You can also specify the width and height in percentage by using the percent (%) symbol after the values.

You can set a background image for a selected cell, row, or column by using the Bg option. You can also set a background color for the selected cell, row, or column by using the Bg Color option. The Brdr option enables you to specify a border color for the selected cells, rows, or columns.

The Split Cells option enables you to split a selected cell into two or more cells. To merge multiple cells into a single cell, you can use the Merge Cells option.

You can select the Header option to format selected rows or columns as table headers. By default, the contents of the table headers are bold and centered.

Generally, if the content in a cell exceeds the size of the cell, the cell wraps the content by expanding either horizontally or vertically. However, if you do not want the text to wrap, you can select the No Wrap option.

Formatting Tables by Using Design Schemes

Apart from designing your own custom tables from scratch, you can use any of the preset design tables UltraDev provides. To view the list of preset design tables, you need to choose Commands, Format Table. The Format Table dialog box with the list of preset design schemes appears, as shown in Figure 11.7.

Figure 11.7
Use the Format Table dialog box to apply formats by choosing from a variety of designs.

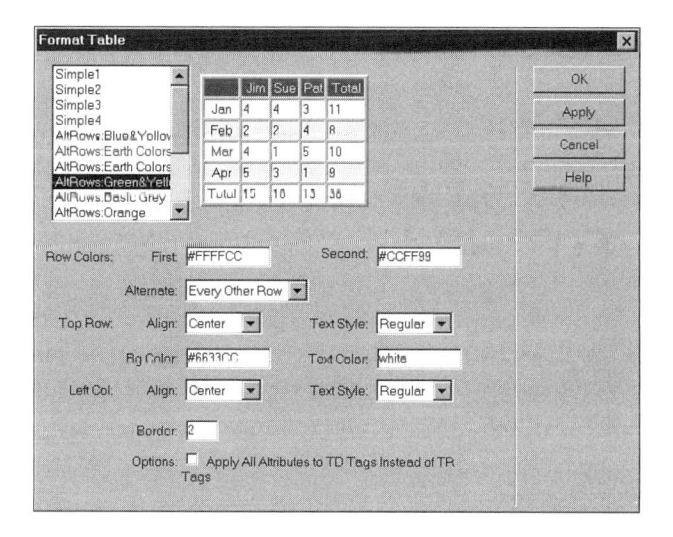

You can select a table design scheme from the list displayed on the left of the Format Table dialog box and further customize the design by making changes to the Row Colors, Top Row, and Left Col options. Select the Apply All Attributes to TD Tags instead of TR Tags option to apply the design of the table to the table cells instead of the table rows.

Resizing Tables, Cells, Rows, and Columns

After you create a table, you might want to resize the entire table or resize individual rows and columns in the table.

To resize an entire table, you must first select the table. After selecting the table, the selection handles around the table are displayed. Drag the selection handles to resize the table to the required dimensions. When you resize an entire table, the size of all the cells in the table change proportionally.

You can also change the width of columns and the height of rows in a table. The easiest way to do this is by selecting and dragging the borders of the rows and the columns. However, you can also use the W and H options in the Property inspector to specify new width and height values. You can also allow the browser or UltraDev to decide the height and width of the rows and columns based on the contents of the rows and columns by leaving the W and H options blank. For example, if you have just two lines of text in a table cell, UltraDev automatically adjusts the height and width of the cell to accommodate those two lines when you leave the W and H options blank.

You can also reset the rows and columns to their original height and width by choosing Modify, Table and selecting the Clear Cell Heights and Clear Cell Widths options.

Inserting and Deleting Rows and Columns

UltraDev enables you to add additional rows and columns to a table or remove existing rows and columns from a table. You can do this by using the Table option of the Modify menu. Alternatively, you can also choose an option from the table context-sensitive menu to add or remove rows and columns.

To add rows or columns to a table, click the cell where you want the new row or column to appear and perform any of the following steps:

- Choose Modify, Table, Insert Row to add a new row. Alternatively, you can right-click the cell and choose Table, Insert Row from the context-sensitive menu that is displayed.
- Choose Modify, Table, Insert Column to add a new column. Alternatively, you can right-click (Windows users) or Ctrl-click (Macintosh users) and choose Table, Insert Column from the context-sensitive menu that is displayed.

You can also add rows and columns to a table by choosing the Modify, Table, Insert Rows or Columns option. This option displays the Insert Rows or Columns dialog box that provides you the option to either add rows or columns. The Insert Rows or Columns dialog box also provides you with options to specify whether the row or column must appear before or after a selected row or column, as well as the number of rows and columns to be added. Figure 11.8 shows the Insert Rows or Columns dialog box.

Figure 11.8
Use this dialog box to add rows or columns to a table.

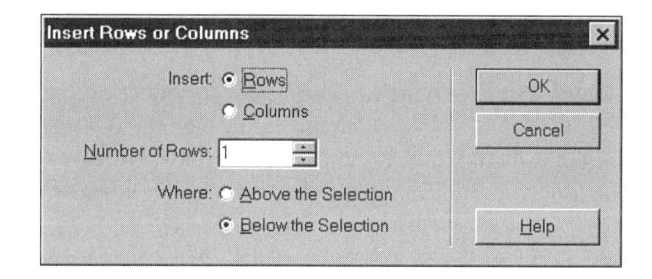

Caution

The Insert Rows or Columns option will not be enabled in the Modify menu if you select the entire table prior to choosing this option. You must either select a cell or cells or place the insertion point within a table cell to enable this option.

Sometimes, you might want to delete rows and columns from a table. To delete a row, click the row you want to delete and choose Table, Delete Row. Similarly, to delete a column, click the column you want to delete and choose Modify, Table, Delete Column. Alternatively, you can choose Table, Delete Row from the context-sensitive menu to delete rows or Table, Delete Column to delete columns.

You can also add or remove rows and columns from a table by selecting the table and modifying the values in the Rows and Cols fields of the Property inspector. However, this method of adding and removing rows and columns always adds or removes rows from the bottom of the table and adds or removes columns from the extreme right of the table.

SPLITTING AND MERGING ROWS AND COLUMNS

Apart from adding, deleting, and resizing cells, you can also split and merge cells in a table. Splitting a cell divides a single cell into multiple rows or columns as specified by you. To split a cell, you must first select the cell or place the insertion point within the cell and choose Window, Properties. In the Property inspector that is displayed, click the Split Cells into Rows and Columns button. The Split Cell dialog box appears, as shown in Figure 11.9.

Figure 11.9
Use this dialog box to split a cell into multiple rows or columns.

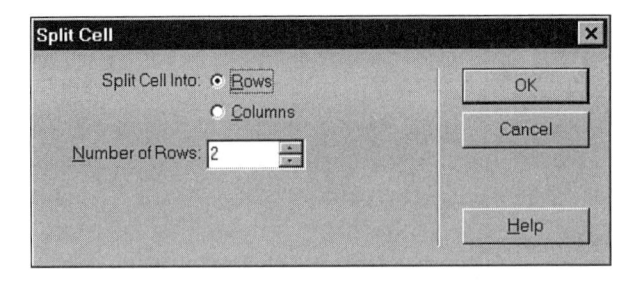

In the Split Cell dialog box, specify whether you want to split the cell into rows or columns and also specify the number of rows or columns into which the cell must be split. After you specify the required information in the Split Cell dialog box, UltraDev splits the cell into the specified number of rows and columns and automatically restructures the table.

> **Tip**
> Windows users can press the Ctrl, Alt, and S keys to split a cell. Macintosh users can press the Command, Option, and S keys.

UltraDev also allows you to merge continuous rows or columns into a single cell. To merge cells, select the cells you want to merge, as shown in Figure 11.10.

Figure 11.10
Select a set of continuous cells to use the merge option.

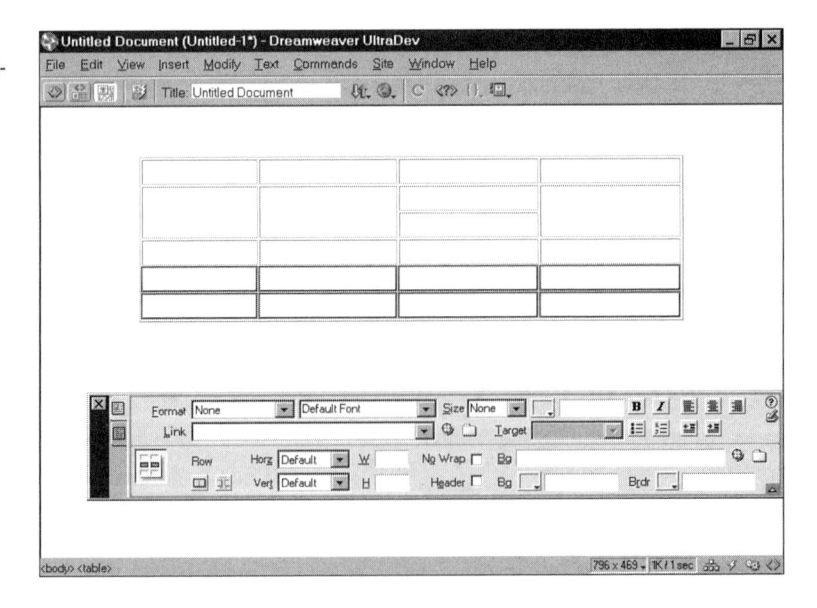

You can only merge continuous cells. You cannot merge cells that are not continuous, such as the ones shown in Figure 11.11. When you select noncontinuous cells, note that the Merge Cells button is disabled in the Property inspector.

Figure 11.11
You cannot merge noncontinuous cells.

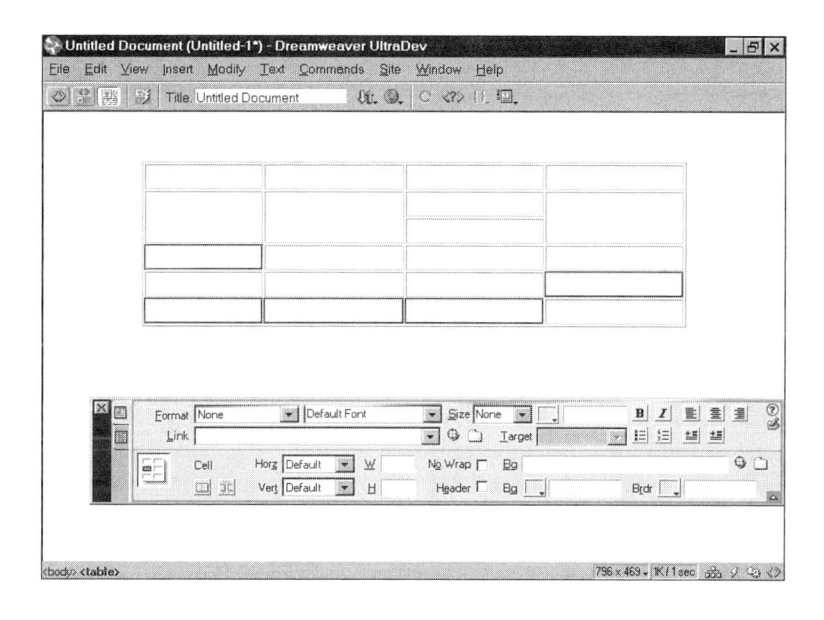

After you select the cells to be merged, click the Merge Cells button in the Property inspector to merge the selected cells into a single cell, as shown in Figure 11.12.

Figure 11.12
The cells in the last row have been merged into a single cell.

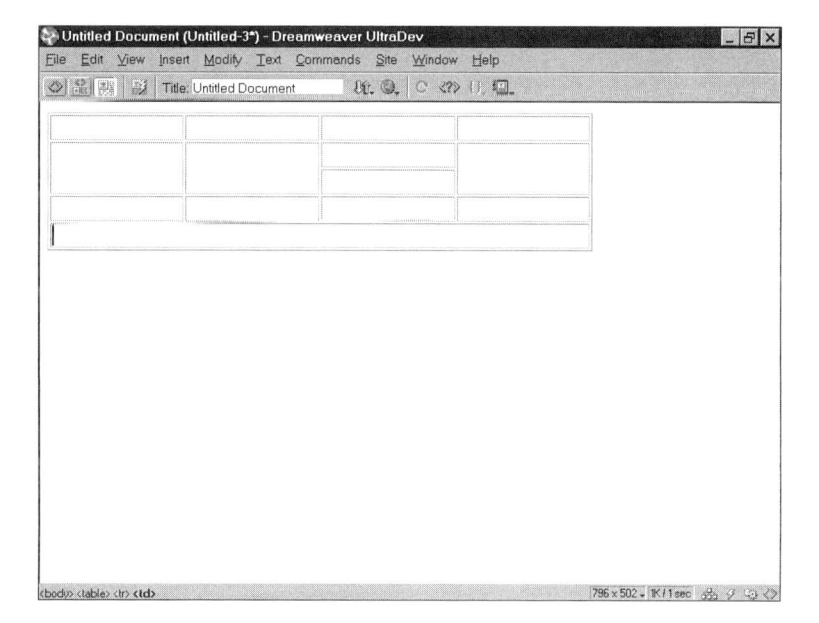

> **Note**
> When you merge multiple cells, the format of the first cell that is selected is applied to the merged cell. The contents of all the selected cells are placed in the merged cell.

> **Tip**
> Splitting and merging cells makes a table complex and difficult to manage. It is always better to use nested tables instead of splitting and merging cells. To split a column into two columns, select the column and insert a table with two columns and one row.

COPYING AND PASTING CELL CONTENT

UltraDev enables you to copy and paste multiple cells. When you copy a cell, you copy the contents and formatting in a cell along with cell splits or merges, if any, within the cell. However, you can copy and paste multiple cells only if the structure of the cells copied matches the structure of the cells in which you want to paste them.

To copy and paste cells, select cells that you want to copy and choose the Copy option from the Edit menu. After you copy the cells, click the cell before or after which you want to paste the selected cells and choose the Paste option from the Edit menu. You can also paste the copied cells anywhere outside the table to create a new table. The cells that want to copy and paste must be continuous, as shown in Figure 11.10.

MANAGING DATA IN A TABLE

UltraDev enables you to manage the contents of a table by sorting them. It also enables you to import information from other applications into a table. In addition, UltraDev allows you to export information from a table to other applications.

SORTING TABLE CONTENTS

You can sort the contents of a table alphabetically or numerically to display the contents in a sequential order. UltraDev enables you to perform a simple sort on a table based on the contents of a single column. You can also perform a more complex sort on a table based on the contents of more than one column. However, you cannot sort a table that contains a merged cell.

To sort the contents of a table, select the table and choose the Sort Table option from the Commands menu. The Sort Table dialog box appears, as shown in Figure 11.13.

From the Sort By drop-down list in the Sort Table dialog box, select the column by which you want to sort the table. The Order By option enables you to specify the order in which you want to sort the contents, alphabetically or numerically.

Figure 11.13
Use the Sort Table dialog box to sort the contents of a table.

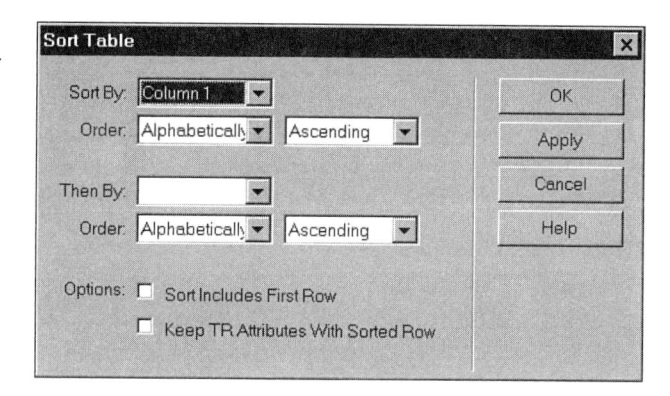

> **Note**
> If you apply an alphabetical sort to a column that contains one or more digits, such as 24, 2, 30, 3, 45, and 4, the sort results in an alphanumerical sort, such that the numbers are sorted as 2, 24, 3, 30, 4, and 45, instead of a numerical sort, which gives the sort result of 2, 3, 4, 24, 30, and 45. In an alphanumeric sort, the numbers are sorted according to the American Standards Code for Information Interchange (ASCII) values of each digit in a number instead of their numerical values. The ASCII value of the first digit in the number 30, which is 3, (the ASCII value of 3 being 51) is less than the ASCII value of 4 (which is 52). Therefore, the number 30 appears ahead of the number 4 in an alphanumeric sort.

You can also specify the order in which you want the data to be sorted, ascending or descending. The Then By drop-down list enables you to perform a secondary sort on a different column. The Sort Includes First Row option enables you to specify whether the first row must be included in the sort. For example, if the first row is the heading row and you do not want to include it in the sort, deselect this option.

IMPORTING TABULAR DATA

You can import data from other applications into UltraDev and display it as a table. However, the data to be imported must be saved in another application in a *delimited format*, in which one piece of data is separated from the other by tabs, spaces, colons, commas, or other characters. To import data from other applications into UltraDev, follow these steps:

1. Choose File, Import, Import Tabular Data. You can also choose Insert, Tabular Data. The Import Table Data dialog box appears, as shown in Figure 11.14. Except for the titles of the dialog boxes, the content of both the dialog boxes is the same.

2. Type the name of the file to be imported in the Data File text box. Alternatively, you can click the Browse button to select the file.

Figure 11.14
Use the Import Table Data dialog box to import a table and set its properties.

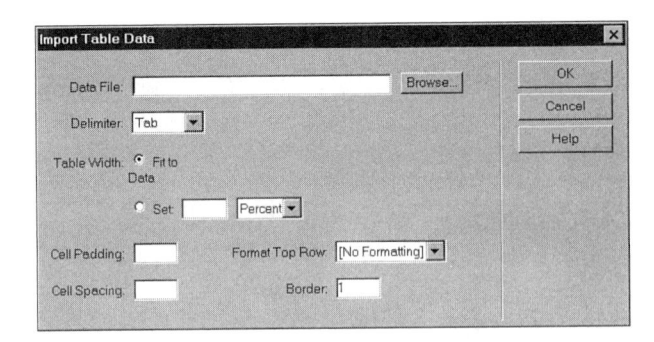

3. From the Delimiter drop-down list, select the delimiter format that matches the delimiter format of the document you are importing. If the Delimiter drop-down list does not contain the delimiter format that you want, you can specify it by using the Other option. Selecting the Other option displays a field to the right of the Delimiter drop-down list enabling you to specify a delimiter.

> **Caution**
> It is essential to specify a delimiter at the time of saving the file. If you do not specify a delimiter, the data will not be imported correctly and UltraDev does not display any warning in this regard.

4. Select the Fit to Data option to adjust the width of the table to fit the data contained in it. Alternatively, you can also select the Set option to set the width of the table in pixels or as a percentage of the browser window.
5. You can specify various formatting options for the table by using the Cell Padding, Cell Spacing, Format Top Row, and Border options.

Exporting Tabular Data

As you import data from other applications into UltraDev, you can also export data stored in a table from UltraDev to other applications. However, you cannot export parts of table data. When you export, the entire table data is exported. To export a part of table data, you can select the required information, create a new table, and export this new table. For example, if you want to export only the names of the books stored in a table, copy the column that contains the names of the books and paste it into the Web page. The column is pasted as a separate table. Select this new table and export its contents.

Exporting table data is very simple. All you have to do is click any of the cells in a table and choose File, Export, Export Table. The Export Table dialog box appears, as shown in Figure 11.15. Specify a delimiter for the table data by selecting a delimiter format from the Delimiter drop-down list. You can specify a line break for the operating system to which you are exporting data by selecting an option from the Line Break drop-down list. After you specify all the details in the Export Table dialog box, click the Export button. The Export Table As dialog box appears, in which you must specify a filename with the extension of your choice and click Save.

Figure 11.15
Use the Export Table dialog box to export tabular data to another file format.

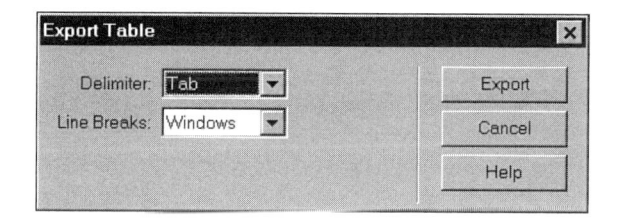

Creating and Managing Layers

Working with tables is not too much fun when it comes to resizing text or an image in a particular cell without affecting the width and height of the other cells in the table. The problems increase if you are trying to alter the size of the rows or columns within a nested table. However, UltraDev enables you to overcome all these tiny but time-consuming problems with the help of layers. You can use layers to move, resize, hide, and display the content of a Web page. In addition, you can use layers to provide other dynamic effects to the contents of your Web Page by animating the layers. For example, by animating layers, you can make a particular text move from one end of the Web page to another when the user clicks a button on the Web page.

Layers are based on stylesheets. The only disadvantage of using layers in your Web pages is that they are supported only by Internet Explorer 4.0, Netscape Navigator 4.0, and the later versions of these browsers, because only these browsers support stylesheets.

Introducing the Layer Panel

To create a layer, click the Document window where you want to insert a layer and choose Insert, Layer. You can also click the Draw Layer button in the Objects panel and drag the pointer on the document to draw a layer. Alternatively, you can also drag the Draw Layer button to the Document window to draw a layer.

Every time you add a layer to a document, the layer is added to the Layers panel, as shown in Figure 11.16. To view the Layers panel, choose Window, Layers. The Layers panel enables you to select a layer, prevent overlaps, and change the visibility and the stacking order of the layer.

Figure 11.16
Use the Layers panel to manage layers.

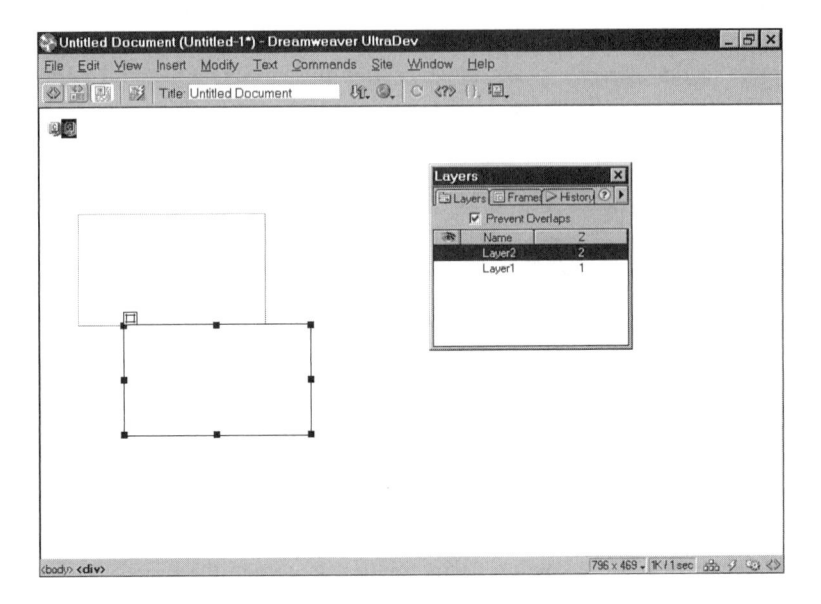

As you create nested tables, you can also create nested layers. A *nested layer* is a layer created within another layer. Creating nested layers is similar to creating layers. The only difference between them is that when you create a nested layer, you need to click the layer within which you want to create the nested layer before using the various methods of creating a layer.

Selecting, Resizing, Moving, and Aligning Layers

To resize, move, or align a layer, first you must select the layer. You can select a layer by clicking the layer name in the Layers panel. You can also hold down the Shift key and click a layer to select the layer. Alternatively, you can click on the border of the layer to select the layer. You can select multiple layers by holding down the Shift key and clicking the layer names in the Layer panel or clicking two or more layers. When you select multiple layers the selection handle of the last selected layer is highlighted in black.

After you select a layer, you can resize the layer by using the selection handles. You can use the Shift and arrow keys to resize the layer by 10 pixels at a time. Alternatively, you can also specify the width and height of the layer in the Property inspector of the layer.

To change the width or height of multiple layers, select the layers and choose Modify, Align, Make Same Width or choose Modify, Align, Make Same Height. However, this option sets the width and height of all the layers to that of the last layer selected. Alternatively, you can also specify the width and height in the W and H options of the Property inspector that appears when you select multiple layers.

> **Caution**
>
> If the Prevent Overlap option is selected in the Layers panel, you will not be able to resize or move layers so that they do not overlap each other.

UltraDev also enables you to move layers. You can easily move layers by dragging them with their selection handles. To move multiple layers, select the layers you want to move and drag the selection handle of the last selected layer. You can also use the Shift and arrow keys to move the layers by 10 pixels at a time.

Apart from resizing and moving layers, you can also align layers. To align layers, select an option from the list of options that appear when you choose Modify, Align. When you select multiple layers, they align to the border of the last layer that is selected.

In addition to these options, you can also resize and move layers with the help of grids. Grids provide a visual tool to resize and move layers. You can view the grids by choosing View, Grid, Show Grid. You can snap the layers to a grid automatically by selecting the Snap to Grid option in the Grid Settings dialog box. You can display the Grid settings dialog box by choosing View, Grid, Edit Grid.

Setting Properties for a Layer

Every layer that you create in your document has a set of characteristics that can be modified and set based on your requirements. You can set these characteristics in the Property inspector, which is shown in Figure 11.17. To view the Property inspector of a layer, select the layer and choose Window, Properties.

Figure 11.17
Use the Property inspector to set the properties of a layer.

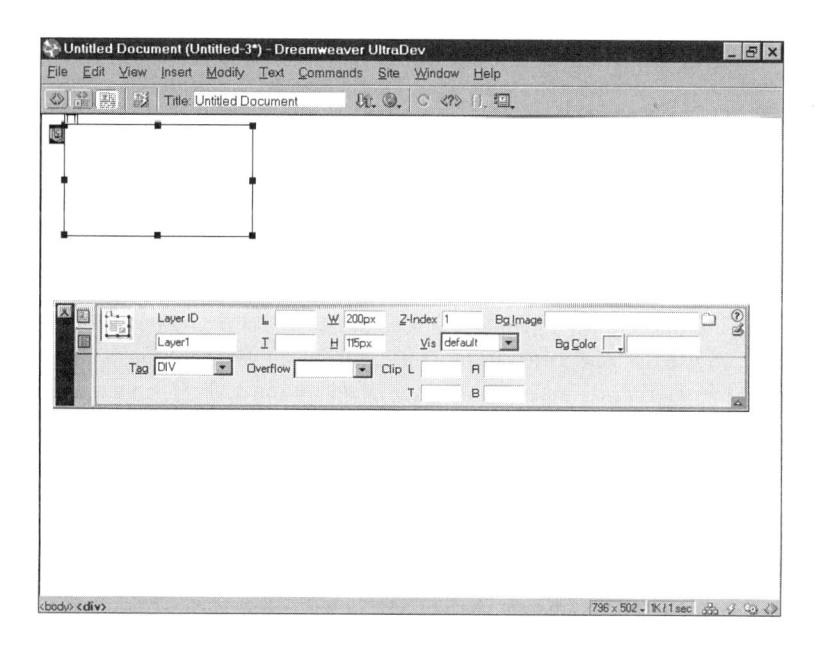

The Layer ID option of the Property inspector enables you to specify a unique name for the layer to identify the layer. The L and T options enable you to specify the position of the layer with respect to the top-left corner of the page or with respect to the parent layer. The W and H options enable you to set the width and height of the layer. The Z-Index option enables you to specify the *stacking order* of the layer. You can also stack layers by moving layers across in the Layers panel. The Vis option enables you to specify the initial visibility status for the layer. The following list summarizes the various visibility options:

- Default—Set the visibility of the layer to the browser default, which is generally set to inherit.
- Visible—Makes the layer visible.
- Hidden—Hides the layer.
- Inherit—Sets the visibility option of the nested layer to that of the parent layer. A *parent layer* is a layer into which another layer is inserted as a nested layer.

The Tag option enables you to specify the tag to be used in HTML code. The Tag option plays an important role with regard to compatibility with different kind of browsers. Generally the `<div>` and `<span>` tags are the most widely used tags as they work in all 4.0 and later browsers. The `<layer>` and `<ilayer>` tags work only with Netscape 4.x browsers.

The Bg Color and Bg Image options enable you to specify a background color and image for the layer, respectively. The Overflow option enables you to specify what needs to be done if the layer's content exceeds its size. The Overflow drop-down list displays the following options:

- Visible—Expands the size of the layer so that all the contents of the layer are visible.
- Hidden—This option does not resize the layer and therefore you cannot view the content that does not fit into the layer.
- Scroll Bars—Adds the vertical and horizontal scroll bars to the layer regardless of whether the contents fit into the layer. However, this option works only with browsers that support scroll bars.
- Auto—Adds scroll bars to the layer only when the content of the layer exceeds the size of the layer. If the content exceeds the layer height, a vertical scroll bar is added. Similarly, if the content exceeds the layer width, a horizontal scroll bar is added.

The Clip option of the Property inspector enables you to set a visibility region for the layer. You can use this option to cut off content from the left, right, top, and bottom edges of the layer by entering the relevant values in pixels in the L, R, T, and B options, respectively. For example, if you have an image within a layer and this image overlaps with the content that is to the right of the layer, you can set the visibility of the image by specifying a pixel value in the R and B options.

You will also find some additional options such as SRC and A/B option in the Property inspector if you select the `<layer>` or `<ilayer>` tags from the Tag drop-down list. The SRC option allows you to specify the HTML document that must be displayed within the layer. You can display HTML documents within a layer only with the `<layer>` and `<ilayer>` tags.

The A/B option allows you to specify the stacking order of the current layer with relation to other layers in the document. For example, you can place the current layer over another layer by selecting the Above option from the A/B drop-down list. The layer above which you want to place the current layer must be selected from the drop-down list next to the A/B drop-down list.

> **Note**
>
> You can mention the stacked order for the layers either in the A/B option or in the Z-Indexed option. However, you cannot specify both simultaneously.

→ To learn more about setting layer preferences, **see** "Setting Layers Preferences," **p. 331**.

For most of the layer properties, you can set default preferences in the Layer category of the Preferences dialog box.

BRINGING LAYERS TO LIFE

UltraDev enables you to add life to your Web pages with the help of timelines. You can create animation effects in your Web page by using timelines with layers. When you create layer animations with the help of timelines, the underlying JavaScript code that actually causes the animation effects is automatically generated. The browser does not require ActiveX controls, plug-ins, or Java applets to display these animation effects. You can create timeline animations by changing the size, color, visibility, and position of layers. Use timeline animations if you plan to design your site for a version 4.0 browser or later, because only these browsers support timeline animations.

The Timeline panel displays the properties of the layers and images over a time. You can open the Timelines panel by choosing Window, Timeline. Figure 11.18 shows the Timelines panel.

Every Timelines window displays a sequential numbering of frames. The current frame number is displayed between the Back and Play buttons. The Playback Head option indicates the frame of the timeline currently displayed on the Web page. Animation Channel displays the Animation bars that contain information about the animated objects, such as the name and duration of the animated object. The circles on the Animation bars represent *keyframes*, which are frames where you specify the properties of the object. Behavior Channel enables you to add behaviors to the animation object. The Rewind button rewinds Playback Head to the first frame in the timeline. The Back button enables you to rewind Playback Head by one frame from the current frame. The Play button enables you to forward Playback Head by one frame. You can hold down the Play and Back buttons to play the timeline forward and backward continuously.

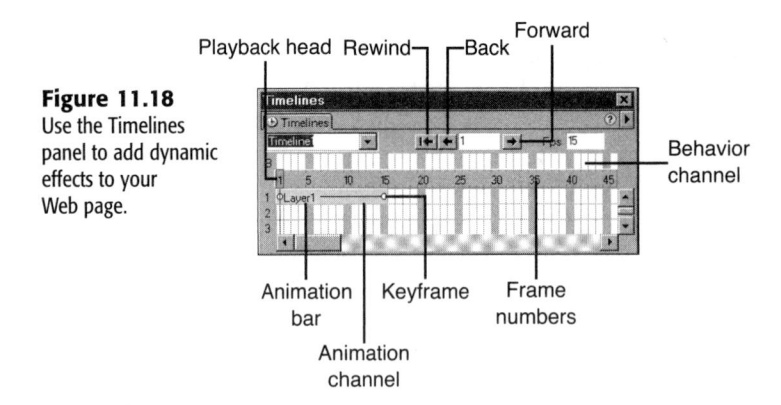

Figure 11.18
Use the Timelines panel to add dynamic effects to your Web page.

(Figure labels: Playback head, Rewind, Back, Forward, Behavior channel, Animation bar, Keyframe, Frame numbers, Animation channel)

CREATING ANIMATIONS WITH TIMELINES

You can create timeline animations only for layers. If you want to create animations for images or text, you must insert them into a layer and create a timeline animation for that layer. To create a timeline animation for a layer, follow these steps:

1. Place the layer at the position where you want it to be at the beginning of the animation.
2. Choose Window, Timelines to display the Timelines panel.
3. Select the layer to be animated.
4. Add the selected layer to the timeline by choosing Modify, Timeline, Add Object to Timeline. A bar with the name of the layer appears at the first channel of the timeline.
5. To specify the position of the layer at the end of the animation, click the keyframe marker at the end of the bar and drag the layer to the position where you want it to be at the end of the animation. A line showing the path of the animation is displayed in the Document window. You can also give a curved path for the layer. To give a curved path for the layer, click a frame in the middle of the animation bar and choose the Add Keyframe option from the context-sensitive menu. After you add the keyframe, drag the layer in a curved path to create a curved path for the layer.
6. Preview the animation by holding down the Play button.

This method of creating a timeline might be too tedious if many keyframes are used for an animation. For example, if the path taken by a layer is too complex, it is better to record the path of the layer as you drag it rather than creating individual keyframes. To record the path of the layer, specify the starting position of the layer by dragging it to the required position. After dragging the layer to the required position, choose Modify, Timeline, Record Path of Layer. Drag the layer in the required path on the Document window to the position where the animation must stop. UltraDev automatically adds an animation bar with keyframes for the layer. You can click the Rewind button to rewind the animation and use the Play button to preview the animation.

Apart from changing the path, you can also change the visibility, stacking order, size, and source of an object in the timeline. To change these properties of an object in the timeline, select the keyframe at which you want to change the property of the object and perform of the following steps:

- Click the Browse button next to the Src field in the Property inspector to change the source file for an image.

> **Tip**
> For multiple image animations, use the Show, Hide layer options instead of the changing the source file, because the load times involved in switching between source files will slow down the animation.

- Select the Hidden, Visible, Inherit, or Default options from the Vis drop-down list in the Property inspector to change the visibility of a layer. You can also use the eye icons in the Layers panel to change the visibility of the layer.
- Drag the resize handles of a layer or enter new value for the W and H options in the Property inspector to resize a layer.

> **Note**
> Dynamic resizing of layers is currently supported by Internet Explorer 4.0 and later versions only.

- Enter a new value in the Z-index text box or use the Layers panel to rearrange the stacking order of the layers.

Use the Play button to preview the timeline animation.

Creating Multiple Timelines

UltraDev enables you to create multiple timelines for your Web page. You can use multiple timelines to control each element in your Web page separately. Multiple timelines are particularly useful if you want to trigger a particular timeline for every user action. To do this, you can use the Behavior panel.

→ To learn more about setting timeline behavior, **see** "Attaching a Behavior to a Layer," **p. 275**.

Modifying Timeline Animations

After creating an animation you can modify the properties of your animation by modifying the timeline.

You can make an animation play longer by dragging the last keyframe to the right. When you drag the last keyframe to the right all the other keyframes adjust to maintain their relative positions. However, you can prevent the other keyframes from moving by pressing the Ctrl key while dragging the end marker.

To make an animation start earlier or later, select all the bars associated with the animation and drag them to the left (earlier) or right (later).

You can add and remove frames in a timeline by choosing the Modify, Timeline, Add Frames or Modify, Timeline, Remove Frames options, respectively.

To make a timeline animation play automatically as soon as the page loads in the browser, select the Auto Play option in the Timeline panel. You can also make a timeline loop continuously by selecting the Loop option in the Timeline window.

Working with Frames

Frames divide a Web page into different HTML pages that enable you to present and organize data effectively. Frames enable you to display more than one Web page at the same time on the browser screen. For example, you can divide a Web page into three different sections: a top portion that displays banner adds, a left portion that displays a set of links, and a third portion, which forms the major part of the Web page, that displays dynamic content based on the link selected by the user from the left portion, as shown in Figure 11.19. Therefore, frames enable you to create a clean and easy to navigate site. Frames also help you to load your site faster. For example, if you have a navigation bar that remains static throughout the site, it is better to place this navigation bar in a frame that loads once instead of inserting the navigation bar in every page of the site. This reduces the download time, because the navigation bar need not be loaded each time you move to a new page.

In UltraDev, you can create multiple frames on a Web page with the help of framesets, which are the main containers for multiple frames. *Framesets* are HTML pages that store information regarding the various definable properties of a Web page, such as the structure, number and size of frames, and so on. For example, Figure 11.19 displays a frameset with two frames in it: a left frame and a right frame.

Every frame can contain and load its own URL independent of the other frames. A frame can also be assigned a name so that it can be targeted by other URLs. However, you need to keep a few points in mind before creating frames on your Web page. Use frames only if they are required and not to enhance the appearance of your Web Page. Use a maximum of only three frames because any number more than this overcrowds the page. Dedicate the major part of the screen area to the frame that displays maximum information about the site.

Creating a Frame

You can create framesets in UltraDev either by selecting a frameset from the predefined set of framesets or by designing it on your own. However, you need to be in the Design view of a document to create a frameset.

Figure 11.19
This page is divided into two sections by the left and right frames.

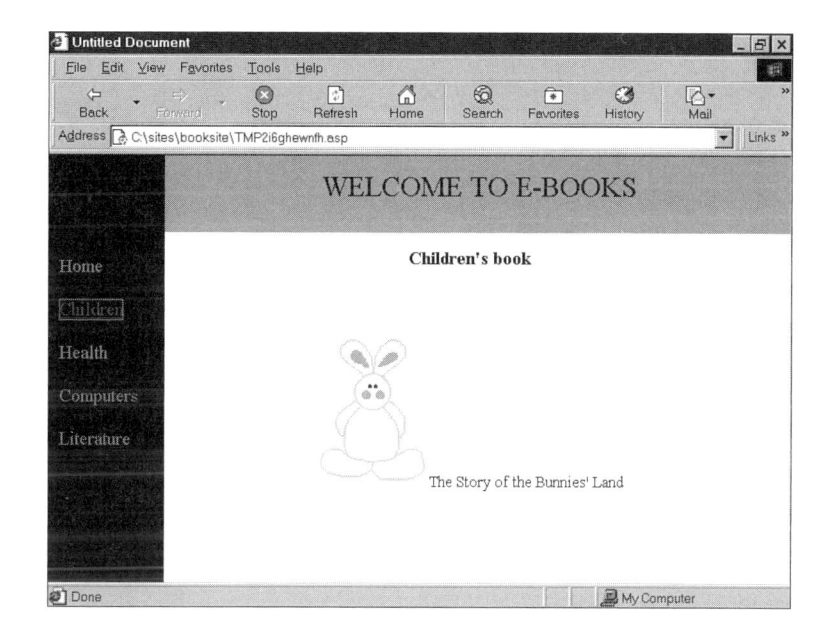

Every frame created in a Web page contains a corresponding HTML document. Apart from these HTML documents, one HTML document is created for the frameset also. For example, a page containing two frames will have three HTML pages. Two pages hold the content that must displayed within individual frames and one holds the frameset information.

CREATING A FRAME WITH A PREDEFINED FRAMESET

Creating a frame from the set of predefined framesets is the easy because the layout of the frameset is already created. To view the set of predefined framesets, select the Frames category of the Objects panel. A visual representation of all the predefined framesets appears in the Frames category, as shown in Figure 11.20.

In the predefined frameset icon, the currently selected page or frame in a document is represented in blue and the new frames are displayed in white. To insert a predefined frameset into a document, place the insertion point in the Document window where you want the frameset to be inserted and click the predefined frameset that you want to insert.

DESIGNING A FRAMESET

Apart from using the predefined framesets, you can also design your own frameset. To design your own frameset, Choose Insert, Frames to display a list of submenu options. Choose any one of the options from this list to insert the frameset. After you insert the frameset, you can drag the frameset borders to split the Document window horizontally or vertically.

To split an inner frame, hold down the Alt key and drag if you are a Windows user. If you are a Macintosh user hold down the Option key and drag.

Figure 11.20
Choose a desired frameset from the Frames category of the Objects panel.

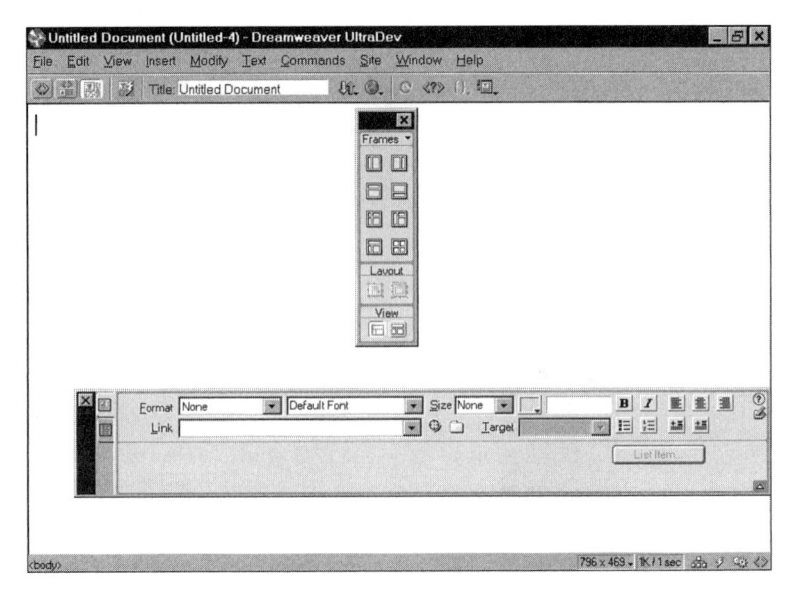

You can also create nested framesets. *Nested framesets* are framesets within other framesets. For example, you can create a main frameset with two frames that divide the frameset horizontally into two portions. You can further divide the lower frame of the frameset into two vertical frames by inserting a frameset in the lower frame, as shown in Figure 11.21.

Figure 11.21
The lower frame is divided into two sections by the two vertical frames.

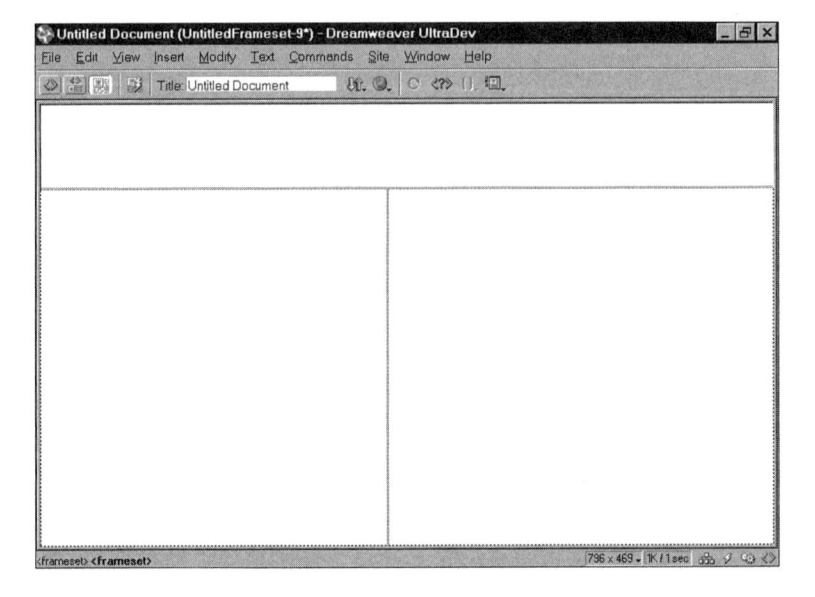

The steps involved in creating a nested frameset are similar to that of creating a normal frameset except that you need to place the insertion point in the frame in which you which you want to insert a nested frameset before inserting it.

You can use the Frameset panel to view the hierarchy of framesets within a document, as shown in Figure 11.22. To view the Frameset panel, choose Window, Frames. The Frameset panel uses a thick three-dimensional border to display a frameset and a thin gray line to display the frames within a frameset. This panel also displays the names of the frames in the frameset.

Figure 11.22
Use the Frameset panel to see the hierarchy of the framesets.

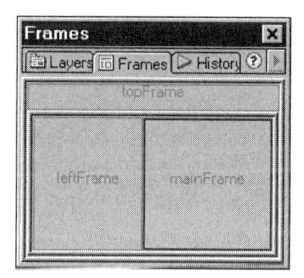

If you want to delete a frame from a frameset, you can drag the border of a page to the border of the parent frame.

SAVING FRAMES AND FRAMESETS

To preview a Web page that contains frames, you must first save all the framesets and frames of that page. To save a frameset or frame, select it from the Frameset panel by clicking it, as shown in Figure 11.23.

Figure 11.23
Use the Frameset panel to select a frameset or frame.

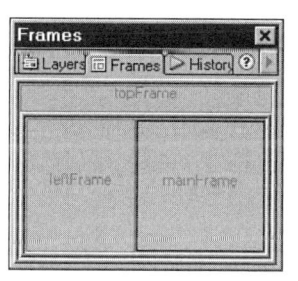

After selecting the frameset or frame, choose File, Save. The Save As dialog box appears, as shown in Figure 11.24.

Enter a name for the frameset or frame in the File name text box. You can also save all framesets and frames in the current document by choosing File, Save All.

Figure 11.24
The Save As dialog box enables you to specify names for the files associated with each frame or frameset.

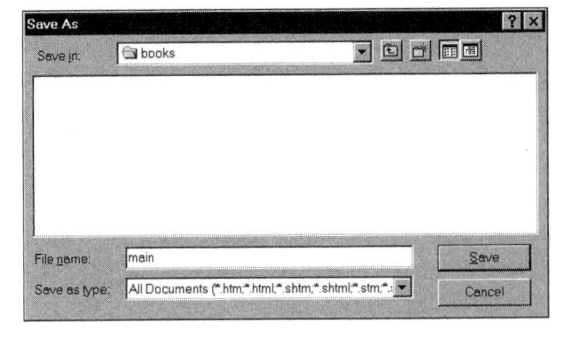

Setting Frameset and Frame Properties

You can set properties for the framesets by using the Property inspector. View the Property inspector of a frameset by selecting the frameset and choosing Window, Properties. The Property inspector displays various options to control the dimensions of frames and set colors for the borders between the frames in the frameset. The Property inspector of a frameset is shown in Figure 11.25.

Figure 11.25
The Property inspector enables you to set properties for framesets.

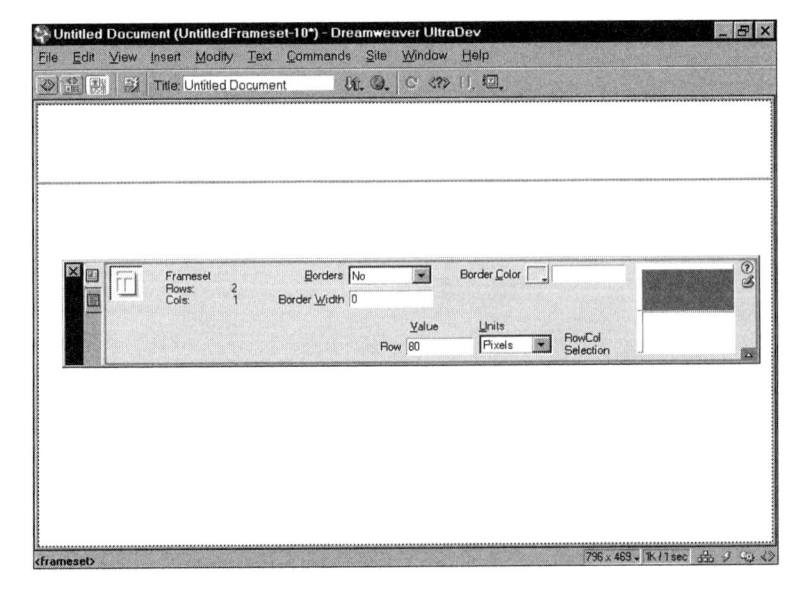

You can also set properties for individual frames in a frameset by using the Property inspector. The Property inspector of a frame displays options that enable you to specify whether a user is allowed to scroll or resize a frame. It also provides options to set the source files, borders, and margins for the frames. The Property inspector of a frame is shown in Figure 11.26.

Figure 11.26
The Property inspector enables you to set properties for a frame.

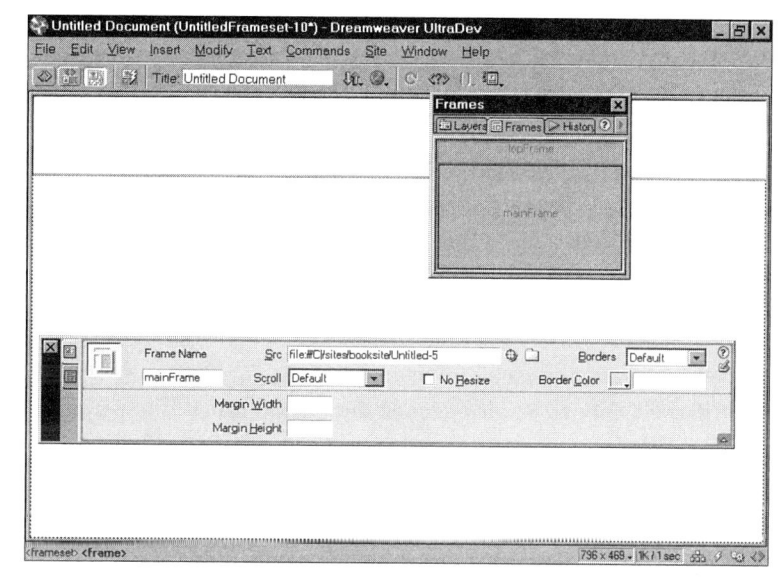

To enhance the appearance of a frame, you might want to specify a background color. To do this, select the frame and choose Modify, Page Properties. In the Page Property window that appears, select a color from the Background drop-down list.

Frame Content and Links

The significance of framesets is best discovered when you use them as a target area to open a linked document. For example, you can have a frame that contains links on the left of the document. You can make the linked documents open in the main content frame by specifying this frame as the target for the links created in the left frame.

→ To learn more about setting target frames for a link, **see** "Creating a Link with the Property Inspector," **p. 193**.

Summary

UltraDev provides various tools such as tables, layers, and frames that enable you to design complex Web sites. You can use combinations of these tools to maintain all aspects of a Web site. Tables, layers, and frames, each one of these has their own advantages and disadvantages. Therefore, it is up to the Web designer to take maximum advantage of each of these tools in the best possible method based on the varied requirements of the Web site.

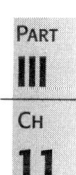

Activity Corner

In this activity corner section, you will create the frames for the `Musichome.asp` file. You will set each of these frames to a source file. You will create layer animations in the `Contentpage.asp` and `Aboutus.asp` files. In addition, you will insert a table in the `Contentpage.asp` file.

To create the frames and set their source to the respective file, follow these steps:

1. Open the `Musichome.asp` file.
2. Choose Window, Objects. From the Objects panel, select the Frames category.
3. Click the Insert Top and Nested Left Frame button in the Objects panel.
4. Choose Window, Frames to open the Frames panel. Choose Window, Properties to open the Property inspector.
5. Select topFrame from the Frames panel. The FrameName textbox of the Property inspector must show topFrame. In the Src text box, browse to select the `Navigation.asp` file.
6. Next, select leftFrame from the Frames panel. In the Src text box of the Property inspector, browse to select `Sidebar.asp`.
7. Select mainFrame from the Frames panel. In the Src text box of the Property inspector, browse to select `Contentpage.asp`.
8. Adjust the size of the frame containing the `Sidebar.asp` file so that the text on this frame becomes fully visible.
9. Choose File, Save All frames. In the Save As dialog box, type **Musichome.asp** in the File name text box. A warning message notifies you that a file named `Musichome.asp` already exists. Click OK in the message box to overwrite the file.

When a user selects a song category from the `Sidebar.asp` file, the `Songfetch.asp` file that each category links to must be loaded in the frame named mainFrame. Similarly, when the user clicks the link Home in the `Sidebar.asp` file, the file named `Contentpage.asp` must be loaded in the frame named mainFrame. So, the target for these links must now be set to mainFrame. To do this, select each link and choose the mainFrame option from the Target drop-down list of the Property inspector.

Creating a Layer Animation

Next, you will create a layer animation in the `Contentpage.asp` document. This animation is used to set the header text for the document. It displays the text "Latest Releases," which scrolls right to left across the screen. The background color for the text scrolls from left to right. When the animation is over, the text is set against the background color. To view the animation, open the `Contentpage.asp` file from the Web and view it in your browser.

To create this animation, follow these steps:

1. Open the Contentpage.asp file in the Design view of the Document window.
2. Insert a layer by choosing the Layer option from the Insert menu.
3. Select the layer and choose Window, Properties to display the Property inspector of the layer. In the Property inspector, specify Releasebg in the Layer ID text box. Specify 44px, 20px, 3px, and 31px in the L, H, T, and W text boxes, respectively. Specify 1 in the Z-index text box of the Property inspector.
4. Set the background color of the layer to blue by typing #000066 in the Bg Color text box of the Property inspector. Select the visible option from the Vis drop-down list.
5. Next, insert another layer in the Contentpage.asp document. Specify the Layer ID as Release in the Property inspector. Type 384px in the L text box, 213px in the W text box, 24px in the T text box, and 23px in the H text box.
6. Specify the Z index of the Release layer as 2. Select the visible option from the Vis drop-down list.
7. Place the cursor within the Release layer and type the text **Latest Release**. Set the font to Verdana, font color to #FF9900, and font size to 4.
8. Next, choose Window, Timelines to display the Timelines panel. Select the layer named Release and choose Modify, Timeline, Add Object to Timeline to add the Release layer to the Timelines panel.
9. In the Timelines panel, by default, the start keyframe begins at frame 1 and end keyframe ends at frame 25. Drag the end keyframe to frame 40.
10. When the keyframe is at frame 40, drag the Release layer to the position of the layer Releasebg.
11. Type 10 in the Fps text box on the Timelines panel to set the speed of the animation to 10 frames per second.
12. Next, select the layer Releasebg. Choose Modify, Timeline, Add Object to Timeline to add the layer to the Timelines panel. In the Timelines panel, drag the end keyframe to frame 40 and click this keyframe to select it.
13. Resize the Releasebg layer such that the L, T, W, and H text boxes of the Property inspector are set to the values 44px, 20px, 504px, and 31px, respectively.
14. Select the Autoplay option in the Timelines panel.
15. Save this document and preview it in the browser to see whether the animation plays correctly.

Repeat steps 1–15 to create a similar layer animation in the About.asp document. Unlike the text "Latest Releases" that is displayed in the Contentpage.asp document, the text to be displayed in the layer animation of the Aboutus.asp is "About Us."

CREATING THE Contentpage.asp DOCUMENT

The Contentpage.asp document displays the list of new releases. To display this list, you will use two tables. To have better control over the positioning of these tables, you will insert the tables within a layer. The first table contains the labels for the list of new songs and the second table contains the actual list of songs. To create these tables and position them with the help of layers, follow these steps:

1. In the Contentpage.asp file, insert a layer below the Releasebg layer.
2. Select the layer and enter **39px**, **92px**, **724px**, and **44px**, respectively, in the L, T, W, and H text boxes of the Property inspector. The Layer ID for this layer is Layer3 by default.
3. Place the cursor inside the layer and choose Insert, Table. In the Insert Table dialog box, specify 1 in the Rows text box and 5 in the Columns text box. Enter 0 in the Cell Spacing and Cell Padding text boxes. Enter 5 in the Border text box.
4. Select the table and specify the border color as #000066 in the Brdr Color text box of the Property inspector of the table. Specify the background color as #FFFFFF in the Bg Color text box. Set the width to 71% and the height to 49 pixels.
5. In the first cell, type **Song**, followed by **Composer**, **Album**, **Listen**, and **Create CD** in the other four cells.
6. Select each text and set the font to Verdana. Specify 3 as the font size and set the font color to #003366. Click the Bold button to make the text bold. Select the Center option from the Horz drop-down list and the Middle option from the Vert drop-down list for each text in every cell.
7. Select each cell in the table and set the border color and background color to #FFFFFF in the Property inspector. Set the bordercolordark attribute to #CCCCCC.
8. Below this table, insert another table. This table must also contain five rows and five columns. Set the cell spacing and cell padding to 0.
9. Select the table and set the width of the table to 71% and the height of the table to 255 pixels using the Property inspector.
10. Specify the border color as #000066 in the Brdr Color text box of the Property inspector. Specify the background color as #FFFFFF in the Bg Color text box.
11. Select every cell in the table and set the background color, bordercolor and bordercolordark attributes to #CCCCCC using the Property inspector. Set the height of every cell to 53 pixels.

The design of the two tables is now complete. Next, you need to add dynamic data to the second table so that it displays the list of new songs. The activity corner sections in Part IV of this book deal with adding dynamic data to this table.

CHAPTER 12

BUILDING USER INTERACTIVITY INTO A PAGE

In this chapter

How Forms Work   238

Using Forms   238

Working with Form Objects   240

Processing Forms on the Server Side   250

Summary   252

Activity Corner   252

How Forms Work

Forms are one of the basic ways in which a user can interact with a Web site. A *form* collects information from the user and submits this information to the server for processing. Forms can contain various objects that enable user interaction. These objects can be list boxes, text boxes, check boxes, radio buttons, and so on. In addition, forms include form tags that contain the path to the application, which processes the user information.

When a user enters some information in the form fields and submits the information, the information is sent to the script or application on the Web server for processing. The Web server responds and sends the requested information to the user. Typically, the user information is passed to a Common Gateway Interface (CGI) application, JavaServer Page (JSP), Active Server Page (ASP), or ColdFusion (CF) page that processes the information and sends the response to the user.

Dreamweaver UltraDev lets you create forms, add objects to the forms, and validate the form information. In this chapter, you will learn how to create a form and add objects to it.

Using Forms

Forms are used to gather various kinds of input from a user. Forms on different Web pages look more or less similar. The three basic components of a form are form objects, the Submit button, and form tags. Form objects let the user enter information. The Submit button lets the user submit the information to the Web server. Form tags contain the URL to the programming script or application at the server end to process the information submitted by the user.

Creating a Form

Dreamweaver UltraDev lets you create a form as well as add objects to it. The Forms category of the Objects panel lets you create a form and add objects such as text fields, buttons, check boxes, radio buttons, and list boxes to the form.

The Insert Form icon in the Forms category of the Objects panel lets you create a form. The Forms category is shown in Figure 12.1.

To create a form, click the Insert Form icon in the Forms category of the Objects panel. You can also click and drag the Insert Form icon to the screen at the position where you want to insert the form. A form is inserted into the Document window. In Design view, the boundary of the inserted form is represented by a red dotted outline.

> **Note:** In Code view, you can view the code generated for the inserted form. This code is written within the `<form>` and `</form>` tags.

Figure 12.1
The Forms category of the Objects panel.

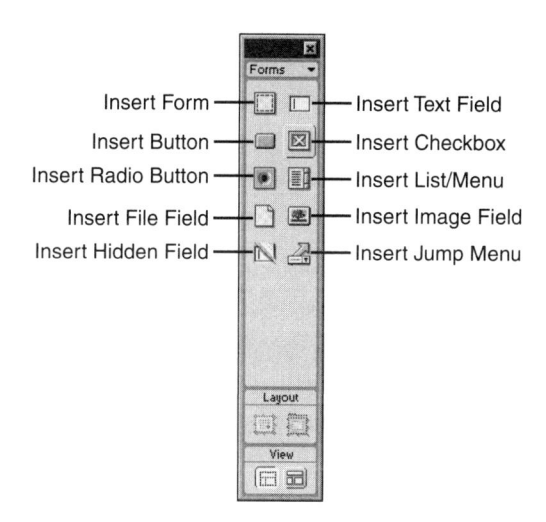

- Insert Form
- Insert Button
- Insert Radio Button
- Insert File Field
- Insert Hidden Field
- Insert Text Field
- Insert Checkbox
- Insert List/Menu
- Insert Image Field
- Insert Jump Menu

> **Tip:** You can also insert a form into a document by choosing Insert, Form.

After you insert a form, the Property inspector of the form is displayed, as shown in Figure 12.2.

Figure 12.2
When you insert a form, the Property inspector of the form is displayed.

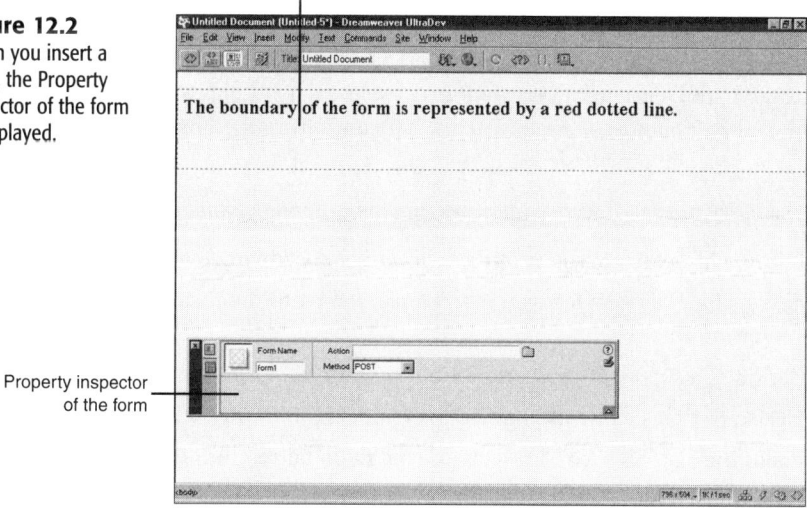

The Property inspector contains three options: Form Name, Action, and Method. These options let you specify the mode for transporting and processing the user information. The options in the Property inspector are summarized in Table 12.1.

TABLE 12.1 DESCRIPTION OF THE OPTIONS AVAILABLE IN THE PROPERTY INSPECTOR OF A FORM

Option	Description
Form Name	Lets you enter a name for the form.
Action	Lets you specify the path to the application, which will accept user information from the form. This application processes the information and sends the response to the user.
Method	Lets you choose a method to handle the information entered in the form.

The Method drop-down list contains the Default, GET, and POST items. When you select the Default item, the form uses the default method of the browser to send the information to the server. Generally, the default method of the browser is the GET method.

When you select the POST item, the form information is embedded in the HTTP headers.

When you select the GET item, the form information is appended to the URL and is sent to the server.

> **Note**
> The data that is sent to the server by using the GET method will be truncated if it exceeds 8,192 characters. This leads to unexpected processing results.

WORKING WITH FORM OBJECTS

Form objects, also known as form fields, are the input types used to accept user information. In Dreamweaver UltraDev, you can create form objects such as fields to enter text, menus to choose items, and radio buttons to select items. The buttons in the Forms category of the Objects panel let you add nine basic form objects.

The Forms category of the Objects panel contains the following icons:

- Insert Form: This icon lets you insert a form into a document.
- Insert Text Field: This icon lets you insert a text field into the form. A text field lets you type or enter information.
- Insert Button: This icon lets you insert a button into the form.
- Insert Checkbox: This icon lets you insert a check box into the form.
- Insert Radio Button: This icon lets you insert a radio button into the form.
- Insert List/Menu: This icon lets you create items in a list or menu.
- Insert File Field: This icon lets you insert a blank text field and a Browse button into the frame. A file field lets you specify the path to/ a file.
- Insert Image Field: This icon lets you insert an Image button into the form, which can be used instead of a Submit button to submit form information to the server.

- Insert Hidden Field: This icon lets you insert a *hidden field*.
- Insert Jump Menu: This icon lets you insert a navigational list or pop-up menu.

CREATING TEXT FIELDS

A text field is one of the nine form objects. It lets you enter alphanumeric information. The three types of text fields are single-line, multiline, and password.

INSERTING A SINGLE-LINE TEXT FIELD

Single-line text fields are the default text fields used in Web pages. These fields are used to accept a single line of text with one or two words, such as a username or user address.

Password fields are a special type of text field that hides the text entered by the user. These fields hide the text by replacing it with asterisks or bullets. These fields can be used to enter passwords. It is not safe to use single-line text fields for password entries, because these text fields do not protect the passwords.

To insert a single-line text field, you need to follow these steps:

1. Choose Insert, Form Objects, Text Field or click the Insert Text Field icon in the Forms category of the Objects panel. You can also click Insert Text Field icon and drag the mouse pointer to the location at which you want to insert a text field into the form. A text field is created in your document, and the text field's Property inspector is displayed.

2. Type a unique name for the text field in the TextField field of the Property inspector. You can also label the text field by typing text next to the text field, as shown in Figure 12.3. In the figure, fname is the name of the text field and "Enter your first name" is the label for the text field. fname is the variable that stores the value of the text field. This value is sent to the server for processing. Label is the prompt displayed on the screen for user reference.

3. Type a number in the Char Width field to specify the length or size of the text field. This number determines how many characters can be displayed on the screen at once. Consider an example in which the character width is 5 and the length of the user's input is 10. In this example, the size of the text field is 5 and the number of characters entered by the user is 10. Although the user enters 10 characters, only five characters will appear on the screen at one time. The default size of the text field is 20 characters.

4. Type a number in the Max Chars field to specify the maximum number of characters the user can type in the text field. This is used for validation and to define the field's size limits.

5. Select Single line from the Type field to insert a single-line text field. The other options in the Type field are Multi line and Password. To create a Password text field, you can select the Password option.

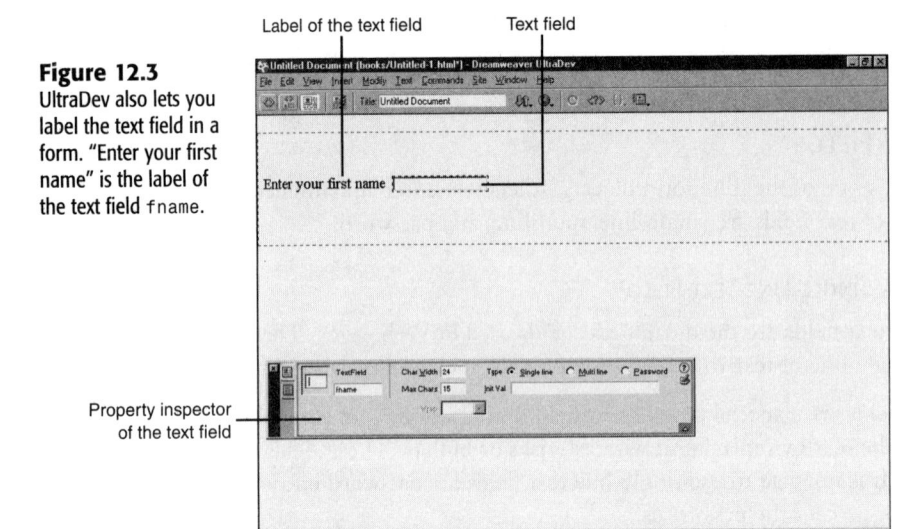

Figure 12.3
UltraDev also lets you label the text field in a form. "Enter your first name" is the label of the text field fname.

6. If you want to set some default text for the text field, type the text in the Init Val field of the Property inspector. For example, suppose you type Don Allen as the `init` value for the text field fname. In this case, each time you open the document containing the form, the fname text field displays the default fname Don Allen. You have an option of overwriting this default text.

INSERTING A MULTILINE TEXT FIELD

Multiple-line text fields let you type multiple lines of text. When you create a multiple-line text field, you can specify the number of rows or lines of text a user can type in the text field.

To insert a multiple-line text field, follow these steps:

1. Choose Insert, Form Objects, Text Field or click the Insert Text Field icon in the Forms category of the Objects panel. A text field is created in your document, and the text field's Property inspector is displayed.
2. Type a unique name for the text field in the TextField field of the Property inspector.
3. Select the Multi line option from the Type field to insert a multiple-line text field. The Num Lines field and the Wrap pop-up menu get activated, as shown in Figure 12.4.
4. Type a number in the Char Width field to specify the number of characters that can be displayed on the screen at one time.
5. Type a number in the Num Lines field to specify the maximum number of lines that can be displayed on the screen at one time.

6. Select an option from the Wrap pop-up menu to define how the user's input will be wrapped in a multiline format. If you want the text in the field to be wrapped to the next line, select Virtual or Physical. If you do not want the text to be wrapped to the next line, choose either Off or Default.

Figure 12.4
The Multi line option in the Type field lets you insert a multiple-line text field.

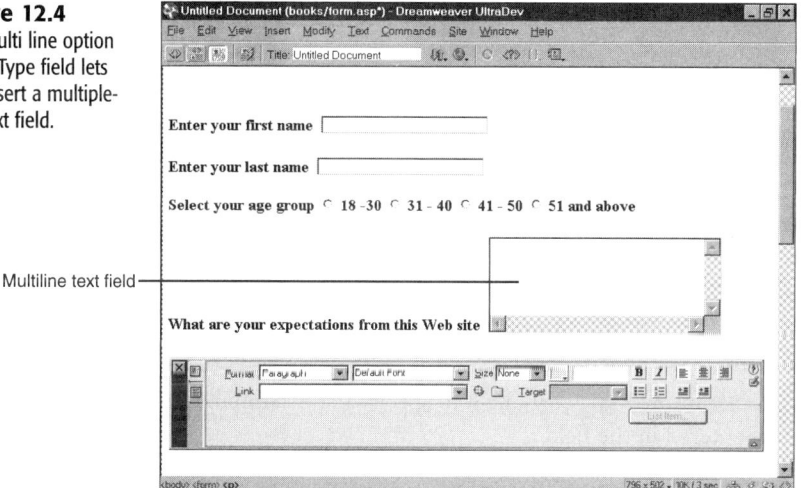

Multiline text field

7. If you want to set some default text for the text field, type that text in the Init Val field of the Property inspector.

INSERTING A FILE FIELD

Consider a situation in which you want the user to send a graphic file or Word document to the Web server for processing. To allow the user to specify the path to the file, you can use a file field. The main difference between a file field and a text field is that a file field has an extra Browse button. The Browse button lets users browse and locate the document they want to send to the server.

Follow these steps to insert a file field:

1. Select the form. The form's Property inspector is displayed. Select POST from the Method list box to send the form information to the target location.
2. Choose Insert, Form Objects, File Field or click the Insert File Field icon in the Forms category of the Objects panel to insert a file field. A Browse button is also inserted along with the file field. This button is placed next to the field. The Property inspector of the file field is displayed, as shown in Figure 12.5.
3. Type the name for the file field in the FileField Name field of the Property inspector.
4. Type a number in the Char Width field to specify the maximum number of characters the field will display.

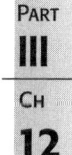

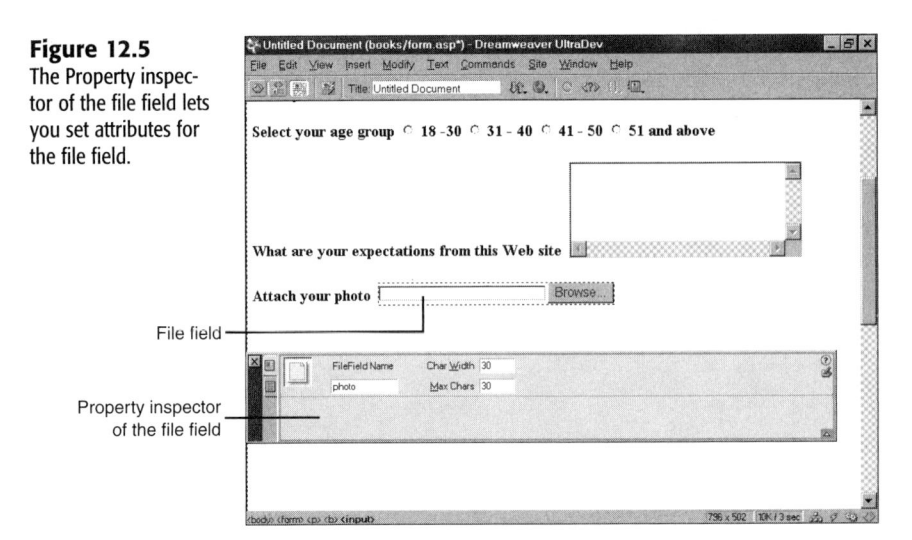

Figure 12.5
The Property inspector of the file field lets you set attributes for the file field.

File field

Property inspector of the file field

5. Type a number in the Max Chars field to specify the maximum number of characters that can be entered in the field.

INSERTING A HIDDEN FIELD

A hidden field is also a text field used to collect user information. Information entered in the hidden field is also sent to the server when the form is submitted. Information entered in the hidden field is not displayed on the page.

To insert a hidden field, follow these steps:

1. Choose Insert, Form Objects, Hidden Field or click the Insert Hidden Field icon in the Forms category of the Objects panel. A hidden field is created in the form, and the hidden field's Property inspector is displayed, as shown in Figure 12.6.
2. Type the name for the hidden field in the HiddenField field of the Property inspector.
3. Type the value to be assigned to the hidden field in the Value field.

CREATING BUTTONS

Dreamweaver UltraDev lets you add different types of buttons, such as text buttons, radio buttons, and image buttons, to your form.

INSERTING A RADIO BUTTON

Radio buttons can be used in a form when you want the user to select only one option from a list of options. Typically, radio buttons are used in groups. A radio button group consists of more than one radio button. The radio buttons in a radio button group have the same name but different values.

WORKING WITH FORM OBJECTS 245

Figure 12.6
The Property inspector of the hidden field enables you to change the properties of the hidden field.

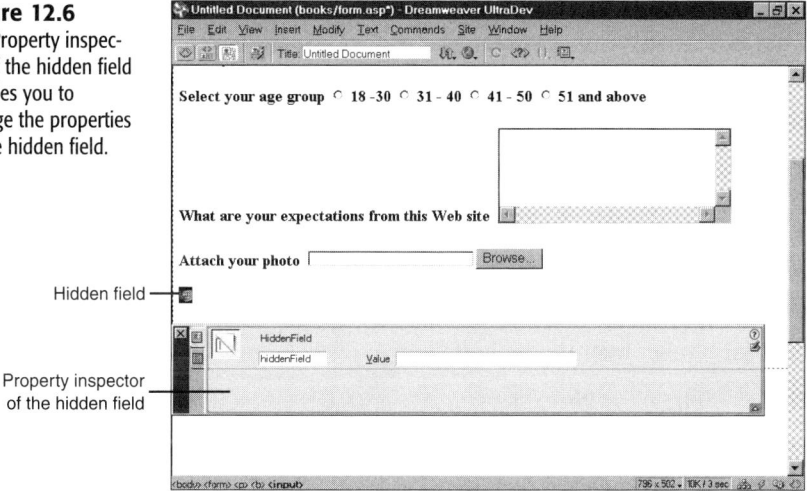

Hidden field

Property inspector of the hidden field

Consider an example in which the user must select his age group on a registration form. As shown in Figure 12.7, the radio button group Age Group consists of four options: 18 - 30, 31 - 40, 41 - 50, and 51 and above. In this example, the options in the radio button group Age Group have a common name but different values.

Figure 12.7
An example of a radio button in a form.

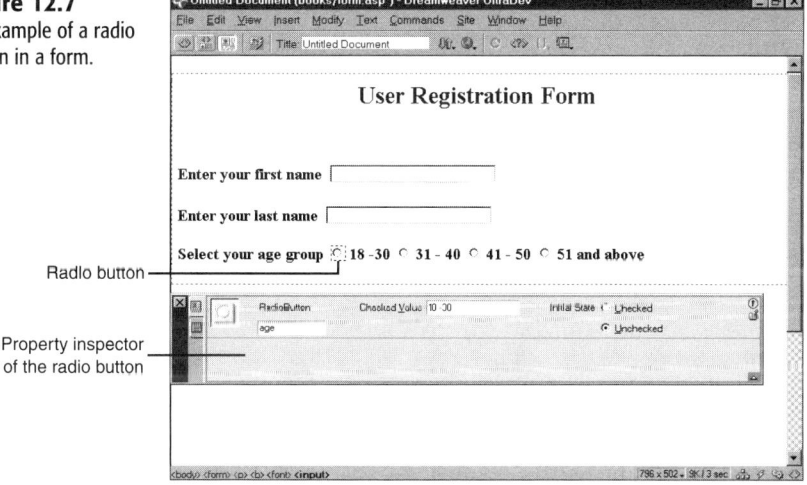

Radio button

Property inspector of the radio button

To insert a radio button, follow these steps:

1. Choose Insert, Form Objects, Radio Button or click the Insert Radio Button icon in the Forms category of the Objects panel. You can also click and drag the Insert Radio Button icon to insert a radio button into the inserted form. A radio button is created in your document, and the radio button's Property inspector is displayed, as shown in Figure 12.7.

2. Type a unique name for the button in the RadioButton field. This name is sent to the server side application for processing.

3. In the Checked Value field, type the value you want to send to the server-side application when a user selects this radio button.

4. The Initial State field has two options: Checked and Unchecked. Select the Checked option if you want the radio button to be selected the first time the user visits the form. The Unchecked option is selected by default.

INSERTING A FORM BUTTON

Any button in a form other than a radio button or an image button is called a form button.

To insert a form button, follow these steps:

1. Choose Insert, Form Objects, Button or click Insert Button icon in the Forms Category of the Objects panel. You can also click and drag the Insert Button icon to insert a form button into the inserted form. A Submit button is created in your document, and the form button's Property inspector is displayed, as shown in Figure 12.8.

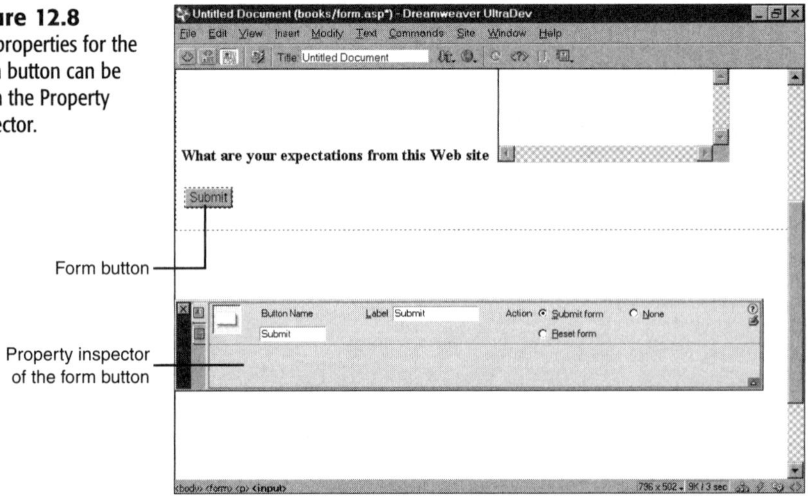

Figure 12.8
The properties for the Form button can be set in the Property inspector.

Form button

Property inspector of the form button

2. Type a unique name for the button in the Button Name field. This name is sent to the server for processing. The most commonly used names for form buttons are Submit and Reset. Submit is the default button.

3. Type the text you want to display on the button in the Label field. Label is the prompt displayed on the button for user reference.

WORKING WITH FORM OBJECTS   247

4. Select one of the three radio buttons in the Action field: Submit form, Reset form, or None. The user selects the Submit form option to submit the form for processing. The user selects the Reset form option to reset the form when the button is clicked. The user selects the None option to activate a different action based on the processing—for example, to calculate the difference between the final value and the initial value entered in the form field. To do such processing tasks, client-side scripts are used.

UltraDev generates the following code for a form button whose name is Submit, whose label is Click to submit, and whose action is Submit form:

```
input type="submit" name="submit" value="Click to submit">
```

INSERTING AN IMAGE BUTTON

The Insert Image Field icon in the Forms category of the Objects panel lets you insert images within a form. If you want a visually appealing Submit button, you can use the Insert Image Field icon to insert an image field. You can also use the image fields as image buttons to let a user perform tasks such as resetting a form or playing an audio file.

If you want an image button to perform any task other than submitting data, you must attach a behavior to this button.

→ To learn more about attaching a behavior to an object, **see** "Adding Client-Side Behaviors," **p. 267**.

To insert a graphical Submit button, follow these steps:

1. Choose Insert, Form Objects, Image Field or click the Insert Image Field icon in the Forms category of the Objects panel to insert an image button. The Select Image Source window is displayed.

2. Select an image for the button, and click OK. An image field is added to your form, and the image field's Property inspector is displayed, as shown in Figure 12.9.

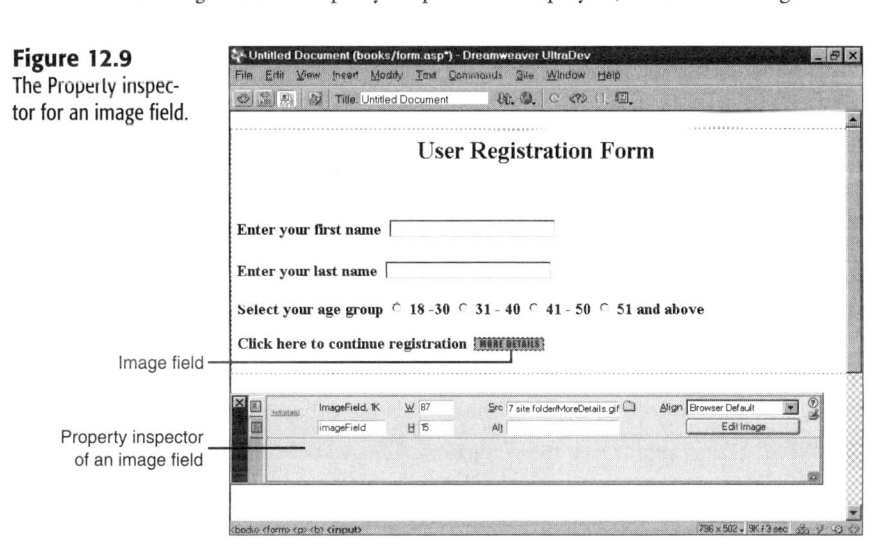

Figure 12.9
The Property inspector for an image field.

Image field

Property inspector of an image field

3. Type the name for the image button in the ImageField, 1K field.
4. The W and H field displays the width and height of the inserted image field. If you want to change the width and height of the image, type the width and height you want in the W and H fields.
5. In the Src field, click the folder icon to browse and find the image you want to insert in the page. The Src field also lets you select an image for the button.
6. For text-only browsers, you can type the text you want to display in place of the image in the Alt field of the Property inspector.

INSERTING A CHECK BOX

A check box can be used in a form when the user can choose more than one option from the list of options displayed.

Follow these steps to insert a check box:

1. Choose Insert, Form Objects, Check Box or click the Insert Checkbox icon in the Forms category of the Objects panel to insert a checkbox. A check box is added to the form, and the check box's Property inspector is displayed, as shown in Figure 12.10.

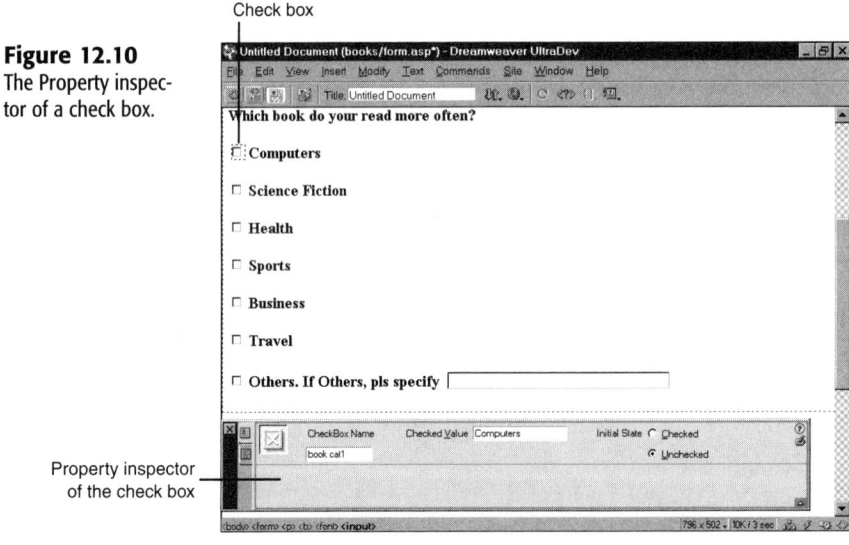

Figure 12.10
The Property inspector of a check box.

2. Type a name for your check box in the CheckBox field.
3. Type the value for the check box in the Checked Value field. This value will be sent to the server-side application when the user selects this radio button.
4. The Initial State field contains two radio buttons: Checked and Unchecked. Select the Checked radio button if you want your check box to be selected by default when the form loads in the browser. The Unchecked radio button is the default value.

Adding Menus and Lists

It is a good practice to add a list or menu to your form if you have many similar options or items to be displayed in limited space. The List/Menu option in Dreamweaver UltraDev lets you create a drop-down list or a scrolling list that can include several options in limited space.

To add a list to a form, follow these steps:

1. Choose Insert, Form Objects, List/Menu or click the Insert List/Menu icon in the Forms category of the Objects panel. A list/menu is added to your form. The list/menu's Property inspector is displayed, as shown in Figure 12.11.

Figure 12.11
The Property inspector of the list/menu.

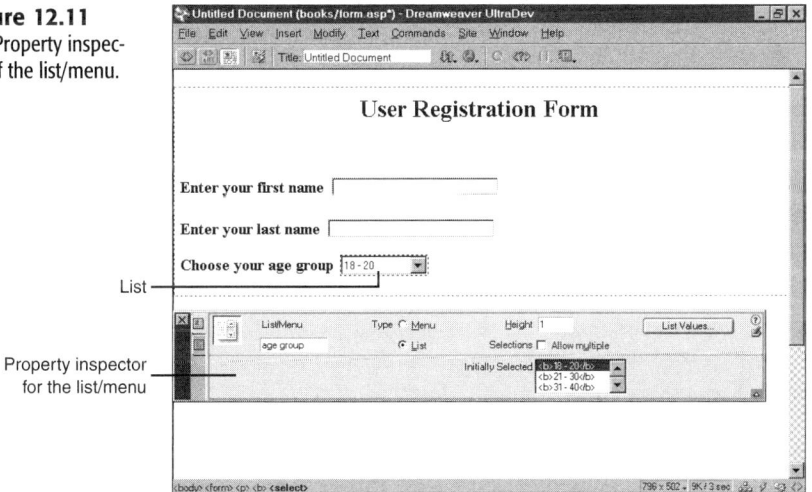

2. Type a name for your list in the List/Menu field. Each list/menu in the form must have a unique name.
3. You can select either the List or Menu radio button, depending on what you want to add. Select the List radio button to add a list to the form.
4. Type a number in the Height field to specify the number of lines in your list. The default height is 4.
5. Sometimes, a user might want to select more than one option from the list. In such cases, to allow the user to select more than one option from the list, check the Allow multiple check box.
6. Click List Values to add items to your list. The List Values dialog box is displayed, as shown in Figure 12.12.

Figure 12.12
The List Values dialog box contains an Item Label field and a Value field.

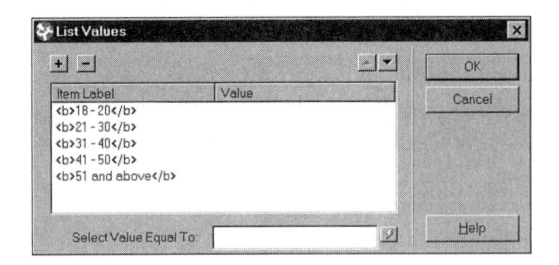

7. Type the items that you want to add to your list in the Item Label field in the List Values dialog box. When you are finished entering the items, type the values for the items in the Value field. Depending on which item is selected, respective values are sent to the server. If you do not include a value, the item labels are used as values.
8. Click the + button to add a new item to the list. Click the – button to delete an item from the list.
9. Click OK to close the List Value dialog box. This takes you back to the list's Property inspector.
10. If you want to display a specific item as selected, specify the name of the item in the Initially Selected field.

Processing Forms on the Server Side

Typically, a Common Gateway Interface (CGI) application, JavaServer Page (JSP), Active Server Page (ASP), or ColdFusion (CF) page processes form information, and the response is sent to the user.

Processing Forms Using ASP

When a Web browser or other client application asks for a page from a Web server, this is called making a request. When the browser makes a request to the server, it not only sends data supplied by the user, but it also sends some additional information. This information can be form data or header data.

The Request object is an ASP object that reads the form field values entered by the user.

→ To learn more about the methods and collections of the Request object in ASP, **see** "The Request Object" **p. 67**.

The Response object sends processed information to the browser. It decides when and how the results should be sent to the browser. The four main methods of the Response object are Buffer, Write, Redirect, and Expiration.

→ To learn more about the methods and properties of the Response object in ASP, **see** "The Response Object" **p. 65**.

Form information can be sent to the server using two methods: GET and POST. To read form data, the ASP page uses the Request object.

Consider the example of a user login form in which the user enters his first name and age, as shown in Figure 12.13.

Figure 12.13
An example of the user login form.

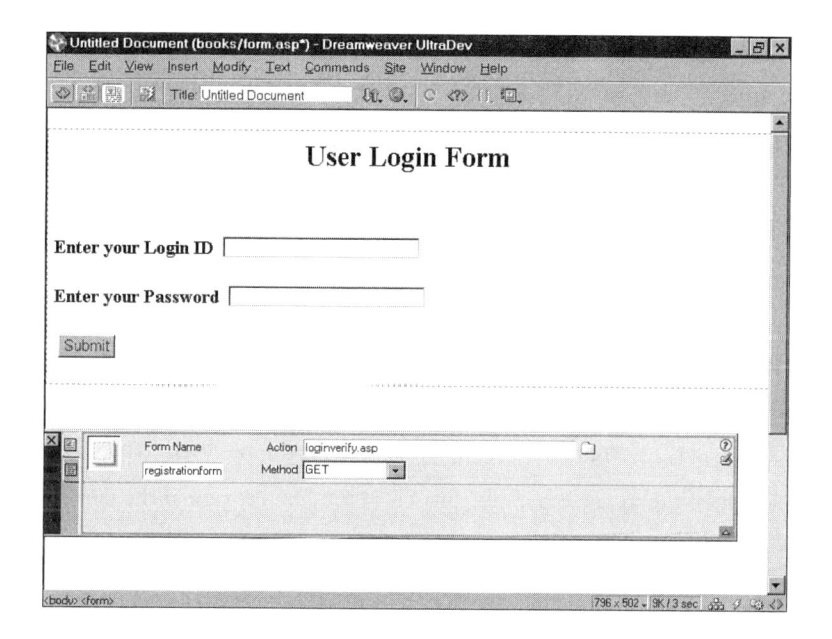

The information that the user enters is submitted through a form on the HTML page. The User Login Form contains two text fields: fname and age. It also contains a Submit button. It is very important to specify the URL to the application in the Action field of the form's Property inspector, as shown in Figure 12.13.

In this example, specify the path to the ASP page, loginverify.asp, in the Action field of the Property inspector of the user login form. Also select the POST method in the Method field.

After the user clicks the Submit button, the browser sends a request to the Web server, indicating that the server should look to the loginverify.asp page, which contains instructions detailing how the user input will be processed. This loginverify.asp code demonstrates the use of the Request and Response object. The ASP code reads the username from the text field, fname. This page contains an ASP code that processes the information and sends the response to the user in HTML format.

ASP uses its Form collection to pass the username and age. The Request.Form command checks to see whether the fname that the user entered is equal to Don Allen. Response.Write displays a welcoming message if the fname is Don Allen. Otherwise, it displays the message No, you are not Authorized. The code in loginverify.asp is shown in Listing 12.1.

LISTING 12.1 THE Request AND Response OBJECTS

```
If Request.Form("fname")="Don Allen" then
        Response.Write ("Hello " & Request.Form("fname") & "!")
        Response.Write ("<h1><u><b>Welcome to our Web page</h1><u></b>")
Else
        Response.Write("<h1><u> <b>No, you are not Authorized</h1></u></b>")
End If
```

SUMMARY

In this chapter, you learned how to create a form in a document. You also learned how to insert form objects, such as text fields, radio buttons, check boxes, lists, and menus. Furthermore, you learned how to set properties for form objects. In addition, you learned how to process forms using the Form collections in ASP.

ACTIVITY CORNER

In this section, you will create the form that allows users to search for songs based on either a composer or song name. To design this form, follow these steps:

1. Open the Sidebar.asp file. Switch to the Layout view if the current view is the Standard view.
2. In the layout table that you have created in the Sidebar.asp file, insert a layout cell after the cell that contains the text Search.
3. Select the inserted cell and set its height to 140 pixels and width to 129 pixels by using the Property inspector.
4. Click inside the cell and select the Forms category from the Objects panel. Click the Insert Form button in the Objects panel.
5. After the form is inserted, type the text **Keyword** and set the font type of the text to Verdana, font size to 1, and color to #CCCCCC by using the Property inspector.
6. Place the cursor after this text and click the Insert Text Field button in the Objects.
7. Select the inserted text field and type **Searchstring** in the Text Field text box in the Property inspector. Type **12** in the Char Width text box.
8. Select the Characters category from the Objects panel and click the Insert Line Break button on the Objects panel. Enable the Invisible Elements option in the View menu to make the line break element visible.
9. Next to the line break, type the text **Select**. Insert a line break after this text.
10. Place the cursor after the line break and select the Forms category from the Objects panel. Click the Insert List/Menu button in the Objects panel.
11. Select the list/menu and select the List option in the Property inspector.
12. Type **selection** in the List/Menu text box in the Property inspector. Type **1** in the Height text box.

13. Click the List Values button in the Property inspector.
14. In the List Values dialog box that is displayed, click the + button. In the Item Label column, type **Composer**. To enter the second value in the list, click the + button again. Type **Album** in the text box that appears in the Item Label column.
15. Click OK to close the List Values dialog box.
16. Next, you need to insert a Go button, which the user must click to submit the form.
17. Place the cursor next to the list item and click the Insert Button icon on the Objects panel. The form button is inserted at the cursor position.
18. Select the form button and type **Go** in the Label text box of the Property inspector.
19. Select the Submit Form option on the Property inspector.
20. Select the form by clicking the <form> tag on the status bar.
21. In the Property inspector of the form, type **Searchform** in the Form Name text box. In the Action text box, type **/Songresults/search.asp**.
22. Select the POST option from the Method drop-down list.

The design of this form is complete. To add the search capability to this form, you need to add more functionality to the form. The steps for completing the search feature will be discussed in the "Activity Corner" section of Chapter 20.

CHAPTER 13

ADDING MULTIMEDIA EFFECTS TO A WEB PAGE

In this chapter

Adding Flash, Generator, and Shockwave Media   256

Adding Fireworks Images to a Page   261

Adding Sound Effects to a Page   264

Inserting ActiveX Controls and Java Applets   266

Adding Client-Side Behaviors   267

Troubleshooting   280

Summary   281

Activity Corner   281

Adding Flash, Generator, and Shockwave Media

In UltraDev, you can create dynamic multimedia content by adding audio and animation effects to your document. You can insert Flash and Shockwave movies, import Generator templates, edit Fireworks graphics, and embed audio files in your document. You can attach client-side behaviors to different page elements, making your Web page interesting and interactive.

To render media files, most browsers require special software known as *plug-ins*. A number of plug-ins on the market help browsers render multimedia content. Plug-ins such as RealPlayer and Windows Media Player allow a browser to play sound files, and you can watch Flash movies using Flash Player. Although some browsers support certain plug-ins, others do not. For example, Internet Explorer does not support all the plug-ins supported by Netscape Navigator.

UltraDev has built-in support for Flash Player and Shockwave Player, with which you can preview Flash and Shockwave content in your documents. You can also add ActiveX controls to your document to view multimedia content in an ActiveX-enabled browser such as Internet Explorer.

Adding Flash Objects to a Document

With Macromedia Flash, you can create *vector-based graphics*. Vector-based graphics download fast and possess high-quality resolution. UltraDev has built-in Flash text and objects that can be customized and added to your page without the need to create them in the Flash authoring environment. To play Flash files, you need the Flash Player plug-in that is available as a Netscape Navigator plug-in and an ActiveX control for Microsoft Internet Explorer.

Files created in Flash can have an extension of .fla, .swf, or .swt. A .fla file can be neither inserted into a document in UltraDev nor viewed in a browser. Therefore, when you create Flash files to insert into an UltraDev document, you need to save them as .swf files. For example, when you create Flash text and button objects to insert into an UltraDev document, you need to save them as .swf files.

In UltraDev, you can add Flash text, button objects, and Flash movies to your document using the Objects panel. You need to click the Insert Flash Text button in the Objects panel to insert a Flash text object in your document. This text object can have text with customized colors and rollover effects. You can also add a link to the Flash text. When you click the Insert Flash Text button in the Objects panel, the Insert Flash Text dialog box is displayed, as shown in Figure 13.1.

Caution Before you can insert Flash text or buttons, you need to save the current document.

ADDING FLASH, GENERATOR, AND SHOCKWAVE MEDIA | 257

Figure 13.1
The Insert Flash Text dialog box lets you customize Flash text by setting the font size, color, rollover color, and background color.

To create a Flash text, follow these steps:

1. In the Insert Flash Text dialog box, select the font type from the Font drop-down list. Type the text in the Text text box. To preview the font type you have set, select the Show Font check box.

2. Select the color of the text by either using the color picker or typing a hexadecimal value in the Color text box. Select a rollover color from the Rollover Color text box. The rollover color that you set will be the color of the text when the mouse pointer points to it.

3. You can also set a background color for the Flash text by choosing a color from the color picker next to the Bg Color text box. This draws a border around the flash text and fills the empty spaces between the text and the border with the background color.

4. To save the Flash text object that you have created as an .swf file, type a name for the text object in the Save As text box.

5. You can attach a link to the Flash text by specifying the URL of the target document in the Link text box.

6. To specify where the target document will be loaded, choose an option from the Target drop-down list text box.

PART
III
CH
13

Note
When you specify the path of the target document in the Link text box, do not use a root-relative path. Use either an absolute path or a document-relative path. When you use a document-relative path, save the Flash file in the same directory as the HTML document to which the Flash file contains a link.

258 CHAPTER 13 ADDING MULTIMEDIA EFFECTS TO A WEB PAGE

To insert a Flash button object, click Insert Flash Button in the Objects panel. The Insert Flash Button dialog box is displayed, as shown in Figure 13.2.

Figure 13.2
Select predefined button styles or download more styles from Macromedia Exchange by using this dialog box.

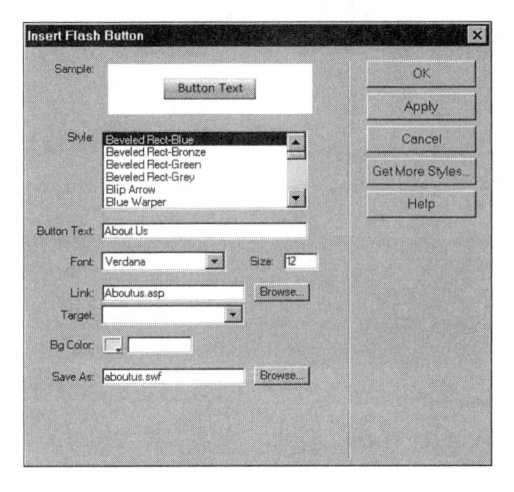

Select the desired button style from the Style drop-down list, and preview it in the Sample area. You can specify properties of the button object, such as the text that will appear on the button, the link to be attached to the text, and the background color of the button, by selecting the appropriate options in the dialog box. Click the Apply button to apply the selected properties to the Flash button object. To download more Flash button styles, click the Get More Styles button.

The rules for saving a Flash text object and for specifying the path of the target document while creating a link also apply to the Flash button object.

When you insert Flash content into a document, UltraDev automatically inserts the `<object>` and `<embed>` tags to make your document cross-browser compatible. The `<object>` tag implants the Flash Player ActiveX control for Internet Explorer, and the `<embed>` tag associates the Flash Player plug-in for Netscape Navigator.

To insert a Flash movie into your document, click Insert Flash in the Objects panel. The Select File dialog box is displayed, as shown in Figure 13.3. Select either the File system option or the Data Sources option to display Flash files.

SETTING PROPERTIES OF FLASH OBJECTS

You can set properties of Flash objects by using the Property inspector. Figure 13.4 shows the Property inspector for a Flash button. Table 13.1 lists the options that are available here.

> **Tip**
> To change the properties of the Flash object by using the dialog box that was displayed when you first created the object, double-click the object.

ADDING FLASH, GENERATOR, AND SHOCKWAVE MEDIA | 259

Figure 13.3
Browse through the folders to select the Flash movie of your choice.

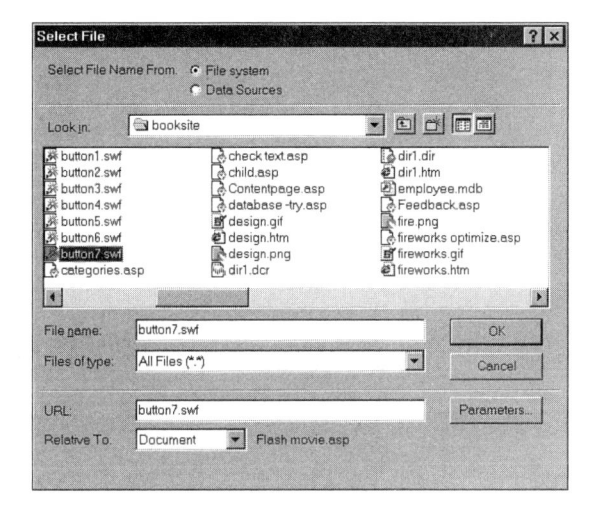

Figure 13.4
Click the Play button in the Property inspector to preview the Flash object in Design view.

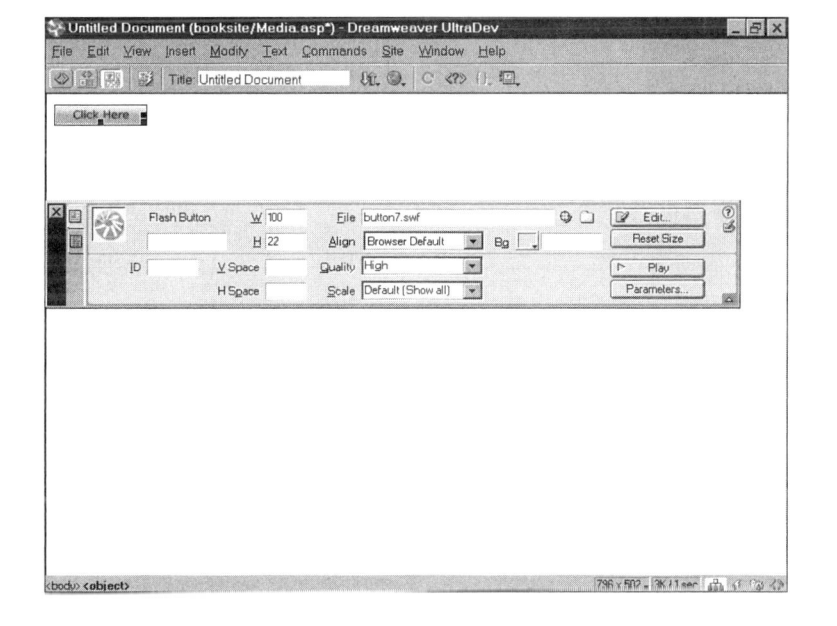

TABLE 13.1   THE PROPERTY INSPECTOR OPTIONS

Option	Usage
The Flash Button text box	Specifies a name for the object.
The W and H text boxes	Specify the width and height of the Flash object in units such as pixels, points, and inches or as a percentage of the parent object.
The Align drop-down list	Aligns the Flash object to the top, middle, bottom, left, or right of the browser screen.

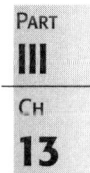

CHAPTER 13 ADDING MULTIMEDIA EFFECTS TO A WEB PAGE

TABLE 13.1 CONTINUED

Option	Usage
The File text box	You can select a Flash button to replace the existing one by specifying the name of the required Flash file in the File text box or by using the folder icon to browse to the file.
The Bg text box and color-picker	You can change the background color of the Flash object by using the color-picker or by typing a hexadecimal value in this text box.
The Edit button	You can edit the Flash object by clicking this button.
The Reset Size button	If you changed the width or height of the Flash object, you can reset its dimensions to the original width and height by clicking the Reset Size button.
The ID text box	You can define an optional ActiveX ID for the Flash object in this text box. This ID is used in scripts to pass information between ActiveX controls.
The V Space and H Space text boxes	Specify the dimensions of the white space around the Flash object in pixels.
The Quality drop-down list	You can give preference to the Flash object's quality of appearance over speed of rendering, or vice versa, by selecting an option from this drop-down list.
The Scale drop-down list	You can specify how the Flash object is displayed within its boundaries defined by the width and height values in the W and H text boxes by selecting an option from this drop-down list.
The Play/Stop buttons	You can preview the Flash object in Design view by clicking the Play button. Click Stop to end the preview.
The Parameters button	You can specify additional parameters for the Flash object using this button.

The Property inspector of a Flash movie has two more options: Autoplay and Loop. The Autoplay check box lets you start playing the Flash movie automatically when the page loads. The Loop check box lets you play the movie indefinitely.

Adding Shockwave Media to a Web Page

Multimedia Web content created in Macromedia Director can be compressed using Macromedia Shockwave for deployment on the Web. Files compressed using Shockwave have .dcr extensions. To play Shockwave movies, you need to have Shockwave Player, which is available as a Netscape Navigator plug-in as well as an ActiveX control for Internet Explorer.

To insert a Shockwave movie, click the Shockwave button in the Objects panel. The Select File dialog box that is displayed is similar to the one that is displayed when you insert a Flash movie. The properties you set for a Shockwave movie are similar to the ones you set for a Flash movie.

Adding Generator Objects to a Web Page

You can use Generator objects to dynamically create Flash movies or images. You can add generator objects created in Flash 4.0 or 5.0 with Generator authoring templates to a document in UltraDev by using the Objects panel.

To insert a Generator object into your document, click the Generator button in the Objects panel. The Insert Generator dialog box is displayed, as shown in Figure 13.5.

Figure 13.5
Specify a Generator template to dynamically create Flash movies.

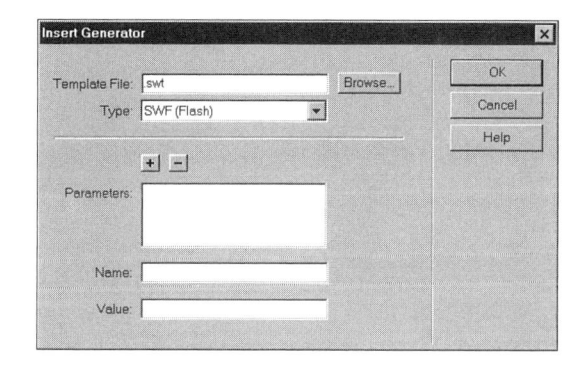

Specify the template file that you want to use in the Template File text box of the Insert Generator dialog box. Select the type of file by choosing an option from the Type drop-down list. You can add parameters to the object by clicking the + button. Specify the name and value for a parameter in the Name and Value text boxes, respectively.

Adding Fireworks Images to a Page

Fireworks 4.0, the solution from Macromedia for developing graphics for the Web, is integrated with UltraDev to allow designers to work on graphics files interchangeably in both environments.

Integration of Fireworks with UltraDev allows you to edit Fireworks files placed in UltraDev by starting Fireworks directly from UltraDev. However, before you can launch Fireworks from UltraDev, you need to first install Fireworks in your system.

Both UltraDev and Fireworks recognize and preserve the HTML generated by the other. Fireworks files have the .png extension. These files can be exported as HTML files and placed in your site's root folder. You can open the .png source file in Fireworks, edit it, and update the corresponding HTML file placed in UltraDev. Fireworks and UltraDev recognize and share the changes made to links, image maps, and table slices in a file.

Inserting Fireworks Files in UltraDev

To be able to insert a Fireworks file into UltraDev, you must first export the file as an HTML file from Fireworks to UltraDev. To do this, choose File, Export in Fireworks. The Export dialog box appears, as shown in Figure 13.6.

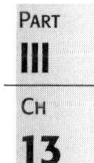

Figure 13.6
You can export the HTML file generated by Fireworks to the desired site folder.

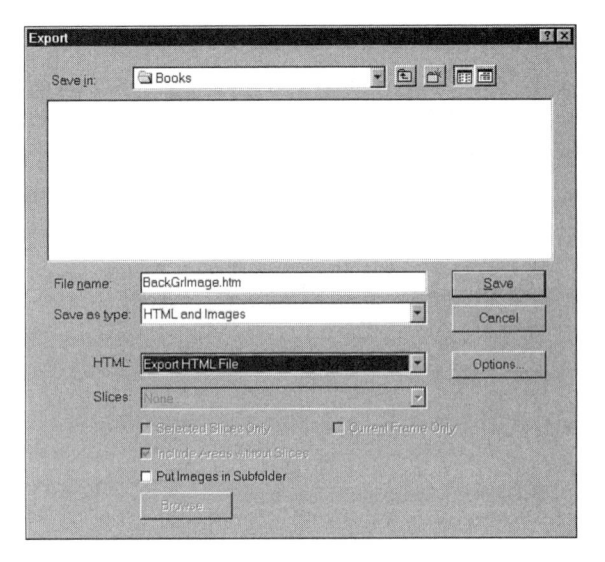

In the Export dialog box, select HTML and Images from the Save as type drop-down list to save the .png file as an HTML file. Select Export HTML File from the HTML drop-down list, and then click Save. The HTML file is saved and can now be opened in UltraDev.

> **Note**
> To export a Fireworks file as an UltraDev library item, select the Dreamweaver Library (.lbi) option from the Save as Type drop-down list in the Export dialog box.

To insert a Fireworks-generated HTML file in UltraDev, choose Insert, Interactive Images, Fireworks HTML. In the Insert Fireworks HTML File dialog box that is displayed, browse to the Fireworks HTML file that you exported from Fireworks. Select the file, and then click OK. You can select the Delete File After Insertion check box to delete the HTML file after inserting. Deleting the HTML file does not delete the source .png file created in Fireworks.

You can also copy Fireworks HTML code and paste it in UltraDev. To do this, choose Edit, Copy HTML Code in Fireworks. This displays a wizard that guides you in copying the images and HTML. For information on using the wizard, refer to the Help menu in Fireworks. After you complete the steps in the wizard, the HTML code is copied to the Clipboard. You can paste this HTML code in UltraDev by choosing Edit, Paste HTML.

EDITING FIREWORKS FILES PLACED IN ULTRADEV

To be able to edit Fireworks files placed in UltraDev, you must designate Fireworks as the primary external image editor. To edit a Fireworks image or table, select the desired Fireworks image or table in UltraDev and choose Windows, Properties. The Property inspector that is displayed recognizes the selected Fireworks image or table and displays the name of the source file in the Image text box. Click the Edit button on the Property inspector to start Fireworks.

After editing the image or table, click the Done button in the document window to return to the UltraDev editing environment.

> **Tip**
>
> If you are working on a source .png file in Fireworks and you want to update the corresponding Fireworks HTML file in UltraDev, choose File, Update HTML in Fireworks.

To optimize a Fireworks image by changing its file type, animation settings, size, and the areas within the image, select the image and choose Commands, Optimize Image in Fireworks.

To change the format of the file and optimize the image in UltraDev, click the Options tab of the Export Preview dialog box. To edit the size and area of the image or to export a selected area of the image, select the File tab. To edit and preview animation frames for the image, click the Animation tab. For help on using the options in these tabs, refer to the Help menu in Fireworks.

CREATING A WEB PHOTO ALBUM BY USING FIREWORKS

You can use Fireworks to create a photo album in UltraDev. The Create Web Photo Album option on the Commands menu in UltraDev lets you do this. This option uses JavaScript that calls Fireworks to create a photo album for the Web. Fireworks creates a thumbnail and a large-sized image for each image in the photo album.

Before you create a photo album, place all the images you want to use for the album in a single folder. To create the album, follow these steps:

1. Choose Commands, Create Web Photo Album. The Create Web Photo Album dialog box is displayed, as shown in Figure 13.7.

Figure 13.7
Specify the folder containing the images, and the album gets created automatically.

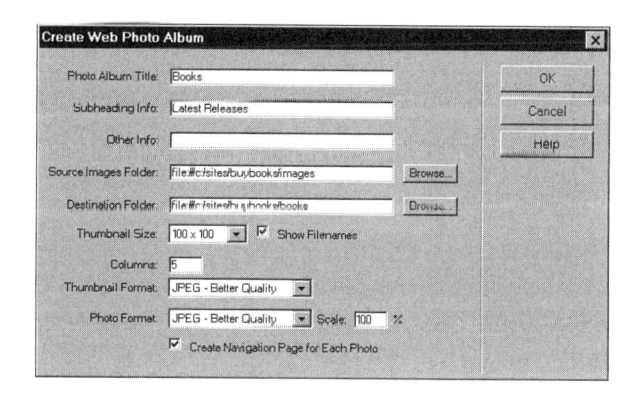

2. Enter a title for the photo album in the Photo Album Title text box. You can enter additional lines of text that will appear beneath the title on your photo album in the Subheading Info and Other Info text boxes.

3. Specify the folder that contains the images in the Source Images Folder text box.
4. Specify the destination folder where the completed album must be placed in the Destination Folder text box. It is better if this destination folder does not already contain a photo album. If it does, creating another photo album might overwrite images that have the same names as the ones used to create the new album.
5. Choose a size for the thumbnail image by selecting an option from the Thumbnail Size drop-down list. If you want to display the name of the image file below each image in the album, select the Show Filenames check box.
6. Specify the number of thumbnail images per row of the album in the Columns text box.
7. Choose the quality of the thumbnail images by selecting the desired format from the Thumbnail Format drop-down list. Select a format for the large-size images by selecting the desired option from the Photo Format drop-down list.
8. Set the scaling percentage of the images to 100% in the Scale text box to produce images that are the same size as the originals. Select the Create Navigation Page for Each Photo checkbox to create navigation links for each photo.
9. Click OK to complete the process.

After you complete the process, Fireworks creates the thumbnail images and the larger-size images. When Fireworks completes the processing, UltraDev creates the Web page containing the Web photo album and displays a dialog box that says "Album Created." Click OK to view the photo album.

Adding Sound Effects to a Page

Adding sound effects to a Web page certainly enhances the page's appeal. However, sound needs to be used with discretion, because it has its inherent drawbacks. Sound effects can sometimes be distracting and might not appeal to everybody's tastes. Audio files take a long time to download, and most audio file formats require a plug-in to be installed. Moreover, different browsers handle audio files differently, resulting in inconsistencies in sound quality.

There are ways to overcome the problems associated with audio files. The problem of slow downloads can be addressed by compression and streaming techniques. Using compression formats such as MPEG (Motion Picture Experts Group) and AIFF (Apple Audio Interchange File Format) results in smaller file sizes that download faster than uncompressed formats. *Streaming* is a technique that allows playback of sound even before the file is completely downloaded. When you use nonstreaming audio, the sound file must download completely before it can start playing. However, when you use streaming audio, the sound player that comes with the browser starts playing the sound even before the file is completely downloaded.

Different audio file formats are available that have different features and requirements. Formats such as .midi (Musical Instrument Digital Interface), .aif (Audio Interchange File Format), and .wav (Waveform Extension) are uncompressed formats that do not require a plug-in to be installed on the browser. However, file formats such as .mp3 (MPEG formats) and .ra (RealAudio formats) are compressed formats that can be streamed. These formats require a plug-in such as QuickTime or Windows Media Player to be able to play them.

To add sound to a page, you can either create a link to a sound file or embed it in a document. Creating a link to a sound file gives users a choice to play sound or not. Embedded audio files can be played only if the required plug-in is present on the user's machine. It is a good idea to link to sound files rather than embed them, because not every browser might have plug-ins installed.

To link to sound files, you can use the Property inspector to create the link. Select the required audio file to which you want to create a link by using the folder icon. Alternatively, you can type the name of the file in the Link text box of the Property inspector.

To embed audio files, click the Insert Plugin button in the Special category of the Objects panel. The Select File dialog box is displayed, and you can select the required audio file by browsing to it.

After you select the file, the plug-in placeholder appears on the document, as shown in Figure 13.8. This placeholder will be replaced by audio controls when the document is viewed in the browser. The audio controls that will appear in the browser occupy more space than the size of the placeholder in Design view. Adjust the width and height of the plug-in placeholder in the Property inspector so that the audio controls are fully visible on the browser screen. To preview the audio controls that will appear in the browser, click the Play button on the Property inspector.

Figure 13.8
Set properties for the plug-in by using the Property inspector.

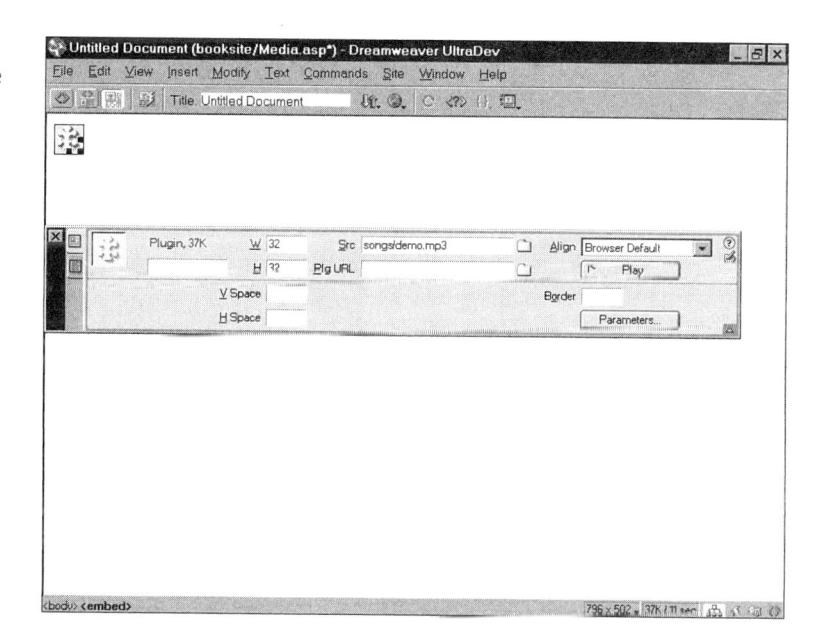

If the plug-in that is required to play the audio file is not installed on the user's machine, you can specify the URL from where the browser can automatically download the plug-in in the Plg URL text box of the Property inspector.

INSERTING ACTIVEX CONTROLS AND JAVA APPLETS

ActiveX controls provide support to an ActiveX-enabled Web browser such as Internet Explorer to play media files much the same way plug-ins provide support to Netscape Navigator. However, ActiveX controls can be used for purposes other than just providing plug-in support to a browser. They can be used to extend the functionality of a Web browser by using any programming language that supports the OLE standard.

If your Web site uses media objects, such as Shockwave files, that need to be viewed in Internet Explorer or any other ActiveX-enabled browser, you need to specify the ActiveX control that must be available on the browser. When you insert an ActiveX object into your document, you need to specify information that tells the browser which ActiveX control is needed to play this object.

To insert an ActiveX object, select the Special category from the Objects panel, and click the ActiveX button. The ActiveX object is displayed in Design view, as shown in Figure 13.9. Open the Property inspector to define the properties for the ActiveX object.

Figure 13.9
Select any type of ActiveX control by using the Property inspector.

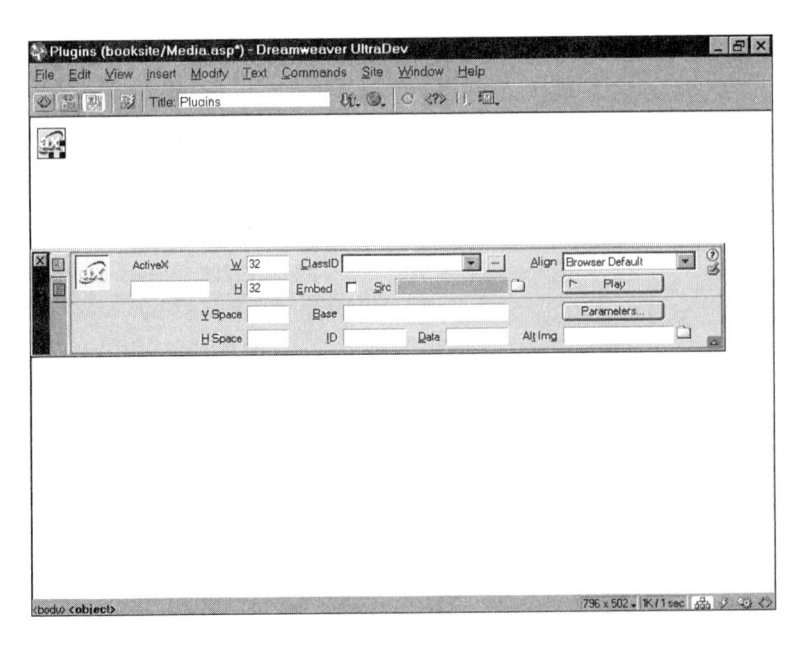

When you insert an ActiveX object into your document, UltraDev automatically detects the ActiveX controls installed on your system. These controls are displayed in the ClassID drop-down list in the Property inspector. Select from this list the ActiveX control that is required to play the inserted ActiveX object. After you select the ActiveX control, the properties in the Property inspector change to reflect the properties of the chosen ActiveX control. In the Base text box, specify the URL that the browser should use to download ActiveX controls in case they are not already installed.

When an ActiveX control is inserted, UltraDev inserts the `<object>` tag in the HTML code. Not all browsers support the `<object>` tag. Therefore, in the Alt Img text box, specify an alternate image that will be displayed. Select the appropriate parameters required for the ActiveX control by clicking the Parameters button. Every ActiveX control comes with a set of predefined parameters. The documentation about the control specifies the parameters that affect the control.

Embedding Java Applets

Java applets are programs written in Java that run within Web pages or in a Java environment. You can embed Java applets within your page by using the Objects panel. To embed a Java applet, select the Special category from the Objects panel and click the Insert Applet button. In the Insert Applet dialog box that is displayed, select the file that contains the Java applet.

You can set properties for an inserted applet by using the Property inspector. Specify a name for the applet in the Applet text box of the Property inspector. The Code text box displays the name of the file that contains the applet. You can click the folder icon to change the file. You can set the applet's width and height by specifying values in the W and H text boxes. The Base text box contains the name of the folder that contains the applet file. You can specify parameters to the applet by clicking the Parameters button.

Adding Client-Side Behaviors

Client-side behaviors make a Web page interactive and dynamic, without having to submit the page to the server. Behaviors allow you to display status messages on the status bar and let users control movies and timeline animations and drag and drop layers. You can also use behaviors to redirect users to a different URL after performing plug-in and browser checks. UltraDev comes with many prewritten *JavaScript* functions that let you add client-side behaviors to your page easily.

→ To learn more about JavaScript functions, **see** "JavaScript Reference," **p. 544**.

Behaviors in UltraDev

The behavior of a Web page is a function of an action performed by a user. When a user performs an action on the browser, such as requesting a Web page, pointing to an image, clicking an image, or stopping a page download, the browser generates an *event*. This event calls a JavaScript function that implements a behavior, such as opening a new browser window, changing an object's property, displaying messages in a dialog box, and so on.

UltraDev saves you from the tedium of writing browser-compatible JavaScript code to implement behaviors. Writing browser-compatible code for every browser is difficult, because the JavaScript implementation on each browser is different. However, by using UltraDev, all you need to do is specify the version of the browser in which you want to use behaviors, and the corresponding browser-specific JavaScript code is generated automatically.

Different browsers generate different events. For example, while Netscape Navigator 4.0 generates the onKeyUp event, Internet Explorer does not. Different versions of a browser support different events. For example, Internet Explorer 5.0 supports a number of events compared to its earlier versions.

Attaching a Behavior

You can attach behaviors to page elements, such as layers, images, text, timelines, and form elements. In addition, you can attach a behavior to an entire document. To attach a behavior, you need to specify both the event and the action that should be performed when the event occurs. For example, if you want to display a status message when a page loads, you must specify the onLoad event and the Set Text of Status Bar action for the event. You can attach a number of actions to a particular event, and you can choose the order in which these actions will occur.

To attach a behavior to a page element, select the element and choose Windows, Behaviors. To attach a behavior to an entire document, select the <body> tag from the Tag selector on the status bar and choose Windows, Behaviors. When you choose Windows, Behaviors, the Behaviors panel is displayed.

From the Behaviors panel, select the action that you want to attach to the element by clicking the + button in the panel. This displays the Actions pop-up menu, from which you can select the desired action. Figure 13.10 shows the actions in the Behaviors panel that are enabled when a layer is selected in the document. Table 13.2 displays a list of the predefined actions available in UltraDev.

Note Not all actions can be applied to all page elements. In Figure 13.10, you can see that some actions are disabled for the layer element.

ADDING CLIENT-SIDE BEHAVIORS | 269

Figure 13.10
Select the action and the event that you want to associate with the page element.

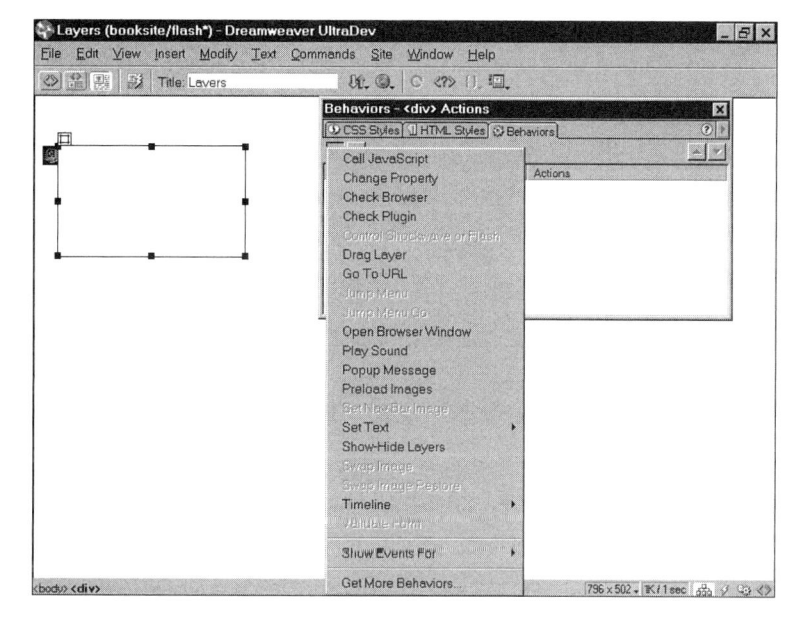

TABLE 13.2 PREDEFINED ACTIONS IN ULTRADEV

Action Name	Description
Call JavaScript	Calls a JavaScript function or code to perform customized functions.
Change Property	Changes the property of an image, form, or layer on your document. The properties of the objects that can be modified by this action are browser-specific.
Check Browser	Checks for the browser type and version. If you have developed different versions of your Web page in order to be browser-compatible, you can send visitors to a page that is supported by the browser type they use.
Check Plugin	Checks whether a plug-in is installed on the browser. It redirects visitors to a different page if they do not have the required plug-in installed on their browser.

PART
III
CH
13

Table 13.2 Continued

Action Name	Description
Control Shockwave or Flash	Lets users play, stop, rewind, or go to a particular frame of a Shockwave or Flash movie.
Drag Layer	Creates movable screen elements by manipulating layers.
Go To URL	Opens a new page in the current window or a specific frame.
Jump Menu	Modifies a jump menu.
Jump Menu Go	Adds a Go button to a jump menu.
Open Browser Window	Opens a page in a new browser window.
Play Sound	Plays sound when a page loads or upon user initiation.
Popup Message	Displays a message box. You can specify a message text or embed a JavaScript function call or expression in this message box.
Preload Images	Loads images that appear on a page after the user initiates. Images that will be swapped in rollover images and timelines can be preloaded into the browser cache with this action.
Set Nav Bar Image	Modifies the display and action of an image in a navigation bar. You can change an existing image into a navigation bar image by using this action.
Set Text of Layer, Set Text of Frame, Set Text of Status	Dynamically sets the text of a layer, a frame, or the status bar.
Show-Hide Layers	Dynamically changes the visibility of layers.
Swap Image	Swaps an image to create rollover effects.
Swap Image Restore	Restores the last swapped image to its original source file.
Play Timeline and Stop Timeline	Lets users control timeline animations.
Validate Form	Validates user entries in a text field on a form.

You can select a browser version for your Web site by choosing the Show Events For option from the Actions menu. Depending on which browser version you select, the events that are available to you will vary. Table 13.3 lists and describes these events.

> **Note**
> Not all events are applicable to all page elements. You might find some events disabled even after you select a browser version. This is because the disabled events are not applicable to the currently selected element.

TABLE 13.3 EVENTS AND THEIR DESCRIPTIONS

Event	Description	Supported by Browser Type and Version
onAbort	This event is generated when the user stops the page from loading.	Netscape Navigator 3.0 and 4.0 and Internet Explorer 4.0 and 5.0
onAfterUpdate	This event is generated after a data element on a page has updated a data source.	Internet Explorer 4.0 and 5.0
onBeforeUpdate	This event is generated when a data element on a page has been changed and is about to update a data source.	Internet Explorer 4.0 and 5.0
onBlur	This event is generated when an element on a page has lost focus.	Netscape Navigator 3.0 and 4.0 and Internet Explorer 3.0, 4.0, and 5.0
onChange	This event is generated when the user changes a value in a page element and then clicks elsewhere on the page.	Netscape Navigator 3.0 and 4.0 and Internet Explorer 3.0, 4.0, and 5.0
onClick	This event is generated when the user clicks a page element.	Netscape Navigator 3.0 and 4.0 and Internet Explorer 3.0, 4.0, and 5.0
onDblClick	This event is generated when the user double-clicks a page element.	Netscape Navigator 4.0 and Internet Explorer 4.0 and 5.0
onError	This event is generated when an error occurs while a page or an image is being loaded.	Netscape Navigator 3.0 and 4.0 and Internet Explorer 4.0 and 5.0
onFocus	This event is generated when a page element gets the user's attention. For example, when a user clicks a text field on a form, this event is generated.	Netscape Navigator 3.0 and 4.0 and Internet Explorer 3.0, 4.0, and 5.0
onHelp	This event is generated when the user clicks the Help button.	Internet Explorer 4.0 and 5.0
onKeyDown	This event is generated when the user presses a key.	Netscape Navigator 4.0 and Internet Explorer 4.0 and 5.0
onKeyUp	This event is generated when the user releases a key after pressing it.	Netscape Navigator 4.0 and Internet Explorer 4.0 and 5.0
onKeyPress	This event is generated when the user presses and releases a key. This event is a combination of the onKeyDown and onKeyUp events.	Netscape Navigator 4.0 and Internet Explorer 4.0 and 5.0
onLoad	This event is generated when a page or image has finished loading.	Netscape Navigator 3.0 and 4.0 and Internet Explorer 3.0, 4.0, and 5.0

Table 13.3 Continued

Event	Description	Supported by Browser Type and Version
onMouseDown	This event is generated when the user presses the mouse button.	Netscape Navigator 4.0 and Internet Explorer 4.0 and 5.0
onMouseMove	This event is generated when the user moves the mouse while pointing to a page element.	Internet Explorer 3.0, 4.0, and 5.0
onMouseOut	This event is generated when the user moves the mouse from one element to point to some other element.	Netscape Navigator 3.0 and 4.0 and Internet Explorer 4.0 and 5.0
onMouseOver	This event is generated when the user points to an element.	Netscape Navigator 3.0 and 4.0 and Internet Explorer 3.0, 4.0, and 5.0
onMouseUp	This event is generated when the user releases the mouse button.	Netscape Navigator 4.0 and Internet Explorer 4.0 and 5.0
onMove	This event is generated when the user moves a window or frame.	Netscape Navigator 4.0
onReadyStateChange	This event is generated when a page element changes states such as uninitialized, loading, and complete.	Internet Explorer 4.0 and 5.0
onReset	This event is generated when the user resets the values in a form.	Netscape Navigator 3.0 and 4.0 and Internet Explorer 3.0, 4.0, and 5.0
onResize	This event is generated when the user resizes a window or frame.	Netscape Navigator 4.0 and Internet Explorer 4.0 and 5.0
onRowEnter	This event is generated when the record pointer in a bound data source changes to point to a row.	Internet Explorer 4.0 and 5.0
onRowExit	This event is generated when the record pointer of a bound data source is about to move to the next row.	Internet Explorer 4.0 and 5.0
onScroll	This event is generated when the user uses the scrollbars to scroll up and down the page.	Internet Explorer 4.0 and 5.0
onSelect	This event is generated when the user selects text in a text field.	Netscape Navigator 3.0 and 4.0 and Internet Explorer 3.0, 4.0, and 5.0
onSubmit	This event is generated when the user submits a form.	Netscape Navigator 3.0 and 4.0 and Internet Explorer 3.0, 4.0, and 5.0
onUnload	This event is generated when the user exits the page.	Netscape Navigator 3.0 and 4.0 and Internet Explorer 3.0, 4.0, and 5.0

ATTACHING A BEHAVIOR TO A LINK

You can attach behaviors to a link to display status messages on the status bar or open a link's target in a new browser window. The Set Text of Status Bar action and the Open Browser Window action are used to perform these actions, respectively.

To attach the Set Text of Status Bar action to a link, follow these steps:

1. Select the link to which you want to attach a behavior.
2. Choose Windows, Behaviors.
3. In the Behaviors panel that is displayed, click the + button to display the Actions pop-up menu.
4. From the Actions pop-up menu, select Set Text, Set Text of Status Bar.
5. In the Set Text of Status Bar dialog box, specify the text that you want to be displayed on the status bar.
6. The default event that triggers the selected action is displayed in the Events drop-down list. Ensure that this event is onMouseOver. If this event is not displayed by default, click the downward-pointing black arrow that appears next to the event name. The Events drop-down list is displayed, as shown in Figure 13.11. Select the onMouseOver option from it.

Figure 13.11
Select the event that you want from the Events drop-down list.

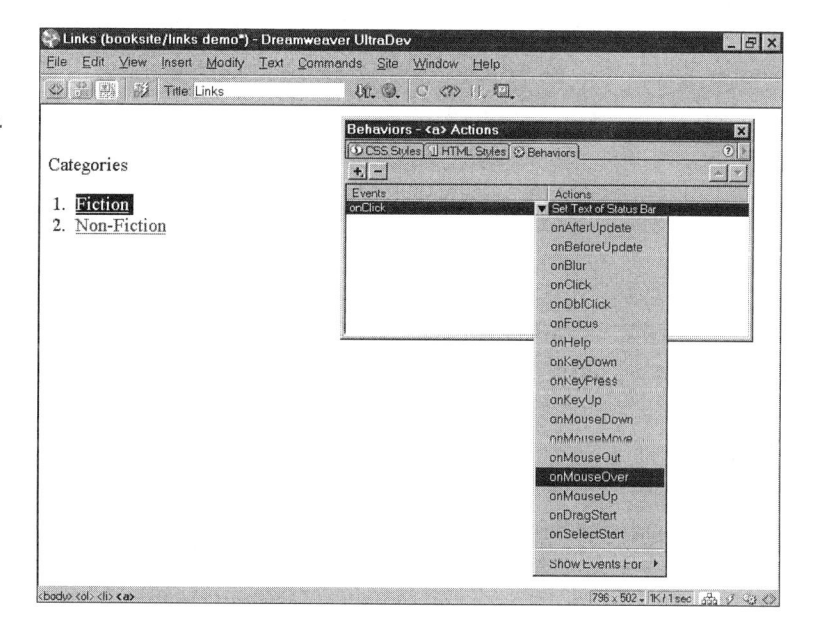

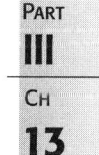

7. Repeat steps 3 through 5 and specify the text that will appear when the mouse pointer is not on the link.
8. Select the onMouseOut event for this action. The Behaviors panel looks like the one shown in Figure 13.12 after the steps have been completed.

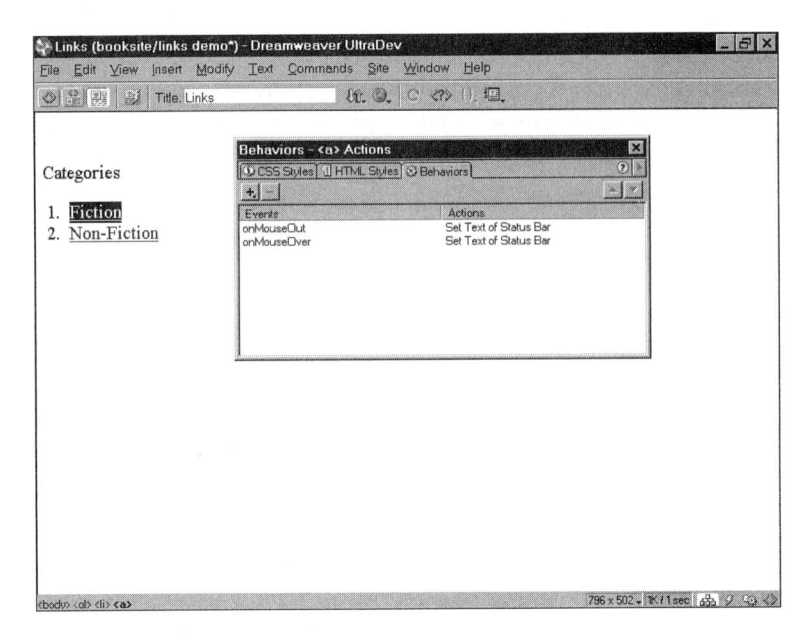

Figure 13.12
This sequence of events displays dynamic messages on the status bar.

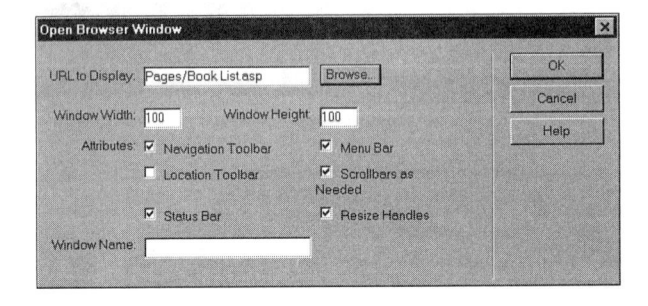

Figure 13.13
Set properties for the new browser window in which you want to open the target document.

THE OPEN BROWSER WINDOW ACTION   When a user clicks a link, you can open the target document in a new browser window using the Open Browser Window action. When you select this option, the Open Browser Window dialog box is displayed, as shown in Figure 13.13.

You can specify the height and width of the new window by using the Open Browser Window dialog box. In addition, you can choose to add the navigation toolbar, the menu bar, the location bar, and the status bar, and resize handles to the new window. You can also give the window a name in case you want to use it as the target window for other links or use the window name in JavaScript functions that you define.

> **Note**
> While visiting sites, you might have come across situations in which, when you access a particular site, new browser windows displaying other related sites open automatically. This is done using the Open Browser Window action with the `onLoad` event attached to the `<body>` tag of the loaded page.

ATTACHING A BEHAVIOR TO AN IMAGE

You can attach behaviors to images to create rollover effects, navigation bars, and jump menu items. You can attach almost any behavior to images, but behaviors such as Swap Image, Swap Image Restore, and Preload Images are applicable only to images. The Swap Image and Swap Image Restore behaviors are used to create rollover effects, and the Preload Images action is used to preload images that appear on the browser only after an event is generated.

To create rollover effects using the Swap Image and Swap Image Restore actions, the Swap Image action must be associated with the `onMouseOver` event, and the Swap Image Restore action must be associated with the `onMouseOut` event.

When you select the Swap Image action from the Actions pop-up menu, the Swap Image dialog box is displayed. In the Swap Image dialog box, select the Preload Images option to load the swap image even before it is actually displayed on the page. Selecting this option speeds up the swap effect by reducing the delay that is caused while the image is downloaded after the `onMouseOut` event occurs. If you select this option, you do not have to again select the Preload Images action from the Actions pop-up menu. In the Swap Image dialog box is another option called Swap Images on MouseOut. Selecting this option is the same as choosing the Swap Restore Image option from the Actions pop-up menu. You can swap more than one image at a time by using the Swap Image action.

You can convert an image into a navigation bar image by using the Set Nav Bar action. If you already have a navigation bar, you can use the Set Nav Bar action to modify the navigation bar.

ATTACHING A BEHAVIOR TO A LAYER

You can attach behaviors to layers to give the user the flexibility to drag and drop elements on the page, selectively show information when the user selects an element, and create other interesting effects such as movable page elements. You can add behaviors to timelines to give users control over playing and stopping timelines.

THE DRAG LAYER ACTION The Drag Layer action is used to drag elements on a page to a specified position on the screen. You can use this action to create simple puzzles and drag-and-drop controls. To create a movable element on a page, first you need to create a layer and then insert an element into the layer.

To insert a Drag Layer action, follow these steps:

1. Select the layer and then select the Drag Layer action from the Actions pop-up menu. The Drag Layer dialog box is displayed, as shown in Figure 13.14.

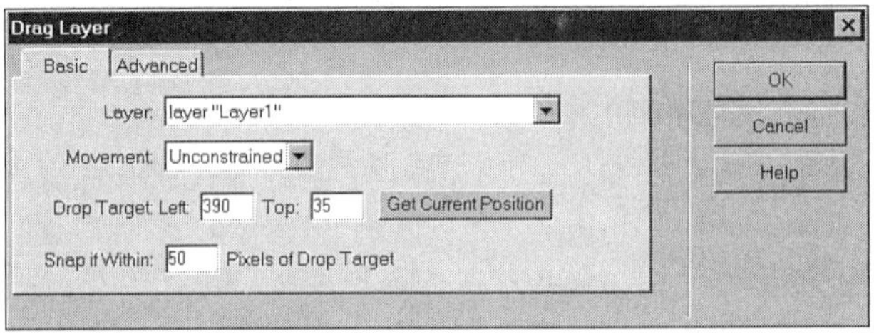

Figure 13.14
Use the Drag Layer action to control the movement of layers on the screen.

2. In the Drag Layer dialog box, select the layer you want to drag from the Layer drop-down list.
3. Specify whether the movement of the layer should be constrained or unconstrained by choosing the appropriate option from the Movement drop-down list. If you want the user to drag the layer to any part of the screen, choose the Unconstrained option, as shown in Figure 13.14. If you want the layer to be dragged in only a specified direction, choose the Constrained option and enter positive values in pixels in the appropriate Up, Down, Left, or Right field. These values are relative to the layer's starting position. For example, to enable only vertical movement, enter 0 in the Left and Right text boxes and enter positive values in the Up and Down text boxes.
4. Specify the destination of the dragged layer in the Drop Target text box. The pixel values that you enter in the Left and Top text boxes will be values at which the layer reaches its destination. These pixel values are relative to the top-left corner of the browser window.

> **Tip**
> You can also specify the target of the dragged layer by placing the layer in the desired position before selecting the Drag Layer action. Then, you can click Get Current Position in the Drag Layer dialog box to set the pixel values automatically.

5. In the Snap if Within: Pixels of Drop Target text box, specify a value in pixels to cause the layer to snap to the target if it is within a certain number of pixels from the target.
6. Click the Advanced tab to specify more properties for the Drag Layer action.
7. To allow the user to drag the layer by using a specific area within the layer, specify the coordinates of that drag area by choosing Area within Layer from the Drag Handle drop-down list. Enter the width, height, and the top and left coordinates of the drag area. Choose the Entire Layer option if you want the user to drag the layer by using any part of the layer.

8. While dragging the layer, you can allow the user to bring the layer to the front of the stacking order while it is being dragged by selecting the Bring to Front check box. While leaving the layer in its destination, you can choose to leave it on top of the stacking order or restore it to its original position in the stacking order by selecting the appropriate option from the drop-down list.

9. To execute a JavaScript code or function as long as the layer is being dragged, enter the JavaScript code or function name in the Call JavaScript text box. You can display messages indicating the user's proximity to the destination in games by using this feature. To execute a JavaScript code when the layer reaches its drop target, enter the name of the function or code in the When Dropped:Call JavaScript text box, and select the Only if Snapped check box.

After you have finished entering the desired properties, check to see if the event is the one you want. It is better to specify an event that will be executed before the user actually starts dragging the layer. For this, choose the onClick or onMouseOver event.

Note
You can attach the Drag Layer action to the <body> tag or to an element within a layer. Use the onLoad event if you are attaching the action to the <body> tag, and use the onMouseOver or onClick events if you are attaching the action to an element within the layer.

THE SHOW-HIDE LAYERS ACTION   The Show-Hide Layers action can be used to show or hide layers when the user interacts with a page. You can also use it to show selected information on a page and simulate ToolTips.

You might have often come across a screen showing a message such as "Loading Page" while the page downloads. Then the screen disappears after the page has fully downloaded. This is achieved by means of a layer that is created to fully cover the page. This layer is made visible before the page downloads and is made invisible as soon as the page is fully loaded.

To attach the Show-Hide action to a layer, select the element to which you want to attach the Show-Hide action. Click the + button in the Behaviors panel and select the Show-Hide Layers action. The Show-Hide Layers dialog box is displayed, as shown in Figure 13.15. Select the layer you want to show or hide, and then click the Show button or the Hide button.

Figure 13.15
Use the Show-Hide Layer behavior to dynamically control the visibility of layers.

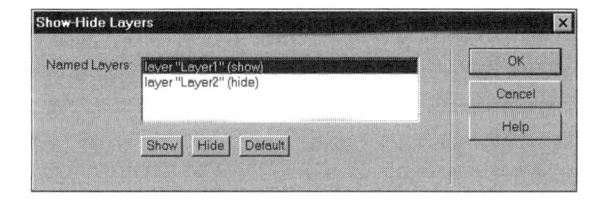

278 | CHAPTER 13   ADDING MULTIMEDIA EFFECTS TO A WEB PAGE

> **Tip**
>
> To make the Show-Hide Layers action work well, you need to attach the appropriate event to this action. For example, to show a layer when the user points to an image, select the image and then attach the Show-Hide Layers action to the onMouseOver event. To display a message while a page loads and to hide the message after the page loads fully, attach the Show-Hide Layers action to the <body> tag and make sure the event is onLoad. The text for this message should be created within a layer that should be made invisible after the page loads.

THE CHANGE PROPERTY ACTION   You can change a layer's properties, such as the background color, visibility, height, and width, by using the Change Property action. If you are familiar with HTML or JavaScript, you can use this action to change a layer's properties. When you select the Change Property action, the Change Property dialog box is displayed, as shown in Figure 13.16.

Figure 13.16
You can change properties of images and form fields apart from layers.

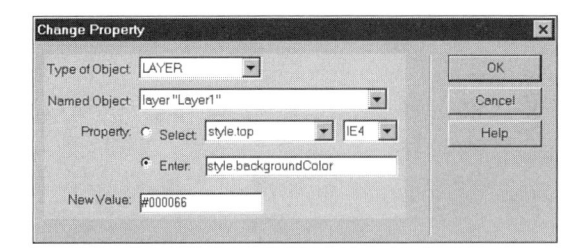

Select the Type of Object drop-down list in the Change Property dialog box to choose the Layer option. In the Named Object drop-down list, choose the name of the layer for which you want to change the property. Select a property by selecting an option from the Select drop-down list, or enter a property name in the Enter text box. You can enter a value for the selected property in the New Value text box.

> **Tip**
>
> If the Select drop-down list in the Change Property dialog box does not display any options, it could be because of the currently selected object or the browser version you have selected. Change the browser version by selecting an option from the drop-down list that is next to the Select drop-down list.

THE SET TEXT OF LAYER ACTION   To change a layer's content dynamically, use the Set Text of Layer action. This replaces the layer's existing content with the content you specified using HTML code or a JavaScript function call. Choose the Set Text, Set Text of Layer option from the Actions pop-up menu. In the Set Text of Layer dialog box that is displayed, select the layer from the Layer drop-down list, and specify the HTML code or the JavaScript function call in the New HTML text box.

> **Note**
> When you use this action, layer attributes such as width and height change only so much to fit the replaced content size. This action does not change layer attributes such as background color or background image.

ATTACHING A BEHAVIOR TO A FORM

You can attach a behavior to a form to validate the values entered by the user or to specify default values for form fields. Two form-specific behaviors are available for this purpose: Validate Form and Set Text of Text Field.

> **Note**
> These behaviors can be attached to only a text field of the form.

To attach the Validate Form behavior to a text field, select the text field and then select the Validate Form action from the Actions pop-up menu. The Validate Form dialog box is displayed, as shown in Figure 13.17.

Figure 13.17
Validate numeric data and e-mail addresses by using this dialog box.

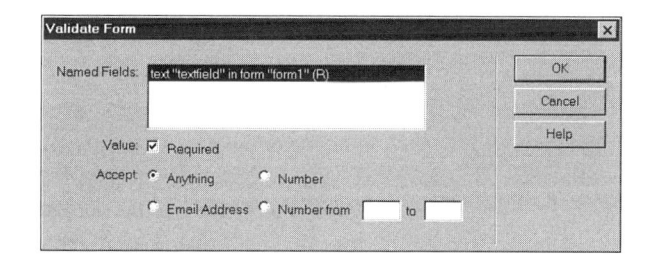

You can select the required text field you want from the Named Fields text box. Select the Required check box if you want the text field to compulsorily contain a value. You can set the text field to accept any value by selecting the Anything option. If you select the Number option, the behavior checks that only numbers are entered in this field. Selecting the Email Address option checks for the presence of the @ symbol in the address. You can also specify the range of numbers that must be entered by giving a range in the Number from and to text boxes. After you close the Validate Form dialog box, ensure that the onBlur or onChange event is selected in the Events drop-down list in the Behaviors panel.

> **Tip**
> You can validate multiple text fields by selecting the <Form> tag and then selecting the Validate Form action. Ensure that this action is associated with the onSubmit event.

You can use the Set Text of Text Field behavior to replace the content of a text field with the text you specify. To do this, choose Set Text, Set Text of Text Field from the Actions pop-up menu. In the Set Text of Text Field dialog box that is displayed, select the text field whose content you want to change from the Text Field drop-down list, and then enter the replacement text in the New Text text box. This content will appear in the text field when an event, such as `onMouseOver`, occurs.

Attaching a Behavior to a Media File

You can add behaviors to your page to let users control media objects. You can use the Control Shockwave or Flash action to let users play or stop a movie. Before attaching this behavior, make sure the movie that you want to control is already present in the document. Insert a form button or an image to indicate the play and stop buttons. Select the button or image, and then click the + button in the Behaviors panel to select the Control Shockwave or Flash action from the Actions pop-up menu.

In the Control Shockwave or Flash dialog box that is displayed, select the movie that you want to control. Then select any of the four options that are displayed in the dialog box to let the user play, stop, rewind, or go to a particular frame.

> **Caution**
> You must create a named movie before you attach this behavior. UltraDev will not allow you to attach the behavior to an unnamed movie.

You can attach the Play Sound behavior to your document by selecting an audio file that is needed to play the sound. Select the Play Sound action from the Actions pop-up menu. The Play Sound dialog box is displayed. You can use it to browse to the required audio file. Attach this behavior to the `onLoad` or `onClick` events.

Troubleshooting

Inserting ActiveX Objects

I can't preview the ActiveX Control in Design View.

While inserting ActiveX controls or plug-ins, sometimes you might not be able to preview the ActiveX object in Design view. Check `UnsupportedPlugins.txt` in the Configuration/Plugins folder to see if it contains an entry about the plug-in or ActiveX control not supported by UltraDev.

Even if you cannot preview the plug-in or ActiveX object in Design view, you can play the object if you preview it in the browser by choosing File, Preview in Browser. If the object does not play in the browser either, install the required plug-in or ActiveX control on your machine.

Summary

This chapter covered some of the important components of a Web page that make it interactive: media and behaviors. You can add media such as Flash and Shockwave movies, Generator objects, Fireworks images, and audio files to a Web page in UltraDev. This chapter also dealt with adding ActiveX controls, plug-ins, and Java applets to a Web page.

You can add behaviors to a Web page to add client-side dynamism to the page. UltraDev implements behaviors by means of prewritten JavaScript code that is generated when you add these behaviors to the page. To add behaviors to a Web page, use the Behaviors panel. This panel lists the actions and events that are used to attach behaviors to a Web page. You can create browser-specific behaviors by choosing the appropriate browser version from the Actions pop-up menu of the Behaviors panel.

Activity Corner

In this section, you will insert Flash buttons into the `Navigation.asp` file. You will then link each of these buttons to a target file. Follow these steps:

1. Open the `Navigation.asp` file.
2. Insert a layer in the `Navigation.asp` file.
3. Select the layer and enter **432x**, **41px**, **301px**, and **23px** in the L, T, W, and H text boxes of the Property inspector, respectively. The Layer ID for this layer is Layer1 by default.
4. Insert a Flash button into Layer1 by choosing Insert, Interactive Images, Flash Button.
5. In the Insert Flash Button dialog box, select the Glass-Silver option from the Style drop-down list.
6. In the Button Text text box, type **About Us**. Select Verdana from the Font drop-down list and specify **12** in the Size text box. Specify **#0033GG** in the Bg text box.
7. In the Link text box, specify the target file as **Aboutus.htm**.
8. Type **Aboutus.swf** in the Save As text box to save the button.
9. Repeat steps 4[nd]6 to insert five more Flash buttons inside Layer1. The labels for these five buttons must be Login, Register, My Profile, My CD, and Help, respectively. The About Us, Login, and Register buttons must appear in one row, whereas the My Profile, My CD, and Help buttons must appear in the next row.
10. The Login button must link to the file `Login.asp` that is in the folder Userdetails. Specify the path to the `Login.asp` file as `\Userdetails\Login.asp` in the Link text box of the Insert Flash Button dialog box of the Login button. Save this button as `\Userdetails\Loginuser.swf`.
11. The Register button must link to the file `Register.asp` that is in the folder Userdetails. Specify the path to the `Register.asp` file as `\Userdetails\Register.asp` in the Link text box. Save this button as `\Userdetails\Register.swf`.

12. When you create the button named My Profile, specify `\Userdetails\Editprofile.asp` in the Link text box of the Insert Flash Button dialog box and save the button as `\Userdetails\Myprofile.swf`. For the My CD button, specify ViewCD in the Link text box and save the button as `Mycd.swf`. For the Help button, specify the `Help.asp` file and save the button as `Help.swf`.

After creating these buttons, open the `Musichome.asp` file. You can now see the `Navigation.asp` file loaded in the top frame with all the buttons you just created. Double-click each button to display the Insert Flash Button dialog box. In this dialog box, select the mainFrame option from the Target drop-down list for every button so that each button loads the target file to which it links in the main frame of the `Musichome.asp` file. Preview the `Musichome.asp` file by launching it from the `Start.htm` file.

COMPLETING THE `Navigation.asp` FILE

The `Musichome.asp` file does not provide you with an option to close the browser window. Therefore, to allow users to close the browser window, you need to attach a Call Javascript behavior to an image. To do this, insert a layer at the top right corner of the `Navigation.asp` file. The Layer ID for this layer is Layer2 by default. Copy the `close.jpg` image to your local folder and insert the image within Layer2. Next, you need to attach the Call Javascript behavior to this image so that when the user clicks the image, the browser window closes. To attach this behavior, perform the following steps:

1. Select the image and choose Window, Behaviors to open the Behaviors panel.
2. Click the + button on the Behaviors panel. Select the Call Javascript option from the pop-up menu.
3. In the Call Javascript dialog box that is displayed, type **window.top.close()** in the Javascript text box.
4. Click OK to close the dialog box.
5. Select the `onClick` event from the Events drop-down list.

Save the `Navigation.asp` file and preview the `Start.htm` file to check whether the behavior works.

CHAPTER 14

Optimizing Your Work

In this chapter

Managing Your Assets   284

The History Panel   289

Templates and Libraries   291

Troubleshooting   297

Summary   297

Activity Corner   297

Managing Your Assets

Assets are elements, such as images, movies, colors, scripts, templates, and library items that are used a site's documents. You can organize and manage these assets by using the Assets panel. The Assets panel is a central location where all the assets in your site are pooled. Finding and editing your site assets in the Assets panel is faster and easier than browsing through folders in the Site window.

The Assets Panel

To display the Assets panel, shown in Figure 14.1, choose Window, Assets.

The Assets panel contains the following categories:

- Images: This category contains image files, such as .gif, .jpeg, or .png files, used across documents in your site.
- Colors: This category contains the colors used in documents and the style sheets used across the documents in your site.
- URLs: This category contains all the links, including script and e-mail links, used across the documents in your site.
- Flash: This category contains all the Flash movies, Flash text, and Flash buttons used across the documents in your site.

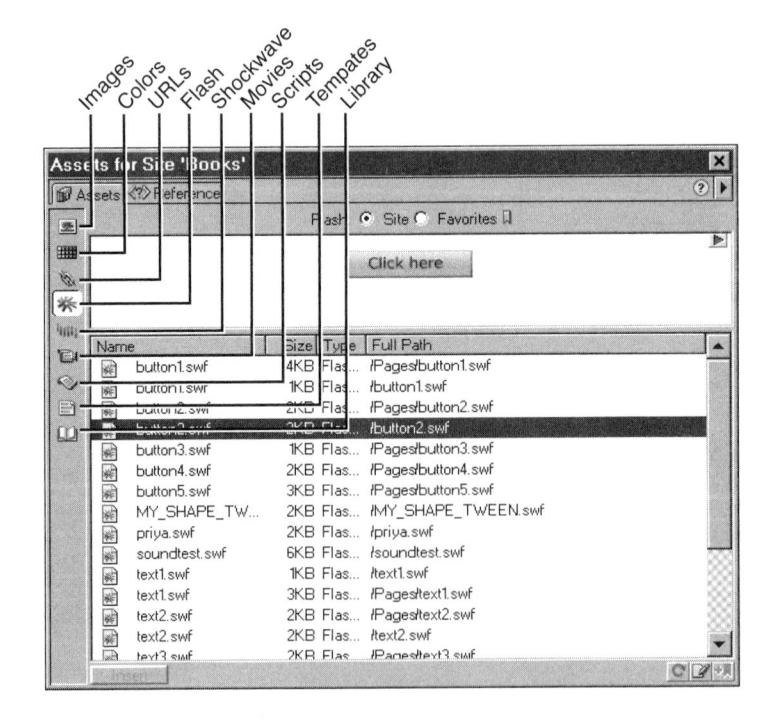

Figure 14.1
Use the categories in the Assets panel to view the assets in your site.

- Shockwave: This category contains all the Shockwave movies used across the documents in your site.
- Movies: This category contains all the movie files, other than Shockwave and Flash, used across documents in your site.
- Scripts: This category contains all the VBScript or JavaScript files used across the documents in your site. Scripts that are embedded within HTML code are not stored in this category.
- Templates: This category contains all the templates used in your site.
- Library: This category contains all the library items in your site. Library items are discussed in the section "Working with Library Items."

USING THE ASSETS PANEL

The Assets panel can display either all the assets in your site or only the selected assets. The Site list of the Assets panel displays all the assets of your site. The Favorites list of the Assets panel displays the selected assets of your site. Although you can view all the assets in your site in the Site list, you can add and organize frequently used assets in the Favorites list. To view all the assets in your site, select the Site option located at the top of the Assets panel. To view the assets in the Favorites list, select the Favorites option, located next to the Site option.

> **Note**
> You can use the Assets panel only if you create a site cache. This is because the Assets panel adds all the assets in the site to the Site list by reading from the site cache. Therefore, you need to ensure that a site cache is created before you use the Assets panel.

To view the assets in a particular category, click the desired category icon in the Assets panel. Figure 14.2 shows the assets that are in the Flash category of the Assets panel. You can select an asset to preview it in the preview area, located below the Site and Favorites options. Figure 14.2 shows the preview of a Flash button in the Assets panel.

If an asset, such as an image or a Flash button, is created within a session, it is not automatically added to the Assets panel. You need to refresh the Assets panel to view the newly created asset. To refresh the Assets panel, click the Refresh Site List button, located at the bottom of the Assets panel. If you do not add the assets to the Assets panel manually, they get added automatically the next time you open the document in UltraDev.

To add an asset to a document, first select the category icon in which the asset is present. Select the asset and drag it to the location where you want it to appear. Alternatively, you can place the insertion point in the document, select the asset from the Assets panel, an click the Insert button [Insert] located at the bottom of the Assets panel..

Figure 14.2
Use the Assets panel to create assets and edit them, too.

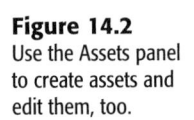

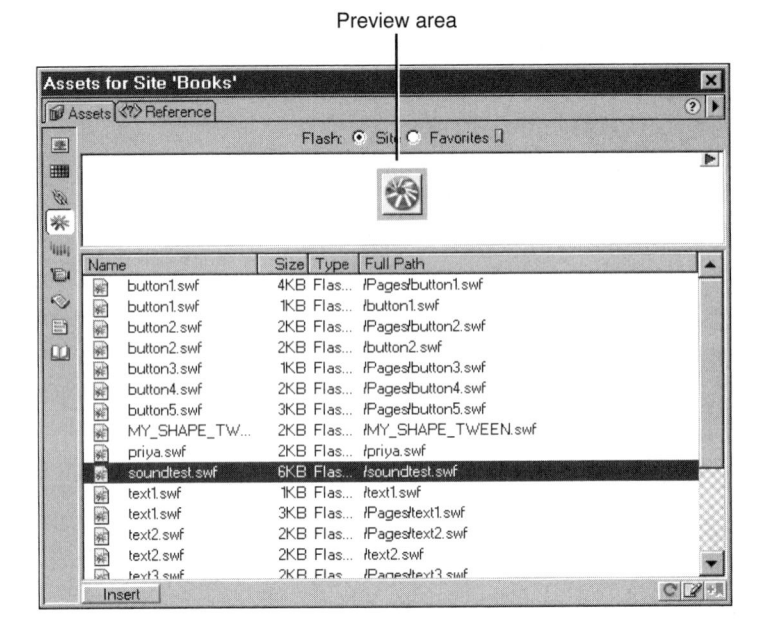

Adding Assets to the Favorites List

When the number of assets on a site becomes large, it becomes difficult to manage them. Grouping frequently used assets and adding them to the Favorites list helps you locate and manage assets easily. Using the Favorites list, you can perform activities that cannot be done in the Site list, such as giving assets nicknames; creating favorites folders colors, URLs, templates, or library items; and editing assets.

To add an asset from the Site list to the Favorites list, select the asset and click the Add to Favorites button ![] located at the bottom of the Assets panel. Click the Favorites option located at the top of the Assets panel to check whether the asset was added to the Favorites list.

> **Note** You cannot add templates and library items to the Favorites list.

Creating Nicknames for Your Assets

You can give descriptive nicknames to your assets in the Favorites list. These nicknames help you identify assets easily. To give a nickname to a favorite asset, select the asset and click after a pause. Type a nickname for the asset in the editing area that appears in place of the asset's name, and press Enter. The nickname is displayed in the Nickname column.

A nickname does not replace the asset's filename. It merely signifies a description of the asset to help you identify it easily.

> **Note**
> You cannot give nicknames to the assets in the Site list.

Within the Favorites list, you can group related assets into folders. These folders do not map to the actual location of the asset files. To create Favorites folders, click the New Favorites Folder button that appears at the bottom of the Assets panel and type the name of the folder in the edit area that appears in the Nickname column. To add an asset to this new folder, drag the asset to the folder. To add multiple assets to a Favorites folder, select a consecutive set of assets by holding down the Shift key, and then drag them to the folder.

CREATING ASSETS IN THE FAVORITES LIST

You can create new colors, URLs, templates, and library items by using the Assets panel. You can create these new assets in the Favorites list but not in the Site list. To create a new color, select a color from the list in the Colors category and click the New Color button located at the bottom of the Assets panel.

The Color palette is displayed, as shown in Figure 14.3. Select a color by using the color picker. The new color is added to the Favorites list. To apply a color from the Favorites list to a text in the Document window, select the text and then select the color from the Assets panel and click the Apply button on the Assets panel.

To create a new URL, select the URLs category and click the New URL button located at the bottom of the Assets panel. The Add URL dialog box is displayed, as shown in Figure 14.4.

Figure 14.3
Use the color picker to select a color from the color palette.

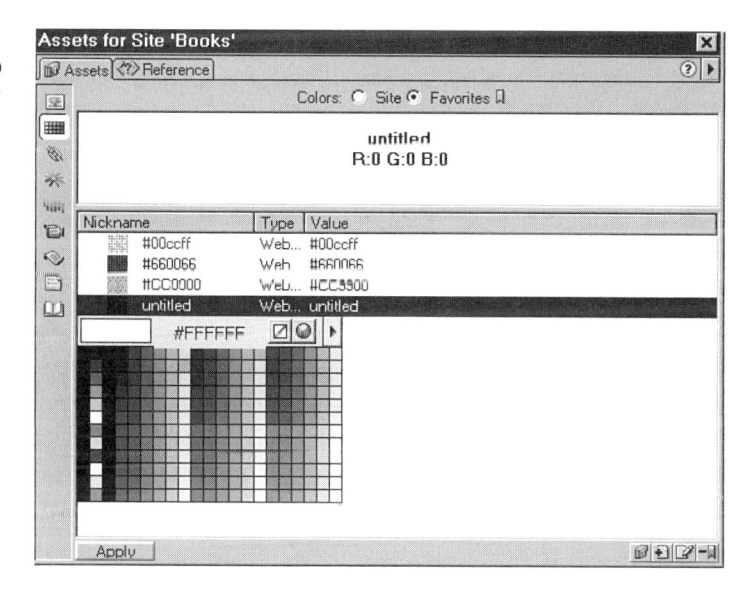

Figure 14.4
Use this dialog box to create a new URL.

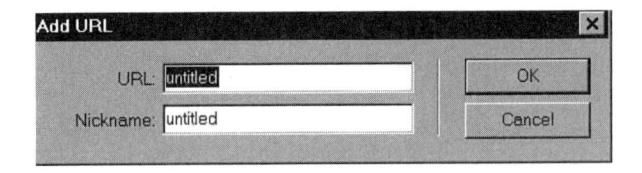

Type the URL in the URL text box. Type a nickname for the URL in the Nickname text box. Click OK. The new URL is added to the Favorites list.

> **Note**
> New URLs, colors, templates, or library items created in the Favorites list cannot be added to the Site list.

Editing Assets in the Favorites List

To edit an asset in the Favorites list, you need to select the asset and click the Edit button located at the bottom of the Assets panel. If you are editing an image or a Flash object, the application associated with the asset is launched for editing. If you are editing a color, the color palette is displayed. The Edit URL dialog box is displayed if you are editing a URL.

Working with Assets and Sites

The Assets panel lists the assets in the current site. The Assets panel lets you locate the file associated with the asset in the Site window. You can copy assets and Favorites folders between sites. To locate the file of an asset in the Site window, right-click the asset and select the Locate in Site option from the context-sensitive menu that is displayed. This displays the file that is associated with the asset in the Site window.

> **Note**
> The Locate in Site option cannot be used for colors and URLs because no files are associated with these assets.

To copy an asset to another site, select the asset and then right-click (Windows users) or Control-click (Mac users) to display the context-sensitive menu. Select the Copy to Site option from the context-sensitive menu. This option, as shown in Figure 14.5, contains the names of the sites that have been created so far in UltraDev. Select the required site from the context-sensitive menu, and the asset is copied to the specified site. If you copy a color or a URL to another site, it is added to the site's Favorites list, not to the Site list.

Figure 14.5
Select the site to which you want to copy the asset from this list of options.

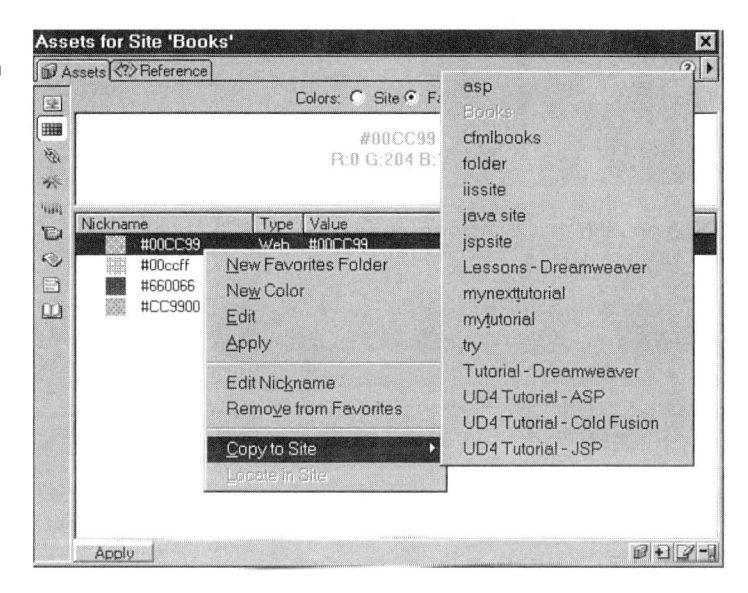

THE HISTORY PANEL

You can use the History panel to repeat or undo sets of recently performed tasks in the current document. The History panel records and displays all the tasks you perform while working on a document, as shown in Figure 14.6.

> **Note**
> A document's History panel does not show the tasks performed in the Site window, other document windows, and frames. It shows only tasks performed in the current document and frames. It does not show steps performed in the Site window.

You can use the History panel to record a series of steps as a command. You can then run this command to replay the steps you recorded. Some steps, such as selecting and dragging page elements, cannot be replayed or recorded as commands. These steps are marked with a red cross in the History panel.

Figure 14.6
Use the History panel to replay steps.

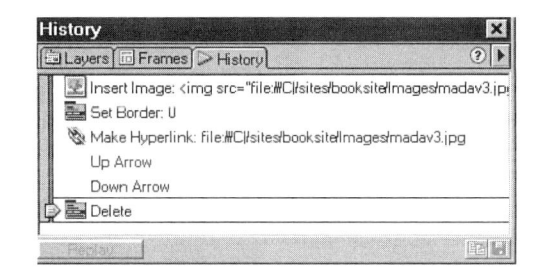

USING THE HISTORY PANEL

To view and replay the steps you performed in the current document, open the History panel by choosing Window, History. The History panel displays a list of the steps that you have performed in the document so far. To replay a step, select the step in the History panel and click the Replay button located at the bottom of the panel. To undo a series of steps, drag the History panel slider up through the steps you want to undo. These steps are highlighted in gray. To redo the steps, drag the slider down through the grayed steps.

You can apply a series of steps to specific objects. Steps involved in formatting an object, such as applying a color or resizing an object, can be applied to multiple objects by using the History panel. To apply the steps to multiple objects, select the required objects to which you want to apply a particular step or series of steps. Select the steps in the History panel, and click the Replay button.

> **Note**
> If you close the current document, the steps in the History panel are cleared.

To be able to use the steps performed in a document in other documents, you can either copy the steps or save them as a command. If you want to copy the steps from one document and use them in another document, follow these steps:

1. Select the steps to be copied from the History panel and click the Copy Steps button located at the bottom of the History panel.
2. Open the other document in which you want to paste the copied steps.
3. Select the object to which you want to apply the steps or place the insertion point where you want to apply the steps.
4. Choose Edit, Paste. The steps are applied to this open document and are made available in the History panel.

SAVING STEPS AS COMMANDS

You can save the steps in the History panel as a command for later use. Saving the steps as a command is better than copying the steps. After you save the steps as a command, the command is added to the Commands menu. You can later select the command name from the menu to apply the steps to objects in different documents.

To save the steps as a command, select the required steps and click the Save Selected Steps as Command button located at the bottom of the History panel. The Save As Command dialog box is displayed, as shown in Figure 14.7.

Type a name for the command in the Command Name text box and click OK. This command is added to the Commands menu. To apply the saved command, select an object to which you want to apply the command, and then choose the command name from the Commands menu.

Figure 14.7
Use this dialog box to save the history steps.

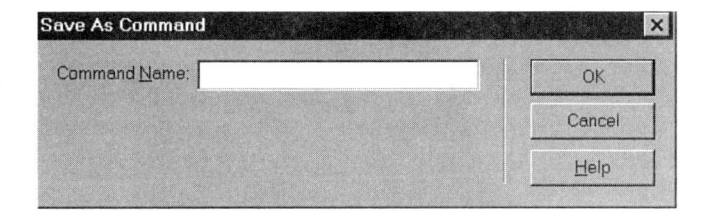

TEMPLATES AND LIBRARIES

Templates and libraries are special categories of assets provided by the Assets panel. A *template* is a document that can be used to create multiple documents with a similar layout. You can easily redesign a Web site that contains multiple pages just by redesigning the templates or library items associated with them. This is possible because templates and library items are linked assets that automatically update all the pages created from them whenever they are changed.

Templates let you define the editable and noneditable regions of your Web page. For example, if you have a Web site offering online software courses, the main layout of the Web site, such as the categories, navigation buttons, FAQ sections, and preassessment sections, will remain the same for all the courses. However, the content, such as the course title, course matter, and questions within the preassessment sections, will vary from course to course. Therefore, you can create a template with the main layout section as a noneditable region and the content section as an editable region. You can use this template to create a new page for every new course you add to the site.

CREATING A TEMPLATE

The first step toward creating a template is to switch to the Design view of the document, because most of the template-related options are available only in this view. After you switch to Design view, you can create a template either by making changes to an existing HTML document or by creating a new template from scratch by using a new HTML document.

All the template files you create in UltraDev are saved in the Template folder in the site's root folder with a .dwt file extension. If the Template folder is not available in the root folder, UltraDev automatically creates it when you save a new template file.

CREATING A TEMPLATE FROM AN EXISTING HTML DOCUMENT

To create a template from an existing HTML document, open the document and choose File, Save as Template. The Save as Template dialog box is displayed, as shown in Figure 14.8.

Select a site from the Site drop-down list, type a name for the template in the Save As text box, and click Save.

Figure 14.8
The Save as Template dialog box can be used to save an existing HTML document as a template file.

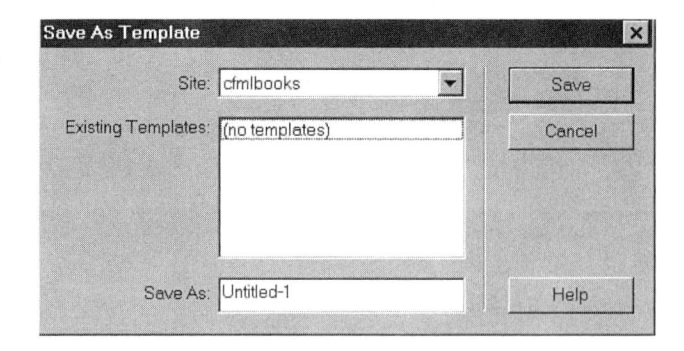

Note

If the HTML document that you want to save as a template is already linked to some other template, you must detach the HTML document from the template before saving it. You can detach an HTML document from a template by choosing Modify, Templates, Detach from Template.

CREATING A BLANK TEMPLATE

You can create a blank template by using the Assets panel. To open the Assets panel, choose Window, Assets. The Assets panel, as shown in Figure 14.9, is displayed, with the Templates category selected by default. To create a new template, click the New Template button in the lower-right corner of the Assets panel. A new untitled template is added to the list of templates. Type a name for the template and press Enter.

You can edit and delete templates by using the Edit and Delete buttons in the lower-right corner of the Assets panel.

Figure 14.9
The Assets panel with the Templates category selected.

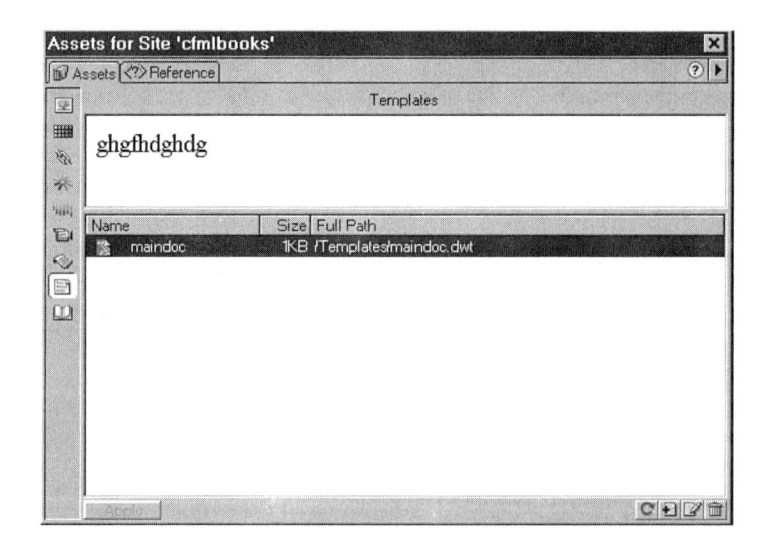

Creating Editable and Noneditable Regions on a Template

When you create a new template, all the template's regions are locked (noneditable). However, you can unlock some of the template's regions and make them editable.

> **Note**
> In a template file, you can make changes to both editable and noneditable regions. However, in a document that is based on a template, you can make changes only to the editable regions.

To define an editable region on a template file, you need to first select the content of the file that needs to be changed to an editable region. After you select the content, choose Modify, Templates, New Editable Region to display the New Editable Region dialog box, shown in Figure 14.10. Enter a unique name for the editable region, and then click OK. UltraDev displays the editable region on the template file with a rectangular outline.

Figure 14.10
Use this dialog box to mark the editable regions in a template.

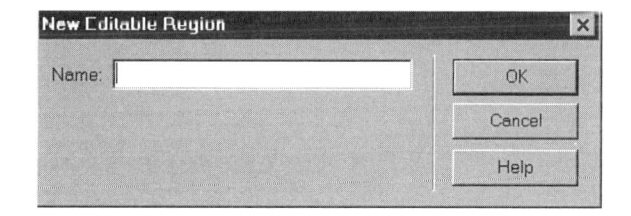

The following are a few points you need to consider while selecting the content for an editable region:

- While setting editable regions for a table, UltraDev considers the table and its contents a single element. You can mark only an entire table or individual cells in a table as a single editable region. You cannot mark multiple cells in a table as a single editable region.
- While setting editable region for layers, UltraDev considers the layer and its contents two separate entities. If you set a layer as an editable region, you can change the layer's position and contents. However, if you set the layer's contents as an editable region, you can change only the contents and not the position of the contents in the layer.

You can also convert an editable region on a template into a noneditable region by choosing Modify, Templates, Remove Editable Region.

Creating Documents Based on Templates

After you design a template file, you can create documents based on that template file. By default, whenever you make changes to a template file, all the documents based on that template file are also updated to reflect the changes. However, you can prevent the documents from getting updated by setting appropriate options in the Select Template dialog box.

Whenever you create a document based on a template, in addition to the editable regions on the template, the entire document is highlighted by an outline, with a tag displaying the name of the template. This additional highlight is used to notify you that you cannot edit any region other than the editable regions in the document.

Creating a New Document Based on a Template

To create a new document based on a template, choose File, New from Template. UltraDev displays the Select Template dialog box with a list of templates in the site, as shown in Figure 14.11. Select a template file from the Templates list. Deselect the Update Page when Template Changes option if you do not want the document to get updated when the template is changed, and click the Select button to create the document.

Figure 14.11
Use the Select Template dialog box to create a new document based on a template.

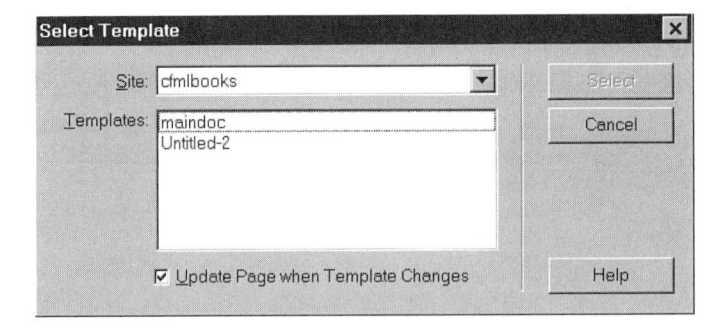

Applying a Template to an Existing Document

You can also apply a template to an existing document by opening the document and choosing Modify, Templates, Apply Template to Page. Select the options in the Select Template dialog box that is displayed, and then click Select.

Exporting and Importing the Editable Regions As XML

UltraDev lets you export editable regions from a document that is based on a template to an XML file. Exporting data to an XML file allows you to work with the data in an external editor or XML editor. You can also import data from an XML document into a document in UltraDev that is based on a template.

→ To learn more about XML and XML tags, **see** "XML Reference," **p. 536**.

To export the content of an editable region as an XML file, you must first open the document that is based on a template, which contains editable regions. After you open the document, choose File, Export, Export Editable Regions as XML. The Export Editable Regions as XML dialog box is displayed, as shown in Figure 14.12. Select the Use Editable Region Names as XML tags option, and click OK. In the dialog box that is displayed, type a name for the XML file, and click Save. An XML file is generated that contains the name of the template and the names of the editable regions in the template. It also contains the contents of the editable regions.

Figure 14.12
The Export Editable Regions as XML dialog box.

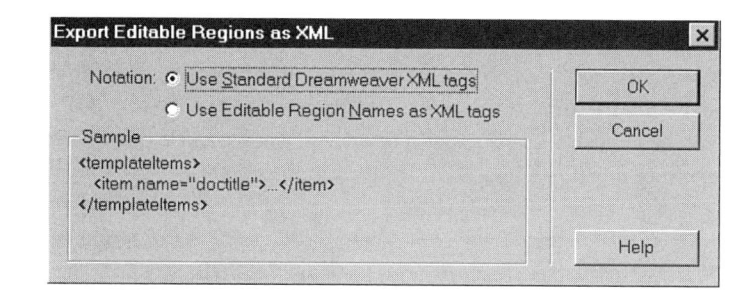

To import XML content into a document, open the document into which you want to import the XML file, and then choose File, Import, Import XML into Template. From the Import XML dialog box that is displayed, select the XML file you want to import, and click Open. The template specified in the XML file is applied to the document, and the contents of the editable regions of the document are replaced with the contents specified in the XML file.

Working with Library Items

Just as templates let you reuse a document's basic layout, libraries let you reuse the objects in a document, such as the text, tables, forms, ActiveX controls, and images. Libraries let you store all the objects you want to use or update frequently. For example, if you want the same navigation button to appear on all the pages of a Web site, you can add this navigation button to the Library panel and use it across pages. You can implement any change to the navigation buttons across pages by just changing the navigation button in the library.

Every site in UltraDev maintains its own library. All of a site's library items are stored in the Library folder, in the local root folder of the site. You can copy library items from one site to another.

Creating a Library Item

To create a library item, you need to select the object in the document that you want to add to the library. After you select the object, choose Window, Library to display the Library category of the Assets panel. Click the New Library Item button in the lower right corner of the Assets panel, and enter a name for the new library item. Every item that you add to the library is saved with a .lib extension.

Note
You can create library items only from the elements that appear in the body section of the document. Therefore, a library item cannot contain style sheets or timelines, because they form a part of the document's head section.

INSERTING A LIBRARY ITEM INTO A DOCUMENT

To insert a library item into a document, you must place the cursor at the location where you want the library item to be inserted and then choose Window, Library. From the Library category of the Assets panel that is displayed, select a library item, and click the Insert button to insert the selected item into the document.

> **Note**
> Right-click the Library items section of the Assets panel and choose Refresh Site List from the context-sensitive menu to refresh the list of library items.

UltraDev inserts the selected item from the library into the document, along with a reference to the library item. It is this reference that lets you update all the pages that contain the library item.

> **Note**
> Whenever you make changes to a library item, UltraDev displays the Update Pages dialog box that prompts you whether pages containing the library item need to be updated. To update the pages, click the Update button in the Update Pages dialog box.

If you do not want the reference to be created while you insert the item into the document, you can hold down the Ctrl key and click the Insert button in the Assets panel.

> **Note**
> You cannot edit an object in the document if it is linked to a library item. However, you can make the object editable by removing the reference to the library item while inserting it into your page.

EDITING A LIBRARY ITEM

To edit a library item, select the item from the Assets panel and click the Edit button in the lower-right corner of the Assets panel. A new window with a gray background is displayed to indicate that you are editing the library item and not the document. After you edit the item, choose File, Save to save the item. When you save the item, the Update Library Items dialog box is displayed, with a list of pages that use the edited library item. Click the Update button in this dialog box to update all the pages. However, if you do not want the pages to be updated immediately, you can click the Don't Update button.

When you click the Update button, the Update Pages dialog box is displayed, as shown in Figure 14.13. The Look in drop-down list provides options to update the pages either in the current site or in all the sites. Choose any one of the options and click the Start button to update the pages.

Figure 14.13
Use the Update Pages dialog box to update the pages by using the edited library item.

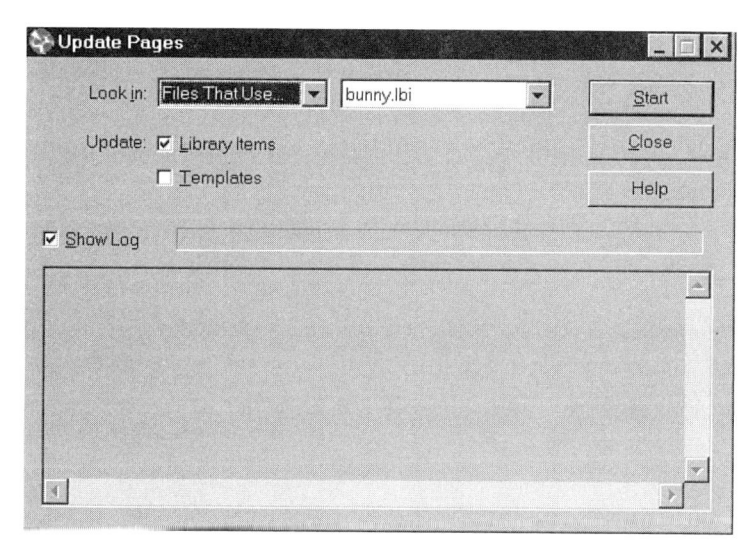

TROUBLESHOOTING

Adding an Asset to the Assets Panel

When you add a new file containing an asset such as an image file outside the Site window, the asset is not added automatically to the Assets panel.

To add an asset from a file that was created outside the Site window, you must manually rebuild the site cache from scratch. To do this, hold down the Ctrl key and click the Refresh Site List button in the Assets panel.

SUMMARY

In this chapter, you learned to create assets in and add assets to the Favorites list and organize and manage these assets by using the Assets panel. You also learned to use the History panel to repeat recently performed tasks in the current document. In addition, you learned to create and apply templates to documents. Finally, you learned to insert library items into a document and edit them if necessary.

ACTIVITY CORNER

In this activity corner section, you will create a template with editable regions from the Contentpage.asp file. You then reuse this template to create new files. To create a template from the Contentpage.asp file, perform the following steps:

1. Open the Contentpage.asp file.
2. Choose the Save as Template option from the File menu. The Save as Template dialog box appears. Specify the name of the template as **Dynamicpage** in the Save As text box and click the Save button to close the dialog box.

3. The template file Dynamicpage.dwt is now displayed in the Document window. Select the layer named Release. This layer must be marked as an editable region.
4. Choose Modify, Templates, New Editable Region.
5. In the New Editable Region dialog box, specify the name of the editable region as **Headingarea**.
6. Select the layer named Layer3 and mark it as an editable region by repeating step 4. Specify the name of the editable region as Contentarea.

The template Dynamicpage.dwt is now ready to be reused. Create two files named Search.asp and Songfetch.asp from the Dynamicpage.dwt template and save them in the Songresults folder.

CHAPTER 15

EDITING AND DEBUGGING IN CODE VIEW

In this chapter

Editing HTML Becomes Easy   300

Debugging JavaScript Code   315

Summary   319

Editing HTML Becomes Easy

UltraDev lets you create and edit Web pages without writing any HTML source code. UltraDev automatically generates the HTML code as you create and design your Web pages in the Document window. If you want to view, delete, or modify the HTML source code, you can use Code view, the Code inspector, or the Quick Tag editor. The Code and Design views in UltraDev let you view both the HTML code and the visual design at the same time.

You can troubleshoot your Web pages by checking the HTML code written for these Web pages in Code view. If you need help understanding and writing HTML code, you can use the Reference panel of UltraDev. If you have cluttered codes and nonstandard tags in the HTML code, you can use the Clean Up HTML and Clean Word HTML commands to clean up the code.

The UltraDev Reference Panel

The Reference panel in UltraDev provides you with an easy reference to HTML tags, JavaScript code, and CSS styles. In the description area of the Reference panel, you can find information, such as a description, functions, syntax, and examples, related to the tags, objects, and styles you are working with in Code view.

Using the UltraDev Reference Panel

If you are writing HTML, JavaScript, or CSS code, and you want to get some help on a particular tag, object, or style, you can use the Reference panel.

To open the Reference panel, choose Window, Reference. You can also open the Reference panel by clicking the Reference button on the toolbar or by choosing Help, Reference. The Reference panel is displayed, as shown in Figure 15.1.

Figure 15.1
The Reference panel.

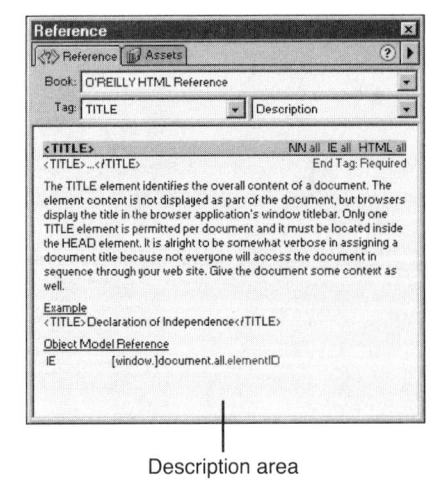

The Reference panel contains the following options:

- **Book:** This drop-down list provides you with three options: O'REILLY HTML Reference, O'REILLY JavaScript Reference, and O'REILLY CSS Reference. Choose the type of reference material depending on the kind of information you need. For example, if you are looking for useful information on tags, choose O'REILLY HTML Reference. Similarly, you choose O'REILLY JavaScript Reference for help with objects and O'REILLY CSS Reference for help with styles.

- **Tag, Object, or Style:** This drop-down list lets you select a tag, object, or style for which you want to find information. The name of this option changes, depending on the type of book selected. If you want to find information about a particular tag, object, or style used in the code, select the tag, object, or style in Code view and then open the Reference panel. The selected tag is displayed in the drop-down list, and a description of the selected tag is shown in the description area. For example, if you select the <TBODY> tag in Code view and then open the Reference panel, this tag is displayed in the Tag, Object, or Style drop-down list. Other information, such as a description and an example of the tag, is displayed in the description area of the Reference Panel, as shown in Figure 15.2.

- **Attributes:** This drop-down list next to the Tag, Object, or Style drop-down list displays the attributes of the tag, object, or style you select. By default, the selection is Description, which displays a description of the chosen tag. For example, if you select the <head> tag in Code view, this drop-down list displays the attributes of the <head> tag, as shown in Figure 15.2. You can select an attribute from this list to view additional information about the selected tag.

Figure 15.2
You can use the Reference panel to find useful information about the selected tag.

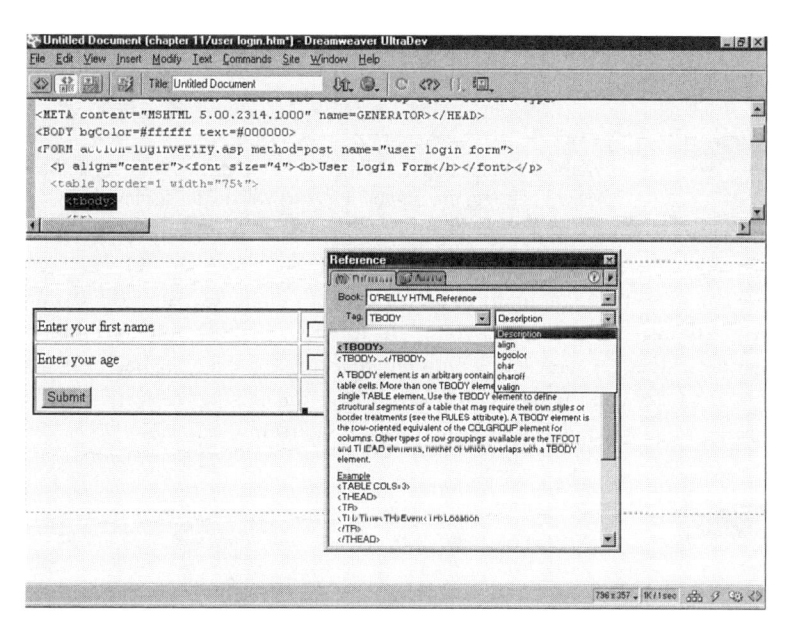

A small arrow at the top-right corner of the Reference panel represents the panel's Options menu. This menu provides you with three options that let you adjust the font size of the text in the Reference panel.

INSERTING COMMENTS

A comment in HTML code lets you explain the code or provide other useful information about it. You can insert a comment in either Code view or Design view. However, you can view the comment only in Code view. Any comment that is inserted will not be displayed in the browser.

To insert a comment in either Code view or Design view, place the cursor where you want the comment to be displayed. After you select the position for the comment, click the Insert Comment button in the Invisibles category of the Objects panel or choose Insert, Invisible Tags, Comment. The Insert Comment dialog box is displayed, as shown in Figure 15.3.

Figure 15.3
Enter the comment in the Comment text box of the Insert Comment dialog box.

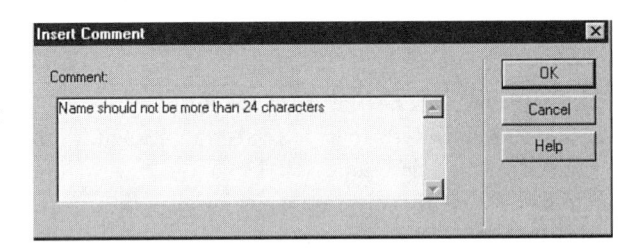

Type the comment in the Comment text box, and click OK. The comment is inserted in Code view, and the comment marker is inserted in the document's Design view, as shown in Figure 15.4.

> **Note**
> If the Comments option in the Invisible Elements category in the Preferences dialog box is not selected, the comment marker will not be displayed.

You can also add a comment to an existing comment by using the comment marker's Property inspector. To add a comment to an existing comment, double-click the comment marker in Design view. The comment marker's Property inspector is displayed, as shown in Figure 15.5. Type the new comment next to the existing comment in the Comment text box. The comment is added to the existing comment in Code view.

> **Note**
> The `<!--Comment text-->` tag is automatically generated in Code view if you add a comment.

EDITING HTML BECOMES EASY 303

Figure 15.4
The comment marker for the comment is inserted in the document's Design view.

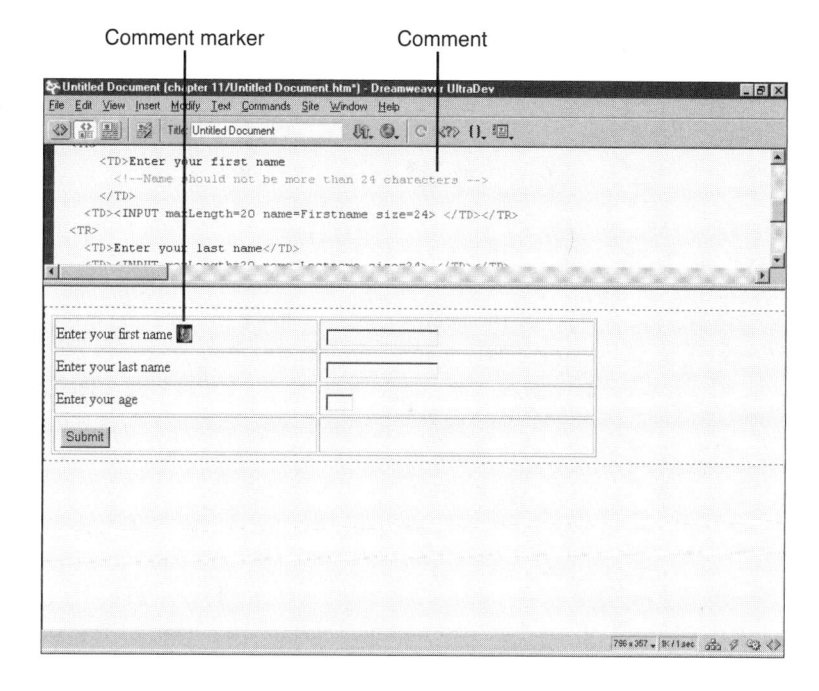

Figure 15.5
The new comment entered in the Comment text box is added to the existing comment.

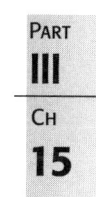

Roundtrip HTML

Roundtrip HTML is a unique feature in UltraDev that lets you copy HTML code from a text-based HTML editor to UltraDev with little or no effect on the code's content and structure.

Some key features of Roundtrip HTML are as follows:

- If you open an existing HTML document that contains any overlapping tags, open tags, or extra closing tags, UltraDev rewrites the code, closes the open tags, and removes the extra closing tags. The options in the Code Rewriting category in the Preferences dialog box let you specify the changes, if any, that UltraDev needs to make to your code when you open an HTML document or script.

→ To learn more about the options in the Code Rewriting category in the Preferences dialog box, **see** "Setting Code Rewriting Preferences," **p. 326**.

- If UltraDev finds an unrecognizable tag overlapping a valid tag, it marks it as erroneous. In this case, it does not rewrite the code.
- If you enter any code or tag not supported by HTML, and if the Highlight Invalid HTML option is selected, UltraDev highlights the invalid code in yellow in Code view as well as in Design view. To select the Highlight Invalid HTML option, choose View, Code View Options, Highlight Invalid HTML. By default, errors are highlighted in Design view and not in Code view. If you double-click an invalid tag in Design view, the Property inspector of the invalid tag is displayed, as shown in Figure 15.6. The Property inspector displays some useful information about how to correct the error.

Figure 15.6
The <tbody> tag is highlighted as invalid because the closing tag is missing.

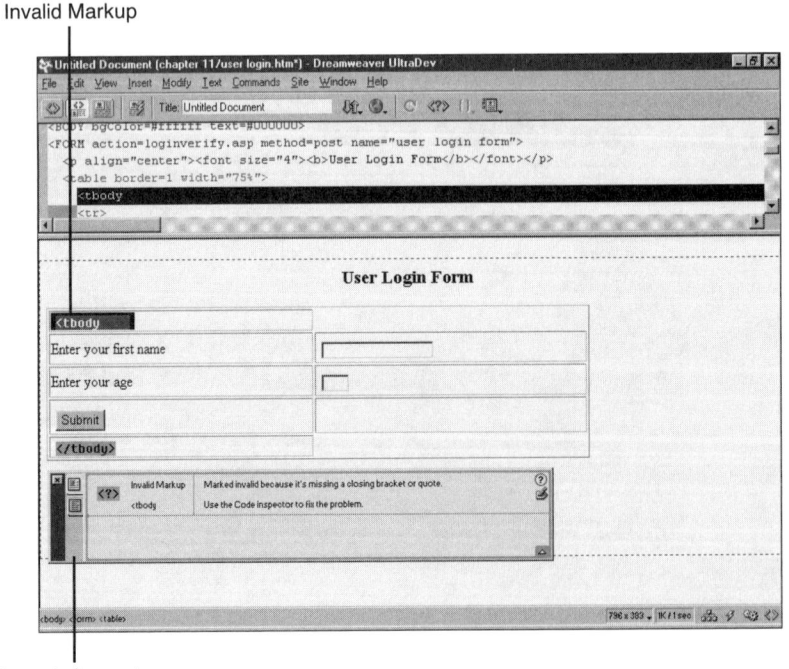

- If you want to edit the code in the current document, UltraDev lets you launch a text-based HTML editor to edit the code.

You can select an external HTML editor in the File Types/Editors category in the Preferences dialog box. In the File Types/Editors category, click the Browse button next to the External Code Editor text box to select the text editor you want to use.

→ To learn more about the options in the File Types/Editors category in the Preferences dialog box, **see** "Setting File Types/Editors Preferences," **p. 328**.

To start an external HTML editor, choose Edit, Edit with (the editor name that you specified in the External Code Editor text box).

INSERTING AND EDITING A SCRIPT

UltraDev lets you insert a script in either Code or Design view. You can view the inserted script in Code view and the script marker in the document's Design view.

INSERTING A SCRIPT

To insert a script in Code or Design view, follow these steps:

1. Place the cursor where you want to insert the script.
2. Click the Insert Script button in the Invisibles category of the Objects panel. The Insert Script dialog box is displayed, as shown in Figure 15.7.

Figure 15.7
The Language drop-down list provides you with four options: JavaScript, JavaScript1.1, JavaScript1.2, and VBScript.

Note
You can also open the Insert Script dialog box by choosing Insert, Invisible Tags, Script.

3. Choose the scripting language from the Language drop-down list.
4. Type the script code in the Content text box.
5. Click OK to insert the script. The script is inserted in Code view, and the script marker is inserted in the document's Design view.

You can also insert an external script file in Code or Design view.

To link to an external script file, open the Insert Script dialog box and click OK without typing anything in the Content text box. A script marker is inserted in Design view of the Document window. Select the script marker and choose Window, Properties. The script marker's Property inspector is displayed, as shown in Figure 15.8.

Figure 15.8
The Property inspector of the script marker.

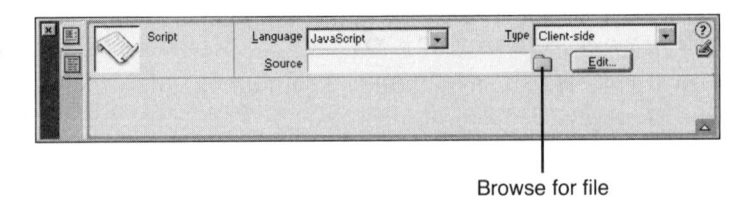

Browse for file

> **Tip**
> You can also open the Property inspector of the script marker by double-clicking the script marker.

To link to an external file, click the Browse for File icon in the script marker's Property inspector and select the external script file. If you know the filename, type it in the Source text box to establish a link to the external script file.

The Language option in the Property inspector lets you specify the script's language, the Edit option lets you make changes to your script, and the Type option lets you specify whether the script is a client-side script or a server-side script.

EDITING A SCRIPT

UltraDev lets you edit a script in either Code view or Design view. To edit a script in Code view, you must open the script in Code view and make changes to the script directly. If you open the script in Design view by selecting the script marker in Design view, the respective part of the script gets highlighted in Code view, and you can edit the script in Code view.

To edit a script in Design view, follow these steps:

1. Choose View, Design to open Design view.
2. Double-click the script marker to open the script marker's Property inspector.
3. Click the Edit button in the Property inspector. The Script Properties dialog box is displayed, as shown in Figure 15.9.
4. Edit the script in the Script text box. If the script is an external script file, clicking the Edit button takes you to the Code view of the script file, where you can make changes to the script.

Figure 15.9
The Script Properties dialog box displays the selected script in the Script text box.

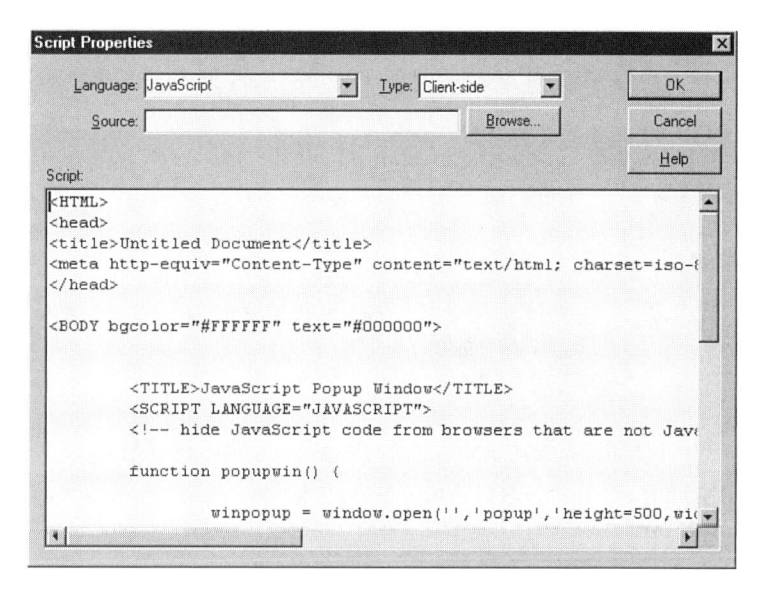

Viewing Script Functions

You can view script functions in your code by opening the code and clicking the Code Navigation button on the toolbar. If any functions are defined in the code, they are displayed in the drop-down list, as shown in Figure 15.10.

Figure 15.10
The Code Navigation drop-down list displays the two script functions defined in the code.

If you want to move to a particular function in your code, click the Code Navigation button and select the function from the drop-down list. The selected function is highlighted in Code view.

If you want to view the code's functions in alphabetical order, hold down the Ctrl key and click the Code Navigation button.

> **Note:** On Macintosh machines, to view the functions in alphabetical order, hold down the Option key and click the Code Navigation button. This step applies to most of the "Right Click" options.

Cleaning Up HTML Code and Microsoft Word HTML

UltraDev lets you clean up HTML files and documents that are saved as HTML files in Microsoft Word.

The Clean Up HTML command in UltraDev lets you clean up a document that contains cluttered HTML code. To do so, choose Commands, Clean Up HTML. The Clean Up HTML dialog box is displayed, as shown in Figure 15.11. Select the required options, and then click OK to complete the cleanup. Table 15.1 lists the options that are available in the Clean Up HTML dialog box.

Figure 15.11
The Clean Up HTML dialog box.

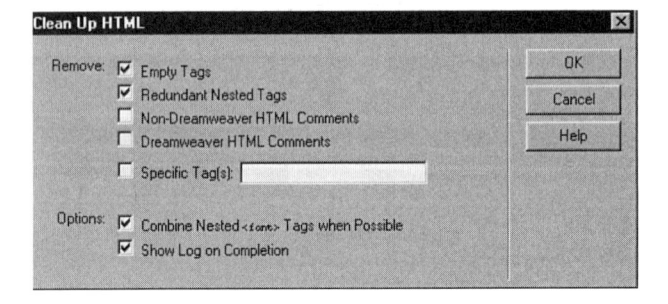

Table 15.1 The Clean Up HTML Dialog Box Options

Option	Description
Remove Empty Tags	Lets you remove tags that do not have content between them.
Remove Redundant Nested Tags	Lets you remove all the redundant occurrences of a tag.
Remove Non-Dreamweaver HTML	Lets you remove Commentsall the HTML comments not inserted by UltraDev.

Table 15.1 Continued

Option	Description
Remove Dreamweaver HTML Comments	Lets you remove all comments that were inserted by UltraDev.
	Note that if you remove the Dreamweaver UltraDev HTML comments, all the template-based documents turn into ordinary HTML documents and all the library items turn into normal HTML code.
Remove Specific Tag(s)	Lets you remove the tags specified in the Word Specific Tag(s) text box.
Combine Nested `<font>` Tags when Possible	Lets you combine two or more `<font>` tags when they are used to control text within the same range.
Show Log on Completion	Lets you display an alert box that gives details about the changes made to the document as soon as the cleanup is complete.

UltraDev also lets you open and clean documents saved as HTML files in Microsoft Word. You can use the Clean Up Word HTML command available in the Commands menu to remove all the irrelevant HTML code generated by Word.

> **Caution**
> Before you clean up a Microsoft Word HTML file, ensure that you preserve a copy of the file. If you do not, you might not be able to reopen the HTML file in Word.

> **Note**
> You can use the Clean Up Word HTML command for all documents saved as HTML files in Word 97 or later.

To clean up a Word document that contains cluttered HTML code, choose File, Import, Import Word HTML. The Select Word HTML File to Import window is displayed. Select the document to be cleaned up, and click OK.

UltraDev opens the selected Word HTML file. The Clean Up Word HTML dialog box is displayed, as shown in Figure 15.12.

The Clean Up Word HTML dialog box contains two tabs: Basic and Detailed. The options on the Basic page are shown in Figure 15.12, and the options on the Detailed page are shown in Figure 15.13. Select the required options, and then click OK to complete the cleanup. All the preferences you enter are saved as default Clean Up Word HTML settings.

Figure 15.12
The Clean Up Word HTML dialog box.

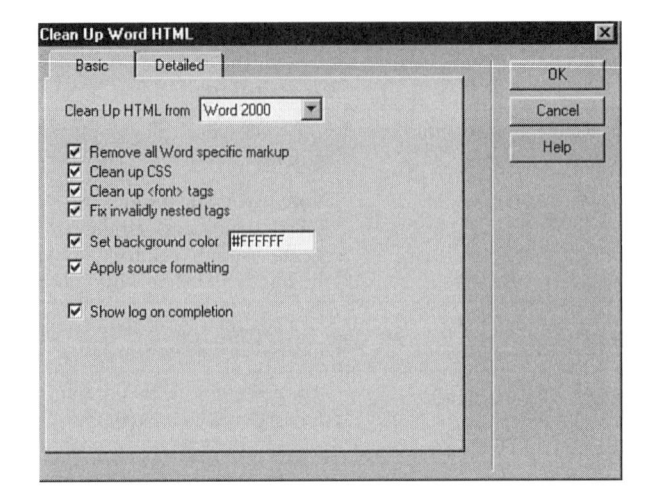

Figure 15.13
The Detailed page of the Clean Up Word HTML dialog box.

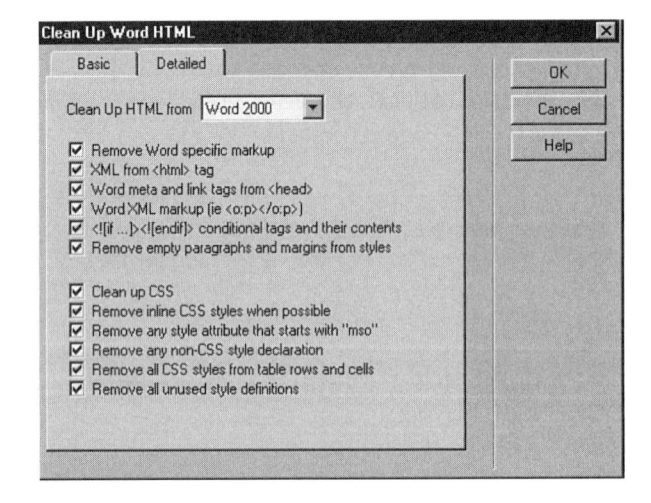

Table 15.2 lists the options that are available in the Clean Up Word HTML dialog box.

TABLE 15.2   THE CLEAN UP WORD HTML DIALOG BOX OPTIONS

Option	Description
Clean Up HTML from	Lets you choose either Word 97/98 or Word 2000.
Remove all Word specific markup	Lets you remove all Word-specific HTML, Word XML markup, and all other options selected on the Detailed page of the Clean Up Word HTML dialog box.
Clean up CSS	Lets you remove all Word-specific CSS and all other options selected on the Detailed page of the Clean Up Word HTML dialog box.

TABLE 15.2 CONTINUED

Option	Description
Clean up `<font>` tags	Lets you remove all the font markup tags inserted by Word outside the paragraph and heading tags.
Fix invalidly nested tags	Lets you remove the font markup tags inserted by Word outside the paragraph and heading (block-level) tags.
Set background color	Lets you set the background color for your document.
Apply source formatting	Lets you apply the source format already specified in the Code Format category of Preferences and the SourceFormat.txt file to the document.
	You will find the file SourceFormat.txt in the Configuration folder, which is within the Dreamweaver UltraDev 4 folder.
Show log on completion	Lets you display an alert box that gives details about the changes made to the document as soon as the cleanup is complete.

FORMATTING THE HTML SOURCE CODE IN EXISTING DOCUMENTS

The options in the Code Format category in the Preferences dialog box let you specify formatting features for the code, such as indentation, line length, tab size, and capitalization of tags and attribute names. If you want to format new documents created within UltraDev, you can use the Code Format category in the Preferences dialog box and the `SourceFormat.txt` file. However, the Apply Source Formatting option in the Clean Up Word HTML dialog box allows you to format new documents as well as existing ones. To apply HTML source formatting to an existing HTML document, choose Commands, Apply Source Formatting in the Document window.

→ To learn more about the options in the Code Format category in the Preferences dialog box, **see** "Setting Code Formatting Preferences," **p. 325**.

The Code Colors category in the Preferences dialog box allows you to specify the color code for the HTML tags, text between the tags, scripts, background, and reserved keywords in the Code view. To open Code Colors category, choose Edit, Preferences, and then select Code Colors.

→ To learn more about the options in the Code Colors category in the Preferences dialog box, **see** "Setting Preferences for Code Colors," **p. 324**.

EDITING COLDFUSION AND ACTIVE SERVER FILES IN ULTRADEV

Active Server Page (ASP) code and ColdFusion code in Code view are represented as markers in Design view. The ASP marker in UltraDev lets you identify blocks of ASP code in the Document window. Similarly, the CFML marker lets you identify blocks of ColdFusion Markup Language (CFML) code.

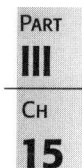

To edit Active Server files, follow these steps:

1. Select the ASP marker in the Document window and then choose Window, Properties. The Property inspector of the ASP marker is displayed, as shown in Figure 15.14.

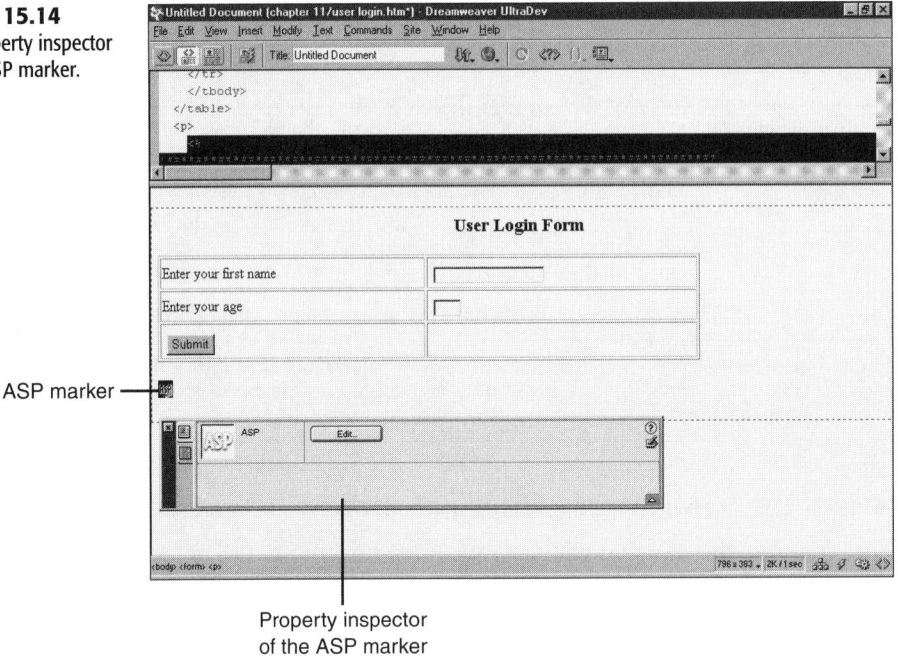

Figure 15.14
The Property inspector of the ASP marker.

ASP marker

Property inspector of the ASP marker

> **Tip**
> You can also open the Property inspector of the ASP marker by double-clicking the ASP marker.

2. Click the Edit button. The Edit Contents dialog box is displayed, as shown in Figure 15.15.
3. View and make changes to the ASP code in the Contents text box, and then click OK.

You can also edit CFML files by using the CFML marker's Property inspector. To edit a CFML file, double-click the CFML marker in Design view. The CFML marker's Property inspector is displayed, as shown in Figure 15.16.

If you want to make changes to a tag's attributes, click the Attributes button in the Property inspector. If you want to make changes to the content that appears between the CFML tags, click the Contents button.

EDITING HTML BECOMES EASY | 313

Figure 15.15
The Edit Contents dialog box.

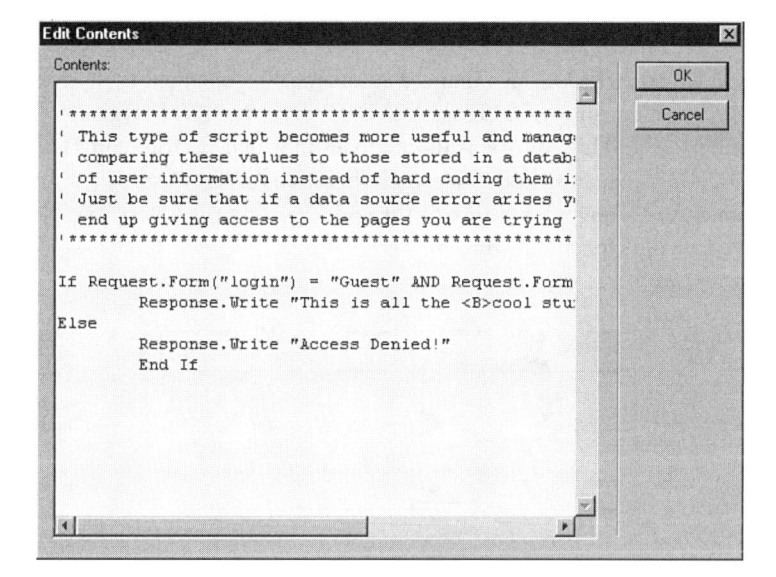

Figure 15.16
The Property inspector of the CFML marker.

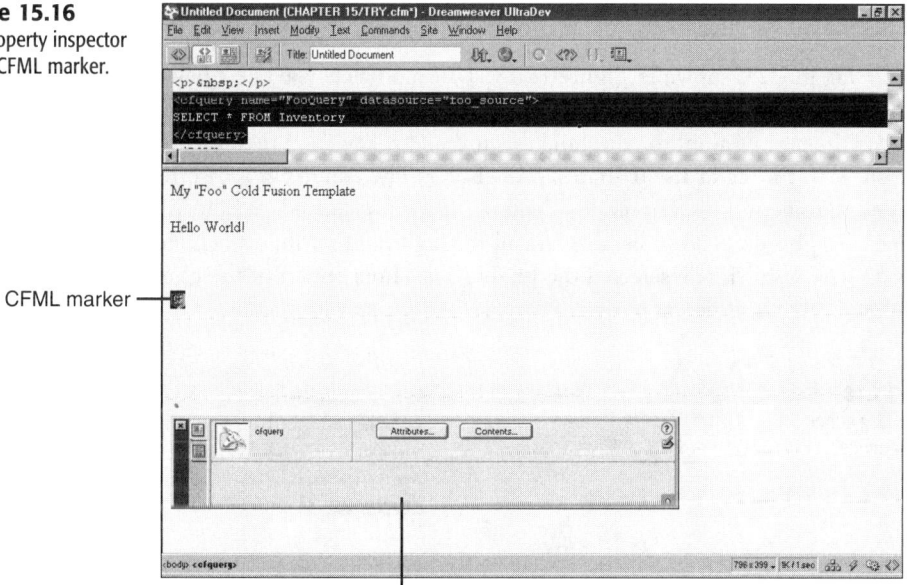

CFML marker

Property inspector of the CFML marker

PART
III
CH
15

Editing an HTML Tag in the Document Window

You can edit the HTML tags that are automatically generated by UltraDev by using the Quick Tag editor, shown in Figure 15.17. To open the Quick Tag editor, hold down the Ctrl key and press T. This editor has three modes in which you can edit HTML tags: Insert HTML, Edit Tag, and Wrap Tag. In all three modes, the basic operation of editing tags is the same. Any changes you make to the code by using the Quick Tag editor are immediately reflected in the Document window.

Figure 15.17
The Quick Tag Editor in Insert mode.

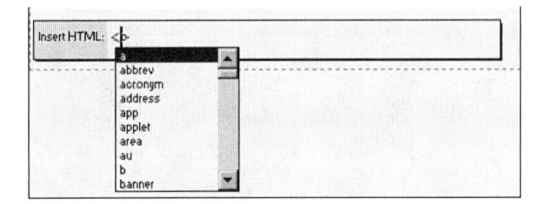

Insert HTML mode, shown in Figure 15.17, is the default mode of the Quick Tag editor. This mode lets you insert new HTML tags into your code. You can type the HTML tag and then press Enter to add the tag to the code.

Edit Tag mode is shown in Figure 15.18. This mode lets you enter new attributes, edit existing attributes, or change the tag's name. To open the Quick Tag editor in Edit Tag mode, select the tag you want to edit, hold down the Ctrl key and press T. After you have made changes to the tag or its attributes, press Enter. The edited tag is inserted into the code. While editing in Edit Tag mode, if you pause for few seconds, a hints drop-down list appears. This drop-down list displays all the tag's valid attributes. The hints drop-down list is displayed only if you selected the Enable Tag Hints option of the Quick Tag Editor item in the Preferences dialog box.

Figure 15.18
The Quick Tag editor in Edit Tag mode.

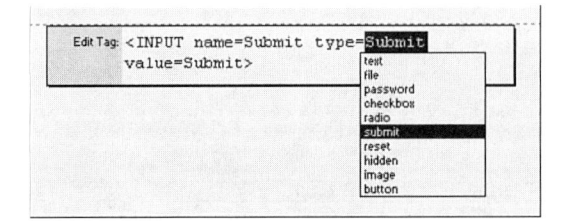

Wrap Tag mode is shown in Figure 15.19. The Quick Tag editor usually starts in Wrap Tag mode if the current selection consists of text other than a complete tag. This mode lets you place the current selection within the new tag of your choice. In this mode, if you enter more than one tag, the Quick Tag editor displays an error message, and the text you entered is ignored.

Figure 15.19
The Quick Tag editor in Wrap Tag mode.

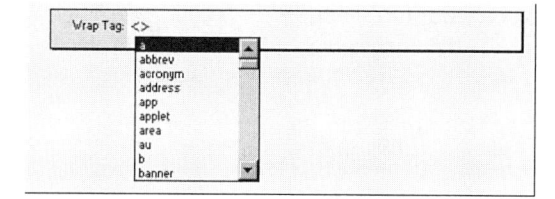

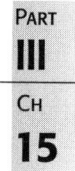

Debugging JavaScript Code

You can write JavaScript code in Code view. While writing JavaScript code, you might make mistakes. If you ignore these mistakes, you will find many bugs when the program is finally executed. JavaScript Debugger is a tool that lets you identify bugs in client-side JavaScript code and helps you fix them before execution.

After you write the JavaScript code, you can run JavaScript Debugger to debug the script and fix the errors. The debugger first checks for syntax errors and then checks for logical errors.

Running JavaScript Debugger to Find Syntax Errors

Syntax errors can include missing brackets around a function, missing quotation marks for strings, missing parentheses, and so on. Whenever a browser comes across any kind of syntax error, it displays an error message. To avoid this, you need to debug the code by finding the syntax errors.

To run the debugger and find syntax errors, follow these steps:

1. Choose File, Debug in Browser, iexplore to run the debugger. The Save Files dialog box, shown in Figure 15.20, prompts you to save the file before you start debugging.

Figure 15.20
The Save Files dialog box.

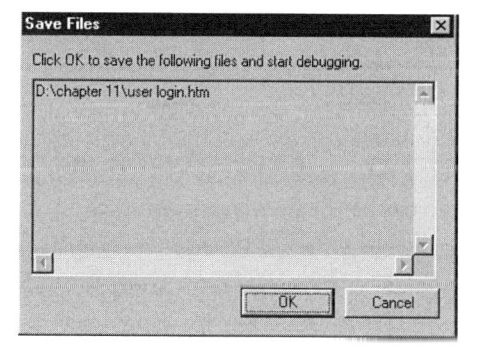

> **Tip**
> You can also run the debugger by clicking the Preview/Debug in Browser button on the toolbar and selecting the Debug in iexplore option.

2. Click OK to save the file and start debugging. The debugger first checks for syntax errors. If the debugger finds syntax errors in the code, it displays the list of errors in the JavaScript Syntax Errors window, as shown in Figure 15.21.

Figure 15.21
The JavaScript Syntax Errors window.

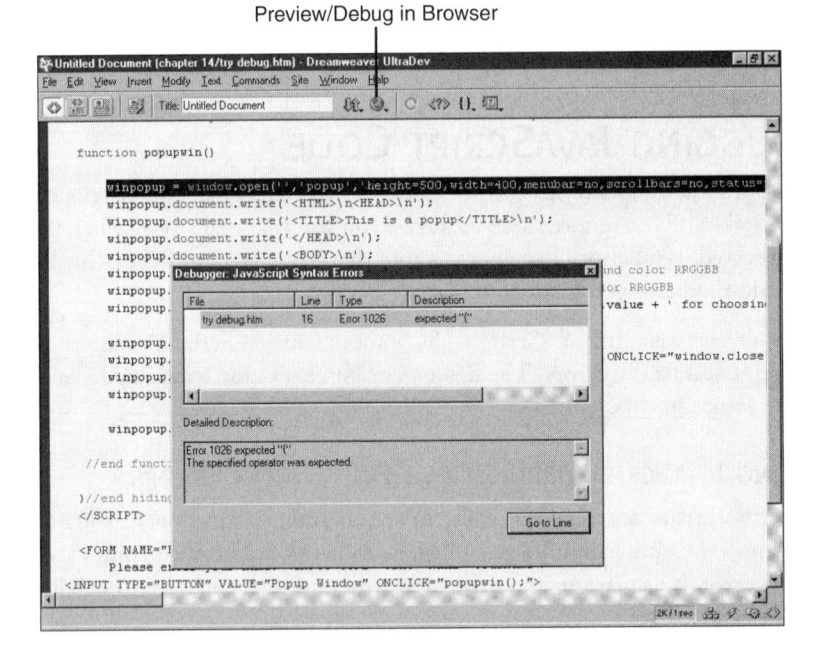

3. To view the description of a syntax error, select the error in the JavaScript Syntax Errors window. The description of the error is displayed in the Detailed Description area in the lower pane of the JavaScript Syntax Errors window.

4. Click the Go to Line button in the JavaScript Syntax Errors window to go to the line that contains the selected error. This line is highlighted in the Code view of the Document window and at this point you correct the error.

USING THE JAVASCRIPT DEBUGGER TO CHECK FOR LOGICAL ERRORS

Logical errors cause the program to function incorrectly. After checking for syntax errors, the debugger starts checking for logical errors. If there are no syntax errors in the code, the debugger starts checking for logical errors.

JavaScript Debugger lets you check for logical errors by using breakpoints. A *breakpoint* is a point in the code at which program execution stops. It is represented by a small red dot in the JavaScript Debugger window.

The options in the JavaScript Debugger window let you identify logical errors in the code. These options are shown in Figure 15.22 and are described in Table 15.3.

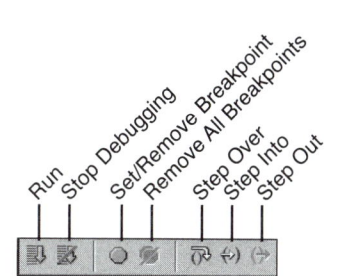

Figure 15.22
Options in the JavaScript Debugger window.

TABLE 15.3 THE JAVASCRIPT DEBUGGER WINDOW OPTIONS

Option	Description
Run	Lets you run the debugger.
Set/Remove Breakpoint	Lets you set or remove a breakpoint.
Remove All Breakpoints	Lets you remove all breakpoints in the code.
Stop Debugging	Lets you stop debugging in the JavaScript Debugger window.
Step Over	Lets you step over a function in the code without executing the function.
Step Into	Lets you move into a function and execute the function one statement at a time.
Step Out	Lets you step out of the function.

The debugger stops at every breakpoint in the code and allows you to view the values of the variables at these breakpoints. Viewing values of variables lets you identify the source of the logical error in the code. To view these values, you need to enter the variable names in the Variable Name column, which is in the bottom pane of the Java Script Debugger window.

You can set breakpoints either between script tags or for a line with an event handler. If you set a breakpoint for an invalid line, a Debugger message box describing the error is displayed. If you click the OK button in this message box, the breakpoint automatically moves to the next valid line of code. You can set or remove a breakpoint in Code view by clicking the Code Navigation button on the toolbar and then selecting the Set Breakpoint or Remove Breakpoint option. Is you have set a breakpoint for an invalid line and if you want to remove this breakpoint, you can use the Remove Breakpoint option to remove the breakpoint.

To run the debugger to find logical errors, follow these steps:

1. Choose File, Debug in Browser, iexplore to run the debugger. The Security Warning dialog box is displayed, as shown in Figure 15.23.

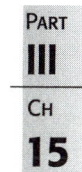

318 CHAPTER 15 EDITING AND DEBUGGING IN CODE VIEW

Figure 15.23
The Security Warning dialog box.

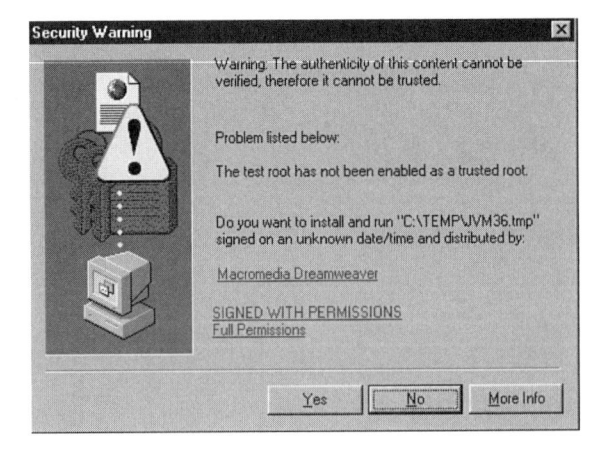

2. If you agree to the condition in the warning dialog box, click the Yes button. If you want to find more information, click the More Info button in the Security Warning dialog box. To proceed further, click Yes in the Security Warning dialog box. After you click the Yes button, the Microsoft Internet Explorer window is displayed. You can start debugging only if you click OK.

3. Click OK in this Microsoft Internet debugger window to start debugging. The JavaScript Debugger window opens, as shown in Figure 15.24.

Figure 15.24
The JavaScript Debugger window.

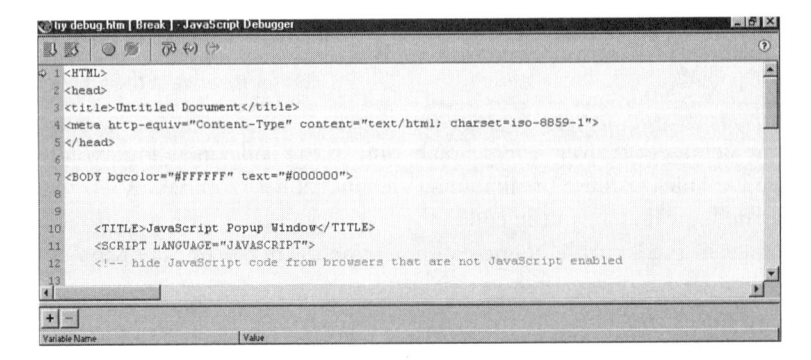

4. Click the Set/Remove Breakpoint button in the JavaScript Debugger window to set a breakpoint.

> **Tip**
> Alternatively, you can also set a breakpoint in the JavaScript Debugger window by right-clicking and selecting the Set Breakpoint option from the context-sensitive menu.

5. Click the Run button in the JavaScript Debugger window to run the debugger and start debugging the JavaScript code.
6. Click the Stop Debugging button to stop debugging in the JavaScript Debugger window.

Summary

The Reference panel in UltraDev provides you with an easy reference to HTML tags, JavaScript code, and CSS styles. You can use the Reference panel to find information about tags, objects, and styles. The Insert Comment button in the Invisibles category of the Objects panel lets you insert comments in HTML code. The Insert Script button in the Invisibles category of the Objects panel lets you insert a script in the code.

You can use the Clean Up HTML command to clean up the HTML code and the Clean Up Word HTML command to clean up the documents saved as HTML files in Microsoft Word. You can find syntax errors and check for logical errors in the JavaScript code by using the JavaScript Debugger.

CHAPTER 16

SETTING INTERFACE PREFERENCES

In this chapter

Choosing Your Style   322

Summary   337

Choosing Your Style

While working with UltraDev, you might come across many instances where you want to change the default settings and appearance of various elements in UltraDev. In such instances, you can make use of the Preferences dialog box to customize UltraDev's various interface-related features. You can view the Preferences dialog by choosing Edit, Preferences. The Preferences dialog box displays a list of categories that let you not only change the general appearance of the UltraDev interface but also change the interface features of specific elements, such as layers, style sheets, external editors, and preview browsers. This dialog box also gives you options to change the display of the HTML and JavaScript code. You can display the Preferences dialog box by choosing Edit, Preferences.

To change any settings in the Preferences dialog box, you must first select the category that you want to customize and then make appropriate changes to the options displayed in that category.

Setting the General Preference

You can control the general appearance and behavior of the UltraDev window by setting the appropriate options in the General category of the Preferences dialog box, shown in Figure 16.1. To view the options in the General category, choose General from the Category list. The General category displays two subcategories of preferences that you can set: File Options and Editing Options.

Whenever you open UltraDev, a blank Document window is displayed by default. However, you can keep the blank Document window from being displayed by selecting the Show Only Site Window on Startup option in the File Options category. This option displays only the Site window and other selected panels whenever UltraDev opens.

Figure 16.1
Use the General category of the Preferences dialog box to control the general appearance and behavior of the UltraDev window.

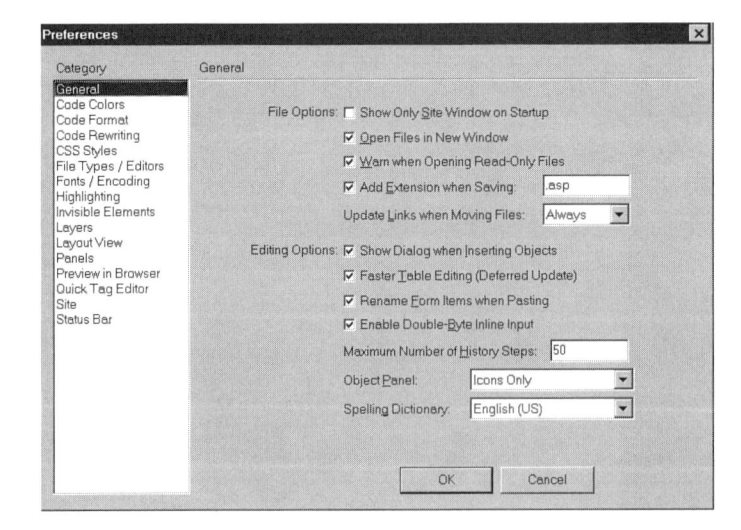

At times, you might have to work with multiple documents at the same time, constantly switching from one document to another. In such situations, you can select the Open Files in New Window option. This option lets you open every document in a new window rather than opening them in the same window. This option is of use only for Windows users, because files on Macintosh machines always open in a new window.

Select the Warn when Opening Read-Only Files option in the File Options category to display a warning whenever you open a read-only file. This warning message displays options that you can use to unlock, check, or view a file.

You can set a default file extension for all the files you save. Select the Add Extension when Saving option and type the required file extension in the text box that follows. For example, if you set .html to be the default file extension, and later you save a file without entering an extension, UltraDev will automatically save the file with an .html extension.

The Update Links when Moving Files option lets you tell UltraDev what must be done when you move files into and out of the site folder. Using this option, you can configure UltraDev to update links automatically, to never update links, or to prompt you to perform an update.

→ To learn more about updating links, **see** "Changing and Updating Links," **p. 196**.

By default, whenever you insert an object, such as an image, a table, or a Shockwave movie, UltraDev displays a dialog box prompting you to enter additional information about the object. You can stop the display of these dialog boxes by deselecting the Show Dialog when Inserting Objects option. If you deselect this option, you must use the Property inspector to specify the additional information for objects you insert. You can also temporarily override this option by holding down the Ctrl key while inserting the object.

> **Note**
> Irrespective of whether the Show Dialog when Inserting Objects option is selected, the Rollover Images and Fireworks HTML dialog box always appears.

By default, whenever you enter content into a cell of a table, the cell's height and width adjust automatically to accommodate the content. However, if you want the cell's height and width to be updated only when you click outside the table and not while you enter the content, you can deselect the Faster Table Editing (Deferred Update) option.

You can rename form items whenever you copy and paste them by selecting the Rename Form Items when Pasting option.

If you are working in a development environment that supports double-byte text, you can allow UltraDev to accept double-byte text by selecting the Enable Double-Byte Inline Input option.

UltraDev's History panel lets you record and replay all the actions performed in a document. By default, the History panel records a maximum of 50 actions. However, you can increase this number by changing the value in the Maximum Number of History Steps option.

The Objects panel displays icons of objects that can be inserted into a document. However, if you find it difficult to identify objects just by looking at their icons, you can change the settings to display text along with the icons or display only text instead of icons by selecting the appropriate option from the Objects Panel drop-down list.

The Spelling Dictionary drop-down list in the General category displays a list of dictionaries available in the Configuration/Dictionaries folder inside the Dreamweaver application folder. The dictionary that you select from this list will be used by the spell checker to check spellings in a document.

Setting Preferences for Code Colors

In any programming language, you can enhance the code's readability by applying different fonts, styles, or colors to various elements in the code. The Code Colors category in the Preferences dialog box, shown in Figure 16.2, provides various options to set different colors for the background, text, tags, and other elements in Code view.

You can change the background color of Code view by setting a color in the Background option of the Code Colors category.

You can specify different colors for the text and comments in the code by setting colors in the Text and Comments options.

You can apply a different color format for the tags in the code by specifying a color in the Tag Default option.

The Reserved Keywords option lets you specify a color for the keywords that are used by the various scripting languages.

The Other Keywords option lets you specify a color for all keywords other than the reserved keywords.

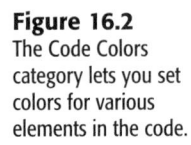

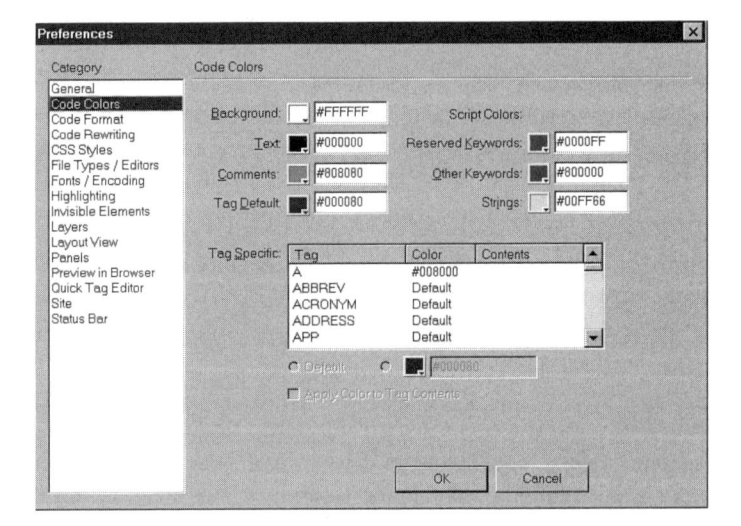

Figure 16.2
The Code Colors category lets you set colors for various elements in the code.

You can differentiate the strings in your code from the other text by specifying a color for strings in the Strings option.

Apart from specifying a common color for all the tags in the code, you can also specify different colors for specific tags in the code by using the Tag Specific option. For example, to identify all the <img> tags in the document, you can specify a particular color for the <img> tag. The tag-specific color overrides all the other color settings. By default, UltraDev applies the selected color only to the opening and closing tag. To specify a tag-specific color, first select a tag from the Tag column of the Tag Specific table. When you select a tag, the Default radio button is selected and the default color for the tag is displayed in the color swatch. However to apply a different color for the tag, select the radio button near the color swatch, and then select a color from the color swatch. Alternatively, you can also enter the hexadecimal value of the color in the text box next to the color swatch. Select the Apply Color to Tag Contents option to apply the selected color to all the text between the opening and closing tags.

SETTING CODE FORMATTING PREFERENCES

The Code Format category of the Preferences dialog box, shown in Figure 16.3, provides options that let you change the code's format, such as indentations, the case of the tags and attributes, line breaks, and the wrapping of text in the code.

You can indent all the tags that are marked as indented in the SourceFormat.txt file by selecting the Indent option. You can specify whether the indentation must be set using tabs or spaces by selecting the appropriate option from the Use drop-down list.

Note: The SourceFormat.txt file is located in the Configuration folder, which is within the Dreamweaver application folder.

Figure 16.3
The Code Format category lets you set preferences for code's format.

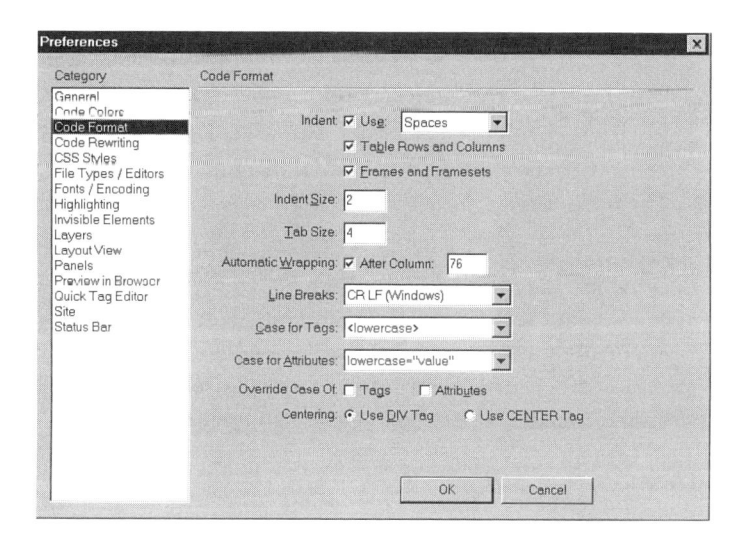

You can indent the contents of a table's rows and columns to enhance readability. To do so, select the Table Rows and Columns option. Similarly, you can also indent the contents of frames and nested frames by selecting the Frames and Framesets option.

The Indent Size and Tab Size options let you specify the size of the indent and the tab, respectively. When you indent code by choosing the Indent Code option from the Edit menu, the code is indented according to the indent size you specify in the Code Format category of the Preferences dialog box. When you indent code by pressing the Tab key, the code is indented according to the tab size you specify in the Code Format category.

The Automatic Wrapping option lets you specify the maximum column width at which the code will wrap automatically. However, UltraDev applies this feature only in places where it does not change the appearance of the document in browsers. Therefore, some lines of code might exceed the specified column width.

The Case for Tags and Case for Attributes options let you specify the case of tags and attributes that are displayed in the Document window when you insert or edit them.

The Override Case Of Tags and Override Case Of Attributes options let you specify whether the case specified in the case options must be applied to open documents. If you want the case of tags and attributes to change in open documents, select the respective Override Case Of options.

The Centering option lets you specify the tag that must be used to center elements on a Web page. This option provides two tag options: DIV and CENTER. Although the functionality of these tags is similar, the CENTER tag is preferable, because a wide range of browsers support it.

Setting Code Rewriting Preferences

The Code Rewriting category of the Preferences dialog box, shown in Figure 16.4, provides options that you can set to allow UltraDev to automatically correct the common errors that you commit while writing HTML code and other scripts. It also provides an option to select the application files to which the corrections must be applied.

The preferences that you set in the Code Rewriting category are applied to HTML and script documents only when you open them, not while you edit them. If you do not set these preferences, UltraDev displays the invalid markup item on the document for the HTML code that has errors in it.

One of the most common errors that is committed while writing HTML code is that of not closing quotation marks or brackets. However, you can overcome this problem by selecting the Fix Invalidly Nested and Unclosed Tags option. This option not only inserts the missing quotations and brackets, but it also rewrites the overlapping tags. For example, the HTML code `<u><i>check this out<u><i>` will be rewritten as `<u><i>check this out<i><u>` when you select the Fix Invalidly Nested and Unclosed Tags option.

You can automatically remove closing tags that do not have corresponding opening tags by selecting the Remove Extra Closing Tags option.

Figure 16.4
Select the various options in the Code Rewriting category to get your common HTML scripting errors corrected automatically.

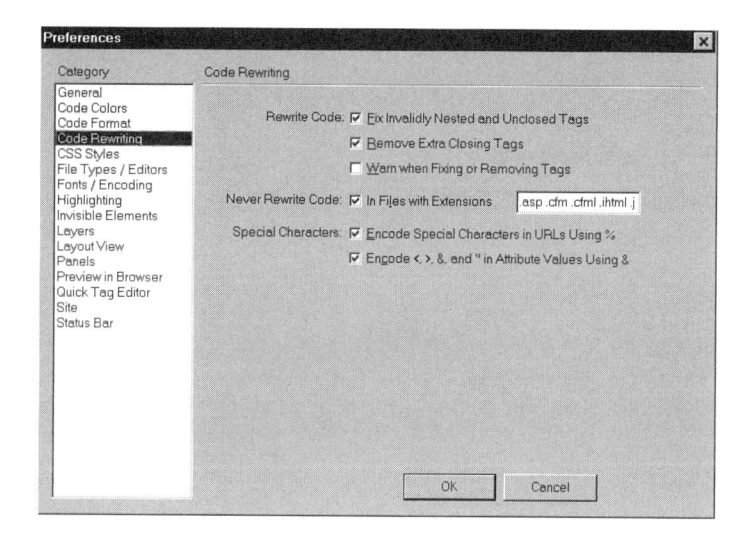

You can opt for a summary of technically invalid HTML to be displayed before UltraDev corrects it by selecting the Warn when Fixing or Removing Tags option.

By default, none of these preferences are applied to files with .asp, .jsp, .cfm, or .php extensions, because UltraDev abstains from modifying such third-party tags. However, you can change this default setting by deselecting the Never Rewrite Code option. You can also add or remove files that you do not want UltraDev to automatically correct by adding or removing the filename extensions from the In Files with Extensions option.

The Special Characters options let you specify whether special characters must be encoded using certain symbols.

SETTING CSS STYLE PREFERENCES

CSS styles can be written using shorthand forms. Although many of the earlier versions of browsers do not properly interpret shorthand forms, many people still use shorthand forms because it is easier to work with them. You can allow UltraDev to write CSS styles in shorthand by using the CSS Styles category of the Preferences dialog box, shown in Figure 16.5.

The Use Shorthand For option lets you select the attributes that you want UltraDev to write in shorthand.

The When Editing CSS Styles Use Shorthand option lets you specify whether existing shorthand code must be rewritten. Select the If Original Used Shorthand option to leave all the shorthand styles as they are. However, if you want the shorthand styles to be rewritten using the attributes specified in the Use Shorthand For option, you must select the According to Settings Above option.

Figure 16.5
Use the CSS Styles category to allow UltraDev to write CSS styles in shorthand.

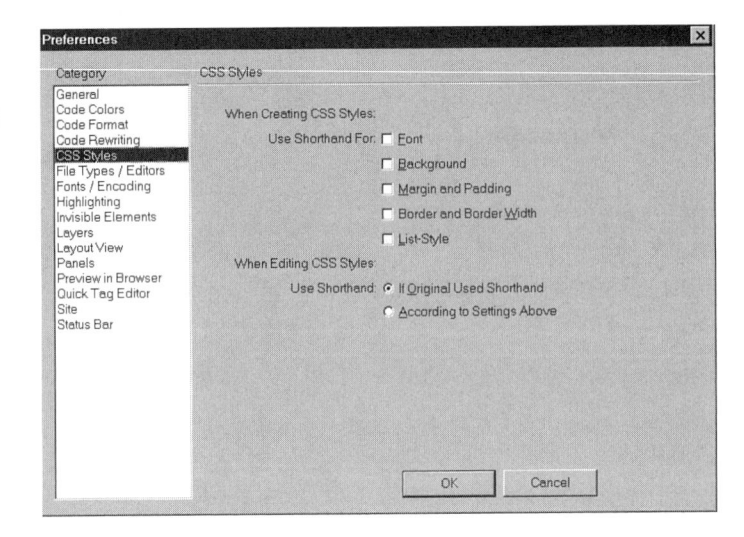

SETTING FILE TYPES/EDITORS PREFERENCES

The File Types/Editors category of the Preferences dialog box, shown in Figure 16.6, lets you specify external editors to edit the various files that you use in UltraDev. It lets you set preferences for external editors based on specific file formats. For example, you can set preferences to start Adobe Photoshop whenever you need to edit GIF images and to start PaintShop Pro whenever you need to edit JPEG images. You can also specify more than one editor for a specific file format.

You need to follow these steps to add an external editor:

1. In the Extensions list box of the File Types/Editors category, select the file type for which you want to set an external editor.

Figure 16.6
Use the File Types/Editors category to set external editors for editing the various types of images.

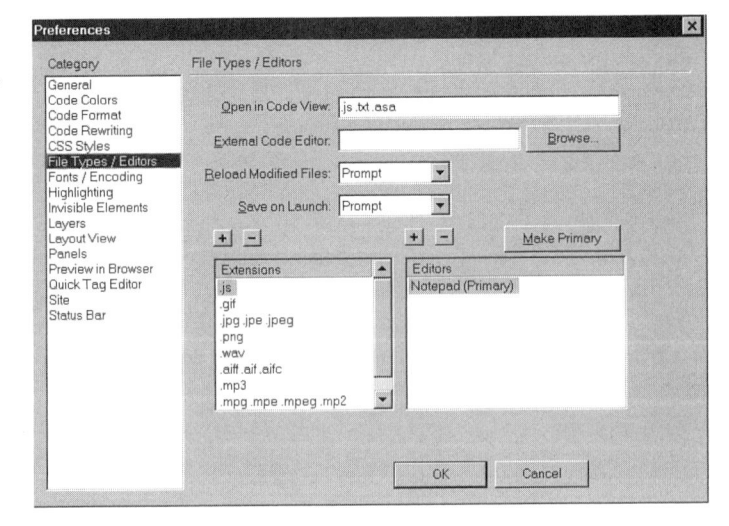

2. Click the + button above the Editors list box to select the graphic editor that must open when you want to edit the specified file type. The Select External Editor dialog box is displayed.
3. In the Select External Editor dialog box, browse and select the application you want to start, and then click Open. The selected editor is added to the Editors list.
4. Click the Make Primary button to specify the selected editor as the primary editor.

You can add multiple editors to the Editors list by repeating steps 1 through 3.

You can also add new file types to the Extensions list. To add a new file type, click the + button above the Extensions list. A text box is displayed in the Extension list that prompts you to enter the new file type for which you want to start an external editor. Enter the file type and follow the steps just given to specify the application that must be started to edit the specified file type.

You can remove extensions and editors from their respective lists by clicking the – buttons above these lists.

You can specify whether the modified files must be reloaded into the document by selecting the appropriate options from the Reload Modified Files option.

The Save on Launch drop-down list lets you specify whether the document needs to be saved before the external editor is launched.

The Open in Code View option lets you specify the file types that can be viewed in Code view.

SETTING FONT/ENCODING PREFERENCES

The Fonts/Encoding category of the Preferences dialog box, shown in Figure 16.7, lets you specify a default font encoding for new documents. It also lets you customize the fonts that UltraDev uses for each of the font encoding schemes. The Font Settings option allows you to customize the font style and size to suit your preferences without affecting how the document is displayed in a browser.

Figure 16.7
Use the Fonts/Encoding category to customize font encoding.

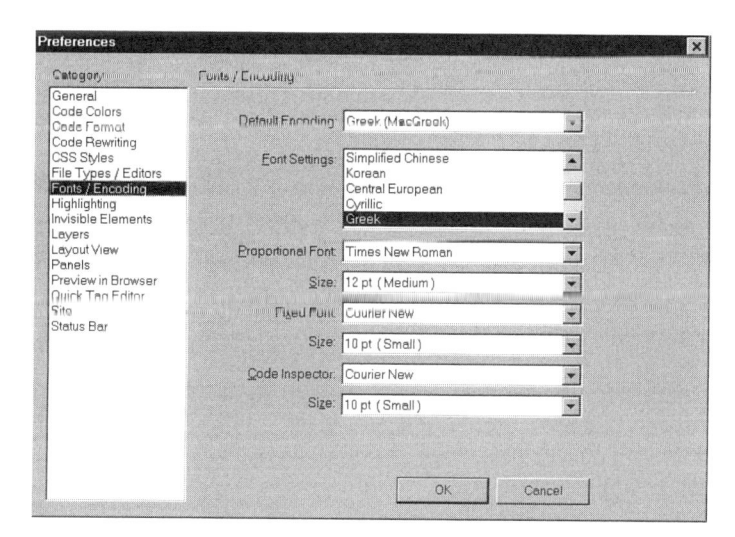

You can specify a default font encoding for new documents by selecting an encoding scheme from the Default Encoding drop-down list. To customize a font encoding provided by UltraDev, you must first select the font encoding from the Font Settings drop-down list. After you select the font encoding, you can select a font for normal text; for text within the pre, code, and tt tags; and for text that appears within the Code inspector by selecting a font from the Proportional Font, Fixed Font, and Code Inspector drop-down lists, respectively. The Size drop-down lists displayed below each of these font lists let you customize the size of the fonts.

Setting Highlight Preferences

The Highlighting category of the Preferences dialog box, shown in Figure 16.8, lets you set the colors used to highlight a document's editable and noneditable regions. It also provides options to set colors for highlighting library items, third-party tags, and live data. You can also specify whether these objects are highlighted at all by selecting or deselecting the Show check boxes next to the objects.

Figure 16.8
You can set colors to highlight the editable and noneditable regions by using the Highlighting category of the Preferences dialog box.

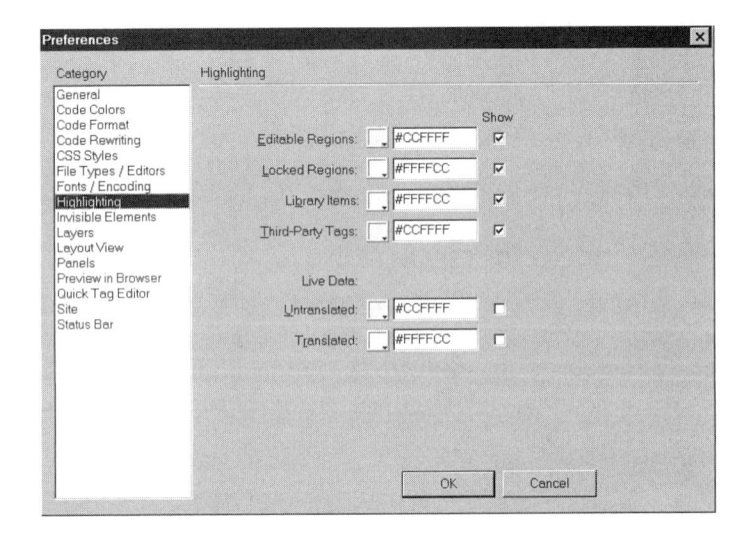

Setting Invisible Elements Preferences

The Invisible Elements category of the Preferences dialog box, shown in Figure 16.9, lets you specify the kinds of elements that must be displayed when you choose View, Visual Aids, Invisible Elements.

To display an element marker, select the element from the list of elements displayed in the Invisible Elements category. To hide an element marker, deselect the element marker from the list.

The Invisible Elements category also lets you set the style in which dynamic content is displayed in the Document window. To set the style of dynamic content, select a style from the Show Dynamic Text As drop-down list.

Figure 16.9
Use the Invisible Elements category to specify the invisible elements that must be displayed in the Document window.

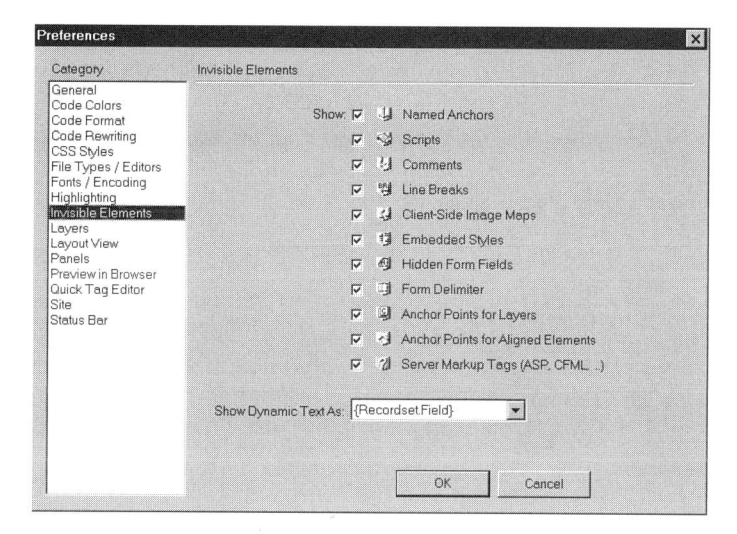

Setting Layers Preferences

The Layers category of the Preferences dialog box, shown in Figure 16.10, lets you change the default settings of layers.

You can set the default HTML tag that must be used for every new layer by selecting an option from the Tag drop-down list in the Layers category.

The Visibility drop-down list in the Layers category lets you set the default visibility option for the layers. The Width and Height options let you change the layers' default height and width. The Background Image and Background Color options let you set a default color and image for the layer's background. The Nesting option lets you specify whether new layers can be nested within an existing layer. Select the Nest when Created Within a Layer option if you want to nest new layers within existing layers.

Figure 16.10
You can change the default settings of the various attributes of layers by using the Layers category.

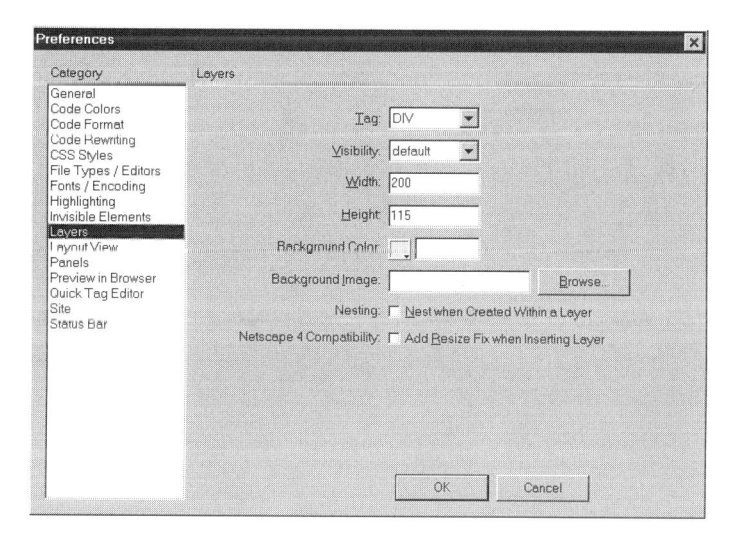

Resizing the Netscape 4.x browser window causes layers in a document to lose their positioning coordinates. However, you can overcome this problem by selecting the Netscape 4 Compatibility option in the Layers category. This option inserts some JavaScript in the head section of the document that fixes this problem in the browser.

Setting Layout View Preferences

The Layout View category of the Preferences dialog box, shown in Figure 16.11, lets you set spacer image files and their locations. It also provides options to change the colors used by layout view to draw tables and cells.

The Autoinsert Spacers option lets you specify whether spacer images must be inserted when you make a column autostretch. Select the When Making Autostretch Tables option if you want spacer images to be inserted. Select the Never option if you do not want spacer images to be inserted.

The Spacer Image option lets you set spacer images for various sites. Choose the site for which you want to set spacer images from the For Site drop-down list. Create a new spacer image for the site by using the Create button, or browse to an existing spacer image in that site by using the Browse button.

The Cell Outline option lets you set a color for drawing a cell outline.

The Cell Highlight option lets you set a color to highlight a cell when you select or point to the cell.

The Table Outline and Table Background options let you set a color for a table's outline and background, respectively.

Figure 16.11
Use the Layout View category to set spacer images.

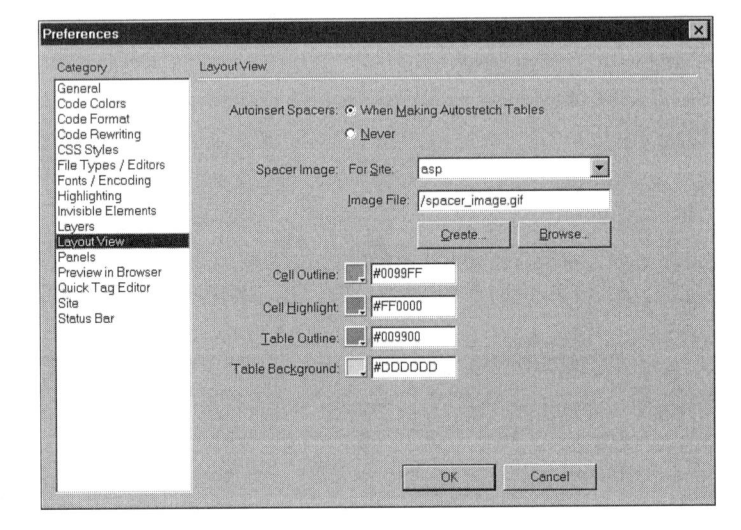

Setting Panels Preferences

The Panels category of the Preferences dialog box, shown in Figure 16.12, lets you select the panels, windows, and inspectors that must always be displayed on the document or Site window. It also lets you add or remove panels that are displayed on the Launcher bar.

Figure 16.12
Use the Panels\ category to organize the UltraDev interface.

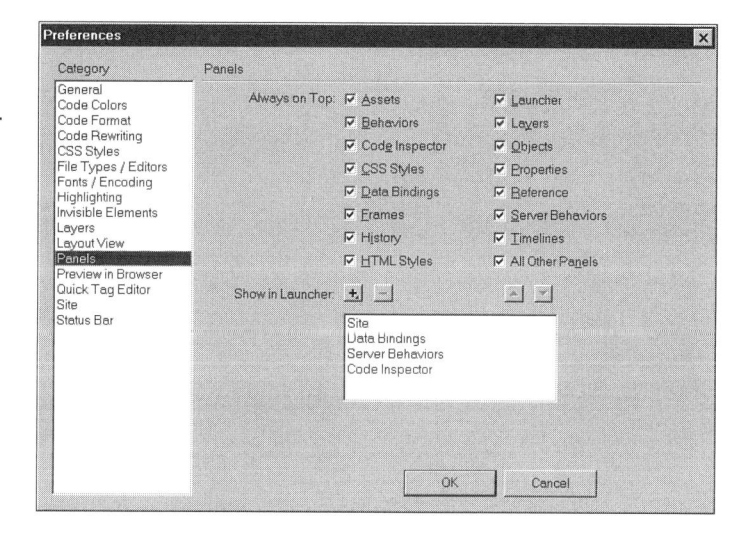

By default, panels, windows, and inspectors are always displayed in the Document or Site window, even if you switch to other objects in the window. However, you can hide the panels, windows, and inspectors in the document by deselecting them from the Always on Top list in the Panels category.

You can add or remove panels from the Launcher bar by using the Show in Launcher option. To add a panel to the Launcher bar, click the + button and select a panel from the drop-down list. To remove a panel from the Launcher bar, select the panel from the list of panels, and then click the – button.

Setting Preferences for Preview in Browser

The Preview in Browser category of the Preferences dialog box, shown in Figure 16.13, lets you set the primary and secondary browsers.

By default, Internet Explorer is set as the primary browser. However, you can add or remove browsers from the Browsers list by clicking the + and – buttons, respectively.

Setting Quick Tag Editor Preferences

You can edit HTML code that is automatically generated by UltraDev by using the Quick Tag Editor, shown in Figure 16.14.

Figure 16.13
Set the primary and secondary browsers by using the Preview in Browser category.

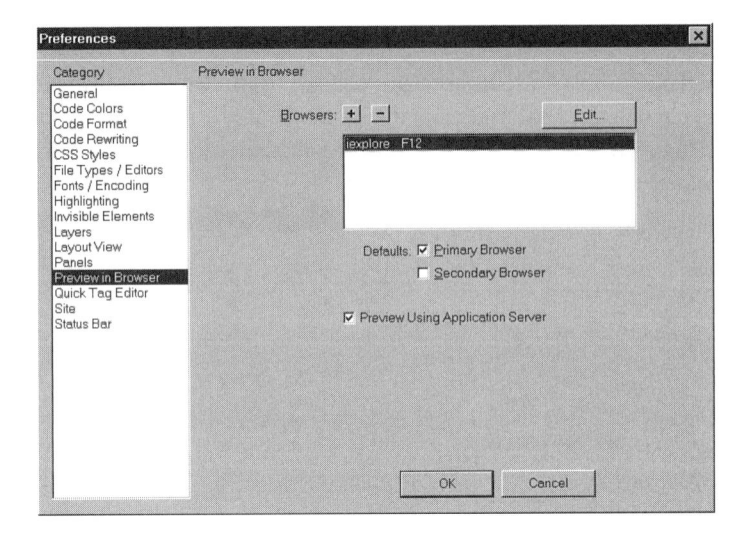

Figure 16.14
Set preferences for the Quick Tag Editor by using the Quick Tag Editor category.

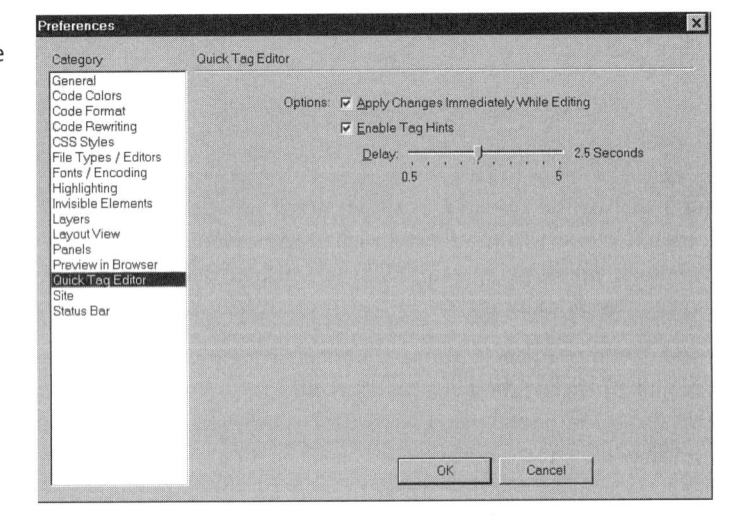

Changes made to the code by using the Quick Tag Editor are immediately reflected in the Document window as you move from one attribute of the object to the other. However, if you want the changes to be reflected in the Document window only when you press the Enter key and not while moving from one attribute to the other, you can deselect the Apply Changes Immediately While Editing option in the Quick Tag Editor category of the Preferences dialog box.

The Quick Tag Editor category also displays options to show or remove hints that are displayed while you edit HTML code in the Quick Tag Editor. Deselect the Enable Tag Hints option to keep tag hints from being displayed while you're typing in the Quick Tag Editor. You can also adjust the delay time for the tag hints to be displayed by using the Delay option.

Setting Site Preferences

The options in the Site category of the Preferences dialog box, shown in Figure 16.15, let you set your preferences for the site's file-transfer features.

The Always Show option lets you designate the pane of the Site window in which local and remote site files must appear.

Whenever you transfer dependent files, such as images and external style sheets, that are referenced in an HTML file, a message box notifying you of the file transfer is displayed by default. However, if you do not want this message to be displayed, deselect the appropriate options in the Dependent Files option of the Site category.

The FTP Connection option lets you determine whether the connection to the remote site needs to be terminated after a specified amount of idle time. If you want the connection to be terminated, select the Disconnect After option and specify the number of minutes after which the connection must be disabled in the Minutes Idle text box. However, if you do not want the connection to be disabled, deselect the Disconnect After option.

The FTP Time Out option lets you specify the number of seconds UltraDev has to connect to the remote server. If the connection with the remote server is not established within the specified amount of time, UltraDev displays a warning that alerts you about this.

If you are behind a firewall, use the Firewall Host option to specify the address of the proxy server through which you like to connect to outside servers. You can leave this option blank if you do not have a firewall.

You can specify the port in your firewall through which you pass to connect to the remote server by entering the appropriate value in the Firewall Port option.

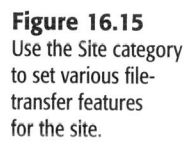

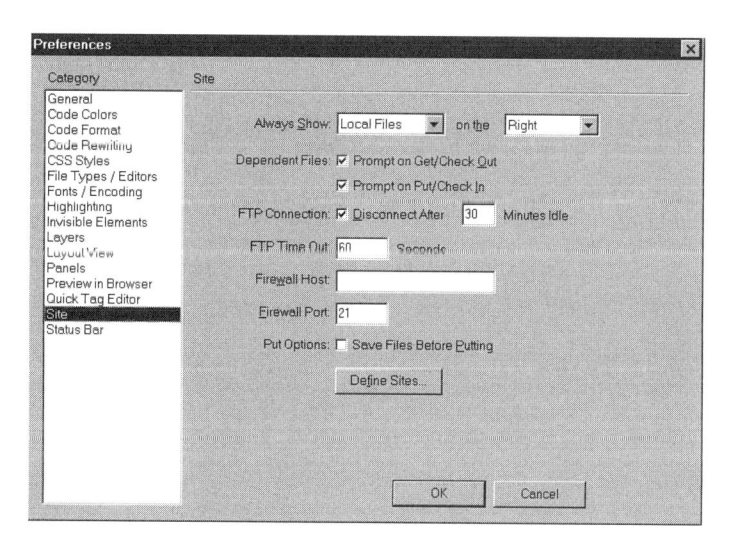

Figure 16.15
Use the Site category to set various file-transfer features for the site.

You can configure UltraDev to automatically save unsaved files before placing them in the remote folder by selecting the Save Files Before Putting option.

The Define Sites button opens the Define Sites dialog box, which lets you create, remove, and edit sites.

Setting Status Bar Preferences

The Status Bar category of the Preferences dialog box, shown in Figure 16.16, lets you customize the various options on the status bar of the Document window.

Figure 16.16
Use the Status Bar category to customize the various status bar options.

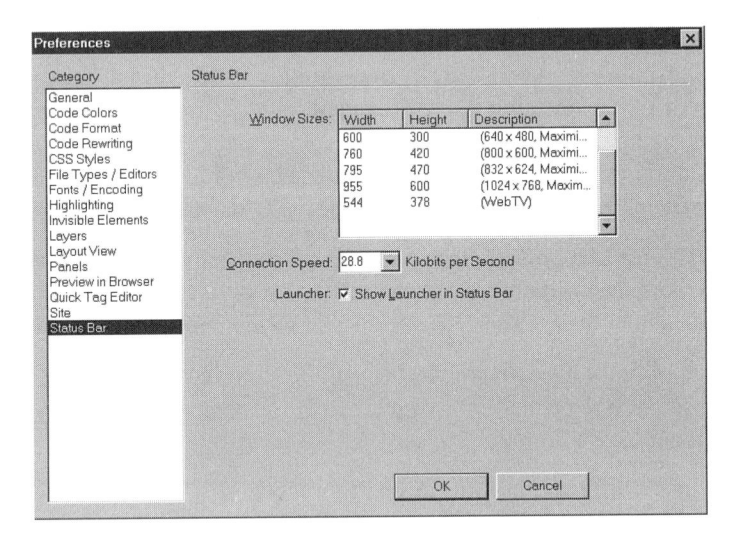

The Window Sizes option lets you customize the window dimensions that are listed on the Window Sizes drop-down menu on the Status bar. By customizing them, you can see how your Web pages will look on various monitors and design them accordingly. You can customize the height, width, and descriptions that are displayed in the list by just clicking them and entering new values. You can also add new values to the list by clicking the end of the list and entering new values in the boxes that appear.

The Connection Speed option lets you specify the connection speed that must be used to calculate the download size of files.

Apart from the window size and connection speed, the status bar also displays the Launcher bar. However, you can remove the Launcher bar from the status bar by deselecting the Show Launcher in Status Bar option.

Summary

UltraDev lets you customize the interface-related features of the various elements in UltraDev by using the Preferences dialog box. The Preferences dialog box provides options to change the default settings and interface-related features of layers, style sheets, the status bar, and the Launcher bar. You can use the Preferences dialog box to add or remove external editors and preview browsers. You can also use this dialog box to change the display of HTML, JavaScript, and other scripting languages.

PART IV

CREATING DYNAMIC WEB PAGES

17 Connecting to a Database 341

18 Dreamweaver UltraDev 4 Data Sources 359

19 Making a Web Page Dynamic 383

20 Building Dynamic Web Applications 407

21 Managing Site Access 431

22 Managing Your Web Site 453

23 Customizing Dreamweaver UltraDev 4 463

CHAPTER 17

CONNECTING TO A DATABASE

In this chapter

Database Connections   342

Creating and Managing Database Connections   344

Troubleshooting   357

Summary   358

Activity Corner   358

Database Connections

ASP, JSP, and CFML applications developed in UltraDev can connect to a wide variety of databases, such as Microsoft Access, Oracle 8i, DB2, Microsoft SQL Server, MySQL, Sybase, and more. UltraDev provides you many methods by which you can connect to the database of your choice. You can choose the method most suitable to you depending on the system you are using to host your Web site (Windows, Macintosh, UNIX, or Linux), the server configuration you have chosen (ASP, JSP, or ColdFusion), and the database you want to access.

UltraDev uses the connections you make to a database to display data at design time as well as at runtime. During design time, UltraDev uses these connections to show dynamic data in Live Data view. Live Data view gives you a preview of data as it appears at runtime. This helps you make necessary changes to the data's presentation before it can be hosted on a Web server.

To be able to connect to a database from UltraDev, you need to have access to a *Web server*, an *application server*, the required database, and a *database driver*. It is not necessary that the Web server, the application server, and the database driver be installed on your development machine. These resources can exist on a remote machine, and you can still access them from UltraDev.

To connect your Web application to a database, you need to use a communication standard such as Open Database Connectivity (ODBC), Object Linking and Embedding Database (OLEDB), or Java Database Connectivity (JDBC).

An Overview of ODBC, OLEDB, and JDBC

In the early days of database connectivity, connecting to a database was not always an easy task. Each database presented data in its own format. To interpret the data available in a database, an application had to make use of an Application Programming Interface (API), which served as an interpreter between the application and the database. Programmers had to know a different API for every database they wanted to access, because there was no common API to access the data that existed in different formats.

The ODBC and OLEDB Standards

ODBC emerged as a solution to provide connectivity between databases and applications. The standards set by ODBC enable connectivity to a wide variety of databases that existed in different formats on different platforms. These standards are implemented in ODBC API, which aims to create a common interface to access databases. A database-specific software program known as a *driver* uses this ODBC API to communicate with a database. The ODBC driver acts as an interpreter between the application and the database. The application communicates with the driver through a set of SQL statements. By using ODBC API, the driver translates these SQL statements into a format the database can understand.

ODBC has rapidly gained widespread acceptance, and a number of databases comply with the ODBC standards. Databases that comply with the ODBC standards are known as ODBC-compliant databases. Oracle, Microsoft Access, Informix, MySQL, and Microsoft SQL Server are some of the popular ODBC-compliant databases available on the market today.

ODBC drivers are developed by Microsoft, Oracle, and a number of third-party software vendors. You can install ODBC drivers on a Windows computer when you install Microsoft Office 2000. These drivers can also be installed when you install Microsoft Data Access Components (MDAC) 2.5. If you already have MDAC 1.5 or 2.0, you need to upgrade, because UltraDev needs at least MDAC 2.1. It is therefore better to install MDAC 2.5. The drivers that come with the MDAC 2.5 package support Microsoft Access, dBASE, SQL Server, and many more. You can download the MDAC 2.5 package from http://www.Microsoft.com/data/download.htm.

Although ODBC has gained widespread acceptance, it still has some shortcomings. It does not completely free the programmer from the task of writing low-level code to access databases. Apart from that, you cannot connect to non-SQL databases with ODBC.

As an enhancement over ODBC, OLEDB evolved as a solution to access data from varied types of data stores without using low-level calls. OLEDB is a set of specifications for designing interfaces based on the Component Object Model (COM). These interfaces let programmers access heterogeneous data from a wide variety of platforms. With OLEDB, you can access data from traditional SQL databases as well as non-SQL databases, such as Active Directory Services Interface (ADSI) directories, Online Analytical Processing (OLAP) servers, log files, and e-mail stores.

Just as you need an ODBC driver to access an ODBC-compliant database, you need an OLEDB provider to connect to an OLEDB-compliant database. An OLEDB provider provides a seamless interface between an application and the database it wants to access. If you want to use an Oracle database with an application, you can use the OLEDB provider for Oracle.

An ASP application connects to an OLEDB provider through ActiveX Data Objects (ADO). An OLEDB provider can understand instructions only if they are written in C++. An ASP application is written in JavaScript or VBScript. Therefore, to create an interface between an ASP application and an OLEDB provider, the ADO model was introduced.

The ADO model consists of a set of objects that encapsulate the low-level details of accessing a database. An ASP application connects to an OLEDB driver by using the ADO objects. The application developer only needs to know how to manipulate these ADO objects to connect with and retrieve data from a database. These objects access the OLEDB provider, which in turn accesses the OLEDB or ODBC database. An ASP application cannot directly connect to an ODBC-compliant database. To connect to an ODBC-compliant database, the ASP application uses a special OLEDB provider that in turn connects to the ODBC driver associated with the database.

OLEDB providers for Microsoft Access and SQL Server are available with the MDAC 2.5 package. The Oracle OLEDB provider comes with the Oracle 8i release 2 for Windows. This Oracle OLEDB provider can be downloaded from http://technet.oracle.com/tech/nt/ole_db.

THE JDBC STANDARD

JDBC is a standard modeled after the ODBC standard to provide universal data access to Java applications. The JDBC standard is implemented in the JDBC API, which is a collection of classes that are used to access data from SQL databases as well as files containing tabular data. The JDBC API builds on the strength of the Java platform, which lets an application run on any kind of platform, by using the same code across platforms. JDBC drivers written using the JDBC API let an application access any kind of database, regardless of the platform on which the application runs. This is how Macintosh users can connect to ODBC databases by means of a JDBC driver.

JSP applications can connect to databases that are JDBC- and ODBC-compliant. JSP applications connect to JDBC-compliant databases by means of a JDBC driver. They connect to ODBC databases by means of a Sun JDBC-ODBC bridge driver that in turn connects to the ODBC driver associated with the ODBC database. When you install the Java 2 SDK, Standard Edition for Windows, the Sun ODBC-JDBC bridge driver is installed automatically. You can download the Java 2 SDK from http://java.sun.com/j2se/.

CREATING AND MANAGING DATABASE CONNECTIONS

In UltraDev, a Web application can use a direct connection to access a database or use an application server to connect to a database. To create a direct connection, you need to have the required database driver on your development machine. UltraDev uses the ODBC, OLEDB, or JDBC drivers installed on your machine to create a direct connection to the database.

If you do not have drivers installed on your development machine, you can use an application server to create a connection to a database. However, ensure that this application server has access to the required drivers.

Note

Macintosh users, who cannot create a direct connection to access a database, will find this a welcome feature. They can connect to databases by using a remote application server.

Before you can use the application server to connect to a database, you must configure UltraDev by using the Site Definition dialog box and specify the location of the application server.

→ For details on configuring UltraDev to connect to an application server, **see** "Application Server Information," **p. 123**.

> **Note**
>
> After you configure UltraDev by specifying an application server, UltraDev creates script files that contain information needed to communicate with a database. These script files are uploaded to a folder called _ _mmDBScripts, which is in the root folder of the Web server. Depending on which application server you specify while configuring your system, these script files will be ASP, JSP, or CFML files.

When you use an application server to connect to a database, UltraDev sends an HTTP request to the Web server the same way a browser sends a request to the Web server. In response to the HTTP request, the Web server sends the connection scripts to the application server for processing. The application server uses the information contained in the connection scripts to connect to the database. After it connects to the database, the application server communicates this information to UltraDev in the form of *XML*. UltraDev reads this XML document to render data in Live Data view. When you use a direct database connection, an HTTP request is not sent to the Web server, because local ODBC, OLEDB, or JDBC connectivity is used.

ODBC Connections: DSN and DSN-less

To connect to an ODBC database from UltraDev, you can use either of the following:

- A Data Source Name (DSN)
- A connection string that uses a DSN-less connection

A DSN is created on a Windows computer to connect to ODBC-compliant databases, and a connection string is used to connect to ODBC- and OLEDB-compliant databases. The best way to connect to a database from a non-Windows platform is by using a connection string.

A DSN is easier to use than a connection string, because the DSN is like a shortcut to connect to a database, whereas a connection string uses elaborate information to connect to a database. However, a connection string is more flexible than a DSN because it does not require a database or its driver to exist on the local machine or the application server, as a DSN does. Each time you use a DSN to connect to a database, the system registry is looked up to find the DSN information. However, a connection string provides a direct connection to the database without using the system registry. Therefore, it works faster than a DSN.

In UltraDev, ASP applications can connect to ODBC databases by using a connection string or a DSN. They can connect to OLEDB databases only by using a connection string. In UltraDev, ColdFusion applications connect to ODBC databases by using a DSN.

A DSN Connection

When you create a connection to a database, you must specify vital information such as the database's name and location and the name of the database driver that supports the database. A DSN encapsulates all this information by providing a name that can be used as a shortcut while creating a database connection. Therefore, when you create a connection using a DSN, you need to specify just the DSN without having to specify all the connection information.

Note

If you want to use a direct connection to connect to a database, the DSN must be defined on the development machine. If you want to use an application server to connect to a database, the DSN must be defined on the machine where the application server is running.

Tip

You can use a clone database of the database on the remote machine to speed up performance while building your site. You can use a direct connection to connect to this clone database. When you host the site, you can use the database on the remote machine. However, when you do this, the connection information that you use when you connect to the clone database must work for connecting to the remote database also. For example, the DSN name that you use to connect to the local database must be the same as the DSN name that you use to connect to the remote database.

ASP and ColdFusion applications can use a DSN defined in Windows to connect to ODBC databases. A ColdFusion application can also use a DSN defined in the ColdFusion administrator to connect to an ODBC database.

The following steps illustrate how to create a DSN to an Access database in Windows:

1. Choose Start, Settings, Control Panel. In the Control Panel window that is displayed, double-click the ODBC Data Sources icon. The ODBC Data Source Administrator dialog box is displayed, as shown in Figure 17.1.

Figure 17.1
Use the ODBC Data Source Administrator dialog box to create and edit DNS.

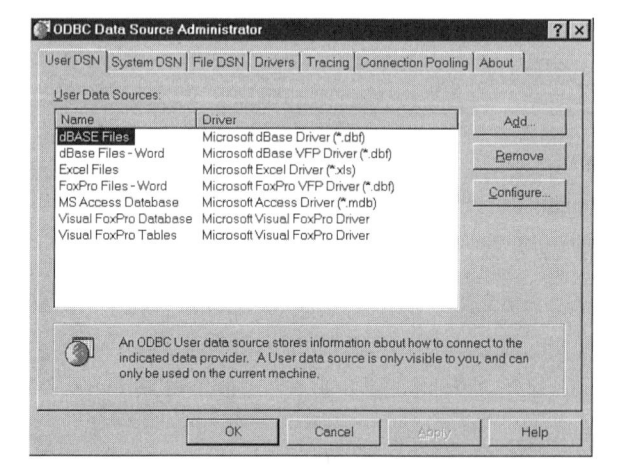

2. Click the System DSN tab. A list of available DSNs is listed here.
3. Click the Add button on the System DSN page. The Create New Data Source dialog box is displayed, as shown in Figure 17.2. You see a list of available drivers.

Figure 17.2
This dialog box lists the drivers that are currently installed on your system.

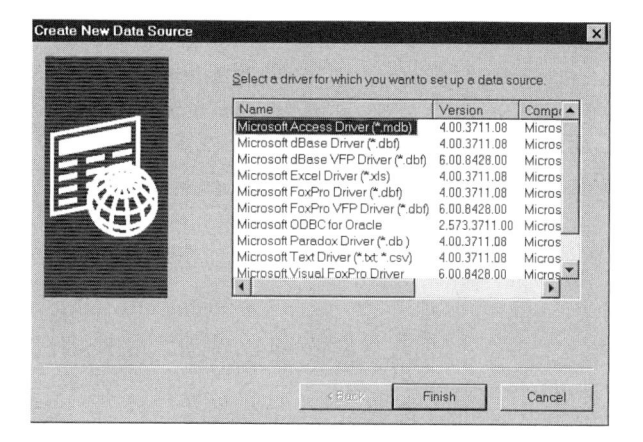

4. Select Microsoft Access Driver from the list, and click the Finish button. The ODBC Microsoft Access Setup dialog box is displayed, as shown in Figure 17.3.

Figure 17.3
Specify the connection parameters in this dialog box to create a DSN.

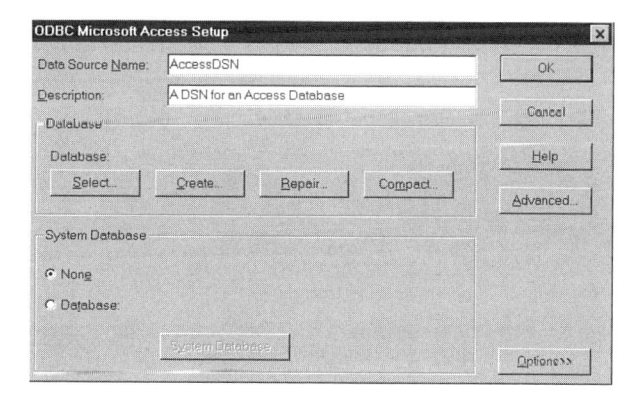

5. Type a name for the data source in the Data Source Name text box. Type an optional description for the DSN in the Description text box.
6. Click the Select button to browse to the database on the local machine or a remote machine.
7. Click the OK button to close the dialog box and return to the ODBC Data Source Administrator dialog box. The DSN that you just created will be listed in this dialog box.
8. Click the OK button.

> **Note**
> A DSN defined in the ColdFusion administrator shows up as a DSN in Windows also.

Creating a DSN Connection to ODBC

After a DSN is defined in Windows, an ASP or ColdFusion application can connect to a database by using this DSN in UltraDev. The steps to be followed to create a DSN connection in UltraDev are the same for both ASP and ColdFusion applications, except for a small change, which will be discussed in the relevant step.

To create a DSN connection to a database from an ASP or ColdFusion application in UltraDev, follow these steps:

1. Choose Modify, Connections. The Connections dialog box is displayed.
2. Click the New button to display a pop-up menu, as shown in Figure 17.4. The pop-up menu that is displayed for an ASP application is slightly different from the one that is displayed for a ColdFusion application. However, both pop-up menus contain the Data Source Name option.

Figure 17.4
You can create either a DSN connection or a custom connection by using the Connections dialog box.

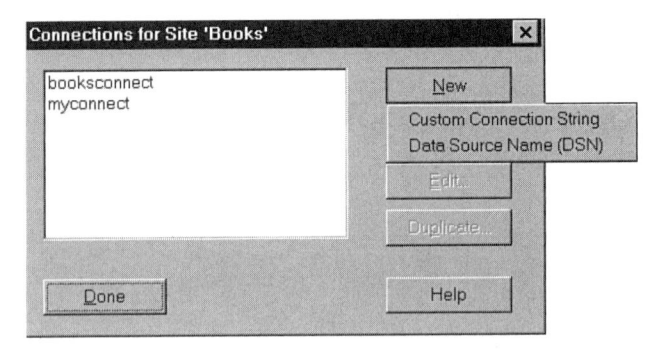

3. Select the Data Source Name option. The Data Source Name dialog box is displayed. If you are creating a connection for an ASP application, the Data Source Name dialog box shown in Figure 17.5 appears. If you are creating a connection for a ColdFusion application, the Data Source Name dialog box shown in Figure 17.6 appears.
4. Enter a name for the connection in the Connection Name text box. It is a good practice to prefix the connection name with conn because it helps to identify the connection name easily.

Figure 17.5
The Data Source Name dialog box for an ASP application.

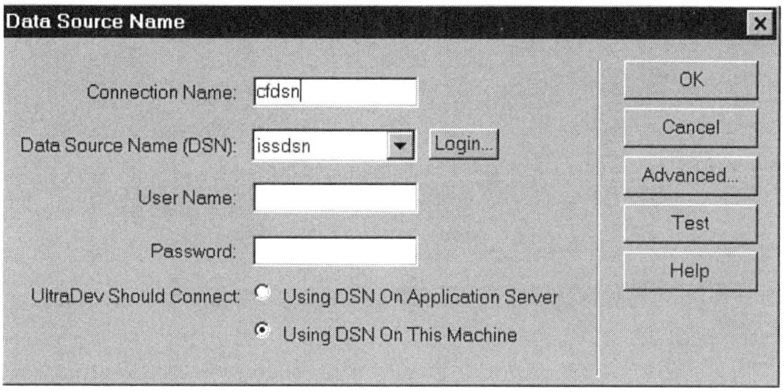

Figure 17.6
The Data Source Name dialog box for a ColdFusion application.

5. Select the Using Local DSN option (for an ASP application) or the Using DSN on This Machine option (for a ColdFusion application) if you want to connect to a database using a direct ODBC connection. Select the Using DSN On Application Server option if you want to create a connection by using an application server.

6. Select a DSN from the list of available DSNs displayed in the Data Source Name drop-down list.

> **Note**
> If you are connecting a ColdFusion application to a database by using a DSN on the application server, you need to log on to the ColdFusion administrator. To do so, click the Login button next to the Data Source Name drop-down list. The DSNs created in the ColdFusion administrator are retrieved and are displayed in the Data Source Name drop-down list.

7. Some databases require a username and password to connect to them. If you need to connect to a database by using a username and password, specify them in the User Name and Password text boxes, respectively.

> **Note**
> Some ISPs display all the DSNs on the server. To prevent other Web developers from accessing your DSN, you should always password protect it.

8. If you want to restrict the number of database items be made available to your Web application, you can create a *schema* or *catalog name* in your database. To create a schema or catalog in your database, consult the database documentation. To specify the schema or catalog name in UltraDev, click the Advanced button to display the Restrict dialog box, as shown in Figure 17.7. Specify the schema or catalog name in the appropriate text box, and then click OK.

Figure 17.7
Restrict access to a database by using this dialog box.

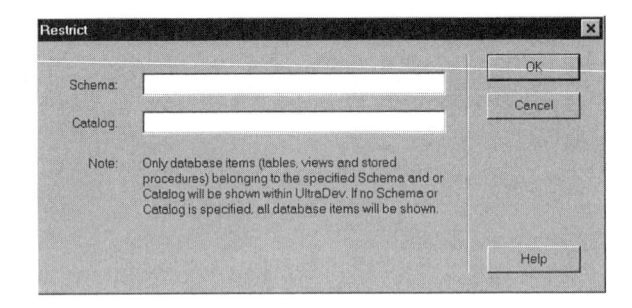

9. Click the Test button in the Data Source Name dialog box to see if the connection is successful. If the connection is established successfully, UltraDev displays a message box telling you that the connection succeeded.
10. Click the OK button in the Data Source Name dialog box. Click the Done button in the Connections dialog box.

USING A CONNECTION STRING TO CONNECT TO ODBC AND OLEDB DATABASES

A connection string consists of sets of parameters with their values. These parameters and their values provide vital information needed by a Web application to connect to a database. A connection string's parameters vary depending on the type of database you want to access. For example, the parameters used to connect to an ODBC database are different from those used to connect to an OLEDB database.

The following list describes some commonly used parameters:

- Driver: This parameter has the name of the ODBC driver as its value. If you want to connect to an ODBC database from an ASP application, you must use this parameter in the connection string.
- Provider: If you are connecting to an OLEDB database, use this parameter. This parameter has the name of an OLEDB provider as its value. If you are connecting to an ODBC database from an ASP application, you can specify the name of the OLEDB provider that must connect to the ODBC driver. If you do not specify the OLEDB provider to connect to the ODBC database, the ASP application will use MSDASQL, which is the default OLEDB provider.
- Server: This parameter has the name of the server where a database resides as its value. Use this parameter only if the database is on a server other than the application server.
- Database: This parameter has the name of a database as its value.
- DBQ: This parameter has the path to a database as its value. If you are connecting to a database on a remote server from an ASP application and you do not know the exact path to the database, you can use the `MapPath` method of the `Server` object in ASP.
- UID: This parameter has the username needed to connect to a database as its value.

- PWD: This parameter has the password needed to connect to a database as its value.
- DSN: This parameter has a DSN as its value. If you use this parameter in a connection string, you do not have to explicitly state the other parameters, such as Database and DBQ, in the connection string.

> **Note**
> To find out the exact parameters needed for your particular database, refer to the database documentation.

SOME SAMPLE CONNECTION STRINGS A connection string consists of sets of parameters and their values, separated by semicolons. The following list shows some sample connection strings:

- An ODBC connection to an Access database:
  ```
  Driver={Microsoft Access Driver (*.mdb)};DBQ=path of the database;
  UID=userid;PWD=password
  ```
- An ODBC connection to a dBASE database:
  ```
  Driver={Microsoft dBASE Driver(*.dbf)};DriverID=driver_id;
  DBQ=path of the database
  ```
- An ODBC connection to an Excel worksheet:
  ```
  Driver={Microsoft Excel Driver (*.xls)};DriverID=driver id;
  DefaultDir=default path
  ```
- An ODBC connection to an Oracle database:
  ```
  Driver={Microsoft ODBC for Oracle};Server=server_name;
  UID=user_id;PWD=password
  ```
- An ODBC connection to a Paradox database:
  ```
  Driver={Microsoft Paradox Driver (*.db)}; DriverID=driver id;
  Fil=Paradox 5.X;DefaultDir=default path; DBQ=path of the database;
  Collating Sequence=ASCII
  ```
- An ODBC connection to a text file:
  ```
  Driver={Microsoft Text Driver (*.txt;*.csv)}; DBQ=path of the database;
  Extensions=asc,csv,tab,txt;Persist Security Info=False
  ```
- An OLEDB connection to a DB2 database:
  ```
  Provider=DB2OLEDB;Network Transport Library=TCPIP;
  Network Address=address;Package Collection=name of the package;
  Host CCSID=host id;Initial Catalog=catalog name;User ID= user_id;
  Password=password
  ```
- An OLEDB connection to an Access database:
  ```
  Provider=MSDASQL;Driver={Microsoft Access Driver (*.mdb)};
  DBQ=path of the database; UID=user_id;PWD=password
  ```

If you are using an ASP application and you are unsure of a database's path, you can use the MapPath method of the Server object. The MapPath method takes the file's virtual or relative path and converts it to the physical path of the file on the server. In the following example, the physical path to an Access database called books.mdb is resolved by using the MapPath method. The username needed to connect to the database is books_user, and the password is my_database. If this database is located in a host directory called booksite, the Server.MapPath method is used in the following manner:

```
Driver={Microsoft Access Driver
(*.mdb)};DBQ=Server.MapPath("/booksite/books.mdb");
UID=books_user;PWD=my_database
```

CREATING A CONNECTION STRING IN ULTRADEV You can use a connection string to connect an ASP application to an ODBC or an OLEDB database from UltraDev. To create a connection using a connection string in UltraDev, follow these steps:

1. Choose Modify, Connections. The Connections dialog box is displayed.
2. Click the New button. Choose the Custom Connection String option from the pop-up menu that is displayed. The Custom Connection String dialog box is displayed, as shown in Figure 17.8.
3. In the Connection Name text box, specify a name for the connection. In the Connection String text box, type the connection string required to connect to the database.
4. If your connection string uses a driver located on your development machine, select the Using Driver On This Machine option. If the connection string uses a driver located on an application server, select the Using Driver On Application Server option.
5. If you have defined a schema for your database, specify it for the connection in the Restrict dialog box. To display this dialog box, click the Advanced button.
6. Click the Test button to see if the connection is established successfully.

Figure 17.8
Use this dialog box to connect to an ODBC or OLEDB database.

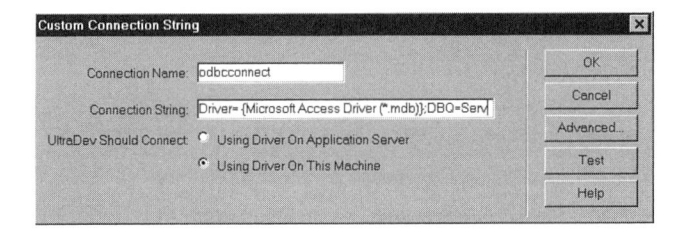

CONNECTING A JSP APPLICATION TO A DATABASE

From UltraDev, you can connect a JSP application to JDBC-compliant databases as well as ODBC-compliant databases by using JDBC driver parameters. UltraDev provides you with a set of default options for connecting to the most commonly used JDBC drivers, such as the Oracle Thin JDBC driver and the Sun JDBC-ODBC Bridge driver. If the driver you use is not listed as an option in UltraDev, you can create a custom connection string to connect to your driver.

To create a JDBC connection from UltraDev, follow these steps:

1. Choose Modify, Connections. In the Connections dialog box that is displayed, click the New button.
2. Select the desired driver from the pop-up menu that is displayed. Figure 17.9 shows the options that are available on this menu.

Figure 17.9
Use this dialog box to connect to a JDBC or ODBC database.

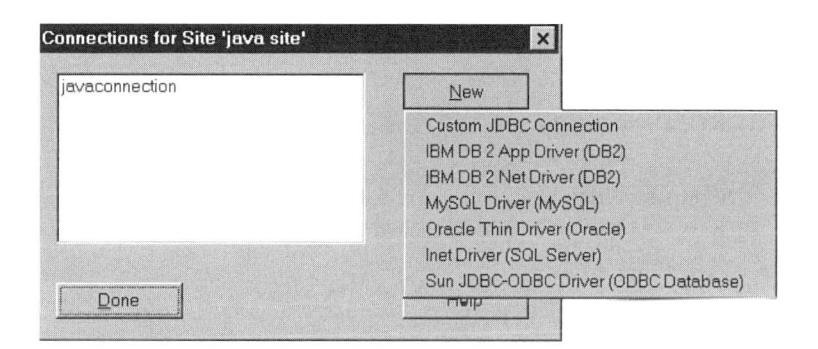

3. If the driver you want to use is not available as one of the options, choose the Custom JDBC Connection option. Depending on the option you choose, the respective dialog box is displayed. Figure 17.10 shows the Sun JDBC-ODBC Driver dialog box.

Figure 17.10
Specify the connection parameters in this dialog box.

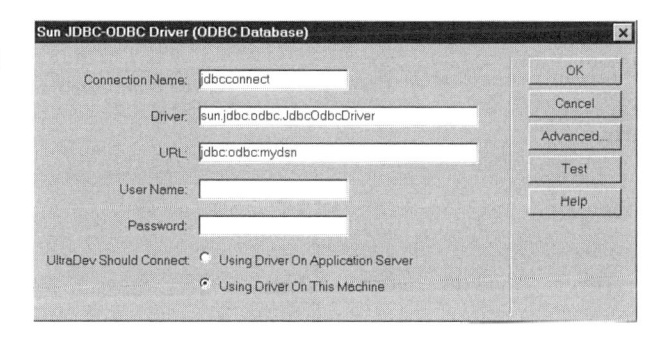

4. Specify a name for the connection in the Connection Name text box.
5. Specify the name of the JDBC driver in the Driver text box.
6. In the URL text box, specify the location of the database.
7. In the User Name and Password text boxes, specify a username and password, if any, needed to connect to the database.

> **Note**
> The values of the URL and Driver parameters depend on which driver you use. Consult the vendor's documentation about the parameter values required to connect to the driver you use.

The following list shows the values of the Driver and URL parameters for some commonly used drivers:

- IBM DB2 driver

  URL parameter value:
  `com.ibm.db2.jdbc.net.DB2driver`

  Driver parameter value:
  `jdbc:db2://database_name`

- I-net JDBC driver

  URL parameter value:
  `com.inet.tds.TdsDriver`

  Drive parameter value:
  `jdbc:inetdae:servername:database_port_number?database=databasename`

- Oracle Thin driver

  URL parameter value:
  `oracle.jdbc.driver.OracleDriver`

  Drive parameter value:
  `jdbc:oracle:thin:@servername:database_port_number:database_system_identifier`

- Sun JDBC-ODBC Bridge driver

  URL parameter value:
  `sun.jdbc.odbc.JdbcOdbDriver`

  Drive parameter value:
  `jdbc:odbc:dsn_name`

- RmiJdbc driver

  URL parameter value:
  `RmiJdbc.RJDriver`

  Drive parameter value:
  `jdbc:rmi://server_name/jdbc:odbc:dsn_name`

- MySQL driver

  URL parameter value:
  `org.gjt.mm.mysql.Driver`

  Drive parameter value:
  `jdbc:mysql://server_name:database_port_number/dsn_name`

Connecting Macintosh Computers to ODBC Databases

Web applications developed on the Macintosh platform connect to ODBC databases by using a JDBC driver called RmiJdbc. A Macintosh computer can access an ODBC data source available on a Windows NT or Windows 2000 computer, as a JDBC data source, by means of the RmiJdbc driver. The RmiJdbc driver has two components: the client driver and the server driver.

The client driver must be installed on the Macintosh machine, and the server driver must be installed on the Windows computer. The Windows computer must have IIS, the ColdFusion application server, and the required ODBC driver. This Windows computer must be networked to the Macintosh computer. The Windows computer acts as a bridge between the JDBC driver installed on the Macintosh computer and the ODBC data source. To install RmiJdbc on the Macintosh and Windows computers, refer to the UltraDev CD, which contains instructions.

After you install the required components and configure the Macintosh and Windows machines, you can open a ColdFusion application on the Macintosh computer and connect it to the required ODBC data source. Follow these steps to connect a ColdFusion application to an ODBC data source:

1. Choose Modify, Connections. The Connections dialog box is displayed.
2. Click the New button. From the pop-up menu that is displayed, select the Data Source Name - Advanced option. The Data Source Name - Advanced dialog box is displayed, as shown in Figure 17.11.

Figure 17.11
Use this dialog box to create a connection from a Macintosh machine.

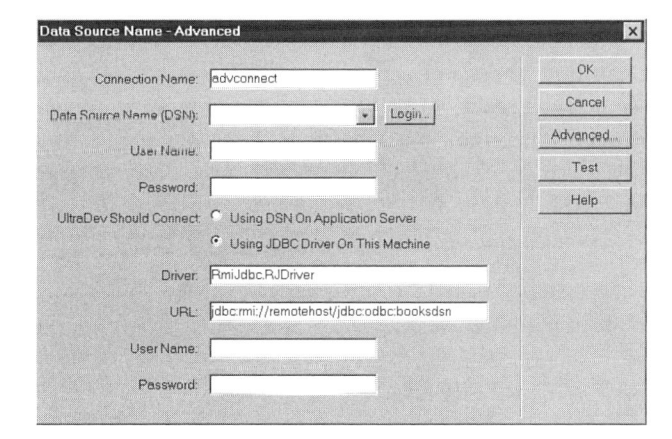

3. In the Connection Name text box, specify a name for the connection.
4. Log on to the ColdFusion administrator by clicking the Login button. The Login to ColdFusion RDS dialog box is displayed. Enter a username and password in the User Name and Password text boxes, respectively.
5. After you log on, the DSNs available in the ColdFusion administrator are retrieved and are displayed in the Data Source Name drop-down list. Select the required DSN from this drop-down list.
6. If required, type a user name and password to connect to the database in the User Name and Password text boxes that appear near the middle of the Data Source Name - Advanced dialog box.
7. Select the Using JDBC Driver On This Machine option to define the connection parameters required for connecting to a JDBC driver.

8. In the Driver text box, type `RmiJdbc.RJDriver`. In the URL text box, type
   `jdbc:rmi://host_name_of_the_NT_Server/jdbc:odbc:DSN_on_Windows NT`.

9. Specify the username and password required to connect to the data source in the User Name and Password text boxes near the bottom of the dialog box.

10. Click the Test button to see if the connection is established successfully.

11. Click OK to close the Data Source Name - Advanced dialog box. In the Connections dialog box, click the Done button to complete the connection process.

> **Note**
>
> After you have created the required connection from your ASP, JSP, or ColdFusion application to a database, UltraDev stores the connection information in a script file. This script file is in the Connections subfolder of the local root folder. Each document that you create will contain an *include directive* that tells the server to include this script file in each document.

Performing a Final Check on the Database Connection

After you create a connection to a database from UltraDev, it displays a message notifying you that the connection was established successfully. However, this does not necessarily mean that the connection really works. UltraDev does not create a database connection until a recordset is defined. Therefore, you will not be able to find out if your connection works until you create a recordset. To double-check whether the connection really works, create a recordset for your Web application.

→ To learn how to create a recordset, **see** "Creating a Recordset," **p. 360**.

After you have successfully created a recordset, you can view the data retrieved from the database, as shown in Figure 17.12.

Managing Database Connections

UltraDev allows you to create many database connections for a single site. This feature helps when you have to access many data sources. During the course of application development, you might want to edit or delete these connections.

To edit or delete a connection, open the Connections dialog box by choosing Modify, Connections. Select the connection you want to edit, and click the Edit button. This displays the dialog box that you used while creating the connection. In this dialog box, you can make necessary changes and then click the OK button. To delete a connection, select the connection and click the Remove button. UltraDev displays the message shown in Figure 17.13. Click Yes to delete the connection.

Figure 17.12
Data retrieved from a database.

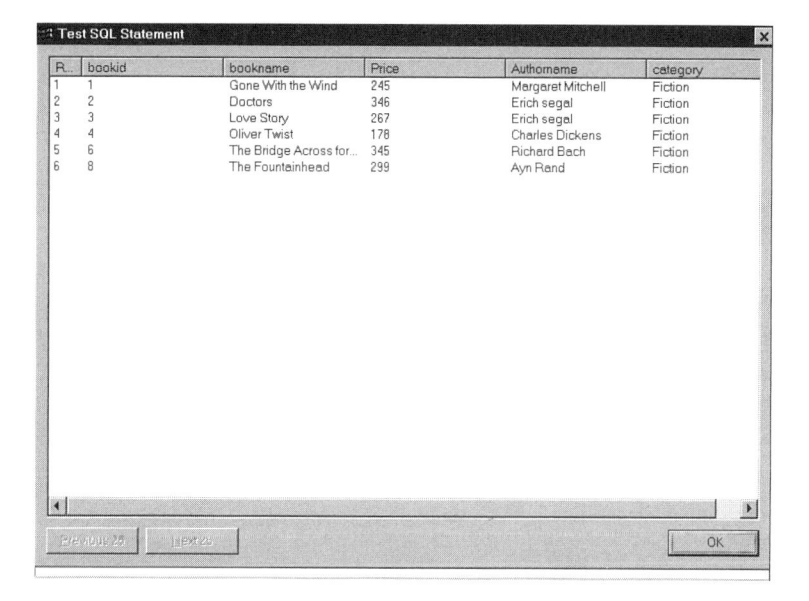

Figure 17.13
You see a confirmation message before you delete a connection.

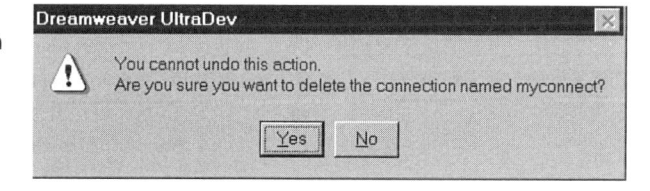

> **Note**
> When you edit a connection, UltraDev updates the connection file in the Connections subfolder. The updated connection information is available to all documents, because this file is included in every document in your site.

TROUBLESHOOTING

Database Connections

I can't establish a connection to the database.

While creating database connections, if you find that the connection is not established successfully, check for the following:

- If you are using a DSN, check to see if the required drivers are installed on the system where you are creating the DSN. If you are connecting to a remote database while creating a DSN, check to see if the network connection is working properly.
- If you are using a connection string, check the connection parameters that have to be specified in the connection string. Refer to the driver's documentation to check whether you specified all the parameters that apply to the particular driver.

- Check the name and path of the database to which you are creating a connection.
- Check to see if you have the required permission to access the database. Check whether the username and password you have supplied are correct.

SUMMARY

This chapter dealt with the various ways in which you can connect to databases from an ASP, JSP, or ColdFusion application in UltraDev. You can create a connection to an ODBC database from an ASP or ColdFusion application by using a DSN. You can also create a connection to an ODBC database and an OLEDB database by using a connection string. To connect to JDBC databases from a JSP application, you need to connect to the appropriate JDBC driver by using the Connections dialog box in UltraDev. Macintosh users can connect to an ODBC database by means of a JDBC driver that they need to install on their systems.

ACTIVITY CORNER

In this section, you will create a connection to a database that helps you implement all the dynamic features in the Tunein.com Web site. The sample Access database named song_master contains all the tables, queries, and sample records necessary to implement and test the dynamic features. If you do not plan to use the song_master database, create a database with the same structure as the song_master database and insert sample records to match the sample records given in the song_master database so that you can follow the activities listed in the following chapters without any problem. Create a database from the Contentpage.asp, Search.asp, and Songfetch.asp files. Name the connection **SongConnect**, regardless of the type of connection you choose to connect to the database.

CHAPTER 18

DREAMWEAVER ULTRADEV 4 DATA SOURCES

In this chapter

Understanding Data Sources   360

Creating and Managing Data Sources   366

Summary   378

Activity Corner   378

Understanding Data Sources

Dynamic Web applications require a data source from which they can retrieve and display the latest information on a Web page. In UltraDev, you can decide to use databases, request variables, URL variables, server variables, form variables, or stored procedures as sources of data.

Before you can use any of these data sources for your Web application, you need to define these data sources for every Web page of the Web application. Defining a data source involves specifying the information that must be retrieved from a database. When you want the information to be retrieved from a database, the data source that is defined in UltraDev retrieves this information. This information is then used to add dynamic content to your Web application.

In UltraDev, when you use a database as a source of data for developing an ASP or a ColdFusion application, the data source that is defined is called a recordset. The same data source is called a resultset if you are developing a JSP application. If you are using other sources of data, such as user input data, the name of the data source that is defined in UltraDev is the same as the data source name itself.

UltraDev gives you many ways to create a data source. The Data Bindings panel in UltraDev is used to create a data source. For ASP, JSP, or ColdFusion applications, you can create as many data sources as required by using the Data Bindings panel. Any new data source that is created is added to the list of existing data sources in the Data Bindings panel. After creating the data source in the Data Bindings panel, you can use it to add dynamic content to your Web page.

→ To learn more about adding dynamic elements to a Web page, **see** "Adding Dynamic Elements to a Web Page," **p. 384**.

Creating a Recordset

When you are using a database as the data source for your Web application developed in UltraDev, you must first create a recordset that will store the retrieved data from the database. The application server uses the data stored in the recordset for faster data retrieval. The server temporarily stores the data in memory and erases it when it is no longer used.

A *recordset* is a collection of columns retrieved from a specified database. It can include all the rows and columns of the database table or only some rows and columns. These rows and columns are retrieved by means of a query that is defined in the recordset. You can create a query by typing SQL statements yourself or by having UltraDev generate the SQL statements. UltraDev uses the SQL builder to generate the SQL statements. This lets you build simple queries and saves time by reducing the amount of typing. If you want to build complex queries, you can build them manually by writing SQL statements in the SQL editor available in UltraDev.

> **Note**
>
> Avoid including unnecessary data in the recordset, and try to create a small recordset. A small recordset occupies less memory space than a large recordset and hence improves server performance.

CREATING A RECORDSET WITHOUT WRITING SQL

To create a recordset, you need to first define a connection to the database. After the connection is made, you can create the recordset to retrieve the data stored in database tables. This recordset can contain either specified rows in a table or an entire table.

The UltraDev simple Recordset dialog box lets you create a recordset without having to type SQL statements.

To create a recordset without writing SQL statements, follow these steps:

1. In the Document window, open the page that will use the recordset created without using SQL.
2. Choose Windows, Data Bindings to display the Data Bindings panel, shown in Figure 18.1.

Figure 18.1
You can use the Data Bindings panel to create a recordset.

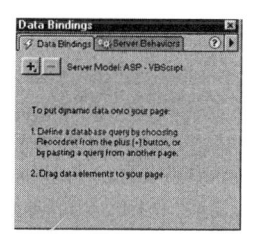

3. Click the + button in the Data Bindings panel. A pop-up menu is displayed, as shown in Figure 18.2.

Figure 18.2
When you click the + button in the Data Bindings panel, it displays the list of options that are used to define data sources.

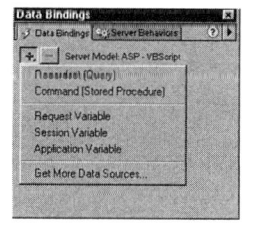

4. Select Recordset (Query) from the pop-up menu. The simple Recordset dialog box is displayed, as shown in Figure 18.3.

Figure 18.3
The simple Recordset dialog box lets you create a recordset without using SQL.

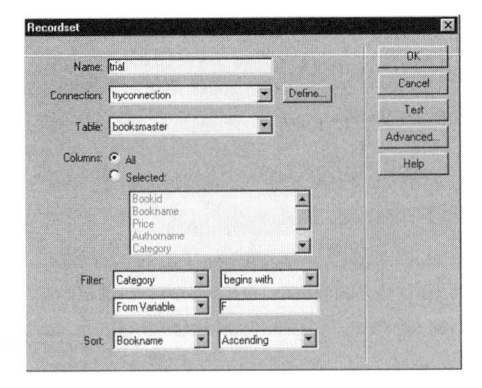

> **Note**
> If the Data Bindings panel opens the advanced Recordset dialog box, click the Simple button to open the simple Recordset dialog box.

5. Type a name for the recordset in the Name text box.

> **Note**
> The recordset name must not contain spaces, underscores, or special characters.

6. Select an existing connection from the Connection pop-up menu. If you do not want to use any of the existing connections, you can create a new connection.

→ To learn more about creating a connection to a database, **see** "Database Connections," **p. 342**.

7. From the Table drop-down list, select a database table, which will send data to or receive data from your recordset. This drop-down list displays a list of all the tables in the connected database.

8. Select the All option if you want to include all the columns from the selected table in the recordset. Select the Selected option if you want to include only some of the columns in the recordset. If you select the Selected option, a list of columns available in the selected table is displayed, as shown in Figure 18.4.

9. Hold down the Ctrl key and select the fields to be included in the recordset.

10. Specify a condition under which a record can be retrieved from a database table to be stored in the recordset. Use the options in the Filter section to specify this condition. From the first drop-down list in the Filter section, select a column in the table that contains values that match a specific value. The records are filtered based on this column.

UNDERSTANDING DATA SOURCES | 363

Figure 18.4
The columns available in the selected table are displayed in the description area.

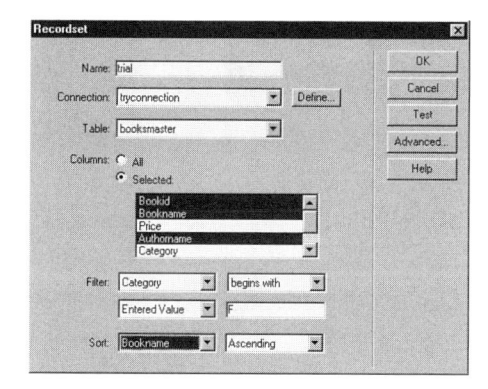

11. From the second drop-down list, select a conditional expression to compare each value of the column to a specified value.
12. Select an appropriate option from the third drop-down list, which indicates the source of the specified value.
13. Finally, specify the value that must be compared to the column values by typing either the value or the variable containing the value in the fourth text box.
14. The Sort section lets you specify whether the records must be sorted in ascending or descending order. Specify the column name to be sorted in the first drop-down list, and specify whether it must be sorted in ascending or descending order in the second drop-down list.
15. Click the Test button to connect to the database and check whether the recordset was created successfully. The Please Provide a Test Value dialog box is displayed, as shown in Figure 18.5.

Figure 18.5
Use the Please Provide a Test Value dialog box to test whether the recordset reads data from the database.

16. Type a test value in the Test Value text box and click OK to test the creation of the recordset. If an instance of the recordset is created successfully, a table showing the data in your recordset is displayed.
17. Click OK to add the recordset to the list of data sources in the Data Bindings panel. The newly defined recordset appears in the Data Bindings panel, as shown in Figure 18.6.

PART
IV
CH
18

Figure 18.6
The specified recordset is defined as a data source in the Data Bindings panel.

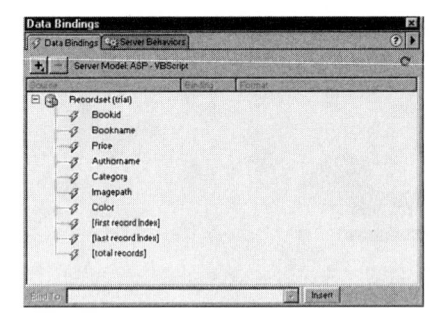

For example, in Figure 18.6, a recordset named trial has been defined to retrieve the Bookid, Bookname, and Authorname columns from a table called bookmaster based on a condition specified in the Filter section. This condition specifies that the recordset must retrieve records in which the Category column contains a value that begins with the entered value, F.

CREATING A RECORDSET BY WRITING SQL

The UltraDev advanced Recordset dialog box lets you create a recordset by writing SQL statements. In the advanced Recordset dialog box, you can access tables, views, and procedures for querying the database, and you can enter SQL statements manually. SQL gives you the option of retrieving the data stored in tables with the help of queries. The set of rows and columns returned after querying a database is called a recordset.

To create a recordset by writing SQL, follow these steps:

1. In the Document window, open the page that will use the recordset.
2. Open the Data Bindings panel. Click the + button in the Data Bindings panel, and select Recordset (Query) from the pop-up menu that is displayed. The simple Recordset dialog box is displayed.
3. Click the Advanced button in the Recordset dialog box. The advanced Recordset dialog box is displayed, as shown in Figure 18.7.
4. Type a name for the recordset in the Name text box.

Note It is a good practice to prefix the recordset name with rs.

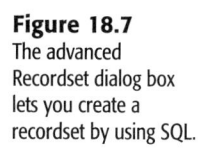

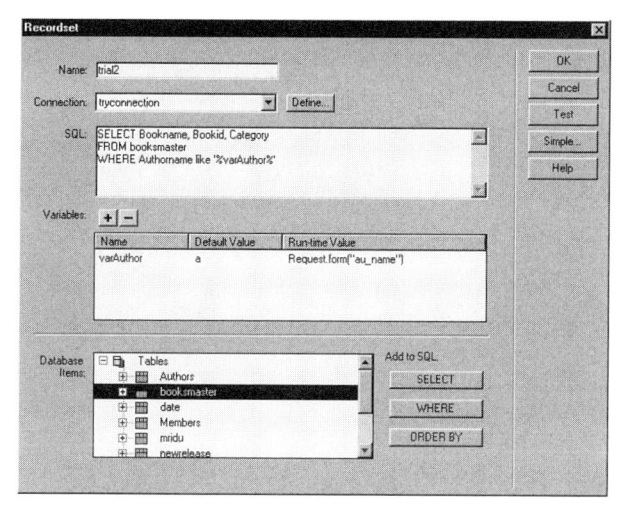

Figure 18.7
The advanced Recordset dialog box lets you create a recordset by using SQL.

5. Select an existing connection from the Connection drop-down menu. If you do not want to use any of the existing connections, you can create a new connection.

→ To learn more about creating a new connection to a database, **see** "Creating and Managing Database Connections," **p. 344**.

6. Type the SQL statement in the SQL text box. You can use the options in the Database Items section and the Add to SQL section in the lower pane of the advanced Recordset dialog box for querying the database. In the Database Items list box, expand the branches in the database tree, and select the database object you need. Click one of the three buttons, SELECT, WHERE, or ORDER BY, in the Add to SQL section to add the selected database object to the SQL statement in the SQL text box.

7. You can define the values for the variables defined in the SQL statement in the Variables list box. Click the + button, and type the variable name in the Name column.

8. Type a default value for the variable in the Default Value column and a runtime value for the variable in the Run-time Value column. The default value is the value assigned to the variable if there is no other incoming value or if you want to test the recordset.

9. Click the Test button to connect to the database and check whether the recordset was created successfully.

10. Click OK to add the recordset to the list of data sources in the Data Bindings panel. The newly defined recordset is added to the list of data sources in the Data Bindings panel, as shown in Figure 18.8.

Figure 18.8
The specified recordset is added to the list of existing data sources in the Data Bindings panel.

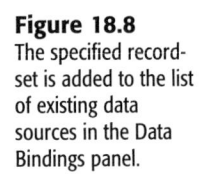

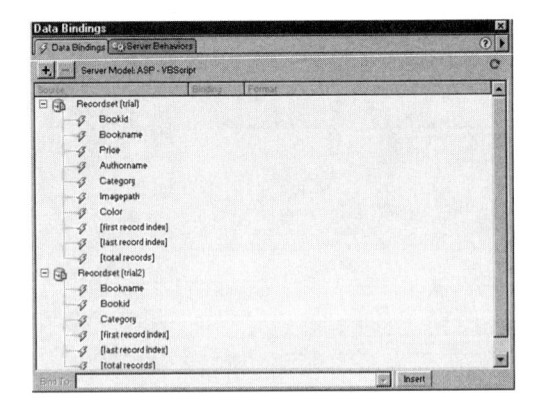

Creating and Managing Data Sources

Dynamic Web applications require a server to process the requests generated dynamically by a browser. In UltraDev, the ASP, JSP, and ColdFusion technologies are used to create dynamic Web applications.

The list of data sources displayed in the Data Bindings panel can be used to provide dynamic content to your Web page. You can use the Data Bindings panel to define data sources such as request, form, session, or URL variables for ASP, JSP, and ColdFusion pages.

Ensure that you have defined and configured the site for dynamic data before you create a data source.

Creating a Data Source for an Active Server Page

To store the information submitted by the browser to the server, you need to create a data source for your ASP page. In ASP, the information submitted by the browser is stored in a request object on the server. You can use a request variable, session variable, application variable, recordset, or stored procedure to create a data source for an ASP page.

Using a Request Object

In ASP, the Request object retrieves the information that a user sends from the browser to the server. Some examples of information that can be sent from a browser are Form data, query string data, and information from cookies.

The Request object in ASP has five collections: Form, QueryString, Cookies, ClientCertificate, and ServerVariables. The Form collection lets you retrieve information that is sent through an HTML form by using the POST method. The QueryString collection lets you retrieve the form information by using the GET method. The Cookies collection lets you retrieve the values of the cookies sent by the browser. The ClientCertificate collection is used to read the values from the certification fields sent by the client. The ServerVariables collection is used to retrieve and store values of environmental variables.

Creating and Managing Data Sources | 367

To display the value of a request variable in an ASP page, you must define it as a data source.

Follow these steps to define a request variable as a data source for an ASP page:

1. Open the ASP page, and then open the Data Bindings panel.
2. Click the + button in the Data Bindings panel. A pop-up menu is displayed, as shown in Figure 18.9.

Figure 18.9
UltraDev lets you create a data source for ASP by using a request variable, session variable, application variable, recordset, or stored procedure.

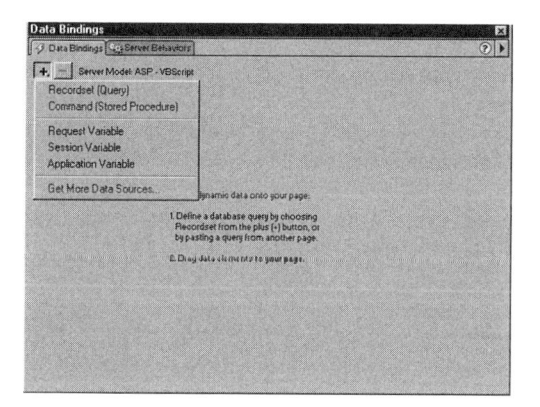

3. Select the Request Variable option from the pop-up menu. The Request Variable dialog box is displayed, as shown in Figure 18.10.

Figure 18.10
Use the Request Variable dialog box to specify a name and a collection for the request variable.

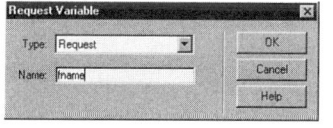

4. Select a collection of the request object from the Type drop-down list. For example, select Request.Form to retrieve information stored in the Form collection.
5. Type a name for the request variable in the Name text box. For example, if you want to retrieve the information from the form variable Request.Form("fname"), type **fname** as the name of the variable.
6. Click OK to close the Request Variable dialog box and add the request variable to the list of data sources. The request variable is defined as a data source for the ASP page and is displayed, as shown in Figure 18.11.
7. Click the Insert button in the Data Bindings panel or drag the data source from the Data Bindings panel to the page to display the value of the request variable on the Web page.

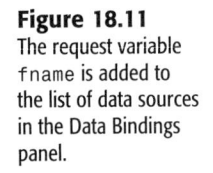

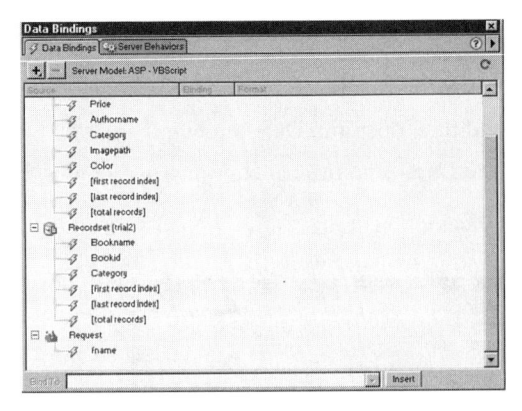

Figure 18.11
The request variable `fname` is added to the list of data sources in the Data Bindings panel.

Using a Session Variable

In ASP, the `Session` object contains session variables, which store the values retrieved from a particular *session*.

Session variables are used to store and display information about the user's interaction with the server, such as the user's name, the duration of the user's visit, the user's preferences, and so on. Apart from storing string variables, the `Session` object can store object variables. The server creates a different `Session` object for each user and maintains the object until it is explicitly terminated.

Assign a value to the session variable in the source code before creating a data source by using that session variable. For example, in the following statement, a session variable called `fname` is created. It contains the value `Ken`:

```
<% Session("fname")="Ken" %>
```

To create a data source for an ASP page by using a session variable, proceed with the following steps:

1. Open the Data Bindings panel.
2. Click the + button and select Session Variable from the pop-up menu. The Session Variable dialog box is displayed, as shown in Figure 18.12.
3. Type a name for the session variable in the Name text box. The name you enter in this text box must be the same as the name defined in the source code.
4. Click OK. The session variable is defined as a data source for ASP and is displayed in the Data Bindings panel, as shown in Figure 18.13.

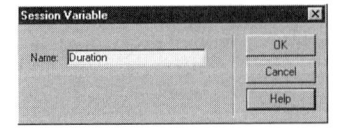

Figure 18.12
Use the Session Variable dialog box to specify a name for the data source.

Figure 18.13
The Data Bindings panel displays the list of data sources created using a recordset, a request variable, and a session variable.

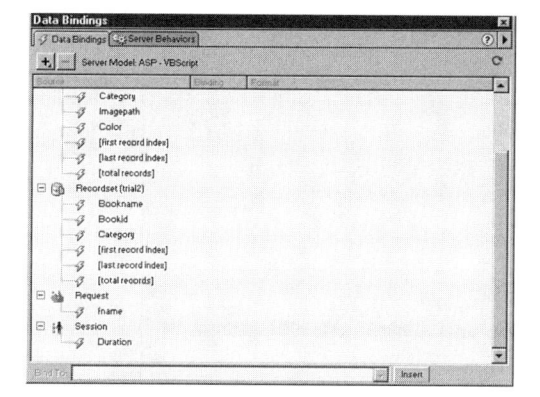

Using an Application Variable

In ASP, application variables contain global information such as the page counter and number of hits for a page. This information can be accessed by all sessions that are running simultaneously on different clients. The information in the application variables is updated every time a user visits the site, and it is made available to all the users who visit the site. Therefore, you can use application variables to store and display information that needs to be maintained for the lifetime of an application.

To create a data source for an ASP page by using an application variable, do the following:

1. Open the Data Bindings panel from the ASP page.
2. Click the + button and select Application Variable from the pop-up menu. The Application Variable dialog box is displayed, as shown in Figure 18.14.

Figure 18.14
Use the Application Variable dialog box to specify the name of the application variable that is used as a data source.

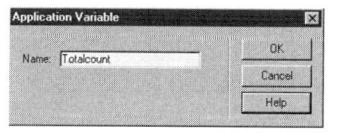

3. Type a name for the application variable in the Name text box. The name of the variable must be the same as the name defined for the variable in the source code.
4. Click OK. The application variable is added to the list of data sources for the ASP page and is displayed in the Data Bindings panel, as shown in Figure 18.15.

Figure 18.15
The Data Bindings panel displays the list of data sources created for the ASP page.

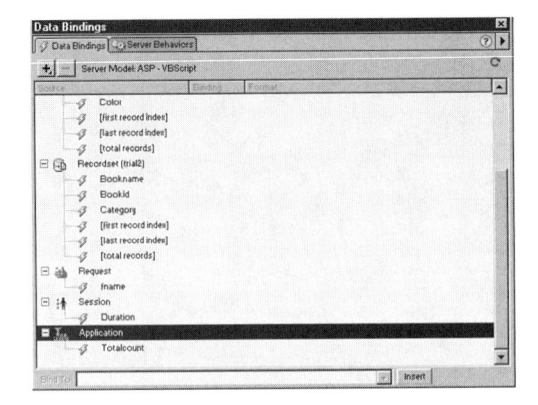

Using a Stored Procedure

A stored procedure consists of one or more SQL statements residing in a database and performing database operations. A stored procedure server object is called a command in ASP. This server object is called a stored procedure in ColdFusion and a callable in JSP. You can use a stored procedure to define a recordset data source.

To create a data source for an ASP page by using a stored procedure, follow these steps:

1. Open a dynamic Web page in UltraDev.
2. Open the Data Bindings panel from this page.
3. Click the + button and select Command (Stored Procedure) from the pop-up menu. The Command dialog box is displayed, as shown in Figure 18.16.

Figure 18.16
The Command dialog box lets you define a stored procedure as a data source.

> **Note**
> Select the Command (Stored Procedure) option from the pop-up menu if you are using an ASP page. If you are using a JSP page, select Callable (Stored Procedure) from the pop-up menu, and if you are using a CFML page, select Stored Procedure.

4. Type a name for the stored procedure in the Name text box.
5. Select a connection from the Connection drop-down list to specify the connection to the database containing the stored procedure.
6. Select Stored Procedure from the Type drop-down list.
7. Select the Return Recordset Named check box and enter a name in the Return Recordset Named text box to specify the recordset to be returned.
8. In the Database Items list box, expand the branches in the database tree, select a stored procedure that returns a recordset, and click the PROCEDURE button. The SQL statement in the stored procedure is displayed in the SQL text box.
9. You can define the values for the parameters defined in the stored procedure in the Variables list box. Click the + button and specify the parameter name in the Name column, the default value for the parameter in the Default Value column, and the runtime value for the parameter in the Run-time Value column.
10. Click the Test button to connect to the database and create an occurrence of the recordset.

Creating a Data Source for a ColdFusion Page

You need to create a data source for your ColdFusion page to store the information submitted by a user. In ColdFusion, most of the information is stored in server variables, such as URL, form, and client. In addition, information can be stored in session, application, cookie, CGI, and local variables.

UltraDev lets you create data sources for ColdFusion pages by using server variables, session variables, application variables, or stored procedures.

Using a URL Variable

URL variables are used to store the retrieved information appended to the URL of the requested page. If a form uses the GET method, the form data is passed through the URL variables. In this case, the query string contains one or more name/value pairs associated with form fields. These name/value pairs are appended to the URL.

> **Note**
> One part of a name/value pair contains the name of a variable, and the other part contains the value of the variable.

> **Note**
>
> If you have more than one name/value pair in a querystring, combine them with ampersands.

For example, consider a form that uses the GET method and has two text fields, fname and lname. When a user types Ken in the fname field and Burton in the lname field and then clicks the Submit button, the URL that is sent to the server is

http://www.myserver.com/loginform.asp?fname=Ken&lname=Burton

In this URL, the querystring is the string that starts with the question mark and contains two name/value pairs. The first name/value pair is represented by fname and Ken, and the second name/value pair is represented by lname and Burton.

The values of fname and lname are stored in the URL.fname and URL.lname variables on the ColdFusion server.

To display the values of the fname variable on the Web page, write the following code in your HTML source code:

```
<CFOUTPUT>
#URL.fname#
</CFOUTPUT>
```

The preceding code reads the value (Ken) contained in the fname field and displays it on the Web page.

To display the value of a URL variable on your Web page, you must define it as a data source in UltraDev and then drag the data source from the Data Bindings panel to the Web page.

Follow these steps to create a data source for a ColdFusion page by using a URL variable:

1. Open the CFML page, and then open the Data Bindings panel.
2. Click the + button in the Data Bindings panel. A list of options that can be used to define a data source for the ColdFusion page is displayed, as shown in Figure 18.17.

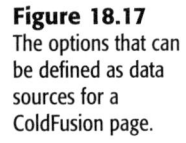

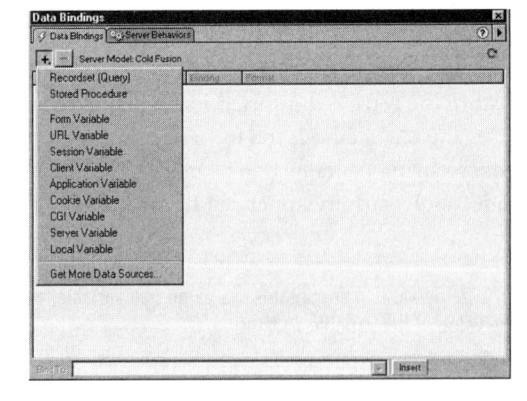

Figure 18.17
The options that can be defined as data sources for a ColdFusion page.

3. Select the URL Variable option from the pop-up menu. The URL Variable dialog box is displayed, as shown in Figure 18.18.

Figure 18.18
Use the URL Variable dialog box to specify the name of the URL variable.

4. Type a name for the URL variable in the Name text box. The name of the variable must be the same as the name given to the variable in the form. For example, if you want to access the information in the URL.fname variable, type **fname** in the Name text box.
5. Click OK. The URL variable is defined as a data source for the ColdFusion page and is displayed in the Data Bindings panel, as shown in Figure 18.19.

Figure 18.19
The data sources list in the Data Bindings panel displays the variable created using the URL variable.

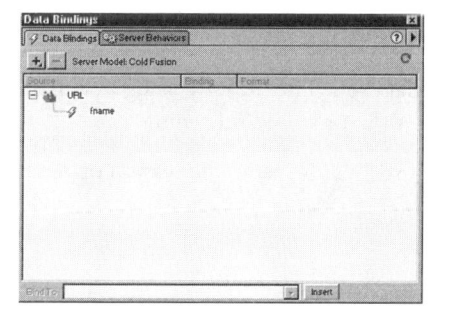

USING A FORM VARIABLE

Form variables included in the body of the HTTP request contain form data. This data is sent through an HTML form by using the POST method.

The steps involved in creating a data source for a ColdFusion page by using a form variable are similar to the steps involved in creating a data source by using a URL variable. The only difference is that you need to select the Form Variable option from the pop-up menu in the Data Bindings panel and type the name of the form variable in the Form Variable dialog box. For example, if you want to access the information in the fname form variable, you need to type **fname** as the variable name in the Name text box.

> **Note**
> Ensure that the HTML form in the search page/client machine uses the POST method. If the form uses the GET method, the form data is passed through the URL variables.

You can also create data sources for ColdFusion pages by using session or application variables. The steps involved in creating these data sources are the same as those involved in creating data sources for ASP pages by using session or application variables.

Similarly, you can define client, cookie, CGI, and local variables as data sources for CFML pages. Figure 18.20 shows an example in which a client, a cookie, a CGI, and a local variable are defined as data sources for a ColdFusion page.

Figure 18.20
The Data Bindings panel displays the list of data sources created for ColdFusion by using a client, a cookie, a session, and a local variable.

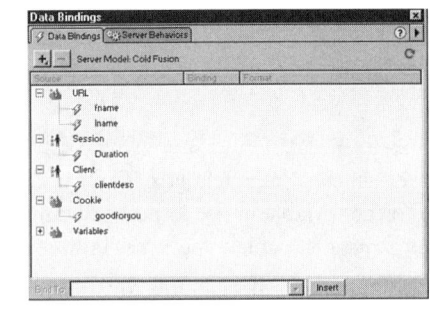

CREATING A DATA SOURCE FOR A JAVASERVER PAGE

In JSP, most of the information submitted by the browser is stored in a request object on the server. UltraDev lets you create a data source for JSP by using a request variable, session variable, JavaBean, JavaBean Collection, or stored procedure.

You can create a data source for a JSP page by using the session or request variable in the same way you did for an ASP page.

USING JAVABEANS

In UltraDev, JavaBeans are treated as data sources. A JavaBean is a reusable and portable software component that is developed using the Java programming language. Its features include properties, methods, and events. When a JavaBean is used with servlets and JSP pages, it forms the business logic of an application.

Follow these steps to create a data source for JSP by using JavaBeans:

1. Open the JSP page and choose Window, Data Bindings to open the Data Bindings panel.
2. Click the + button in the Data Bindings panel. A pop-up menu is displayed, as shown in Figure 18.21. It shows the options that can be defined as data sources for a JSP page.

Figure 18.21
You can create a data source for a JSP page by using a request variable, session variable, JavaBean, JavaBean collection, recordset, or stored procedure.

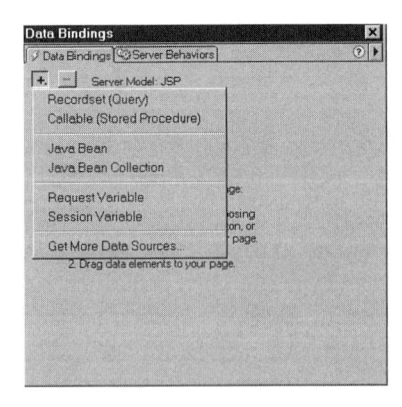

3. Select the Java Bean option from the pop-up menu. The Java Bean dialog box is displayed, as shown in Figure 18.22.

Figure 18.22
Use the Java Bean dialog box to define a data source for a JSP page.

4. Specify a name for the JavaBean in the Name text box.
5. Select the scope of the bean from the Scope drop-down list. This attribute of the <jsp:usebean> tag sets the scope of the associated bean to a page, a request, a session, or an application.

→ To learn more about the scope of a bean, **see** "The <jsp:usebean> Tag," **p. 96**.

6. Select the class of the JavaBean from the Class drop-down list, or click the Browse button to select the bean class from the Select Java Archive File dialog box, shown in Figure 18.23. In this dialog box, you can view the list of classes in a .zip file or a .jar file.

Figure 18.23
Select a .zip file or a .jar file containing the bean class from the list displayed in the Select Java Archive File dialog box.

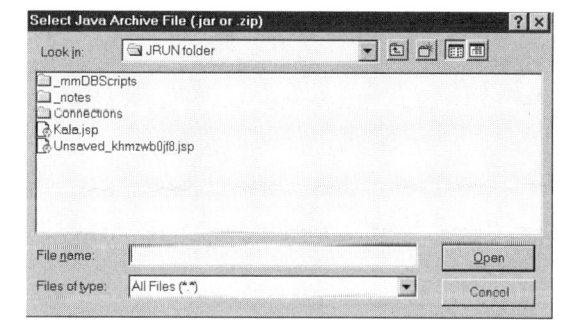

7. If you want to give a default value to one of the bean's properties, in the Java Bean dialog box, select the property from the Property column in the Properties list box, and type the default value for the property in the Default Value text box that is located below the list box. You can click the lightning bolt icon beside the Default Value text box to set the default value of the property to a dynamic value.

8. Click OK. The newly defined data source created for the JSP page is displayed, as shown in Figure 18.24.

Figure 18.24
JavaBean is defined as a data source for the JSP page in the Data Bindings panel.

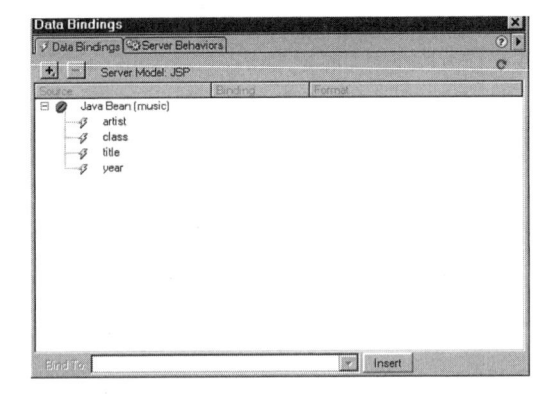

After defining the JavaBean as a data source, you can drag the data source from the Data Bindings panel to the Web page to view the value of the JavaBean component on your Web page.

USING A JAVABEANS COLLECTION

You can also create a data source for a JSP page by using a JavaBeans collection. A *JavaBeans collection* is a set of beans.

Follow these steps to define a JavaBeans collection as a data source:

1. Open the JSP page. Select Java Bean Collection from the pop-up menu that is displayed when you click the + button in the Data Bindings panel. The Java Bean Collection dialog box is displayed, as shown in Figure 18.25.

Figure 18.25
Use the Java Bean Collection dialog box to define a JavaBean Collection as a data source for a JSP page.

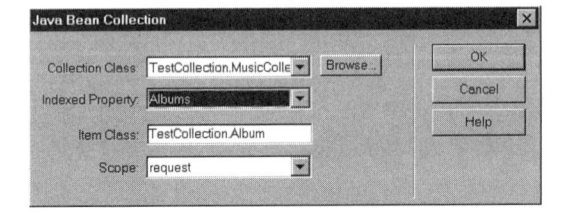

> **Note**
> The dialog box that is displayed for a JavaBean is slightly different from the one that is displayed for a JavaBean collection. In the Java Bean Collection dialog box, you cannot assign default values to the bean's properties, whereas in the Java Bean dialog box, you can. However, the option for defining the scope is present in both dialog boxes.

2. Select the class of JavaBean from the Collection Class drop-down list, or click the Browse button to select the class from the Select Java Archive File dialog box that is displayed. In this dialog box, you can view the list of classes in a .zip file or a .jar file.

3. Select an indexed property for the JavaBean class from the list of properties displayed in the Indexed Property drop-down list in the JavaBean Collection dialog box.
4. By default, UltraDev displays a default name in the Item Class text box. If you want to change the default name, type the new name in the Item Class text box.
5. Select the scope of the bean from the Scope drop-down list.
6. Click OK. The JavaBean collection is defined as a data source for the JSP page and is displayed, as shown in Figure 18.26.

Figure 18.26
The Java Bean collection is added to the list of data sources in the Data Bindings panel.

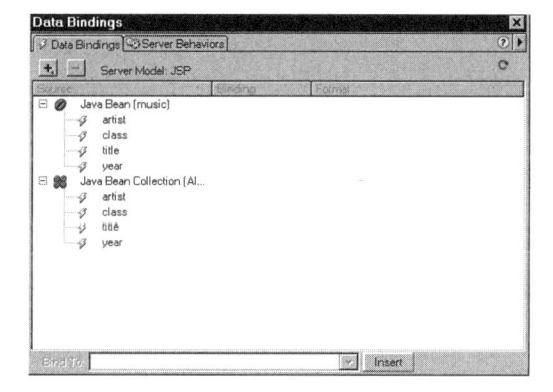

Caching, Changing, and Deleting Data Sources

In UltraDev, all the data sources that are created for a Web page are listed in the Data Bindings panel. You can cache, change, or delete any of these data sources. You can also cut, copy, or paste them.

In UltraDev, you can cache the data sources defined in the Data Bindings panel to store them temporarily on the hard disk. After you have cached a data source, you can continue working on it irrespective of whether the connection to your database or server exists. If you want to retrieve any information from the data source, you can get it from the cache instead of from the original server. Caching a data source speeds up development and saves time. To cache a data source, select the data source and click the arrow button in the top-right corner of the Data Bindings panel. A pop-up menu is displayed, as shown in Figure 18.27.

Select the Cache option from the pop-up menu to cache the data source. If you make any changes to a cached data source, you must refresh the data source to store the latest information. You can refresh the cached data source by clicking the circle arrow icon in the Data Bindings panel.

You can edit a data source listed in the Data Bindings panel. To do so, double-click the name of the data source in the list. The dialog box for that data source is displayed. After making the required changes in the dialog box, click OK.

You can delete a data source from the list of data sources available in the Data Bindings panel by selecting the data source and clicking the – button in the Data Bindings panel.

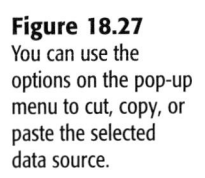

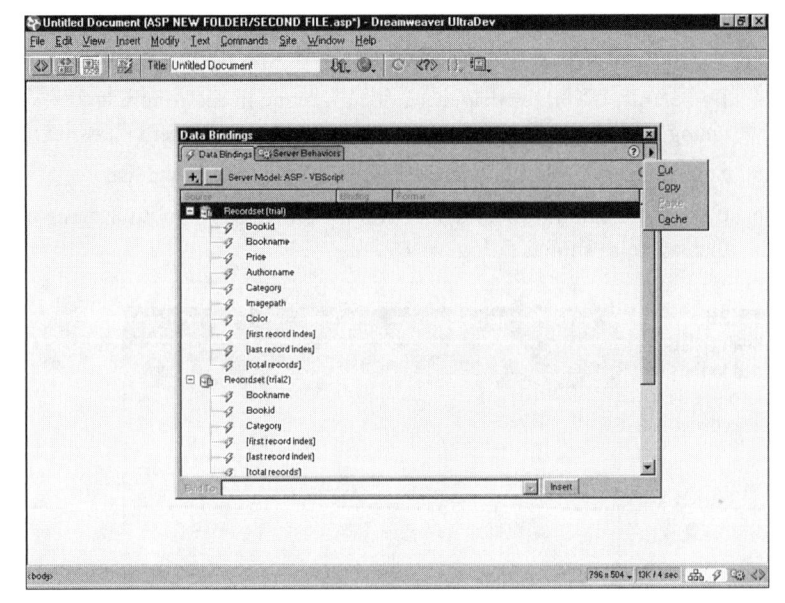

Figure 18.27
You can use the options on the pop-up menu to cut, copy, or paste the selected data source.

Summary

If you want to build a dynamic Web page in UltraDev, it is essential to use one or more data sources that allow you to display data dynamically. In UltraDev, the Data Bindings panel lets you create a recordset to display dynamic data. Displaying dynamic data means you can display the information stored in the database table on a Web page. You can also use the Data Bindings panel to create other data sources, such as request, form, or URL variables. You can create data sources for ASP, JSP, and ColdFusion pages by using request variables, form variables, URL variables, and so on.

Activity Corner

In this chapter, you will create recordsets in the `Contentpage.asp`, `Songfetch.asp`, and `Search.asp` files.

Creating a Recordset in the `Contentpage.asp` File

The `Contentpage.asp` file lists the songs that are newly released. Therefore, in this file, you will create a recordset to holds all the records from the table LatestSongs. This recordset will be created using a simple query, without your having to type out SQL statements. To create this recordset in the `Contentpage.asp` file, follow these steps:

1. Open the `Contentpage.asp` file.
2. Choose Window, Data Bindings to open the Data Bindings panel.

3. Click the + button on the Data Bindings panel. Choose the Recordset option from the pop-up menu.
4. In the Recordset dialog box that is displayed, type **LR** in the Name text box.
5. Select SongConnect from the Connection drop-down list.
6. Select LatestSongs from the Table drop-down list.
7. Select the All option. Click the Test button to see whether all the records from the table LatestSongs are displayed.
8. Click OK to close the Recordset dialog box.

CREATING A RECORDSET IN THE Songfetch.asp FILE

When the user clicks a music category in the `Musichome.asp` file, the `Songfetch.asp` file is called. This file must display those songs that belong to the category selected by the user. To do so, you must create a recordset in this file, which will retrieve those records that match the link selected by the user. Before creating the recordset, take a brief look at how you can implement this feature. When the user clicks a link on the `Musichome.asp` file, the music category that corresponds to the link selected by the user must be passed as a URL parameter to the `Songfetch.asp` file. You then create a recordset in the `Songfetch.asp` file that will compare the Category field of the AllDetails query with the value passed from the `Sidebar.asp` file through the URL parameter. So, before you create a recordset, create a URL parameter called search in the `Sidebar.asp` file. To create this URL parameter, follow these steps:

1. Open the `Sidebar.asp` file.
2. Select the link "Merry" in the `Sidebar.asp` file.
3. Open the Property inspector of the link. The Link text box in the Property inspector shows the target file as Songresults/Songfetch.asp. Type **?search=Merry** following Songresults/Songfetch.asp. The Link text box must now show Songresults/Songfetch.asp?search=Merry.
4. Select each of the other links and type **?search=** after the target file in the Link text box of the Property inspector, followed by the values FootTapping, SoulStirring, Mystical, and Melancholy, for each of the other links respectively.

After creating the URL parameter named search, you can now create the recordset in the `Songfetch.asp` file. To do this, perform the following steps:

1. Open the `Songfetch.asp` file.
2. Open the Data Bindings panel and click the + button on the Data Bindings panel. Choose the Recordset option from the pop-up menu.
3. In the Recordset dialog box, type Links in the Name text box. From the Connection drop-down list, select SongConnect. From the Table drop-down list, select AllDetails.
4. Select the All option.

5. In the Filter area, select Category from the first drop-down list. From the second drop-down list, select the = option. Select URL Parameter from the third drop-down list. In the text box next to the third drop-down list, type **select**.

6. Click the Test button to see whether the recordset displays the required records. When you click the Test button, a dialog box named Please Provide a Test Value appears. Type a test value for the URL parameter named search and see whether the recordset works correctly.

7. Click OK to close the Recordset dialog box.

CREATING A RECORDSET IN THE Search.asp FILE

To implement a search feature in the Search.asp file, you need to create a recordset by building a complex query in the Search.asp file. Recall that the form Searchform in the Sidebar.asp file calls the Search.asp file to display the list of songs that match the search criteria entered by the user. Therefore, you will create a recordset in the Search.asp file that will retrieve the records that match the search criteria entered by the user. To create this recordset, follow these steps:

1. Open the Search.asp file.

2. Open the Data Bindings panel and click the + button to display the pop-up menu. Choose Recordset from the pop-up menu. In the Recordset dialog box that is displayed, click the Advanced button to display the SQL query editor.

3. In the Name text box, type **SR**.

4. Select SongConnect from the Connection drop-down list.

5. In the Variables area, click the + button. In the Name column, type **searchParam**. In the Default Value column, type **Album**. In the Run-time Value column, type **Request("selection")** if you are using ASP. If you use JSP, type **request.getParameter("selection")**. ColdFusion users need to type **#form.selection#** in the Run-time Value column.

6. Click the + button in the Variables area again to create another variable. In the Name column, type **valueParam**. In the Default Value column, type a default value such as a. In the Run-time Value column, type **Request("Searchstring")** if you are using ASP. If you use JSP, type **request.getParameter("Searchstring")** and if you use ColdFusion, type **#form.Searchstring#** in the Run-time Value column.

7. In the SQL area, type the following SQL statement:
```
SELECT *
FROM AllDetails
WHERE searchParam LIKE '%valueParam%'
```

8. Click the Test button to see whether the recordset works properly. When you test this SQL query, the query compares the Album field of the AllDetails query with the value a and displays those records in which the Album field contains the letter a. At runtime,

the field name is obtained from the selection text field on the `Sidebar.asp` file and the value with which the values of the field must be checked is obtained from list/menu item named Searchstring on the `Sidebar.asp` file.

9. After checking whether the query works correctly, click OK to close the Recordset dialog box.

MODIFICATIONS TO THE `Sidebar.asp` FILE

Open the `Sidebar.asp` file and select the list/menu form object named selection. Click the List Values button on the Property inspector of the list/menu form object. In the List Values dialog box, you can see the item labels for each of the options in the list/menu form object. In the Value column of the item label Composer, type **ComposerName**. In the Value column of the item label Album, type **Album**. Note that these two values are the names of the fields in the `AllDetails` query, which contain values that match the search keyword entered by the user.

CHAPTER 19

MAKING A WEB PAGE DYNAMIC

In this chapter

Adding Dynamic Elements to a Web Page   384

Adding More Functionality to the Dynamic Content   401

Summary   404

Activity Corner   404

Adding Dynamic Elements to a Web Page

UltraDev's simple menu-driven interface lets you develop dynamic Web applications without having to write extensive code. You can add dynamism to a Web page by using the Live Objects and Server Behaviors options available in UltraDev. These options let you make text, images, and form objects dynamic. They also let you make HTML attributes and the parameters of ActiveX controls, Flash, and other objects dynamic. When you add a server behavior to a page, such as an `.asp`, `.jsp`, or `.cfm` page, UltraDev inserts a server-side script in the page's source code. This script instructs the server to transfer data from the data source to the page's source code.

Adding Dynamic Text to a Page

Displaying dynamic text on a Web page means that you can display the information stored in a database table or in a server object on the Web page. For example, consider an online bookstore called Buybooks. It stores the details of all its books in a database table called `Books`, as shown in Figure 19.1. You can display the name, price, description, and other details of the books that are stored in this table as dynamic content on a Web page.

Figure 19.1
The `Books` table with information on various books.

Books Table

Book Id	Bookname	Price	Authorname	Category	Imagepath	Color
1	Chocolate Days	245	Anne Willie	Literature	Images/Chocolate days.jpg	Red
2	Nuts and Bolts	175	Richard Robinson	Literature	Images/Nuts & bolts.jpg	White
3	Winter Musings	120	Dalreen Rand	Literature	Images/Winter musings.jpg	Blue
4	Solitude	75	Anne Willie	Literature	Images/Solitude.jpg	Red
5	Rhythms	90	Susan Ward	Literature	Images/Rhythms.jpg	White
6	A Face in the Moonlight	125	Nancy Jones	Literature	Images/Moonlight.jpg	Blue

To display the dynamic content, you must first create a recordset that contains the required columns from the database table.

→ To learn more about creating recordsets, **see** "Creating a Recordset," **p. 360**.

You can display dynamic data on a Web page by following these steps:

1. Place the cursor on the Web page at the position where you want to display the dynamic data.
2. From the Data Bindings panel, select the recordset whose column values must be displayed on the Web page.

3. From the list of columns in the recordset, select the column whose value must be displayed on the Web page, and then click the Insert button. Alternatively, you can also drag the column to the required place on the document. Figure 19.2 shows the Data Bindings panel with a column selected from a recordset.

Figure 19.2
Use the Data Bindings panel to select the column from the recordset whose value must be displayed on the Web page.

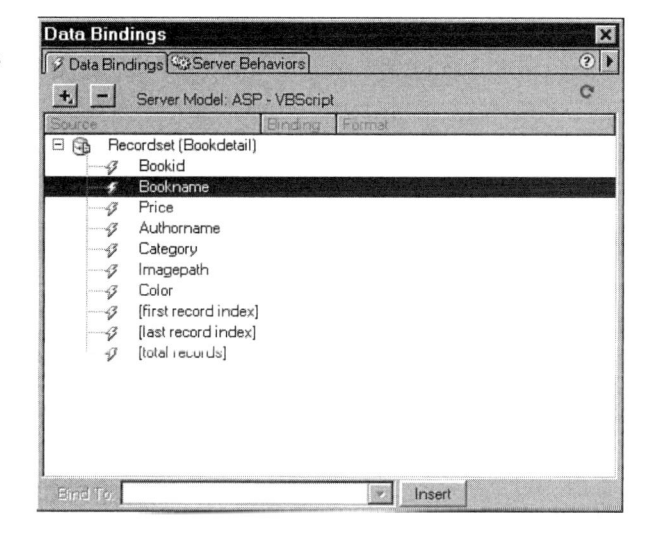

Repeat the preceding steps for all the columns you want to display on the Web page.

When you click the Insert button in the Data Bindings panel, UltraDev inserts a placeholder on the page, as shown in Figure 19.3. The placeholder displays the name of the recordset and the column as {Recordset name.Column name}. For example, if you insert a column called Bookname from a recordset called Bookdetail, the placeholder on the Web page will be {Bookdetail.Bookname}. You can view the placeholder on the page only in Design view.

You can also customize the syntax of the placeholders on the Web page by using the Invisible Elements category of the Preferences dialog box.

→ To learn how to customize the display of placeholders on a Web page, **see** "Setting Invisible Elements Preferences," **p. 330**.

After you follow the steps required to display the dynamic data on the Web page, preview the page in Live Data view or in a browser. To switch to Live Data view, choose View, Live Data. By default, Live Data view displays only one record from the recordset, as shown in Figure 19.4. If you want to display all the records in the recordset, you can do so by using the Repeat Region server behavior. Alternatively, you can create a recordset navigation bar to browse through the records in the recordset.

Figure 19.3
A sample Web page of the Buybooks site with columns inserted into a table from a recordset called `Bookdetail`.

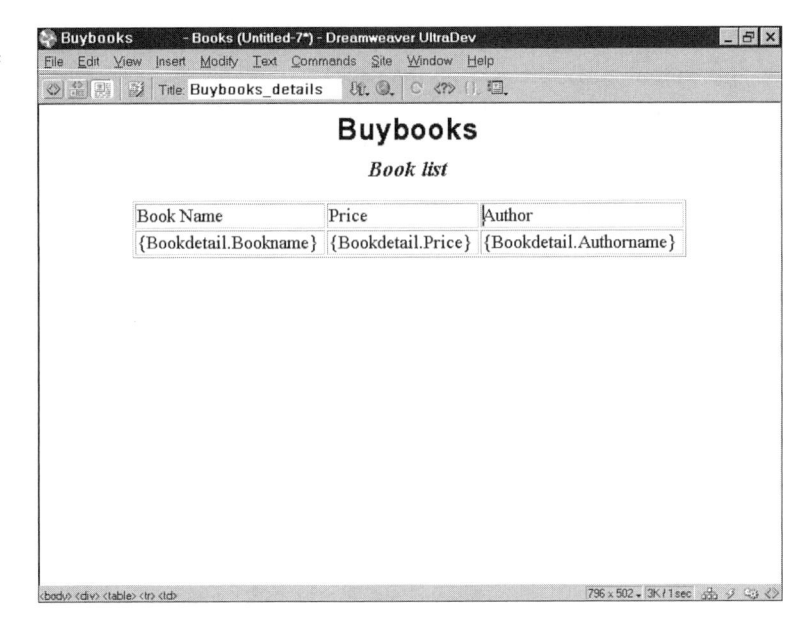

Figure 19.4
The sample Web page of the Buybooks site displaying only one record from the recordset.

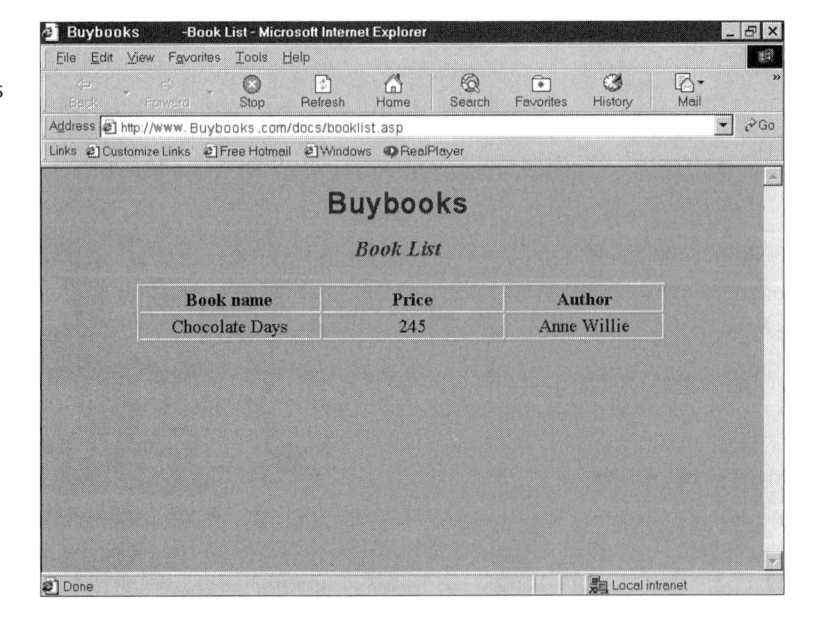

You will learn about the Repeat Region server behavior and the recordset navigation bar in the following sections.

In addition to adding new dynamic content, you can replace the existing regular content on the Web page with dynamic data. To replace the regular existing content, select the content and follow steps 2 and 3 given earlier. All the styles and formats applied to the existing content are adopted by the new dynamic content.

CREATING A RECORDSET NAVIGATION BAR

In Live Data view, UltraDev displays only one record, regardless of the number of records in the recordset. You can view the other records in the recordset by creating a recordset navigation bar. The recordset navigation bar provides links from the current record to the recordset's first, last, next, and previous records.

> **Note**
> A single page can have any number of recordset navigation bars, provided that all of them operate on the same recordset. However, it is not a good practice to have more than one navigation bar per page.

You can create a recordset navigation bar by following these steps:

1. Place the cursor at the location where you want to insert the recordset navigation bar, and choose Insert, Live Objects, Recordset Navigation Bar. The Insert Recordset Navigation Bar dialog box is displayed, as shown in Figure 19.5.

Figure 19.5
Use the Insert Recordset Navigation Bar dialog box to specify various features for the recordset navigation bar.

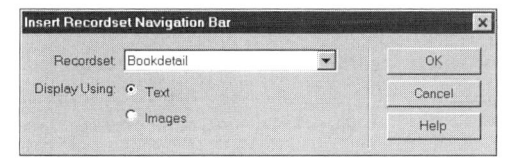

2. From the Recordset drop-down list, select the recordset you want to navigate.
3. From the Display Using section, select the format in which the navigation links must be displayed on the Web page. Select the Text option if you want the navigation links to be displayed as text. Select the Images option if you want the navigation links to be displayed as images. After selecting the format, click OK.

UltraDev displays the recordset navigation bar with text or images as the navigation links. These links do not work in Live Data view. To check the navigation bar links, you must view them in a browser. Figure 19.6 displays a sample Web page with a recordset navigation bar.

By default, the recordset navigation bar lets you browse through only one record at a time. However, if you apply the Repeat Region server behavior to the dynamic data to view multiple records, the recordset navigation bar is automatically customized to browse through multiple records.

Figure 19.6
The sample Web page of the Buybooks site with a recordset navigation bar.

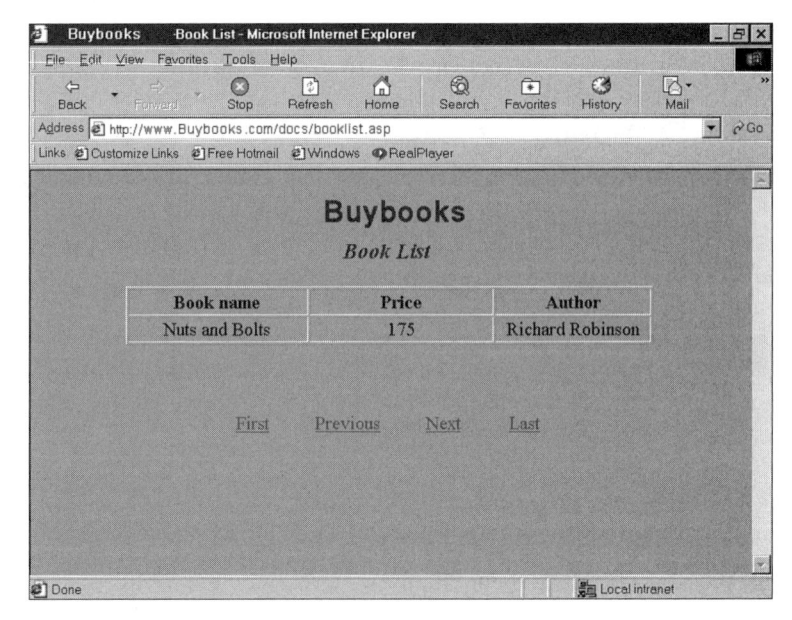

Adding the Repeat Region Server Behavior

If the recordset has a large number of records, it might be tedious to browse through the recordset by using the recordset navigation bar, because by default it allows you to browse through only one record at a time. In such situations, you can make use of the Repeat Region server behavior, which displays more than one record on a page. The Repeat Region server behavior lets you specify the number of records that are displayed on the Web page.

Before you implement the Repeat Region server behavior on a page, you must create a recordset for the page. Along with the recordset, you must also create a page layout to display the recordset on the page. After you create the recordset and the page layout, you can follow these steps to create a repeat region:

1. On the page layout, select the region that has the dynamic content that must be repeated. For example, if you have dynamic content within a row of a table, select the row. You can also select an entire table or a series of rows in a table and apply the Repeat Region server behavior.
2. Choose Window, Server Behaviors to open the Server Behaviors panel.
3. In the Server Behaviors panel, click the + button and choose Repeat Region from the pop-up menu. The Repeat Region dialog box is displayed, as shown in Figure 19.7.

Figure 19.7
Use the Repeat Region server behavior to display multiple records on a Web page.

4. From the Recordset drop-down list, select the recordset whose data must be displayed in the repeated region.
5. Specify the number of records that must be displayed on a page by selecting an option from the Show section. If you want a specific number of records to be displayed per page, select the Records option and enter the number of records in the text box. If you want all the records in the recordset to be displayed on the page, select the All Records option and click OK.

When you view the Web page in Live Data view or in the browser, UltraDev uses the Repeat Region server behavior and repeats the selected region as many times as there are records in the recordset. Each region displays a new record from the recordset, as shown in Figure 19.8.

Figure 19.8
A sample Web page of the Buybooks site displaying multiple records after the Repeat Region server behavior has been applied.

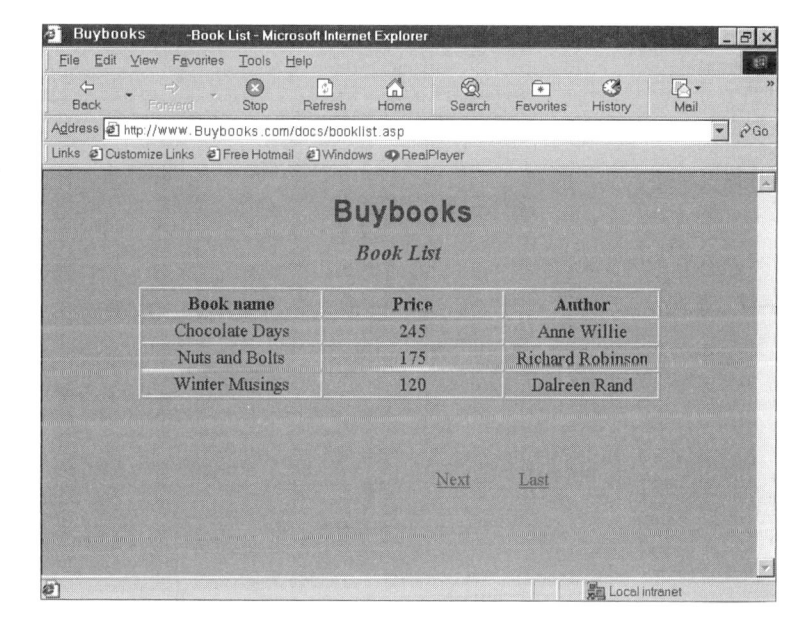

> **Note**
>
> If you are placing dynamic data directly in the Document window and not within a table, remember to put line breaks at the end of each line of dynamic data. By doing this, you can keep all the records from being displayed on the same line.

APPLYING FORMATS FOR DYNAMIC DATA

When you display the dynamic content stored in a field of a table, the content is displayed as it appears on the Web page. For example, if the Price field in the Books table holds the value 245, as shown in Figure 19.1, this value is displayed on the Web page as shown in Figure 19.8. However, if you want to change the display format of the price on the Web page to $245.00, in the Data Bindings panel, select Format, Currency, 2 Decimal Places.

You can apply various formats to dynamic data by following these steps:

1. Select the placeholder of the dynamic content to which you want to apply a format. The column to which this content is bound is automatically selected in the Data Bindings panel.
2. Click the down arrow in the Format column of the Data Bindings panel.
3. From the Format drop-down list, select the data format category you want. A list of formats in the selected category is displayed, as shown in Figure 19.9.

Figure 19.9
Change the display format of the dynamic data on the Web page by using the Format drop-down list.

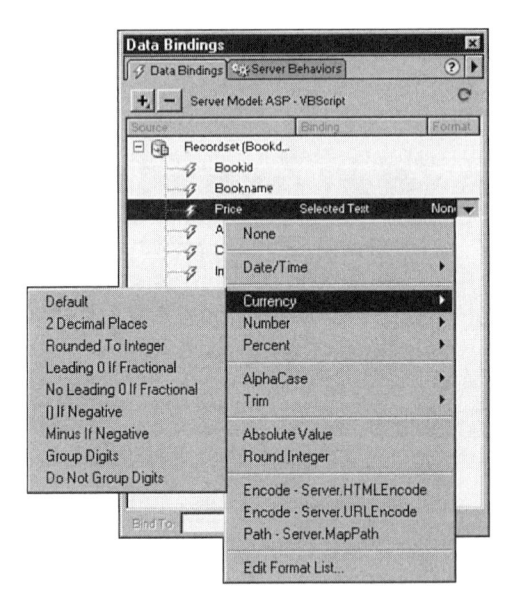

4. Choose a format that you want to apply to the dynamic data.

ADDING DYNAMIC ELEMENTS TO A WEB PAGE | 391

> **Note**
>
> The format that you select for a field must be appropriate for the field. For example, the AlphaCase format can be applied only to text fields, not to numeric or currency fields. Similarly, the Date/Time format can be applied only to date or time fields, not to text or numeric fields.

Verify whether the selected format is applied to the dynamic data by previewing the page in Live Data view or in the browser, as shown in Figure 19.10.

Figure 19.10
The sample Web page of the Buybooks site with the new display format applied to the price of the books.

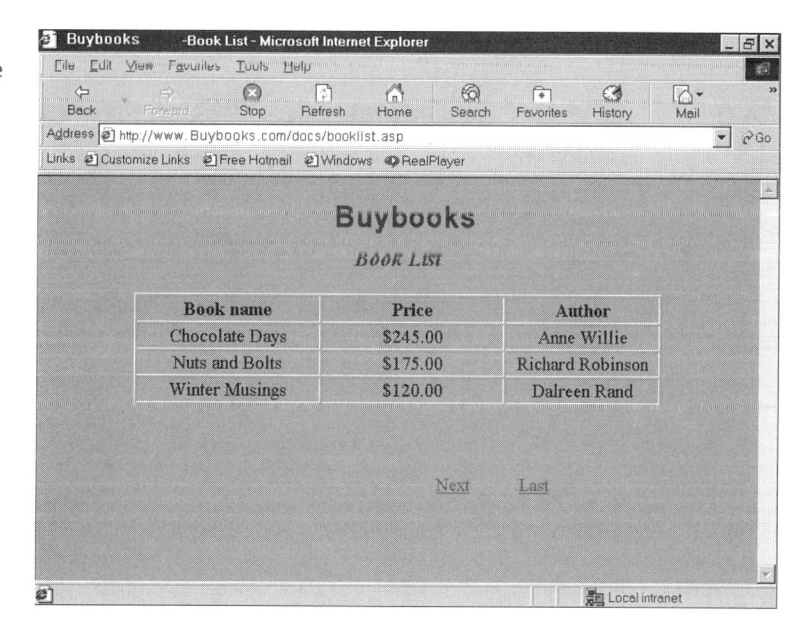

If the format that you require is not available in the Format drop-down list, choose the Edit Format List option from the list. This option displays the Edit Format List dialog box, which lets you add a new format or edit or remove an existing format.

→ To learn how to use the Edit Format List dialog box, **see** "Customizing Data Formats," **p. 472**.

DISPLAYING DYNAMIC IMAGES ON A WEB PAGE

Similar to displaying dynamic text, you can also display dynamic images on the Web page. For example, on the Buybooks site, along with the other details of a book, you can also display a photograph of the book's cover page. To do this, you must first create a recordset that contains the field in the table that stores URLs to the image files. For example, in the Books table shown in Figure 19.1, the Imagepath field stores the URL to an image file for each record. Therefore, you must include this field in the recordset to display dynamic images for each book.

PART
IV
CH
19

> **Caution**
>
> While storing the URL to an image in a field of a database table, make sure that you specify only the relative path of the image. In addition, you also need to make sure that the image file is stored in the specified location.

After you create the recordset, place the cursor at the location where you want to display the dynamic image, and choose Insert, Image. The Select Image Source dialog box is displayed, as shown in Figure 19.11. In this dialog box, select the Data Sources option from the Select File Name From section. A list of recordsets along with the list of columns in each recordset is displayed. Select the column that contains the URLs to the image files, and click OK.

Figure 19.11
From the recordset, select the column that contains the path to the image files.

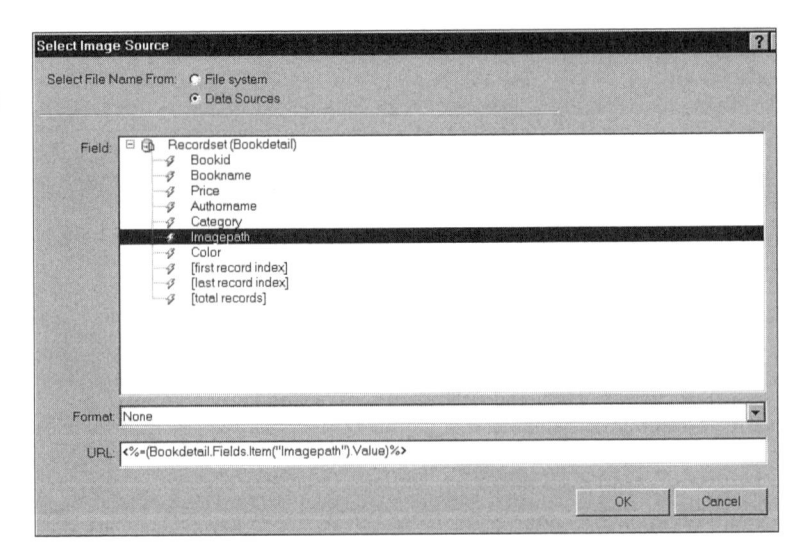

UltraDev inserts a small image icon in the Document window to represent the dynamic image, as shown in Figure 19.12.

Preview the Web page in Live Data view or in the browser to view the dynamic images, as shown in Figure 19.13.

Displaying Dynamic Data Within Form Objects

With e-commerce becoming popular, most Web sites use online forms for business transactions. Online forms are forms with various form objects that are linked to the fields in a database through a recordset. Consider the example of a database table called Members, shown in Figure 19.14, which stores the details of all the members of the Buybooks online bookstore.

ADDING DYNAMIC ELEMENTS TO A WEB PAGE | 393

Figure 19.12
An image icon is inserted at the location where you want to display the dynamic image.

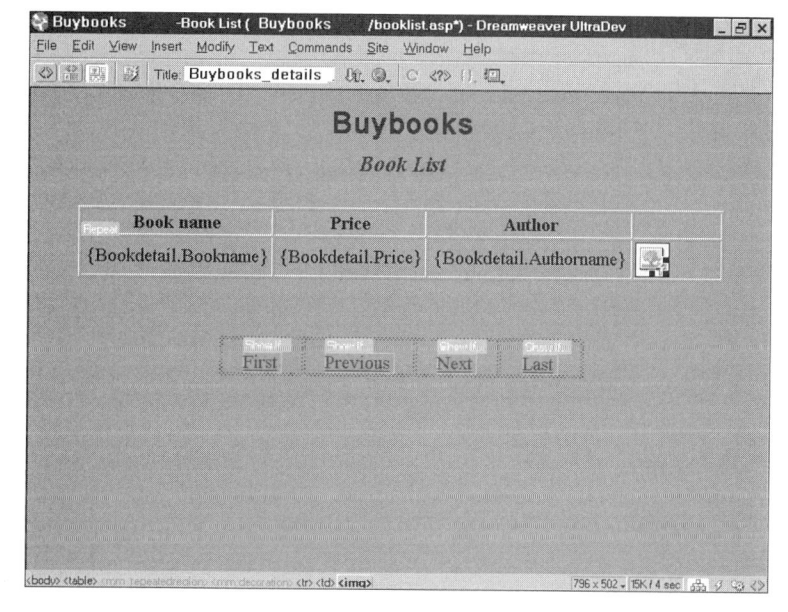

Figure 19.13
The sample Web page of the Buybooks site with the cover of each book displayed dynamically.

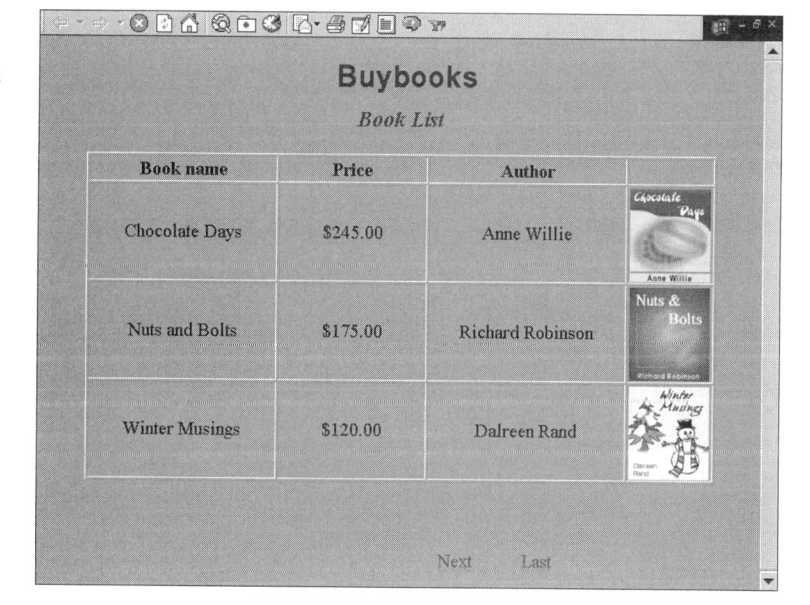

PART
IV
CH
19

Figure 19.14
The Members table with information on the various members of the Buybooks online bookstore.

Members Table

Memberid	Name	City	Sex	Remind
M001	Ken Burton	New York	Male	Yes
M002	Edith Jones	Las Vegas	Female	No
M003	Pat Greene	Boston	Male	Yes
M004	Steve Irving	Florida	Male	Yes
M005	Ron Floyd	Alaska	Male	Yes
M006	Mary Peterson	New York	Female	Yes

You can display the records stored in this table on the Buybooks Member form, shown in Figure 19.15, by binding each of the form objects to the respective fields in the table through a recordset.

Figure 19.15
The Buybooks Member form displaying the records of the members of the bookstore.

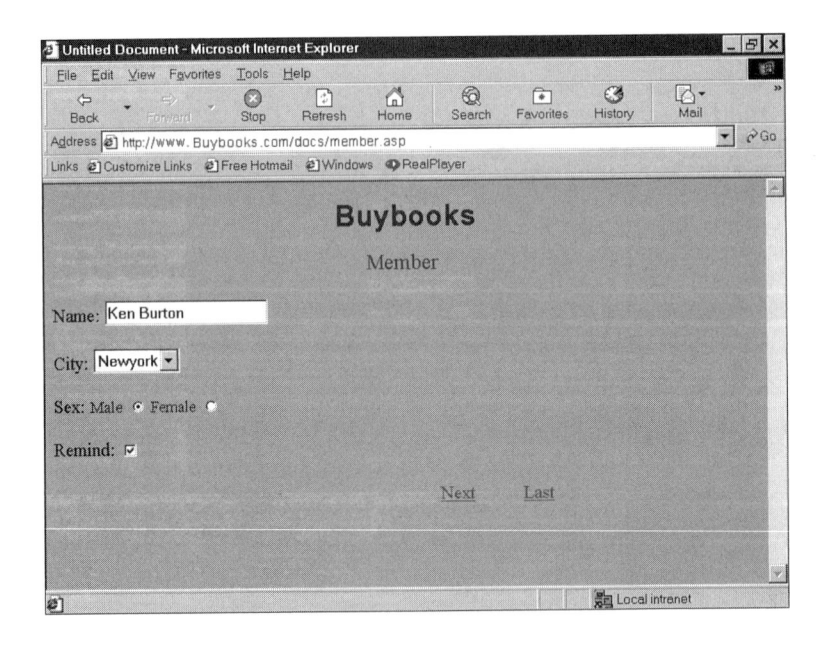

In the following sections, you will learn how to make the form objects dynamic by binding them to the various columns of a recordset.

DYNAMIC TEXT FIELDS

You can make text fields on a form dynamic by binding them to the columns in a recordset. For example, to display the names of the members of the Buybooks bookstore in the Name text field of the Buybooks Members form, as shown in Figure 19.15, you must bind the text field to the column in the recordset that stores the members' names.

Follow these steps to bind a text field to a recordset column:

1. Select the text field on the HTML form that must be bound to a column in a recordset.
2. In the Data Bindings panel, from the recordset, select the column that must be bound to the text field, as shown in Figure 19.16.

Figure 19.16
Use the Data Bindings panel to bind a text field to a column in a recordset.

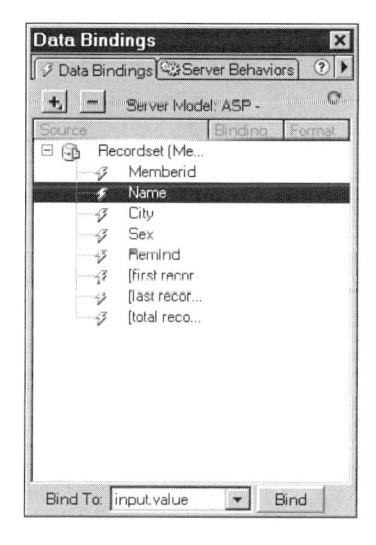

3. In the Bind To option, check whether the `input.value` value attribute is selected, and then click Bind.

Repeat these steps for all the text fields that must display dynamic data.

After you bind the text fields to the recordset columns, the placeholders are displayed in the text boxes. Switch to Live Data view or preview the page in the browser to view the dynamic data on the Web page.

DYNAMIC CHECK BOXES

There might be times when you want a check box to be selected or deselected when a column in a record equals a certain value. For example, you can cause the Remind check box in the Buybooks Members form (see Figure 19.15) to be automatically selected if the value in the Remind field of the Member table is Yes. This field indicates whether the user has opted to receive reminders about the latest books that have been released.

Follow these steps to make a check box dynamic:

1. Select the check box on the HTML form that must be made dynamic.
2. In the Data Bindings panel, click the Server Behaviors tab, and then click the + button to view a list of server behaviors.

3. From the Server Behaviors pop-up menu, select the Dynamic Elements option. From the list of options that are displayed, select the Dynamic Check Box option. The Dynamic Check Box dialog box is displayed, as shown in Figure 19.17.

Figure 19.17
You can use the Dynamic Check Box dialog box to apply dynamic features to check boxes.

4. From the Check Box drop-down list, select the check box to which you want to apply the dynamic feature.
5. Click the lightning bolt icon next to the Check If option. The Dynamic Data dialog box is displayed, as shown in Figure 19.18.

Figure 19.18
You can use the Dynamic Data dialog box to specify the column for which the check box must be made dynamic.

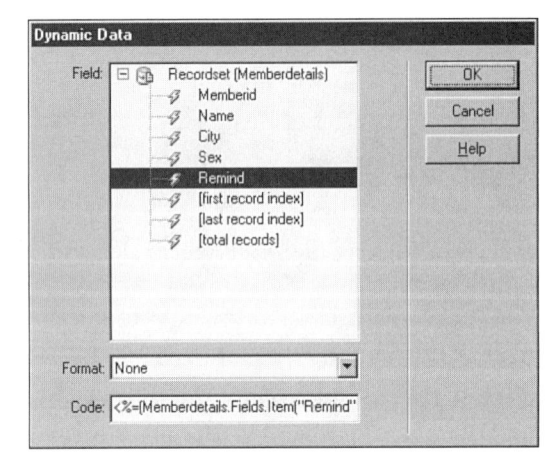

6. In the Dynamic Data dialog box, select the column from the recordset for whose value the check box must be selected or deselected. Then click OK.
7. In the Equal To text box of the Dynamic Check Box dialog box (see Figure 19.19), specify the value that the column must have for the check box to be selected. Then click OK.

Preview the Web page in Live Data view or in the browser to view the dynamic data. As you browse through the records, the check box gets selected or deselected dynamically based on the value contained in the column that is bound to the check box.

Figure 19.19
The Dynamic Check Box dialog box with sample values entered.

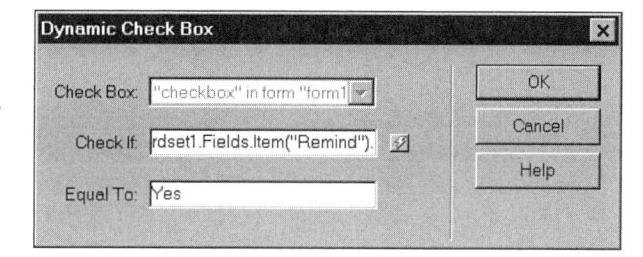

Dynamic Radio Buttons

As in the case of text boxes and check boxes, you can also make radio buttons dynamic. For example, based on the value entered in the Sex field of the Member table, one of the radio buttons, either Male or Female, is automatically selected, as shown in Figure 19.15.

To create a dynamic radio button, you must have at least one group of radio buttons on the page. You can create a group of radio buttons by giving the same name to a set of radio buttons. Follow these steps to make a radio button dynamic:

1. Click the + button in the Server Behaviors panel, and choose Dynamic Radio Buttons from the Dynamic Elements submenu. The Dynamic Radio Buttons dialog box is displayed, as shown in Figure 19.20.

Figure 19.20
You can use the Dynamic Radio Buttons dialog box to create dynamic radio buttons.

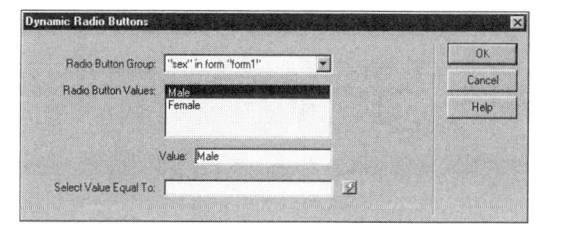

2. From the Radio Button Group drop-down list, select the radio buttons group to which you want to add the dynamic feature.
3. Select a radio button from the Radio Button Values list box, and enter a value for the radio button in the Value text box to specify a value for each radio button. The value that you specify for the radio button will be inserted into the column to which the radio button is bound when you insert a record.
4. In the Select Value Equal To text box, enter a value equal to the value of the radio button that must be selected when you display the records in a form. You can also display this value dynamically for each record by clicking the lightning bolt icon next to the Select Value Equal To text box. When you click the lightning bolt icon, the Dynamic Data dialog box is displayed. From this dialog box, select the column from which the value must be retrieved dynamically, and click OK.

Irrespective of the method you adopt, the value you specify in the Select Value Equal To text box must match the value of one of the radio buttons.

Switch to Live Data view or preview the page in the browser to view the dynamic data on the Web page. As you browse through the records, the radio buttons get selected or deselected dynamically based on the value contained in the column that is bound to the radio button.

DYNAMIC LIST BOXES

Lists boxes are used to display a list of options from which the user chooses one. For example, the Buybooks Member form, shown in Figure 19.15, uses a list box to display the city to which a member belongs. You can make the list of options in the list box, including the default option that is selected, dynamic by binding the list box to a column in the recordset.

Follow these steps to make list boxes dynamic:

1. In the page, select the list box to which you want to apply the dynamic feature.
2. Click the + button in the Server Behaviors panel, and choose Dynamic List/Menu from the Dynamic Elements submenu. The Dynamic List/Menu dialog box is displayed, as shown in Figure 19.21.

Figure 19.21
You can use the Dynamic List/Menu dialog box to make list boxes dynamic.

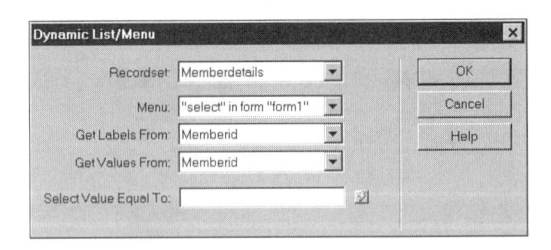

3. From the Recordset drop-down list, select the recordset that contains the list box information.
4. From the Menu drop-down list, select the list box to which you want to apply the dynamic feature.
5. From the Get Labels From drop-down list, select the column from the recordset that contains the labels for the items in the list box.
6. From the Get Values From drop-down list, select the column from the recordset from which the list box must fetch values to display in the list.
7. In the Select Value Equal To text box, enter the list item that must be selected by default when the list is displayed on the Web page. However, if you want this default value to be set dynamically based on the value that is already entered in the recordset column, click the lightning bolt icon next to the Select Value Equal To text box. In the Dynamic Data dialog box that is displayed, select the column for whose value the default list item must be selected, and click OK.

Irrespective of the method you adopt, the value you specify in the Select Value Equal To text box must match the value of one of the list items.

Switch to Live Data view or preview the page in the browser to view the dynamic data on the Web page. As you browse through the records, the selected value in the list box changes automatically based on the value contained in the column that is bound to the list box.

Creating Dynamic HTML Attributes

Apart from making text, images, and form objects dynamic, you can also add dynamic features to the HTML attributes in a Web page. For example, you can dynamically change a table row's background color by binding the row's background color attribute to a column in the recordset that stores various colors. The Color field in the Books table shown in Figure 19.1 is used to specify the color for each record. You can include this field in your recordset and bind it to the table row's `bgcolor` attribute to dynamically change its background color.

To make HTML attributes dynamic by using the Property inspector, follow these steps:

1. Select the object on the document whose HTML attribute must be made dynamic. For example, to make the background color of a row in a table dynamic, select the row.
2. Open the Property inspector and switch to List view.
3. From the list of attributes that are displayed, select the attribute you want to make dynamic. If the attribute you require is not listed, click the + button. A text box with a down arrow is displayed. Click the down arrow and select an attribute from the displayed list. For example, to make the background color dynamic, select the bgcolor attribute from the drop-down list.
4. To apply the dynamic feature to the selected attribute, click the lightning bolt icon at the end of the attribute row. From the Dynamic Data dialog box that is displayed, select the column from the recordset that must be bound to this attribute.
5. Save the document and view it in the browser to see the dynamic feature of the HTML attribute, as shown in Figure 19.22.

Creating Dynamic Flash and ActiveX Controls

By using UltraDev, you can make the parameters of Java applets, plug-ins, ActiveX, Flash, Shockwave, Director, and Generator objects dynamic. However, to make these objects dynamic, you must have columns in a recordset that hold data appropriate for the object parameters you want to bind them to.

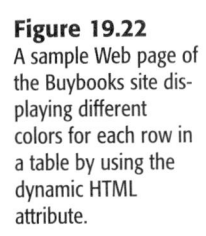

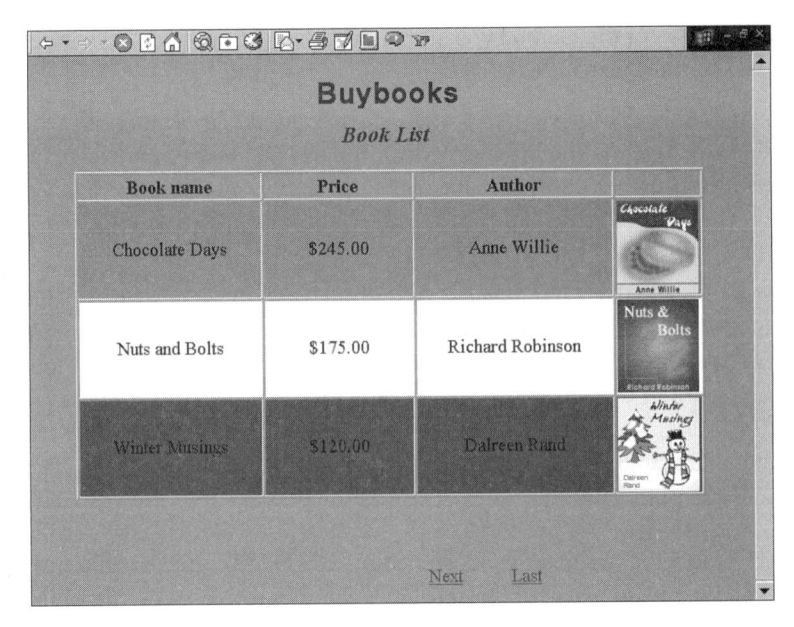

Figure 19.22
A sample Web page of the Buybooks site displaying different colors for each row in a table by using the dynamic HTML attribute.

You can make object parameters dynamic by following these steps:

1. Select the object in the document whose parameters must be made dynamic, and click the Parameters button in the Property inspector. The Parameters dialog box is displayed, as shown in Figure 19.23.

Figure 19.23
Use the Parameters dialog box to make object parameters dynamic.

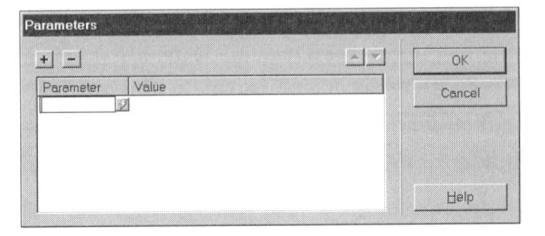

2. Select a parameter from the list of parameters that is displayed, or click the + button and enter a parameter name in the Parameter column.
3. In the Value column, click the lightning bolt icon. In the Dynamic Data dialog box that is displayed, select a column from the recordset that must be bound to the specified parameter, and then click OK.

Adding More Functionality to the Dynamic Content

In addition to adding dynamic features to the various objects on a Web page, you can add more functionality to the Web page by adding record counters and master-detail pages.

Displaying Record Counters

Record counters on a Web page give users an idea of which set of records they are currently working on with reference to the total number of records in the recordset. Record counters are especially useful for pages that display records from large recordsets.

To create a record counter for a page, you must first create a recordset for the page. After you create a recordset, you must create a page layout. You must also create a recordset navigation bar for the page so that you can browse through the recordset.

After you create the recordset and the page layout, you can create a record counter for the page by following these steps:

1. Place the mouse cursor at the location where you want to insert the record counter.
2. Choose Insert, Live Objects, Recordset Navigation Status. The Insert Recordset Navigation Status dialog box is displayed, as shown in Figure 19.24.

Figure 19.24
You can use the Insert Recordset Navigation Status dialog box to add a record counter for a Web page.

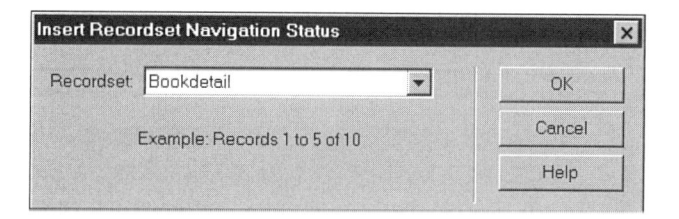

3. From the Recordset drop-down list, select the recordset for which you want to display the record counter, and then click OK.

The recordset navigation status bar is inserted into the document. Preview the document in the browser, and navigate through the records by using the recordset navigation bar. The recordset navigation status bar displays a counter for the current set of records displayed on the page, as shown in Figure 19.25.

The Master-Detail Page

While designing a Web page, it is not a good practice to populate all the information regarding a product on a single page. For example, if you want to provide information regarding some of the latest books that have been released, you can just list the names of the books in the main page, called the master page. From this master page, you can provide a link to another page, called the detail page, which gives detailed information on the book you select in the master page. This method gives users the flexibility to decide whether they want to view all of a book's additional details.

Figure 19.25
The recordset navigation status bar with a counter for the current set of records is displayed on the Web page.

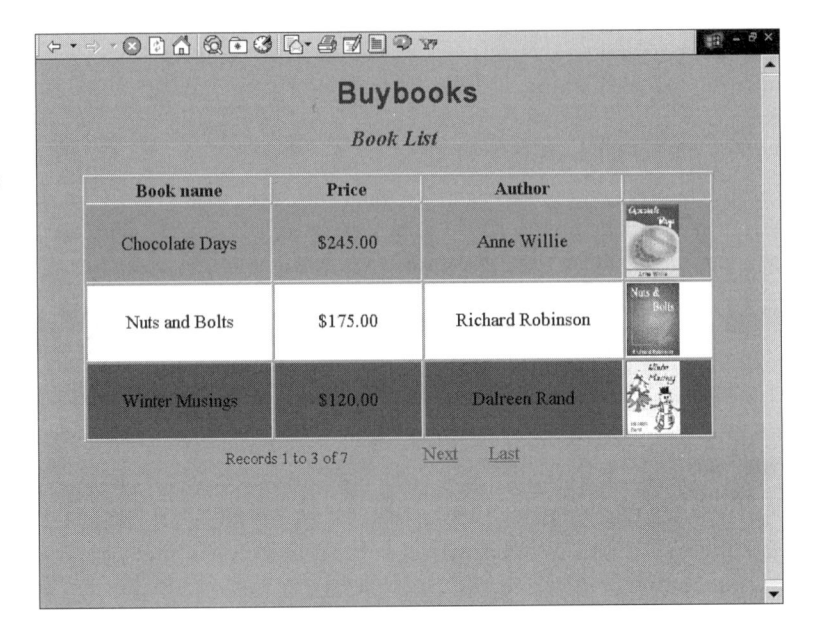

Figure 19.26 shows a sample master page for the Buybooks online bookstore. This page displays only the names of some of the latest books that have been released.

Figure 19.26
A sample master page for the Buybooks online bookstore.

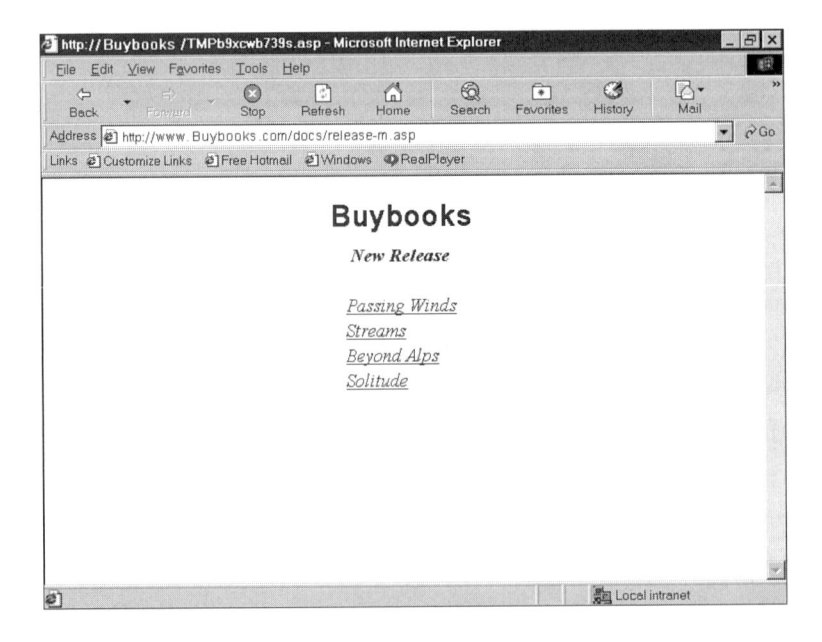

When users click the name of a book, they are taken to the detail page, which displays the book's name, price, and description. The detail page can also display the book's cover, as shown in Figure 19.27.

Figure 19.27
A sample detail page for the Buybooks online bookstore.

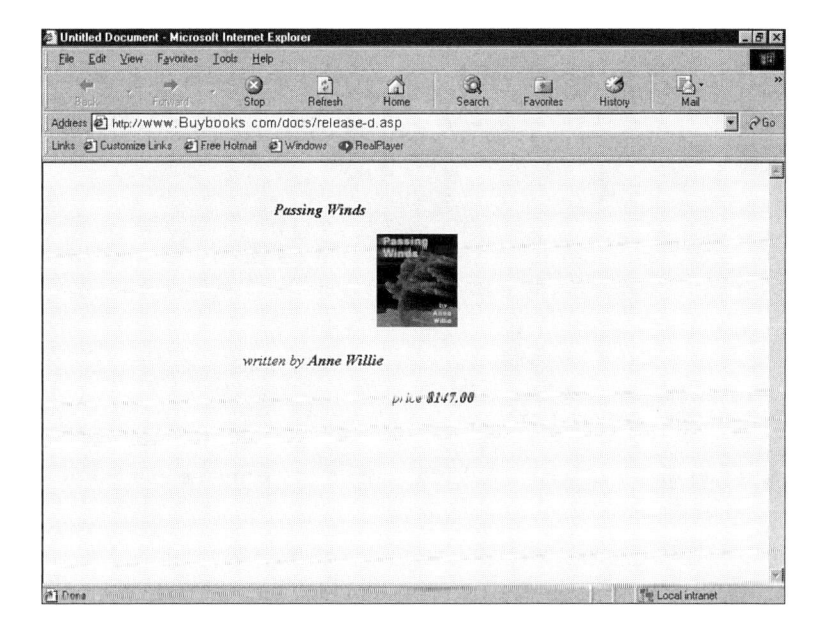

To create a master page, you must first create a recordset and a page layout to display the dynamic data from the recordset. The recordset you create for the master page must include the fields that must be displayed not only on the master page but also on the detail page. After you create the recordset and page layout for the master page, you can follow these steps to complete the master page:

1. Choose Insert, Live Objects, Master-Detail Page Set. The Insert Master-Detail Page Set dialog box is displayed, as shown in Figure 19.28.
2. From the Recordset drop-down list, select the recordset that must be used by the master page.
3. From the Master Page Fields list box, select the fields that must be displayed on the master page. By default, this list box displays all the fields from the selected recordset. However, if you do not want to display one of the listed fields in the master page, select the field and click the – button to remove the field from the list. You can also change the order in which the fields will be displayed on the page by using the up and down arrow buttons.
4. From the Link To Detail From drop-down list, select the field whose value will be used as a link to the detail page.
5. From the Pass Unique Key drop-down list, select the field that will act as a primary key. The detail page uses this field to identify the record that the user selected in the master page.

Figure 19.28
Use the Insert Master-Detail Page Set dialog box to specify the columns that must be displayed on the master page and the detail page.

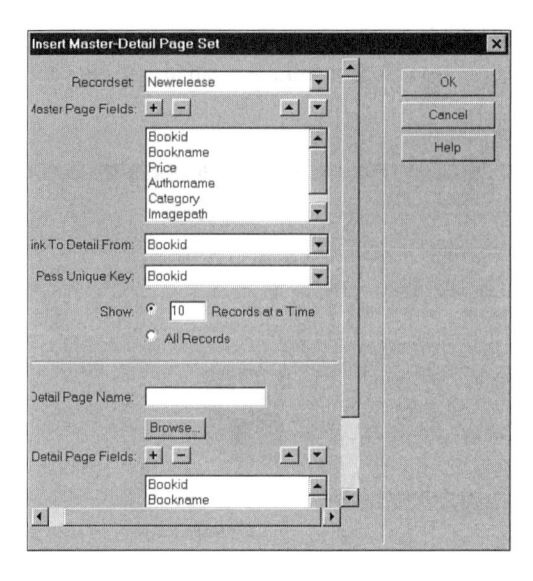

6. From the Show section, select an option to specify the number of records that you want to be displayed on the master page.
7. Click the Browse button under to the Detail Page Name text box to browse to the detail page file. Alternatively, you can also enter the name of the detail page file in the Detail Page Name text.
8. From the Detail Page Fields list box, select the fields that you want to display on the detail page, and then click OK.

You can view the master page in the browser to check its functionality.

SUMMARY

You can apply dynamic features to the objects on a Web site by using the various server behaviors that UltraDev provides. By using server behaviors, you can make text, images, and form objects such as text boxes, radio buttons, check boxes, and list menus dynamic. UltraDev also lets you add functionality to a Web page by creating recordset navigation bars, record counters, and master-detail pages.

ACTIVITY CORNER

In this activity corner section, you will add dynamic elements to the `Contentpage.asp`, `Search.asp`, and `Songfetch.asp` files. For each of these files, you will do the following:

- You will bind the SongName, ComposerName and Album columns from the recordset to the second table in each file.

- You will add the Repeat Region server behavior to the dynamic data in each file.
- You will add the Recordset Navigation Bar and Recordset Navigation Status live objects to each file.

Perform the following steps to add these features to the `Contentpage.asp` file:

1. Open the `Contentpage.asp` file.
2. Choose Windows, Data Bindings to open the Data Bindings panel.
3. The Data Bindings panel contains a recordset by the name LR. Drag the SongName column from the recordset to the cell below the cell containing the text Song Name.
4. Drag the ComposerName column from the recordset to the cell below the cell containing the text Composer.
5. Drag the Album column from the recordset to the cell below the cell containing the text Album.
6. Copy the image `playsong.gif` to your root folder and insert this image in the cell below the cell containing the text Listen.
7. Select the image and type `<%=(LR.Fields.Item("SongFile").Value)%>` in the Link text box of the Property inspector of this image. JSP users must type `<%=(LR.getObject("SongFile"))%>` and ColdFusion users must type `<cfoutput> #LR.SongFile# </cfoutput>`.
8. Type the text Add to CD in the cell below the cell containing the text Create CD.
9. Select the Add to CD text and type /Userdetails/Login.asp in the Link text box of the Property inspector.
10. Create an HTML style by the name dynamic_style. Set the font to Verdana, font size to 2, and text color to #000066. Apply this style to the dynamic data as well as the Add to CD link.
11. Next, you need to add the Repeat region server behavior to the cells. To do this, select the five cells of the second table and select the Repeat Region server behavior from the Server Behaviors panel.
12. In the Repeat Region dialog box, select the LR option from the Recordset drop-down list and type five in the text box next to the Show option button so that the number of records to be displayed in the repeat Region is 5.
13. Next, you need to add the Recordset Navigation Bar and Recordset Navigation Status live objects below the second table. To do this, select the Live category from the Objects panel and click the Insert Recordset Navigation Bar button.
14. In the Recordset Navigation Bar dialog box that is displayed, select the LR option from the Recordset drop-down list and select the Display Using Text option.
15. To add the Recordset Navigation Status, click the Insert Recordset Navigation Status button on the Objects panel. Select the LR option from the Recordset drop-down list and click OK. Change the display on the Recordset Navigation Status live object from Records to Songs. Apply the `dynamic_style` HTML style to the entire live object.

Repeat steps 1–15 to apply the same to the `Search.asp` and `Songfetch.asp` files. The recordset in the `Search.asp` file is SR and that in the `Songfetch.asp` is Links. Select the appropriate recordset while applying the Repeat Region server behavior and the Recordset Navigation Status and Recordset Navigation Bar live objects.

ADDING THE SHOW REGION SERVER BEHAVIOR

You also need to add a Show Region server behavior to the Search.asp file. If there are no records matching the search initiated by the user, an appropriate message must be displayed. This message must be created within a layer and the Show Region server behavior must be applied to the layer. To do these, perform the following steps in the `Search.asp` file:

1. Insert a layer in the editable region of the file. Adjust the width and height of this layer such that it hides the layer containing the table.

2. Set the background color of the layer to #CCCCCC. Type a message such as "Sorry !! Currently, there are no matching songs…". Apply the `dynamic_style` HTML style to this message.

3. After creating the message, select the layer and click the + button on the Server Behaviors panel to display the pop-up menu.

4. Select Show Region If Recordset Is Empty from the Show Region option of the pop-up menu. In the dialog box that is displayed, select the required recordset from the Recordset drop-down list and click OK.

Save the Search.asp file and preview the `Start.htm` file to see if the dynamic elements are displayed in the `Contentpage.asp`, `Search.asp`, and `Songfetch.asp` files.

CHAPTER 20

BUILDING DYNAMIC WEB APPLICATIONS

In this chapter

Adding a Search Feature to a Page   408

Adding, Updating, and Deleting Data in a Database   417

Troubleshooting   429

Summary   429

Activity Corner   430

Adding a Search Feature to a Page

The search feature is one of the most important features of a dynamic Web application. The search feature lets a user search for specific information in a Web page. The user searches for specific information by entering a search parameter in a form on the Web page. The Web application responds to the user's request by querying a database and retrieving records that match the search parameters that the user entered. You can build a search feature in your Web application by using the form objects, server behaviors, and live objects available in UltraDev.

To build a search feature in UltraDev, you need to create the following pages:

- A search page
- A results page
- An optional detail page

The search page contains a form to accept a search parameter from the user. The user specifies the search parameter on this form. After the user specifies the search parameter, the search page calls the results page, which accepts the search parameter from the form.

The results page searches the database for records that contain column values matching the search parameter. After the matching records are found, they are displayed on the results page. If there are many columns in the resultant records, displaying all these columns can clutter the screen. To avoid this, create a detail page. This detail page contains the columns of the retrieved records that cannot be fit into the results page. It is always a good design practice to display the most important part of the retrieved information on the results page and create a link to the detail page, where the rest of the information can be viewed if desired.

A Sample Search Feature

Assume that the user wants to search for books in a particular category, such as fiction or computers. To build a search feature in this case, create a database named books.mdb in Microsoft Access that contains information about books. Create a table called booksmaster in the database books.mdb that contains the information about the categories to which these books belong. Figure 20.1 shows the fields and their data types in the booksmaster table.

> **Caution**
> In the booksmaster table, the bookid column is the primary key that uniquely identifies every record in the table.

Figure 20.1
The Design view of the booksmaster table shows the fields in the table.

To implement this search feature, the following pages are required:

- A search page where the user enters the books' category.
- A results page that displays all the books that belong to the category specified by the user. Every book that is listed in the results page contains a link to a detail page where the rest of the information about the book is displayed.
- A detail page that displays additional information about the book, such as the name of the author and the book's price.

Create a connection called sampleconnection to connect to the books.mdb database. After creating the connection, create the search page, the results page, and the detail page.

THE SEARCH PAGE

A search page contains a form with the necessary form objects to accept search parameters from the user and pass them to the results page. The user can search a database by supplying one or more search keywords. If you want the search feature in your Web application to allow the user to specify a single search parameter, you can create a form object, such as a text field or menu, to accept the search parameter. To allow the user to specify multiple search parameters, you need to create as many form objects as there are search parameters.

> **Note**
> The form on a search page must necessarily contain a form button. This button is used to submit the search parameters to the results page.

The following steps illustrate how to create a search page:

1. Create a form, and add the required form objects to it. To implement the search feature just discussed, create a form called form1 that contains a text field named form_category and a form button named Submit. Give a descriptive label to the Submit button, such as Go or Click Here to Search.

→ To learn how to create form objects, **see** "Working with Form Objects," **p. 240**.

2. In the form button's Property inspector, select the Submit form option, as shown in Figure 20.2.

Figure 20.2
This form lets the user enter the search parameter.

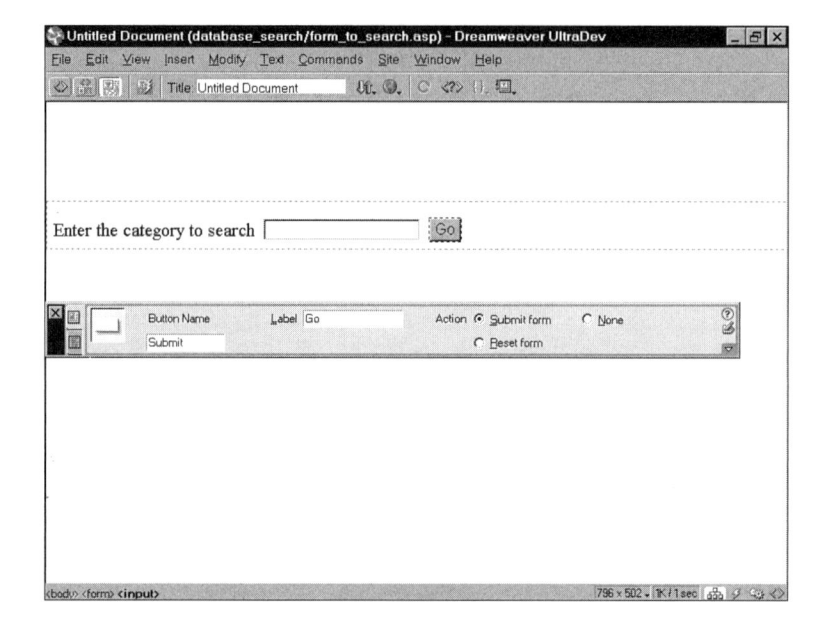

3. After you create the form and the form objects, click the <form> tag in the Tag selector on the status bar. In the <form> tag's Property inspector, specify the name of the results page in the Action text box.

4. From the Method drop-down list of the form's Property inspector, select the GET or POST method. If you select the GET method, the search parameters entered by the user are submitted through a querystring. If you select the POST method, they are submitted through the body of the message. If you choose the Default option, the browser's default method is used.

→ For more information on the GET and POST methods, **see** "The Request Object," **p. 67**.

Figure 20.3 shows the form's Property inspector, which contains the name of the results page as display_results.asp in the Action text box and has the GET method selected in the Method drop-down list.

The search page is now complete. The next step in creating the search feature is to create the results page.

Figure 20.3
This form calls the results page to process the search request.

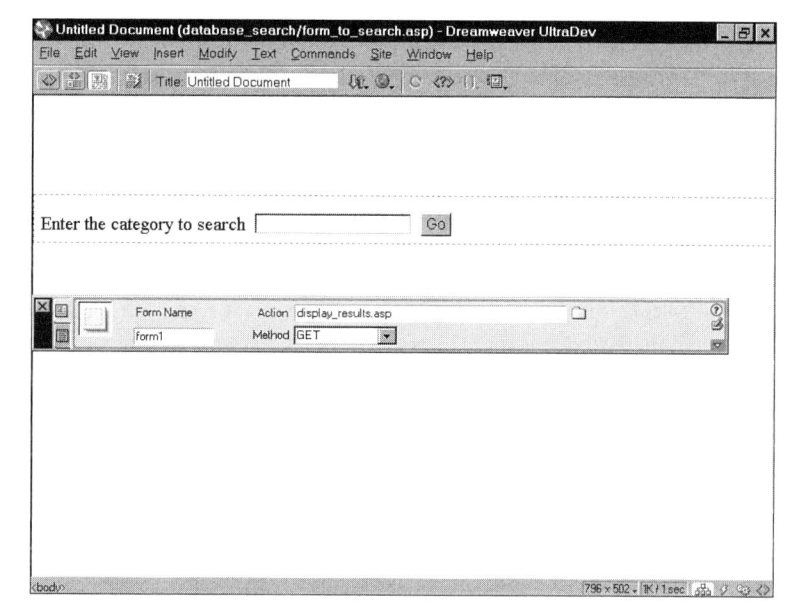

THE RESULTS PAGE

A results page accepts the search parameters from the search page and searches a database to find records that contain the column values that match the search parameter. After it finds these records, it retrieves and displays them. The results page must contain a recordset that will hold the results retrieved from the database. Creating a results page involves the following two steps:

1. Designing the page's layout
2. Creating a recordset

DESIGNING THE RESULTS PAGE

The design of the results page determines the extent of information that can be displayed on this page. When you design the results page, you determine how much space is allocated to display the retrieved information. If the information that is retrieved from the database is huge and the space allotted is not, you must decide how much of the retrieved information can be displayed in the allocated space. Depending on the space available, you can choose to display only those columns that fit into the allocated space and create the recordset accordingly. You can then create a detail page that will display the rest of the information. You can create a link to the detail page by attaching the Go to Detail Page server behavior in the results page (see the later section "Attaching the Go to Detail Page Server Behavior").

Creating a Recordset to Hold the Results

A recordset is the most important component of the results page. It retrieves the required records from a database and holds them. The recordset can be used to search a database with a single search parameter or multiple search parameters. To search with a single parameter, the recordset uses a filter. To search with multiple search parameters, the recordset uses a SQL query.

→ To learn how to create a recordset by using a filter and a SQL query, **see** "Creating a Recordset," **p. 360**.

USING A SINGLE SEARCH PARAMETER If you want to search for records based on a single search parameter, fill the appropriate fields in the recordset filter. In the sample search feature we discussed earlier, you need to create a recordset that allows the user to search for books that belong to a specific category. To do so, you must define the recordset filter so that it retrieves only those records that match the category that the user specifies in the search page.

Figure 20.4 shows the Recordset dialog box of the display_results.asp page, where a recordset filter is defined to retrieve records that match the category that the user entered.

The options in the Filter section of the Recordset dialog box define the recordset filter in the following manner:

- In the first drop-down list, the category field is selected from the list of fields in the booksmaster table. This is the column whose values must be compared to the search parameter entered by the user in the form_category text field on the form1 form.

Figure 20.4
This recordset retrieves records that match the search parameter.

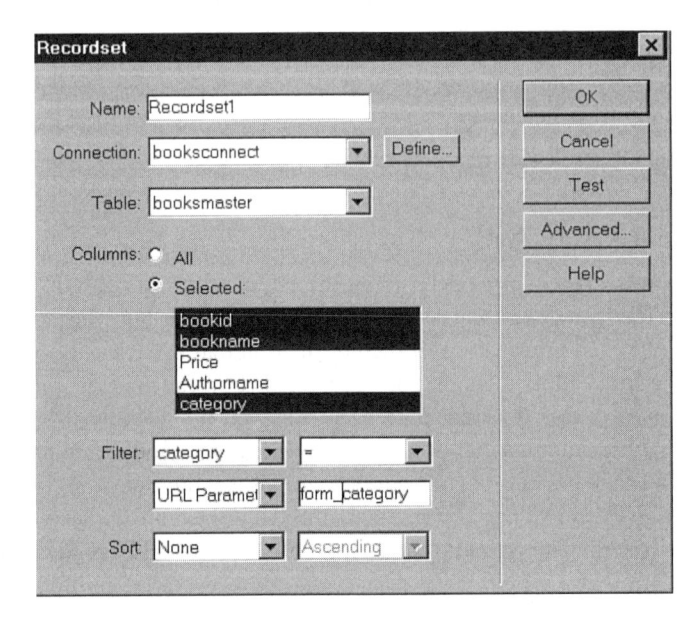

- In the second drop-down list, the = option is selected. This specifies that only those records in which the value in the category column equals the value entered by the user must be retrieved.
- In the third drop-down list, the URL Parameter option is selected because the form1 form submits the data by using the GET method.
- In the fourth drop-down list, form_category is specified because this is the name of the text field on the form where the user enters the search parameter.

SEARCHING WITH MULTIPLE SEARCH PARAMETERS When you want to search a database based on multiple search parameters entered by the user, you need to write a SQL query to retrieve the matching records.

For example, if you want to allow the user to search for books in a particular category written by a particular author, you can create two text fields on a form that will accept two search parameters from the user—the book's category and the author's name. Assume that one text field is named category and the other is named authorname.

To retrieve records that match the search parameters entered by the user, you must create a recordset by using SQL. Figure 20.5 shows the recordset defined by using the advanced Recordset dialog box.

After creating the recordset for the results page, bind the required columns to the results page.

Figure 20.5
Create advanced SQL queries in this dialog box.

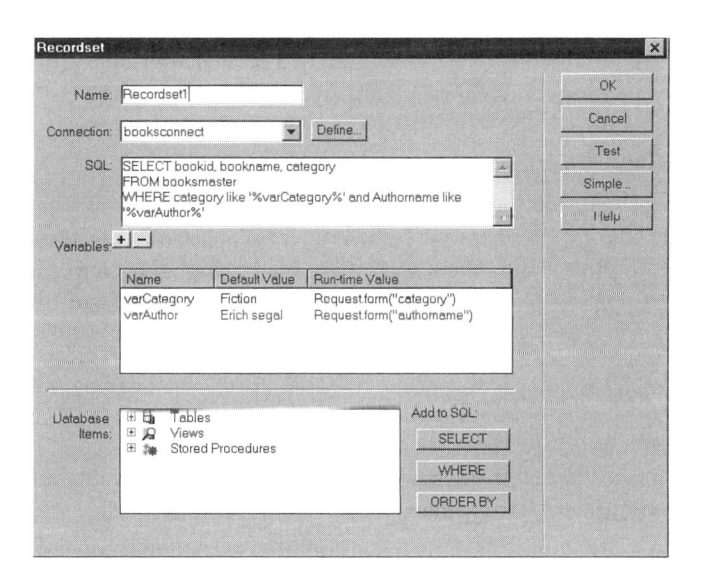

> **Tip**
> To make your results page as informative as possible and to allow users to easily browse through the results, add the Repeat Region server behavior and the Recordset Navigation Bar and Recordset Navigation Status live objects. (These topics are covered in Chapter 19, "Making a Web Page Dynamic.")

Figure 20.6 shows the bookname column of the recordset bound to a text element of the results page. A Repeat Region server behavior is attached to this bound column.

Figure 20.6
This page displays the books that belong to the category entered by the user.

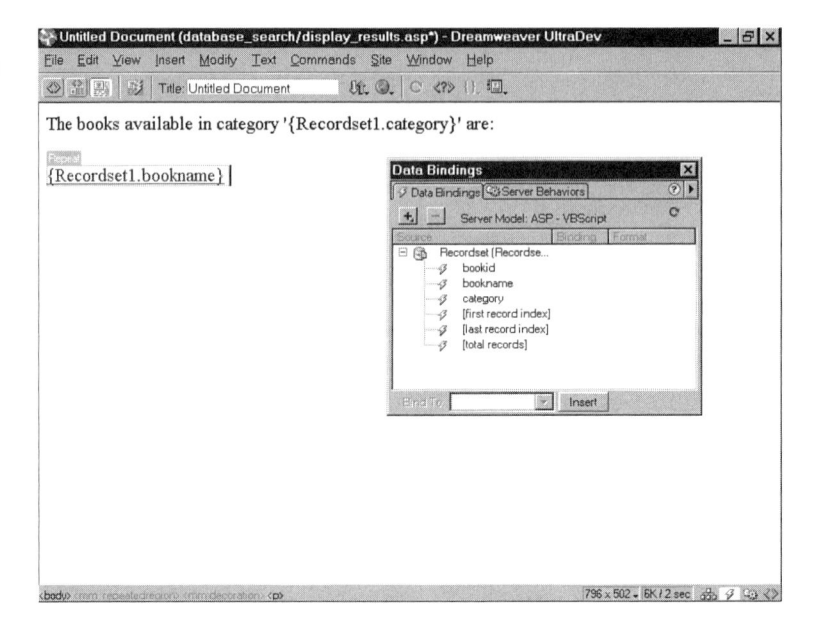

When the user searches for books belonging to a particular category, the titles of all the books that belong to that category are displayed in the results page.

CREATING A DETAIL PAGE

After you create a results page, you can create a detail page that displays the rest of the information about the records displayed on the results page. In the example just discussed, the results page showed only the names of the books belonging to the user-specified category. To display the author's name and the price of the book selected by the user, you need to create a detail page.

The following list is an overview of the steps. To create the detail page, do the following:

1. Decide on the detail page's layout.
2. Create a recordset on the detail page. This recordset must contain the columns that need to be displayed on the detail page.
3. The required columns from the recordset must be bound to the page elements of the detail page. It is not mandatory to bind the unique column to either the results page or the detail page. Figure 20.7 shows the authorname and price columns of the recordset bound to the elements of the detail page.

ADDING A SEARCH FEATURE TO A PAGE | 415

> **Note**
> The recordset defined in the detail page and the recordset defined in the results page must have at least one column in common. This common column must be a unique identifier for the records in the recordsets of the results and detail pages. Usually, this column is the primary key column. When a user selects a result in the results page, the value of the unique column associated with the selected result is passed from the results page to the detail page. In our example, when the user clicks a book name, the value of the bookid column associated with the bookname column is passed from the results page to the detail page.

Figure 20.7
The detail page lists more information about the retrieved records.

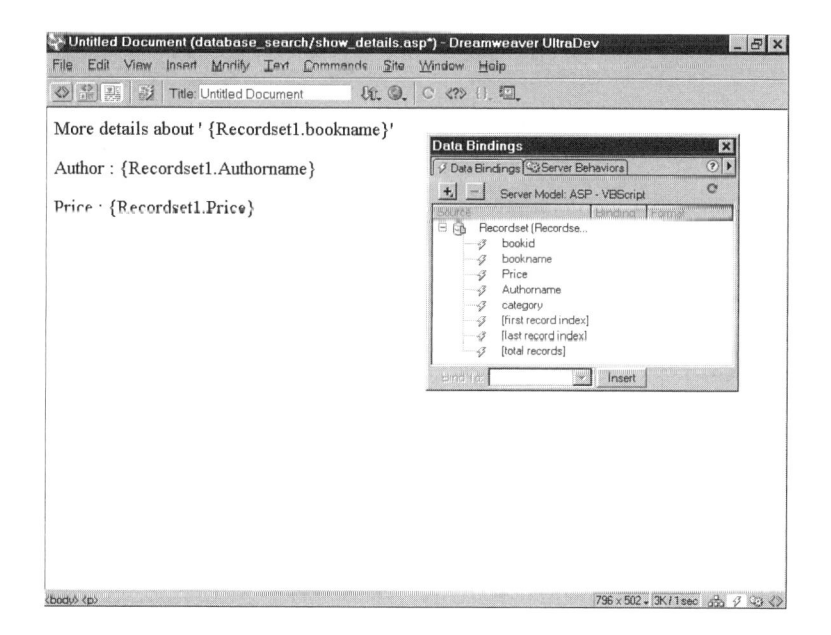

4. In the results page, the results must be displayed in a repeat region. The Go to Detail Page server behavior must be attached to the results displayed in the repeat region (see the next section). When the user selects a particular result in this region, the Go to Detail server behavior passes the unique column associated with the selected result to the detail page.

5. In the detail page, the Move to Specific Record server behavior (discussed in a moment) must be defined. This server behavior accepts the column value passed by the results page and displays the record that matches this value.

6. After the Move to Specific Record server behavior is attached to the detail page, the columns of the recordset defined for the detail page must be bound to the elements of the detail page.

ATTACHING THE GO TO DETAIL PAGE SERVER BEHAVIOR

To attach the Go to Detail Page server behavior to a results page, follow these steps:

1. Open the results page. Select the columns that are displayed in the repeat region.
2. Choose Windows, Server Behaviors to open the Server Behaviors panel. Click the + button and choose Go to Detail Page from the pop-up menu. The Go To Detail Page dialog box is displayed, as shown in Figure 20.8.

Figure 20.8
Specify the detail page in this dialog box.

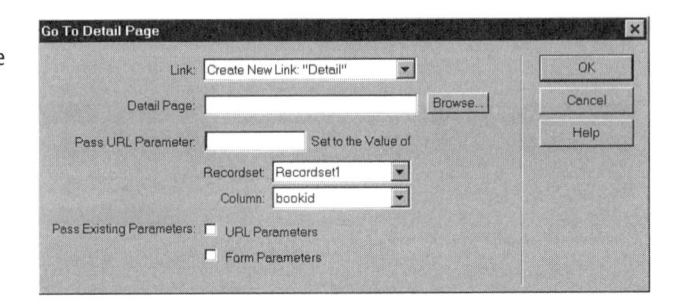

3. In the Link drop-down list, the link associated with the repeat region is displayed automatically. In the Detail Page text box, specify the name of the detail page.
4. In the Pass URL Parameter text box, type the name of the unique column associated with the result.
5. From the Recordset drop-down list, select the recordset of the results page that holds the results.
6. From the Column drop-down list, select the unique column in the recordset.
7. If additional information is passed from the form to the detail page, select the URL Parameters and Form Parameters check boxes.
8. Click OK after you have specified the required information.

In the search example discussed earlier, when the user clicks a book name in the results page, the bookid of the selected book name is passed to the detail page. Figure 20.9 shows the Go to Detail Page dialog box, where bookid is entered in the Pass URL Parameter text box.

Figure 20.9
Use this dialog box to pass the information to the detail page.

ATTACHING THE MOVE TO SPECIFIC RECORD SERVER BEHAVIOR

To add the Move to Specific Record server behavior to the detail page, follow these steps:

1. Open the detail page, and choose Windows, Server Behaviors to open the Server Behaviors panel. Click the + button in the Server Behaviors panel, and choose Move to Record, Move to Specific Record.
2. The Move To Specific Record dialog box is displayed, as shown in Figure 20.10. From the Move to Record In drop-down list, select the recordset that will contain the record to be displayed on the detail page.

Figure 20.10
Use this dialog box to retrieve a specific record that matches the search parameter.

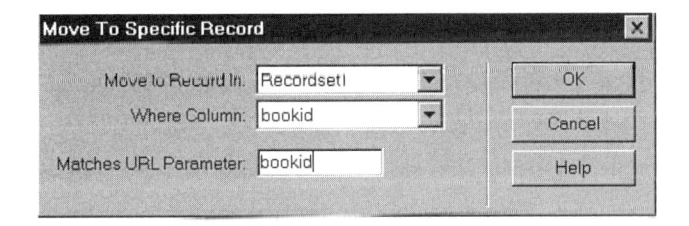

3. From the Where Column drop-down list, select the column of the recordset that contains the values that must be compared with the column value passed by the results page.
4. In the Matches URL Parameter text box, specify the column name whose value is passed from the results page.

In the dialog box shown in Figure 20.10, the bookid value passed by the results page is compared with the values of the bookid column of the recordset. After a matching record is found, the recordset holds the values of the matching record.

After you attach the Move to Specific Record server behavior, the search feature is complete. Preview the feature by opening the search page and pressing F12.

ADDING, UPDATING, AND DELETING DATA IN A DATABASE

In UltraDev, you can build a dynamic Web application that can add, update, and delete records in a database. You can use the server behaviors and live objects available in UltraDev to easily add these capabilities to your Web application.

To add, update, or delete records, an appropriate page, such as the insert, update, or delete page, is created, and the required server behavior is defined and attached to the page. For the insert and update pages, a form must be created in the page to allow the user to enter the data that is to be inserted or updated in the database. After the form is created, the required server behavior is added to the form.

UltraDev provides you with live objects for creating the insert and update pages. When you use these live objects, you do not have to manually create the forms and define the server behaviors. The live object automatically generates the form and adds the required server behavior to it.

INSERTING RECORDS INTO A DATABASE

To insert records into a database, first you need to create an insert page containing a form that will allow users to enter the data that is to be added to the database. Next, you have to attach the Insert Record server behavior to this insert page.

To create an insert page, add the required form objects, which are needed to capture the user's data, to the page. The form on this page must contain a button that will submit the form data to the server. Ensure that the Submit Form option is selected in the form button's Property inspector. Figure 20.11 shows an insert page with a form that accepts data from the user.

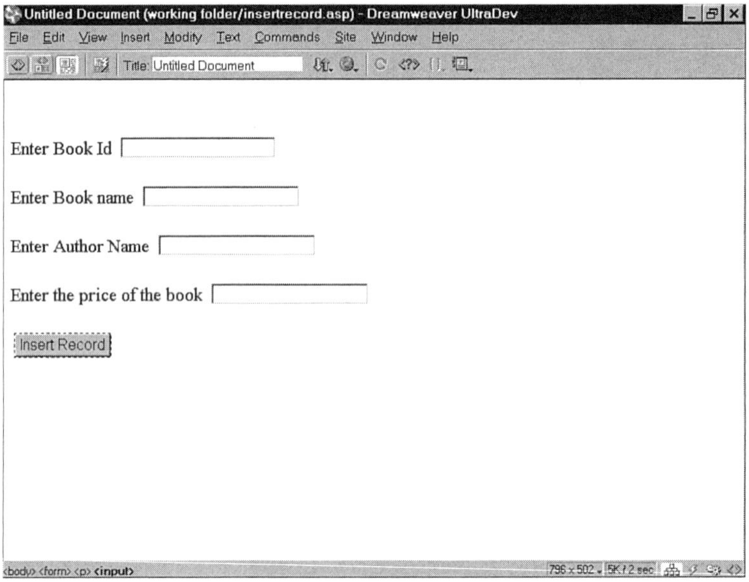

Figure 20.11
The form on the insert page allows the user to input data to insert in a database.

ADDING THE INSERT RECORD SERVER BEHAVIOR

After you have created the insert page, you need to add the Insert Record server behavior to the page. This server behavior accepts the data submitted by the form button and inserts this data into the required columns in the table.

ADDING, UPDATING, AND DELETING DATA IN A DATABASE | 419

> **Note**
> When you define the Insert Record server behavior, you don't need to worry about manually attaching this behavior to the form. This server behavior gets attached to the <form> tag as soon as you create it. You also don't need to specify whether the form should use the GET method or the POST method to submit the data or specify the page it should call to process the submitted data. This server behavior takes care of all these details.

To add the Insert Record server behavior, follow these steps:

1. Choose Windows, Server Behaviors.
2. Click the + button in the Server Behaviors panel. A pop-up menu is displayed.
3. Choose the Insert Record option from the pop-up menu. The Insert Record dialog box is displayed, as shown in Figure 20.12.

Figure 20.12
Use this dialog box to insert form data into a table.

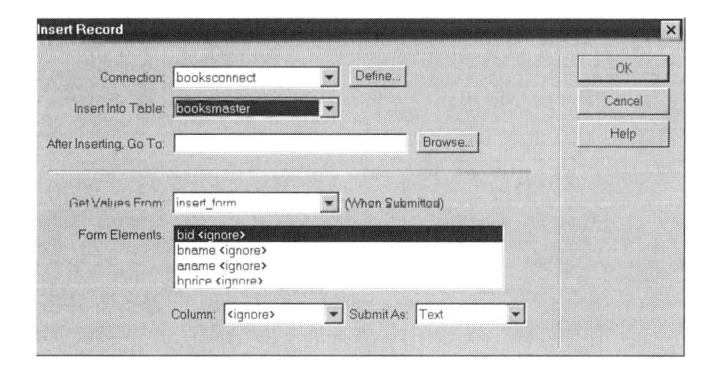

4. From the Connection drop-down list, select the connection that connects to the database in which you want to insert records.
5. From the Insert Into Table drop-down list, select the table in which you want to insert records.
6. In the After Inserting, Go To text box, specify the page that must be displayed when the insertion process is complete. For example, in online registration forms, after the user enters all the details and submits the form, the next page that is usually displayed is one that informs the user that the registration was successfully completed. If you have created such a page, specify the name of the page in this text box.

> **Note**
>
> You can also specify the name of the insert page in this text box. In such a case, the same insert page is displayed after the user submits the form. Although this feature is allowed in UltraDev, it is not a good design practice to display the same registration page.

7. From the Get Values From drop-down list, select the insert form from where the user input data is to be accepted.
8. The next step is to bind every form object on the insert page to the column in the table so that the data contained in the form object can be inserted into the respective column of the table. To do so, from the Form Elements list box, select the form object that contains data submitted by the user.
9. From the Column drop-down list, select the column in which the data contained in the form object must be inserted. From the Submit As drop-down list, select a data type for the value that will be entered by the user in the form object. This data type must match the data type of the column in which the data entered by the user is inserted.
10. Repeat steps 8 and 9 to bind every form object to the respective column in the table. A sample Insert Record dialog box with completed details is shown in Figure 20.13.
11. Click OK to close the Insert Record dialog box.

Figure 20.13
Data from the insert page is inserted into the booksmaster table by using this dialog box.

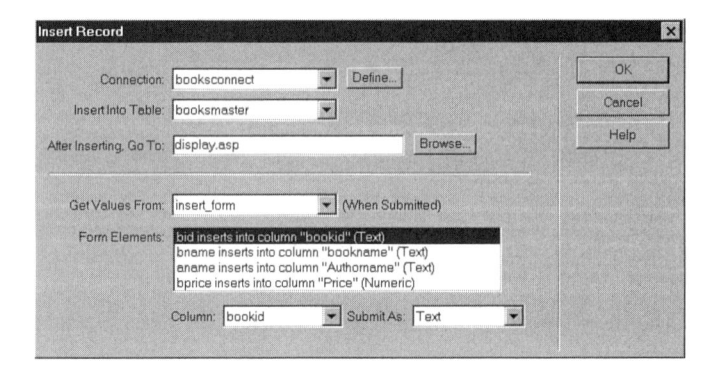

> **Tip**
>
> After inserting the records into a database through a Web application, you can check whether the data was successfully inserted by creating a page that displays all the table's records. Specify the name of this page in the After Inserting, Go To text box. To see whether the form works correctly, press F12 to preview the form in the browser. After checking, you can edit the Insert Record server behavior by double-clicking the Insert Record server behavior and changing the name of the next page that must be displayed in the After Inserting, Go To text box.

USING THE RECORD INSERTION FORM LIVE OBJECT

You can use the Record Insertion Form live object to create an insert page without having to manually create an insert form and add an Insert Record server behavior to the form.

The following steps illustrate how to build an insert page by using the Record Insertion Form live object:

1. Choose Insert, Live Objects, Record Insertion Form. The Insert Record Insertion Form dialog box is displayed, as shown in Figure 20.14.

Figure 20.14
Use this dialog box to create a form and add the Insert Record server behavior at the same time.

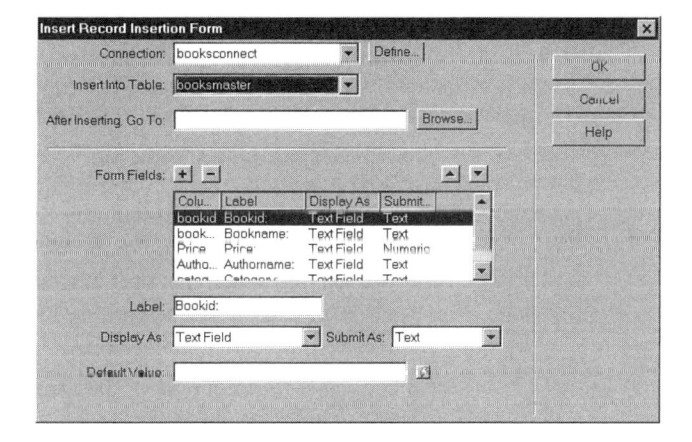

2. Select the connection that connects to the required database from the Connection drop-down list.
3. Select the table in which the records must be inserted from the Insert Into Table drop-down list.
4. Specify the page that must be displayed after the records are inserted in the After Inserting, Go To text box.
5. In the next section of the Insert Record Insertion Form dialog box, specify information that is needed to create the insert form. All the columns from the selected table are listed in the Form Fields list box. Each column in the Form Fields list box is associated with a form object that accepts user input for inserting values into that column. For every column you select in the Form Fields list box, the corresponding form object is created on the insert form. If you do not want to allow the user to insert data into a certain column, remove that column from the list by selecting it and clicking the – button located at the top of the Form Fields list box. After removing the required columns, select the column for which you want to create a form object.

> **Tip:** An alternative way to restrict a user from inserting values into a specific column is to associate the column with the Text form object. The usage of the Text form object is discussed in step 7.

6. After selecting the required column, specify the information about the form object that is associated with the selected column. The first information is a label that will be displayed next to the form object. Specify this label in the Label text box that appears below the Form Fields list box.

7. From the Display As drop-down list, select the type of form object that will accept user input. You can choose to create a text field, a text area, a menu, a check box, or a radio button group to accept user input. If you choose the Text Field or Text Area option, specify a default value in the Default Value text box. This default value is inserted into the respective column if the user does not input a value. The Text option displays data and does not allow the user to edit it. Use this option for columns in which you do not want the user to insert values. If you choose the Menu or Radio Group option, a button appears below the Display As drop-down list. Click this button to set the properties for the menu or radio group. If you select the Check Box option, decide on the initial state of the check box by selecting the Checked or Unchecked option.

8. From the Submit As drop-down list, select the data type of the form object. This data type must match the data type of the column in which user input is inserted.

9. Repeat the steps 5 through 8 to define the properties for all the form objects you want to display on the insert page.

10. Click OK to close the dialog box. The insert page is automatically created with the insert form, as shown in Figure 20.15.

Updating Records in a Database

To allow users to update a particular record in a database, a Web application must have the following two pages:

- A page in which the user specifies the information about the record that needs to be updated
- An update page that displays the record that the user wants to update and allows the user to edit that record

An update page accepts information about the record the user wants to update from the page where the user specifies this information. The information passed to the update page must be a column value that uniquely identifies each record. The update page contains a recordset that retrieves the record that contains the column value passed to it.

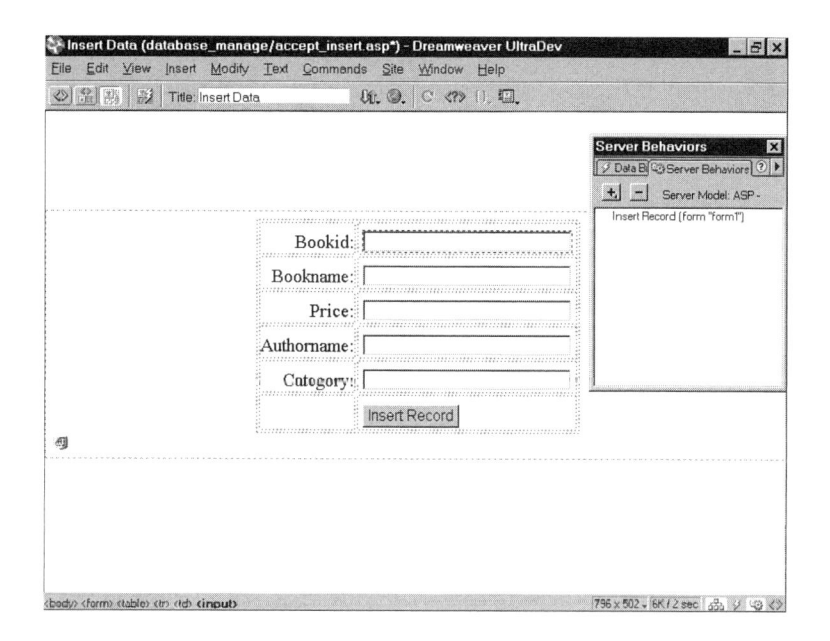

Figure 20.15
The insert form created using the Record Insertion Form live object.

This record is displayed on a form on the update page. This form also allows the user to enter the new values that need to be updated in the database. It contains a server behavior called the Update Record server behavior that updates the database with the new values entered by the user.

The page that calls the update page can be either a search page or a results page. If it is a search page, the update page must be called through the form button. If it is a results page, the Go to Detail Page server behavior must be attached to the results page. The name of the update page must be specified in the Detail Page text box of the Go to Detail Page server behavior.

After you create the appropriate user input screen, you can proceed to create the update page. The first part of creating an update page is to create a recordset that will retrieve the record that the user wants to update.

After you create a recordset, you can create the update page by manually creating the form to accept data that is to be updated from the user and attaching the Update Record server behavior to the form. You can also create the form and attach the server behavior at the same time by using the Record Update Form live object.

Using the Update Record Server Behavior

After you create a recordset, create a form for the update page by using form objects. Add a form object for every column that you want to allow the user to update. Ensure that the form has a submit button with an appropriate label, such as Update Record.

After creating the form, follow these steps to add the Update Record server behavior to the update page:

1. Choose Windows, Server behaviors. Select the Update Record server behavior from the pop-up menu that is displayed when you click the + button in the Server Behaviors panel.
2. The Update Record dialog box is displayed, as shown in Figure 20.16.

Figure 20.16
Use this dialog box to specify the columns that must be updated.

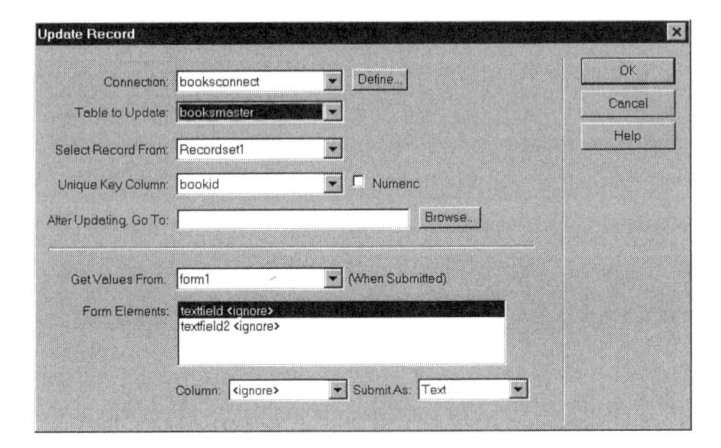

3. Select the connection name from the Connection drop-down list.
4. Select the table that must be updated from the Table to Update drop-down list.
5. From the Select Record From drop-down list, select the recordset that contains the record that matches the information entered by the user.
6. From the Unique Key Column drop-down list, select the unique column that is used to identify records.
7. In the After Updating, Go To text box, specify the name of the page that must be displayed after a record is updated.

> **Tip**
> Create a page that will display the updated record. Specify this page in the After Updating, Go To text box to check whether the update was successful. After checking, you can specify the name of the page that must appear after the update page.

8. From the Get Values From drop-down list, select the form that will be used to allow the user to update the data.
9. The Form Elements list box displays a list of all the form objects in the form. Select the form object in which the user will update the data. This form object must be bound to the corresponding column in the table that must be updated with the value entered by the user.

10. From the Column drop-down list, select the column that corresponds to the selected form object.
11. From the Submit As drop-down list, select the data type of the form object. This data type must match the data type of the column that is updated.
12. Repeat steps 9 through 11 for every form object in the Form Elements list box. After you bind every form object to the respective column in the table, the Update Record dialog box looks like Figure 20.17.

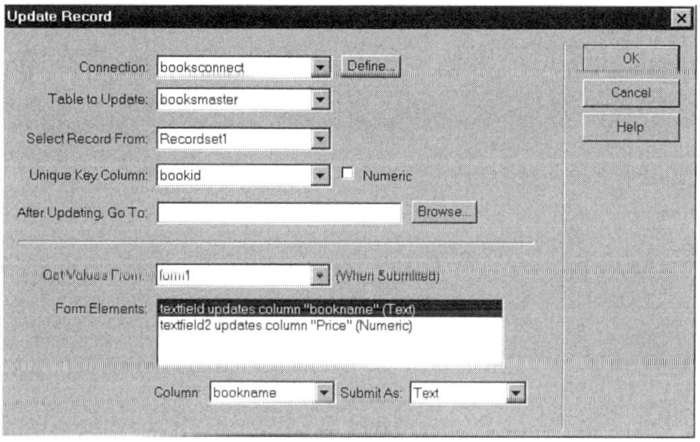

Figure 20.17
Data from form1 updates the bookname and price columns of the booksmaster table.

13. Click OK to close the dialog box. The update page is now complete.

To preview the update page to see whether it works successfully, press F12.

USING THE RECORD UPDATE FORM LIVE OBJECT

The Record Update Form live object is similar to the Record Insert Form live object in terms of providing a single interface to build a form and add an appropriate server behavior to it. It creates the form that allows the user to update the data and adds the Update Record server behavior to the form.

To use the Record Update Form live object to automatically create a form and add the Update Record server behavior to it, follow these steps:

1. Choose Insert, Live Objects, Record Update Form. The Insert Record Update Form dialog box is displayed, as shown in Figure 20.18.
2. Select the connection name and the table to be updated from the Connection and Table to Update drop-down lists, respectively.
3. From the Select Record From drop-down list, select the recordset that contains the record that matches the information entered by the user.
4. From the Unique Key Column drop-down list, select the unique column that is used to identify records. This is usually the table's primary key.

Figure 20.18
Create the update form and add the Update Record server behavior by using this dialog box.

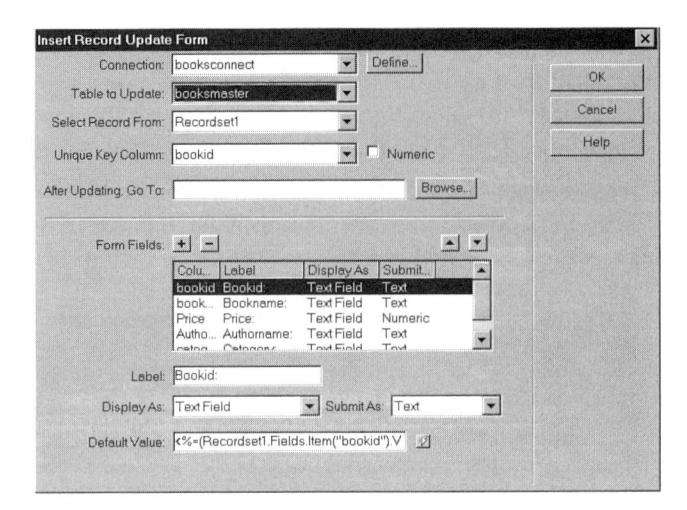

5. In the After Updating, Go To text box, specify the name of the page that must be displayed after a record is updated.
6. All the table's columns are automatically listed in the Form Fields list box. Select the column that you want to display on the form.
7. In the Label text box, specify a label that will be displayed next to the form object.
8. From the Display As drop-down list, select the type of form object that will accept the data entered by the user. For example, if you want to allow the user to edit a book's category, you can select the Menu option from the Display As drop-down list and specify the values to be displayed on the menu.
9. From the Submit As drop-down list, select the data type of the form object. This data type must match the data type of the column that is updated.
10. Repeat steps 6 through 9 to define the properties for all the form objects you want to display on the update page.
11. Click OK to close the dialog box. The update page is automatically created, with the form appearing in a table, as shown in Figure 20.19.

DELETING RECORDS IN A DATABASE

The Delete Record server behavior is used to delete records from a database. The procedure for creating a delete page sis similar in many respects to the procedure used for creating an update page. A delete page requires information from the user about the record that the user wants to delete. This information can be obtained from the user by means of a search page or a results page. The delete page must contain a recordset that will retrieve the record that is to be deleted. After you create a recordset, you can display the details of the record to be deleted on the delete page and prompt the user for a confirmation to delete the record.

Figure 20.19
This update page allows the user to update a record.

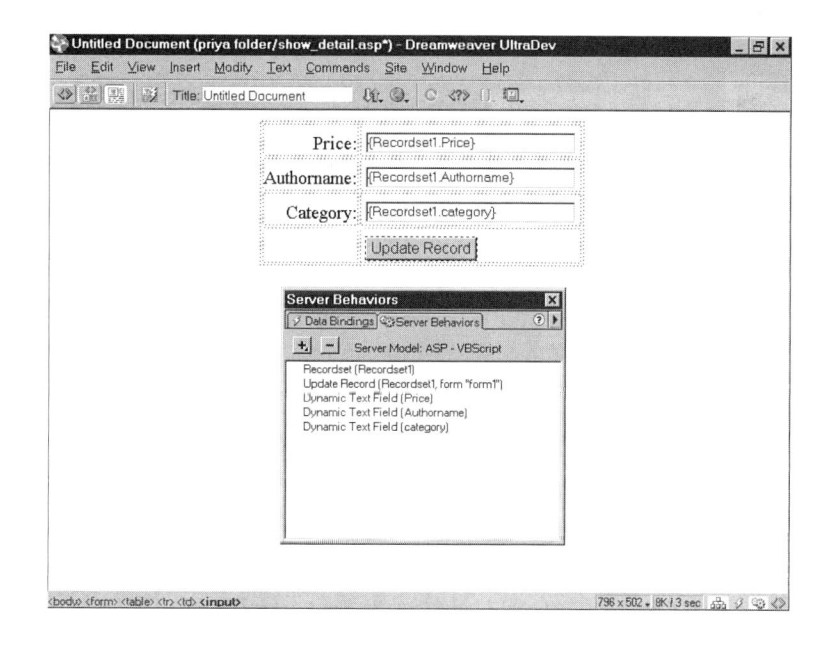

To display the record to be deleted, you can create a form on the delete page and bind the columns of the recordset to the form objects. You need to use a form button on this form that has an appropriate label that prompts the user for confirmation before deleting the record. Figure 20.20 shows a sample delete page that displays the record that the user wants to delete and prompts for confirmation.

Figure 20.20
A delete form that displays the record to be deleted.

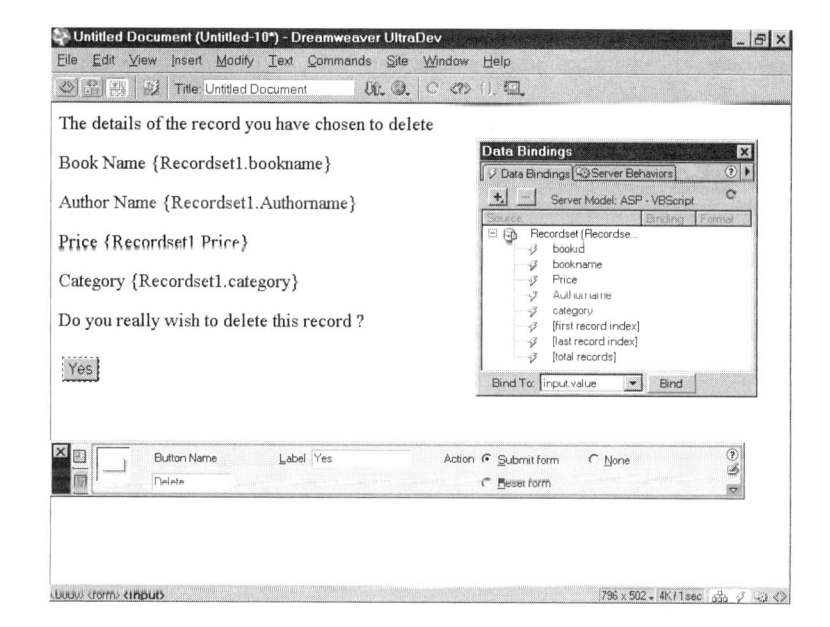

> **Note:** The page to which you attach the Delete Record server behavior must necessarily have a form button. The action associated with the form button must be Submit Form.

After you create a recordset and a form on the delete page, the next step is to attach the Delete Record server behavior to the form. To attach the Delete Record server behavior to the form, follow these steps:

1. Choose Windows, Server behaviors. Select the Delete Record server behavior from the pop-up menu that is displayed when you click the + button in the Server Behaviors panel.
2. The Delete Record server behavior is displayed, as shown in Figure 20.21.

Figure 20.21
Use this dialog box to delete the record specified by the user.

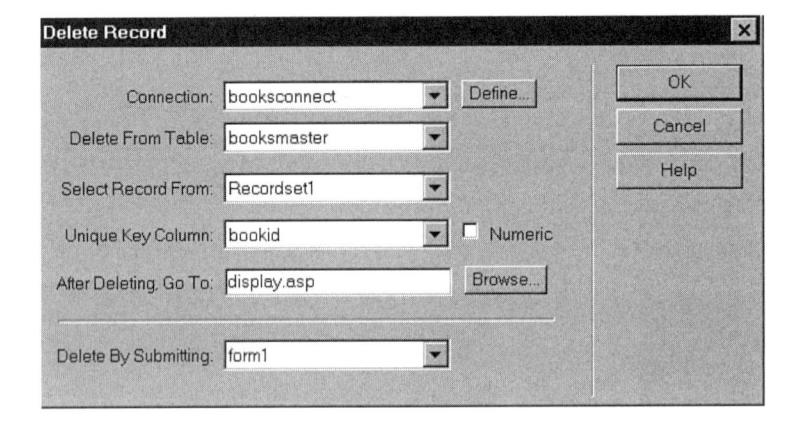

3. Select the connection name from the Connection drop-down list.
4. Select the table from which you want to delete the required record from the Delete from Table drop-down list.
5. From the Select Record From drop-down list, select the recordset that contains the record that must be deleted.
6. From the Unique Key Column drop-down list, select the unique column that is used to identify records. This is usually the table's primary key.
7. In the After Deleting, Go To text box, specify the name of the page that must be displayed after a record is deleted.
8. From the Delete By Submitting drop-down list, select the form name that contains the button that the user clicks to delete the record.
9. Click OK to close the Delete Record dialog box.

Preview the delete page by pressing F12 to see whether it works properly.

Troubleshooting

Errors in the search and results pages

My search and results pages are not working properly.

Check the following:

- Check whether the connection you have defined in the Connections dialog box works properly.
- Check whether the name of the form object in the search page is the same as the name specified in the recordset filter or the SQL query of the results page.
- Check whether the method you selected to submit the form data corresponds to the method you specified to accept the submitted data in the recordset filter. For example, if you used the GET method to submit the form and you selected Form Variable in the recordset filter, the results page will not work properly.
- If you bound the columns of the recordset to the page elements in the results page and then modified the recordset filter, the change will not take effect while records are displayed. Therefore, you need to bind the columns again to see the changes.

Error Messages

I keep getting an error message when I preview a page.

The following error message appears when a record containing the search parameter is not found in the table:

```
' ADODB.Field error '800a0bcd' ,
Either BOF or EOF is True, or the current record has been deleted;
the operation requested by the application requires a current record.
```

The following error message appears when you try to insert duplicate records into a database:

```
Microsoft OLE DB Provider for ODBC Drivers error '80040e14'
[Microsoft][ODBC Microsoft Access Driver] The changes you requested
to the table were not successful because they would create duplicate
values in the index, primary key, or relationship. Change the data in
the field or fields that contain duplicate data, remove the index, or
redefine the index to permit duplicate entries and try again.
```

Summary

This chapter dealt with building a search feature in a Web application. It also dealt with adding, updating, and deleting records in a database. You can build a search feature into a Web application by using a form that accepts search parameters from a user. This form calls a results page that retrieves the record matching the search parameter by using a recordset.

You can build an insert page by using a combination of a search page and a results page along with the Insert Record server behavior. You can use the Record Insert Form live object to build the insert page. You can build an update page by using the Record Update Form live object. You can also build the update page by using a combination of the search page and the results page along with the Update Record server behavior. You can implement a delete operation using the Delete Record server behavior.

ACTIVITY CORNER

In this activity corner section, you will create a registration page that allows users to register with your site. After a user registers with the site, the registration details must be added to the UserDetails table. To add the details to the table, you need to add an Insert Record server behavior to the registration page. To add the Insert Record server behavior, follow these steps:

1. Copy the `Register_base.asp` file to the Userdetails folder in your local root folder. After copying, rename the `Register_base.asp` file as `Register.asp`.
2. Open the `Register.asp` file and select the form button labeled Register.
3. Open the Server Behaviors panel and select the Insert Record server behavior from the pop-up menu.
4. In the Insert Record dialog box, select SongConnect from the Connection drop-down list.
5. Select UserDetails from the Insert Into Table drop-down list.
6. The name of the form appears automatically in the Get Values From drop-down list. The Form Elements list box shows all the form objects bound to the table fields, except the `fName` and `lName` form objects. Select fName from the Form Elements list box, FirstName from the Column drop-down list, and Text from the Submit As drop-down list.
7. Select the lName option from the Form Elements lsit box, LastName from the Colunm drop-down list, and Text from the Submit As drop-down list.
8. Click OK to close the dialog box.

Preview the page to check if the details you enter have been added to the UserDetails table.

CHAPTER 21

MANAGING SITE ACCESS

In this chapter

Preventing Unauthorized Access to a Site   432

Copying and Pasting Access Rights to Other Pages   441

Logging Out of a Web Page   441

Summary   442

Activity Corner   442

Preventing Unauthorized Access to a Site

A Web site's registration and login pages play an important role in guarding the Web site. These pages are used to restrict unauthorized users from accessing personalized Web pages that contain information specific to a user. They validate user information by using server behaviors.

You can build registration and login pages in your Web application by using the icons in the Forms category of the Objects panel and the server behaviors available in UltraDev.

You can add a server behavior to these forms by using the options in the Server Behavior panel. When you add a server behavior, UltraDev inserts a server-side script in the page's source code. This script instructs the server to transfer data from the data source to the page's source code. UltraDev provides you with four server behaviors: Log in User, Restrict Access to Page, Check New Username, and Log out User.

With e-commerce becoming popular, most Web sites use online registration forms to register to a Web site.

> **Note**
> Online forms are forms with various form objects that are linked to the fields in a database through a recordset.

Consider an online bookstore called Cyberscrolls.com. This bookstore stores the details of all the books in its bookstore in a database table called Books and details of all the registered users in a database table called Registered Users.

The Web site consists of some Web pages that display book details such as the book name, book price, and descriptions of the books that are accessible to all the users. In addition, it contains some Web pages that display user details such as the user ID, the password, and the credit card number that are accessible only to specific users. To restrict unauthorized users from accessing these personalized Web pages, you can create registration and login pages that enable user authentication.

Creating a Registration Page

The registration page lets the user register by specifying user information, such as the user ID and password, and become a member of the Web site.

A registration page consists of a registration form, which is a simple HTML form with a specific name. This form contains the basic fields to collect user information, such as the user ID and the password, a Submit button, and a Reset button. Figure 21.1 shows the registration form of an online bookstore.

Preventing Unauthorized Access to a Site | 433

Figure 21.1
The registration form of a Web site lets users register themselves to become members of the site.

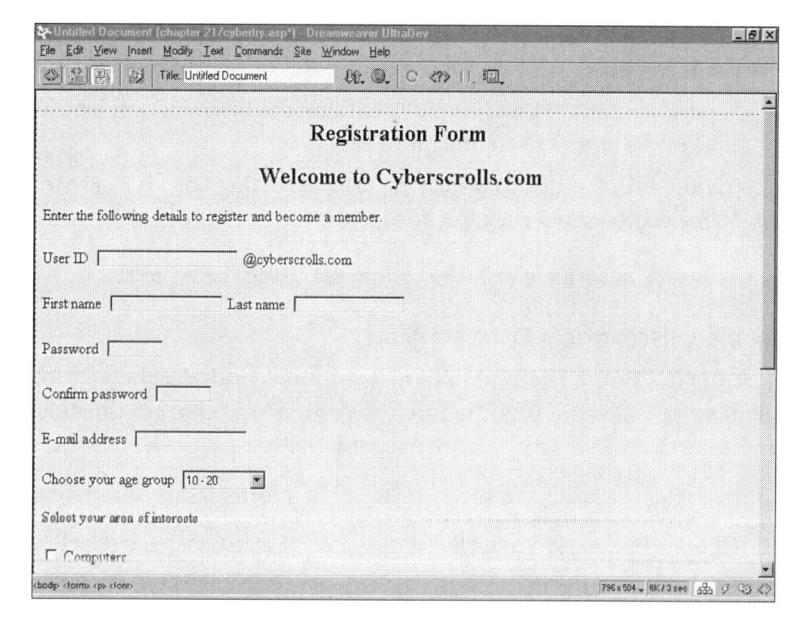

[Screenshot of Dreamweaver UltraDev showing a Registration Form titled "Welcome to Cyberscrolls.com" with fields for User ID (@cyberscrolls.com), First name, Last name, Password, Confirm password, E-mail address, Choose your age group (10-20), Select your area of interests, and a Computers checkbox.]

To design a registration form similar to the sample registration form shown in Figure 21.1, follow these steps:

1. Click the Insert Form icon in the Forms category of the Objects panel. A form is inserted into the Document window.

2. Specify the name of the form as Registration in the Form Name text box of the form's Property inspector.

3. Click the Insert Text Field icon in the Forms category of the Objects panel. A text box is created in your document, and the text box's Property inspector is displayed.

4. To name the text box userid, type `userid` in the TextField text box of the Property inspector.

5. Label the text box in the form by typing User ID next to the text box. In this example, userid is the variable that stores the value entered in the text box, and User ID is the label for the text box. The value stored in the variable userid is sent to the server for processing.

6. Type 24 in the Char Width text box to specify the length of the User ID text box.

7. Type 24 in the Max Chars text box to specify the maximum number of characters a user can type in the text box. This is used to validate and define the size limits of the text box.

8. Similarly, insert text boxes for obtaining user details such as the username, age, and e-mail address.

9. In addition to these text boxes, insert a password field for obtaining the password from the user. To insert a password field, you need to switch to the Code View and type
   `<input type ="password" name="password">`.

PART
IV
CH
21

10. After inserting the text fields, insert a Submit button by clicking the Insert Button icon in the Forms category of the Objects panel. By default, the Submit button is labeled Submit.
11. Similarly, insert a Reset button by clicking the Insert Button icon and changing the label of the button from Submit to Reset.
12. Choose File, Save As to display the Save As dialog box. Type Registration in the File Name text box, and click OK to save the form.

→ To learn how to create forms and form objects, **see** "Using Forms," **p. 238**.

Adding a Record to a Database Table

After you design the registration form, the form is ready for the user to enter information. UltraDev provides you with the Insert Record server behavior, which lets you add records entered in the registration form to a database table.

To attach the Insert Record server behavior to a form, follow these steps:

1. Choose Windows, Server Behaviors. The Server Behaviors panel is displayed.
2. Click the + button in the Server Behaviors panel and choose the Insert Record option from the pop-up menu. The Insert Record dialog box is displayed, as shown in Figure 21.2.

Figure 21.2
The Insert Record dialog box lets you insert the registration details entered in a registration form into a database table.

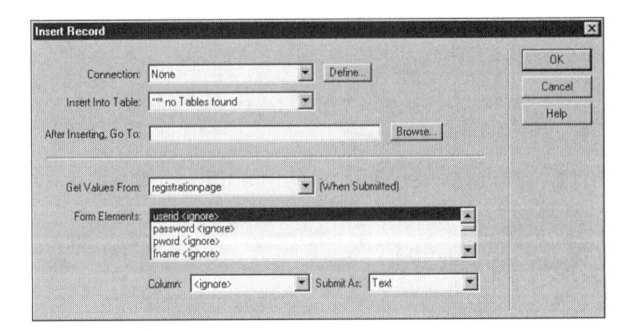

3. Select a connection from the Connection drop-down list. This connection lets you connect to the database containing the table of registered users. If you do not want to use any of the existing connections, you can create a new connection.

→ To learn more about creating a connection to a database, **see** "Creating and Managing Database Connections," **p. 344**.

4. From the Insert Into Table drop-down list, select the database table that you want to use to store the data entered in the registration form. This drop-down list displays a list of all the tables in the connected database. Consider the online bookstore example, in which the user fills out a registration form to become a member of the bookstore. The details of this form are added to the Registered Users database table specified in the Insert Into Table drop-down list.

5. Specify the path to the Web page that will be displayed to the user after the record is inserted in the After Inserting, Go To text box. You can also click the Browse button to select the path from the Select File dialog box.
6. From the Get Values From drop-down list, select the name of the registration form from which the registration details are to be taken. The Form Elements list box displays a list of all the fields in the selected form.
7. To specify what each form object on the registration form will update in the database table, first select the form object in which the user will update data, and then select the table column that corresponds to that form object from the Column drop-down list.
8. Select the data type of the selected column from the Submit As drop-down list.
9. Click OK to close the Insert Record dialog box. The Insert Record server behavior is applied to the form, and the form color changes to blue.

Validating Registration Form Information

After you design the registration form, it is ready for the user to enter information. Before you add the form information to a database table, you must add a server behavior to the form to validate the form information. Apart from this validation, you can incorporate client-side validations, such as checking the maximum character limit of the user ID and so on.

Each time a user enters details into the registration form and then submits it, the database table associated with this page is updated with the latest information entered by the user. You cannot have two identical user IDs in a database table. Therefore, to ensure that the user ID is unique, you can use the Check New Username server behavior. This server behavior compares the user ID entered by the user in the form with the user IDs stored in the database table. If the user ID does not match any value in the user ID field of the database table, the record is inserted into the database table. If it matches, the record is not inserted, and the user is redirected to an error page that prompts the user to specify a different user ID.

Consider the registration page of the `Cyberscrolls.com` site, to which the Check New Username server behavior is attached. When a user enters `KenBurton` as the user ID in the Userid text field and `pass1` as the password in the Password text field and clicks the Submit button, registration details are submitted to the server. The Check New Username server behavior automatically creates a recordset that compares the user ID, `KenBurton`, with the user IDs stored in the Registered Users table. If the table does not contain any record with the same user ID, the registration is successful, and the record is inserted into the table. However, if the database table already contains a record with that user ID, the user is directed to an error page that prompts him to enter a different user ID. Figure 21.3 shows a sample error page.

Figure 21.3
The error page prompts the user to try a different user ID and redirects him to the registration page.

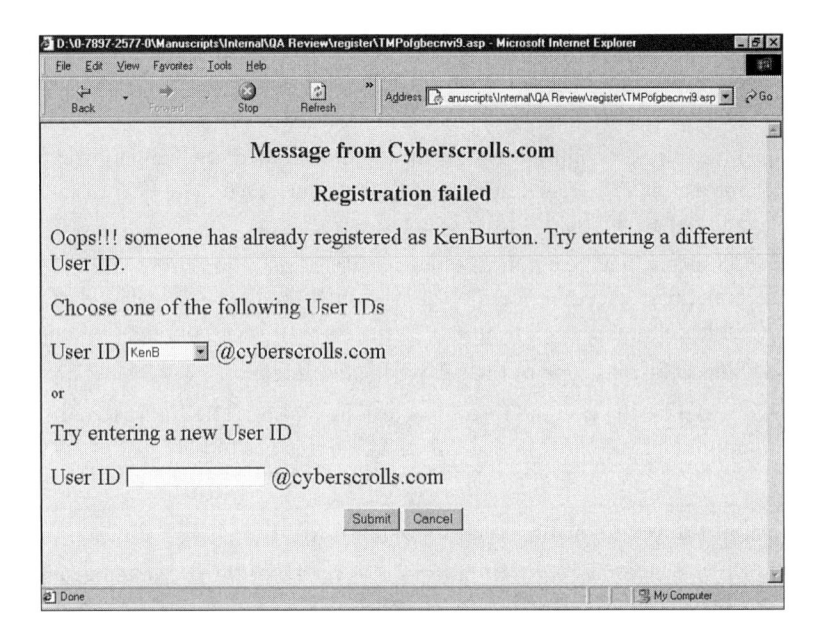

In UltraDev, the Check New Username server behavior allows you to ensure the uniqueness of user IDs.

Follow these steps to ensure that the username entered in the registration form is unique:

1. Choose Windows, Server Behaviors to open the Server Behaviors panel.
2. Click the + button in the Server Behaviors panel. A pop-up menu is displayed, as shown in Figure 21.4.

Figure 21.4
When you click the + button in the Server Behaviors panel, it displays the list of server behaviors.

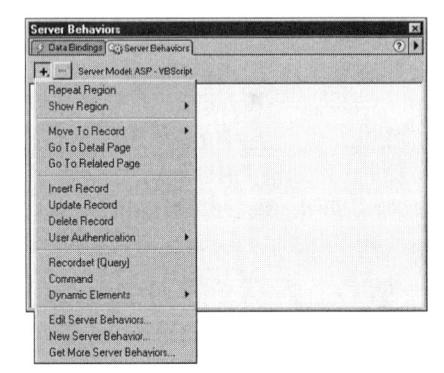

3. Choose User Authentication, Check New Username from the pop-up menu. The Check New Username dialog box is displayed, as shown in Figure 21.5.

Figure 21.5
The Check New Username dialog box lets you ensure that the name entered by the user is unique.

4. Specify the name of the text field that accepts the user ID from the registration form in the Username Field text box.
5. Specify the path to the Web page that the user will be redirected to if the user ID already exists in the If Already Exists, Go To text box. You can also click the Browse button to select the path to the Web page from the Select File dialog box.
6. Click OK to close the Check New Username dialog box. The Check New Username server behavior is applied to the form, and the form color changes to blue.

CREATING A LOGIN PAGE

A Web site's login page ensures that the user is a registered member of the Web site. This page lets all the site's registered users log in to the site and access the content pages. Typically, a login page consists of a login form that contains two text fields for the user to enter the user ID and the password, as well as a Submit button. For example, the login page of the Cyberscrolls.com online bookstore contains the User ID and Password text boxes and a Login button, as shown in Figure 21.6.

Figure 21.6
A login form lets a registered user log on to a Web site and redirects a new user to the registration page.

The Forms category of the Objects panel lets you create a login form and add objects to the form. For example, you can design a login form similar to the login form of the `Cyberscrolls.com` site by using the icons in the Forms category of the Objects panel and save it as loginform.

After you design the login form, the next step is to attach a server behavior to the form to validate the login information. In UltraDev, you can use the Log in User server behavior to ensure the validity of the login information. Attach the Log in User server behavior of the Server Behaviors panel to ensure that only registered users log on to the Web site.

Each time a registered user enters the details in the login form and submits it, the Log in User Server behavior compares the user ID and password entered by the user with the user IDs and passwords stored in the database table. If the values match, the user is redirected to the contents page. Otherwise, the user is redirected to a page that displays an error message, such as `Login failed, try again`.

Follow these steps to attach the Log in User server behavior to a login form:

1. In the Document window, open the login form to which you want to attach the Log in User server behavior.
2. Choose Windows, Server Behaviors to open the Server Behaviors panel.
3. Click the + button in the Server Behaviors panel and choose User Authentication, Log In User from the pop-up menu that is displayed. The Log In User dialog box is displayed, as shown in Figure 21.7.

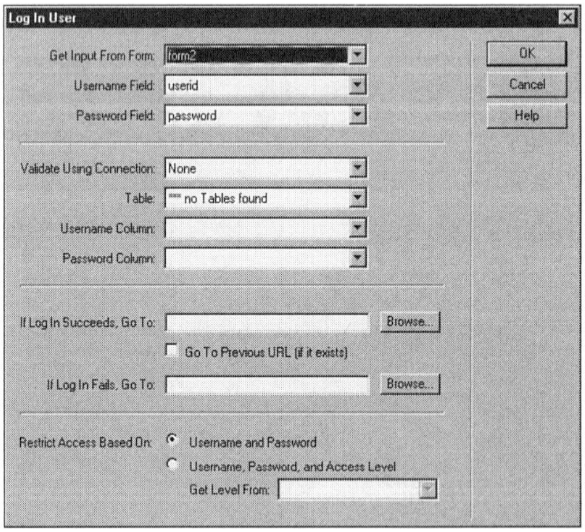

Figure 21.7
The Log In User dialog box lets you validate the login information entered in the login page of a restricted Web site.

4. Select the login form that submits the login information from the Get Input From Form drop-down list.
5. Select the name of the form field that submits the user ID data entered in the login form from the Username Field drop-down list.

6. Similarly, select the name of the form field that submits the password data entered in the login form from the Password Field drop-down list.

7. Select the database connection you want to use from the Validate Using Connection drop-down list.

8. Select the database table from the list of tables available in the Table drop-down list.

9. Select the column name of the database table that corresponds to the user ID field in the login form from the Username Column drop-down list. The server behavior compares the values entered in the user ID and password fields in the login page with the values stored in these columns.

10. Similarly, select the column name in the database table that corresponds to the password field in the login form from the Password Column drop-down list.

11. Specify the path to the Web page that will be displayed if the login is successful in the If Log In Succeeds, Go To text box. Generally, this Web page is the site's Welcome page.

12. Specify the path to the Web page that will be displayed if the login fails in the If Log In Fails, Go To text box. Generally, this is the site's Errors page.

13. Specify the condition on which you want to restrict access to the page in the Restrict Access Based On option. If you want to restrict access based on the user ID and password, choose the Username and Password option. If you want to restrict access based on the user ID, password, and access level, choose the Username, Password, and Access Level option, and then select the appropriate access level from the Get Level From drop-down list.

14. Click OK to close the Log In User dialog box.

Redirecting Unauthorized Users to Another Page

The Restrict Access to Page server behavior in UltraDev lets you prevent unauthorized users from accessing a restricted page.

Consider the example of the online bookstore, `Cyberscrolls.com`. This bookstore contains some restricted Web pages that contain information related to the books in the bookstore. These pages can be accessed only by authorized users, such as database administrators. You can restrict access to these Web pages to database administrators by adding the Restrict Access to Page server behavior to these pages. Any unauthorized user can only view these pages, not modify them. If a user attempts to access these protected pages and update them, an error message is displayed, and the user is redirected to another page.

Follow these steps to redirect an unauthorized user to a different page:

1. In the Document window, open the page that you want to protect.

2. Open the Server Behaviors panel and click the + button in the Server Behaviors panel.

3. Choose User Authentication, Restrict Access To Page from the pop-up menu that is displayed. The Restrict Access To Page dialog box is displayed, as shown in Figure 21.8.

Figure 21.8
The Restrict Access To Page dialog box lets you set authorization levels for various pages of a Web site.

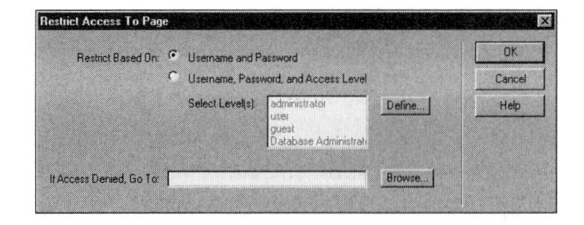

4. If you want to restrict access based on the user ID and password, choose the Username and Password option.

5. If your Web site has some protected Web pages and if you plan to use some authorization levels for these pages, select the Username, Password, and Access Level option. This option lets you provide access to registered users who have certain special access privileges to view the page.

6. After you select the Username, Password, and Access Level option, the items in the Select Level(s) list box are activated. Select the authorization level from the list of items displayed in this list box.

> **Note**
>
> You can set more than one authorization level by holding down the Ctrl key and clicking the authorization level in the Select Level(s) list box.

7. Click the Define button if you want to define a new level. The Define Access Levels dialog box is displayed, as shown in Figure 21.9.

Figure 21.9
The Define Access Levels dialog box lets you add authorization levels to the list of existing authorization levels displayed in the Select Level(s) list box.

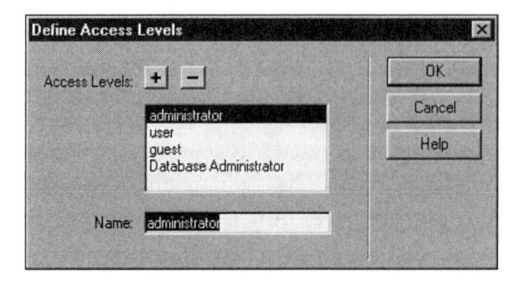

8. Click the + button in the Define Access Levels dialog box, and enter the new authorization level in the Name text box. For example, if you want to authorize only users who have the Database Administrator privilege to view a particular page, click the + button and type Database Administrator in the Name text box. Click OK to add the new authorization level to the list.

9. In the Restrict Access To Page dialog box, specify the page to which an unauthorized user will be redirected in the If Access Denied, Go To text box. You can also click the Browse button to select the path to the page from the Select File dialog box. Consider the example in which only the database administrator is given the privilege of viewing the protected Web page. If users other than the database administrator try to access the protected Web page, they are redirected to the page specified in the If Access Denied, Go To text box.

10. Click OK to close the Restrict Access To Page dialog box.

Copying and Pasting Access Rights to Other Pages

In UltraDev, all the server behaviors that are created for a Web page are listed in the Server Behaviors panel. You can cut, copy, or paste any of these server behaviors. To copy and paste access rights assigned to a Web page to other Web pages, you need to copy and paste the Restrict Access to Page server behavior.

If you want to copy an access right from one page to another page, first open the page that is protected. Open the Server Behaviors panel by choosing Window, Server Behaviors.

Select the Restrict Access to Page server behavior from the list of server behaviors displayed in the Server Behaviors panel. After selecting the server behavior, click the arrow button in the top-right corner of the Server Behaviors panel. Select the Copy option from the pop-up menu to copy the server behavior.

Open the Web page you want to protect using the same server behavior. Open the Server Behaviors panel by choosing Window, Server Behaviors. Click the arrow button in the top-right corner of the Server Behaviors panel, and select the Paste option from the pop-up menu to paste the Restrict Access to Page server behavior in this Web page.

Logging Out of a Web Page

In UltraDev, the Log Out User server behavior lets you log out a user of a Web page without exiting the browser. Whenever a user logs on successfully, a session variable for that user is created on the user's browser. Session variables are used to store and display information about the user's interaction with the server. The session variable is cleared when the user logs out of the site.

Note: If the user quits Netscape or Internet Explorer to exit the browser, the session variable is automatically discarded. In this case, there is no need to use the Log Out User behavior.

Follow these steps to let the user log out from a Web site without exiting the browser:

1. In the Document window, open the page where you want to add a link for logging out.
2. Choose Windows, Server behaviors to open the Server Behaviors panel.
3. Click the + button in the Server Behaviors panel and choose the User Authentication, Log Out User option from the pop-up menu that is displayed. The Log Out User dialog box is displayed, as shown in Figure 21.10.

Figure 21.10
The Log Out User dialog box lets you specify when the user must log out.

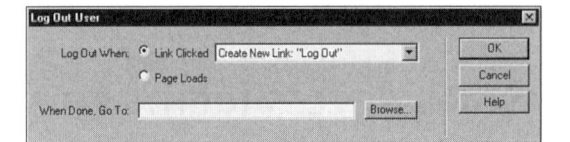

In the Log Out User dialog box, specify when the user must log out by choosing one of the options, Link Clicked or Page Loads, in the Log Out When radio button group. If you want the user to log out when a particular link is selected, select the Link Clicked option. If you want the user to log out when a specific page loads, select the Page Loads option. Specify the page to which the user will be redirected after logging out in the When Done, Go To text box. Click OK to close the Log Out User dialog box.

SUMMARY

This chapter dealt with building a registration page and a login page for a Web application. These pages restrict unauthorized users from accessing personalized Web pages that contain information specific to a user. You can design the registration and login pages by using the icons in the Forms category of the Objects panel and various server behaviors provided by UltraDev. The Log in User server behavior lets you ensure that only registered users log on to the restricted Web page. The Restrict Access to Page server behavior lets you prevent unauthorized users from accessing a restricted page. The Log out User server behavior lets you log out a user of a Web page. The Check New Username server behavior lets you ensure that the user IDs in the database table are unique.

ACTIVITY CORNER

In this activity corner section, you will complete the web application that you have been developing. The tasks that you need to do to complete the Web application are

- Complete the registration page by adding a Check New Username server behavior.
- Create a login page.
- Complete the `Contentpage.asp`, `Search.asp`, and the `Songresults.asp` files.
- Create two e-commerce pages, `ViewCD.asp` and `Placeorder.asp`.
- Create the `Editprofile.asp` page that allows the user to edit her profile.

Completing the Registration Page

To complete the registration page, you must add the Check New Username server behavior to the `Register.asp` page. This behavior checks whether the login name chosen by the user is unique. Before adding this server behavior to the `Register.asp` file, copy the `Failregister.asp` page to the Userdetails folder in your local root folder. The `Failregister.asp` file displays an error message if a duplicate user name is found.

Open the `Register.asp` file and add the Check New Username server behavior. In the Check New Username dialog box, select the LoginID option from the Username Field drop-down list. In the If Already Exists, Go To text box, browse to the `Failregister.asp` file.

Creating the Login Page

To create the login page, follow these steps:

1. Copy the `Login_base.asp` and `Loginfail.asp` files to the Userdetails folder in your local root folder. Rename the `Login_base.asp` file in the Userdetails folder as `Login.asp`.
2. Open the `Login.asp` file and select the Log In User server behavior from the Server Behaviors panel.
3. In the Log In User dialog box that is displayed, select form1 from the Get Input From Form drop down list.
4. Select loginId from the Username Field drop-down list and password from the Password Field drop-down list.
5. Select SongConnect from the Validate Using Connection drop-down list. Select UserDetails from the Table drop-down list.
6. Select LoginID from the Username Column drop-down list. Select Password from the Password Column drop-down list.
7. In the If Log In Succeeds, Go To text box, specify the Contentpage.asp file. In the If Login Fails Go To text box, specify the Loginfail.asp file.
8. Select the Username and Password option.
9. Click OK to close the Log In User dialog box.

The login page is now complete. As soon as a user logs on to a site, her login name is maintained in a session variable named `MM_Username`. Create a session variable called `MM_Username` in the Login page. This session variable is available across all pages in your site. The `MM_Username` session variable is used in the e-commerce pages to determine if a user can add songs to a CD and place an order for the CD. ColdFusion users must enable session management to use the session variable. To enable session management, ColdFusion users must include the following code in their pages:

```
<CFAPPLICATION NAME="SearchApp"
CLIENTMANAGEMENT="Yes"
SESSIONMANAGEMENT="Yes">
```

JSP users must enable session management by modifying their page directive to set the value of the session attribute to true as follows:

```
<%@page contentType="text/html; charset=iso-8859-1"
    language="java" import="java.sql.*" session = "true"%>
```

COMPLETING THE Contentpage.asp, Search.asp, AND Songfetch.asp PAGES

The e-commerce in this Web application are the Contentpage.asp, Search.asp, and Songfetch.asp files, apart from two other files, the ViewCD.asp and Placeorder.asp files.

The Contentpage.asp, Search.asp, and Songfetch.asp pages allow a user to add songs to a CD. Adding these songs to a CD is similar to adding products to a shopping cart. The songs that a user adds to a CD will be available in the shopping cart (or, in this case, the CD) even after the user terminates her session.

The ViewCD.asp displays all those songs in the CD for which the user did not place an order. The shopping cart scenario in this sample web application allows a user to place a total of 10 songs in the CD. If there are less than 10 songs, the user is asked to add more songs before placing an order. If there are more than 10 songs, the user is asked to remove some songs. The ViewCD.asp file implements these features.

The Placeorder.asp file contains a form that a user must fill to place an order for the CD. When a user fills out the form to place an order, a unique order ID is generated. The order ID and other order details are inserted in the Orderdetails table in the song_master database.

The Contentpage.asp, Search.asp, and Songfetch.asp files allow a user to add songs to a CD, but only after she logs on to the site. Therefore, a check needs to be built in these pages. This check can be built by checking the contents of the session variable that you created in the Login.asp file.

In the Contentpage.asp, Search.asp, and Songfetch.asp files, a form button with a label Add to CD must be displayed if a user has logged on. Otherwise, a link text Add to CD must be displayed. When the user clicks the link text Add to CD, the Login.asp file is displayed, so that a user can log on before proceeding.

To allow a user to add songs to the CD only after she logs on, you need to add some code to the Contentpage.asp, Search.asp, and Songfetch.asp files. Switch to the Code View in each of these files and replace the code between the <td> ... </td> tags, which contain the link text Add to CD, with the following code, depending on which server technology you are using:

Code for ASP users:

```
<% If Session ("MM_Username") <> "" then %>
<form METHOD="POST" name="form1" >
<input type="hidden" name="username" value="<%= Session("MM_Username") %>">
<input type="submit" name="addsong" value="Add to CD" style="10">
</form>
<% End If %>
<% If  Session("MM_Username") = "" then %>
<a href="/Userdetails/Login.asp"> <font face="Verdana" size="1"
color="#000066">Add
```

```
to CD</font> </a>
<% End If %>
```

Code for JSP users:

```
<% If (session.getValue("MM_Username")!= " " ){%>
<form METHOD="POST" name="form1" >
<input type="hidden" name="username" value="<%= Session.getValue("MM_Username")
%>">
<input type="submit" name="addsong" value="Add to CD" style="10">
</form>
<% } %>
<% If (session.getValue("MM_Username") == " ") {%>
<a href="/Userdetails/Login.asp"> <font face="Verdana" size="1"
color="#000066">Add
 to CD</font> </a>
<% } %>
```

Code for ColdFusion users:

```
<CFIF Session.MM_Username NEQ " " >
<form METHOD="POST" name="form1" >
<input type="hidden" name="username" value="<%= Session.getValue("MM_Username")
%>">
<input type="submit" name="addsong" value="Add to CD" style="10">
</form>
<CFELSEIF Session.MM_Username EQ " " >
<a href="/Userdetails/Login.asp"> <font face="Verdana" size="1"
color="#000066">Add
 to CD</font> </a>
</CFIF>
```

The preceding code creates a form button named addsong within a form named form1 and displays this form button only if the session variable MM_Username is not empty. In the preceding code, a hidden field named username is also created. This hidden field contains the value of the session variable MM_Username, which is the login name specified by a user when she logs on to the site.

You also need to create another hidden field named songId within form1 in each of these three files. This hidden field will contain the SongId column when a user selects a song. To create the songId hidden field in form1, switch to using the Design View, choose Insert, Form Objects, Hidden Field, and specify the name of the hidden field as songId in the Property inspector of the hidden field. Bind the SongId field from the recordset to this hidden field.

Next, you need to attach the Insert Record Server behavior to the form button named addsong on form1 in each of the three files. To do this, follow these steps:

1. Select the addsong form button on form1 and select the Insert Record server behavior from the Server Behaviors panel.

2. In the Insert Record server behavior dialog box, select SongConnect from the Connection drop-down list.

3. Select CartInfo from the Insert Into Table drop-down list. In the Get Values From drop-down list, select form1.

4. The Form Elements list box automatically shows the hidden field username bound to the UserName recordset column and the songId hidden field bound to the SongID recordset column.

5. Click OK to close the dialog box.

Next, you need to create two links in all the three files, one that links to the `ViewCD.asp` file and another that leads the user to the previous page. Create a link text named Continue Shopping and link this text to the `ViewCD.asp` file. Create another link text named Back and type `javascript:history.back()` in the Link text box of the Property inspector of this text. Apply the HTML style named `Text_style` to the link text.

CREATING THE `ViewCD.asp` PAGE

The `ViewCD.asp` file displays the contents of the CD selected by the user. It also allows the user to remove some songs from the CD.

Copy the `ViewCD_base.asp` file to the local root folder. Then, rename the file as `ViewCD.asp`. Open the `ViewCD.asp` file. Create a recordset called ShowCart by using the Advanced option of the Recordset dialog box. Type the following SQL statement:

```
SELECT CartInfo.SongID, CartInfo.UserName, CartInfo.CartID, SongDetails.SongName
FROM CartInfo, SongDetails
WHERE CartInfo.SongID = SongDetails.SongId
      AND CartInfo.UserName LIKE '%loginName%' AND CartInfo.OrderID = 0
```

In the Variables section of the Recordset dialog box, create a variable called `loginName`. ASP users specify the run-time value for the loginName variable as `Session("MM_Username")`. JSP users need to specify the runtime value as `session.getValue("MM_Username")` and ColdFusion users need to specify `#session.MM_Username#`.

The ShowCart recordset contains those records where the UserName column of the CartInfo table matches the user's login name that is contained in the session variable `MM_Username`.

The CartInfo table contains a column called OrderID. Until a user places an order, the orderID field of the CartInfo table does not contain a value. So, the SQL statement also checks for those records whose orderID columns are empty.

Bind the SongName column from the ShowCart recordset to the first cell in the `ViewCD.asp`. Add a repeat region server behavior to the cells containing the recordset column SongName and the Remove Song form button. Insert a recordset navigation bar and a recordset navigation status live object below the table.

REMOVING SONGS FROM THE CD

To allow a user to remove songs from the CD, you need to attach the Delete Record server behavior to the form removeSong. To attach the Delete Record server behavior to the form button named Remove Song, follow these steps:

1. Select the Remove Song form button and select the Delete record server behavior from the Server Behaviors panel.
2. In the Delete Record server behavior that is displayed, select SongConnect from the Connection drop-down list.
3. Select CartInfo from the Delete From Table drop-down list.
4. Select ShowCart from the Delete From Table drop-down list. Select CartID from the Unique Key Column drop-down list.
5. Select removeSong from the Delete By Submitting drop-down list.
6. Click OK to close the Delete Record dialog box.

Adding the Show Region If Recordset Is Empty Server Behavior

If the user has not added any songs to the CD, but tries to view the ViewCD.asp page, a message must be displayed, informing the user that there are no songs in the CD. To add this feature, insert a layer called MessageLayer. Type a message such as "You have not added any songs to the CD" in this layer. Adjust the size of this layer such that it completely covers the layer named CDSongs that contains the table and the links below the table. Select MessageLayer and apply the Show Region If Recordset Is Empty server behavior to it.

Checking for the Number of Songs in the CD

The ViewCD.asp file checks if the total number of songs selected by the user equals 10. If the number of songs selected by the user exceeds 10, the user is asked to remove some songs from the CD. If the number of songs is equal to 10, the user is led to the Placeorder.asp page where she can place the order for the CD.

To implement this feature in the ViewCD.asp file, you need to create a recordset that contains a count of the number of songs selected by the user. Name this recordset CheckSongs and type the following SQL query in the SQL area of the Recordset dialog box:

```
SELECT count(UserName) as countCD
FROM CartInfo
WHERE UserName = 'loginName' AND OrderID = 0
```

In the Variables section of the Recordset dialog box, create a variable called loginName. ASP users must specify the runtime value as Session("MM_Username"). JSP users need to specify the runtime value as session.getValue("MM_Username") and ColdFusion users need to specify #session.MM_Username#.

The recordset now has a column called countCD that contains the number of songs selected by the user. Next, switch to the Code View and paste the following code after the last </table> tag.

Code for ASP users:

```
<%
dim count
count= checkSongs.Fields.Item("countCD").Value %>
<% If count = 10 Then %>
<p><font face="Verdana" size="2" color="#000066"><b> <a href="/getorder.asp">
Proceed to place order</a> </b></font></p>
<% End If %>
<% If count > 10 Then %>
<br>
<p> <font size="2" face="Verdana" color="#000066">You have added more than 10
songs to the CD. <br>
</font></p>
<p><font size="2" face="Verdana" color="#000066">Remove some songs before
proceeding
to place the order.</font></p>
<p> </p>
<% End If %>
<% If count < 10 Then %>
<p><font face="Verdana" size="2" color="#000066">
You need to have 10 songs to place an order for the CD </font></p>
<p><font face="Verdana" size="2" color="#000066"><b>
<a href="javascript:history.back()">Go
back</a> </b></font></p>
<% End If %>
```

Code for JSP users:

```
<%
int count;
count = checkSongs.getObject("countCD")%>
If (count == 10) {%>
<p><font face="Verdana" size="2" color="#000066"><b> <a href="/getorder.asp">
  Proceed to place order</a> </b></font></p>
<% } If (count > 10) { %>
<br>
<p> <font size="2" face="Verdana" color="#000066">You have added more than 10
  songs to the CD. <br>
  </font></p>
<p><font size="2" face="Verdana" color="#000066">Remove some songs before
proceeding
  to place the order.</font></p>
<p> </p>
<% } If (count < 10) { %>
<p><font face="Verdana" size="2" color="#000066">
  You need to have 10 songs to place an order for the CD </font></p>
  <p><font face="Verdana" size="2" color="#000066"><b>
<a href="javascript:history.back()">Go
  back</a> </b></font></p>
<% } %>
```

Code for ColdFusion users:

```
<CFSET count = checkSongs.countCD>
<CFIF count EQ 10 >
<p><font face="Verdana" size="2" color="#000066"><b> <a href="/getorder.asp">
```

```
    Proceed to place order</a> </b></font></p>
</CFIF>

<CFIF count GT 10 >
<br>
<p> <font size="2" face="Verdana" color="#000066">You have added more than 10
  songs to the CD. <br>
  </font></p>
<p><font size="2" face="Verdana" color="#000066">Remove some songs before
proceeding
  to place the order.</font></p>
<p> </p>
</CFIF>

<CFIF count LT 10 >
<p><font face="Verdana" size="2" color="#000066">
  You need to have 10 songs to place an order for the CD </font></p>
  <p><font face="Verdana" size="2" color="#000066"><b><a
href="javascript:history.back()">
  Go back</a> </b></font></p>
</CFIF>
```

RESTRICTING ACCESS TO THE ViewCD.asp PAGE

You must attach the Restrict Access to Page server behavior to the ViewCD.asp file. Recall that this file can be accessed from the ViewCD flash button that you created in the Navigation.asp file. If a user tries to view the contents of the CD without logging in, she must be taken to the login page. Add the Restrict Access to Page server behavior to add this feature to the ViewCD.asp file. To add this server behavior, select the Restrict Access to Page server behavior from the Server Behaviors panel and select the Restrict Based on Username and Password option in the Restrict Access to Page dialog box. In the If Access Denied Go To text box, specify the path to the Login.asp file.

CREATING THE Placeorder.asp PAGE

The Placeorder.asp file allows the user to specify order details, which include shipping and billing information as well as payment details. After a user specifies these details, an order ID is generated and this order ID is inserted into the Orderdetails table along with the details specified by the user. The order ID is generated by incrementing the order ID that was generated in the previous order.

The CartInfo table contains those songs that the user added to the CD before placing an order. After the user places the order, the songs in the CartInfo table must have the corresponding order id to reflect the confirmed order status. Therefore, the CartInfo table must be updated with the order id that was generated by a user while placing the order.

Copy the Placeorder_base.asp file to your local root folder and rename it as Placeorder.asp. Copy the Thankyou_base.asp file and rename it as Thankyou.asp in your local root folder.

Create a recordset called orderRec such that it retrieves the record from the UserDetails table whose LoginID column matches the login name of the user. This recordset is used to provide the address details of the user so that she can fill out the order form quickly. The SQL for this recordset is as follows:

```
SELECT *
FROM UserDetails
WHERE LoginID = 'loginName'
```

In the Variables section of the Recordset dialog box, create a variable called `loginName`. ASP users must specify the run-time value as `Session("MM_Username")`. JSP users need to specify the run-time value as `session.getValue("MM_Username")` and ColdFusion users need to specify `#session.MM_Username#`.

After you create the recordset, bind each column of the recordset to the each form field in the form named billform in the `Placeorder.asp` file. You need to bind the address-related columns, such as Address, City, State, Country, and ZipCode to the form fields in the billing information section of the form and to the form fields in the shipping information section. Create a hidden field named loginId and bind the LoginId column from the orderRec recordset to this hidden field.

Next, you need to attach the Insert Record server behavior to the form button labeled Place Order. Select the form button and select the Insert Record server behavior from the Server Behaviors panel. From the Connection drop-down list of the Insert Record dialog box, select SongConnect. Select Orderdetails from the Insert Into Table drop-down list. Specify the path to the `Thankyou.asp` file in the After Inserting, Go To text box. Select billform from the Get Values From drop-down list. In the Form Elements list bind the form elements to the appropriate columns of the Orderdetails table. Click OK to close the dialog box.

To generate the order ID for each order, you need to create a recordset that retrieves the last order number that was generated in the preceding transaction from the Orderdetails table. Name this recordset as Recordset1. The SQL for this recordset is as follows:

```
Select max(OrderId) as ID from Orderdetails
```

Because the OrderId is a numeric field, its value can be retrieved using the `max()` function and incremented. Before trying out this SQL statement, insert the first record in the Orderdetails table by typing 1 in the OrderId field.

After the last order ID is retrieved, you must increment it. Switch to the Code View and type the following code, depending on which server technology you are using.

ASP users should locate the code block that contains instructions for creating the INSERT statement. Type the following code just above the line of containing the INSERT statement stored in `MM_editQuery`:

```
ordID = Recordset1.Fields.Item("ID").Value
ordID = ordID + 1
```

JSP users should declare an integer variable below the comment `// *** Edit Operations: declare variables` as follows:

```
int ordID = 0;
```

Next, type the following code just above the comment `// *** Insert Record: set variables`:

```
<%
String orderStr = Recordset1_data.toString();
ordID = Integer.parseInt(orderStr);
ordID = ordID + 1;
%>
```

ColdFusion users should use the following code:

```
<cfset ordID = #Recordset1.ID# + 1>
```

Next, you need to modify the `insert` statement generated by UltraDev when you added the Insert Record server behavior. The modified INSERT statement includes the generated order ID as well as the price of the CD, which is $20. Type the following code in place of the INSERT statement that is stored in `MM_editQuery`, depending on which server technology you are using.

Code for ASP users:

```
MM_editQuery = "insert into " & MM_editTable & "
➥(Amount, OrderId, " & MM_tableValues & ")
➥values ('$20', ' " &ordID &" ', " & MM_dbValues & ")"
```

Code for JSP users:

```
MM_editQuery= new StringBuffer("insert into " + MM_editTable);
MM_editQuery.append(" (OrderId,Amount,").append(MM_tableValues.toString())
➥.append(") values (").append(ordID).append(",'20',");
MM_editQuery.append(MM_dbValues.toString()).append(")");
```

Code for ColdFusion users:

```
MM_editQuery = "insert into " & MM_editTable & "
➥(Amount, OrderId, " & MM_tableValues & ")
➥values ('$20', ' " &ordernum &" ', " & MM_dbValues & ")";
```

Next, you need to add an UPDATE statement that updates the CartInfo table with the order ID that is generated for each order. Type the following code to add the UPDATE statement, depending on your server technology.

ASP users should type the following code just below the line of code containing the INSERT statement:

```
Set PlaceOrder = Server.CreateObject("ADODB.Command")
PlaceOrder.ActiveConnection = MM_editConnection
PlaceOrder.CommandText = " UPDATE CartInfo SET OrderID= '"& ordID &"'
  WHERE UserName = '"&Session("MM_Username")&"' AND OrderID = 0 "
PlaceOrder.Execute
PlaceOrder.ActiveConnection.Close
```

Code for JSP users:

```
<%
String Prepared1__s = null;
if(session.getValue("MM_Username") != null)
➥{ Prepared1__s = (String)session.getValue("MM_Username");}
%>
<%
Driver DriverPrepared1 = (Driver)Class.forName
➥(MM_musicconnection_DRIVER).newInstance();
Connection ConnPrepared1 = DriverManager.getConnection
➥(MM_musicconnection_STRING,MM_musicconnection_USERNAME,
➥MM_musicconnection_PASSWORD);
PreparedStatement Prepared1 = ConnPrepared1.prepareStatement
➥("UPDATE CartInfo  SET OrderID = '"+ordID+"'
WHERE UserName = '"+ Prepared1__s + "' AND  OrderID = 0 ");
Prepared1.executeUpdate();
%>
```

Code for ColdFusion users:

```
<cfquery name="MM_editCmd" datasource=#MM_editDatasource#
➥username=#MM_editUserName# password=#MM_editPassword#>
Update CartInfo set OrderID = #ordID#
➥where UserName = '#Session.MM_Username#' and OrderID = 0
</cfquery>
```

CREATING THE Editprofile.asp PAGE

The Editprofile.asp file allows a user to edit her profile. However, a user can edit her profile only if she is already registered with the site and has logged on to the site after the registration. To allow a user access to this page only if she has logged on to the site, attach the Restrict Access to Page server behavior to the page.

To create the Editprofile.asp file, perform the following steps:

1. Copy the Editprofile_base.asp file to the Userdetails folder in your local root folder. Rename the Editprofile_base.asp file in the Userdetails folder as Editprofile.asp.

2. Open the Editprofile.asp file. Select the Restrict Access to Page server behavior from the Server Behaviors panel and select the Restrict Based on Username and Password option in the Restrict Access to Page dialog box. In the If Access Denied Go To text box, specify the path to the Login.asp file.

3. Copy the orderRec recordset from the Placeorder.asp file and paste it in the Data Bindings panel in the Editprofile.asp file. Rename the copied recordset as editProfile. Bind each column in the editProfile recordset to the appropriate field in the form named updateProfile in the Editprofile.asp file.

4. Attach the Update Record server behavior to the form button in the updateProfile form. In the Update Record dialog box, specify the connection as SongConnect, the recordset as editProfile, the table to be updated as UserDetails, the unique key column as LoginID, and the form from which to obtain the data as updateProfile. In the Form Elements list box, bind the appropriate form elements to the required columns in the UserDetails table.

CHAPTER 22

MANAGING YOUR WEB SITE

In this chapter

File Transfer and Synchronization   454

Working in a Team   455

Checking Links and Fixing Broken Links   461

Summary   462

File Transfer and Synchronization

In the course of site development, you might have to copy the files that you modified in the local site to the remote site and similarly transfer the latest version of the files from the remote site to the local site. You can carry out these activities of transferring files smoothly with the help of the Get File(s), Put File(s), and Synchronize options available in UltraDev. These options let you match the contents of the remote site with the local site.

File Transfer Between the Remote and Local Sites

When you work on your local machine, you might want to access files that exist on the remote site to view, add, or modify its content. Similarly, you might want to transfer any new file or a modified file from your machine to the remote site. To transfer files between the local and remote sites, use the Get File(s) and Put File(s) buttons on the Site Window toolbar.

→ To learn more about local sites and remote sites, **see** "Server Information," **p. 121**.

> **Note**
>
> Sometimes, you might find that a particular host you want to connect to does not support Dreamweaver UltraDev's FTP utility. Similarly, the FTP tool in Dreamweaver UltraDev does not support some hosts such as VMS or VAX. In such cases, you can use a third-party utility, such as WS_FTP.

To transfer a file from your machine to the remote site, select the file from the Local Folder pane of the Site window and click the Put File(s) button. To transfer a file from the remote site to your local site, select the file from the Local Folder pane and click the Get File(s) button. If other developers add or modify some files on the site that you are working on, you can update your Site window with the latest set of files on the remote site by using the Refresh button.

Synchronizing Files

When you transfer files between the local and remote sites, it is possible that you might overwrite the latest version of some files with an older version. For example, you might overwrite the latest version of a file on the remote site with an older version existing on your local machine. To overcome this problem, you need to synchronize the files between the remote and local sites. Synchronizing allows you to maintain the latest versions of files on both the remote and local sites. In UltraDev, you can synchronize the files between the local and remote sites by using the Site, Synchronize command. To synchronize files between the remote and local sites, follow these steps:

1. From the Remote Site or Local Folder pane in the Site window, select the file that you want to synchronize and choose Site, Synchronize. The Synchronize Files dialog box is displayed, as shown in Figure 22.1. If you want to synchronize all the files within a folder, select the folder from the Remote Site or Local Folder pane.

Figure 22.1
Use the Synchronize Files dialog box to synchronize the files between the local and remote sites.

2. From the Synchronize drop-down list, select the Entire Site option if you want to synchronize the entire site. However, if you want to synchronize only selected files, select the Selected Local Files Only option.

3. From the Direction drop-down list, select the direction in which you want to synchronize the files. Select the Put newer files to remote option if you want to upload all the files from the local site that were modified more recently than the files on the remote site. Select the Get newer files from remote option if you want to download all the files from the remote site that were modified more recently than the files on the local site. Select the Get and put newer files option if you want to place the latest version of the files on both the remote and local sites.

4. Select the Delete remote files not on local drive check box if you want to delete all the files from the local site that do not have corresponding files on the remote site, or vice versa. These files are deleted from the local or remote site based on the option you selected from the Direction drop-down list. For example, if you selected the Put newer files to remote option from the Direction drop-down list, selecting the Delete Remote files not on local drive option deletes all the files from the remote site that do not have corresponding files on your local site.

5. Click Preview.

The list of files that will be deleted, uploaded, or downloaded based on the criteria specified by you is displayed in the Synchronize dialog box. From this list, you can deselect the files that you do not want to be deleted, uploaded, or downloaded, and then click OK. However, if the version of the files in the remote and local sites matches, UltraDev displays a message box to inform you that no synchronization is required.

UltraDev synchronizes the files between the remote and local sites and displays the results in the Synchronize dialog box. Click the Save Log button in the Synchronize dialog box if you want to save the results. The results are saved in a .txt file.

WORKING IN A TEAM

If you are a Web developer, you realize that most Web sites are not created by one person. It is always a team effort, with each member of the group contributing to one or more features of a site. In such a team scenario, many people might try to simultaneously work on a file, which might lead to confusion. Therefore, it is essential to have proper coordination within the team so that you do not interfere with each other's work. UltraDev provides you with excellent features that make collaborative Web development easier. In the following sections, you will learn about some UltraDev features that let you develop Web pages with absolute coordination with the team.

Checking Files In and Out

The most common problem that you might face while working in a collaborative environment is that of simultaneous access and modifications to files on the local and remote site. Many members of a team might try to access the same file at the same time. In such cases, it is possible that some of the major changes that you incorporated into a page might be overwritten by small changes made by your coworkers because they saved their version of the file after you saved your changes. This will end up causing the entire job to be redone. To avoid this, you can use the Check In/Check Out option provided by UltraDev. This option lets you notify your team members whether you are working on a file in the remote or local site.

Checking out a file signifies that you are currently working on the file and therefore you do not want anybody else to edit the file. Whenever you check out a file, UltraDev creates a file with an .lck extension and uses this file to inform others that the file is checked out. When you check out a file, UltraDev displays a green mark next to it. If any other team member checks out a file, a red mark is displayed. UltraDev also displays the name and e-mail ID of the person who checked out the file so that you can get in touch with that person in case any clarification is needed.

One of the drawbacks of checking out a file is that it does not make that file read-only on the remote site. It just acts as a visual aid to notify you that the file is in use by one of the team members. For example, when you open a file for editing that is checked out by any other team member, you see a message box warning you that the file is checked out. However, if you still want to edit the file, you can do so by clicking the Yes button in the message box. Another drawback of the Check Out option is that applications other than UltraDev cannot recognize the .lck file created by UltraDev. Therefore, anybody using an application other than UltraDev can easily overwrite the checked-out files.

Note
To implement strict version control for files, you must use source- and version-control products. In UltraDev, you can implement source control by connecting to SourceSafe databases and servers or by connecting to source control systems that support *WebDAV protocol*. To connect to SourceSafe databases, you must have Visual SourceSafe client version 6.0 (for Windows users) or MetroWerks SourceSafe client version 1.1.0 (for Macintosh users) installed on your system. To make UltraDev connect using WebDAV, you must have access to a system that supports the WebDAV protocol. You can contact your network administrator for these requirements.

Checking in a file signifies that you are not using the file anymore and therefore it is available to the other team members for editing. As soon as you check in a file, UltraDev makes that file available to other team members for editing and makes the local copy of that file read-only. UltraDev also displays a lock next to the checked-in file so that you do not make any changes to the file when others are editing it.

You can enable the Check In/Check Out option for various sites by using the Site Definition dialog box. Before enabling this option, you must link your local site with a remote FTP or network server.

→ To learn how to link your site to an FTP or network server, **see** "Server Information," **p. 121**.

Follow these steps to enable the Check In/Check Out option:

1. In the Site window, choose Site, Define Sites. The Define Sites dialog box is displayed.
2. In this dialog box, select the site for which you want to enable the Check In/Check Out option, and click Edit. The Site Definition dialog box is displayed.
3. From the Category list, select Remote Info. The Remote Info page is displayed.
4. In the Remote Info page, select the Enable file check in and check out option.
5. Select the Check out files when opening option if you want a file to be automatically checked out when you open it. The Check out files when opening option checks out only those files that you open by double-clicking, not the files that you open by choosing File, Open.
6. Enter your name and e-mail ID in the Check out name and Email address text boxes, respectively. The name you specify will be displayed as a link beside the file you check out. Clicking this link opens the default e-mail program with a new message box containing your e-mail ID. This lets your team members contact you in case you are using the file that they require. If you are working from multiple machines, you can use the Check out name text box to specify the name of the machine from which you checked out a file.

After you enable the Check In/Check Out options for a site, you can check in and check out files from the remote site by using various menu and toolbar options in the Site window or Document window.

To check out a file, select the file on the remote site from the Site window and click the Check Out File(s) button on the toolbar. Alternatively, you can choose Site, Check Out. If you want to undo the check-out of a file, you can choose Site, Undo Check Out. When you undo a check-out, the local copy of the file becomes read-only, and any change that you made to the file is not saved.

To check in a file, select the file and click the Check In button on the toolbar. Alternatively, you can choose Site, Check In.

Integrating UltraDev with SourceSafe Databases and the WebDAV Protocol

You can integrate UltraDev with SourceSafe databases or with systems that support the WebDAV protocol for implementing version control features. To do this, you can use the Remote Info category of the Site Definition dialog box.

To connect UltraDev to SourceSafe databases, follow these steps:

1. Select SourceSafe Database from the Access drop-down list in the Remote Info category of the Site Definition dialog box, and click the Setting button. The Open SourceSafe Database dialog box is displayed.
2. In the Database Path text box, enter the path to the SourceSafe database.
3. In the Project text box, enter the name of the project that is assigned in SourceSafe. This will be the root directory of the remote site.
4. Enter the username and password for the selected database in the Username and Password text boxes, respectively, and click OK.

The steps involved in connecting UltraDev to the WebDAV protocol are similar to the steps involved in connecting to a SourceSafe database. After you configure a server to support the WebDAV protocol, select the WebDAV option from the Access drop-down list in the Remote Info category of the Site Definition dialog box, and click the Setting button. In the WebDAV Connection dialog box that is displayed, enter the URL of the WebDAV server, username, password, and e-mail ID in the respective text boxes, and then click OK. You can contact your network administrator to obtain the required information that must be filled in the various fields of the Open SourceSafe Database and WebDAV Connection dialog boxes.

Creating Design Notes

Apart from the Check In/Check Out option, UltraDev provides you with another tool called design notes. This tool allows members of a team to update and share information regarding changes in files, new features, or any urgent attention that is required for a file.

The first step toward implementing and sharing design notes for a site is to enable the design notes feature for the site. To enable the design notes feature, follow these steps:

1. Choose Site, Define Sites. The Define Sites dialog box is displayed.
2. In the Define Sites dialog box, select the site for which you want to enable the design notes feature, and click Edit.
3. In the Site Definition dialog box that is displayed, select the Design Notes option from the Category list.
4. In the Design Notes page, select the Maintain design notes option to enable the creation of design notes for the files in the site.
5. Select the Upload design notes for sharing option if you want to share the design notes with the rest of your team members.

After you enable the design notes feature for the site, you can add design notes to the files by using the Design Notes option on the File menu.

Note

You cannot directly add design notes to the files on the remote site. To do so, you must transfer the file to the local site or check out the file, select it from the local site, and add design notes to it.

When you select File, Design Notes, the Design Notes dialog box is displayed, as shown in Figure 22.2. The Basic Info tab is selected by default.

Figure 22.2
Use the Design Notes dialog box to share information with the rest of the team members.

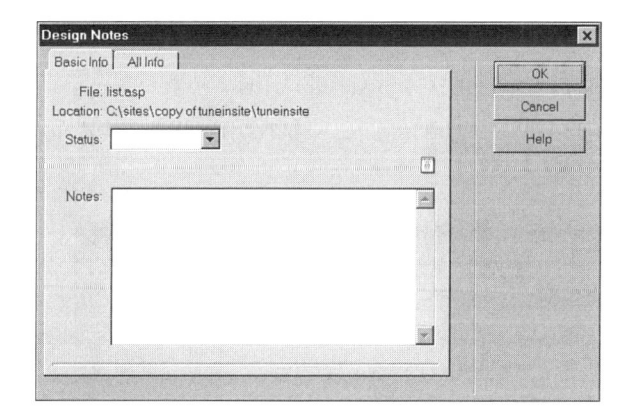

You can add your comments to design notes by typing them in the Notes section. If you want to specify the current status of the file, you can select an option from the Status drop-down list. This drop-down list displays various statuses, such as Alpha, Beta, Need attention, and so on. You can specify the time when you entered the comments by clicking the date icon. You can select the Show while file is opened check box in the Design Notes dialog box if you want the design notes to be automatically displayed every time you open the file. The status and the notes that you specify for each note are displayed as a paired list in the All Info page. You can add items to or remove items from the All Info page by using the + and – buttons. For example, you can add a status that does not exist in the Status drop-down list by clicking the + button, entering the name of the status in the Name text box, and entering a value for the status in the Value text box. The new status you added is displayed in the Status drop-down list.

The design notes that you add to a file are saved in a subfolder called _notes with an .mno extension in the same folder as that of the current file. You can view the design notes added to a file by either opening the file and choosing File, Design Notes or by clicking the yellow design notes icon in the Notes column of the Site window.

In addition to adding design notes to files, you can add design notes to the objects in the site. To add design notes to an object, select the object and choose File, Design Notes. However, the design notes that you add to an object are saved in a subfolder called a_notes, which is within the folder where the object's source file exists.

If you do not require a design note anymore and you want to remove it, you can do so by clicking the Clean Up button in the Design Notes category of the Site Definition dialog box.

REPORTS

You can obtain a consolidated report on the check in and check out status of the files on your site with the help of Workflow reports. You can also use these reports to get a list of files based on the design notes attached to them.

To create a Workflow report for your site, follow these steps:

1. In the Document window, choose Site, Reports. The Reports dialog box is displayed, as shown in Figure 22.3.

Figure 22.3
Use the Reports dialog to view the check in and check out status of files.

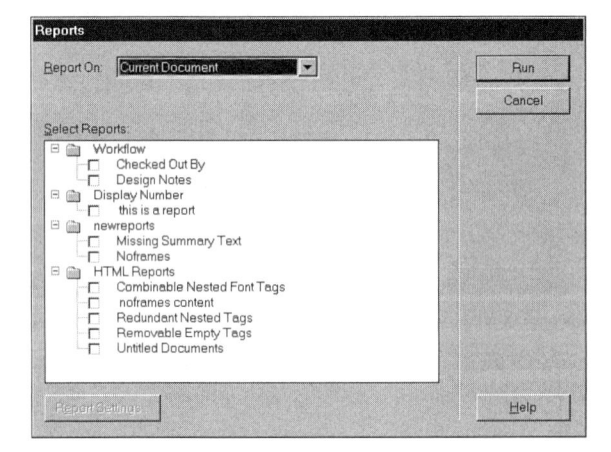

2. From the Report On drop-down list, select the folder, site, or document for which you want to generate the report.
3. From the Workflow list, select the Checked Out By option. If you want to display only the list of files locked by a specific team member, click the Report Settings button and enter the name of the team member in the Checked By dialog box.
4. If you want the Workflow report to display files based on the information in the design notes, such as files that contain the status "Need attention," select the Design Notes option from the Workflow list and click Report Settings.
5. In the Design Notes dialog box that is displayed (see Figure 22.4), specify the values that must be checked in the design notes while generating the report. For example, if you want to view the list of files whose design notes contain the status "Need attention," you can specify this in the Design Notes dialog box.

Figure 22.4
Use this dialog box to specify the Design Notes information that you want the report to contain.

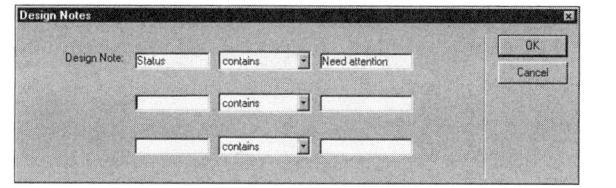

After you specify various options for the Workflow report, click Run to view the report.

CHECKING LINKS AND FIXING BROKEN LINKS

A site is a collection of individual files that are linked to each other. If the link between any of these files breaks, the site loses its impact. Links in a site are broken for various reasons, such as moving files from one location to another and deleting files that are linked. It is essential to fix these broken links and remove all those files, which are not linked to any other file, to maintain the site's integrity. The files that are not linked to any other file are called *orphaned files*. You should delete them, because they occupy disk space.

You can solve all the problems arising from broken links by using the Check Links option available in UltraDev. The Check Links option lets you search for broken links and unreferenced files in an entire site, in certain portions of a site, or in a particular document. To check for links in an entire site, follow these steps:

1. Open the Site window and choose Site, Check Links Sitewide. The Link Checker dialog box is displayed.

2. From the Show drop-down list, select the type of link for which you want to view the report. You can choose to view a report on broken links, external links (files that are linked to other files outside the site), or orphaned files. Based on the option you select in the Show drop-down list, the list of files that fall under the selected option is displayed in the Link Checker dialog box. If you want to delete the orphaned files from your system, you can directly remove them using the Link Checker dialog box by selecting the files and pressing the Delete key. You can also save the report for future use by clicking the Save button.

You can also use the Link Checker dialog box to check for links in specific portions of the site. To do this, select the files or folders in the site for which you want to check links, and then choose File, Check Links in the Site window. In the Link Checker dialog box that is displayed, follow the steps described in the "Reports" section to view the reports. However, you cannot view reports on orphaned files, because they can be viewed only when you check links for the entire site.

After the report on the files with broken links is displayed in the Link Checker dialog box, you can fix the broken links directly in this dialog box. To fix a broken link, select the link from the Broken Links column of the Link Checker dialog box and type the correct path or filename. Alternatively, you can also click the folder icon that is displayed next to the broken link to browse to the file that you want to link to. As soon as you fix a broken link, it is automatically removed from the broken link list in the Link Checker dialog box. A

Summary

Site maintenance requires as much care and attention as site creation, because a single careless action can lead to a lot of rework. The need for site maintenance becomes even more crucial if more than one person is involved in the site's development. UltraDev provides excellent features that you can use for site maintenance and collaboration with other team members.

CHAPTER 23

CUSTOMIZING DREAMWEAVER ULTRADEV 4

In this chapter

Modifying the UltraDev Interface   464

Using the Keyboard Shortcut Editor   464

Customizing the Objects Panel   466

Customizing the Menu System   467

Customizing Dialog Boxes   470

Customizing Data Formats   472

Customizing Server Behaviors   473

Summary   479

Modifying the UltraDev Interface

You can customize the UltraDev environment by modifying the existing features or creating new ones. To customize the UltraDev interface, you can use tools available in UltraDev, such as the Keyboard Shortcut editor and the server behavior builder. This chapter focuses on the ways in which you can modify the UltraDev interface to suit your needs.

You can modify the UltraDev interface by changing the keyboard shortcuts for the menu options, adding new menus to the menu system, customizing the appearance of dialog boxes, creating new data formats for dynamic data, and so on.

Using the Keyboard Shortcut Editor

All the menu options in UltraDev have keyboard shortcuts. For example, in the earlier chapters, you saw that you can invoke the Preview in Browser menu option by pressing F12 and that you can open a file by using the Ctrl and O keys. If you want to change any of these existing keyboard shortcuts or create new ones, you can use the Keyboard Shortcut editor.

UltraDev 4 ships with predetermined keyboard shortcut sets that define shortcut keys for the menu systems in Dreamweaver 3, HomeSite, and BBEdit. Users familiar with the shortcuts in Dreamweaver 3 can choose the Dreamweaver 3 shortcut set, which includes shortcut keys for the features in both Dreamweaver 3 and Dreamweaver UltraDev 4. You can choose the default set or create customized shortcut sets in the Keyboard Shortcut editor.

To use the Keyboard Shortcut editor, choose Edit, Keyboard Shortcuts. The Keyboard Shortcuts dialog box is displayed, as shown in Figure 23.1.

Figure 23.1
Use the Keyboard Shortcuts editor to create your own shortcut keys.

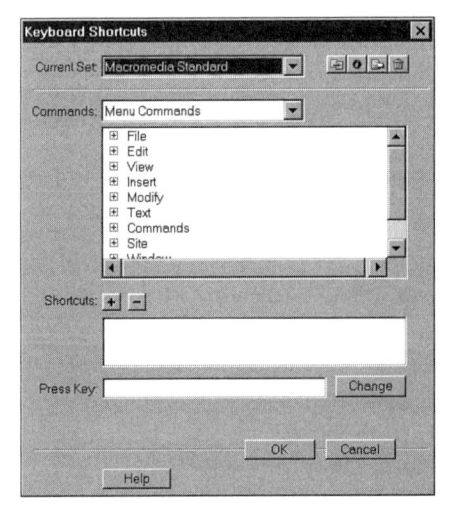

Creating a Customized Shortcut Set

You can create a customized keyboard shortcut set by changing the shortcut keys assigned to the menu options of predetermined shortcut sets. You can create shortcuts to menu options that do not have any shortcuts in the predetermined shortcut sets, remove shortcuts, and modify existing shortcuts. Before you can create, remove, or modify a keyboard shortcut for any of the predetermined sets, you need to create a copy of the predetermined shortcut set. To create a copy, select the predetermined set from the Current Set drop-down list in the Keyboard Shortcuts dialog box and click the Duplicate Set button.

The Duplicate Set dialog box is displayed. Type a name for this set in the dialog box. Click OK to create the new set. You can customize this set depending on your requirements by adding or removing keyboard shortcuts.

To add a keyboard shortcut associated with a menu option, follow these steps:

1. From the Current Set drop-down list, select the copy of the shortcut set that contains the menu option for which you want to set the shortcut key.

2. From the Commands drop-down list, select the category of the menu command you want to edit. For example, if you want to set the keyboard shortcut for the Open option on the File menu, select the Menu Commands category from this list. In addition to this category, this list contains four other categories: Site Menu commands, Code Editing, Document Editing, and Site window.

3. Depending on the command category you have selected, the menus available in that category are displayed in the Commands list box. Select the menu that has the option for which you want to set the shortcut key.

4. Click the + sign next to the menu. The list of options on the menu is displayed. The keyboard shortcut associated with each option is displayed in the Shortcuts list box. You can see that only some options on this menu have shortcut keys.

5. If you want to add a shortcut key to a menu option, select the option in the Commands list box and click the + button above the Shortcuts list box. Press the key or keys that you will use as shortcut key for the selected menu option.

6. If you want to assign a different shortcut key to the option, position the cursor in the Press Key text box and press the key or keys that you will use to invoke the selected menu option. If you want to assign number or letter keys, you must press them in combination with the Ctrl key.

7. If you want to remove the shortcut for a menu option, select that option and click the – button above the Shortcuts list box.

> **Tip**
> After you modify your keyboard shortcut set, you can save this set as an HTML file, which later can be printed or viewed in a browser.

Customizing the Objects Panel

The Objects panel consists of objects grouped into categories, such as Characters, Common, Forms, Frames, Head, Invisibles, and Special. You can customize the Objects panel by adding new objects to the panel, moving objects from one category to another, removing objects, and renaming the categories in the Objects panel.

For each of the categories in the Objects panel, a corresponding folder exists in the Objects subfolder of the Configuration folder. The Configuration folder is found in the folder where the UltraDev application is installed. In the Objects subfolder, you can find a folder for each category of object. Each of these folders contains an HTML file, a GIF file, and an optional JavaScript file for every object. When you insert an object into a document, the HTML code associated with the object is inserted into your Web page. In the case of objects that contain an HTML file as well as a JavaScript file, the JavaScript file generates the HTML to be inserted into the document. By manipulating these files, you can customize the Objects panel.

Creating an Object

You can create an object by using either JavaScript or HTML. In this section, you will see how to create a simple object by using HTML.

→ To learn how to create objects by using JavaScript, **see** "Extending Objects," **p. 496**.

You can create an object to insert commonly used text or images into your document by using HTML. For example, to insert a commonly used image into your document, follow these steps:

1. Create a file in a text editor, such as BBEdit or Notepad.
2. Add the `<img>` tag to this file. Set the `src` attribute to the path of the file. This HTML file represents the object that you want to add to your Web page.
3. If you want to add this object to an existing category of the Objects panel, save this file in the subfolder of the Objects folder that corresponds to this category. If you want to add the object to a new category, create a subfolder in the Objects folder and save the file in the new subfolder.
4. Create an image file that will act as an icon for the newly created object. This image file must be an 18×18 GIF image. If you do not create an icon, UltraDev automatically creates a generic icon for the new object. The name of this image file must be the same as that of the HTML file that you created for the object.
5. To view the newly created object in the Objects panel, press Ctrl. From the pop-up menu that appears, select the Reload Extensions option. The newly created object appears at the bottom of the Insert menu as well as in the Objects panel.

Moving and Deleting an Object

You can move an object from one Objects panel to another by moving the files associated with the object from its folder to another folder within the Objects folder. For example, to move an ActiveX object to the Common category, you need to move the `ActiveX.gif` and `ActiveX.htm` files from the Special folder to the Common folder.

To see the ActiveX object in the Common category of the Objects panel, you need to reload these files of the ActiveX object. After the files are reloaded, you see small black arrows on the top and bottom of the Objects panel. Click the down arrow to view the Insert ActiveX button in the Common category.

To rename a category in the Objects panel, you simply need to rename the folder that corresponds to that category. To remove an object from the Objects panel, you need to move the files associated with the object from the respective folder.

> **Caution**
>
> To remove an object, you might think that you should delete the files associated with the object. However, deleting the files of the object that you want to remove from the Objects panel is not a good idea. If you delete these files, you cannot access the object even from the Insert menu. Therefore, it is always better to move the files corresponding to the object to another folder so that you can move them back if you need the object again.

CUSTOMIZING THE MENU SYSTEM

The key to the menu system in UltraDev is in the menus.xml file, located in the Menus subfolder of the Configurations folder. By making a few changes to this file, you can customize your menu system by rearranging, moving, or renaming menu options or customizing keyboard shortcuts. To edit the `menus.xml` file, you need to use an ordinary text editor. Editing this file in an XML editor or UltraDev results in error messages.

> **Caution**
>
> Before editing this file, make a backup copy of it. If you do not have a backup copy, you can revert to the previous menu system by replacing the modified `menus.xml` file with the `menus.bak` file, which is the default backup for the file.

Before you can edit the `menus.xml` file, it is necessary to understand the structure of the file.

READING THE `menus.xml` FILE

The menus.xml file contains tags for menu bars, menus, menu options, separators, keyboard shortcuts, and shortcut lists. The `<menubar>` and `</menubar>` tags are for the menu bars in the Document window, the Site window, and the context menus, such as the ones that appear in the CSS Styles panel. Menu bar menus, such as File and Edit, are represented by the `<menu>` and `</menu>` tags. Each of these `<menu>` `</menu>` tag pairs contains a `<menuitem>` tag for every menu option. For example, the Open option on the File menu is represented by a `<menuitem>` tag, which is within the `<menu>` `</menu>` tag pairs of the File menu. The following code from the menus.xml file represents the File menu on the menu bar of the Site window that is available only on a Windows platform:

```xml
<menubar name="Site Window" id="DWMainSite" platform="win">
    <menu name="_File" id="DWMenu_MainSite_File">
        <menuitem name="New _Window" key="Cmd+N"
        enabled="true"
        command="dw.createDocument()" id="DWMenu_MainSite_File_New" />
        <menuitem name="New from Template..."
        domrequired="false" enabled="true" command="dw.newFromTemplate()"
        id="DWMenu_MainSite_File_NewFromTemplate" />
        <menuitem name="_New File"
        key="Cmd+Shift+N"
        enabled="dw.getFocus() == 'site' && site.canMakeNewFileOrFolder()"
        command="site.makeNewDreamweaverFile()"
        id="DWMenu_MainSite_File_NewFile" />
        <menuitem name="New _Folder"
        key="Cmd+Opt+Shift+N"
        enabled="dw.getFocus() == 'site' &&
        site.canMakeNewFileOrFolder()"command="site.makeNewFolder()"
        id="DWMenu_MainSite_File_NewFolder" />
        <menuitem name="_Open..."
        key="Cmd+O"
        enabled="true"
        command="dw.openDocument()" id="DWMenu_MainSite_File_Open" />
        <menuitem name="Open _Selection"
        key="Cmd+Opt+Shift+O"
        enabled="site.canOpen()"
        command="site.open()" id="DWMenu_MainSite_File_OpenSelection" />
        <menuitem name="_Close"
        key="Cmd+W" enabled="true"
        command="dw.setFloaterVisibility('site', false)"
        id="DWMenu_MainSite_File_Close" />
        <menuitem name="Save Site Map..."
        enabled="dw.getFocus() == 'site' && site.getFocus() == 'site map'"
        command="site.saveAsImage('bmp')"
        id="DWMenu_MainSite_File_SaveSiteMap" />
        <separator />
        <menuitem name="_Rename"key="F2"enabled="site.canRename()
        "command="site.renameSelection()"
        id="DWMenu_MainSite_File_Rename" />
        <menuitem name="
        Delete"key="Del"enabled="dw.canDeleteSelection()
        "command="dw.deleteSelection()" id="DWMenu_MainSite_Edit_Clear" />
        <menuitem name="Turn Off R_ead Only"
        enabled="site.canMakeEditable()" command="site.makeEditable()"
        id="DWMenu_MainSite_File_MakeEditable" />
        <separator />
        <menu name="_Preview in Browser" id="DWMenu_MainSite_PIB">
            <menuitem dynamic name="No Browsers Selected"
            file="Menus/MM/PIB_Dynamic.htm"
            arguments="'No Browsers'" id="DWMenu_MainSite_File_PIB_Default"
/>
```

```
            <separator />
            <menuitem name="_Edit Browser List..."
            enabled="true" command="dw.editBrowserList()"
            id="DWMenu_MainSite_File_PIB_EditList" />
        </menu>
</menu>
</menubar>
```

In the preceding code, the `<menu> </menu>` tag pairs for the File menu are within the `<menubar> </menubar>` tag pairs of the Site window. The submenu of the Preview in Browser option is also enclosed within the `<menu> </menu>` tag pairs of the File menu. The first `<separator />` tag indicates the separator between the Save Site Map and Rename options on the File menu.

Apart from the tags for menus and menu options, the menus.xml file also contains tags for keyboard shortcuts. The `<shortcutlist> </shortcutlist>` tags specify the shortcut list for menu options. These tags include a `<shortcut/>` tag, which is an empty tag that defines a shortcut key. The following code snippet shows the definition for the F12 key, which invokes the Preview in Browser option:

```
<shortcutlist id="DWMainWindow">
<!-- other shortcut keys here -- >
<shortcut key="F12"
file="Menus/MM/PIB_Dynamic.htm" arguments="'primary'"
id="DWShortcuts_Main_PIBPrimary"
name="Preview in Primary Browser"/>
<!-- other shortcut keys here -- >
</shortcutlist>
```

In this example, the `id` attribute of the `<shortcutlist>` tag contains the ID of the menu bar, `DWMainWindow`, as its value. When you use a keyboard shortcut, the associated JavaScript code is executed. The value in the `file` attribute of the `<shortcut/>` tag contains the name of the file that includes this JavaScript code. The `arguments` attribute contains the arguments that need to be passed to the JavaScript code. The `id` attribute of the `<shortcut/>` tag contains a unique identifier for the shortcut. The `name` attribute contains the name of the menu option that is invoked when you use this shortcut.

EDITING THE menus.xml FILE

You can edit the menus.xml file to rearrange menu options within a menu or move a menu option to a different menu. You can also create a submenu within a menu and insert a separator between two menu items by editing this file. Before you open the menus.xml file for editing, you need to quit UltraDev.

To move a menu option from one menu to another, cut the `<menuitem>` tag that contains the particular menu option and paste it between the `<menu> </menu>` tag pair of the menu in which you want the menu option to appear. For example, suppose you want to move the

Exit menu option from the File menu and place it after the Restore All option on the Window menu. Between the

```
<menu name="_File" id="DWMenu_MainSite_File">
```

and

```
</menu>
```

tags, find and cut the following code:

```
<menuitem name="Exit" key="Cmd+Q"
enabled="true" command="dw.quitApplication()" id="DWMenu_MainSite_File_Exit" />
```

Insert this code between the

```
<menuitem name="_Restore All" key="Opt+Shift+F23" platform="Win" enabled="true"
command="dw.minimizeRestoreAll(false)" id="DWMenu_Window_RestoreAll" />
```

and

```
<separator />
```

tags within the `<menu>` `</menu>` tags defined for the Window menu.

To create a submenu for a newly created menu option, create a `<menu>` `</menu>` tag pair inside the `<menu>` `</menu>` tag pair of the parent menu and then insert the `<menuitem/>` tag inside this pair.

To insert a separator between two menu options, insert the `<separator/>` tag between two `<menuitem>` tags.

To change the name of a menu option or a menu, change the value of the name attribute of the `<menuitem>` or `<menu>` tag.

To add a keyboard shortcut to a menu option, add key=" " inside the `<menuitem>` tag of the menu option. Inside the double quotes, enter the key combination. You can edit a menu option's keyboard shortcut by changing the key attribute in the `<menuitem>` tag of the menu option. To remove a shortcut key, remove the key attribute from the menu option's `<menuitem>` tag.

Customizing Dialog Boxes

You can customize the appearance of a dialog box by changing the width, height, and other attributes pertaining to the layout of the dialog box. For each dialog box, an HTML file exists. This file specifies the layout of the dialog box by using an HTML form. You can find this HTML file in the respective subfolder within the Configuration folder. You can edit the HTML form attributes in this file to change the appearance of the dialog box.

> **Caution**
>
> When you edit the HTML form associated with a dialog box, you must edit only those attributes that determine the appearance of various form elements. If you change the name attribute of a form element or remove any of the form elements, UltraDev will not be able to use the dialog box to accept the intended information.

To modify the appearance of a dialog box, you need to first locate the file that corresponds to the dialog box. For example, the Change Property.htm file associated with the Change Property dialog box is located in the Actions folder, which is in the Behaviors subfolder of the Configuration folder. To see how this dialog box uses the HTML form in this file, open the file in UltraDev. When you view the file in Design view, it appears as shown in Figure 23.2.

Figure 23.2
The Change Property dialog box is built using a table and a form.

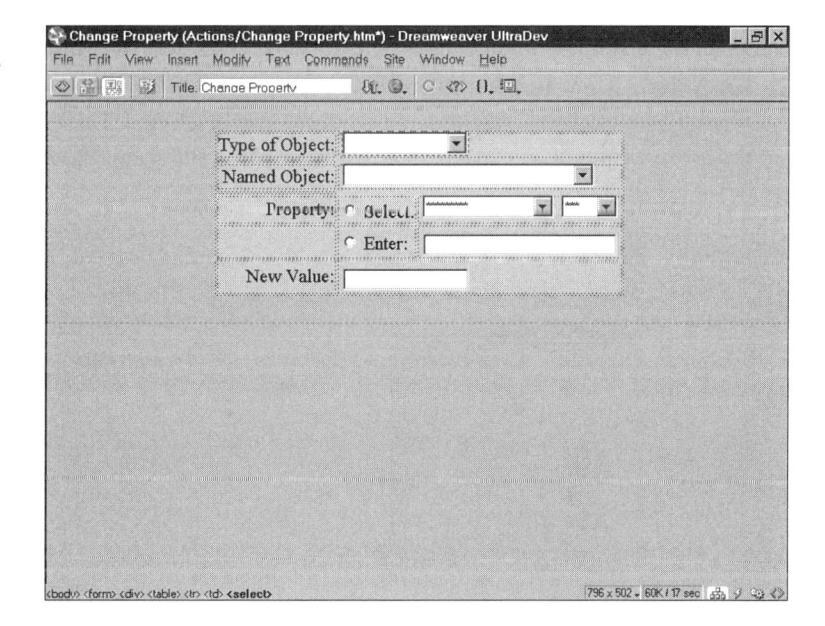

Switch to Code view to see the form elements of the Change Property dialog box, such as text boxes and list boxes, which are embedded within a table. The <input> tag and the <select></select> tag pair are embedded within the <td></td> tag pair.

One way you can change the appearance of the Change Property dialog box is by changing the background color of the table. To do so, follow these steps:

1. Make a copy of the Change Property.htm file in a folder outside the Configuration folder so that you can revert to the original file later if necessary.
2. Open the Change Property.htm file in UltraDev.
3. In Design view, change the table's background color by using the table's Property inspector.

4. Save the file and reload the changed file by using the Reload Extensions option in the Objects panel. You can also quit UltraDev and restart to reload the file.
5. Check the Change Property dialog box by using the Behaviors panel.

Customizing Data Formats

You can display dynamic data on a Web page in a customized and user-friendly format by applying various data formats to the dynamic data. UltraDev has a set of predefined data formats that you can apply to the dynamic data. For example, you can apply a format to currency data that places a specific number of digits after the decimal point in the currency.

You can create your own data formats as well as edit them. To create a new data format for dynamic text, follow these steps:

1. Open the document that contains dynamic text. Open the Data Bindings panel.
2. Select the dynamic text for which you want to create the new data format. In the Data Bindings panel, the corresponding bound column is selected. Click the down arrow in the Format column. A pop-up menu is displayed, as shown in Figure 23.3.

Figure 23.3
A list of available data formats is shown in this pop-up menu.

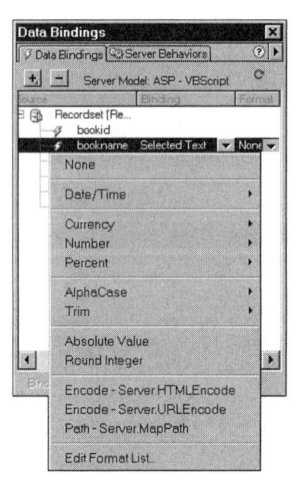

3. Select the Edit Format List option from the pop-up menu. The Edit Format List dialog box is displayed, as shown in Figure 23.4.
4. Click the + button and select the format type you want to create. The dialog box for creating the new format is displayed. For example, if you select the Percent option, the Percent dialog box is displayed, as shown in Figure 23.5.

Figure 23.4
Use this dialog box to create new data formats.

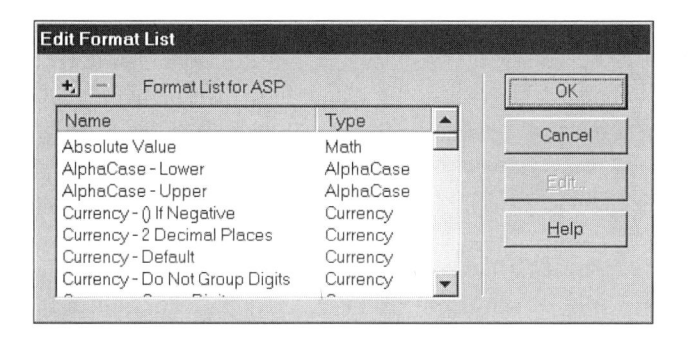

Figure 23.5
Specify the required details in this dialog box to create the data format for the percent format type.

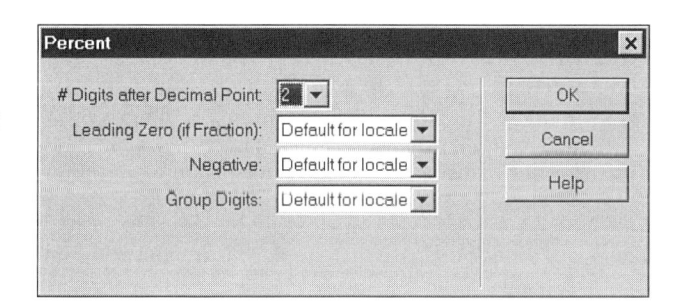

5. Set the properties for the new data format. For the percent format type, you can choose the number of digits that will appear after the decimal point. You can also choose whether there must be leading zeros for fractional values and how negative values are specified. A new data format for the percent format type is created after you complete the details in the Percent dialog box.

6. The new data format is displayed in the Edit Format List dialog box. You can change the name of the data format by clicking, pausing, and then clicking again to edit the name.

7. Click OK to complete the process of creating the data format. The newly created data format appears as an option in the respective format type.

To edit an existing data format, select the data format from the Edit Format List dialog box. Double-click the data format to display its dialog box. Specify the new format details in this dialog box. UltraDev does not allow you to edit the format for all format types. For example, you cannot edit the format for the AlphaCase - Lower, AlphaCase - Upper, and Absolute Value format types.

CUSTOMIZING SERVER BEHAVIORS

UltraDev ships with a set of predefined server behaviors that allow you to easily add server-side scripts to your Web applications. If you want to have more flexibility in terms of the features of these server behaviors, you can edit these server behaviors to suit your needs by using UltraDev's server behavior builder. You can also create new server behaviors using the server behavior builder. For example, if you want to display the current date in your HTML document, you can create a server behavior that inserts the current date. Whenever you want to display the current date in your document, you can simply apply the server behavior.

Using the Server Behavior Builder

You can create server behaviors in UltraDev's server behavior builder by using any of the scripting languages used to write server-side code, such as VBScript, CFML, or Java.

Typically, the code for building a server behavior consists of several code blocks or tags. When you create a server behavior in the server behavior builder, you need to create a code block for every tag or logical code block. After creating each code block, you need to specify the location where each code block must be inserted in your HTML code.

To create a server behavior by using the server behavior builder, follow these steps:

1. Choose New Server Behavior from the pop-up menu in the Server Behaviors panel. The New Server Behavior dialog box is displayed, as shown in Figure 23.6.

Figure 23.6
Use this dialog box to create server behaviors for any server model.

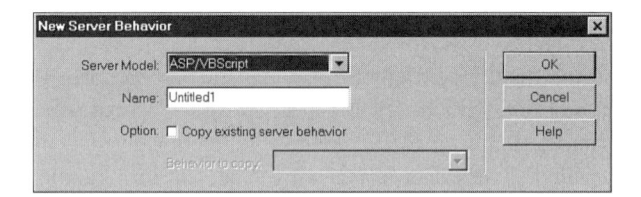

2. From the Server Model drop-down list, select the server model for which you are developing the server behavior.

3. Type a name for the server behavior in the Name text box. For example, to create a server behavior that inserts the current date in your document, you can name the server behavior as Show Current Date.

4. If you want to copy an existing server behavior and add to the server behavior you are creating, select the Copy existing server behavior check box. When you select this check box, a list of available server behaviors is displayed in the Behavior to copy drop-down list. Select the required server behavior from this drop-down list.

5. Click OK to display the Server Behavior Builder dialog box, shown in Figure 23.7. The name of the server behavior appears on the title bar of this dialog box.

6. To add a code block to the server behavior, click the + button. The Create a New a Code Block dialog box is displayed, as shown in Figure 23.8.

CUSTOMIZING SERVER BEHAVIORS | 475

Figure 23.7
Use this dialog box to build a new server behavior.

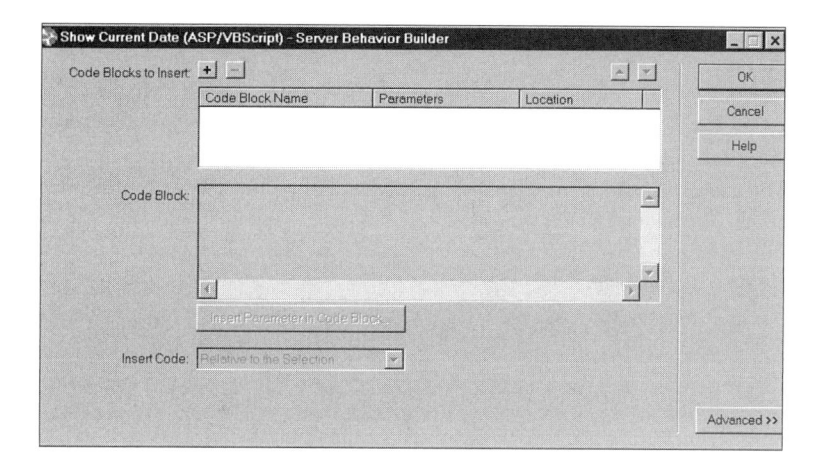

Figure 23.8
Specify a name for the new code block in this dialog box.

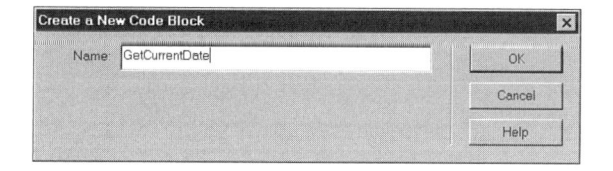

7. Type a name for the code block in the Name text box. Click OK to return to the Server Behavior Builder dialog box. Figure 23.8 shows the name of the code block as GetCurrentDate.

8. In the Code Block list box, type the code that contains instructions for implementing the server behavior. When you write code in this section, you can include only a single tag or a single code block. If you want to include multiple tags or code blocks, you need to create that many code blocks in the Server Behavior Builder dialog box. For example, to write the code for a server behavior that generates the current date in an ASP application, insert a line of VBScript code such as `<% Response.Write Date() %>`, as shown in Figure 23.9.

9. If you need to supply some parameters at runtime, include them in the code that you write in the Code Block section by clicking the Insert Parameter In Code Block button. The Insert Parameter In Code Block dialog box is displayed, as shown in Figure 23.10.

10. Specify a name for the parameter in the Parameter Name drop-down list, and then click OK to close this dialog box. The parameter that you just created is inserted into the code block at the point where you placed the cursor before defining the parameter.

Figure 23.9
Specify the code in this dialog box.

Figure 23.10
Specify the parameters for your code blocks in this dialog box.

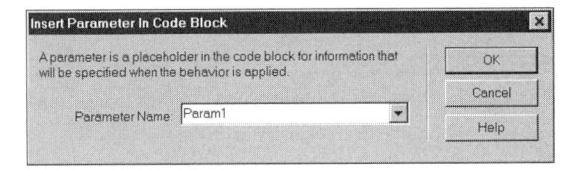

11. Select an option from the Insert Code drop-down list in the Server Behavior Builder dialog box to specify the location in which to embed the newly created code block in the HTML code of your Web page. You can embed the code either above the `<html>` tag or below the `</html>` tag, relative to a specific tag or a selected tag. When you select one of the first two options, a drop-down list named Relative Position and a text box named Position appear near the Insert Code drop-down list. If you select Custom Position from the Relative Position drop-down list, you need to specify a number of 99 or less in the Position text box. The code block will be inserted at the position signified by the number. The Custom Position option is also used to decide the order in which multiple code blocks will be inserted at a particular location. For example, if you need to insert two code blocks after the opening `<html>` tag in a particular order, you need to specify their position numbers in the Position text box. If you specify 55 for one code block and 60 for the other, the code with lower position number is inserted first. To insert the Show Current Date server behavior at a specific position in your HTML document, select the Relative to the Selection from the Insert Code drop-down list and the After the Selection option from the Relative Position drop-down list.

12. If you want to specify additional information about the server behavior you are building, click the Advanced >> button in the Server Behavior Builder dialog box. The Server Behavior Builder dialog box with some additional options is displayed, as shown in Figure 23.11.

Figure 23.11
Specify advanced settings for your server behavior in this dialog box.

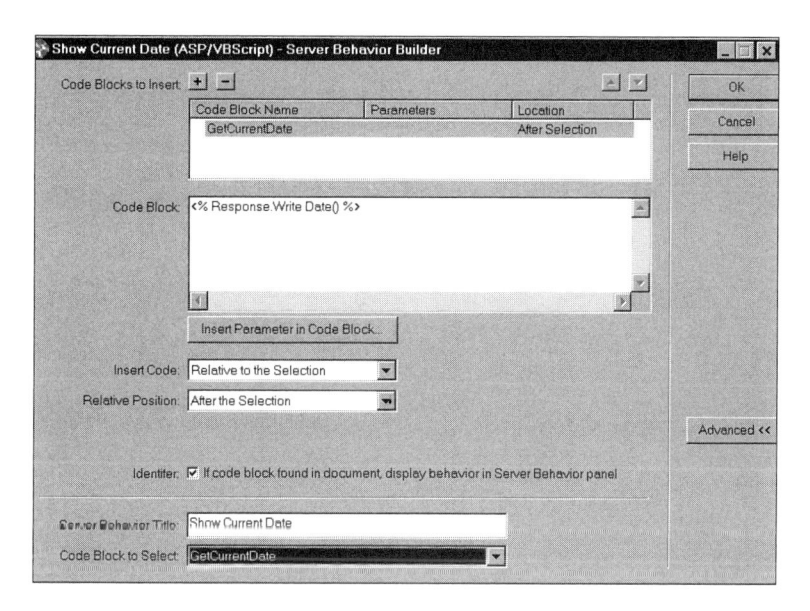

13. In Figure 23.11, you see a check box named Identifier that is checked. When you create a server behavior, UltraDev treats every code block in that server behavior as an identifier. You can remove the identifier for a code block that is used by other server behaviors by deselecting the Identifier check box. However, you need to ensure that at least one code block in your server behavior is an identifier, because UltraDev lists the newly created server behavior in the Server Behaviors panel only if it finds at least one identifier code block per server behavior.

14. In the Server Behavior Title text box, specify the title for the server behavior as you want it to appear in the Server Behaviors panel. If your server behavior requires parameters to be supplied by a user, the title of the behavior includes the parameter name and the server behavior name by default. This default title is not very user-friendly. Therefore, you can change the title to represent the server behavior more clearly.

15. Whenever you select an element in Design view of a Web page, the HTML code associated with the element is also selected in Code view. Similarly, when you attach a server behavior to your Web page and select the behavior in the Server Behavior panel, the code block associated with the server behavior is selected in Code view. To specify a code block that must be selected when you select the server behavior, select that code block from the Code Block to Select drop-down list. For the Show Current Date server behavior, select the GetCurrentDate option.

16. In the Server Behavior Builder dialog box, create more code blocks by repeating steps 6 through 15.

17. If you have specified parameters for the server behavior, you need to generate a dialog box that accepts the parameters from the developer. To generate this dialog box, click the Next button in the Server Behavior Builder dialog box. The Generate Behavior dialog box is displayed, as shown in Figure 23.12.

Figure 23.12
Use this dialog box to generate a dialog box for a server behavior.

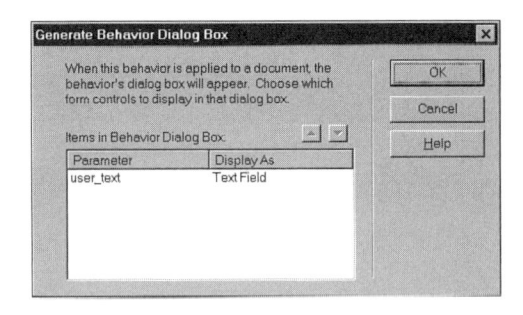

18. In the Items in Behavior Dialog Box list box, the parameters that you specified in all the code blocks of the newly created server behavior are displayed, along with their display type. To change a parameter's display type, select the parameter, click the down arrow next to the default display type, and select an option from the drop-down list. Click OK after you have specified the display types for each parameter.

19. Click OK in the Server Behavior Builder dialog box to complete the process of building the server behavior.

After you create a server behavior, it is listed in the Server Behaviors panel. Apply the server behavior. If the server behavior requires the developer to supply parameters, specify the same in the dialog box that you generated.

Editing a Server Behavior

To edit a server behavior, select the Edit Server Behavior option from the pop-up menu in the Server Behaviors panel. The Edit Server Behaviors dialog box is displayed, as shown in Figure 23.13.

Figure 23.13
Use this dialog box to edit existing server behaviors.

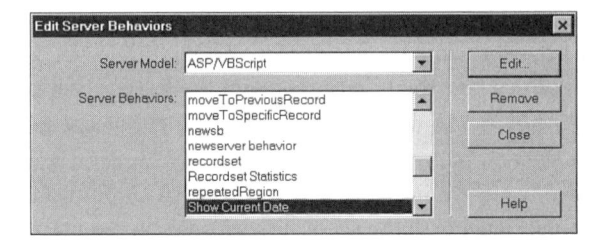

From the Server Behaviors list box, select the server behavior you want to edit, and click the Edit button. The Server Behavior Builder dialog box is displayed. For example, if you want to edit the title of a server behavior, make the necessary changes in the Server Behavior Title text box of the Server Behavior Builder dialog box, and then click OK. After you return to the Edit Server Behaviors dialog box, click OK to complete the editing process.

> **Caution**
>
> If you edit an existing server behavior, you will no longer be able to use the previous version of this server behavior. Therefore, it is better to make a copy of a server behavior before editing it. To make a copy of an existing server behavior, choose New Server Behavior from the pop-up menu in the Server Behavior panel. In the New Server Behavior dialog box, select the Copy existing server behavior check box.

Summary

This chapter dealt with customizing the UltraDev interface. You can customize the menu system in UltraDev by editing the `menus.xml` file. You can modify keyboard shortcuts by using the Keyboard Shortcut editor. You can create an object by using HTML as well as JavaScript. You can customize the Objects panel by changing the file associated with an object in the Configuration/Objects folder.

You can customize dialog boxes by changing their appearance. You can customize data formats by editing them and creating new ones. You can customize server behaviors by using the server behavior builder.

PART V

EXTENDING THE CAPABILITIES OF DREAMWEAVER ULTRADEV 4

24 Introducing Extensions 483

25 Interface Extensions 495

CHAPTER 24

INTRODUCING EXTENSIONS

In this chapter

The Concept of Extensions   484

The Document Object Model   485

JavaScript in Extensions   489

Summary   493

The Concept of Extensions

Extensions are programs added to UltraDev to extend its functionality. You can write these programs by using a combination of HTML, JavaScript, and the UltraDev API, which is based on JavaScript. In addition, you can write extensions in C or C++. With extensions, you can customize the UltraDev interface by adding new objects, menu commands, floating panels, Property inspectors, server behaviors, data sources, and so on. By adding extensions to UltraDev, you reduce the time and effort spent in creating Web applications. For example, if you want to add to your Web application a feature that allows users to filter results of a search operation based on some criteria, you can create a server behavior extension. This extension creates a server behavior that implements this feature. You can add this new server behavior to the UltraDev interface and reuse this server behavior in other Web applications you create. This saves the time spent writing code to implement this feature every time.

In UltraDev, you can create extensions to

- Add objects to the Object panel
- Add custom commands and menus to the menu bar
- Create custom floating panels
- Create custom client-side behaviors
- Create custom Property inspectors
- Create new server behaviors
- Create new data sources for data source connectivity
- Create new server models

You can also download extensions, which are contributed by the developer community, from Macromedia Exchange at `http://www.macromedia.com/exchange/ultradev/`.

UltraDev lends itself to customization because it is based on the Document Object Model (DOM), which allows you to access and modify any part of an HTML document. The features of UltraDev, such as objects and Property inspectors, are implemented by means of an HTML file and a JavaScript file. Most of the features have a user interface to accept user input on how the feature must be implemented. This interface is designed as an HTML document, which is then accessed by a JavaScript file to get the user input and implement the feature as per user input. For example, the `Named Anchor` object is implemented by using an HTML file and a JavaScript file. When you select the `Insert Named Anchor` object from the Objects panel, the Insert Named Anchor dialog box appears. This dialog box is an HTML form. When users input data, such as the name of the anchor, in this form, the JavaScript file associated with the Named Anchor object accesses this user input and inserts a named anchor into the document the user is designing. The UltraDev DOM lets you access user input values from the HTML document associated with a feature of UltraDev. Therefore, to create an extension, all you need to do is design the interface for the extension and create a JavaScript file to implement the extension as per user input.

The files associated with all the features of UltraDev are located in the folders within the Configuration folder, which is in the folder where UltraDev is installed. When you create extensions, you need to place these extensions in the folders corresponding to the category of these extensions. For example, if you create an object extension, you need to place it in the Objects subfolder of the Configuration folder. The folder structure within the Configuration folder is shown in Figure 24.1.

Before you begin writing extensions, it is necessary to understand DOM and how the UltraDev DOM is implemented.

Figure 24.1
You can view the directory structure of the Configuration folder in the program directory of UltraDev 4.

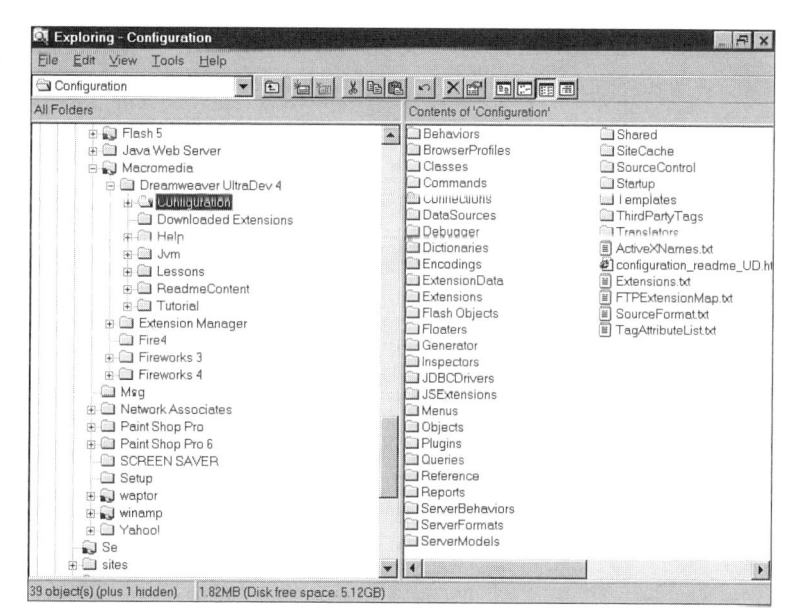

The Document Object Model

Web pages or documents consist of many objects, such as text, buttons, forms, images, and so on. Each of these objects has some associated properties that define how the object appears and associated behaviors that determine what actions must happen when a user interacts with that object. For example, the page shown in Figure 24.2 contains some text and some form elements, such as text boxes, a check box, and a form button. The form button in the page has an associated property that contains the name that must be displayed on the button. This button also has an attached behavior that specifies that the form must be submitted to the server when the user clicks the button. Similarly, all the objects on a Web page have properties and behaviors associated with them.

It is easy to specify the properties of objects on a Web document by using HTML tags, because each tag represents an object. An HTML tag contains attributes whose values when set determine the properties of that object. For example, when you want to display a table with a certain height and width, you use the `<table>` tag with its height and width attributes set to that value.

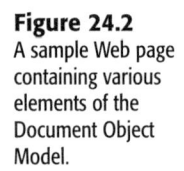

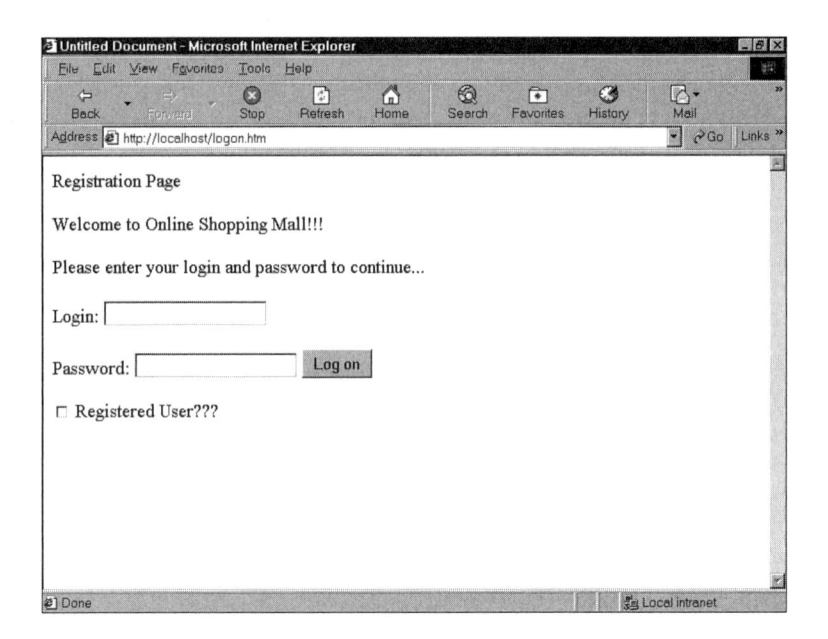

Figure 24.2
A sample Web page containing various elements of the Document Object Model.

Although HTML is sufficient to decide on the appearance of an object on a Web page, it is limited in terms of being able to decide on the object's behavior. JavaScript lets you attach behaviors to document objects. It does this by using the DOM. In fact, the DOM was developed when there was a requirement to port Java and JavaScript programs across Web browsers. However, DOM has evolved as a specification and an Application Programming Interface (API) that allows developers to access the objects in an HTML document and attach behaviors to these objects, irrespective of the platform or programming language they use.

W3C specifies various levels for the DOM. DOM Level 1 categorizes DOM as DOM Core and DOM HTML. DOM Core is a set of specifications for XML documents that are widely used to represent data. DOM HTML, as defined by W3C, is a superset of all the document object models. DOM HTML brings in a new way of referencing HTML elements. For example, a document object represents the scope of an entire HTML document, whereas a document.head object represents the scope of the head objects in the document. The DOM API is scalable across platforms and applications. This scalability is achieved by W3C by providing a language-independent interface definition language called OMG IDL.

DOM describes a document in terms of a tree, in which the objects in the document are arranged in a hierarchical fashion. The DOM hierarchy for HTML documents starts with the document object, which is at the root of the document tree. The rest of the objects in the document stem from the document object. You can refer to each object in the document by using the object name and a dot notation. For example, to refer to a button named button1 that exists on a form named accept_form, you must use the dot notation shown in the following syntax:

```
document.accept_form.button1
```

Multiple objects with same name are grouped into an array. You can use array indexes to refer to individual objects rather than referring to each by its name. Consider a page that has a form named form1 that has three text boxes with the same name. To refer to the second text box on the form, you must use the dot notation shown in the following syntax:

```
document.form1.mytextboxes[2]
```

THE DOCUMENT OBJECT MODEL IN ULTRADEV

The UltraDev 4 DOM is a combination of the Netscape Navigator 4 DOM and W3C DOM Level 1. The working of the UltraDev engine is based on Netscape DOM. Therefore, extensions for UltraDev 4 are developed on the Netscape DOM specification.

The DOM architecture in UltraDev is shown in Figure 24.3.

Figure 24.3
The DOM architecture represents the document hierarchy in UltraDev.

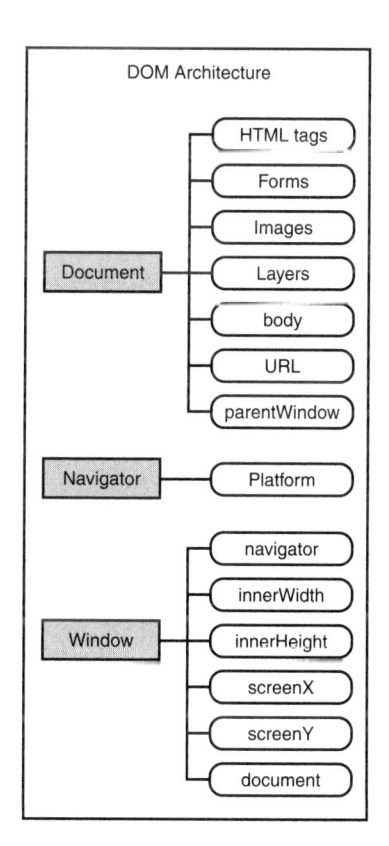

The W3C DOM Level 1 represents documents as a hierarchy of node objects. A *node* is an element container in a DOM document. For example, each of the HTML start and end tag pairs is a node. In addition, all single tags, such as <HR>, are also nodes. Some nodes have more than one type of child node, and others do not have any. Nodes without any child nodes are called *leaf nodes*. DOM specifies the NodeList interface to handle ordered lists of Node objects. The NamedNodeMap interface is used to handle unordered sets of nodes. You must use the dot notation to access a node's properties. For example, to access the src attribute of an Image node, you need to specify document.formname.Image.src. The following is a list of node types for UltraDev DOM:

- DOCUMENT_NODE—Lets you access an entire document.
- ELEMENT_NODE—Lets you access nodes, such as <BODY>.
- COMMENT_NODE—Lets you access HTML comments.
- TEXT_NODE—Lets you access HTML text on a page.

Listing 24.1 shows a sample document with various types of tags.

LISTING 24.1 NODE TYPES IN DREAMWEAVER ULTRADEV 4

```
<HTML>
<HEAD>
<TITLE>First Page</TITLE>
<!--This is commented-->
</HEAD>
<BODY>
<FORM>
Book Name: <INPUT TYPE=LABEL>
</FORM>
</BODY>
</HTML>
```

In Listing 24.1, the <HTML> node is the DOCUMENT_NODE and the <BODY> node is the ELEMENT_NODE that has child nodes. The block within the <HEAD> tag contains the COMMENT_NODE.

You can use the tagName property of the <BODY> tag to find a particular node. You can create a new element node by using the createElement() method of the document object. The createElement() method takes the tag for the element as a parameter. The following example creates a new element called NEWBR:

```
var myele = document.createElement("NEWBR");
```

The new element created does not have any attributes or methods. You use the setAttribute() method of the DOM element to assign properties to the element. You use the following syntax to assign an ID attribute for the newly created element:

```
NEWBR.setAttribute("id", "NEWBRID");
```

You can use other document object methods to assign text to the element and append child nodes to it. After creating the extensions for UltraDev by using the DOM structure, you can access the properties, methods, and events of any object by using dot notation.

UltraDev DOM incorporates the objects defined by W3C. In addition to these objects, it incorporates two specific objects, dreamweaver and site. The dreamweaver object exposes two read-only properties, appName and appVersion. These properties check for the application name and the version of UltraDev.

API Methods

You can use DOM methods to specify the attributes, methods, and events of an extension. You've already learned how to use the `setAttribute()` method to assign attributes. Some of the other methods are discussed in the following sections.

THE `getElementsByTagName(tagName)` METHOD The `getElementsByTagName(tagName)` method accepts a tag name and returns the elements for the tag. For example, you can use the following code to search for all input elements on a page:

`var inputele = dreamweaver.getDocumentDOM.getElementsByTagName("input");`

THE `hasChildNodes()` METHOD The `hasChildNodes()` method returns a Boolean value depending on whether the node has child nodes. For example, you can use this method when you want to perform a set of actions on a node depending on whether the node has child nodes.

THE `removeAttribute(attrName)` METHOD The `removeAttribute(attrName)` method removes the attribute specified as a parameter for the tag. For example, you can use the following syntax to remove the ID attribute of the NEWBR tag:

`NEWBR.removeAttribute("id");`

JavaScript in Extensions

The DOM for a browser interprets the JavaScript code in an HTML document and displays the page in the browser. The DOM for UltraDev interprets the JavaScript code written for extensions. UltraDev compiles and executes any JavaScript code written between the <SCRIPT> tags in an HTML document, as well as scripts written in external .js files.

You can create advanced extensions by using the basic HTML form elements and adding the JavaScript code. You can even create new custom controls by using JavaScript. The UltraDev architecture provides two built-in controls created using JavaScript—the tree and color button controls.

Using Tree Controls

You can use the tree control to display data in a hierarchical structure. One good example of a tree control is Windows Explorer, available in Windows 95 and 98. The tree control is made up of nodes that you can expand and collapse to view the data in the nodes. Each node can have many child nodes, which you can further expand and collapse. A tree control used in UltraDev is shown in Figure 24.4.

> **Note** The buttons that identify nodes are represented as + or – signs in the Windows environment and as inverted triangles in the Macintosh environment.

Figure 24.4
An example of a custom tree control.

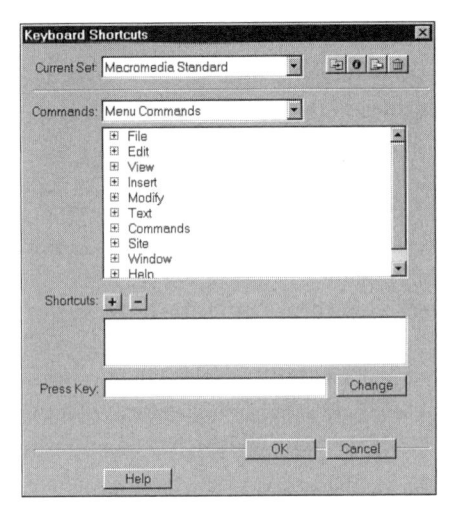

In a tree control, the topmost node is called a *root node*. A node that contains other nodes is called a *data node*. The nodes within a data node are called *child nodes*. The nodes at the end of the tree structure are *leaf nodes*. These do not contain any child nodes.

You can create a tree control by using the new tags provided by UltraDev:

- MM:TREECONTROL
- MM:TREECOLUMN
- MM:TREENODE

You use the <MM:TREECONTROL> tag to identify the tree control. If you want to create a column in the tree control, use the <MM:TREECOLUMN> tag. You use the <MM:TREENODE> tag to create a node for the tree control. Each of these tags has a set of attributes, events, and methods.

You can use the following code to create a tree control and set attributes for it:

```
<MM:TREECONTROL name="sampletreectrl"
size="10"
multiple
style="width=200px;height=200px"
noheaders>
</MM:TREECONTROL>
```

In this example, the attributes, such as `name`, `size`, and `style`, are used with the <MM:TREECONTROL> tag. The `multiple` attribute allows multiple selections in the tree control. The `size`, `multiple`, `style`, and `noheaders` attributes are optional and take a default value. You must have at least one <MM:TREECOLUMN> tag for each tree column to create a tree control.

To add columns to the tree control, use the following code:

```
<MM:TREECONTROL name="sampletreectrl"
size="10"
multiple
```

```
style="width=200px;height=200px"
noheaders>
<MM:TREECOLUMN name="col1" width=50 state=visible value="bookstores" align=center>
<MM:TREECOLUMN name="COL2" width=50 state=visible value="locations" align=center>
</MM:TREECONTROL>
```

The `<MM:TREECOLUMN>` tags are embedded within the `<MM:TREECONTROL>` tag. After you create the columns for the tree control, you can use `<MM:TREENODE>` tags to create nodes for individual columns.

Listing 24.2 creates a tree control with two columns and two nodes in the first column.

LISTING 24.2 CODE TO CREATE A SAMPLE TREE CONTROL

```
<MM:TREECONTROL name="sampletreectrl"
size="10"
multiple
style="width=200px;height=200px"
noheaders>
<MM:TREECOLUMN name="col1" width=50 state=visible value="bookstores" align=center>
<MM:TREENODE name=node1 value="bookmark" state=collapsed selected=false icon=4>
    </mm:treenode>
<MM:TREENODE name=node2 value="crossroads" state=collapsed selected=false icon=4>
    </mm:treenode>
<MM:TREECOLUMN name="col2" width=50 state=visible value="locations" align=center>
</MM:TREECONTROL>
```

A node can have attributes, such as `name`, `value`, `state`, `selected`, and `icon`. The `icon` attribute takes numeric literals from 0 to 10 for the images to be displayed for the nodes created. The tree control created in Listing 24.2 is shown in Figure 24.5.

Figure 24.5
A sample tree control created in UltraDev.

The `<TREECONTROL>` and `<TREENODE>` tags are similar to any other document object. You can manipulate these tags by using DOM functions to add, delete, move, modify, and traverse nodes.

INSTALLING EXTENSIONS

You can download the extensions available at Macromedia Exchange and install them on your machine by using Extension Manager, which comes installed with UltraDev. The extensions from Macromedia Exchange are downloaded as extension package files with an .mxp extension. To open Extension Manager in UltraDev, choose Commands, Manage Extensions. Extension Manager of UltraDev 4 is shown in Figure 24.6.

Figure 24.6
You can use the built-in Extension Manager of UltraDev 4 to install and submit extensions.

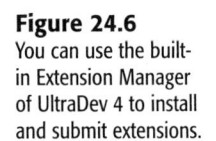

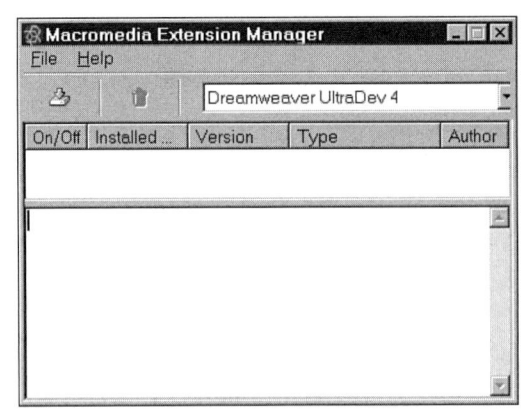

Installing Extensions in UltraDev

Using Extension Manager, you can add the extension of your choice to UltraDev. The files to be used for the extensions are available in the .mxp file.

Follow these steps to install an extension:

1. Open Extension Manager by choosing Commands, Manage Extensions.
2. Choose File, Install Extension in Extension Manager. The Select Extension to Install dialog box is displayed.
3. Browse and select the name of the .mxp file you want to install as an extension.
4. Click Install. The extension is installed in UltraDev.

Sharing Extensions

Macromedia accepts user-defined extensions. You can create an extension, package it, and submit it to the Macromedia Web site. These extensions are distributed and made available to all users.

Packaging and Submitting an Extension

You must use Extension Manager to package an extension and submit it for sharing. To package an extension, you need to first create an extension installation file. This file has a name that ends in .mxi.

To package an extension, follow these steps:

1. Choose File, Package Extension from Extension Manager.
2. Select the .mxi file from the Select Extension to Package dialog box. Click OK.
3. The dialog box changes to the Save Extension Package As dialog box. Select the location where you want to store the packaged extension file. Click Save after selecting the file. The extension is now packaged.

After you package the extension, test it by installing it. After testing, submit it by choosing File, Submit Extension in Extension Manager.

Summary

Extensions are powerful pieces of software code used to build new features into UltraDev. You can create extensions by using plain HTML or JavaScript. UltraDev parses and interprets the extensions by using DOM. You can create extensions in various ways. You can create a simple extension just by adding commands to a menu or create complex extensions such as a shopping cart or a date stamp. The DOM for Dreamweaver determines how the JavaScript code in extensions is parsed and interpreted by browsers.

CHAPTER 25

INTERFACE EXTENSIONS

In this chapter

Extending Objects   496

Extending Commands   505

Extending Property Inspectors   508

Extending Floating Panels   514

Summary   515

Extending Objects

Objects are the most indispensable interface features you need when creating Web applications. Objects let you easily add HTML elements to your document. To add an element, such as a table, to your document, you click the Table icon in the Common category of the Objects panel. The table object associated with this icon accepts properties for the table from you by means of the Insert Table dialog box. It then creates a table according to the properties you set and inserts the <table> tag into your document with the required attributes set to the values you specify. You can write your own object extensions to create custom-made objects or add more features to existing objects. These object extensions are the simplest to write.

To be able to write object extensions, you need to know what goes into creating an object and how these objects work in UltraDev. You learned in Chapter 23, "Customizing Dreamweaver UltraDev 4," that every object has an HTML file, a GIF file, and an optional JavaScript file associated with it. To write an object extension, all you need to do is create the HTML, JavaScript, and GIF files and place them in the folder that corresponds to the category of the object in the Objects folder that is in the Configuration folder. The JavaScript file is optional, so you can choose not to create a separate JavaScript file. Instead, you can embed the JavaScript code in the object's HTML file. The GIF file must contain the image of the object that appears next to the object name in the Objects panel. If you do not create a GIF file, UltraDev creates a GIF file for the object you create.

The HTML and JavaScript files associated with an object hold the key to the functioning of the object. These two files contain the necessary code needed to implement the object. To create an object, you need to implement two components. The first and most important component is the HTML component that needs to be inserted into the HTML code at the current selection or insertion point in the document so that the object appears in the current document.

> **Note**
> A *selection* refers to an element that is highlighted in the Document window. An *insertion point* is the place where the cursor is currently located in the Document window.

For example, if you insert an object, such as an image, the object's corresponding HTML code, which is the <img> tag, is inserted into the document.

The second component of an object is optional but is no less important than the first. In fact, most objects need to have this component to be fully qualified as objects. This component is also an HTML component. It determines the object's interface, which is required to accept user input regarding the object's properties. If the object needs user input to define its properties, it must have this interface component. For example, the interface of the table object is the Insert Table dialog box, which accepts properties of the table, such as the number of rows and columns, as user input. This interface is designed using an HTML form. The controls that you see in the dialog box, such as the Rows and Columns text boxes, are form fields.

> **Note**
> When you want to create an object to implement a desired feature, you need to examine the feature to see if it really qualifies as an object. For example, if you want to insert a custom image, such as a logo, into your documents, you can place it in the library rather than create an object extension for that logo. Such features that do not require user input need not be implemented as object extensions, because what really differentiates an object from a library item is its ability to allow users to set its properties at the time it is inserted. For example, a table qualifies as an object because the user decides its properties, such as width, height, and the number of rows and columns at the time the table is inserted.

The two components discussed in the preceding paragraphs are not implemented in the same HTML file of the object. You implement the interface component in the HTML file of the object. For example, if you want to create a marquee object that accepts the marquee text, the color of the text, the font size, and so on from the user, you need to create an HTML form that accepts these user input values. You must create this HTML form in the HTML file that you create for the object. You must then place this HTML file in the subfolder of the Objects folder that corresponds to the object's category.

The first component of the object, the HTML tag that is needed to display the object on the document, is not predetermined. It is created when the object's attributes are specified. To implement this component, you need to use the functions of the JavaScript API and UltraDev API. These functions, which are discussed in the following sections, comprise the JavaScript file that you create for the object. You can include these functions in the same HTML file that contains the HTML code for designing the object's interface if you do not want to create a separate JavaScript file for the object.

> **Note**
> The HTML, JavaScript, and GIF files associated with an object must have the same name, because UltraDev can associate the object with these files only if the names are the same. This is the name that appears for the object in the Objects panel. For example, the files associated with an image object are named `Image.htm` and `Image.js`. This name appears in the Objects panel next to the image icon.

To understand object extensions better, you need to learn about what happens when a user clicks the object icon in the Objects panel or chooses an option that corresponds to an object from the Insert menu. When the user chooses the required object, UltraDev searches for the object's corresponding HTML file in the subfolders of the Objects folder. UltraDev then parses this HTML file to any form tag. If it finds this HTML file, the form is displayed as a dialog box to allow users to enter values that will determine the object's properties. After the user enters the values, they are accessed from the form by using the methods of the DOM. These values are then concatenated with appropriate HTML tags or attributes as a string. This string contains the complete HTML tag or tags for displaying the object as per user-defined properties. For example, when you want to insert a named anchor into your document, you click the Named Anchor icon in the Objects panel. The Insert Named Anchor dialog box appears. You can implement this dialog box by using the `<form>` tag, as follows:

```
<form name="theform">
<table border=0>
<tr>
<td NOWRAP>  Anchor Name:<br>
<input type="text" name="anchorname" size="30"></td>
</tr>
</table>
</form>
```

When you specify the name of the anchor in the form's anchorname text box, this name is accessed from the form by using the dot notation specified by DOM, as follows:

```
document.forms[0].anchorname.value
```

To retrieve the form values and to create a string from these values, you need to use JavaScript. The following code that is part of the `objectTag()` function of the `Anchor.js` file shows how the anchor tag is created with the value specified in the anchorname text box of the Insert Anchor dialog box:

```
{
...
return '<A NAME="' + document.forms[0].anchorname.value + '"></A>';
}
```

FUNCTIONS TO IMPLEMENT OBJECTS

To create object extensions, you need to use standard JavaScript API and Dreamweaver JavaScript API functions. Apart from these, some exclusive functions for object extensions exist. These functions form the Object API. In this section, you will learn about the API functions that are specifically used to create object extensions. The flexibility that you get in creating object extensions stems from the fact that these functions are not predefined and do not belong to the `dreamweaver`, `site`, or `dom` objects. Therefore, they neither take predefined arguments like the standard JavaScript and UltraDev API functions nor return values that are generated automatically. The user has total control over these object API functions. Therefore, the user can determine what arguments are needed for these functions and what goes into the body of these functions and generates the return values. More importantly, these functions are not called explicitly in the script. UltraDev calls these functions automatically when it finds them in the script file associated with the object. The only requirement for these object API functions is that you need to specify a return value if the function requires one. This return value must be of the same type as the return value required by the function.

THE `displayHelp()` FUNCTION

It is a good practice to include a Help button in the interface you create for your extension. When a user clicks this Help button, a help file is displayed. This help file can be any HTML page or a series of pages containing information about the form or the object. You can use the `displayHelp()` function to do this.

No matter where this function is defined in your extension, UltraDev inserts the Help button below the OK and Cancel buttons on your object's interface. When the user clicks this button, the `displayHelp()` function is invoked.

In this function, you can use the `browseDocument()` function of the `dreamweaver` object, as follows:

```
function displayHelp()
{
Dreamweaver.browseDocument(helpFilePath);
}
```

This `browseDocument()` function takes the path of a file as an argument and opens the file in a new browser window. In the preceding code, `helpFilePath` can be the absolute path of the help file on your local machine, or it can be a URL.

You need to give the full path in the `browseDocument()` function. Otherwise, it will fail to work. The `Dreamweaver.getConfigurationPath()` function returns the path of the Configuration folder. It is generally a good practice to place the extension's help file in a folder inside the Shared folder of the Configuration folder so that you can locate its full path by using the `getConfigurationPath()` function, as follows:

```
var helpFilePath = dw.getConfigurationPath()+ "/Shared/ExtHelp/ExtHelp1.htm"
```

This `helpFilePath` can be passed as an argument to the `browseDocument()` function.

THE `isDomRequired()` FUNCTION

This function determines whether the object extension you create requires a valid DOM to function properly. In case the function is not defined anywhere in your extension, by default UltraDev assumes that the object requires a valid DOM to function properly.

This function returns a Boolean value. The usage of this function varies from extension to extension, because it entirely depends on what the extension is intended to do.

You can use the `isDomRequired()` function as shown in the following code:

```
function isDomRequired()
{
return true;
}
```

THE `objectTag()` FUNCTION

The `objectTag()` function is the root of the object extension, because this function inserts the string containing the HTML tags that correspond to the object into the UltraDev document at the current insertion point or selection. This function accepts no arguments and returns the string specified after the `return` statement.

The greatest advantage that you get from using this function is that it inserts the HTML code into the document as a string. This means that the tag you insert can be appended with parameters that a user inputs in the form.

For example, suppose you want to create a marquee object for IE. Here is the code for creating the string containing the `<marquee>` tag to insert the marquee object:

```
function objectTag()
{
return '\n'+'<marquee>'+document.userinp.txtfld.value+ '<'+'/marquee>';
}
```

In this example, `userinp` is the name of the form that accepts the user input, and `txtfld` is the name of the text field in which the user enters the text for the marquee. The `document.userinp.txtfld.value` statement returns the text entered in the text field. You need to encapsulate the text for the marquee inside the `<marquee>` and `</marquee>` tags. The `\n` inserts a new line after the current selection in the document.

You have to be very careful while formulating the string that is inserted. It should not contain any tags that will conflict with the tags that are in the document. For example, the string that you format must not ideally have any `<head>`, `<body>`, or `<html>` tags, because if the string is inserted with these tags, they will be a repetition of the existing `<head>`, `<body>`, and `<html>` tags that are present in the current document.

After you finish creating the object, you can see that the object is added automatically to the bottom of the Insert menu. You can change the object's location on the Insert menu by making a few modifications to the `menus.xml` file.

→ To learn how to use the menus.xml file to determine the positioning of menu items, **see** "Customizing the Menu System," **p. 467**.

THE windowDimensions() FUNCTION

The `windowDimensions()` function determines the size of the user input dialog box that UltraDev displays when a user clicks an object. This function is optional.

> **Note**
> Even if you have defined the `windowDimensions()` function, UltraDev does not display a dialog box unless the Show dialog when inserting objects check box in the General category of the Preferences dialog box is checked.

This function must be defined inside your extension either in the HTML file or in the `.js` file. The following is a sample `windowDimensions()` function:

```
function windowDimensions()
{
return "650,500";
}
```

> **Note**
> UltraDev automatically computes the dimensions of the object's dialog box if the `windowDimensions()` function is not defined. You need to define this function if you want the size of the dialog box to exceed 640×480 pixels.

EXTENDING OBJECTS   501

IMPLEMENTING THE Marquee OBJECT

In this section, you will learn to use the object API and the JavaScript API to implement a sample object that inserts a marquee into your document. This object accepts user-defined parameters for setting the marquee's attributes, such as the marquee's text, the font attributes for the text, and the marquee's background color. These attributes are combined with the <marquee> tag to insert the HTML for displaying the marquee as per user specifications. The <marquee> tag that is inserted into the document to implement the marquee is as follows:

```
<marquee bgcolor="user_defined color"><font face="user_defined font type"
color=" user_defined color "size=" user_defined size"> text_entered_by user
</font></marquee>
```

To implement this object, you need to create the interface component using HTML and the processing component using API functions.

Figure 25.1 shows the dialog box that accepts user input to define the properties of the marquee.

Figure 25.1
You use this interface to accept input from the user for the marquee object.

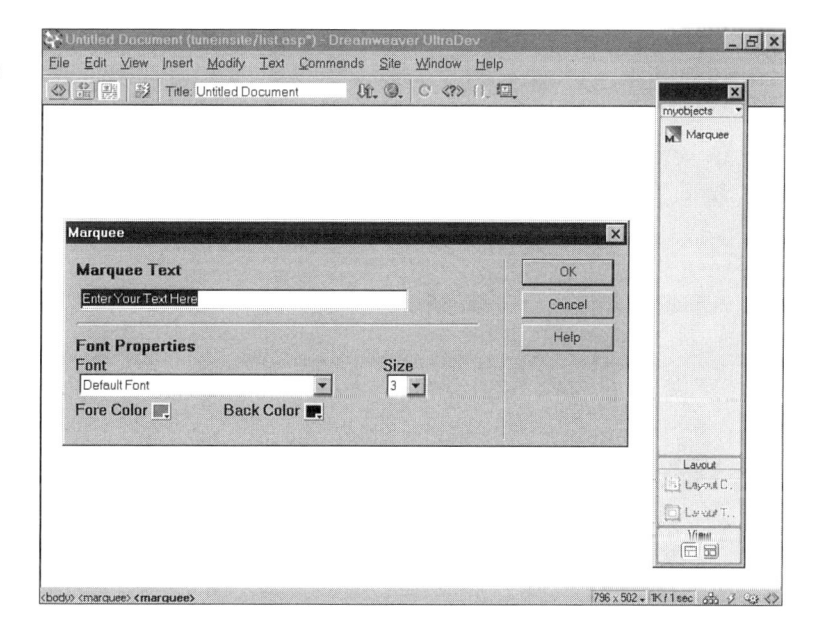

PART
V
CH
25

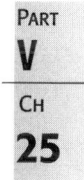

In Figure 25.1, the Marquee Text text box is a text field form object, the Font and Size drop-down lists are list/menu form objects, and the Fore Color and Back Color palettes are UltraDev built-in controls for a special form object known as mmcolorbutton. You can use this object as a value for the type attribute of the <input> tag. When used this way, the mmcolorbutton object instantiates the color button control and displays the color palette on the form. To set the initial color of the color palette, you can use the value attribute of the <input> tag to specify the color value. The following code shows how to instantiate a color button control to create a color palette with the name `mycolorpalette` and an initial green color:

```
<input type = "mmcolorbutton" name="mycolorpalette" value="#009900">
```

The HTML code for implementing the dialog box displayed in Figure 25.1 is shown in Listing 25.1.

LISTING 25.1 THE HTML INTERFACE FOR THE Marquee OBJECT

```
<html>
<head>
<title> My Marquee </title>
<meta http-equiv="content-type" content="text/html; charset=iso-8859-1">
</head>
<body>
<form name="parametersForm" action="" method="post">
<table cellspacing="0" cellpadding="0" border="0" width="433">
    <tr>
            <td width="3" height="3" valign="top"></td>
            <td width="134" height="3" valign="top"></td>
            <td width="120" height="3" valign="top"></td>
            <td width="25" height="3" valign="top"></td>
            <td width="74" height="3" valign="top"></td>
            <td width="4" height="3" valign="top"></td>
            <td width="26" height="3" valign="top"></td>
    </tr>

    <tr>
            <td width="3" height="32" valign="top"></td>
            <td height="32" colspan="5" valign="top">
            <font face="MS Sans Serif" size="2"><b>
            Marquee Text
            <input type="text" name="textfield"
            size="50" value="Enter Your Text Here"></b></font>
            </td>
            <td width="26" height="32" valign="top"></td>
    </tr>

    <tr>
            <td width="3" height="25" valign="top"></td>
            <td height="25" colspan="6" valign="top">
            <hr>
            </td>
    </tr>

    <tr>
            <td width="3" height="20" valign="top"></td>
            <td height="20" colspan="6" valign="top">
            <font face="MS Sans Serif" size="2"><b>Font Properties</b></font>
            </td>
    </tr>

    <tr>
            <td width="3" height="32" valign="top"></td>
```

LISTING 25.1 CONTINUED

```html
            <td height="32" colspan="2" valign="top">
            <font face="MS Sans Serif" size="2">Font</font>
            <select name="fontSelect" size="1">
            <option value=" " selected>Default Font</option>
            <option value="Arial, Helvetica, sans-serif">Arial, Helvetica,
            sans-serif</option>
            <option value="Times New Roman, Times, serif">Times New Roman, Times,
            serif</option>
            <option value="Courier New, Courier, mono">Courier New, Courier,
            mono</option>
            <option value="Georgia, Times New Roman, Times, serif">Georgia, Times
            New Roman, Times, serif</option>
            <option value="Verdana, Arial, Helvetica, sans-serif">Verdana, Arial,
            Helvetica, sans-serif</option>
            </select></td>
            <td width="25" height="32" valign="top"></td>
            <td width="74" height="32" valign="top">
            <font face="MS Sans Serif" size="2">Size
            <select name="sizeSelect" size="1">
            <option value="1">1</option>
            <option value="2">2</option>
            <option value="3" SELECTED>3</option>
            <option value="4">4</option>
            <option value="5">5</option>
            <option value="6">6</option>
            <option value="7">7</option>
            </select></font></td>
            <td width="4" height="32" valign="top"></td>
            <td width="26" height="32" valign="top"></td>
        </tr>

        <tr>
            <td width="3" height="26" valign="top"></td>
            <td width="134" height="26" valign="top">
            <font face="MS Sans Serif" size="2">Font
            Color
            <input type="mmcolorbutton" name="fontColor" value="red">
            </font></td>
            <td width="120" height="26" valign="top">
            <font face="MS Sans Serif" size="2">Back
            Color
            <input type="mmcolorbutton" name="backColor" value="black">
            </font></td>
            <td width="25" height="26" valign="top"></td>
            <td width="74" height="26" valign="top"></td>
            <td width="4" height="26" valign="top"></td>
            <td width="26" height="26" valign="top"></td>
        </tr>
</table>
</form>
</body>
</html>
```

Create the HTML code in Listing 25.1 and place it in a file called marquee.htm. However, the marquee is not complete as it is now. You need to add API functions to the marquee object to complete the rest of the functionality. Create the following API functions and add them to the marquee.htm file. You need to place the code shown in Listing 25.2 just after the `<meta>` tag and before the closing `</head>` tag.

LISTING 25.2 THE API FUNCTIONS TO IMPLEMENT THE Marquee OBJECT

```
<script language="JavaScript">
var finalText="";
function isDomRequired()
      {
              return true;
      }
function tagSpec()
      {
              if (document.parametersForm.textfield.value == ""){
              alert("Please  Enter The Text");
              return finalText; }
              else {
              var fontColorValue = ' color="' +
              document.parametersForm.fontColor.value + '"';
              var selectedNumber=document.parametersForm.fontSelect.selectedIndex;
              var fontStyle='face="' +
              document.parametersForm.fontSelect.options[selectedNumber].value +
➥'"';
              var fontSize='size="' +
              document.parametersForm.sizeSelect.options
              [document.parametersForm.sizeSelect.selectedIndex].value + '"';
              var bgColor = 'bgcolor="'+ document.parametersForm.backColor.value +
➥'"';
              var fontStyleHtmlTag='<Font ' + fontStyle + fontColorValue + fontSize+
              '>'+ document.parametersForm.textfield.value + '</' + 'font>';
              finalText = '\n' + '<marquee ' + bgColor + '>' + fontStyleHtmlTag +
              '<' + '/marquee>';
              return finalText;}
      }
function displayHelp()
      {
              var helpFilePath = dw.getConfigurationPath() +
              "/Shared/myHelp/MarqueeHelp.htm";
              dreamweaver.browseDocument(helpFilePath);
      }
function objectTag()
      {
              return (tagSpec());
      }
</script>
```

In Listing 25.2, two key functions are used to implement the object—tagSpec() and objectTag().The tagSpec() function retrieves the values from the form and concatenates them to create the string named finalText. It returns this text to the objectTag() function, which in turn inserts this text into the document. The other two API functions, `isDomRequired()` and `displayHelp()`, are also included in Listing 25.2. `isDomRequired()` returns true, indicating that the object requires a valid DOM to operate properly. `displayHelp()` uses the `browseDocument()` function of the Dreamweaver object to locate the help file whose path is specified in the `helpFilePath` variable.

Create a new folder called My Objects in the Objects folder, and place the marquee.htm file in it. In addition to this folder, create a GIF file with the name `marquee.gif`, and place it in the My Objects folder.

When you reload extensions, a new category called My Objects appears in the pop-up menu of the Objects panel. Click this category to view the object named `My Marquee` listed in the Objects panel, with the GIF image appearing next to it.

EXTENDING COMMANDS

You can use commands for a variety of purposes. You can use them to add HTML code to the page, edit existing HTML code, open files stored on the hard disk, and perform site manipulations that make them very powerful extensions. Commands can also be called by other extensions. Commands are stored in the Commands folder inside the Configuration folder.

You can implement command extensions just as you implement object extensions. To implement a command extension, use a combination of an HTML file and a JavaScript file or just an HTML file that contains the required script functions to execute the command. A command can be based on user input, or it might not require user input, but instead something like a selection in a document. An example of a command that requires user input is the Create Web Photo Album command, which displays a dialog box for accepting information from the user. If you create a command to justify text onscreen, the command does not require any user input, but it does require a selection, which means that the user needs to select the text onscreen before justifying it.

If a command needs user input to specify values for executing the command, you must design a form and place it in an HTML file. The head section of the HTML file contains the script that manipulates input specified by the user and performs the intended operations.

> **Note**
> One main difference between a command and an object is that each file associated with the object is displayed in the Objects panel. However, you can keep the command from being listed on the Commands menu by using the Edit Commands List option of the Commands menu.

A command is executed when a user selects the menu option corresponding to that command or when the command is explicitly called by the `runCommand()` function of the `dreamweaver` object. The `runcommand()` function takes as its argument the name of the file that contains the command instructions.

Functions to Implement Command Extensions

Just as you have API functions for writing object extensions, you also have API functions for commands. The API functions used for command extensions are discussed in the following sections.

The `canAcceptCommand()` Function

This is an optional function that can be defined by the user to verify whether the selection on the document is valid for the command to be operated. You need to use this function only when a command needs to be applicable to certain selections on the screen. This function returns a Boolean value. The menu option corresponding to the command is enabled or disabled depending on whether the return type is true or false, respectively. If this function is not defined, the command is enabled at all times, regardless of the selection on the screen.

For example, if you want the command to be performed only on a specific tag, such as the `<form>` tag, you must write the script as follows:

```
function canAcceptCommand()
{
var getDOM= dw.getDocumentDOM();
var selectedtag = getDOM.getSelectedNode();
return (selectedtag.nodeType == Node.ELEMENT_NODE &&
selectedtag.tagName=="FORM");
}
```

In this example, the `getDocumentDOM()` function of the Dreamweaver object is used to return the document tree as an object. The `getDOM` variable contains the document object. The `getSelectedNode()` function of the document object returns the tag that is currently selected from the variable `getDOM` and stores it in the variable `selectedtag`. This `selectedtag` variable is checked to see whether it is a `<form>` tag. If it is, a true value is returned by the `canAcceptCommand()` function, thereby enabling the command.

The `commandButtons()` Function

You can use the `commandButtons()` function to specify which buttons appear in a dialog box that accepts user input. This function returns an array of elements. The first element of the array specifies the label that will appear on the button, and the second element specifies the JavaScript code that will be executed when the user clicks the button. The array can contain as many elements as there are buttons, but the number of elements must be even. To create a close button in a dialog that closes the dialog when the user clicks it, use the following syntax:

```
function commandButtons()
{
return new Array("Close" , "window.close()");
}
```

In the preceding syntax, the `window.close()` function of the JavaScript API is called when the user clicks the close button. This function closes the dialog box.

Apart from the `commandButtons()` and `canAcceptCommand()` functions, you can use other API functions such as `isDomRequired()` and `windowDimensions()` in writing command extensions.

If the command requires a valid DOM to operate, you can use the `isDomRequired()` function. If the command uses a form to accept user values, you can use the `windowDimensions()` function to determine the size of the dialog box.

If the command you use contains a form to accept user input, the dialog box to accept user input is displayed. After the user finishes entering the required values, he or she must click the appropriate buttons defined by the `commandButtons()` function to execute the command.

> **Note**
> If a command does not have a form to accept user input, it cannot be called from any of the event handlers associated with the form controls. In such a case, it can be executed only by calling the `onLoad()` event handler of the `<body>` tag.

THE JUSTIFY TEXT COMMAND

In this section, you will create a command that justifies text that appears within a layer. The flow of logic for implementing this command is to first determine when the command must be enabled. You can do this by using the `canAcceptCommand()` function, which determines whether the selection on the document is text within a layer. If it is, the command must be executed. This command does not have an interface to accept user input. Therefore, it is attached to the `onLoad()` event handler of the `<body>` tag. Create a `justify.htm` file that contains the code to implement the Justify Text command, and include it in the Commands subfolder of the Configuration folder. This file will automatically be listed on the Commands menu.

Listing 25.3 illustrates how the Justify Text command can be implemented.

LISTING 25.3 THE CODE TO IMPLEMENT THE JUSTIFY TEXT COMMAND

```
<HTML>
<HEAD>
<TITLE>Text Justify</TITLE>
<script language="javascript" src="..\Shared\MM\Scripts\CMN\docInfo.js"></script>
<SCRIPT LANGUAGE="javascript">
function canAcceptCommand()
    {
        return(selectionInsideTag("div"));
    }
function justifyText()
    {
        var theDOM = dw.getDocumentDOM();
        // Get the offsets of the selection
        var theSel = theDOM.getSelection();
        // Get the outerHTML of the HTML tag (the
        // entire contents of the document)
        var theDocEl = theDOM.documentElement;
        var theWholeDoc = theDocEl.outerHTML;
        // Extract the selection
        var selText = theWholeDoc.substring(theSel[0],theSel[1]);
        // Re-insert the modified selection into the document
        theDocEl.outerHTML = theWholeDoc.substring(0,theSel[0]) +
```

Listing 25.3 Continued

```
                '<p align=' + '"' + 'justify">' + selText + '</' + 'p>'+
                theWholeDoc.substring(theSel[1]);
                // Set the selection back to where it was when you started
                theDOM.setSelection(theSel[0],theSel[1]);
    }
</SCRIPT>
</HEAD>
<BODY onLoad="justifyText()">
</BODY>
</HTML>
```

In Listing 25.3, the `selectionInsideTag()` function is called from the `canAcceptCommand()` function. This `selectionInsideTag()` function takes div as its argument to check whether the selection on the document is within the `<div>` tags. If it is, the Justify Text command is enabled. After the user selects the text within a layer and chooses the Justify Text command from the menu, the `justifyText()` function is called. It retrieves the selected text from the document and wraps a `<p>` tag around it, with the `align` attribute of the `<p>` tag set to justify. It then inserts this `<p>` tag back into the document by using the `outerHTML` attribute of the selected text.

Extending Property Inspectors

Property inspectors are the most common floating panels in the Dreamweaver UltraDev interface. They provide a GUI that lets you change an object's attributes in the document without having to go to Code view for editing.

As in the case of objects, a Property inspector is an HTML file that is stored in the Inspectors subfolder of the Configuration folder. The Property inspectors that you find in Dreamweaver are part of the Dreamweaver core and therefore are not stored in this folder. However, you can create custom Property inspectors to override the built-in Property inspectors.

These custom Property inspectors are implemented using HTML files, just as objects and commands are implemented. To create a Property inspector, first you need to design the inspector's interface. The interface of the Property inspector must conform to the specifications given by Macromedia with respect to its size and appearance. The size of a Property inspector must be fixed. It is not dockable like other floating panels, and it has two states, expanded and collapsed. You cannot have OK or Cancel buttons in the Property inspector.

To design a Property inspector, you can use layers and a tracing image. You can get the exact size of a Property inspector by using an existing Property inspector as a tracing image and then designing your Property inspector based on that layer. Layers give you more control over the positioning of elements in the Property inspector.

An important component of the Property inspector HTML file is the header. This component contains vital information that must be specified for every Property inspector you create. This information is enclosed in a comment tag. This comment tag must appear in the first line of every Property inspector HTML file. The comment tag contains the following attributes:

- `tag`—Specifies the tag that the Property inspector must inspect. It takes the name of an HTML tag as its value. It can also take any of the `*comment*`, `*locked*`, or `*asp*` values. The `*comment*` value is for inspecting comments, the `*locked*` value is for locked regions, and the `*asp*` value is for inspecting ASP code.

- `priority`—Determines the precedence of the Property inspector with respect to other inspectors that can be used for the same tag as this inspector. It can take values from 1 to 10, where 1 indicates low precedence and 10 indicates that this Property inspector precedes all other inspectors.

- `selection`—Determines how the selection must be made so that the inspector is enabled. It can take two values, `within` or `exact`. A value of `within` indicates that the Property inspector must be enabled only if the selection is within a tag, whereas a value of `exact` indicates that the selection must contain the tag that surrounds it.

- `vline`—This is an optional attribute that indicates that a vertical gray line must separate the `name` attribute of the selected tag and the rest of the tag's attributes.

- `hline`—This is also an optional attribute. It indicates that a horizontal gray line must appear in the center of the inspector when it is in the expanded mode.

- `serverModel`—This is also an optional attribute. It specifies the server model you use to create your Web site. The server model that you specify in this attribute must be the same as the server model you specify in the Site Definition dialog box for the current document. If the server models differ, the Property inspector will not appear when you make a selection.

The following code shows a completed comment tag that specifies that a Property inspector must be invoked for the `<marquee>` tag with a priority of 10, the `selection` attribute set to `exact`, and with the `hline` and `vline` attributes set:

```
<!-- tag:marquee,priority:10,selection:exact,hline,vline-->
```

After the comment tag is inserted into the Property inspector, the `<body>` tag of the inspector file must contain the `<form>` tags that determine the interface of the Property inspector. The difference between how Property inspector and object or command extensions are displayed is that the form elements are not displayed in a dialog box.

FUNCTIONS TO IMPLEMENT PROPERTY INSPECTORS

The `canInspectSelection()` and `inspectSelection()` functions are the two API functions that are required to implement Property inspectors.

The `canInspectSelection()` function specifies whether the selection contains the appropriate tag that the Property inspector can inspect. This function is similar to the `canAcceptCommand()`

function that is used in command extensions. UltraDev considers the selection for inspecting only if the `canInspectSelection()` function returns true. The following code shows that a Property inspector is applicable to the current selection only if the selection contains a `<marquee>` tag:

```
function canInspectSelection()
    {
            var mySelection =   dreamweaver.getDocumentDOM().getSelectedNode();
            return (mySelection.nodeType == Node.ELEMENT_NODE &&
            mySelection.tagName =="MARQUEE");
    }
```

The next important function is `inspectSelection()`, which determines the contents of the Property inspector. It retrieves the attributes of the current selection and sets the corresponding attributes in the Property inspector with these values. For example, Listing 25.4 indicates that the `behavior` attribute in the Property inspector must be set to the `behavior` attribute of the current selection.

LISTING 25.4 **AN EXAMPLE OF THE `inspectSelection()` FUNCTION**

```
function inspectSelection()
{
     var formSelectedIndex;
     if (selectionInsideTag('marquee'))
            {
                    var marqueeTag=getSelectedObj();
                    var behaveProperty=marqueeTag.getAttribute('behavior');
                    if (behaveProperty=='alternate'){formSelectedIndex=0;}
                    if (behaveProperty=='scroll'){formSelectedIndex=1;}
                    if (behaveProperty=='slide'){formSelectedIndex=2;}
                    alert(formSelectedIndex);
                    document.form1.behaviorSelect.selectedIndex=formSelectedIndex;
            }
}
```

Apart from these two functions, you can include the `displayHelp()` function. When you include this function, a small question mark icon appears in the top-right corner of the inspector. You can access the help file by clicking this icon.

When a user selects an element in the document, UltraDev determines which Property inspector to display according to two criteria. First, only Property inspectors that have their selection attributes set to a value of `within` are selected first. If no Property inspectors have a `within` value, Property inspectors with the `exact` value are selected. Next, UltraDev determines whether the Property inspector can inspect the selection by executing the `canInspectSelection()` function. If many Property inspectors can be called by the `canInspectSelection()` function, the Property inspector with the highest priority among the potential inspectors is selected. After the Property inspector is selected, the `inspectSelection()` function is selected.

A Property Inspector for the Marquee Object

In this section, you will learn to create a Property inspector with a few sample controls for the marquee object created earlier. Create an HTML file called marquee.htm that contains the interface for the Property inspector and the API functions that implement the functionality of the Property inspector. Save this file in the Inspectors subfolder of the Configuration folder.

You can use the <form> tag to design the interface for the Property inspector, as shown in Listing 25.5.

LISTING 25.5 THE HTML INTERFACE FOR THE Marquee PROPERTY INSPECTOR

```html
<body leftmargin="0" topmargin="0">
<form name="form1" method="post" action="">
<table cellspacing="0" cellpadding="0" border="0" width="134">
        <tr>
                <td width="1" height="1" valign="top"></td>
                <td width="5" height="1" valign="top"></td>
                <td width="59" height="1" valign="top"></td>
                <td width="1" height="1" valign="top"></td>
                <td width="1" height="1" valign="top"></td>
                <td width="60" height="1" valign="top"></td>
                <td width="14" height="1" valign="top"></td>
        </tr>
        <tr>
                <td width="1" height="19" valign="top"></td>
                <td height="19" colspan="3" valign="top"> Behavior</td>
                <td width="1" height="19" valign="top"></td>
                <td height="19" colspan="2" valign="top">
                <select name="behaviorSelect" onChange="behaviorUpdate()">
                <option value="alternate">Alternate</option>
                <option value="scroll" selected>Scroll</option>
                <option value="slide">Slide</option>
                </select>
                </td>
        </tr>
        <tr>
                <td width="1" height="3" valign="top"></td>
                <td width="5" height="3" valign="top"></td>
                <td width="59" height="22" rowspan="2" valign="top"> Direction
➥</td>
                <td width="1" height="3" valign="top"></td>
                <td width="1" height="3" valign="top"></td>
                <td width="60" height="3" valign="top"></td>
                <td width="14" height="3" valign="top"></td>
        </tr>
        <tr>
                <td width="1" height="19" valign="top"></td>
                <td width="5" height="19" valign="top"></td>
                <td width="1" height="19" valign="top"></td>
                <td width="1" height="19" valign="top"></td>
                <td width="60" height="19" valign="top">
                <select name="directionSelect" onChange="directionUpdate()">
```

LISTING 25.5 CONTINUED

```
                <option value="down">Down</option>
                <option value="up">Up</option>
                <option value="left" selected>Left</option>
                <option value="right">Right</option>
                </select>
                </td>
                <td width="14" height="19" valign="top"></td>
        </tr>
</table>
Bgcolor
<input type="mmcolorbutton" name="marqueeBgcolor" value="red"
onChange="bgcolorUpdate()">
</form>
</body>
```

The interface that you create for the Property inspector using the code in Listing 25.5 is shown in Figure 25.2.

Figure 25.2
The interface of the Property inspector for the `marquee` object.

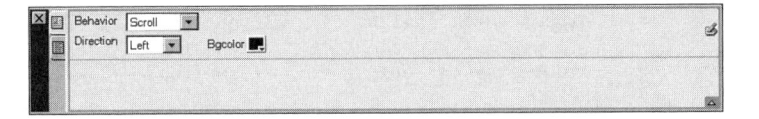

After creating this form, create the code shown in Listing 25.6 and place it before the `</head>` element in the marquee.htm file.

LISTING 25.6 THE API FUNCTIONS TO IMPLEMENT THE Marquee PROPERTY INSPECTOR

```
<!-- tag:marquee,priority:10,selection:exact,hline,vline-->
<HTML>
<HEAD>
<TITLE>Marquee Inspector</TITLE>
<script language="javascript" src="..\Shared\MM\Scripts\CMN\docInfo.js"></script>
<SCRIPT LANGUAGE="JAVASCRIPT">
function canInspectSelection()
        {
                return true;
        }
function inspectSelection()
        {
                var behSelectedIndex;
                var dirSelectedIndex;
                var colorIntial;
                if (selectionInsideTag('marquee'))
                        {
                                var marqueeTag=getSelectedObj();
                                var behaveProperty=marqueeTag.getAttribute('behavior');
                                var direcProperty=marqueeTag.getAttribute('direction');
                                colorInitial=marqueeTag.getAttribute('bgcolor');
```

LISTING 25.6 CONTINUED

```
                                 if (behaveProperty=='alternate'){behSelectedIndex=0;}
                                 if (behaveProperty=='scroll'){behSelectedIndex=1;}
                                 if (behaveProperty=='slide'){behSelectedIndex=2;}
                                 if (direcProperty=='down'){dirSelectedIndex=0;}
                                 if (direcProperty=='up'){dirSelectedIndex=1;}
                                 if (direcProperty=='left'){dirSelectedIndex=2;}
                                 if (direcProperty=='right'){dirSelectedIndex=3;}
                                 document.form1.behaviorSelect.selectedIndex=
                                 behSelectedIndex;
                                 document.form1.directionSelect.selectedIndex=
                                 dirSelectedIndex;
                                 document.form1.marqueeBgcolor.value=colorInitial;
                         }
                 }
         function behaviorUpdate()
                 {
                         var marqueeTag=getSelectedObj();
                         var selectedValue=document.form1.behaviorSelect.selectedIndex;
                         var behaviorValue=
                         document.form1.behaviorSelect.options[selectedValue].value;
                         marqueeTag.setAttribute('behavior',behaviorValue);
                 }
         function directionUpdate()
                 {
                         var marqueeTag=getSelectedObj();
                         var selectedValue=document.form1.directionSelect.selectedIndex;
                         var directionValue=
                         document.form1.directionSelect.options[selectedValue].value;
                         marqueeTag.setAttribute('direction',directionValue);
                 }
         function bgcolorUpdate()
                 {
                         var marqueeTag=getSelectedObj();
                         var selectedValue=document.form1.marqueeBgcolor.value;
                         marqueeTag.setAttribute('bgcolor',selectedValue);
                 }
</script>
</head>
```

In Listing 25.6, the canInspectSelection() function checks whether the current selection contains a marquee tag. If it does, the Property inspector is called. The control next passes to the inspectSelection() function, which reflects the attributes of the current selection in the controls in the Property inspector. When the user changes an attribute in the Property inspector, the changes are immediately reflected on the selected element in the document, because the function that updates the selection is called by the onChange() event handler associated with the control in the Property inspector. For example, if a user selects a behavior from the Behavior drop-down list, the onChange() attribute of the <select> tag containing the name behaviorSelect calls the behaviorUpdate() function of JavaScript API. This function updates the behavior of the selection by using the SetAttribute() function of the JavaScript API.

Extending Floating Panels

You can use floating panels to set properties for document elements similar to the way you use Property inspectors. However, floating panels differ from Property inspectors in two main aspects. They do not have restrictions on size and layout as Property inspectors do. In addition, they need to be called explicitly, unlike Property inspectors, which get invoked automatically when placed in the Inspectors folder of the Configurations folder.

You can create custom floating panels if you want to add more room and flexibility to an interface that is used to set the properties of document elements. You can incorporate the same features of a Property inspector in a floating panel and add more features and functionality to the floating panel. For example, if your custom Property inspector lets you set only certain attributes for an object, you can use a floating panel that has more space to allow you to set more attributes for the same object.

To create a custom floating panel, you need to create an HTML file that determines the floating panel's interface. This file contains a form that specifies what controls must appear on the interface by means of form elements. You can use a combination of UltraDev and JavaScript API functions to implement the functionality of a floating panel. These functions can be placed inside the HTML file of the floating panel just as you do for any other extension, such as an object or a Property inspector. A floating panel needs to have the two basic features found in a Property inspector. First, it must reflect the attributes of the current selection when it appears in the Document window. Second, it must allow users to specify properties for the selection in the interface and then update the selection with these properties.

Functions to Implement Floating Panels

To invoke a floating panel, you must use one of the three UltraDev API functions—`toggleFloater()`, `getFloaterVisibility()`, or `setFloaterVisibility()`—of the Dreamweaver object. These three functions take the name of the floating panel's HTML file as their arguments. One of these functions must be explicitly called by a menu item or from another extension. When one of these functions is called, UltraDev locates the floating panel's HTML file from the Floaters folder of the Configuration folder.

> **Note**
> The built-in floating panels of the UltraDev interface are not placed in the Floaters folder because they are part of the core of the UltraDev code.

After UltraDev locates the required HTML file associated with the floating panel, it searches for any of the floating panel's API functions. One of these functions is the `initialPosition()` function, which determines the initial default position of the floating panel on the screen. This function is optional. It takes the computer's platform as its argument. You can determine the position of the floating panel by returning the position as a string that contains the number of pixels from the left and top of the screen. If UltraDev finds the `initialPosition()` function, it displays the floating panel depending on the value returned by the `initialPosition()` function.

As mentioned earlier, the floating panel needs to have the same two main functions that a Property inspector does. First, it needs to reflect the changes made to a selection. To do this, you must use the `selectionChanged()` function and define its functionality such that the floating panel tracks the selection. The next functionality you must add is to update the selection's attributes, depending on the values you specify in the floating panel. To do this, you can use JavaScript functions that contain code to update the values and call these functions from the event handlers of the form elements in the floating panel interface.

After creating a floating panel, you can call it from any other extension. You can even attach the floating panel to a button in the Property inspector. You can also call a floating panel from a menu by creating a `<menuitem>` tag in the `menus.xml` file. To do this, you need to set the `command` attribute of the `<menuitem>` tag to the `dw.toggleFloater()` function in the `menus.xml` file. If you want to include the floating panel on the Window menu, you need to include the `<menuitem>` tag within the `<menu name="_Window" id="DWMenu_Window"> </menu>` tag pair in the `menus.xml` file.

Summary

You can implement interface extensions such as objects, Property inspectors, floating panels, and commands by using a combination of HTML and JavaScript. You use HTML to design the interface of the extension you create and then implement the extension's functionality by using JavaScript and UltraDev API functions. Each extension comes with its own set of API functions whose return values are predetermined. The body of the function is not predetermined. This allows developers to custom-code these functions to implement the functionality they require. The interface extensions are easy to add to the UltraDev environment, because you just need to place them in their respective folders in the Configuration folder, and UltraDev automatically calls them. The floating panel extension is an exception. It needs to be called explicitly from a menu item or another extension.

PART VI

APPENDIXES

- **A** Installing and Configuring Supporting Technologies 519
- **B** Dreamweaver UltraDev Web Sites and References 529
- **C** XML, HTML, and JavaScript Reference 535
- **D** Creating a Database Using Microsoft Access 551

  Glossary 559

APPENDIX A

INSTALLING AND CONFIGURING SUPPORTING TECHNOLOGIES

In this appendix

Internet Information Server (IIS) 4.0 520

Installing SQL Server 7.0 521

ColdFusion Server 4.5 522

Dreamweaver UltraDev 4.0 524

Allaire JRun 3.0 526

Windows DSN 528

Internet Information Server (IIS) 4.0

To test the ASP or ColdFusion application developed locally, you need a Web server. The Web servers you can use are Personal Web Server (PWS) or IIS 4.0. The choice depends on the operating system you installed on the machine. Windows 9*x* supports PWS, and Windows NT 4.0 Server supports IIS 4.0. You can install IIS 4.0 from the Windows NT 4.0 Option Pack. If your operating system is Windows 2000, the IIS 5.0 service is integrated with the operating system. In this case, you need to install IIS by using Control Panel.

Installing IIS 4.0

Follow these steps to install and configure IIS 4.0 on Windows NT Server:

1. Insert the Windows NT 4.0 Option Pack CD into the CD-ROM drive. The Welcome page for the Windows NT 4.0 Option Pack setup is displayed. Click Install.
2. In the page that is displayed, click the Install Windows NT 4.0 Option Pack link.
3. The File Download dialog box is displayed. Select the Run This Program from Its Current Location option, and click OK.
4. The Security Warning dialog box is displayed. Click Yes. If Windows Service Pack 4.0 is installed, a message box is displayed. Click Yes to continue.
5. The Welcome screen for the Option Pack setup is displayed. Click Next.
6. The End User License Agreement dialog box is displayed. Click Accept, and then click Next.
7. The setup options are displayed. Choose the Typical option.
8. The Select Components dialog box is displayed, as shown in Figure A.1. Ensure that the Internet Information Server (IIS) option is selected, and then click Next.

Figure A.1
Specify the services to be installed using the Select Components dialog box.

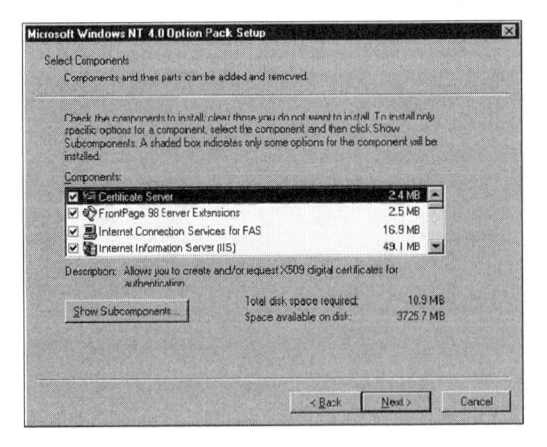

9. The default folders for WWW publishing home directory, FTP publishing home directory, and application files are displayed. You can accept default folders and click Next to continue.
10. The Completing Installation dialog box is displayed. Click Finish to complete the installation of IIS 4.0. A message box prompting you to restart the system is displayed. Click Yes to restart.

> **Note:** If you selected other services in the Setup Components dialog box, such as MTS, the respective services might require additional options to be configured.

After the system is restarted, the IIS service is configured to run on your system. You can use the Internet Service Manager management console to manage the IIS service.

INSTALLING SQL SERVER 7.0

To install SQL Server 7.0, follow these steps:

1. Insert the Microsoft SQL Server 7.0 CD into your CD drive. The Autorun.exe file executes automatically, and the Microsoft SQL Server screen is displayed.
2. From the list of options that is displayed, select Install SQL Server 7.0 Components. The Install SQL Server 7.0 Components screen is displayed.

> **Note:** If your operating system is Windows 95, select SQL Server 7.0 Prerequisites, and click Install Common Controls Library Update.

3. From the list of options displayed, select the Database Server-Standard Edition option.
4. In the Select Install Method dialog box that is displayed, select the Local Install-Install to the Local Machine option to install SQL Server on the local machine, and then click Next. If you want to perform remote installation, select the Remote Install-Install on the Remote Computer option, and type the name of the remote computer or click Browse to locate the remote computer.
5. The Welcome dialog box is displayed, warning you to close all Windows-based programs before you run the setup. Click Next.
6. The Software License Agreement dialog box is displayed. Click Yes to accept the agreement.

7. In the User Information dialog box that is displayed, enter your name and the name of your organization, and then click Next.
8. In the Setup dialog box that is displayed, enter the CD key number, and click OK. The Setup dialog box displays your Product ID. Click OK.
9. The Setup Type dialog box is displayed. From the list of setup options that is displayed, select the Typical option to install SQL Server with all the most common options. In the Destination Folder section, specify the location where you want to save the program files and data files. Click Next.
10. The Service Accounts dialog box is displayed. You need to set a domain password in this dialog box. Accept other default settings, and click Next.
11. The Start Copying Files dialog box is displayed, informing you that the setup files will be copied after you click Next. Click Next to start copying the setup files.
12. The Choose Licensing Mode dialog box is displayed. Choose the options according to the license agreement, and then click Continue. This begins your SQL Server 7.0 installation.
13. The Setup Complete dialog box is displayed. Select Yes I want to restart my computer now, and click Finish.

ColdFusion Server 4.5

Macromedia's ColdFusion 4.5 Server is a cross-platform Web application server. You can get a copy of both UltraDev 4 and ColdFusion 4.5 in the ColdFusion 4.5 UltraDev 4 Studio pack. You can download the evaluation copy of ColdFusion 4.5 UltraDev 4 Studio from http://www.macromedia.com/software/ultradev/special/coldfusion/. You can install the ColdFusion server only on a Web server, such as Microsoft PWS or IIS.

Installing ColdFusion Server 4.5

To set up ColdFusion Server on your Windows system, you need to ensure that you satisfy the following system requirements:

- Windows 95, 98, Windows NT 4.0, Windows 2000, or Windows ME
- Intel Pentium or above
- 128MB RAM (recommended is 512MB)
- 150MB of free hard disk space

After you ensure that these requirements are satisfied, follow these steps to install ColdFusion Server 4.5:

1. Run the ColdFusion installation .exe from the CD. In the Welcome screen that is displayed, click Next.
2. Click Yes in the Software License Agreement dialog box that is displayed.

3. In the User Information dialog box, enter the required information, such as your name and the name of your organization, and then click Next.

4. In the Choose Destination Location dialog box, specify the folder in which to install ColdFusion Server 4.5, and then click Next.

> **Note** If you do not specify the folder, ColdFusion Server will be installed in the CFUSION folder, which is on the root drive of your local machine.

5. In the Select Web Server dialog box, select the Microsoft IIS Peer Web Server or Personal Web Server option, depending on the server you installed. If you installed other Web servers, such as Apache Web Server, select the Other Server option. After selecting the server, click Next.

6. In the Select Web Server Document Directory dialog box, specify the default directory of your Web server, and then click Next.

7. The Select Install Options dialog box is displayed, as shown in Figure A.2. Select the necessary options, and then click Next.

Figure A.2
Use the Select Install Options dialog box to specify the components that can be installed with ColdFusion server.

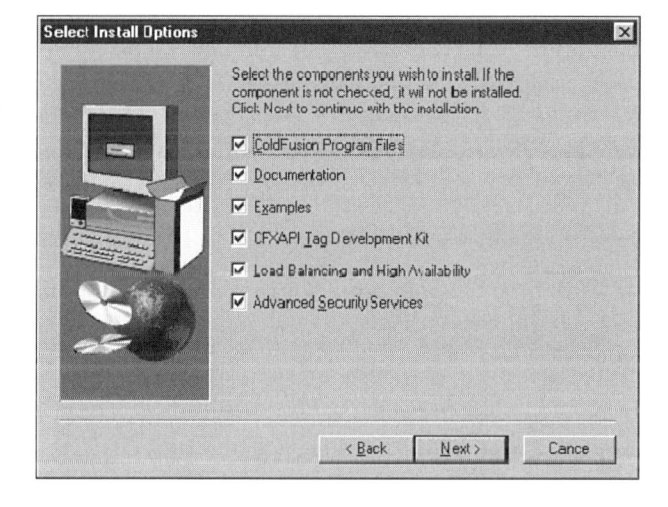

8. The Server High Availability dialog box is displayed. If the Yes option is enabled, ColdFusion assumes that the server will act as a failover server in case any cluster members in the Web farm fail. Click Next.

9. In the Select Administrator Password dialog box, type the password for ColdFusion Administrator, and confirm it in the Confirm text box. Click Next.

10. The Select ColdFusion Studio Password dialog box is displayed. Type the password, confirm it, and click Next. The ColdFusion studio requires this password before you can access the ColdFusion server.
11. The Select Program Folder dialog box is displayed. Program icons are added to the specified folder. Click Next.
12. The Start Copying Files dialog box is displayed. Click Next.
13. You see a warning message informing you that ColdFusion Active Directory Services Interface (ADSI) Installer will run. Click OK.
14. A message box is displayed, informing you that the ADSI 2.0 services are installed. Click Yes to continue.
15. You see a message box prompting you to restart the system. Click Yes to restart.

After the system restarts, ColdFusion displays the Welcome page in the Web browser. Click Test Your Installation Under Installation option and follow the instructions to test the installation. After testing, you can use the local Web server to publish ColdFusion pages that are created in UltraDev.

Dreamweaver UltraDev 4.0

In addition to the features of Dreamweaver 4.0, UltraDev 4.0 provides support for building Web applications by using ASP, JSP, and ColdFusion.

System Requirements for Dreamweaver UltraDev

You can install Dreamweaver UltraDev on a Windows system or on a Macintosh system.

Here are the system requirements to install UltraDev on a Windows platform:

- 166MHz or faster Intel Pentium processor on Windows 9*x*, Windows Me, Windows NT 4.0 with Service Pack 5.0 or above, or Windows 2000
- 64MB of RAM
- 170MB of free hard disk space
- Macromedia Flash Player. This is available with the UltraDev CD, or you can download it from http://www.macromedia.com/software/flashplayer/downloads/.

Here are the system requirements to install UltraDev on a Macintosh platform:

- Power Macintosh running Mac OS 8.6 or higher
- 64MB of RAM
- 130MB of free disk space
- Macromedia Flash Player

> **Note:** If you install UltraDev on a Macintosh system, you must use the JDBC driver to connect to a database on a server.

INSTALLING DREAMWEAVER ULTRADEV

To install Dreamweaver UltraDev, follow these steps:

1. Insert the Dreamweaver UltraDev CD into the CD-ROM drive.
2. Run the UltraDev installer file on the CD to launch InstallShield Wizard.
3. The Extracting Files dialog box is displayed. After the file is extracted completely, click Next.
4. The Macromedia Dreamweaver UltraDev Welcome screen is displayed. Click Next.
5. The License Agreement dialog box is displayed. Click Yes.
6. In the Choose Destination Location dialog box, select the destination directory in which to install UltraDev, and then click Next.
7. The Default Editor dialog box is displayed, as shown in Figure A.3. This dialog box displays a list of files that can use UltraDev as their default editor. If you do not want any or some of these files to use UltraDev as the default editor, deselect them and click Next.

Figure A.3
Use the Default Editor dialog box to specify the file types that use UltraDev as the default editor.

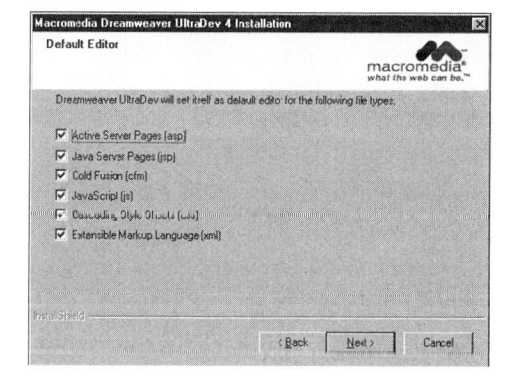

8. The Select Program Folder dialog box is displayed. Click Next.
9. The Start Copying Files dialog box is displayed. Click Next.
10. The Setup Status dialog box is displayed. The files are copied to the specified destination folder.
11. The final screen of InstallShield Wizard is displayed. Click Finish. The UltraDev Resources of Interest page is displayed. Macromedia Dreamweaver UltraDev is now ready to use.

Allaire JRun 3.0

Allaire's JRun 3.0 is a Java application server. You can use JRun to deploy e-commerce solutions. Four editions are available for JRun 3.0: Enterprise, Advanced, Professional, and Developer.

Requirements for Allaire JRun 3.0

You can install the JRun server on Windows 9*x*, Windows NT, Windows 2000, Red Hat Linux 6.x, and HP-UX 11.0. The following system requirements must be satisfied to install the JRun server:

- A minimum of 32MB of RAM
- 20MB of free disk space
- Java Runtime Environment (JRE) 1.1

> **Note:** JRE 1.2.2 or later is required for EJB, JTA, and JMS applications.

- Microsoft Internet Explorer 4.0 or later or Netscape Communicator 4.0

Installing JRun Server 3.0

Follow these steps to install JRun 3.0 Developer Edition:

1. Run the JRun installation file from the CD.
2. Click Next in the Welcome to JRun Setup screen.
3. The JRun License Agreement dialog box is displayed. Click Yes to accept the terms of the agreement and continue.
4. The JRun Product Serial Number dialog box is displayed. Enter a serial number for JRun Developer edition, and then click Next.
5. The JRun Installation Folder is displayed. Click Next to accept the default destination directory and continue.
6. The Setup Type dialog box is displayed. Select the Full, Minimal, or Custom option, and then click Next.
7. The Select Program Folder dialog box is displayed. Click Next.
8. The installation files are copied. The Install JRun Services dialog box is displayed, with the Install JRun Services option selected. This option enables the autostart of JRun services along with the operating system. Click Next.
9. The Select a Java Runtime dialog box is displayed. If your applications require EJB support, select Java Runtime 1.2, and then click Next.

10. The JVM Advisor dialog box is displayed, with JVM (Java virtual machine) settings for your machine already selected. Click Next.
11. The JRun Management Console dialog box is displayed. Specify the port to be used to access JMC in the JRun Admin Service Port Number text box, and then click Next.
12. In the next screen, you need to specify the admin password for the JMC admin account used to administer JRun.
13. The JRun Product Information dialog box is displayed. Enter the required details if you want to receive information on JRun updates. Click Next.
14. The JRun Setup Complete dialog box is displayed. Click Finish to complete the configuration process.

Configuring JRun Application Server

After installing JRun, you need to configure the server by using JRun Application Management Console. To configure JRun for deploying Web applications, do the following:

1. In the first screen of the JRun Application Management Console, the user login dialog box is displayed, as shown in Figure A.4. Enter the JRun administrator's username and password, and then click login.

Figure A.4
You can use the JRun Application Management screen to log in by specifying the username.

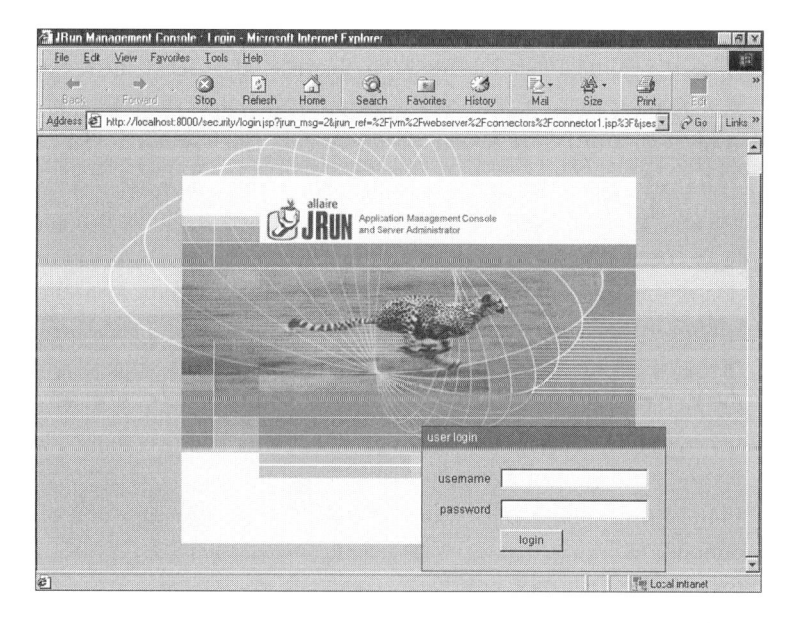

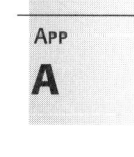

2. In the JRun Server Information dialog box that is displayed, select JRun Admin Server from the JRun Server Name list box.

3. Select Microsoft Internet Information Server from the Web Server Type drop-down list to use it as the Web server for the JRun Application server. Click Next.
 4. The JRun Server Connection Module Settings Information dialog box is displayed. Specify the JRun Server IP address in the JRun Server IP Address text box. This IP address must be the local host IP address. Specify the connector port in the JRun Server Connector Port text box. Click Next.
 5. In the Directory dialog box, specify the default directory for IIS scripts. This directory is used to install the JRun Connection Module. Click Next.
 6. The Installation Status dialog box is displayed. Click Done to complete the JRun setup and open Application Management Console and Server Administrator.

Windows DSN

You can use Windows DSN to establish a database connection. The DSN contains information that is used by ODBC Driver Manager to connect to an ODBC database. The DSN can be stored in a file or in the Windows System Registry.

Configuring Windows DSN for SQL Server Databases

Follow these steps to configure DSN for SQL Server databases on a Windows NT system:

 1. Open the Control Panel window. Double-click the ODBC Data Sources icon.
 2. In the ODBC Data Source Administrator dialog box, click the System DSN tab. It displays a list of DSNs created on the system. Click Add to add a new DSN.
 3. The Create New Data Source dialog box is displayed. A list of data sources and drivers loaded on your system appears. Select SQL Server from the list, and then click Finish.
 4. In the Create New Data Source to SQL Server dialog box, type the name and description of the data source. Select the name of the SQL server from the Server list box. Click Next.
 5. In the Microsoft SQL Server DSN Configuration dialog box that is displayed, specify the kind of authentication you are using to connect to the SQL server. Click Next.
 6. In the Create a New Data Source to SQL Server dialog box, the default database options are displayed. Click Next.
 7. In the Create a New Data Source to SQL Server dialog box, the language settings options are displayed. Accept the default values, and click Finish.
 8. The ODBC Microsoft SQL Server dialog box is displayed. Click OK. The DSN is created. You can test the created DSN by clicking Test Data Source.
 9. In the ODBC Data Source Administrator dialog box, click OK to finish configuring the DSN for a SQL Server database.

APPENDIX B

DREAMWEAVER ULTRADEV WEB SITES AND REFERENCES

In this appendix

JSP Sites   530

ASP Sites   531

ColdFusion Sites   532

Dreamweaver UltraDev Sites   533

HTML and XML Sites   534

This appendix contains links to Web sites that provide useful information on Dreamweaver UltraDev, extensions in UltraDev, and server technologies supported by UltraDev.

JSP Sites

TABLE B.1 Synopsis of JSP Web Sites

Site	Synopsis
http://www.apl.jhu.edu/~hall/java/Servlet-Tutorial	Provides an online tutorial on servlets in JavaServer Pages 1.0. In addition, it provides information about the JSP architecture and tags, and syntax and examples for each JSP tag.
http://developer.java.sun.com/developer/onlineTraining/JSPIntro/contents.html	Provides a short course written by Java Software licensee jGuru that helps you learn how to use Java Server Pages to develop dynamic Web sites by exploring the syntax and components of JSP development. In addition, it provides information about the advantages of the JSP technology, JSP tags and syntax, the life cycle of a JSP page, and the use of JavaBean components in JSP pages.
http://java.sun.com/products/jsp	Provides detailed information about the JSP server technology. Sun Microsystems owns this site.
http://www.jspin.com	Provides links to Web sites containing information about JSP pages. In addition, it provides a directory of JSP tutorials, applications, scripts, books, references, and articles for different audiences, beginner to advanced.
http://www.allaire.com/products/jrun/	Provides detailed information about JRun 3.0.
http://www.devbeach.com	Provides online tutorials on ASP, C++, ColdFusion, Java, JavaScript, Palm, Perl, PHP, and Visual Basic.
http://www.jsptut.com	Provides an online tutorial on JSP. This tutorial includes both simple and complex examples of JSP.
http://jsptags.com	Provides a directory of JSP tags, tag libraries, and bean libraries.
http://www.jspinsider.com	Provides articles, tutorials, sample code, and general information on JSP.
http://www.burridge.net/jsp/jspinfo.html	Provides online information about JSP and useful books and links to Web sites on JSP. In addition, it provides online articles on JSP.

ASP Sites

Table B.2 Synopsis of ASP Web Sites

Site	Synopsis
`http://www.stardeveloper.com`	Provides articles and tutorials on ASP and JSP. In addition, it provides tutorials on creating and using COM components.
`http://hotwired.lycos.com/webmonkey/98/39/index2a.html?tw=programming`	Provides an introduction by Kevin Cooke to Active Server Pages and syntax used in ASP.
`http://www.aspin.com`	Provides information, reference books, and Web sites on ASP pages. The information in this Web site caters to different audiences, beginner to advanced.
`http://www.4guysfromrolla.com`	Provides the latest updates and reference Web sites on ASP. It also provides articles on ASP, some ASP coding tips, and FAQs about ASP.
`http://msdn.Microsoft.com/workshop/server/asp/ASPover.asp`	Provides information about the Microsoft server technology, ASP. It also provides information about the built-in COM objects and methods supported by ASP.
`http://www.w3schools.com/asp`	Provides information about how the ASP server technology lets you create dynamic and interactive Web pages. On this site, you will find complete information about built-in COM objects and components and their properties and methods. In addition, this site includes a quiz on ASP to test your level of understanding. You can refer to this site for simple examples of the objects in ASP.
`http://www.trainingtools.com/online/ASP/index.htm`	Provides an introduction to the ASP technology and the Common Gateway Interface (CGI). In addition, it provides information about the commonly used built-in objects in ASP, VBScript, and server side scripting.
`http://www.asptoday.com`	Provides recent updates on ASP. This site is a daily knowledge site for professional ASP programmers.
`http://www.asp101.com`	Provides detailed information about ASP. In addition, it provides articles, tutorials, and FAQs on ASP and sample code on ASP and related technologies.
`http://www.Chilisoft.com/products/`	Provides information about ChiliSoft ASP.

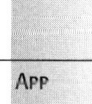

Table B.2 Continued

Site	Synopsis
http://www.learnasp.com	Provides a list of free ASP components, book reviews, tutorials, links to other ASP sites, and popular database tutorials.
http://www.asphole.com	Provides tutorials, articles, and reference materials on ASP.
http://www.cfvault.com/index.cfm/mode/DisplayTutorial/TuUUID/402546EF-8CF1-11D4-93D100D0B765C726	Provides a guide to Cold Fusion error handling by Stephen Tual.

ColdFusion Sites

Table B.3 Synopsis of ColdFusion Web Sites

Site	Synopsis
http://www.allaire.com/Products/ColdFusion/productinformation	Provides information about the ColdFusion server technology in a structured manner. This site belongs to Allaire.
http://www.cfvault.com	Provides the most popular hands-on ColdFusion training. This site also provides links to jobs, forums, events, news, tutorials, and articles on ColdFusion.
http://cc-www.oulu.fi/cfpro/tutorial/tutorial.htm	Provides a tutorial on the basics of using ColdFusion.
http://www.sims.berkeley.edu/courses/is213/s99/Readings/cold-fusion-tutorial/tutorial	Provides detailed information about the basics of ColdFusion, the ColdFusion architecture, and ColdFusion Data Input Forms.
http://forestry.msu.edu/cfpro/getstart.htm	Provides an interactive introduction to the use of ColdFusion. In addition, it provides examples of applications that illustrate ColdFusion development techniques, and an online information and technical support forum.
http://www.allaire.com/products/ColdFusion	Provides detailed information about Macromedia ColdFusion 5.
http://www.defusion.com	Provides news, articles, links, and good reference guides on ColdFusion.

Dreamweaver UltraDev Sites

Table B.4 Synopsis of Dreamweaver UltraDev Web Sites

Site	Synopsis
http://www.macromedia.com/software/dreamweaver	Provides detailed information about Dreamweaver UltraDev. This site belongs to Macromedia.
http://www.dreamweaverfever.com	Provides valuable information about Dreamweaver and Dreamweaver UltraDev.
http://hotwired.lycos.com/webmonkey/01/01/index1a.html	Provides an overview of the Dreamweaver interface and other features of Dreamweaver.
http://www.basic-ultradev.com/	Provides a complete reference on UltraDev 4 and its related server technologies.
http://www.projectseven.com	Provides tools for learning Dreamweaver. In addition, it provides information on Dreamweaver Web tutorials, extensions, and resources.
http://www.udzone.com	Provides links, tutorials, and updates on the latest extensions in UltraDev. It also provides FAQs on Dreamweaver UltraDev.
http://www.ultradeviant.co.uk	Provides a tutorial on Dreamweaver UltraDev by Owen Palmer.
http://www.macromedia.com/support/dreamweaver/ts/documents/dream_websites.htm	Provides links to books and Web sites that contain useful information for Web designers using Dreamweaver.
http://hotwired.lycos.com/webmonkey/98/27/index1a.html	Provides a tutorial on Dreamweaver by Taylor.
http://www.macromedia.com/support/dreamweaver/ts/documents/quick_tips.htm	Provides tips for Dreamweaver users.
http://idm.internet.com/articles/200002/dream_index.html	Provides a tutorial on Dreamweaver 3 by Troy Dreier.
http://wally.rit.edu/instruction/web/drw3	Provides basic tutorials, archived Dreamweaver tutorials, and Dreamweaver reference sites.
http://www.learnthat.com/courses/viewlets/dreamweaver/index.shtml	Provides tutorials and courses on DreamWeaver.
http://illinois.online.uillinois.edu/stovall/DreamWorkshop	Provides tutorials on how to use styles, layers, behaviors, and frames in Dreamweaver.
http://www.macromdia.com/support/dreamweaver/	Provides information on application building in Dreamweaver UltraDev. This is an UltraDev support center.
http://www.macromdia.com/support/ultradev/	Provides information and support on Web site creation and Web page design in Dreamweaver UltraDev. This is a Dreamweaver support center.

Table B.4 Continued

Site	Synopsis
http://www.macromedia.com/support/ultradev/ts/documents/ultradev_newsgrp.htm	Provides information on accessing the UltraDev discussion group on the Macromedia site. This is a very useful site because you can discuss technical issues and share useful tips and tricks with other UltraDev users.
http://hotwired.lycos.com/webmonkey/99/11/index2a.html	Provides an introduction to Dreamweaver extensions.
http://hotwired.lycos.com/webmonkey/authoring/tools/tutorials/tutorial1.html	Provides lessons on creating forms, images, and tables. It also contains information about style sheets.
http://www.dreamweaver-extensions.com	Provides instructions for installing Dreamweaver extensions.

HTML and XML Sites

Table B.5 Synopsis of HTML and XML Web Sites

Site	Synopsis
http://w3.one.net/~jhoffman/sqltut.htm	Provides a comprehensive tutorial on Structured Query Language (SQL).
http://www.iboost.com/build/programming/html/index.html	Provides the basics of HTML and XML and gives URLs and links to HTML tutorials.
http://www.xml.com	Provides information about XML tags and links to XML tutorials.
http://davesite.com/webstation/html	Provides a hands-on tutorial on HTML. This site also provides some exercises to test your HTML skills.
http://www.gorin.com/class/class.html	Provides a quick tutorial on the basics of writing Web pages by using HTML.
http://www.stardeveloper.com/html.asp	Provides a tutorial on the basics of HTML. This tutorial covers information about the structure of an HTML document, basic HTML tags, text basics, multimedia, hyperlinks, formatted lists, tables, and frames in HTML.

APPENDIX C

XML, HTML, AND JAVASCRIPT REFERENCE

In this appendix

    XML Reference   536

    HTML Reference   541

    JavaScript Reference   544

XML Reference

Information is transmitted over the Web in the form of documents containing structured data ranging from plain text to vector graphics, mathematical equations, and so on. Two major concerns exist in handling the information contained in these documents. The most prevalent concern is rendering these documents on heterogeneous computer systems. The second and growing is allowing these heterogeneous computer systems to intelligently interpret and process this information. Although HTML is sufficient to indicate how data must be formatted and displayed on various computer systems, it has no provision for describing this data such that Web applications can interpret and process the data. XML is a solution that describes and identifies structured data. This feature of XML enables the interpretation and exchange of data between applications.

XML is a meta-markup language that offers a set of rules that you can apply to documents containing structured data. Applying this set of rules standardizes the way data is described and allows applications to identify and interpret data easily. XML lets you describe the data in documents by using tags. If you want to highlight an important piece of information in your document that needs to be processed in a particular way, you can describe that information by creating your own customized tags and enclosing that information within the customized tag you create.

An XML document differs from an HTML document in the number and variety of tags you can create. HTML tags are restricted in number and type, whereas XML tags are user-defined, which means that you can create as many tags as you want. However, these tags must follow the syntax rules specified by the W3C, the most important of which are described in the next section. The data in an XML document is enclosed within the user-defined tags. For example, in the menus.xml file, the <menubar>, <menu>, and <menuitem> tags are customized XML tags that describe the menu system in UltraDev. After you create an XML document, you can create applications to recognize and read the data contained within these tags.

The main advantage of using XML to mark up documents is that it provides a simple standard format for describing data that enables easy interchange of data between applications running on heterogeneous systems. XML documents are essentially text files. Therefore, they are independent of various file and database formats present in different computer systems. XML is extensible, which means that you can create as many tags as required to describe data and also create nested tags to any desired level of complexity. The power of XML's extensibility is such that you can create your own markup language by using XML. For example, VoxML is an XML-based markup language that was created by Motorola for developing voice applications.

Another advantage of using XML is that it separates the format-related information about data from the data itself. This frees the application from format-related issues, which lets it focus on interpreting and processing the data. Applications have greater flexibility in deciding how the data must be displayed, because XML does not indicate how data must be formatted. To tackle format-related issues, applications can use the XML Stylesheet Transformation Language (XSLT). XSLT is an application written in XML that is used to create style sheets. These style sheets provide information about how the data in an XML document must be converted to any other format, such as an HTML or ASP page. The process of converting the data in an XML document to another format is known as *transformation*.

Applications use XSLT to format the data that must be displayed, and they use scripting languages to interpret and process this data.

CREATING XML DOCUMENTS

You can create and edit an XML document in any text editor. XML documents consist of the following main components:

- Elements
- Content
- Attributes
- Comments
- Prolog
- Document Type Definition
- Entities

ELEMENTS

Elements denote pieces of data in a document. They describe data by means of tags. For example, if your document contains information about books, you can create an element called BOOK to denote the information contained in a document as belonging to a book. This BOOK element can then be translated to a paired tag called <BOOK>, which has a starting tag and an ending tag. Elements that are represented by starting and ending tags are called container elements. Apart from container elements, there are also empty elements. These elements are represented by empty tags, which are not written in pairs.

The following is an XML document that contains three elements: BOOK, TITLE, and AUTHOR. Each element is a container element with a starting tag and an ending tag:

```
<BOOK>
<TITLE> Far From the Madding Crowd </TITLE>
<AUTHOR> Thomas Hardy </AUTHOR>
</BOOK>
```

CONTENT

Content refers to the information contained between a tag pair. In the preceding example, the information regarding books constitutes the content of that XML document.

Attributes

Attributes further define an element by specifying additional information about that element. For example, you can further define the BOOK element by specifying the language in which the book is written. To do this, you can add an attribute called LANGUAGE to the <BOOK> tag that takes the language in which the book is written as its value.

The following XML document shows the LANGUAGE attribute of the <BOOK> tag:

```
<BOOK LANGUAGE = "English">
<TITLE> Far From the Madding Crowd </TITLE>
<AUTHOR> Thomas Hardy </AUTHOR>
</BOOK>
```

Comments

Comments are similar to the comment tags in HTML documents. The syntax of a comment tag in an XML document has the same syntax as a comment tag in an HTML document, in which a comment is enclosed within the <!-- and --> tags.

Prolog

The prolog indicates the version of the XML specification to which the XML document conforms. If the XML document you create conforms to version 1.0, the prolog is written as follows:

```
<? xml version="1.0"?>
```

Document Type Definition

An XML document can have a Document Type Definition (DTD) that helps applications understand the structure of the XML document. A DTD provides vital information about an XML document, such as the elements that are present in the document, the nesting between the elements in the document, the attributes an element can have, and so on. This DTD is an optional component of an XML document. However, if you are planning to use a DTD, you must have a declaration for it in your XML document. The following XML document contains a DTD called books.dtd that is included for the example discussed earlier:

```
<? xml version="1.0"?>
<!doctype BOOK SYSTEM "books.dtd">
<BOOK LANGUAGE = "English">
<TITLE> Far From the Madding Crowd </TITLE>
<AUTHOR> Thomas Hardy </AUTHOR>
</BOOK>
```

Entities

Entities are pieces of text or whole XML documents that you can use in other XML documents. For example, if you want to use the title of a book throughout a document, you can create an entity called `title` that refers to the title of the book. You can then refer to the title of the book by just mentioning this entity name preceded by an & symbol, as shown in the following example:

```
<!doctype showexample
[
<!entity title " Far From the Madding Crowd">
]>
<showexample>
<BOOK LANGUAGE = "English">
<TITLE> &title </TITLE>
<AUTHOR> Thomas Hardy </AUTHOR>
<BLURB> &title is a     </BLURB>
</BOOK>
</showexample>
```

RULES FOR CREATING XML DOCUMENTS

Although XML lets you create as many user-defined tags as you desire, you must adhere to certain specifications laid down by W3C while creating XML documents. These specifications let an XML document have a standardized syntax that in turn lets applications interpret and process them. XML documents that adhere to the W3C specifications are called *well-formed documents*.

Well-formed XML documents adhere to the following basic rules specified by W3C:

- Every XML document must have a *root element*. A root element is an element that has opening and closing tags.
- Tags must be stated explicitly, and all starting tags must have ending tags. For example, an HTML document with the following syntax is a valid HTML document:
  ```
  <table>
  <tr>
  <td> element 1
  <td> element 2
  </tr>
  <tr>
  <td> element 3
  <td> element 4
  </table>
  ```
  However, in XML documents, you cannot imply tags in this manner. They need to be explicitly stated. In addition, tags must be nested properly. For example, the following XML syntax is invalid:
  ```
  <BOOK>
  <TITLE> Far from the Madding Crowd <PRICE> 121$ </TITLE> </PRICE>
  </BOOK>
  ```
  The correct syntax is as follows:
  ```
  <BOOK>
  <TITLE> Far from the Madding Crowd </TITLE>
  <PRICE> 121$ </PRICE>
  </BOOK>
  ```

- Empty tags in XML documents are slightly different from those in HTML documents. An empty XML tag must have a / before the tag's closing angle bracket (>). For example, the following tag is an empty tag:
  `<MYEMPTYTAG/>`
- Tag names cannot contain spaces. For example, you cannot have a tag name such as `<MOVIE TITLE>`.
- The values for attributes must be enclosed within double quotation marks.
- Tags are case-sensitive in XML. Therefore, the start and end tags must have the same case in order to be correct.
- All entities must be declared before they are used.

Defining the Document Structure

A DTD defines the structure of an XML document. Although a DTD is an optional component, it is an invaluable component that helps an application validate an XML document. The process of checking the content and structure of an XML document is called *validation*. Validating an XML document helps an application process the data in the document properly. A DTD is especially useful while creating markup languages where you can specify the syntax and semantics for the language in the DTD.

A DTD must consist of the following minimum information:

- It must specify the elements that you can use in an XML document. You need to use the `<!element>` tag to specify the elements that can appear in an XML document.
- It must specify the attributes that an element might have and the values that the attributes must take. You need to use the `<!ATTLIST>` tag to specify information about attributes.

Apart from this information, the DTD must also specify information about empty tags, if any.

The following DTD shows the structure of an XML document:

```
<!ELEMENT BOOK (TITLE, AUTHOR, BLURB?)>
<!ELEMENT TITLE  (#PCDATA)>
<!ELEMENT AUTHOR (#PCDATA)>
<!ELEMENT BLURB  (#PCDATA)>
<!ATTLIST BOOK LANGUAGE #REQUIRED>
```

In this DTD, the first line indicates that the BOOK element must have the TITLE and AUTHOR elements and might or might not have a BLURB element. The next three lines indicate that the TITLE, AUTHOR, and BLURB elements must contain text data as their content. The last line indicates that the BOOK element must have an attribute called LANGUAGE.

The XML Parser

When XML documents are processed by applications, they are first checked to see whether they are well-formed. A software program known as an XML parser checks an XML document for syntax errors. XML parsers are of two types—validating and nonvalidating.

A validating parser checks whether an XML document is well-formed and also checks whether it conforms to the DTD specified along with the document. The XML parser for Java version 3.1.1 release, `XML4J-3_1_1`, is a validating parser.

A nonvalidating parser just checks whether a document is well-formed and conforms to the rules laid down by XML specifications. It does not check with the DTD to see whether the document conforms to the rules specified in the DTD. An example of a nonvalidating parser is the jXML parser for Java.

HTML Reference

HTML stands for Hypertext Markup Language. It is a standard tag-based language that you can use to display information on a Web page. The following is a list of HTML tags used to display information on a Web page:

- `<a> </a>`—Lets you specify anchors and links.
- `<abbr> </abbr>`—Lets you specify an abbreviation.
- `<address> </address>`—Lets you specify an address. The text between the `<address>` tags is displayed in italics.
- `<applet> </applet>`—Lets you execute a Java applet.
- `<area> </area>`—Lets you create a client-side image map. You must use this tag pair with the `<map>` tag. The `<area>` tag must be placed within the map element.
- `<b> </b>`—Lets you display text in bold.
- `<base>`—Lets you specify the base URL for the HTML document. You must place the `<base>` tag between the `<head>` tags. The `<base>` tag does not have closing tags.
- `<basefont> </basefont>`—Lets you set the appearance of the font for a specific block of text. If the `<basefont>` tag is placed between the `<head>` tags, the font values are set for the entire document. The closing tag for the `<basefont>` tag is optional.
- `<blockquote> </blockquote>`—Lets you display text quoted from another source. This tag pair causes a paragraph break and provides space above and below the quote.
- `<br>`—Lets you put a line break at the end of a sentence. There is no closing tag for the `<br>` tag.
- `<center> </center>`—Lets you place blocks of text or elements, such as tables and images, in the center of the document.
- `<cite> </cite>`—Lets you display a citation in a font that is different from the normal text—typically italics. Unlike the `<blockquote>` tag, the `<cite>` tag does not insert paragraph breaks before and after the text.
- `<code> </code>`—Lets you display a part of a program or some code in the HTML document.
- `<col>`—Lets you specify the text alignment for the columns in a table. There is no closing tag for the `<col>` tag.

- `<dl> </dl>`—Lets you display terms and definitions in the HTML document. This tag is used along with two more tags, `<dt>` and `<dd>`. The `<dt>` tag lets you specify the term that must be defined, and the `<dd>` tag lets you specify the term's definition. The `<dd>` and `<dt>` tags do not have any closing tags.
- `<em> </em>`—Lets you emphasize certain text in a document by making it look different form the rest of the text in the document.
- `<font> </font>`—Lets you specify the face, color, and size of the characters in text.
- `<form> </form>`—Wraps all form elements and acts as a container for all form controls (fields). All form controls are placed within the `<form>` and `</form>` tags.
- `<frame> </frame>`—Lets you create a frame. A frame is a window in an HTML document in which another HTML document is displayed.
- `<frameset> </frameset>`—Acts as a container that describes all the frames in an HTML document.
- `<h#> </h#>`—Lets you define the style of the text in a document's headings. The `<#h>` tag displays text in six different sizes, ranging from h1 to h6.
- `<head> </head>`—Acts as a container for the tags that control the appearance of the document's main body.
- `<hr>`—Lets you display a horizontal line. The `<hr>` tag does not have a closing tag.
- `<html> </html>`—Informs the browser that the document is an HTML document containing an HTML encoded program.
- `<i> </i>`—Lets you display text in italics.
- `<iframe> </iframe>`—Lets you display a floating frame. A floating frame is similar to a frame, except that you can place it anywhere on the HTML document.
- `<img>`—Lets you insert an image into the HTML document. You can use this tag pair to set various properties for the image, such as size and alignment. The `<img>` tag does not have a closing tag.
- `<input>`—Lets you create various form controls, such as buttons, text boxes, list boxes, and check boxes. The `<input>` tag does not have a closing tag.
- `<kbd> </kbd>`—Lets you specify text that the user needs to enter.
- `<label> </label>`—Lets you specify labels for an element (control) in a form.
- `<li> </li>`—Lets you display a list of items on the Web page.
- `<link>`—Lets you define a relationship between documents. The `<link>` tag does not have a closing tag.
- `<map> </map>`—Lets you create a client-side image map.
- `<meta>`—Lets you provide information (metadata) about the current HTML document, such as its author and subject matter. The `<meta>` tag does not have a closing tag.

HTML Reference 543

- `<noframes> </noframes>`—Lets you display an alternative message to users who have browsers that do not recognize frames.
- `<noscript> </noscript>`—Lets you display alternative text to users who have browsers that do not recognize the `<script>` tag.
- `<object> </object>`—Lets you insert ActiveX components, applets, image maps, media players, plug-ins, and other objects into an HTML document. You can also use this tag pair to specify various attributes of the object inserted into the document.
- `<ol> </ol>`—Lets you display an ordered list.
- `<option> </option>`—Lets you add items to a drop-down list.
- `<p> </p>`—Lets you mark the beginning and end of a paragraph.
- `<param> </param>`—Lets you specify the parameters that might be required by the objects in the `object` tag, such as a Java applet.
- `<samp> </samp>`—Lets you display some sample output.
- `<script> </script>`—Lets you place JavaScript or VBScript code in an HTML document
- `<select> </select>`—Lets the user select an option from the list of options displayed in a drop-down list.
- `<strong> </strong>`—Lets you put strong emphasis on specific text in the document.
- `<style> <style>`—Lets you create and define style sheet rules for a document.
- `<sub> </sub>`—Lets you display subscripts, which are widely used for mathematical and scientific calculations.
- `<sup> </sup>`—Lets you insert superscripts into the text.
- `<table> </table>`—Wraps all the table tags. All the tags that are used to define a table's properties are enclosed within this tag pair.
- `<tbody> </tbody>`—Lets you specify the body portion of a table in which the data is displayed.
- `<td> </td>`—Lets you create the cells that contain the information in a table.
- `<text area> </text area>`—Lets you create a text box in a form.
- `<tfoot> </tfoot>`—Lets you define a footnote for a table.
- `<th> </th>`—Lets you create header cells for a table.
- `<thead> <thead>`—Lets you define the header section of a table.
- `<title> </title>`—Lets you specify the title for the HTML document. This title appears on the title bar of the Web page.
- `<tr> </tr>`—Lets you create a row in a table.
- `<ul> </ul>`—Lets you display an unordered list of items.
- `<var> </var>`—Lets you specify that a particular word is a variable name used in code.

JavaScript Reference

JavaScript is a scripting language that you can use to implement both server-side and client-side components of a Web application. JavaScript files are saved with a .js extension. You can embed JavaScript within HTML by using the `<script>` and `</script>` tags. The `<script>` tag is the opening tag for JavaScript statements. To specify that the language used is JavaScript, you need to use the `language` attribute with the `<script>` tag:

```
<HTML>
<head>
<title>Introduction to JavaScript </title>
<body>
<script language="javascript">
document. write("Welcome to javascript")
</script>
</body>
</html>
```

The `</script>` tag is used to identify the end of JavaScript statements.

Browsers that support JavaScript tags extract the JavaScript tags and execute them. However, browsers that do not support these tags display the JavaScript code as it is on the screen. You can overcome this problem by using the following code:

```
<html>
<head>
<title>Introduction to JavaScript </title>
</head>
<body>
<script language="JavaScript">
<!--start hiding JavaScript
document. write("Welcome to JavaScript")
stop hiding JavaScript-- >
</script>
</body>
</html>
```

In the preceding code, the JavaScript code is hidden within the HTML comment. Therefore, browsers that do not recognize JavaScript ignore this part of the code, because it is enclosed in the HTML comment tag. Browsers that recognize JavaScript code execute the code and display the text in the comment statement on the screen. To avoid this, you can designate these comment statements as JavaScript comments by using //, as shown in the following code:

```
<script language="JavaScript">
<!--start hiding JavaScript
document. write("Welcome to JavaScript")
//stop hiding JavaScript-- >
</script>
```

You can also have browsers that support JavaScript ignore JavaScript code by using the `<noscript>` tag.

You can place the JavaScript code in the head or body section of the HTML document. If you want the JavaScript code to be executed as soon as the page loads, you need to place the code in the body section of the HTML document. If you want the JavaScript code to be executed only when it is called or when an event is triggered, place the code in the head section of the HTML document.

Instead of embedding the JavaScript code into the HTML file, you can place the HTML and JavaScript code in two different files and refer to the JavaScript file in the HTML file by using the SRC attribute, as shown in the following code:

```
<html>
<head>
<title>Introduction to JavaScript </title>
</head>
<body>
<script language="JavaScript" SRC=javas1.js>
</script>
Welcome to JavaScript
</body>
</html>
```

In the preceding example, the JavaScript file used is javas1.js. If the content of this file is as follows

```
document. write("Hi!")
```

the output of the preceding HTML code is as follows:

```
Hi!
Welcome to JavaScript
```

The first line of the output is generated by the JavaScript code, and the second line is generated by the HTML code.

VARIABLES

You use variables to store values used in a program. In JavaScript, variable names can start with a letter or an underscore (_). Variable names can consist of letters, digits, and special characters, such as _. Variable names in JavaScript are case-sensitive. In JavaScript, it is not necessary to specify a variable's data type. JavaScript automatically handles different types of values assigned to the same variable. The data type is implicitly defined based on the literal values assigned to the variable. JavaScript supports data types such as number, boolean, string, and null.

You can declare variables in JavaScript by using the var statement, as shown in the following syntax:

```
var name="Myname"
```

The var keyword in the preceding syntax is optional. You can declare a variable and assign a value to it without the var keyword, as shown in the following syntax:

```
Name="Myname"
```

Similar to the variables used in other programming languages, the variables in JavaScript are of two types—local and global. Local variables are declared within a function and can be accessed only from within that function. These variables are destroyed as soon as you exit the function. Global variables are declared outside the function. These variables can be accessed by all the functions in the page in which they are declared. Global variables are destroyed after you close the Web page.

Operators

JavaScript supports various operators, such as arithmetic operators, assignment operators, logical operators, comparison operators, and string operators.

Table C.1 lists the arithmetic operators supported by JavaScript.

TABLE C.1 ARITHMETIC OPERATORS

Operator	Description
+	Addition
-	Subtraction
*	Multiplication
/	Division
%	Returns the remainder after dividing two integers
++	Increment
--	Decrement

Table C.2 lists the assignment operators supported by JavaScript.

TABLE C.2 ASSIGNMENT OPERATORS

Operator	Description
+=	Increments the value of the variable on the left side of the operator by the value of the expression on the right side. For example, a+=b is the same as a=a+b.
-=	Decrements the value of the variable on the left side of the operator by the value of the expression on the right side. For example, a-=b is the same as a=a-b.
*=	The value of the variable on the left side of the operator is multiplied by the value of the expression on the right side. For example, a*=b is the same as a=a*b.

Table C.3 lists the logical operators supported by JavaScript.

TABLE C.3 LOGICAL OPERATORS

Operator	Description
&&	And
||	Or
!	Not

Table C.4 lists the comparison operators supported by JavaScript.

TABLE C.4 COMPARISON OPERATORS

Operator	Description
==	Equal
!=	Not equal
<	Less than
<=	Less than or equal to
>	Greater than
>=	Greater than or equal to

Apart from the operators just mentioned, JavaScript uses the string operator, +, to concatenate two strings. The following code shows the usage of the string operator, +:

```
text1= "Hello"
text2="World"
text3=text1+text2
```

The text3 variable contains the value HelloWorld. If you want to put a space between the words Hello and World, you can use the following code with a space included in the expression:

```
text1= "Hello"
text2="World"
text3=text1+" "+text2
```

JAVASCRIPT ENTITIES

JavaScript entities let you assign the value of a JavaScript variable to an HTML attribute. JavaScript entities begin with an ampersand (&) and end with a semicolon (;). The following code uses the value of the JavaScript variable to specify the value for the table border and cell spacing in HTML:

```
<html>
<head>
<script language="JavaScript">
a=5;
b=2;
</script>
</head>
<body>
<TABLE BORDER =&{a}; CELLSPACING = &{b};>
<CAPTION>JavaScript Entities</CAPTION>
</TABLE>
</body>
</html>
```

Programming Constructs

JavaScript supports most of the programming constructs supported by other programming languages:

- `if-else`—Executes a set of statements based on a condition. If the condition is true, the set of statements after the `If` statement is executed. If the condition is false, the set of statements after the `Else` statement is executed. Following is the syntax for the `If-Else` construct:

```
if(condition)
{
the statements to be executed if the condition is true
}
else
{
the statements to be executed if the condition is false
}
```

- `while`—Executes a set of statements repeatedly as long as a condition is true. Following is the syntax for the `While` construct:

```
while(condition)
{
statements
}
```

- `do-while`—This construct is similar to the `While` construct, except that the condition is checked only after the statements are executed. Therefore, even if the condition is false, the set of statements is executed at least once. Following is the syntax of the `do-while` construct:

```
do
{
statements
}while(condition)
```

- `for`—Executes a set of statements a specific number of times. The `For` construct also alters the value of a variable each time it loops back to the condition. Following is the syntax of the `For` construct:

```
For(initial value, condition, value alteration)
{
statement to be executed
}
```

- `switch-case`—Executes a specific block of code based on a condition. The `switch` statement compares the value in the expression with the value in each `case` statement. If they match, it executes the set of statements that follow the `case` statement. Otherwise, it executes the default set of statements. The following is the syntax for the switch-case construct:

```
switch (expression)
{
case value1:
      statements to be executed if expression= value1;
```

```
    break;
case value2:
    statements to be executed if expression= value2;
    break;
case value3:
    statements to be executed if expression= value3;
    break;
default:
    statements to be executed if expression is not equal to value1, 2 or 3;
    break;
}
```

The break keyword is used to prevent the execution of the next case statement.

FUNCTIONS

A function is a set of statements that are executed whenever the function is called. Functions in JavaScript can take parameters and return values as in any other programming language. Unlike other programming languages, a function's return data type is not specified at the time the function is declared.

OBJECTS AND METHODS

JavaScript provides a list of objects and methods (functions that operate on an object are called methods in JavaScript) that you can use to display dynamic data on a Web page. JavaScript provides objects such as string, date, and math.

STRING OBJECTS

You use a string object to work with text data. The following are some of the methods that operate on the string object:

- Length()—Returns the length of a string
- Tolowercase()—Converts a string from uppercase to lowercase.
- Touppercase()—Converts a string from lowercase to uppercase.
- Substr()—Extracts a specified number of characters from a specified location in a string.

DATE OBJECTS

You use date objects to work with date and time values. The following are some of the methods that operate on the date object:

- Date()—Returns the current date, along with the month and year.
- Time()   Returns the current time in hours, along with minutes and seconds.
- getDate()—Returns the date part (1 through 31) of the date object.
- getDay()—Returns the day part (0 through 6, where 0 is Sunday, 1 is Monday, and so on) of the date object.
- getMonth()—Returns the month (0 is January, 1 is February, and so on) of the date object.

- `getHour()`—Returns the hour part of the date object.
- `getMinutes()`—Returns the minutes part of the date object.
- `getSeconds()`—Returns the seconds part of the date object.

Math Objects

Math objects contain methods that perform mathematical calculations. The following are some of the methods that operate on the math object:

- `Max()`—Returns the highest number from a specified set of numbers.
- `Min()`—Returns the lowest number from a specified set of numbers.
- `Random()`—Returns a random number between 0 and 1.

Event Handling

Most of the objects or elements that are displayed on a Web page have events associated with them. For example, some of the events associated with the window object are error, focus, move, and resize. For these events associated with the window object, JavaScript provides a list of event-handling attributes, such as OnError, OnResize, OnFocus, and OnMove. JavaScript provides a list of standard methods to connect these event-handling attributes to user-defined JavaScript code. Table C.5 lists some of the methods that you can use with the objects used on a Web page.

TABLE C.5 JavaScript Methods Used for Event Handling

Method	Description
Alert()	Displays an alert dialog box.
Blur()	Removes focus from an object.
Open()	Opens a new window.
Prompt()	Displays a prompt dialog box.
Close()	Closes a window.
Confirm()	Displays a confirmation dialog box.
Focus()	Puts the focus on the specified object.
Scroll()	Scrolls a window to a specific location.

APPENDIX D

CREATING A DATABASE USING MICROSOFT ACCESS

In this appendix

Creating a Database   552

CREATING A DATABASE

Access is a DBMS that lets you store, modify, and retrieve data stored in a database. Although Access is a DBMS, it supports most of the features of RDBMS. The databases that you create in Access are stored as files with an .mdb extension.

In this appendix, you will learn how to create a sample database, Schoollibrary, in Access. This database is used to maintain the transaction of books in a school library. The Schoollibrary database contains two tables, Studentdetail and Bookdetail, which are used to store information about the students and the books in the library, respectively.

CREATING A TABLE

To create a database in Access, you must first start Access by choosing Start, Programs, Microsoft Access. As soon as you start Access, the window shown in Figure D.1 is displayed.

Figure D.1
Use the Microsoft Access dialog box to create a blank database.

From the Create a new database using section, select the Blank Access database option, and click OK. In the File New Database dialog box that is displayed, type a name for your database, save it in the required location, and click the Create button to create the database. Access saves the database as a file with an .mdb extension. For example, if you create a database called Schoollibrary, the database is automatically stored by Access as Schoollibrary.mdb.

After you specify the name of the database and click the Create button, the Database window is displayed, as shown in Figure D.2.

Select the Tables option from the Objects list box in the Database window, and click the New button on the toolbar. The New Table dialog box appears, as shown in Figure D.3. It has a list of options to create a new table.

Creating a Database 553

Figure D.2
Use the Database window to create various database objects, such as tables, queries, forms, and reports.

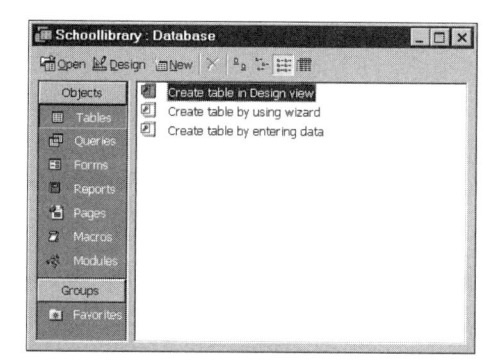

Figure D.3
The New Table dialog box provides various options with which you can create a new table.

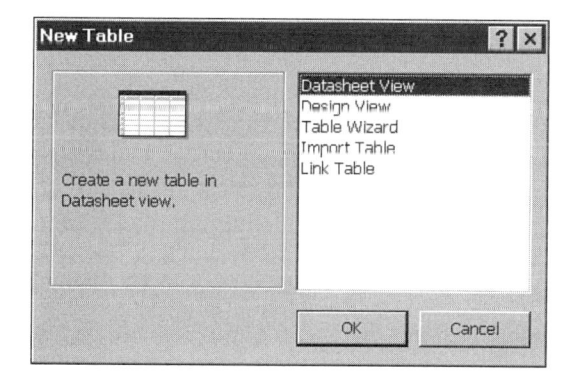

Select the Design View option, and click OK. The Design View option lets you create customized tables with full control over the table structure. You can define relationships, data validations, and rules using Design view. After you select the Design View option and click OK, the Table window is displayed. It is divided into two sections. The upper section, which is the Field pane, lets you enter the names and data types of the fields in a table. The lower section, which is the Field Properties pane, lets you set the properties of each of the fields in the table.

The Field pane of the Table window is further divided into three columns: Field Name, Data Type, and Description.

You can use the Field Name column to specify the name of a field in a table. Names given to fields and other objects in Access, such as tables and queries, must not contain more than 64 characters, leading spaces, and control characters (ASCII values 0 to 31). The names can contain a combination of letters, numbers, spaces, and special characters except for a period (.), an exclamation mark (!), a grave accent (`), and brackets ([]). It is always a good practice to use short and easy-to-understand field names, because long names are difficult to remember.

You can use the Data Type column to specify the data type of each field in a table. The Data Type column displays a drop-down list of data types supported by Access. They are as follows:

- **Text**—Stores alphanumeric characters (letters, a combination of letters and numbers, or numbers that are not used for any calculation such as a phone number). For example, you can store the student ID, name, and address fields as text fields. This data type can hold up to 255 characters. The default size of a text data type is 50. You can change this default size by entering the new field size in the Field Size column of the Field Properties pane. The field size that you specify is allocated to all the values in that field, irrespective of whether all the values are of that size. For example, if you set the field size of the Studentname field to 50 characters, 50 bytes is allocated to all the values in that field. If a student name occupies only 15 characters, 35 characters of space is wasted because it is left unoccupied.

- **Memo**—Stores alphanumeric characters. The Memo field can store up to 64,000 characters, so you can use it to store a huge amount of information, which might exceed 255 characters. For example, if you want to store some general comments and feedback on a student in a field of a table, you can use the Memo field. Unlike the text data type, which allocates the same space for all the values in the field, the memo data type allocates only the amount of space that is required by each value in the field. For example, if a student's name has 15 characters, only 15 bytes of memory is allocated to that data. Therefore, you can use the memo data type for all fields that have values of varying lengths.

- **Number**—Stores numeric values that might require calculations to be performed on them. For example, you can store the marks scored by the students in a field that is of the number data type.

- **Currency**—Stores monetary data. For example, you can specify the field that stores the course fee paid by the students as a currency data type.

- **Date/Time**—Stores date and time values. For example, you can store the Date of Birth field as a date/time data type.

- **Auto number**—Stores a number that is incremented or decremented automatically every time you add or delete a record in a table.

- **Yes/No**—Stores values that can contain only one or two values, such as yes or no or true or false. For example, if you have a field that is used to store the information as to whether a student is a graduate or not, you can specify this field as a yes/no field.

- **OLE object**—Stores objects such as video clips and pictures. For example, if you want to store pictures of the students along with other details, you can create a field of the OLE object data type.

The Description column is optional. You can use it to store any additional information about a field, such as the rules that need to be followed for the field at the time of data entry.

After you enter the field names, data types, and descriptions for all the fields in a table, you can set the table's *primary key*. The field that uniquely identifies every record in a table is an ideal choice for a primary key. To specify a primary key, click the field that you want to set as the primary key, and click the Primary Key button on the toolbar. Access displays a key next to the primary key field, as shown on the StudentID line in Figure D.4.

Figure D.4
Use Design view to create a customized table structure.

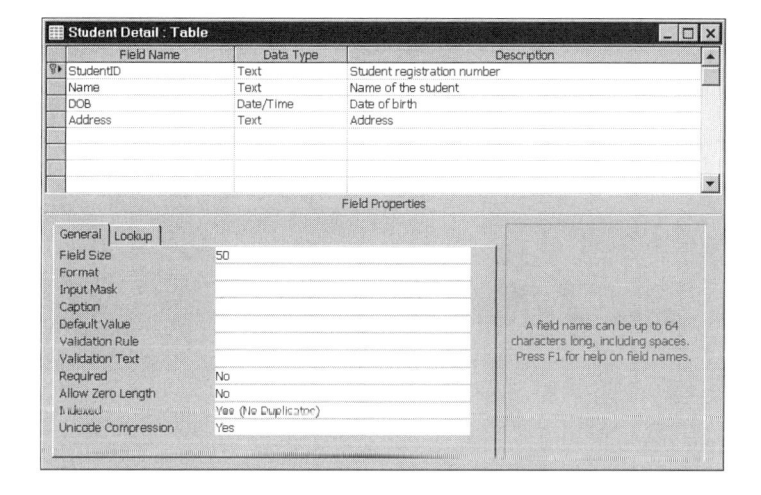

Save the table by choosing File, Save. In the Save As dialog box that is displayed, enter a name for the table, and click OK. Access creates the table with the structure defined by you. Close the Design View window to view the table in the Database window.

After you save the table structure, you can enter records into the table. To enter records into the table, you must open the table by double-clicking the table name in the Database window. The table is displayed in the form of a datasheet. Enter the values in the various fields, and then close the window.

LINKING TABLES

Linking two tables helps you to obtain information that is spread across the two tables. In Access, you can link two tables when the primary key in one table is a foreign key in another table. For example, assume you have a table called Employee Master that contains the employee code (primary key), employee name, address, and salary details such as basic pay and allowances, and another table called Employee Pay Details that contains the employee code (foreign key) and monthly leave details. To get information that contains the employee name and monthly leave details, you need to link the two tables based on the employee code field.

You can link the tables that you create in Access to each other by using the Relationship option on the Tools menu. Follow these steps to create a relationship between tables:

1. Choose Tools, Relationship. The Show Table dialog box is displayed, with the Tables tab selected by default.
2. From the list of tables, double-click the tables that you want to link, and click the Close button. The selected tables are displayed in the Relationships window, as shown in Figure D.5.

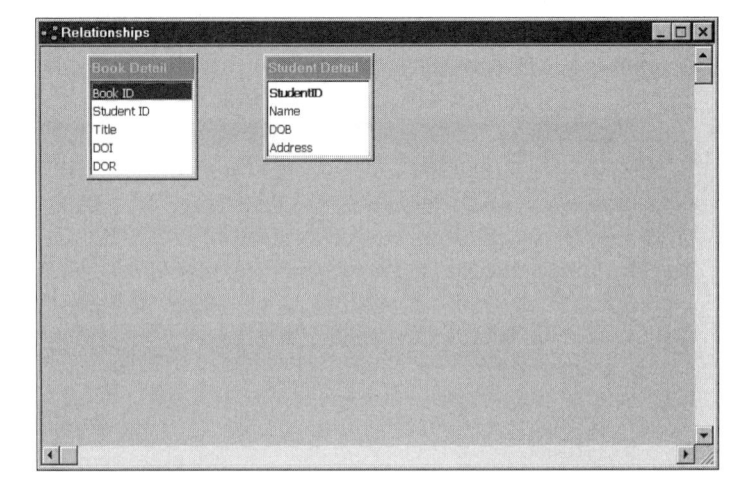

Figure D.5
Use the Relationships window to link the tables in a database.

3. Select the field that you want to link, and drag it to the field in the other table to which you want to link. For example, if you want to link the Studentid column of the Bookdetail table to the Studentid column of the Studentdetail table, drag the Studentid column of the Bookdetail table to the Studentid column of the Bookdetail table.
4. After you drag the field, the Edit Relationships dialog box is displayed, as shown in Figure D.6.

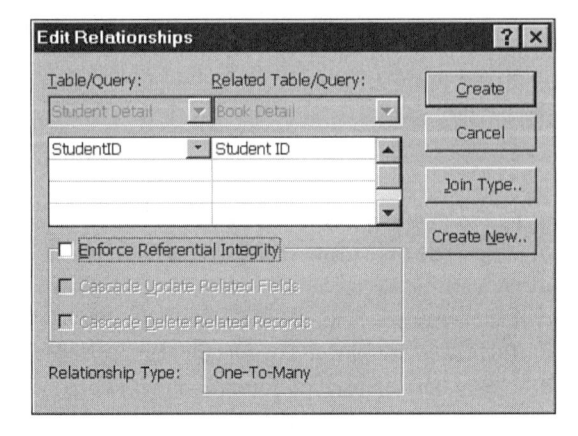

Figure D.6
Use the Edit Relationships dialog box to specify the referential integrity constraints between tables.

Select the Enforce Referential Integrity option if you want to maintain referential integrity between the tables. For example, for every Student ID field you enter in the Bookdetail table, you must have a corresponding Student ID field in the Studentdetail table. To check this referential integrity feature, select the Enforce Referential Integrity option.

Select Cascade Update Related Records Fields if you want the changes made to the values of a particular field in a table to be reflected in the other table to which it is linked. For example, if a student's ID is changed from S003 to S033 in the Studentdetail table, all the records in the Bookdetail table that contain the old student ID, S003, must be changed to S033. To enforce this check, select the Cascade Update Related Fields option.

Select the Cascade Delete Related Records option if deleting a record in one table must result in the deletion of the corresponding record in the related table. For example, if deleting a student's record from the Studentdetail table must result in the deletion of the corresponding student record from the Bookdetail table, select the Cascade Delete Related Records option.

5. After you specify various referential integrity constraints, click the Create button in the Edit Relationships dialog box to create the relationship. Access displays the link between the linked fields, as shown in Figure D.7.

Figure D.7
Use the Relationships window to view the relationship between the tables in a database.

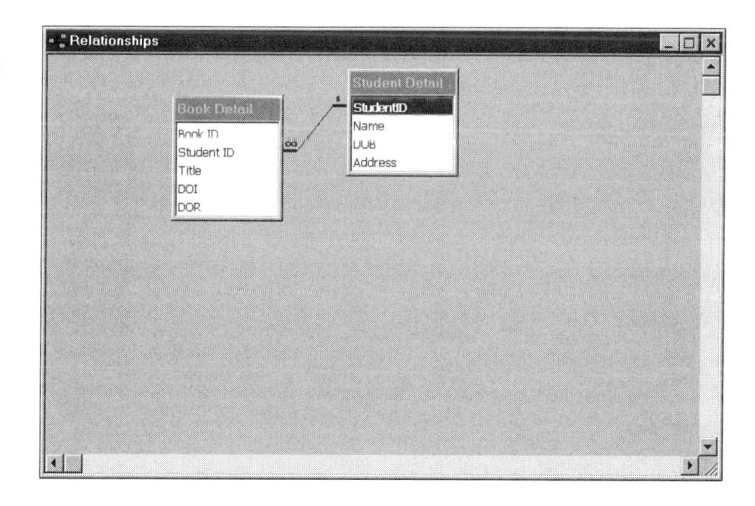

You can edit or delete the relationship between the tables. To edit a relationship, select the connecting arrow between the tables and choose Tools, Relationship. In the Edit Relationships dialog box that is displayed, you can edit the relationship. To delete a relationship, select the connecting arrow between the tables and press the Delete key.

QUERYING A DATABASE

Access lets you retrieve data stored in a database by using queries. For every query you create in Access, the corresponding SQL statements are generated automatically. However, you can edit the SQL statements that are automatically generated using Access.

To create a query in Access by using SQL statements, follow these steps:

1. Choose Insert, Query. The New Query dialog box is displayed, with a list of different methods you can use to create a query.
2. Select the Design View option, and click OK.

3. In the Show Table dialog box that is displayed, double-click the table or tables from which you want to retrieve the data, and then click Close. The selected table or tables are displayed in the Select Query window.

4. Choose View, SQL View to switch to SQL view, in which you can type SQL statements. Type the SQL statement for the query you want to perform, and then choose File, Save.

5. In the Save As dialog box that is displayed, type a name for the query, and then click OK. Close the Select Query window.

You can execute the query by double-clicking it in the Database window.

GLOSSARY

absolute path   A path that contains the complete URL of the linked document. This path contains the protocol used to request the document, followed by the complete path of the target document. An example of an absolute path is `http://www.example.com/folder/targetfile.htm`.

Active Server Pages   See *ASP*.

API   Application Program Interface, an interface between the operating system and application programs that specifies how the operating system and the programs communicate with each other.

Application Program Interface   See *API*.

application server   Also called appserver. An application server is a program that lets Web applications connect and retrieve information from a database. In other words, application servers serve applications to end users.

application variable   A variable that contains global information, such as the page counter and number of hits for a page, that can be accessed by all sessions that are running simultaneously on different clients. These variables are reset only when the *Web server* is restarted. See *user session*.

ASP   Active Server Pages, a product of Microsoft. This technology is used to create dynamic Web applications, which require a server to process requests generated dynamically by a browser. ASP is a server-side technology with which you can combine HTML tags, scripts, and reusable ActiveX server components to create dynamic Web applications.

attribute   A property of an *entity* that describes the entity.

bean   See *JavaBean component*.

breakpoint   A point in code at which program execution stops. It pinpoints the logical errors and lets you fix them.

Cascading Style Sheets   See *CSS*.

cell padding   The space between the border of a cell and the contents of the cell in a table.

cell spacing   The space between the cells in a table.

CFML   ColdFusion Markup Language, a product of Allaire Corporation. This application development environment lets you build dynamic Web sites. In *ColdFusion*, you can create Web applications by using CFML. The pages you create using CFML are similar to HTML pages, except that CFML pages contain *server-side scripts* that dynamically control data integration and presentation.

CGI   Common Gateway Interface, a *server-side script* that runs on a server. A CGI script is written in a programming language such as C or Perl. It is a standard for external gateway programs to interface with information servers such as an HTTP server.

client/server model   A model that allows information transfer between the local computer and the remote computer. This model has two parts, the client program and the server program. The client program runs on the local computer, and the server program runs on the remote computer that provides the information. In this model, the local computer (the client) requests information from the remote computer (the server). The server receives the request, processes it, and sends it in a standard format to the client. The client displays the information.

client-side script   A program that is executed by a Web browser. A server does not process client-side scripts. It simply passes the page containing these scripts to the browser, which takes care of processing the code in the scripts.

ColdFusion   A product of Allaire Corporation, this Web application server lets you build dynamic Web sites. ColdFusion is now owned by Macromedia.

ColdFusion Markup Language   See *CFML*.

collection   A set of information represented as a name and value pair. An example of a name and value pair is the string that you can see in a browser's URL text box. For example, in the string ?fname=Don&lastname=Allen, the name and value pair is represented by fname and Don, respectively.

COM   *Component Object Model*, developed by Microsoft. This model is a software architecture that lets the components created by various software vendors be combined to create a variety of applications.

Common Gateway Interface   See *CGI*.

Component Object Model   See *COM*.

component-centric model   A Web development model in which the logic for dynamic content generation is not embedded within a page but is implemented through *servlets* or *beans*.

continuous shading tone image   An images that contains an unlimited range of color or shades of gray.

controller   A component of the second JSP application model. This component is also known as the front component and is responsible for creating any *beans* or *objects* used by the *presentation component*. A controller can be either a servlet or a JSP page.

cookie   Information bits written on the client computer by the Web server. These information bits contain information about a *user session*, which can be used when the user visits the Web site again.

CSS   Cascading Style Sheets, external text files that contain styles and formatting details that let Web designers apply text and page formatting. CSS define the formatting for all text in a particular class. You can also use these styles to redefine the formatting for a particular tag.

data source A source from which dynamic Web applications can retrieve and display the latest information on a Web page. An UltraDev data source is a store of information from which you can retrieve data to include in your Web page.

database A collection of data stored in an organized manner for easy access, management, and modification.

Database Management System See *DBMS*.

DBMS Database Management System, a computerized record-keeping system that lets you organize, store, and retrieve the data stored in a *database*.

debugger A tool that lets you identify bugs in code, if any, and helps you fix them before the execution of the code.

docking A process of combining one or more panels to form a single tabbed panel. Docking helps you keep from cluttering the workspace with too many panels.

document A page of a Web site that contains text, images, animations, links to other documents, audio, and so on. A document can contain static elements, such as text, images, and links, as well as dynamic content, such as Flash movies, rollover images, and recordset navigation bars.

DSN A name that can be used as a shortcut while creating a database connection. This name encapsulates information that is needed to connect to a database.

dynamic Web site A Web site on which the content changes daily, hourly, or even by the second. The content is generated dynamically as the user browses the site.

entity An object for which you need to store data. An object can be a person, place, thing, or concept.

event A browser generates an event when a user performs an action on the browser, such as requesting a Web page, pointing to an image, clicking an image, or stopping a page download.

Extensible Markup Language See *XML*.

firewall configuration A combination of hardware and software buffer that many companies or organizations have in place between their internal networks and the Internet. It allows only specific kinds of messages from the Internet to flow in and out of the internal network.

foreign key A field in a table that exists as a *primary key* in another table.

form An HTML document that is used to collect information from the user in the form of a request.

form button A button other than a radio button or an image button in a form.

form object An input type used to accept user information. A form object can be a field to enter text, a menu to choose items, or a radio button to select an item. A form object is also called a form field.

form variable A variable included in the body of the *HTTP* request containing form data.

frameset   An HTML page that stores information regarding various characteristics of a Web page, such as the Web page's properties and structure, the number and size of the frames in the Web page, and so on.

freeware   Software that is available on the Net and that you can download free of cost.

grayscaling   A process of converting a *continuous shading tone image* to an image that a computer can manipulate.

hexadecimal color   A color code used to create colors that can be displayed on browsers. This hexadecimal color code is represented by six digits, of which the first two digits represent red, the second two represent green, and the last two represent blue. Each digit can take a hexadecimal value from 0 to F. The hexadecimal representation of a color is preceded by a # symbol. For example, the hexadecimal representation of a dark blue color is #000099.

hidden field   A text field used to collect user information that is not displayed on the page. Password fields are a type of hidden field that hide text entered by a user. These fields hide the text by replacing it with asterisks or bullets.

horizontal rules   Rules used to split and divide long pages into sections.

HTML   Hypertext Markup Language, a language used to create Web sites and Web pages that can be accessed over the World Wide Web. The HTML code in a Web page tells the Web browser how to display the Web page and its elements. The HTML code consists of text files that contain links to other documents.

HTML entity   An HTML tag. In UltraDev, special characters, such as the copyright, registered, trademark, and ampersand symbols, are displayed in the form of HTML entities in Code view. See *HTML*.

HTML style   A style that consists of a combination of several standard HTML tags.

HTTP   A communication protocol that defines a set of rules to enable the transfer of hypertext documents on the World Wide Web.

HTTP header   The *request* and *response headers* together are called an HTTP header.

hyperlink   A link on a Web page that takes a user to other pages on the Web site or to a different Web site.

Hypertext Markup Language   See *HTML*.

image map   An image used in Web page development that can be divided into various regions called hot spots, where each hot spot points to a different URL.

IP address   A unique identifier for a computer or a device on a TCP/IP network.

Java Server Pages   See *JSP*.

JavaBean component   A reusable and portable software component that is developed using the Java programming language.

JSP Java Server Pages, a product of Sun Microsystems. JSP is a technology for creating dynamic Web applications, which require a server to process requests generated dynamically by a browser. JSP makes working with HTML easier and faster.

JSP core tag The standard tag used in JSP 1.0. Most of the processing in JavaServer Pages is implemented through these tags, which are XML-based.

JSP declaration A declaration that lets you define a *method* or a global variable. JSP declarations are similar to the declarations used in Java.

JSP page A page similar to any HTML page, except that it contains additional bits of code that execute application logic.

JSP scriptlet A small block of Java code included in JSP pages. In other words, it is a code fragment executed at the time of a client request.

JSP tag An elements that performs server-side tasks without using any code. These tags are also called JSP actions or JSP bean tags. Java Web servers use JSP tags to generate dynamic content. JSP tags are case-sensitive. You can use them to perform a variety of functions, such as calling a *bean*, connecting to a *database*, or executing standard Java codes.

keyframe A strategic frame in which an object or an image changes its direction or action. You can use a keyframe as a guide to create intermediate frames automatically.

log file A file that lists all the actions that occurred. For example, a log file on a Web server stores a list of the requests made to the server.

logical error An error in a program that causes it to function incorrectly.

many-to-many relationship A relationship that exists between two *entities* when for each instance of the first entity there can be multiple instances of second entity and for every instance of the second entity there can be multiple instances of the first entity.

metatag A tag used in the header of an HTML or XML page to provide information about the page. Each metatag includes the name of the information and the content that supports that name.

method The functionality or behavior associated with the objects in ASP and JSP.

Microsoft Visual SourceSafe The leading version-control system. In UltraDev 4, your Web development process can be streamlined by connecting to Microsoft Visual SourceSafe.

Motion Picture Experts Group compression See *MPEG compression*.

MPEG compression Motion Picture Experts Group compression, an international standard for compression formats. Files compressed with MPEG compression have smaller file sizes when compared to the uncompressed formats. MPEG files, although small in file size, produce high-quality sound.

multiple-line text field A field that lets a user type multiple lines of text. When you create a multiple-line text field in UltraDev, you can specify the number of rows or lines of text that a user can type in the text field.

nested layer   A layer created within another layer.

object   A block of generalized programs modeled after an *entity*.

Object Linking and Embedding   See *OLEDB*.

ODBC   Open Database Connectivity, an interface that is used to connect a database to an application by using a *DSN*.

OLAP server   A high-capacity multiuser data manipulation engine specifically designed to support and operate on multidimensional data structures.

OLEDB   Object Linking and Embedding, an application program interface that lets you access data from different data sources.

one-to-many relationship   A relationship that exists between two *entities* when, for each instance of the first entity, there can exist zero or more instances of the second entity, and for every instance of the second entity, there is only one instance of the first entity.

one-to-one relationship   A relationship in which for each instance of one *entity* there exists only one instance of the other entity.

Open Database Connectivity   See *ODBC*.

orphaned file   A file that is not linked to any other file in a site.

page-centric model   A Web development model in which all information, including data and the logic for the layout, design, and content display of a specific page, is embedded within the page.

Perl   A programming language developed by Larry Wall. It is one of the most popular languages for writing CGI scripts. See *CGI*.

plug-in   A special kind of software used by most browsers to render media files. A number of plug-ins are available today in the market to allow browsers to render multimedia content. Plug-ins such as Real Player and Windows Media Player let a browser play sound files. You can watch Flash movies by using Flash Player.

POP   Post Office Protocol. POP3 is the most recent version of a standard client/server protocol in which e-mail is received and held for you by your Internet server.

Post Office Protocol   See *POP*.

presentation component   One of the two components in the second JSP architecture model. This component is a JSP page that generates HTML or XML content as output. Therefore, this component is responsible for the presentation of the content and the user interface.

primary key   A field or combination of fields that lets you enforce the uniqueness of every record in a table.

radio button   A button used in a form that lets a user select only one option from a list of options.

RDBMS Relational Database Management System, a database management system that lets you organize and manage the data stored in a *relational database*.

recordset A set of rows and columns returned after a database has been queried. These rows and columns are retrieved by means of a query that is defined in the recordset. An application server uses a recordset for faster retrieval of data. A recordset can include all the rows and columns of a database table or only some rows and columns.

relational database A database in which the data is stored in the form of tables that are related to each other. You can query and view the information stored in these tables in different ways without changing their structure.

Relational Database Management System See *RDBMS*.

relationship A logical connection between two separate *entities*.

relative path A path that does not specify the complete path to the target document. It contains the path from a specific folder in the folder hierarchy. Depending on the starting point specified in the relative path, which can be either the current document folder or the site root folder, the path can be called document-relative or root-relative.

request header A header that includes additional information about the client, such as the name of the browser, the operating system on which it is running, and the page's URL, which requests the ASP page.

response header A header that includes information about the page that is processed by a server. For example, *cookies* are sent to the client computer through response headers.

roundtrip HTML A unique feature in UltraDev that lets you copy HTML code from a text-based HTML editor to UltraDev with little or no effect on the code's content and structure. See *HTML*.

schema The structure of a *database* that includes the name of the database and the names of the columns in the database. It is also called *metadata*.

search parameter A parameter that a user enters in a *form* on a Web application to search for specific information on the Web. The Web application responds to the user's request by querying a *database* and retrieving records that match the search parameter entered by the user.

server-side script A script that runs on the Web server in a *client/server model*. JSP and ASP scripts are some examples of server-side scripts. These scripts are processed completely on the Web server. The output, in the form of HTML pages, is sent to the Web browser.

servlet A server-side Java application. A servlet is invoked by a user request, and it responds to the request with an HTML reply. Servlets use Servlet Application Program Interface (Servlet API) and its classes and methods to modify a Web page before it is sent to the user. Servlets are loaded and run on a Web server and are similar to applets that run on a browser on the client side. Servlets provide a platform-independent way to develop Web applications.

session variable   A variable used to store and display information about the user's interaction with the Web server, such as the user's name, the duration of the user's visit, user preferences, and so on.

shareware   Software that is available for free download. Shareware software is available for distribution on a trial basis on the Net so that a user can buy the software after using the trial version.

single-line text field   The default text field used in Web pages. This field is used to accept a single line of text.

spacer image   A transparent 1-pixel-by-1-pixel GIF image that controls the spacing in autostretch tables and cells. This image maintains the width that has been set for a layout table and cell.

SQL statement   A statement used to add, modify, and delete the data stored in a *database*. SQL statements also let you modify and delete data based on specific conditions. Furthermore, they let you fetch summarized data from various databases.

stacking order   The order in which the layers are placed in a stack of layers. In computer terminology, *stack* refers to the buffer used to store requests, and *stacking order* refers to the order in which the requests are handled.

stateless transaction   A transaction in which the information obtained from a user from an earlier page is lost when the next page is served in the same session. See *user session*.

static Web site   A Web site on which the content remains static. Static Web sites do not contain any scripts that need to be executed on a server.

stored procedure   A procedure that consists of one or more SQL statements that reside in a database and that perform database operations. A stored procedure is called a *command* in ASP, a *stored procedure* in ColdFusion, and a *callable* in JSP.

streaming   A technique that allows playback of sound even before the file download is complete. With streamed audio, the sound player that comes with the browser starts playing the sound even before the file is completely downloaded.

style   A set of formatting attributes that controls the appearance of the text in a document. Using a style, you can change various formatting properties at the same time. *HTML styles* and *CSS styles* are some examples of styles.

style sheet   A page template where all the styles and formatting specifications are stored.

template   A document that you can use to create multiple documents with a similar layout. You can easily redesign a Web site that contains multiple pages by just redesigning the templates associated with them. This is possible because templates are linked assets that automatically update all the pages created from them whenever they are changed.

true color Another name for 24-bit color or 16.7 million colors that looks realistic in a video or a photograph on your screen.

URL variable A variable used to store the retrieved information appended to the URL of the requested page.

user session The amount of time that a user remains connected to a particular Web site.

vector-based graphic A graphic image consisting of groups of basic shapes, such as lines, arrows, callouts, rectangles, and other geometric shapes. Such images are grouped to form a single picture. Vector-based graphics download fast and possess high-quality resolution. You can create vector-based graphics by using Macromedia Flash.

W3C World Wide Web Consortium, a group that develops specifications, standards and guidelines, software, and tools. W3C set the W3C standards for Web pages when the need to standardize HTML was felt strongly by the Web development community.

Web server A computer that delivers Web pages. By installing server software on a computer and connecting the computer to the Internet, you can convert the computer to a Web server. Every Web server has an IP address and possibly a domain name.

Web site A collection of Web pages that are called *documents*. The first page of a Web site is called the *home page*.

Web-based Distributed Authoring and Versioning protocol See *WebDAV protocol*.

WebDAV protocol Web-based Distributed Authoring and Versioning protocol, a protocol used on the Web that lets multiple users edit and manage files on remote Web servers collaboratively. WebDAV is a set of standard extensions to HTTP to manage metadata, namespaces, and versions, and prevent overwrites.

Web-safe color A color that does not change its shade when viewed on different monitors and browsers.

World Wide Web A collection of interlinked text and multimedia files and other network services that work together using a specific Internet protocol called *HTTP*.

World Wide Web Consortium See *W3C*.

XML Extensible Markup Language, a markup language that provides features to define and deliver structured data on the Web. It offers a flexible way to express data.

INDEX

Symbols

+ (addition) arithmetic operator, 57, 546
&& (and) operator, 546
/ (division) arithmetic operator, 57, 546
= (equal to) comparison operator, 55, 547
> (greater than) comparison operator, 55
>= (greater than or equal to) comparison operator, 55
++ increment operator, 546
< (less than) comparison operator, 55, 547
<= (less than or equal to) comparison operator, 55, 547
* (multiplication) arithmetic operator, 57, 546
! (not) operator, 546
!= (not equal to) comparison operator, 55, 547
!> (not greater than) comparison operator, 55
!< (not less than) comparison operator, 55
|| (or) operator, 546
% (remainder/wildcard) operator, 57, 546
- (subtraction) arithmetic operator, 57, 546
^ (wildcard) string operator, 57
[] (wildcard) string operator, 57
_ (wildcard) string operator, 57

A

<A HREF> tag, 110
Abandon method (Session object), 72
abbreviations, HTML, 541
abort event, 271
Aboutus.asp file, HTML styles, 170
Absolute Bottom option (alignment), 183
Absolute Middle option (alignment), 183
absolute paths, 191, 560
absolute URLs, 121
Access, *see* Microsoft Access
access rights
    copying and pasting, 441
    information access points, 190
    JSP models, 83–84
    restricting, 432
    ViewCD.asp file, 449
    Web pages, 439–441
Action option (Property inspector), 239–240
actions
    Call JavaScript, 269
    Change Property, 269, 278
    Check Browser, 269
    Check Plugin, 269
    Control Flash, 270
    Control Shockwave, 270
    Drag Layer, 270, 275–277
    <forward> tag, 93
    <getProperty> tag, 98–99
    Go To URL, 270
    <include> tag, 95–96
    <jsp> tag, 93
    Jump Menu, 270
    Jump Menu Go, 270
    Open Browser Window, 270, 274–275
    Play Sound, 270
    Play Timeline/Stop Timeline, 270
    <plugin> tag, 94–95
    Popup Message, 270
    Preload Images, 270
    Set Nav Bar Image, 270
    Set Text of Frame, 270
    Set Text of Layer, 270
    Set Text of Status, 270
    Set Text of Status Bar, 273
    <setProperty> tag, 98
    Show-Hide Layers, 270, 277–278
    Swap Image, 270
    Swap Image Restore, 270
    <usebean> tag, 96–97
    Validate Form, 270
Active Server Pages, *see* ASP
ActiveX Data Objects, *see* ADO
Add Extension when Saving option (Preferences dialog box), 323
Add URL dialog box (Assets panel), 287
Add/Remove Netscape Resize Fix option (Commands menu), 35
addCookie() method (JSP), 86
AddHeader method (Response object), 66
adding
    ActiveX controls, 266
    assets, 285–287, 297
    behaviors, 267
    check boxes, 240, 248
    columns, 210
    counters, 401
    databases, 52–53
    dates, 146–147

dynamic content, 25, 384–385, 404–406
extensions, 15
external editors, 328–329
file fields, 243–244
file types, 329
Flash effects, 17, 281–282
form buttons, 240, 246–247
frames, 228
hidden fields, 244
image buttons, 247–248
images, 174–176
Insert Record server behavior, 418–420
keyboard shortcuts, 465, 470
lists, 249–250
log files, 66
menus, 249–250
navigation bars, 177–180
objects, 238, 261
panels, 333
radio buttons, 240, 244, 246–248
records, 434–435
Repeat Region server behavior, 388–390
rollover images, 176–177
rows, 209–210
searches, 408–409
server behaviors, 26
Shockwave, 260
Show Region server behavior, 406
sound, 264–266
special characters, 147–148
text, 209
text fields, 240–243
addition (+) arithmetic operator, 57, 546
AddNew method (Recordset object), 77–78
addresses, HTML, 541
ADO (ActiveX Data Objects)
adding, 266
creating, 399–400
databases, 74
objects, 74
previewing, 280
troubleshooting, 280
aggregate functions, 58
AIFF (Apple Audio Interchange File Format), 264
Alert() method (JavaScript), 550

Align option
Modify menu, 33
Property Inspector, 259
Text menu, 151
alignment
cells, 212
fonts, 168
images, 181–184
layers, 222–223
layout tables, 139
navigation bars, 180
objects, 259
tables, 210
text, 151
Allaire, 13, 526–528
alpha channels, 173
Always Show option (Preferences dialog box), 335
anchors, 198, 541
AND logical operator, 55–56
and operator, 546
animation, 39
layers, 226–227, 234–235
rewinding, 227
starting, 228
ANSI SQL, 54
Apache, 83
API (application programming interface), 73, 560
AppendToLog method (Response object), 66
Apple Audio Interchange File Format (AIFF), 264
applets, 94–95, 267
Application object, 64, 72–73, 86
application program interface (API), 73, 560
applications, *see* Web applications
Apply button option (CSS Styles panel), 162–163
Apply Source Formatting option (Clean Up Word HTML dialog box), 35, 311
Apply To option (Define HTML Style dialog box), 160
applying
CSS styles, 164
formats, 390–391

HTML styles, 161–162, 169–170
steps to objects, 290
styles, 163
templates, 294
architecture, DOM, 487–488
arithmetic operators, 57, 546
Arrange option (Modify menu), 33
ascending sort, 59
ASP (Active Server Pages), 10, 560
application variables, 369
CDs, songs, 444, 448
code, 62
creating, 366–370
data, 68
databases, 74–75
DSN connections, 346, 348–349
dynamic Web applications, 8
files, 73, 311
forms, 250–252
IIS, 62
ODBC, 73, 352
objects, 63
OLEDB, 352
PWS, 62
Recordset object, 75–77
Request object, 67–69, 366–367
scripts, 63
session variables, 368
sites, 14
stored procedures, 370–371
syntax coloring, 15
ViewCD.asp file, 450–451
ASPError object, 65
assets
adding, 285–287, 297
copying, 288
creating, 287–288
displaying, 285
editing, 288
grouping, 287
location, 288
naming, 286–287
sites, 288
troubleshooting, 297
viewing, 285
see also images; objects
Assets panel, 18
configuration, 285
options, 284–285, 287–288
refreshing, 285

Assets panel (Window menu), 38

assignment operators, 546

Attach Style Sheet option (CSS Styles panel), 163

attaching behaviors, 200, 268–275, 278–280

attributes, 88, 560
- beans, 98
- case, 326
- CSS styles, 165
- HTML tags, 314, 399
- jsp tags, 93-94, 96, 98
- Property inspectors, 509
- relational databases, 47
- tree controls, 490
- XML documents, 538, 540

Attributes option (Reference panel), 301

audio, *see* sound

Auto Apply check box option, 161, 163

auto-indenting, 12

Autoinsert Spacers option (Preferences dialog box), 332

Automatic Wrapping option (Preferences dialog box), 326

automating
- layout tables, 138
- local file lists, 120
- scroll bars, 224
- style selection, 161, 163
- timelines, 228

Autoplay check box (Property Inspector), 260

autostretching layout tables, 139

B

background color
- code, 311, 324
- documents, 129, 131–132
- images, 213, 331
- layers, 224
- objects, 260
- Preferences dialog box, 331
- tables, 139, 210, 332

Background option (Preferences dialog box), 324

Balance Braces option (Edit menu), 30

baseline alignment, 182

BEA WebLogic, 13

beans
- attributes, 98
- dynamic content, 98–99
- initiating, 96–97
- naming, 96, 99
- properties, 98
- scopes, 97

behaviors, 267
- attaching, 200
- client-side, 267
- documents, 268
- forms, 279–280
- images, 275
- layers, 275–278
- links, 273–275
- media files, 280
- Web pages, 268–272

Behaviors panel (Window menu), 38

BETWEEN range operator, 56

Bg color-picker (Property Inspector), 260

Bg text box (Property Inspector), 260

BinaryWrite method (Response object), 66

_blank option (Target list), 195

blur event, 271, 550

body sections, 135

BOF property (Recordset object), 76

bold text, 150, 541

Book option (Reference panel), 301

Border option (Insert Table dialog box), 208

borders
- images, 182
- pixels, 208
- tables, 210

bottom alignment, 182

boxes, 395–399

brackets, 326

breakpoints, 316–317, 560

broken links, 461

browseDocument( ) function, 499

Browser Default option (alignment), 183

browsers
- client-side image maps, 185
- compatibility, 140
- events, 271–272
- HTML tags, 73
- JavaScript, 544
- plug-ins, 256, 269
- tables, 15
- versions, 269
- windows, 270, 282

Buffer property (Response object), 66

Buffer( ) method (Response object), 250

buffers, 66, 96

building sites, 14

bulleted lists, 154–155

buttons
- adding, 240
- Flash Player, 256, 258
- forms, 246–247
- image, 247–248
- radio, 244, 246, 397–398

C

caching
- data sources, 377
- enabling, 121

Call JavaScript action, 269

canAcceptCommand( ) function, 506

CancelUpdate method (Recordset object), 78

canInspectSelection( ) function, 509–510

Cascading Style Sheets, *see* CSS

case, 326

catalog names, 349

categories, 467

CDs, songs, 446–449

cellpoints, 560

cells
- alignment, 212
- background images, 213
- copying, 218
- height, 137, 323
- highlighting, 332

HTML, 543
layout tables, 136–137
merging, 213, 215–218
moving, 137
outlining, 332
padding, 139, 208, 210
pasting, 218
resizing, 137, 214
selecting, 137, 210–211
spacing, 139, 208, 210, 560
splitting, 213, 215–218
text, 209
width, 136, 323

Centering option (Preferences dialog box), 326

CFELSE tag, 111

CFIF tag, 111

CFINSERT tag, 111

CFML (ColdFusion Markup Language), 14, 311, 560
coding, 102
data, 110–112
records, 112–113
server-side scripts, 102
SQL statements, 102
syntax coloring, 15
tags, 107–112

CGI (Common Gateway Interface), 10, 82, 238, 560

Change Link option (Site menu), 198

Change Property action, 269, 278

char (#) data type, 51

check boxes, 240, 248, 395–396

Check In/Check Out option, 36, 456–457

check outs, remote servers, 36

checking
browsers, 269
files, 122, 456–457
links, 29, 37, 461
plug-ins, 269
spelling, 152
target browsers, 29
usernames, 443
see also troubleshooting

child node, 490

circles, fonts, 168

circular hotspots, 185

citations, HTML, 541

classes, JavaBean, 96

clauses, 55–58

clean up, HTML code, 18, 35, 308–311

clearing buffers, 66

clicking, 271

client drivers, RMiJdbc, 354

client-side processing, 10–12
behaviors, 267
image maps, 184–185
scripts, 62, 82, 561

client/server models, 10, 67–69, 561

ClientCertificate collection (Request object), 69, 366

Clip option (Property inspector), 224

clone databases, 346

Close method (Recordset object), 75, 77

Close( ) method (JavaScript), 550

closing
files, 28
quotation marks, 326
recordsets, 77
windows, 282

code
color, 324–325
debugger, 18
editing, 16
font, 150
formatting, 325
HTML clean up, 308–310
JavaScript, 544
server behaviors, 474
tabs, 326
writing, 62

Code and Design option (View menu), 31, 154

Code Colors category (Preferences dialog box), 324–325

Code Format category (Preferences dialog box), 325

Code Inspector panel (Window menu), 38

Code Rewriting category (Preferences dialog box), 326–327

Code View option (View menu), 31, 238, 306

CodePage property (Session object), 72

coding CFML, 102

ColdFusion, 8, 10, 13, 561
Administration, 102
application servers, 124
CD songs, 445, 448
data sources, 371–373
DSNs, 104, 106, 346–349
files, 311
forms, 238
HP-UX, 102
installation, 142
Linux, 102
ODBC, 104, 355
queries, 108–109
scalability, 119
Server, 102–103, 522–524
sessions, 443
Solaris, 102
Studio, 102
variables, 110
ViewCD.asp file, 451–452
Windows 95/98, 102
Windows NT, 102
see also CFML

collections, 64, 561
JavaBeans, 376–377
Request object, 69, 366
Session object, 72

color
Assets panel, 284
background, 311, 324
code, 324–325
configuration, 35
continuous shading tone, 173
documents, 129, 131–132
editing, 288
flat colors, 173
fonts, 168
frames, 233
hexadecimal, 563
indexed, 173
layers, 224
objects, 260
tables, 139, 210
text, 149
true, 568
Web-safe, 568

columns
adding, 210
background images, 213
deleting, 214–215
HTML, 541
indenting, 326

CREATING

inserting, 208, 214–215
merging, 215–218
resizing, 214
selecting, 210–211
site maps, 128
splitting, 215–218
table headers, 213
tree controls, 490
values, 422
width, 210, 214

COM (Component Object Model), 561

Combine Nested Tags option (Clean Up HTML dialog box), 309

commands
ADO, 74
buttons, 506–507
extensions, 505
functions, 506–507
Justify Text, 507–508
menus, 35, 218
saving, 290

comments, 302, 488, 538

Common Gateway Interface (CGI), 10, 82, 238, 560

comparison operators, 55, 547

compatibility
browsers, 140
tables, 15

Component Object Model (COM), 561

component objects, 73, 82–84, 496, 563, 565

compression
lossless, 172
MPEG, 140, 264, 564

computer systems, 536

conditional searches, 55

configuration
application servers, 123–125
Assets panel, 285
code, 324–325
color, 35
CSS styles, 327
data sources, 360
documents, 128
frames, 232–233
general preferences, 322–324
home pages, 144
JRun 3.0, 527–528
JSP, 86
keyboard shortcuts, 15

layers, 223–225
lists, 156
Objects panel, 466
Quick Tag Editor, 333
Site window, 125
tables, 209
Web servers, 121–122
Windows DSN, 528

Confirm( ) method (JavaScript), 550

connections
databases, 8, 74–75, 104
  creating, 344
  deleting, 356
  editing, 356
  JDBC, 344, 353–354
  JSP applications, 352, 354
  Macintosh computers, 354, 356
  ODBC, 342–344
  OLEDB, 342–344
  recordsets, 356
  script files, 345, 356
  SourceSafe, 456, 458
  troubleshooting, 357
  Windows computers, 355
  XML, 345
DSN, 345–346, 348
FTP servers, 122–123, 142, 335
ODBC, 73
remote databases, 12
remote servers, 141
speed, 140
strings, 37, 350–352
Web servers, 122
WebDAV protocol, 458

Connections option (Modify menu), 34

content, framesets, 233, 537

Contentpage.asp file, 236, 378, 405, 444–446

Contents collection (Session object), 72

ContentType property (Response object), 66

context menu option (HTML Styles panel), 161, 163

continuous shading tone images, 173, 561

Control Flash action, 270

Control Shockwave action, 270

controllers, 84, 561

controls, ActiveX, 266

Convert option, 29, 33

converting CSS styles to HTML tags, 168

cookies, 561
reading, 69–70
Request object, 69, 366
Response object, 67
writing, 70

Copy HTML option (Edit menu), 30

copying/pasting
access rights, 441
assets, 288
cells, 218
HTML source code, 148
keyboard shortcuts, 465

counters, record, 401

CREATE DATABASE statement, 50

CREATE PROCEDURE statement, 59

creating
assets, 287–288
Contentpage.asp file, 236, 444–446
CSS styles, 164–167
data sources, 25, 366–377
databases, 50–52, 74–75, 344, 552
delete pages, 426
design notes, 458–460
detail pages, 414
documents, 125–126, 129
DSNs, 104, 106
Editprofile.asp file, 452
extensions, 484
files, 143–144
Flash Player, 257
floating panels, 514
folders, 143–144
forms, 238–240, 252–253
frames, 228–229, 234
home pages, 126
HTML styles, 160
images, 172, 185
intranets, 21
jump menus, 202–203
layers, 221, 227, 234–235
libraries, 295
links, 205
  e-mail, 201
  Make Link option, 193
  named anchors, 198–200

Property inspector, 193–195
site maps, 196–197
UltraDev, 193
login pages, 437–439, 443–444
objects, 73, 466, 497
photo albums, 35, 263–264
Property inspectors, 508–509
record navigation bars, 387
recordsets, 356, 360–365, 378–380
registration pages, 432–434, 443
rollover effects, 275
root folders, 142
Search.asp file, 444–446
server behaviors, 474–475, 477–478
shortcut sets, 465
Songfetch.asp file, 444–446
tables, 208–209, 552–555
templates, 291–294, 297
URLs, 287
ViewCD.asp file, 446, 449–452
Web sites, 119
XML documents, 537, 539–540

CSS (Cascading Style Sheets), 11, 561
applying, 164
attributes, 165
configuration, 327
creating, 164–167
documents, 131
editing, 165
formatting, 162–163
HTML tags, 168
Internet Explorer, 163
Netscape Navigator, 163, 168
Preferences dialog box, 327
removing, 310
W3C standards, 17
Windows, 38, 163

custom tags, 90

customizing, *see* **configuration**

D

data
copying, 218
exporting, 220–221
formats, 472–473
importing, 219–220
inserting, 110–112
nodes, 490
objects, 549
pasting, 218
reading, 68
retrieving, 75–76, 85, 106–107
sorting, 218–219
types, 554
Web pages, 107–108

Data Bindings panel (Window menu), 38

Data Manipulation Language (DML) statement, 52

data sources, 355, 562
Active Server Page, 366–371
caching, 377
ColdFusion, 371–373
configuration, 360
creating, 25
deleting, 377
editing, 377
JavaServer, 374–377
recordsets, 360–365
see also DSN

Database Management System (DBMS), 46, 562

databases, 562
application servers, 8
catalog names, 349
clones, 346
connections, 8, 74–75, 104, 342–345, 352–357
creating, 50, 552
data, 75–76, 106–107, 110–112
drivers, 104, 352
naming, 552
parameters, 350
queries, 557
records
  adding, 52–53
  deleting, 50, 54, 77–78, 426, 428
  duplicating, 429
  editing, 112–113
  inserting, 77–78, 418–422
  retrieving, 54–57
  sorting, 58
  summary values, 58
  updating, 53–54, 77–78, 422–426
recordsets, 76–77
relational, 566
requests, 103
schemas, 349
song_master, 358
stored procedures, 59–60
tables, 48, 51–52, 434–435, 555–557
using, 50
Web applications, 13

Date( ) object (JavaScript), 549–550

dates, 51, 146–147, 554

DB2, 351

dBASE, 351

DBMS (Database Management System), 46, 562

DBQ parameter, 350

debuggers, 18, 29, 316, 562

declaring
JSP, 90
variables, 545

decrement operator, 546

default configuration, 224, 240

defining Web sites, 36, 119, 127, 142–143
application servers, 123–125
documents, 125–126
FTP servers, 122–123
home pages, 126
HTML, 160–161, 542
local folders, 120–121
Site window, 125
Web servers, 121–122

Delete method (Recordset object), 78

DELETE statement, 54

deleting
breakpoints, 317
columns, 214–215
data sources, 377
databases, 50, 54, 356
frames, 228, 231
objects, 466–467
pages, 426
records, 77–78, 426, 428, 446
relationships, 557
rows, 214–215
styles, 162–163
text, 209

delimited format, 219

dependent files, 128

descending sort, 59

design notes, 18, 29, 458–460

Design view, 31, 130–131, 306

designing
framesets, 229, 231
pages, 24–25
relational databases, 46
Web sites, 118–119

detail pages, 415–417
dialog boxes
    displaying, 323
    editing, 470–471
    Link Checker, 461
    Preferences, 322
dictionaries, 152, 324
directives, 87–90, 356
directories, home, 126
discussion forums, 20
displaying
    assets, 285
    Define HTML Style dialog box, 160
    dialog boxes, 323
    dynamic data, 472–473
    element markers, 330
    General category list, 322
    Help, 498–499, 505
    hints, 334
    History panel, 290
    HTML tags, 73
    images, 181, 391–392
    layers, 224, 270
    links, 190
    objects, 260
    properties, 156
    Site window, 322
    Web pages, 10, 107–108, 228
division (/) arithmetic operator, 57, 546
DMS (Data Manipulation Language) statement, 52
do-while programming construct (JavaScript), 548
docking panels, 26, 39, 562
DOCUMENT NODE type, 488
Document Size and Estimated Download Time indicator, 40
documents, 26, 146, 562
    assets, 285
    behaviors, 268
    body sections, 135
    color, 129, 131–132
    configuration, 128
    creating, 125–126, 129
    CSS styles, 131, 164–168
    elements, 134
    Flash Player, 257
    fonts, 149–150
    frames, 128
    grids, 133
    head sections, 135
    history, 323
    HTML, 159–162, 169–170, 311
    languages, 133
    links, 190
    lists, 153–156
    margins, 132
    opening, 129
    paths, 191
    properties, 131–133
    rulers, 133
    saving, 130
    size, 40
    special characters, 147–148
    templates, 291–294
    text, 148–153, 156–159
    titles, 131
    tracing images, 133
    type definition (DTD), 538, 540
    well-formed, 539
    Word, 129
    XML, 536–540
DOM (Document Object Model), 485
    architecture, 487–488
    form buttons, 485
    levels, 486
    methods, 488–489
    nodes, 488
    trees, 486
double-byte text, 323
double-clicking, 271
Down state (navigation bars), 178
downloading
    button styles, 17
    Flash Player, 258
    plug-ins, 94
Drag Layer action, 270, 275–277
drawing layout tables, 136–137
Dreamweaver 3, 464
drivers, 342, 350, 354
DSN (System Data Source Name), 74, 104, 106, 345–346, 348
DTD (document type definition), 538, 540
duplicating records, 429
dynamic content, 384
    ActiveX controls, 399–400
    adding, 25, 384–385
    applications, 8
    beans, 98–99
    check boxes, 395–396
    data, 472–473
    elements, 404–406
    files, 95
    Flash controls, 399–400
    form objects, 392, 394
    formats, 390–391
    HTML attributes, 399
    images, 391–392
    JSP, 82
    list boxes, 398–399
    pages, 24
    radio buttons, 397–398
    replacing, 386
    scriptlets, 92
    text fields, 394–395
    viewing, 15
    Web sites, 10–11, 562

E

e-commerce sites, 20
e-mail links, 201
Edit menu, 30
editing
    Active Server files, 311
    assets, 288
    buttons, 260
    code, 16
    ColdFusion files, 311
    color, 288
    command lists, 35
    CSS styles, 163, 165, 327
    data formats, 472–473
    data sources, 377
    database connections, 356
    dialog boxes, 470–471
    external editor, 30
    Fireworks, 262–263
    Flash Player, 258
    format lists, 472
    graphics, 17
    HTML, 300, 302, 306, 314
    images, 182, 186
    interface, 464
    items in libraries, 296
    jump menus, 203, 270
    layers, 227–228
    libraries, 296
    links, 196–197
    menus, 467–470
    navigation bars, 179
    objects, 260
    options, 322

EDITING

profiles, 452
properties, 269
recordsets, 112–113, 381
relationships, 557
server behaviors, 473, 478–479
site maps, 125, 128
templates, 293
text, 148, 280

editions, ColdFusion Server, 102

editors, 186, 188, 328–329

educational sites, 20

ELEMENT NODE type, 488

elements
centering, 326
documents, 134
hiding, 134, 330
invisible, 199
XML documents, 537

embedding, 258
ASP scripts, 63
Java applets, 267
JavaScript, 544
sound, 265

employee information management, 20

enabling/disabling
cache, 121
Check In/Check Out option, 457
invisible elements, 199
Table option, 208

encoding fonts, 329

End method (Response object), 66

Enterprise JavaBeans (EJB), 82

Enterprise Server, 13

entities, 562
HTML, 563
JavaScript, 547
relational databases, 46
XML documents, 538, 540

EOF property (Recordset object), 76

equal to (=) comparison operator, 55

errors
ADO, 74
handlers, 271, 550
HTML, 326–327
logical, 316–319

messages, 429
site reporting feature, 18
syntax, 315–316

onFocus event, 271

onHelp event, 271

onLoad event, 271

onMove event, 272

onReset event, 272

onScroll event, 272

onSelect event, 272

onSubmit event, 272

events, 11, 64, 267, 271–272, 562

Excel spreadsheets, 129, 351

exception object (JSP), 86

executing
applets, 94–95
.asp files, 73

expiration dates, 66, 250

ExpiresAbsolute property (Response object), 66

exporting
data, 220–221
Fireworks files, 262
options, 28
tables, 221
template regions, 294–295

expressions, 90–91

Extensible Markup Language, see XML

extensions
adding, 15
commands, 505
creating, 484
Extension Manager, 15
files, 187, 323
Flash Player, 256
installation, 491–492
objects, 496–497
packaging, 492–493
page, 124
removing, 329
sharing, 492
submitting, 492–493

external editors, 186, 188, 328–329

external style sheets, 163

eye-dropper (color picker), 132

F

failover, ColdFusion Server, 102

Faster Table Editing (Deferred Update) option, 323

Favorites lists, 286–288

fields, 49
ADO, 74
forms, 238
hidden, 241–244, 563
text, 394–395

File Options (Preferences dialog box), 322

File Transfer Protocol (FTP), 18, 122–123, 142

File Types/Editors category (Preferences dialog box), 328

files
Active Server, 311
checking, 122
checking in/out, 456–457
ColdFusion, 311
compression, 140
creating, 143–144
dependent, 128
extensions, 187, 323
fields, 243–244
Flash Player, 256
hiding, 128
JSP, 89
links, 204
menus, 28–29, 129–130, 219, 221
objects, 260
opening, 129, 323
orphaned, 461, 565
previewing, 120
read-only, 323
remote servers, 36
reports, 460–461
saving, 336
sound, 264
synchronizing, 454–455
transferring, 454
types, 328–329
uploading, 123

filters, searches, 412

Find and Replace dialog box, 157–158

findAttribute() method (JSP), 86

firewalls, 123, 335, 562

Fireworks 4.0, 261–264

hasChildNodes( ) method (DOM) 577

Fix invalidly nested tags option, 311, 326

Flash buttons, 259, 270
adding, 281–282
controls, 399–400
downloading, 17

Flash Player, 256–260

flat colors, 173

floating frames, 542

floating panels, 26, 508, 514–515

flushing buffers, 66, 96

focus event, 271, 550

folders
creating, 143–144
links, 191
root, 142
Web sites, 118

fonts, 140, 149–150, 161, 168, 329, 541–542

footnotes, HTML, 543

for programming construct (JavaScript), 548

foreign keys, 49, 562

formats
applying, 390–391
code, 325
CSS styles, 162–163
delimited, 219
HTML, 311
images, 172
GIF, 172–173
JPEG, 173
PNG, 173–174
layout tables, 138–139
tables, 35, 213–214

forms, 238, 562
ASP, 250–252
behaviors, 279–280
buttons, 240, 246–247, 485, 562
CGI, 238
check boxes, 240, 248
Code view, 238
ColdFusion, 238, 373
collection, 69, 366
controls, 542
creating, 238–240, 252–253
default configuration, 240
fields, 238, 241–244
image buttons, 240, 247–248

items, 323
lists, 240, 249–250
menus, 240, 249–250
names, 239–240
objects, 238, 240–241, 392, 394, 562
passwords, 241
POST method, 68
radio buttons, 240, 244, 246–248
Submit button, 238
text fields, 240–243
user login, 251
validation, 270, 279–280
variables, 562

frames, 38
adding, 228
color, 233
creating, 234
deleting, 220, 231
documents, 128
HTML, 542–543
links, 233
properties, 232–233
saving, 231
splitting, 229
text, 270
Web pages, 228

framesets, 33, 228, 563
creating, 228–229
designing, 229, 231
links, 233
nested, 230
properties, 232–233
saving, 231

Freehand, 17

freeware, 563

FTP servers, 18, 122–123, 142, 335

functions
aggregate, 58
commands, 506–507
Dreamweaver object, 514
floating panels, 514–515
JavaScript, 269, 549
objects, 498–500, 504–505
Property inspectors, 509–510
scripts, 307–308

G

General category (Preferences dialog box), 322–323

Generator, 17, 261

GET method, 373

Get More Commands option (Commands menu), 35

Get option (Site menu), 36

getAttributes( ) method (JSP), 86

getDate( ) object (JavaScript), 549

getDay( ) object (JavaScript), 549

getElementsByTagName (tagName) method (DOM), 489

getFloaterVisibility( ) function, 514–515

getHour( ) object (JavaScript), 550

getMessage( ) method (JSP), 86

getMinutes( ) object (JavaScript), 550

getMonth( ) object (JavaScript), 549

getSeconds( ) object (JavaScript), 550

getServletName( ) method (JSP), 86

GIF images, 172–173, 184, 497

global data, 72

Go to Detail Page server behavior, 416, 423

Go To URL action, 270

graphics, 17, 256–258, 568

grayscaling, 563

greater than (>), 55, 547

greater than or equal to (>=) comparison operator, 55, 547

Grid option (View menu), 32

grids, 32, 133

grouping assets, 287

H

H Space text box (Property Inspector), 260

H text box (Property Inspector), 259

hand coding, 12

hasChildNodes( ) method (DOM), 489

H

Head Content option (View menu), 31
headers, 135, 542
  columns, 213
  HTML, 543
  HTTP, 563
  Property inspectors, 508
  request, 566
  response, 566
  rows, 213
height
  cells, 137, 323
  images, 180–181
  layers, 222, 279, 331
  layout tables, 138
  objects, 259
  rows, 210, 214
  windows, 274
Help Menu, 39, 170, 271
hexadecimal colors, 139, 563
hidden fields, 241, 244, 563
hiding, 32
  elements, 134, 330
  files, 128
  layers, 224
  panels, 39
hierarchies, tree controls, 489–491
highlighting
  cells, 332
  HTML, 304
  text, 330
hints, displaying, 334
History panel, 18, 38, 289–290, 323
hline attribute (Property inspector), 509
home directories, 124, 126, 144
horizontal alignment, 139, 212
horizontal rules, 542, 563
hotspots, 184–186
HP-UX, ColdFusion, 102
HTML (Hypertext Markup Language), 8, 541, 563
  abbreviations, 541
  addresses, 541
  anchors, 541
  attributes, 399
  bold text, 541
  cells, 543
  citations, 541
  code, 308–310
  columns, 541
  comments, 302
  CSS styles, 168
  definitions, 542
  dialog boxes, 470
  editing, 300, 302
  entity, 563
  errors, 326–327
  External Code Editor, 305
  fonts, 541–542
  footnotes, 543
  forms, 111, 542
  frames, 542–543
  headers, 542–543
  highlighting, 304
  horizontal lines, 542
  image maps, 541–542
  italic text, 542
  items, 542
  Java applets, 541
  JSP, 99
  labels, 542
  line breaks, 541
  links, 541–542
  maps, 542
  metadata, 542
  objects, 466
  options, 543
  ordered lists, 543
  paragraphs, 543
  parameters, 543
  Roundtrip, 304–305, 566
  rows, 543
  scripts, 305–306
  source code, 148, 311
  strong text, 543
  style sheets, 38, 159–162, 169–170, 543, 563
  subscripts, 543
  superscripts, 543
  syntax coloring, 15
  tables, 543
  tags, 73, 314, 497, 541–543
  templates, 291–292
  titles, 543
  views, 130
  W3C standards, 17
HTMLEncode method (Server object), 73
HTTP (Hypertext Transfer Protocol), 12, 69, 563
hyperlinks, 563
Hypertext Markup Language, see HTML

I

I-net JDBC driver, 354
IBM DB2 driver, 354
IBM WebSphere, 13
icons, objects, 324
ID text box (Property Inspector), 260
if-else programming construct (JavaScript), 548
IIS (Internet Information Server), 13, 62, 83, 520–521
images
  adding, 174–176
  alignment, 181–184
  alpha channels, 173
  background, 131
  behaviors, 200, 275
  borders, 182
  buttons, 247–248
  compression, 172
  continuous shading tone, 173
  creating, 172
  displaying, 181, 391–392
  editing, 182
  external editors, 186, 188
  flat colors, 173
  formats, 172
  forms, 240
  GIF, 172–173
  height, 180–181
  HTML, 542
  indexed colors, 173
  JPEG, 173
  links, 181
  maps, 184–186, 541, 563
  navigation bar, 270, 275
  Navigation.asp file, 188
  PNG, 173–174
  preloading, 270
  properties, 180
  resizing, 184
  restoring, 270
  rollover, 176–177
  Sidebar.asp file, 188
  source files, 181
  spacing, 181
  swapping, 270
  targets, 181
  tracing, 133
  Web sites, 35
  width, 180–181
Images option (Assets panel), 284

I

IMG tag, 110
implementing command extensions, 505
implicit objects, *see* objects
importing, 28
    data, 219–220
    Excel spreadsheets, 129
    template regions, 294–295
    Word documents, 129
include directive, 89, 356
increment operator, 546
indenting, 149, 325
    code, 30
    columns, 326
    rows, 326
indexed colors, 173
information access points, 190
Informix, 8
inheriting layers, 224
initialPosition() function, 514
initiating beans, 96–97
insert pages, 418, 420
inserting, 32, 52–53
    buttons, 240
    check boxes, 240
    columns, 214–215
    data, 110–112
    fields, 240–241
    Flash Player, 256, 258
    forms, 238, 240
    HTML, 302, 305–306
    jump menu, 241
    Layers panel, 221–222
    libraries, 296
    menus, 241
    options, 146–147
    records, 77–78, 418–422, 434
    rows, 214–215
    tables, 208
insertion points, 496
inspectSelection() function, 509–510
installation
    ColdFusion, 142, 522–524
    Dreamweaver UltraDev 4.0, 524–525
    extensions, 491–492
    IIS 4.0, 520–521
    JRun 3.0, 526–527
    JSP, 142
    SQL Server 7.0, 521–522

instance component objects, 73
int data type, 51
interactive Web sites, 10–11, 20
interface, 8–9, 464
international languages, 133
Internet, 9–10
Internet Explorer
    cross-browser compatibility, 140
    CSS styles, 163
    events, 271–272
    Flash Player, 256, 258
    logging out, 441
    Shockwave, 260
Internet Information Server (IIS), 13, 62, 83, 520–521
intranets, 20–21
invisible elements, 199, 330
invoking floating panels, 514–515
IP addresses, 563
isDomRequired() function, 499, 505
italic fonts, 150, 168, 542
items
    HTML, 542
    libraries, 296

J

Java
    applets, 266–267, 541
    Blend components, 84
    plug-ins, 94
    Web Server, 83
Java Database Connectivity (JDBC), 342, 344, 353–354
JavaBean
    classes, 96
    collections, 376–377
    components, 82, 563
    data sources, 374–375
JavaScript
    application servers, 124
    ASP, 62
    assets, 285
    browsers, 544
    code, 544
    Debugger, 18, 315–319
    embedding, 544

    entities, 547
    extensions, 491–493
    functions, 269, 549
    links, 200
    location, 544
    methods, 550
    objects, 497, 549–550
    opening, 129
    operators, 546–547
    programming constructs, 548–549
    SRC attribute, 545
    syntax coloring, 15
    tree controls, 489–491
    variables, 545–546
JavaServer, 8, 10, 87, 374–377
JDBC (Java Database Connectivity), 342, 344, 353–354
JPEG images, 173, 184
JRun 3.0 (Allaire), 526–528
JScript, 62
JSP (JavaServer Pages), 564
    access, 83–84
    actions, 93–99
    Apache, 83
    CD songs, 448
    database connections, 352, 354
    declarations, 90, 564
    directives, 87–90
    dynamic content, 82, 95
    expressions, 90–91
    files, 89
    HTML, 99
    IIS, 83
    installation, 142
    Java Web Server, 83
    language, 88
    methods, 86
    objects, 85–86
    pages, 564
    scriptlets, 91–93, 564
    servlets, 85
    sessions, 444
    sites, 14
    static files, 95
    syntax, 85
    syntax coloring, 15
    ViewCD.asp file, 451–452
    Web sites, 119
jump menus
    actions, 270
    links, 190, 202–203
justifying text, 507–508

K

key events, 271
keyboard shortcuts, 30
   adding, 465
   copying, 465
   customizing, 15
   Dreamweaver, 464
   Editor, 464
   menus, 470
keyframes, 564
keywords, 56
knowledge management, 20

L

labels, 542
languages
   international, 133
   JSP, 88
   scripts, 306
Launcher bar, 40, 333
layers, 38, 331
   aligning, 222–223
   animation, 234–235
   behaviors, 275–278
   color, 224
   creating, 221
   displaying, 224, 270
   dragging, 270
   height, 222, 279
   hiding, 224
   moving, 222–223
   naming, 224
   nested, 222
   Netscape 4.x, 332
   parent, 224
   paths, 226
   properties, 223–225
   resizing, 222–223, 227
   scroll bars, 224
   selecting, 222–223
   stacked order, 224–225
   tables, 236
   text, 270
   timelines, 222, 225–228, 279
layout
   site maps, 128
   views, 130–131, 332
layout tables, *see* tables
LCID property (Session object), 72
leaf nodes, 487, 490
Length( ) object (JavaScript), 549
less than (<) comparison operator, 55, 547
less than or equal to (<=) comparison operator, 55, 547
libraries, 34, 38, 285–286, 295–296
Library panel (Window menu), 38
LIKE keyword, 56
line breaks, 541
links
   behaviors, 273–275
   checking, 37, 461
   creating, 193–197, 205
   displaying, 190
   documents, 190
   e-mail, 201
   editing, 196–197
   external style sheets, 163
   folders, 191
   framesets, 233
   HTML, 541–542
   images, 181
   information access points, 190
   jump menus, 190, 202–203
   master-detail page, 401, 403–404
   named anchors, 198–200
   null, 200
   orphaned files, 461
   paths, 190–192
   removing, 198
   scripts, 200, 306
   sound, 265
   sources, 197
   tables, 555–557
   target files, 33, 192, 194
   troubleshooting, 204
   UltraDev, 190
   updating, 196, 323
Linux, 102
list boxes, 398–399
List Properties dialog box, 153, 156
listings
   commands, 507
   cookies, 70
   inspectSelection( ) function, 510
   marquee object, 502–504
   Property inspectors, 511–513
   records, 77–78
   Request object, 68
   ServerVariables collection, 69
   session variables, 71
   tree controls, 491
   Write method, 65
lists
   adding, 249–250
   configuration, 156
   forms, 240
   nesting, 153, 155
   ordered, 153–154
   unordered, 154–155
live data feature, 15, 31
live objects, 421–422, 425–426
load balancing, 102
loading Web sites, 228, 271
local folders
   documents, 126
   files, 120
   root foldes, 119, 142
   Web site files, 120–121
Locate in Local/Remote Site options, 37, 288
location
   assets, 288
   JavaScript, 544
   target files, 194
log files, 66, 564
logical errors, 564
   breakpoints, 316
   troubleshooting, 316–319
logical operators, 55–56, 546
login/logout pages
   creating, 437–439, 443–444
   user forms, 251
   Web pages, 441–442
Loop check box (Property Inspector), 260
lossless compression, 172
low-level APIs, 73

M

Macintosh computers, 198, 354, 356
   assets, 288
   cells, 216
   documents, 126
   files, 323
   font sizes, 140
   frames, 229

NONSTANDARD TAGS 581

layout tables, 137
ordered lists, 154
script functions, 308
UltraDev, 524
Macromedia Flash, 17
Make Link option (Modify menu), 33, 193
Manage Extensions option (Commands menu), 35
management, sessions, 443–444
Many-to-Many relationships, 48, 564
maps, 542
margins, 132
markers, 306, 311
marquee object, 501–505, 511–513
Master database, 50
master-detail page, 401, 403–404
math objects, 550
Max() object (JavaScript), 550
maximizing Site windows, 195
Maximum Number of History Steps option (Preferences dialog box), 323
media files
  behaviors, 280
  plug-ins, 256
memo data type, 554
menus
  adding, 249–250
  editing, 467
  forms, 240
  keyboard shortcuts, 465, 470
  menus.xml file, 467–470
  options, 470
  pop up, 241
  separators, 470
merging table cells, 213, 215–218
metadata, 542
metatags, 564
Method option (Property inspector), 239–240
methods, 64, 564
  Application object, 73
  DOM, 488–489
  JavaScript, 550

pageContext object (JSP), 86
Recordset object, 75–78
Response object, 65–66, 86, 250
Server object, 73
Session object, 72, 86
Microsoft Access
  databases, 552
  DSN connections, 346
  ODBC, 351
  tables, 552–557
Microsoft Visual SourceSafe, 564
MIME (Multi-Purpose Internet Mail Extensions), 69
Min() object (JavaScript), 550
modeling
  database tables, 48
  JSP access, 83–84
Modify menu, 33–34, 193
money data type, 51, 554
Motion Pictures Expert Group (MPEG), 140, 264, 564
mouse
  events, 272
  rollover images, 176–177
Move methods (Recordset object), 76
Move recordnumber method (Recordset object), 76
Move to Specific Record server behavior, 417
movies, 258, 285
moving, 272
  cells, 137
  hotspots, 186
  layers, 222–223
  objects, 466–467
  target files, 192
MPEG (Motion Pictures Expert Group), 140, 264, 564
Multi-Purpose Internet Mail Extensions (MIME), 69
multiple-line text fields, 242–243, 564
multiplication (*) arithmetic operator, 57
multiplication operator, 546
Musichome.asp file, 170
MySQL driver, 354

N

naming
  anchors, 198–200
  assets, 286–287
  beans, 96, 99
  databases, 552
  forms, 240
  HTML styles, 160
  layers, 224
  objects, 98, 259
  parameters, 96
navigation bars, 33
  adding, 177–180
  alignment, 180
  editing, 179
  Flash buttons, 281–282
  images, 188, 270, 275
  recordsets, 387
  state, 178
navigational lists, 241
nesting
  framesets, 230
  layers, 222, 565
  layout tables, 136, 139
  lists, 153, 155
  tags, 311
Netscape Enterprise Server, 13
Netscape Navigator, 332
  cross-browser compatibility, 140
  CSS styles, 163, 168
  DOM, 487–488
  events, 271–272
  Flash Player, 256, 258
  images, 182
  logging out, 441
  Shockwave, 260
New from Template option (File menu), 28
New option (File menu), 28, 129
New Server Behavior option, 479
New Site option (Site menu), 36
New Style option, 162–163
nicknames, 286–287
nodes, 488
non-HTML files, 16
non-SQL statements, 361–364
noneditable regions, 293
nonstandard tags, 18

nonvalidating XML parsers, 540

NOT BETWEEN range operator, 56

not equal to (!=) comparison operator, 55, 547

not greater than (!>) comparison operator, 55

not less than (!<) comparison operator, 55

NOT logical operator, 55–56, 546

null links, 200

numbered lists, 153–154, 543

numeric data type, 554

O

Object Linking and Embedding Database (OLEDB), 73–74, 104, 342–344, 350, 352, 554, 565

Object option (Reference panel), 301

objects, 258, 565
    ActiveX, 260, 280
    adding to forms, 238
    ADO component, 74
    alignment, 259
    ASP, 63
    color, 260
    components, 496
    creating, 466
    deleting, 466–467
    design notes, 460
    displaying, 260
    editing, 260
    extensions, 496–497
    files, 260
    Flash Player, 258, 260
    forms, 238, 240–241, 392, 394
    functions, 498–500, 504–505
    Generator, 261
    GIF files, 497
    height, 259
    HTML tags, 497
    icons, 324
    JavaScript, 497
    JSP, 85–86
    libraries, 295–296
    marquee, 501–505
    moving, 466–467
    naming, 98, 259
    parameters, 260

    previewing, 260
    properties, 269
    Request, 252
    resetting, 260
    Response, 250, 252
    servlets, 85
    steps, 290
    storing, 72
    timelines, 227
    whitespace, 260
    width, 259

Objects panel (Window menu), 38
    categories, 467
    configuration, 466
    Insert Flash Text option, 256
    Insert Form option, 238
    objects, 466–467
    options, 240–241

ODBC (Open Database Connectivity), 352, 565
    Access, 351
    APIs, 73
    ASP, 73
    ColdFusion, 104
    data source, 355
    databases connections, 342–344
    DB2, 351
    dBASE, 351
    DSN connections, 345, 348
    Excel, 351, 354, 356
    Oracle, 351
    Paradox, 351
    parameters, 350
    text files, 351
    Windows computers, 355

OLAP servers, 565

OLEDB (Object Linking and Embedding Database), 73–74, 104, 342–344, 350, 352, 554, 565

on events, 271–272

One-to-Many relationships, 47, 565

One-to-One relationships, 47, 565

Open Database Connectivity, *see* **ODBC**

opening, 75
    browser windows, 270, 274–275
    documents, 129
    external editors, 188
    files, 129, 323

    frames, 28
    JavaScript, 129, 550
    linked pages, 33, 198
    Musichome.asp file, 170
    Quick Tag Editor, 134
    sites, 36
    windows, 37, 270

operators
    BETWEEN, 56
    comparison, 55
    JavaScript, 546–547
    precedence, 57
    range, 56

Optimize Image in Fireworks option (Commands menu), 35

options
    Assets panel, 284–288
    Check In/Check Out, 456–457
    Check Links, 461
    Clean Up HTML dialog box, 308–309
    Clean Up Word HTML dialog box, 310–311
    CSS Styles panel, 163
    Define HTML Style dialog box, 160–161
    Edit Format List, 472
    Edit Server Behavior, 478
    Flash Player, 259–260
    HTML Styles panel, 161–162, 543
    Insert menu, 146–147
    interface, 9
    JavaScript Debugger, 317
    List Properties dialog box, 153
    menus, 470
    Modify menu, 193
    New Server Behavior, 479
    Objects panel, 240–241, 256
    Reference panel, 301
    Site menu, 198
    Target list, 195–196
    Text menu, 149–152
    View menu, 154, 199

OR logical operator, 55–56, 546

Oracle, 8, 351, 354

ORDER BY clause, 58

ordered lists, 153–154, 543

orders, placing, 449–452

orphaned files, 461, 565

out object (JSP), 86

Outdent options, 30, 149

outlining, 332

output of ColdFusion queries, 108–109
Over state (navigation bars), 178
Override Case Of options (Preferences dialog box), 326

P

packaging extensions, 492–493
padding cells, 139, 208, 210
page-centric Web development, 83, 565
pages
   context, 86
   designing, 24–25
   detail, 414–417
   directives, 87–88
   elements, 200
   expiration dates, 66
   extensions, 124
   insert, 418, 420
   layout, 25, 135
   objects, 86
   previewing, 429
   properties, 33
   results, 411–414, 423
   searches, 408–410, 423
   updates, 422
panels, 333
   docking, 26, 39
   floating, 26
   hiding, 39
   Window menu, 38–39
panes, Site window, 335
Paradox, 351
paragraphs
   attributes, 161
   HTML, 543
   text, 149
parameters
   ADO, 74
   database, 350
   DBQ, 350
   driver, 350
   dynamic content, 400
   HTML, 543
   naming, 96
   objects, 260
   ODBC, 350
   OLEDB, 350
   provider, 350
   searches, 412–414

   server, 350
   stored procedures, 59
   UID, 350
   values, 96
parent layers, 224
_parent option (Target list), 195
parsing XML documents, 540
passing parameters, 59
passwords, 123, 241
pasting, see copying/pasting
paths
   absolute, 560
   layers, 226
   links, 190–192, 204
   relative, 566
Perl, 565
PerlScript, 62
Personal Web Server (PWS), 62, 520
personalized Web sites, 19
photo albums, 263–264
pixels, 208
placing orders, 449–452
plain-text files, 129
platforms, see Macintosh; Windows
Play button (Property Inspector), 260
Play Recorded Command option (Commands menu), 35
Play Sound action, 270
playing timelines, 270
plug-ins, 32, 94, 256, 269, 565
PNG images, 173–174, 184
Point-to-File icon, 195, 197, 199
pointers, 76
POP (Post Office Protocol), 104, 565
pop-up menus, 241
Popup Message action, 270
Portable Network Graphics (PNG images), 173–174, 184
ports, 335
POST method, 68, 373
Post Office Protocol (POP), 104, 565
precedence, 57

predefined framesets, 229
preferences, external editors, 186
Preferences dialog box, 30, 322
   Code Colors Category, 324–325
   Code Format category, 325
   Code Rewriting category, 326–327
   CSS Styles category, 327
   File Types/Editors category, 328
   Fonts/Encoding category, 329
   General category, 322–323
   Highlighting category, 330
   Invisible Elements category, 330
   Layers category, 331
   Layout View category, 332
   Panels category, 333
   Preview in Browser category, 333
   Site category, 335
   Status Bar category, 336
Preload Images action, 270
presentation components, 84, 565
preset design tables, 213–214
Preview in Browser option, 29, 333
previewing
   ActiveX objects, 280
   files, 120
   objects, 260
   pages, 429
   update pages, 425
   Web sites, 170
primary keys, 49, 554, 565
printStackTrace() method (JSP), 86
priority attribute (Property inspector), 509
procedures, see stored procedures
processing, 10, 12–14
product management, 20
profiles, 452
programming constructs, 548–549
prologs, XML documents, 538
Prompt() method (JavaScript), 550

properties
  beans, 98
  documents, 131–133
  editing, 269
  Flash Player, 258–260
  frames, 232–233
  images, 180
  layers, 223–225
  Recordset object, 76
  Response object, 66
  Session object, 72
  tables, 209
Properties panel (Window menu), 38
Property inspector
  Action option, 239–240
  attributes, 509
  creating, 508–509
  Form Name option, 239–240
  functions, 509–510
  headers, 508
  HTML attributes, 399
  jump menus, 203
  links, 193–195, 199–201
  marquee objects, 511–513
  options, 195, 239–240, 259
  viewing, 209
provider parameter, 350
Put option (Site menu), 36
PWS (Personal Web Server), 62, 520
Python, 62

Q–R

Quality drop-down list (Property Inspector), 260
queries
  ColdFusion, 108–109
  databases, 557
  recordsets, 54
  strings, 67, 69, 366
  see also retrieving
Quick Tag Editor, 16, 33, 134, 314, 333
QuickTime, 17
quotation marks, 326

radio buttons, 565
  adding, 240
  creating, 397–398
  forms, 244, 246–248

Random( ) object (JavaScript), 550
range operators, 56
RDBMSs (relational database management systems), 46, 566
read-only files, 323
reading
  cookies, 69–70
  data, 68
  menus.xml file, 467–469
  recordsets, 76–77
  session variables, 71
Real content, 17
Record Insertion Form live object, 421–422
Record Update Form live object, 425–426
recording layers, 226
records, 49
  adding, 52–53, 434–435
  counters, 401
  deleting, 54, 77–78, 426, 428
  duplicating, 429
  editing, 112–113
  inserting, 77–78, 418–422
  navigation bars, 387
  retrieving, 54–57, 413
  sorting, 58
  summary values, 58
  updating, 53–54, 77–78, 422–426
recordsets, 25, 54, 566
  ADO, 74
  closing, 77
  creating, 378–380
  data sources, 360–365
  databases, 356
  editing, 381
  methods, 75–78
  pointers, 76
  properties, 76
  reading, 76–77
  results pages, 412–414
Redirect( ) method (Response object), 66, 250
Reference panel, 38, 300–302
referential integrity, 49, 556
Refresh Design Views option (View menu), 31
refresh rates
  Assets panel, 285
  local file lists, 120

regions, templates, 293–295
registration, 142, 430, 432–437, 443
relational databases, 566
  attributes, 47
  deleting, 557
  designing, 46
  entities, 46
  management systems (RDBMSs), 46, 566
  Many-to-Many, 48, 564
  One-to-Many relationship, 47, 565
  One-to-One relationship, 47, 565
  relationships, 47, 566
  tables, 557
relative paths, 191–192, 566
Reload Modified Files option (Preferences dialog box), 329
remainder operator, 546
remote databases, 12
Remote Method Invocation (RMI), 82
remote root folders, 142
remote servers, 36, 141
remote sites, 37
removing, 73
  attributes, 86, 489
  breakpoints, 30, 317
  connection scripts, 37
  CSS, 310
  editors, 329
  empty tags, 308
  extensions, 188, 329
  external editors, 188
  HTML comments, 308–309
  links, 33, 198
  markup, 310
  nested tags, 308
  panels, 333
  songs from CDs, 446
renaming
  categories, 467
  form items, 323
  menus, 470
  target files, 192
Repeat Region server behavior, 388–390
replacing
  dynamic content, 386
  text, 152

reports, 460–461
Reports option (Site menu), 36
request headers, 68–69, 563, 566
Request object, 64, 252, 366–367
    client/server models, 67–69
    collections, 69
    cookies, 69–70
    JSP, 85
requests, 103
Reset Count To option (List Properties dialog box), 153
resetting objects, 260, 272
resizing
    cells, 137, 214
    columns, 214
    events, 272
    hotspots, 186
    images, 184
    layers, 222–223, 227
    rows, 214
    tables, 138, 214
    see also sizing
resolution, screens, 141
response headers, 68, 563, 566
Response object, 252
    cookies, 67
    methods, 64–66, 250
    properties, 66
response object (JSP), 85
restoring images, 270
restricting access rights, 432, 439–441, 449
results pages, 423
    search parameters, 411–414
    troubleshooting, 429
retrieving
    data, 75–76, 85, 106–107
    databases, 54–57
    records, 413
    see also queries
rewinding animation, 227
RmiJdbc driver (JDBC), 354
rollover effects, 275
rollover images, 176–177, 323
roman fonts, 168
root elements, 539
root folders, 123, 142
root node, 490

root-relative paths, 192
Roundtrip HTML feature, 16, 304–305, 566
rows, 272
    adding, 209–210
    background images, 213
    deleting, 214–215
    height, 210, 214
    HTML, 543
    indenting, 326
    inserting, 214–215
    merging, 215–218
    resizing, 214
    selecting, 210–211
    splitting, 215–218
    table headers, 213
Rows option (Insert Table dialog box), 208
rulers, 32, 133
rules, horizontal, 563
Run option (JavaScript Debugger), 317

S

sales management, 20
saving, 28, 130
    commands, 290
    documents, 130
    files, 336
    Flash Player, 257
    frames, 28, 231
    passwords, 123
    queries, 158
    templates, 28
    text searches, 158–159
scalability, 119
Scale drop-down list (Property Inspector), 260
schemas, 349, 566
scopes, 97
screens, resolution, 141
scriptlets, 91–93
scripts, 285
    ASP, 63
    CGI, 10
    client-side, 11, 62, 82, 561
    connections, 37
    files, 345, 356
    functions, 307–308
    HTML, 305–306
    language, 124, 306

    links, 200, 306
    markers, 306
    server-side, 82, 560, 566
scroll bars, 224, 272
search pages, 409–410, 423
searches
    conditional, 55
    creating, 444–446
    multiple parameters, 413–414
    operators, 55–57
    pages, 408–409
    parameters, 412–413, 566
    recordsets, 380
    Show Region server behavior, 406
    text, 156–159
    troubleshooting, 429
SELECT statement, 54–55
selecting, 272
    cells, 137, 210–211
    child, 30
    columns, 210–211
    image source, 174
    layers, 222–223
    objects, 496
    parent tags, 30
    rows, 210–211
selection attribute (Property inspector), 509
Selection Properties option (Modify menu), 33
selectionChanged( ) function, 515
self option (Target list), 196
semicolons, 91–92
sendRedirect( ) method (JSP), 86
separators, menus, 170
server behaviors, 38
    adding, 26
    Check New Username, 443
    code, 474
    creating, 474–475, 477–478
    Delete Record, 426, 428, 446
    editing, 473, 478–479
    Go to Detail Page, 416, 423
    Insert Record, 418, 420, 434
    Log in User, 438
    Log Out User, 441–442
    Move to Specific Record, 417
    Repeat Region, 388–390
    Restrict Access to Page, 439–441, 449
    Show Region, 406

Show Region If Recordset Is
  Empty, 447
Update Record, 423–425
servers
  applications, 342
  drivers, 354
  forms, 250–252
  image maps, 184–185
  models, 509
  objects, 64, 73
  OLAP, 565
  parameters, 350
  processing, 10, 12–14
  scripts, 82, 102, 560, 566
  Web, 342, 568
servlets, 82, 566
  APIs, 83
  JSP, 85
  objects, 85
  variables, 69, 366
sessions, 64, 71
  IDs, 72
  management, 443–444
  objects, 72, 86
  scopes, 97
  user, 568
  variables, 71–72, 368, 567
setting
  attributes, 86, 488
  breakpoints, 30, 317
  color, 35, 311
  dates, 86
  floaters, 514–515
  headers, 86
  navigation bars, 270
  text, 270, 273
sharing extensions, 492, 567
Shockwave, 17, 260, 270, 285
shortcut sets, 465
shorthand forms, 327
Show Dialog when Inserting Objects option (Preferences dialog box), 323
Show Log on Completion option (Clean Up HTML dialog box), 309, 311
Show Only Site Windows on Startup option (Preferences dialog box), 322
Show Region If Recordset Is Empty server behavior, 447
Show Region server behavior, 406

Show-Hide Layers action, 270, 277–278
Sidebar.asp file, 188, 381
single search parameters, 412–413
single-line text fields, 241–242, 567
Site category (Preferences dialog box), 335
site maintenance
  design notes, 458–460
  files, 454–457, 460
  links, 461–462
  teams, 455–460
  see also Web sites
site maps
  columns, 128
  editing, 125
  layout, 128
  links, 196–198
Site menu, 36–37, 198
site reporting feature, 18
Site windows, 18
  configuration, 125
  displaying, 322
  documents, 125–126
  files, 36
  FTP, 18
  maximizing, 195
sites, *see* **Web sites**
sizing
  documents, 40
  fonts, 140, 149–150, 168
  windows, 40, 336
  see also resizing
Solaris, 102
Songfetch.asp file
  creating, 444–446
  dynamic content, 405
  recordsets, 379
songs, CDs, 446–449
song_master database, 358
sorting
  data, 218–219
  databases, 58
  tables, 35, 218
sound, 264–266, 270, 280
source code, 148, 181, 311
SourceFormat.txt file, 325

sources
  controls, 456
  links, 197
SourceSafe databases, 456, 458
spacer images, 139, 181, 332, 567
spacing cells, 139, 208, 210
special characters, 147–148, 327
Specific Tag option (Find and Replace dialog box), 157
speed of connections, 140
spell checking, 151–153, 324
splitting
  cells, 213, 215–218
  columns, 215–218
  frames, 229
  rows, 215–218
  views, 16
spreadsheets, 129
SQL (Structured Query Language), 8, 49
  aggregate functions, 58
  arithmetic operations, 57
  CFML, 102
  installation, 521–522
  recordsets, 364–365
  statements, 567
  stored procedures, 59–60
  string operators, 56–57
squares, fonts, 168
SRC attribute, 110, 545
stacking order, 224–225, 567
standard view, 130–131
standards, W3C, 17
starting animation, 228
Starting Recording option (Commands menu), 35
state/stateless transactions, 70, 178, 272, 567
statements, 50, 52–55, 59
static files, 95
static Web sites, 9–10, 567
StaticObjects collection (Session object), 72
Status bar, 39, 270, 336
Status property (Response object), 66
Step Into/Out/Over options (JavaScript Debugger), 317

steps, History panel, 290
Stop button (Property Inspector), 260
Stop Debugging option (JavaScript Debugger), 317
Stop Timeline action, 270
stopping timelines, 270
stored procedures, 567
  data sources, 370–371
  databases, 59–60
  SQL statements, 59–60
storing data, 72, 162
streaming, 264, 567
strikethrough fonts, 168
strings
  objects, 549
  operators, 56–57
  queries, 67
strong text, 543
structure, Web sites, 118–119
Structured Query Language, *see* SQL
Style option (Reference panel), 301
style sheets, 159, 162, 543, 567
  see also CSS
submitting extensions, 238, 272, 492–493
subscripts, 543
Substr( ) object (JavaScript), 549
subtraction (-) arithmetic operator, 57, 546
summary values, 58
Sun JDBC-ODBC Bridge driver, 354
superscripts, 543
swapping images, 270
Switch Views option (View menu), 31
switch-case programming construct (JavaScript), 548
Sybase, 8
synchronizing files, 454–455
syntax
  coloring, 12, 15
  JSP, 85
  syntax errors, 315–316
System Data Source Name, *see* DSN

T

T-SQL, 54
tables
  alignment, 139, 210
  autostretching, 139
  background, 332
  borders, 208, 210
  browsers, 15
  cells, 136–137, 139, 323, 332
  color, 139, 210
  columns, 214–215, 326
  configuration, 209
  creating, 51–52, 208–209, 552–555
  data, 218–221
  formatting, 35, 138–139, 213–214
  headers, 213
  height, 138
  HTML, 543
  layers, 236
  linking, 555–557
  modeling, 48
  nested, 136, 139
  options, 33, 208, 214
  outlines, 332
  primary key, 554
  properties, 209
  records, 52–58
  referential integrity, 556
  relationships, 557
  resizing, 138, 214
  rows, 209, 214–215, 326
  sorting, 35
  spacer images, 139
  text, 209
  viewing, 31
  width, 138, 208, 210
tabs, 326
taglib directive (JSP), 89–90
tags
  A HREF, 110
  attribute, 509
  case, 326
  CFELSE, 111
  CFIF, 111
  CFINSERT, 111
  CFOUTPUT, 107–109, 112
  CFQUERY, 107, 111
  CFSET, 107
  forms, 238
  HTML, 314, 541–543
  IMG, 110
  nested, 311
  options, 301
  Quick Tag Editor, 333
  selecting, 40
  SRC, 110
  text searches, 157–158
  tree controls, 490
  XML documents, 536, 539
tagSpec( ) function, 504
target files
  images, 181
  listing, 195
  location, 194
  moving, 192
  renaming, 192
teams, 456–460
templates, 18, 38, 567
  creating, 297
  documents, 291–294
  Favorites list, 286
  options, 34, 285
  regions, 293–295
text
  adding, 240
  alignment, 151
  auto numeric, 554
  behaviors, 200
  bold, 541
  cells, 209
  color, 149
  data type, 554
  deleting, 209
  double-byte, 323
  editing, 148, 280
  fields, 394–395
  files, 351
  Flash Player, 256–257
  forms, 240–241
  frames, 270
  highlighting, 330
  indenting, 325
  italic, 542
  justifying, 507–508
  layers, 270
  menus, 149, 151–152
  multiple-line, 242–243
  paragraphs, 149
  replacing, 152
  searches, 156–159
  single-line, 241–242
  spell checking, 151–153
  status bar, 270
  wrapping, 326
TEXT NODE type, 488

Text Top option (alignment), 183
text-only browsers, 140
Time( ) object (JavaScript), 549
timelines, 34, 39, 225–228, 270
Timeout property (Session object), 72
titles, 131, 543
togglerFloater( ) function, 514–515
Toolbar option (View menu), 32
ToolTips, 277
_top option (Target list), 196
Touppercase( ) object (JavaScript), 549
Tracing Image option (View menu), 32, 133
transactions, stateless, 70, 567
transferring files, 454
transformation, XML documents, 537
tree controls, 486, 489–491
troubleshooting
　ActiveX objects, 280
　assets, 297
　database connections, 357
　FTP servers, 142
　links, 204, 461–462
　logical errors, 316–319
　remote servers, 141
　results pages, 429
　searches, 429
true colors, 568
tutorials, 39

U

UID parameter, 350
UltraDev, 12
　Active Server Pages (ASP), 8
　ColdFusion, 8
　files, 456–457
　installation, 524–525
　JavaServer Pages, 8
　links, 190
　　creating, 193
　　e-mail, 201
　　editing, 196
　new features, 13–19
　upgrading, 9

underlining fonts, 150, 168
Undo Check Out option (Site menu), 36
Uniform Resource Locators, *see* URLs
unloading, 272
unordered lists, 154–155
Up state (navigation bars), 178
UPDATE statement, 53
updating, 271
　databases, 53–54
　links, 196, 204, 323
　pages, 422, 425
　records, 77–78, 422–426
upgrading UltraDev 4.0, 9
uploading
　files, 123
　links, 204
URLEncode method (Server object), 73
URLs (Uniform Resource Locators), 10, 270
　absolute paths, 121, 191
　Assets panel, 284
　creating, 287
　prefixes, 124
　variables, 371–373, 568
　see also links
users
　interactivity, 10–11
　login forms, 251
　registration, 142
　sessions, 568
　Web sites, 10–11, 430
using databases, 50

V

V Space text box (Property Inspector), 260
validation
　forms, 270, 279–280
　registration forms, 435–437
　XML documents, 540
values
　columns, 422
　parameters, 96
varchar data type, 51
variables
　application, 560
　applications, 369

ColdFusion, 110
declaring, 545
form, 373
JavaScript, 545–546
sessions, 368, 567
URLs, 371–373, 568
VBScript
　application servers, 124
　ASP, 62
　assets, 285
　records, 77–78
　Request object, 68
　ServerVariables collection, 69
　session variables, 71
vector-based graphics, 184, 256–258, 568
versions
　browsers, 269
　files, 456
vertical alignment, 213
View menu, 31–32, 154, 199
ViewCD.asp file, 446, 449–452
viewing
　assets, 285
　data, 15
　grids, 133
　HTML, 130
　layers, 227
　layout, 130–131
　page layout, 25
　Property inspector, 209
　rulers, 133
　scripts, 307–308
　songs from CDs, 447–449
　standard, 130–131
　WYSIWYG, 130
visibility, *see* displaying
Visual aids option (View menu), 31
vline attribute (Property inspector), 509

W

W text box (Property Inspector), 259
W3C (World Wide Web Consortium), 11, 17, 568
Warn when Fixing or Removing Tags option, 327

Warn when Opening Read-Only Files option (Preferences dialog box), 323
Web applications, 9, 19
  Active Server Pages (ASP), 8
  Contentpage.asp file, 444–446
  data sources, 369
  database-driven, 13
  development, 83
  Editprofile.asp file, 452
  login pages, 443–444
  registration pages, 443
  Search.asp file, 444–446
  servers, 8, 123–125, 342, 560
  Songfetch.asp file, 444–446
  variables, 560
  ViewCD.asp file, 446, 449–452
Web pages
  access rights, 439–441
  behaviors, 267–272
  data, 107–108
  displaying, 228
  dynamic content, 384
    ActiveX controls, 399–400
    adding, 384–385, 404–406
    check boxes, 395–396
    displaying, 472–473
    Flash controls, 399–400
    form objects, 392, 394
    formats, 390–391
    HTML attributes, 399
    images, 391–392
    list boxes, 398–399
    radio buttons, 397–398
    replacing, 386
    text fields, 394–395
  Generator, 261
  images, 174–176, 261–263
  logging out, 441–442
  master-detail page, 401, 403–404
  navigation bars, 177–180
  photo albums, 263–264
  record counters, 401
  registration pages, 432–434
  rollover images, 176–177
  server behaviors, 26
  Shockwave, 260
  sound, 264–266, 280
Web servers, 142, 342, 568
  configuration, 121–122
  connections, 122
  files, 122
  requests, 103

Web sites, 146, 568
  access rights, 432
  application servers, 123–125
  creating, 119
  defining, 119, 127, 142–143
  designing, 118
  discussion forms, 20
  documents, 125–126
  dynamic, 10–11, 562
  e-commerce sites, 20
  educational sites, 20
  files, 143–144
  folders, 143–144
  FTP servers, 122–123
  home directory, 124
  home pages, 126
  images, 35
  interactive, 20
  JSP, 119
  loading, 228
  local folders, 120–121
  login pages, 437–439
  personalized, 19
  previewing, 170
  registration, 430
  Site window, 125
  static, 9–10, 567
  structure, 118–119
  Web servers, 121–122
WebDAV protocol, 13, 19, 456, 458, 568
weight of fonts, 168
well-formed documents, 539
What You See Is What You Get (WYSIWYG), 11
When Applying option (Define HTML Style dialog box), 160
WHERE clause, 55–56
while programming construct (JavaScript), 548
whitespace, 260
width
  cells, 136, 323
  columns, 210, 214
  images, 180–181
  layers, 222, 279, 331
  layout tables, 138
  objects, 259
  tables, 208, 210
  windows, 274
Width option (Insert Table dialog box), 208

wildcard string operators, 57
Window Sizes option (Preferences dialog box), 336
windowDimensions() function, 500
Windows
  assets, 288
  cells, 216
  computers, 355
  documents, 126
  DSN, 528
  files, 323
  font sizes, 140
  frames, 229
  layout tables, 137
  menus, 38–39
  UltraDev installation, 524
windows
  closing, 282
  height, 274
  HTML tags, 314
  opening, 37, 270
  size, 40
  width, 274
Windows 95/98, 102, 521
Windows NT, 102
Word documents, 129, 309–310
Workflow reports, 460
World Wide Web Consortium (W3C), 11, 17, 568
wrapping text, 326
Write() method (Response object), 65–66, 250
writing
  code, 62
  cookies, 70
  object extensions, 496
WYSIWYG (What You See Is What You Get), 11, 130

X–Z

XML (Extensible Markup Language), 568
  attributes, 538, 540
  comments, 538
  computer systems, 536
  contents, 537
  database connections, 345
  documents, 537, 539–540

XML (Extensible Markup Language)
  DTD, 538, 540
  elements, 537
  entities, 538, 540
  parsing, 540
  prologs, 538
  root elements, 539
  tags, 536, 539
  templates, 294–295
  transformation, 537
  validation, 540
  well-formed documents, 539
XSLT, 537

yes/no value data type, 554

Hey, you've got enough worries.

Don't let IT training be one of them.

Get on the fast track to IT training at InformIT,
your total Information Technology training network.

InformIT | **www.informit.com** | **Que**

- Hundreds of timely articles on dozens of topics
- Discounts on IT books from all our publishing partners, including Que Publishing
- Free, unabridged books from the InformIT Free Library
- "Expert Q&A"—our live, online chat with IT experts
- Faster, easier certification and training from our Web- or classroom-based training programs
- Current IT news
- Software downloads
- Career-enhancing resources

InformIT is a registered trademark of Pearson. Copyright ©2001 by Pearson.
Copyright ©2001 by Que Corporation.